MACROECONOMICS

MACROECONOMICS

Roger LeRoy Miller

Center for Policy Studies
and
Department of Economics
Clemson University

Robert Pulsinelli

Western Kentucky University

1817

HARPER & ROW, Publishers, New York

Cambridge, Philadelphia, San Francisco,
London, Mexico City, São Paulo, Singapore, Sydney

Sponsoring Editor: John Greenman
Project Editor: Susan Goldfarb
Text Design: Robert Bull/Design
Cover Design: Robert Bull/Design
Text Art: Vantage Art, Inc.
Production: Debra Forrest
Compositor: Ruttle, Shaw & Wetherill, Inc.
Printer and Binder: R. R. Donnelley & Sons Company

Macroeconomics

Library of Congress Cataloging-in-Publication Data

Miller, Roger LeRoy.
  Macroeconomics.

  Includes indexes.
  1. Macroeconomics.   I. Pulsinelli, Robert W.
II. Title.
HB172.5.M543   1986   339   85-16460
ISBN 0-06-044497-5

86 87 88 89 9 8 7 6 5 4 3 2 1

BRIEF CONTENTS

DETAILED CONTENTS

DETAILED CONTENTS

PREFACE

Perhaps more than any other area of economics, macroeconomics is studied because of its governmental policy implications. Indeed, for at least the last few decades macroeconomic analysis—albeit in simplified forms—has appeared in the platforms of incumbents as well as political hopefuls. Media coverage of federal budget deficits, import and export problems due to either the falling or the rising dollar, tax reform, and inflation and disinflation seems never to cease, at least not for more than a few days.

GENERAL APPROACH

We believe that understanding even the rudiments of macroeconomic policymaking requires a knowledge of the history of macroeconomic theory and problems. Consequently, we have developed a historical approach to meet the following objectives:

1. Present theories in the order in which they developed historically
2. Demonstrate that new theories often result from economic events that call into question the extant wisdom (i.e., theories do not exist in a vacuum)
3. Present the origins of modern theories and controversies
4. Lead the student from less complicated to more complicated models
5. Establish a microeconomic foundation to macroeconomics

Within this framework, we concentrate on economic policy throughout the text and explore the policy implications of every model that we present. We also devote an entire chapter (Chapter 16) to monetary policy and an entire chapter (Chapter 17) to fiscal policy.

PEDAGOGICAL FEATURES OF THIS TEXT

Keeping the student in mind at all times, we have added a number of useful pedagogical features to this book.

Policy Controversy Sections

At the end of many chapters there is a Policy Controversy section. These sections indicate that experts can disagree. Our experience has been that students love controversy and like to know when there is disagreement about particular areas of macroeconomic theory.

Chapter Summaries

Every chapter contains a point-by-point summary that provides the student with a useful overview of the main topics presented in the chapter.

Glossaries

All important terms appear in boldface the first time they are used in the text, and their definitions are provided at the end of the chapter in which they are introduced. An index to glossary terms listing the pages on which their definitions may be found is provided at the end of the book.

End-of-Chapter Questions and Problems for Review

All chapters (except Chapter 1) contain end-of-chapter questions and problems. Answers to half of these questions appear at the end of the book; answers to the other half are in the Instructor's Manual.

Mathematical Appendixes

In discussing mathematical concepts, we have attempted to take into consideration the students' varying levels of sophistication. In Chapters 6, 7, and 17, rather than letting mathematics get in the way of students' understanding of the content we have placed the math in chapter appendixes, where it can be more easily absorbed as a unit unto itself. When we do use mathematical equations in the text, we develop them patiently, step by step, keeping the student with minimal math training in mind.

Measuring Economic Variables

Since policymakers derive much of their impetus from the results of measuring economic variables, we look at such variables very carefully in Chapter 2. In that chapter we emphasize that economic variables are difficult to measure, and then we stress the importance of this fact throughout the text. *The imprecise measurement of economic variables is one of the unifying themes of the text*, and we point out repeatedly how this imprecision

  1. Creates difficulties for policymakers;
  2. Opens the door to ideological disputes;

3. Creates controversies; and

4. Makes it difficult to resolve rival hypotheses by "looking at the data."

Since we do not believe that the intermediate course in macroeconomic theory and policy should be overconcerned with the manipulation of data, we do very little of it.

A NOTE ON SUPPLEMENTS

We are very fortunate to have Robert C. Bingham, Professor of Economics at Kent State University, write the Study Guide to accompany this text. Robert Bingham is best known for his work on the supplements to the McConnell *Principles of Economics* package. He has also written the Student Guide to our *Modern Money and Banking* (McGraw-Hill Book Company, 1985). We believe that Professor Bingham's superb pedagogical skills will contribute a great deal to the overall usability of our text as part of a complete teaching/learning system.

Included in the Study Guide are the following (for each chapter of the text):

1. An introduction to the topic being covered

2. A checklist of behavioral objectives for the chapter

3. An outline of the chapter in statement form

4. A list of the glossary terms defined at the end of the chapter

5. Numerical problems

6. True-false questions, multiple-choice questions, and fill-in questions, all with answers given

7. Short-answer questions, without answers given

Another part of the teaching/learning system is the Instructor's Manual, written by Robert Pulsinelli. It includes the following:

1. An overview of the contents of each chapter

2. Questions for class discussion

3. Answers to the end-of-chapter questions

4. At least 20 multiple-choice questions for each chapter

ACKNOWLEDGMENTS

An extremely fine group of reviewers helped us at all stages with the manuscript for *Macroeconomics*. We are most grateful to these reviewers:

Saul Z. Barr
  University of Tennessee at Martin

Robert C. Bingham
  Kent State University
W. Carl Biven
  Georgia Institute of Technology
Melvin Borland
  Western Kentucky University
Michael Conti
  University of New Hampshire
Donald S. Elliott
  Southern Illinois University at Edwardsville
Jorge L. Martinez
  Georgia State University
R. Keith Miller
  Pennsylvania State University, Beaver Campus
Thomas P. Potiowsky
  Portland State University
R. K. Russell
  Southwestern Oklahoma State University, Weatherford
Case M. Sprenkle
  University of Illinois, Urbana/Champaign
Darrel Young
  University of Texas at Austin

    We also wish to thank Lavina Leed for her typing and editing assistance and for her coordination of this entire project. We welcome any comments or criticisms (no matter how harsh) from instructors or students.

ROGER LeROY MILLER

ROBERT PULSINELLI

MACROECONOMICS

PART I

INTRODUCTION TO MACROECONOMICS

1

OVERVIEW

This is an exciting time to be studying macroeconomics. Economic events of the 1970s and the early 1980s have created turmoil and have led to new theorizing in an area of economics that was in danger of becoming stylized. Today economists are happily embroiled in controversies surrounding the interpretation, analysis, and policy prescriptions regarding such events as

1. The periodic outbreaks of *stagflation* (the simultaneous existence of both high rates of inflation and high unemployment rates) that occurred in the mid- and late 1970s
2. The appearance of *supply shocks* (equilibrium-disturbing events emanating from the factors that determine the position of an economy-wide supply curve), such as the Arab oil embargo and the subsequent rapid rise in the price of oil and other energy sources that occurred in the 1970s
3. The slowdown in the rate of growth of productivity (a measure of output per unit of input) that has occurred since 1965
4. The emergence of huge federal government deficits in the $170 billion-per-year range and a public debt (the value of federal government outstanding debt) of over $8 trillion
5. The growth in debt owed by less-developed countries to economically advanced countries to more than $700 billion

These and other important economic events will be analyzed in this text. In the ensuing chapters you will learn that the interpretation of the importance of these events and the analysis of their causes and effects are subject to much controversy among economists. It is important to realize, however, that these controversies are merely the most recent manifestations of centuries-old issues that have not been resolved. Indeed, the issues may be unresolvable. Because of this relationship between past and current economic issues and controversies, in this introductory chapter we will attempt to provide a historical framework within which the current issues can be better understood. We will look at the old issues and then relate them to the controversies surrounding the interpretation and analysis of current events. In the process, we hope to show that (1) although economic events change, the major issues remain; (2) nevertheless, the social science of economics progresses as old theories and old debates are refined or are replaced by newer theories that are more general (in that they can explain past *and* current events) or are better able to explain current economic events.

ENDURING MAJOR ECONOMIC ISSUES

Since 1776, when Adam Smith published his masterpiece, *The Wealth of Nations,*[1] there have been at least three discernible major macroeconomic issues. These issues have focused on the following three questions:

1. Is a private enterprise economy inherently stable or unstable?
2. What is the proper *role* of government in a free enterprise economy?
3. What is the proper *size* of government?

Is a Private Enterprise Economy Inherently Stable or Unstable?

Economists have long debated the issue of whether a free enterprise (or capitalistic) economy is stable. Let us assume that there are four initial equilibrium conditions, all of which are considered to be desirable, in an economy:

1. Full employment exists.
2. The price level is stable.
3. An international payments equilibrium (defined and analyzed in Chapter 20) exists.
4. The economy is growing at its "usual" or "natural" rate (defined precisely in Chapter 3).

Now assume that this desirable equilibrium situation is disturbed by some shock, such as a change in the money supply, or by a worsening of profit expectations. Will the economy eventually regain the four equilibrium conditions listed above? If so, *how long* will it take for equilibrium to be restored?

Classical and Neoclassical Economists   Classical economists and neoclassical (*neo* means "new") economists, whose work spanned the period from the late eighteenth century to the early twentieth century (and whose models are analyzed in Chapters 4 and 5), maintained that capitalistic economies contain mechanisms that do in fact restore the economy to an equilibrium consistent with the four conditions listed above. They contended that the prices of goods and services, wage rates, and interest rates are sufficiently flexible to assure that the four desirable conditions will be achieved, *eventually*. To many of the classical and neoclassical economists, then, a free enterprise economy is stable.

---

[1] Adam Smith, *An Enquiry into the Nature and Causes of Wealth of Nations* (London, 1776).

Of course, other economists writing in that period were less sanguine about a capitalistic economy's self-regulating capabilities, and these economists disputed the contentions of the classical and neoclassical economists. Still, the latter group was more influential.

The policy prescription for many—but certainly not all—of the classical economists was encapsulated in the doctrine of *laissez-faire*, which literally means "allow to do." That is, people should be allowed economic freedom to do what they want, within broad ranges, and the government should not intervene in the economy. (Smith's *Wealth of Nations* documented countless examples of governmental actions that led to a misallocation of resources or to inefficiency.) Their typical policy prescription, then, was *to do nothing*, and that is a reasonable policy if the economy is expected to produce around its full-employment output level anyway.

The Great Depression, Keynes, and the Neo-Keynesians The worldwide Great Depression of the 1930s, however, seemed to provide the evidence that something was amiss. In the United States and England that depression was both severe and protracted; neoclassical admonitions to governments to not "interfere" with the economy, and their exhortations to wait until the "long run," when the economy would again be stabilized around the full-employment level, just didn't seem to ring true anymore. In 1936 John Maynard Keynes, an economist in Cambridge, England, and a colleague and former student of the great neoclassical economist Alfred Marshall, wrote a book called *The General Theory*,[2] which proved to be as revolutionary and influential as Smith's *Wealth of Nations*.

Despite its title, John Maynard Keynes's book contained a theory about how aggregate (economywide) equilibrium is established in an economy characterized by depression conditions—excess capacity for producers, mass unemployment, and (allegedly) inflexible prices (for goods and services, labor, credit, and so on). Keynes was able to demonstrate theoretically the simultaneous existence of both general *equilibrium*, in the sense that there is no tendency for change, and *involuntary unemployment*; in essence, he maintained that there are no mechanisms in capitalism that assure full employment. (Keynes's model is discussed at length in Chapters 6 and 7.)

From the 1940s to the mid-1970s Keynesian and neo-Keynesian economists held the reins of economic influence. Of course, many *non-*

---

[2] John Maynard Keynes, *The General Theory of Employment, Interest and Money* (London: Macmillan, 1936).

Keynesians clung to the neoclassical tradition of a belief in a self-regulating, inherently stable economy. But most of the economic profession—and most of the population at large—believed that a free enterprise economy was unstable. Keynesians and neo-Keynesians convinced many influential politicians and citizens that a free enterprise economy *needs* to be stabilized and *can* be stabilized, and therefore it *should* be stabilized.

In particular, neo-Keynesians believe that free enterprise economies suffer from chronic unemployment and that such economies are inherently unstable. [The extent to which (1) household consumption expenditures, (2) business investment expenditures, and (3) household and business demand for money are stable or unstable is assessed in Chapters 9, 10, and 11, respectively.] Neo-Keynesians also believe that the business cycle (discussed in Chapter 3) can be eliminated by using monetary policy and fiscal policy in just the right amounts at just the right times and that a fully employed, price-stable equilibrium can be attained.

Stagflation, Monetarism, Rational Expectations, and Supply-Side Economics Recently, the pendulum of economic thought seems to have swung again. The periodic bouts of stagflation during the 1970s, the productivity slowdown, and a federal budget that seems to be out of control have been humbling experiences for the economics profession. Apparently, it is not as easy to finely tune an economy as the neo-Keynesians have led us to believe.

Monetarism The *monetarist* economic school of thought developed as a counterrevolution[3] to the Keynesian revolution and grew out of an attempt to explain stagflation. Monetarists include Milton Friedman (Hoover Institute at Stanford University), Karl Brunner (University of Rochester), Allan H. Meltzer (Carnegie-Mellon University), and Beryl W. Sprinkel (Undersecretary of the Treasury for Monetary Affairs) in their ranks. In the long run, stagflation will prove to be as damaging to the Keynesian model as the Great Depression was to the neoclassical model. We analyze the monetarist model in detail in Chapter 18; here we merely indicate the main contentions of the monetarists:

1. Money supply growth is an important determinant of economic activity in the short run, but it determines only the price level in the long run.
2. A private enterprise economy is inherently stable, and the level of

---

[3] See Harry G. Johnson, "The Keynesian Revolution and the Monetarist Counter-Revolution," *American Economic Review*, Papers and Proceedings (May 1971), pp. 1–4, for a fascinating historical account.

national income eventually returns to the *natural output level* (that output level that is consistent with the *natural rate of unemployment*, which is the rate of unemployment to which the economy eventually returns), as discussed in Chapter 14.

3. Most unemployed workers are *voluntarily* unemployed and are searching for jobs; such unemployment is said to be *frictional*. The job search model is an exciting innovation and is analyzed in Chapter 14. The natural rate of unemployment includes frictional unemployment and the unemployment that results from wage rigidities or from restrictions on labor mobility.

4. Monetary policy and fiscal policy affect only frictional unemployment by changing the *duration* of employment, and then only *to the extent that such policies can fool people into, say, underestimating the true rate of inflation*. Consequently, monetary policy and fiscal policy can affect such real variables as national output and national employment only in the short run. In the long run, those values return to their natural levels. The relationship between inflation and unemployment is also explored in Chapter 14.

Rational Expectations   A (perhaps) more radical branch of the monetarist school has proposed the *rational expectations* hypothesis, discussed in Chapter 15. Proponents of this hypothesis include Robert Lucas (University of Chicago) and Thomas Sargent and Neil Wallace (both of the University of Minnesota). These proponents accept the monetarist notion of a natural rate of output and a natural rate of unemployment, but they reject the monetarist conception of how people form their expectations and how economic agents make forecasts of future events. Their model assumes (1) that people take into account *all* relevant information (including stabilization policy itself!) when they forecast the future state of the economy, and (2) that people will not make *systematic* forecasting errors about, say, the future rate of inflation. Because policymakers cannot systematically induce people to underestimate or overestimate the rate of inflation in the future, *policymakers cannot systematically affect real output and real employment even in the short run*. The implications of the rational expectations hypothesis are truly startling, but this hypothesis has not gained widespread acceptance; the less-radical monetarist model, however, has gained general (but not universal) acceptance.

Supply-Side Economics   *Supply-side economics* gets its name from the fact that its proponents stress the importance of aggregate supply, which neo-Keynesians (following Keynes) have seriously neglected. Supply-siders trace their origins, especially with respect to the emphasis on the importance of economic incentives to economic growth, to the classical economists. Conservative supply-siders include Martin Feldstein

(Harvard), Michael K. Evans (president and founder of Evans Econometrics, Inc.), and Michael Boskin (Stanford). Supply-side economists blame stagflation on the allegedly inflationary and antibusiness policies of the neo-Keynesians; inflation has increased marginal tax rates for individuals and businesses, and governmental regulations have hindered commercial transactions. Consequently, their cure for stagflation is to reduce marginal tax rates drastically.

The more radical supply-siders include Jude Wanniski, Arthur Laffer (Stanford), Alan Reynolds, George Gilder, and Paul Craig Roberts. The radical supply-siders were very influential in the Reagan administration and helped to frame "Reaganomics." They maintained that a drastic *reduction* in marginal tax rates would increase the tax base by so much [as income rose, and as incentives to (1) hide income from the IRS in the underground economy or (2) seek tax shelters were reduced] that tax revenues would actually *rise.* Consequently, they alleged that the nation could simultaneously experience lower taxes, more consumption and investment, and more government expenditures on social welfare and national defense.

Because the free lunch that radical supply-siders promised did not materialize, their influence waned by the time President Reagan was reelected in 1984. We analyze supply-side economics and the productivity slowdown in Chapter 19.

What Is the Proper Role of Government in a Free Enterprise Economy?

The previous section demonstrated that economists have long disagreed about the extent to which a free enterprise economy stabilizes around a desirable level. Occasionally, some dramatic economic event seems to settle the issue once and for all in favor of one set of the disputants. But then another dramatic event occurs, and the battle rages anew.

In this section we analyze briefly the second major enduring macroeconomic issue: What is the proper role of the government in a free enterprise economy? This issue is clearly related to the first issue, which is concerned with the degree of stability or instability of the private sector. To the extent that an economy is inherently stable, there is less of a role for government, other things constant. On the other hand, if a free enterprise economy is essentially unstable, then an important stabilization role exists for government. The government must pursue an activist stabilization policy through the mechanisms of monetary policy (analyzed in Chapter 16) or fiscal policy (analyzed in Chapter 17). These two major enduring economic issues are analyzed in depth in the discussion of the monetarist-nonmonetarist debate in Chapter 18.

The issue concerning the proper role of government goes beyond the role of stabilization of the economy, however. Even if the economy were inherently stable, there might be an important role for government to play. Nearly all economists believe that *some* role for government exists in

1. Maintaining competition or regulating natural monopolies
2. Enforcing private property rights and enforcing voluntary contracts
3. Providing internal security and providing security from external forces
4. Redistributing income from higher-income groups to those unable (or *less* able) to compete in the marketplace
5. Providing goods and services that would not otherwise be provided by a free enterprise economy in sufficient quantities (for example, correcting for the positive externality problem)
6. Correcting such negative externalities as pollution

Even though there is general agreement that at least *some* government role is desirable in each of these areas, there is tremendous disagreement concerning *how much*. In general, those who believe that the economy is inherently stable also maintain that the government's role should be *minimal* in most of these areas. Those who maintain that the economy is inherently unstable tend to favor a very active role for the government in most of these areas.

In recent years a major development in the area of government activism in the economy has emerged. The *public choice* school of economics maintains that government bureaucrats, regulators, and politicians behave much like people in the private sector: they usually (but not always) make decisions that are in their *own (and not necessarily society's)* interest. The public choice model has very profound implications for the major issues we have looked at in this chapter; we discuss the public choice model in Chapter 17. We merely point out here that proponents of the public choice school favor a very small role for government in the economy.

In Chapter 18 we analyze the rules-versus-discretion debate, which concerns the extent to which the government should pursue an activist stabilization policy through monetary and fiscal policies. This debate questions whether the behavior of economic agents should be constrained by a set of *rules*, or by people with (government) authority. It may be viewed as the latest round in the never-ending battle over the proper role of government in a private enterprise economy.

What Is the Proper Size of Government?

This third issue is closely related to the first two issues. Those who believe that a private enterprise economy is inherently unstable and that government has important roles to play in providing public goods and services, maintaining competition, assuring "social justice," and so on, will doubtless favor a relatively large share of national output being allocated to the government or public sector. Many government agencies will be viewed as essential for the correction of an inadequate free enterprise economy.

On the other hand, those who believe that the private sector is inherently stable and who favor a minimal role for government will view a small government sector as not only desirable but necessary to the preservation of economic (and, some say, political) freedom.

In Chapter 17 we analyze the burden of the public debt. Whether a large public debt is or is not a burden on society depends largely on what we feel is the "proper" size of the government. After all, if we *desire* a large government share of national output, then what real difference does it make if government spending is financed by *borrowing* (which generates a high public debt) or by taxing (which generates a large tax burden)? Some economists want to solve the public debt "problem" by reducing government expenditures; others want to solve the problem by increasing taxes. The former group may be viewed as favoring a smaller government in terms of size; the latter group probably favors a larger share of national output for the government sector.

CONCLUSION

The three major issues discussed above continue to be debated by economists (and philosophers). Each of these issues is related to the others, and specific economists tend to take predictable and consistent sides concerning each of the issues.

Through time, dramatic economic events occur that set off the debate or settle the debate—for a short time. Recent economic events in the 1970s and early 1980s have made the study of modern macroeconomics interesting and exciting. In order to put the economic debates concerning these events in the proper perspective, however, it is important to realize that even the most recent debates have centuries-old origins. One way to understand the rich tapestry of modern macroeconomics is to follow the thread of the major enduring issues outlined in this chapter. If you ever lose sight of the overall picture and become bogged down in a specific chapter, it may help you to reread this first chapter.

Another important fact to keep in mind is that economic variables are difficult to measure. This point is made convincingly in Chapters 2 and 3 and is stressed again in later chapters. Because measurement is difficult, ideology tends to creep into economic analyses, as specific economists sometimes *define* variables in a manner that suits their personal ideology. By redefining variables, new problems can be created or old problems may seem to disappear. Throughout this text we try to show how a problem is created or how a problem seemingly disappears because economic measurement is such a difficult task. Moreover, we try to point out that because economic *measurement* is difficult, economic *policy* also is difficult to conduct. A good rule is to make sure a problem exists before devising and implementing policies to cure it.

CHAPTER SUMMARY

1. Recent events, such as stagflation, supply shocks, the productivity slowdown, huge federal deficits and an enormous public debt, and the rapid growth in the debt owed by less developed countries have stirred centuries-old economic controversies.
2. Although economic events change, the main macroeconomic issues remain. Nevertheless, the social science of economics advances as the main issues in the debates are refined to incorporate new events.
3. Three major enduring macroeconomic issues are: (*a*) Is a private enterprise economy inherently stable or unstable? (*b*) What is the proper role of government in a private enterprise economy? (*c*) What is the proper size of government?
4. Classical and neoclassical economists believed that such mechanisms as flexible prices, wage rates, and interest rates assure that a private enterprise economy will eventually be restored to a desirable equilibrium situation.
5. The Great Depression seemed to demonstrate that a private enterprise economy is inherently unstable and needs to be stabilized by government economic policy.
6. John Maynard Keynes waged a successful revolution against the classical-neoclassical model. He demonstrated the simultaneous existence of involuntary unemployment and equilibrium and provided a framework for stabilization policy.
7. The economic events of the 1970s and early 1980s have launched a counterrevolution to the Keynesian revolution. The Keynesian model cannot adequately explain high inflation or stagflation; also, the effectiveness of stabilization policies has been called into question.
8. One's point of view regarding the proper role of government depends on one's position regarding the inherent stability of a free enterprise system and on one's assessment of the ability of such an economy to attain other desirable goals. It is also tempered by one's opinion regarding the ability of *government* to achieve desirable results.
9. The proper size of government depends on whether or not a private enterprise economy is inherently stable or unstable and on the proper role of government in such an economy. Recent controversies re-

garding the size of the federal deficit and the size of the public debt are essentially about the proper size of government.

10. Because economic variables are difficult to measure, ideology can creep into the operational definitions of such variables and in the interpretation of data. By redefining variables and reinterpreting data, new problems may seem to arise or old problems may seem to disappear. Economic policy is difficult under such circumstances.

REFERENCES

Harry G. Johnson, "The Keynesian Revolution and the Monetarist Counter-Revolution," *American Economic Review*, vol. 61 (1971).

John Maynard Keynes, *The General Theory of Employment, Interest, and Money* (New York: Harcourt Brace Jovanovich, 1964).

Paul W. McCracken, "Has Macro-Theory Failed Economic Policy?" *Southern Economic Journal*, vol. 51 (1984).

Robert Reich, *The Next American Frontier* (New York: Time Books, 1982).

Lionel Robbins, "Economics and Political Economy," *American Economic Review*, vol. 71 (1981).

Adam Smith, *An Inquiry into the Nature and Cause of the Wealth of Nations* (New York: Random House, 1937).

Herbert Stein, "Are Economists Getting a Bum Rap?" *Southern Economic Journal*, vol. 51 (1984).

Lester Thurow, *The Zero Sum Society* (New York: Penguin Books, 1981).

Melville J. Ulmer, "What Economists Know," *Commentary* (July 1982).

———, "Our Egalitarian Economists," *Commentary* (September 1982).

———, "The War of the Liberal Economists," *Commentary* (October 1983).

2

MEASURING ECONOMIC

PERFORMANCE

conomics is sometimes called the "queen of the social sciences" because many of its key variables lend themselves readily to measurement. In this chapter we are concerned with:

1. Indicating the key macroeconomic variables
2. Defining these variables
3. Explaining how they are measured
4. Explaining problems in measuring them

One important theme of this chapter is that, in practice, it is very difficult to measure the important macroeconomic variables. Perhaps that is why only *economists* refer to economics as the queen of the social sciences.

WHAT IS MACROECONOMICS ALL ABOUT?

The term *macro* is derived from the Greek word meaning "large"; **macroeconomics** is thus the study of economic aggregates.[1] A list of economic aggregates with which we will deal in this text includes such variables as gross national product (GNP), the general price level, the unemployment rate, the money supply, and national wealth.

Economic Performance

In this chapter we are concerned primarily with measuring the economic performance of an entire economy between two points in time, and we will concentrate on three important indicators of an economy's macroeconomic performance:

1. The annual rate of growth of real GNP
2. The rate of inflation
3. The unemployment rate

Stabilization Policy

A rising GNP, price stability, and full employment have been official goals of government policy since the Employment Act of 1946. The Full Employment and Balanced Growth Act of 1978 (the Humphrey-Hawkins

---

[1] *Micro* is a term derived from a Greek word meaning "small," and thus microeconomics analyzes relationships concerning individual households and businesses, or such well-defined groups as cartels and unions.

Act) reaffirms these goals. Throughout this text we will examine theories that purport to explain the levels—and changes in the levels—of these aggregated variables (and such other variables as interest rates and wage rates). Macroeconomic analysis is also vitally concerned with **stabilization policy:** What can be done to make the macroeconomic aggregates move in more desirable directions?

There are three major categories of stabilization tools that can be used to achieve national economic goals:

1. **Monetary policy**—which includes control over such **policy instruments** as the money supply and interest rates
2. **Fiscal policy**—which includes changes in government expenditures and tax rates; tax rates are policy instruments of fiscal policy
3. A miscellaneous category—which includes such diverse things as price-wage controls, incomes policy, and manpower policy

Disagreement Among Economists

There is, and always has been, considerable disagreement among economists over what determines the levels and rates of growth of GNP, general prices, and unemployment. No uniformity of opinion exists regarding their interrelationships either. Perhaps even more controversy surrounds specific *policy* choices; one's favorite policy is intimately related to one's favorite theory. For example, those who believe that inflation is usually caused by "too much money chasing too few goods" are likely to recommend a monetary policy that reduces the rate at which the money supply is rising. Those who view inflation as a situation in which aggregate attempted real expenditures exceed the economy's ability to supply goods will probably recommend a fiscal policy that reduces government expenditures and increases tax rates. Those who see inflation as resulting from the economic power of big business and/or big unions would probably recommend price-wage controls. In short, controversy over stabilization policy can result because economists do not agree on the underlying theory.

Specific stabilization policies also generate disagreements among those who agree on the underlying theory. For example, suppose it were agreed that the correct stabilization policy is decreased government spending and increased taxes. A falling-out is bound to arise with respect to (1) what the proper mix of increased taxes and decreased government expenditures should be, (2) whose taxes should be raised (those with low, middle, or high income), and (3) what kinds of governmental expenditures should be reduced (welfare, national defense, or education).

Finally, we should point out that ideology plays an important role in stabilization policy—and, indeed, in framing economic theory itself.[2] Thus, if it can be demonstrated that national economic goals can be attained by judicious use of any of the three types of policy, most economists will have a preference for one method over the other two because of such other criteria as the effect of the policy on the distribution of income or the effect of the policy in relation to economic freedom. A good rule to remember is that if ideology *can* enter economic analysis and policy formation, it *will*. Because economic concepts are often difficult to define (in such a way that they permit measurement), science is often mixed with ideology.

MEASURING GROSS NATIONAL PRODUCT

The **gross national product,** or **GNP,** is defined as the market value of all final goods and services currently produced per year or time period. Note that, as the definition suggests, for an item to be included in GNP it must meet several criteria:

1. *The item must be sold through the marketplace.* As will be seen, there are exceptions to this rule, but for now it will suffice to say that the value of final goods is reflected by their market price because buyers make their purchases voluntarily. Buyers will pay more for a Mercedes than for a tie because they value the former more highly than the latter.
2. *The item must be a final good.* This means that the item must not be resold in the current period. An intermediate good—such as coal that is to be used in the production of steel during the current period, or steel that is to be used in the production of automobiles in the current period—is not counted in GNP in order to avoid double-counting. There are exceptions to this rule also.
3. *The item must be currently produced.* This requirement automatically excludes sales of items that were produced in previous periods. The period is usually one year, although GNP estimates are made quarterly (every three months) and annualized. Clearly, sales of goods produced in previous periods (such as used cars or previously owned

---

[2] The important influence of ideology on theory and policy is not peculiar to economics; it is widespread in other social sciences as well. Indeed, it seems to be endemic in the natural sciences. Witness the controversies among scientists with respect to whether acid rain is made by humans or nature, whether "yellow rain" in Afghanistan and Cambodia is a result of chemical warfare or bees' excrement, whether or not nuclear waste can be treated safely, whether a nuclear war will bring about a "nuclear winter," or whether President Reagan's "Star Wars" defense system is feasible. These and many other scientific controversies in which certain scientists consistently take sides along ideological lines lead us to suspect that economists are not the only scientists who let ideology influence their thinking.

houses) are not eligible for inclusion in the current GNP. Private **transfer payments**—money receipts that are not accompanied by the *production* of a good or service (such as purchases of financial assets like stocks and bonds)—are also excluded from GNP. Gifts from one person to another are private transfers and hence are excluded.

The Components of GNP

The components of GNP are broken down into personal consumption expenditures, gross private domestic investment, government purchases of goods and services, and net exports of goods and services.[3] This particular method of aggregation reflects the influence of John Maynard Keynes's analysis, which we discuss in Chapter 4.[4] Such an aggregation procedure results also from an attempt to categorize purchases by type of buyer (rather than by type of product) for the sake of simplicity. Think of the enormity of the task of trying to measure the value of total expenditures on each of the millions of individual goods and services produced in a modern economy.

Personal Consumption Expenditures (C)   These expenditures are defined as the value of the goods and services purchased by individuals and the operating expenses of nonprofit institutions per year or time period; they include the value of food, fuel, clothing, rent of dwellings, and financial services received in kind by individuals. *Net* purchases of used goods are also included. (The difference between, say, what a used car dealer pays for a used car and what he or she sells the car for would be a "net purchase"; double-counting is thus avoided.) Note that "in kind" payments for services rendered are counted as a personal consumption expenditure (and are therefore included in GNP), even though such payments do not satisfy the rule of being sold through the market. The three major components of consumption are

1. Durables (items that last longer than one year)
2. Nondurables
3. Services

Gross Private Domestic Investment (I_g)   This component includes the value of fixed capital goods purchased per year or time period by private

---

[3] The definitions in this section can be found in any recent edition of *Business Conditions Digest*, a publication of the U.S. Department of Commerce—the department now responsible for GNP accounting.

[4] Lovers of GNP accounting can thank Simon Kuznets, a 1971 Nobel Prize winner, who played a dominant role in the early development of national income accounting.

businesses and nonprofit institutions (including private purchases of dwellings used for rental purposes), the value of the change in the physical inventories held by private businesses, and the value of purchases of dwellings used for personal use.[5] Also included in this category are *net* purchases of used goods. The major investment categories are

1. Fixed nonresidential
2. Fixed residential
3. Changes in business inventories

Government Purchases of Goods and Services (G) This represents the compensation of government employees and government purchases from domestic businesses and from abroad. Note that "government" includes federal, state, and local governments and that this category excludes such government transfers as Social Security payments and unemployment compensation. This category includes gross investment by government enterprises but excludes their current outlays; it includes net purchases of used goods but excludes sales and purchases of land and financial assets.

Because most governmental goods and services are provided free of charge, this component also violates the "sold through a market" rule; in effect, the *cost* of these goods and services is used to represent their *value*.

Net Exports of Goods and Services (X − M) This component represents the value of exported goods and services X minus imports M. Exports are expenditures by foreigners for goods and services produced domestically; export production creates income locally, but exports are not a part of domestic consumption or investment. Imports are expenditures by domestic residents for goods and services produced by foreigners; imports do *not* create domestic income. If exports exceed imports, then the income created from exports exceeds domestic income spent on imports, and the *net* effect is a higher level of domestic production (and income). Net exports, therefore, are a component of GNP. Viewed alternatively, the value of imports is *already* counted under investment and consumption expenditures, so imports must be subtracted.

---

[5] The treatment of home ownership deserves special attention because it is a little confusing. When an individual purchases a new house for personal use, this transaction is treated as an investment. From then on, an imputed rental value on the house is estimated and treated as a consumption expenditure; it is *as if* a houseowner were a businessperson who charges himself or herself rent. The home owner is also treated as receiving an income equal to the rent he or she is paid.

We can summarize the above definitions in the following GNP identity:[6]

$$GNP \equiv C + I_g + G + (X - M) \qquad (2.1)$$

Table 2.1 shows GNP and its components for the years 1929 to 1984.

GNP and National Income

GNP is a measure of the value of *expenditures* made by various aggregated components. In the process of producing and selling goods and services, equal-valued *incomes* are created automatically. Firms hire labor and other factors of production, and they combine these resources in order to produce and sell goods for a profit (they hope). There is, therefore, a link between production and income. This link is demonstrated more clearly in the following section, which shows that there are two approaches to national income accounting—an expenditures approach and an income approach.

The Value-Added Technique   Let's consider a very simple economy that produces only one final good—the consumer good automobiles—and does so in four (simplified) distinct stages. Table 2.2 shows the four stages of production and the **value added,** or income created, at each stage. Coal companies extract $5 million worth of coal and sell it to steel companies. The coal companies have added $5 billion to the value of the final good and have thereby created $5 billion of income in the form of wages, rent, interest, and profit. The steel companies purchase this coal (which is an intermediate good and a cost to them) and transform it into $20 billion worth of steel. The steel companies have created incomes via value added in the sum of $15 billion. This process continues. Note that the market value of the final goods and services created in this simple economy—GNP equals $60 billion—is equal to the total expenditures on final goods and services *and* is also equal to the value of income created from this production.

A careful examination of Table 2.2 will help you to understand some very important national income accounting concepts.

1. GNP equals the value of total expenditures, *E*, on final goods and services. In the simple economy depicted in Table 2.2,

$$C = GNP \equiv E \qquad (2.2)$$

---

[6] Note that three bars imply an identity, a mathematical statement that is always true; two bars, an equals sign, imply only an equality of the left-hand side and the right-hand side.

TABLE 2.1. GROSS NATIONAL PRODUCT (GNP) AND ITS COMPONENTS, 1929–1983 (billions of dollars)

	GNP	Personal Consumption Expenditures	Gross Private Domestic Investment	Government Purchases of Goods and Services	Net Exports
1929	103.4	77.3	16.2	8.8	1.1
1933	55.8	45.8	1.4	8.2	.4
1939	90.9	67.0	9.3	13.5	1.2
1940	100.0	71.0	13.1	14.2	1.8
1941	125.0	80.8	17.9	24.9	1.5
1942	158.5	88.6	9.9	59.8	.2
1943	192.1	99.4	5.8	88.9	−1.9
1944	210.6	108.2	7.2	97.0	−1.7
1945	212.4	119.5	10.6	82.8	−.5
1946	209.8	143.8	30.7	27.5	7.8
1947	233.1	161.7	34.0	25.5	11.9
1948	259.5	174.7	45.9	32.0	6.9
1949	258.3	178.1	35.3	38.4	6.5
1950	286.5	192.0	53.8	38.5	2.2
1951	330.8	207.1	59.2	60.1	4.4
1952	348.0	217.1	52.1	75.6	3.2
1953	366.8	229.7	53.3	82.5	1.3
1954	366.8	235.8	52.7	75.8	2.5
1955	400.0	253.7	68.4	75.0	3.0
1956	421.7	266.0	71.0	79.4	5.3
1957	444.0	280.4	69.2	87.1	7.3
1958	449.7	289.5	61.9	95.0	3.3
1959	487.9	310.8	78.1	97.6	1.4
1960	506.5	324.9	75.9	100.3	5.5
1961	524.6	335.0	74.8	108.2	6.6
1962	585.0	355.2	85.4	118.0	6.4
1963	596.7	374.6	90.9	123.7	7.6
1964	637.7	400.5	97.4	129.8	10.1
1965	691.1	430.4	113.5	138.4	8.8
1966	756.0	465.1	125.7	158.7	6.5
1967	799.6	490.3	122.8	180.2	6.3
1968	873.4	536.9	133.3	199.0	4.3
1969	944.0	581.8	149.3	208.8	4.2
1970	992.7	621.7	144.2	220.1	6.7
1971	1077.6	672.2	166.4	234.9	4.1
1972	1185.9	737.1	195.0	253.1	.7
1973	1326.4	812.0	229.8	270.4	14.2
1974	1434.2	888.1	228.7	304.1	13.4
1975	1549.2	976.4	206.1	339.9	26.8
1976	1718.0	1084.3	257.9	362.1	13.8
1977	1918.3	1204.4	324.1	393.8	−4.0
1978	2163.9	1346.5	386.6	431.9	−1.1
1979	2417.8	1507.2	423.0	474.4	13.2
1980	2631.7	1668.1	401.9	537.8	23.9
1981	2954.1	1857.2	474.9	595.7	26.3
1982	3073.0	1991.9	414.5	649.2	17.4
1983	3304.8	2155.9	471.6	685.5	−8.3
1984	3661.3	2342.3	637.3	748.0	−66.3

Source: Economic Report of the President, 1985.

2. In such a simple economy, where only consumer goods are produced, GNP and E also equal the value of national income, Y, created. In Table 2.2 the total value added, or the total value of incomes created (in the form of wages, interest, rent, and profit earnings), also equals $60 billion.[7] In such a simple economy,

$$C \equiv \text{GNP} \equiv E \equiv Y \qquad (2.3)$$

3. The value-added method allows national income accountants to avoid double-counting when using the expenditures approach, while still allowing them to count the incomes earned by people producing intermediate goods when using the income approach.

Adding Investment   Consider now an economy that produces two types of final goods: consumption goods and capital goods. At first blush, this should not affect the conclusion that $E \equiv Y$, reached in number 2 above, because when people produce capital goods, they are performing a productive activity, and they also earn income in the form of wages, interest, rent, and profits. A problem does exist, however. If we now make the realistic assumption that consumer goods are often produced with the aid of capital goods, expenditures on final goods and services will now exceed the income generated by their production; or

$$C + I_g \equiv \text{GNP} \equiv E > Y \qquad (2.4)$$

This is true because in the process of producing consumer goods there will be a certain amount of wear and tear—depreciation—on capital

---

[7] This is true because of the way profit is defined. For a national income accounting statistician, profit is a residual; profit is what is left over from total business receipts after wages, interest, and rents have been paid. Profit, therefore, can be positive, zero, or negative.

TABLE 2.2. RELATING PRODUCTION TO INCOME CREATION VIA THE VALUE-ADDED APPROACH (billions of dollars)

Stage of Production	Sales Receipts	− Cost of Intermediate Goods	= Value Added (Wages, Rent, Profits, Interest)
1. Coal extraction	$ 5	$ 0	$ 5
2. Steel production	20	5	15
3. Auto manufacturing	50	20	30
4. Sale by dealer to customer	60	50	10
TOTAL			$60

equipment. This depreciation is subtracted from the income statements of businesses as a business expense. And rightly so; otherwise, profit would be overstated (see footnote 7). Depreciation is not a wage, an interest, a rent, or a profit, and therefore GNP (or total expenditures in this more realistic economy) now exceeds national income.

Which method—the expenditure approach or the income approach— is a better measure of "the market value of all final goods and services currently produced"? Actually, the income approach is better because GNP overstates the value of goods *currently* produced. This is because some of the goods produced in the current period require the use of capital that was produced in a *previous* period. If we subtract from current output the value of capital that is used up during the process of production—depreciation—we get a better measure of current output. For this reason some economists believe that a better measure of the market value of all final goods and services currently produced is **net national product,** or **NNP,** which equals GNP minus an estimate of depreciation (or capital consumption allowances) D. Thus,

$$NNP \equiv GNP - D \tag{2.5}$$

In the simple economy in this section, where only consumer goods and capital goods are produced,

$$C + I_n \equiv NNP \equiv Y \tag{2.6}$$

where $I_n \equiv I_g - D$; that is, net investment equals gross investment minus an estimate of depreciation.

Because NNP is net of depreciation, the economy can continue to produce at that level. While NNP might be a measure that is preferable to GNP, in practice GNP is widely used because depreciation is difficult to estimate and is conceptually different from the depreciation estimates recorded by business firms. The latter reflect tax laws more than the actual wear and tear on capital goods.

Adding Government Activities   Governments complicate our analysis because they not only purchase goods and services (consumer and capital goods), but they tax households and businesses and provide government transfers to households and businesses. Government purchases of goods and services create incomes in the same way that household purchases and business purchases do. Indirect business taxes (which include sales, excise, and business property taxes and tariffs), however, create a discrepancy between the market price and the prices received by producers; GNP (and NNP) is valued at a market price that reflects a sales tax, but the value of the sales tax is not a wage, an interest, a rent, or a profit

TABLE 2.3. RELATING GROSS NATIONAL PRODUCT (GNP) TO NATIONAL INCOME FOR THE UNITED STATES, FIRST QUARTER 1985 (billions of dollars)

Gross national product		$3817.1
Minus		
Capital consumption allowance	$422.5	
Equals		
Net national product		$3394.6
Minus		
Indirect taxes	$318.1	
Other (net)	$ 1.1	
Equals		
National income		$3075.4

Source: *Survey of Current Business*, May 1985

receipt. Again, the value of expenditures exceeds the value of the income generated from production. Table 2.3 shows the relationships among GNP, NNP, indirect business taxes, and *Y* (national income), using actual first-quarter 1985 data for the United States.

National Income and Factor Shares

National income is divided into its individual (pre–income tax) factor shares in Table 2.4, which also uses actual 1985 data for the United States. Note that wages and salaries (compensation to employees) account for 74 percent of national income and that this percentage has remained relatively constant over the past 100 years or so; however, it rises during periods of recession and falls during boom periods. Proprietors' income is income from unincorporated businesses. Rental income

TABLE 2.4. THE ALLOCATION OF NATIONAL INCOME TO FACTOR SHARES FOR THE UNITED STATES, FIRST QUARTER 1985 (billions of dollars)

National income	$3075.4	
Compensation of employees	2272.9	73.90%
Proprietors' income	154.1	5.00
Rental income of persons	64.8	2.10
Corporate profits	294.0	9.58
Net interest	289.6	9.42

Source: *Survey of Current Business*, May 1985

of persons includes income from patents, royalties, and imputed income of owner-occupied buildings. Net interest consists of interest payments by domestic businesses and others to individuals and firms who have lent to them.

National Income and Personal Income

Table 2.5 shows how national income is adjusted to reach personal income. The adjustment requires (1) subtracting earnings from the corporate sector, net interest (net interest paid by businesses to domestic households and net interest from abroad), and contributions for social insurance, and (2) adding net transfer payments received by the personal sector, personal interest income, and personal dividend income.

The Allocation of Disposable Personal Income   In a later chapter we will be concerned with the determinants of household consumption expenditures and household saving. Here we will only point out that not all personal income is available to households for spending and saving. Table 2.6 shows how personal income is adjusted to become personal disposable income and then how personal disposable income is allocated.

Nominal GNP versus Real GNP   To this point we have been concerned only with **nominal GNP,** which measures the market value of all final

TABLE 2.5. DERIVING PERSONAL INCOME FROM NATIONAL INCOME FOR THE UNITED STATES, FIRST QUARTER 1985 (billions of dollars)

National income		$3075.4
Minus		
Corporate profits with inventory valuation	$294.0	
Net interest	$289.6	
Contributions for social insurance	$330.0	
(Other)	$ 0.1	
Plus		
Government transfers to persons	$420.8	
Personal interest income	$458.7	
Personal dividend income	$ 81.4	
Business transfer payments	$ 18.5	
Equals		
Personal income		$3141.1

Source: *Survey of Current Business,* May 1985

TABLE 2.6. DERIVING AND ALLOCATING PERSONAL DISPOSABLE INCOME FOR THE UNITED STATES, FIRST QUARTER 1985 (billions of dollars)

Personal income		$3141.1
Minus		
Personal tax and nontax payments	$ 487.7	
Equals		
Disposable personal income		$2653.4
Minus		
Personal consumption expenditures	$2446.1	
Personal net transfer payments to foreigners	$ 1.2	
Interest paid by consumers to businesses	$ 87.8	
Equals		
Personal saving		$ 118.3

Source: *Survey of Current Business,* May 1985

goods and services produced during the current period—*at the prices prevailing in that period.* Nominal GNP (also referred to as GNP measured in current dollars), however, is not a very good measure of economic performance. Consider a situation in which the output of final goods and services remains constant year after year, but the price level rises. It would appear that the economy is performing admirably because GNP is apparently rising. Yet, in fact, the level of production (by assumption) remains constant. In periods during which the price level is rising, nominal GNP overstates production. Conversely, during the periods of deflation, when the price level falls, nominal GNP understates production. As a rule, we can say:

When inflation occurs, nominal GNP overstates production and national income; when deflation occurs, nominal GNP understates production and national income.

Because we want a true measure of output and national income, and because stabilization policy requires better information than is afforded by nominal GNP, economists have attempted to measure real GNP. **Real GNP** is nominal GNP adjusted for changes in the price level. Clearly, what is required is a definition of inflation and a method of measuring inflation. Such a measure will not only help us to evaluate the economy's performance with respect to the production of goods and services, but the rate of inflation itself is a measure of an economy's performance. This takes us to the next section. (We will return to an analysis of some problems in measuring GNP in the Policy Controversy section at the end of this chapter.)

MEASURING INFLATION

Inflation is a sustained increase in the aggregate price level over time. While there are numerous measures of inflation, we will confine ourselves to a brief discussion of two: the implicit GNP price deflator and the Consumer Price Index (CPI).

The Implicit GNP Price Deflator

In the previous section we said that nominal GNP measures the value of output in current dollars. For example, nominal GNP in 1985 measures the value of all final goods and services produced in the United States during 1985 at the prices that prevailed in 1985; nominal GNP in 1980 measures the value of all final goods and services produced in 1980 valued at the prices that prevailed in 1980, and so on.

Real GNP (or constant-dollar GNP) measures changes in physical output through time by valuing the goods and services produced in each period by using the prices that existed in some arbitrarily chosen base year. The year 1972 is currently used as the base year; thus, real GNP in 1984 is a measure of the value of the output of 1984 evaluated in terms of the prices that prevailed in 1972. In equation form, 1984 nominal GNP can be written as follows:

$$\text{GNP}_{1984} = P_{1984}Q_{1984} \tag{2.7}$$

where P_{1984} equals the price level in 1984 and Q_{1984} represents the quantity of final goods and services in 1984.[8] Real GNP[9] in 1984 can be written, in equation form, as follows:

$$\text{gnp}_{1984} = P_{1972}Q_{1984} \tag{2.8}$$

---

[8] $PQ = P_1q_1 + P_2q_2 + \cdots + P_nq_n$, where P_1 represents the price of good number one, P_2 represents the price of good number two, and so on. q_1 represents the quantity of good number one, q_2 represents the quantity of good number two, q_n represents the quantity of the nth good. Note that p_1q_1 represents the value of expenditures on good number one.

[9] Hereafter, we will let lowercase letters represent real variables and capital letters represent nominal values.

TABLE 2.7. NOMINAL GNP, REAL GNP, AND THE GNP PRICE DEFLATOR, 1970–1984 (billions of dollars)

Year	Nominal GNP	Real GNP (1972 dollars)	GNP Implicit Price Deflator
1970	992.7	1085.6	91.45
1971	1077.6	1122.4	96.01
1972	1185.9	1185.9	100.00
1973	1326.4	1254.3	105.75
1974	1434.2	1246.3	115.08
1975	1549.2	1231.6	125.79
1976	1718.0	1298.2	132.34
1977	1918.3	1369.7	140.05
1978	2163.9	1438.6	150.42
1979	2417.8	1479.4	163.42
1980	2631.7	1475.0	178.42
1981	2957.8	1512.2	195.60
1982	3069.3	1480.0	207.38
1983	3304.8	1534.7	215.34
1984	3661.3	1639.0	223.38

Source: *Economic Report of the President,* 1985.

The **implicit GNP price deflator** equals nominal GNP divided by real GNP[10] multiplied by 100 (to remove the decimal). Thus, the implicit GNP price deflator in 1984 equals

$$\frac{\text{GNP}_{1984}}{\text{gnp}_{1984}} = \frac{P_{1984}Q_{1984}}{P_{1972}Q_{1984}} \times 100$$

Table 2.7 shows nominal GNP, real GNP, and the price deflator for the U.S. economy for the years 1970 to 1984.

Note that the price deflator is indeed a measure of inflation because it gives an indication of the amount by which prices have changed since the base year.[11] Table 2.7 shows that in 1975 the implicit GNP deflator was 125.79; this means that, on average, prices increased 25.79 percent from 1972 to 1975. The annual rate of inflation during the period 1974

---

[10] Actually, the GNP price deflator is derived by constructing price deflators for individual components of GNP, "in as fine a breakdown as practicable," and weighting the sum of these component deflators based on their relative share of GNP. Thus, the GNP deflator is derived *first* and real GNP is then derived. See the 1979 *Statistical Supplement to the Survey of Current Business.*

[11] If the implicit GNP price deflator for 1985 equals

$$\frac{\text{GNP}_{1985}}{\text{gnp}_{1985}} = \frac{P_{1985}Q_{1985}}{P_{1972}Q_{1985}} \times 100$$

can you see why the 1972 implicit deflator is the number 100?

to 1975 was 9.3 percent $[0.093 = (125.79 - 115.08)/115.08$, or $(125.79/115.08) - 1]$; each of these is multiplied times 100 to remove the decimal.

The Consumer Price Index

Recall that the GNP price deflator is a measure of the increase of the prices of all final goods and services through time. The concern *here*, however, is only with a specific subset of all prices: consumer prices. The **Consumer Price Index (CPI)** is an index of the prices of a fixed market basket of goods and services in 85 urban areas. The data are collected by personal surveys of about 18,000 tenants, 18,000 housing units, and about 24,000 business establishments. The index is a representation of the prices of goods that are typically purchased by "representative" (urban working-class) families. Because some goods and services are more important than others, in the sense that they require a higher percentage of the budget outlays of representative people, this index (as is the GNP price deflator) is a weighted average. The CPI includes indirect taxes (sales, excise, and so on) but does not include income taxes or Social Security taxes. In effect, the CPI measures the cost through time of a *given basket of goods and services.* It equals the ratio of a base-year market basket valued at current-year prices to the base-year market basket valued at base-year prices—times 100 to remove the decimal.

Of course, the goods purchased in the "representative basket" change through time. For example, for a number of years the CPI representative basket was based on a 1960-to-1961 survey of consumer purchases. More recently, the representative basket has been changed to represent the results of a 1972-to-1973 survey of consumer purchases. The Bureau of Labor Statistics has continued to publish an Index for Urban Wage Earners and Clerical Workers, who represent approximately 40 percent of the total noninstitutional (not living in mental institutions or jails) civilian U.S. population. In addition, an Index for All Urban Consumers is published, which reflects the purchasing habits (representative bundle of goods and services) of some 80 percent of the total noninstitutional civilian population.

The CPI and the implicit GNP price deflator differ in three important ways:

1. The implicit GNP price deflator measures price changes in a much wider basket of goods and services; the CPI basket includes only goods consumed by a typical urban consumer, while the GNP deflator basket includes investment goods and publicly (government) provided goods as well.

2. The basket of goods included in the implicit GNP price deflator changes annually, whereas the basket of goods included in the CPI is unchanged—except for infrequent, periodic changes.

3. The implicit GNP price deflator excludes imported goods because it measures the value of *domestically* produced goods; the CPI includes imported goods in its basket.

Problems with Measuring Inflation

Inflation is not easy to measure. Both the implicit GNP deflator and the CPI implicitly assume that the relative importance (weights) and quality of the goods and services that are being measured remain constant during the measurement period.

The implicit GNP deflator is a weighted average of price indices devised for the various components of GNP. If, say, the relative share of government purchases of goods and services rises, then eventually this component's prices will be given a higher weight; in the meantime, the old weights will give an inaccurate estimate of inflation. Similarly, if household tastes change, then *eventually* the relative weights of individual goods in the CPI will change; but in the meantime inflation will be measured inaccurately.[12]

Another problem common to the implicit GNP deflator and the CPI lies in determining how to treat changes in the quality of goods. Although "a rose is a rose is a rose," the quality of durable goods seldom remains constant. For example, manual typewriters have evolved into electric typewriters and now into word processors. Surely some of the higher price of modern "typewriters" should be attributed to better quality; if that is the case, the implicit GNP price deflator overstates inflation. Even though economists now are attempting to measure quality (in automobiles, for example), this is a recent advance, and quality changes are not measured for all goods.

At times the quality change for a good that performs some function is so great as to amount to a change in the product. Are color TVs the same as black-and-white TVs? Indeed, was black-and-white TV the same "good" as radio? This is a particularly difficult problem for the CPI measure, which estimates the cost of an *unchanging* basket of goods and services through time. Although the "representative" basket *is changed* on occasion to reflect these new goods, the problem exists in the meantime. Moreover, by adding new products, a new problem emerges: How

---

[12] Roughly every 10 years or so the U.S. Bureau of Labor Statistics conducts a survey of consumer expenditures from which it gains information as to the proper weights to use for individual goods. In general, the higher the percentage of income spent on a good, the higher its relative weight.

do we compare price index numbers over *long* periods of time when the representative basket itself is changing?

MEASURING UNEMPLOYMENT

It may seem cut-and-dried to decide whether or not someone is employed or unemployed, but the measurement of unemployment is at least as difficult as the measurement of GNP and the measurement of inflation.

Statistics on the employment status of the population, the personal, occupational, and other characteristics of the employed, of the unemployed, and of persons not in the labor force, and related data are gathered for the Bureau of Labor Statistics (BLS) by the Bureau of the Census in its Current Population Survey.[13] Monthly surveys of the population are conducted by using a sample designed to represent the civilian noninstitutional population aged 16 and over.[14] The monthly survey solicits information related to activity or status during the calendar week, Sunday through Saturday, that includes the twelfth day of each month. This period is referred to as the *survey week*. Data on the members of the Armed Forces stationed in the United States are obtained from the Department of Defense.

Definitions

The following definitions are taken verbatim from the May 1984 issue of *Employment of Earnings*, U.S. Department of Labor, Bureau of Labor Statistics, pages 160–161.

> *Employed persons* are (*a*) all civilians who, during the survey week, did any work at all as paid employees, in their own business, profession, or on their own farm, or who worked 15 hours or more as unpaid workers in an enterprise operated by a member of the family; and (*b*) all those who were not working but who had jobs or businesses from which they were temporarily absent because of illness, bad weather, vacation, labor-management disputes, or personal reasons, whether they were paid for the time off or were seeking other jobs. Members of the Armed Forces stationed in the United States are also included in the employed total.
>
> Each employed person is counted only once. Those who held more than one job are counted in the job at which they worked the greatest number of hours during the survey week.
>
> Included in the total are employed citizens of foreign countries who are

---

[13] A detailed description of this survey appears in *Concepts and Methods Used in Labor Force Statistics Derived from the Current Population Survey*, Bureau of Labor Statistics, report no. 463.

[14] Data are also collected separately for 14 and 15 year olds.

temporarily in the United States but not living on the premises of an embassy. Excluded are persons whose only activity consisted of work around the house (painting, repairing, or own home housework) or volunteer work for religious, charitable, and similar organizations.

Unemployed persons are all civilians who had no employment during the survey week, were available for work, except for temporary illness, and (a) had made specific efforts to find employment sometime during the prior 4 weeks, or (b) were waiting to be recalled to a job from which they had been laid off, or (c) were waiting to report to a new job within 30 days.

The *civilian labor force* comprises all civilians classified as employed or unemployed in accordance with the criteria described above. The "labor force" also includes members of the Armed Forces stationed in the United States.

The *overall unemployment rate* represents the number unemployed as a percent of the labor force, including members of the Armed Forces stationed in the United States.

The *unemployment rate for all civilian workers* represents the number unemployed as a percent of the civilian labor force. This measure can also be computed for groups within the labor force classified by sex, age, race, ethnic origin, marital status, etc.

Not in the labor force includes all persons who are not classified as employed or unemployed. These persons are further classified as engaged in own home housework, in school, unable to work because of long-term physical or mental illness, retired, and other. The "other" group includes individuals reported as too old or temporarily unable to work, the voluntarily idle, seasonal workers for whom the survey week fell in an off season and who were not reported as looking for work, and persons who did not look for work because they believed that no jobs were available in the area or that no jobs were available for which they could qualify—*discouraged workers*. Persons doing only incidental, unpaid family work (less than 15 hours in the specified week) are also classified as not in the labor force.

As should be clear from reading these definitions, it is not an easy task to categorize someone's employment status.

Calculations

Consider Table 2.8, which shows how the (seasonally adjusted) unemployment rate was calculated for April of 1984. Start with a noninstitutional population of 177.662 million aged 16 and over and subtract from it the 62.724 million not in the labor force. This leaves a total labor force of 114.938 million. Subtracting 8.843 million unemployed gives a total employed figure of 106.095 million. Subtracting the 1.693 million resident Armed Forces gives a total civilian employment future of 104.402 million. The overall unemployment rate is 7.7 percent, and the unemployment rate for all civilian workers is 7.8 percent (8.843/113.245). Table 2.9 shows these data for the years 1951 to 1983.

TABLE 2.8. EMPLOYMENT STATUS OF THE NONINSTITUTIONAL POPULATION 16 YEARS AND OVER, APRIL 1984, SEASONALLY ADJUSTED (millions)

Noninstitutional population	117.662
Less Not in the labor force	62.724
Equals Total labor force	114.938
Less Unemployed	8.843
Equals Total employed	106.095
Less Resident Armed Forces	1.693
Equals Total civilian employment	104.402
Overall unemployment rate	7.7%
Unemployment rate for all civilian workers	7.8%

Source: *Employment and Earnings*, U.S. Department of Labor, Bureau of Labor Statistics, May 1984, p. 11.

Problems with Measuring Unemployment

As indicated earlier, it is a very tricky business to define employment and unemployment. Critics of the current method of measuring unemployment fall into two basic categories—those who believe that the present method overstates true unemployment and those who believe that the present method understates true unemployment.[15]

Those who think that the current method *overstates* unemployment point out that there are probably hundreds of thousands (maybe even millions) of people who are working in the underground economy and who are either categorized as "not in the labor force" or even as "unemployed persons." Equally important is the large number of homemakers who are unquestionably performing productive activities but who are classified as "not in the labor force."

There are also some economists who maintain that the unemployment rate, even if it were adjusted to account for household services and for those working in the underground economy, would still overstate the degree of suffering and hardship associated with unemployment because the overall unemployment rate does not indicate the extent to which at

---

[15] There are doubtless some nonideologically motivated economists who are not yet sure. We just don't know any such economists.

TABLE 2.9. EMPLOYMENT STATUS OF THE NONINSTITUTIONAL POPULATION 16 YEARS AND OVER, 1951 TO 1983 (thousands)

Year and Month	Noninstitutional Population Number	Percent of Population	LABOR FORCE Total	Resident Armed Forces	EMPLOYED Total	CIVILIAN Agriculture	Nonagricultural Industries	UNEMPLOYED Number	Percent of Labor Force	Not in Labor Force
Annual Averages										
1951 . . .	106,764	60.1	62,104	2,143	59,961	6,726	53,235	2,055	3.2	42,604
1952 . . .	107,617	60.0	62,636	2,386	60,250	6,500	53,749	1,883	2.9	43,093
1953a . .	109,287	59.7	63,410	2,231	61,179	6,260	54,919	1,834	2.8	44,041
1954 . . .	110,463	59.6	62,251	2,142	60,109	6,205	53,904	3,532	5.4	44,678
1955 . . .	111,747	60.0	64,234	2,064	62,170	6,450	55,722	2,852	4.3	44,660
1956 . . .	112,919	60.7	65,764	1,965	63,799	6,283	57,514	2,750	4.0	44,402
1957 . . .	114,213	60.3	66,019	1,948	64,071	5,947	58,123	2,859	4.2	45,336
1958 . . .	115,574	60.1	64,883	1,847	63,036	5,586	57,450	4,602	6.6	46,088
1959 . . .	117,117	59.9	66,418	1,788	64,630	5,565	59,065	3,740	5.3	46,960
1960* . . .	119,106	60.0	67,639	1,861	65,778	5,458	60,318	3,852	5.4	47,617
1961 . . .	120,671	60.0	67,646	1,900	65,746	5,200	60,546	4,714	6.5	48,312
1962* . . .	122,214	59.5	68,763	2,061	66,702	4,944	61,759	3,911	5.4	49,539
1963 . . .	124,422	59.3	69,768	2,006	67,762	4,687	63,076	4,070	5.5	50,583
1964 . . .	126,503	59.4	71,323	2,018	69,305	4,523	64,782	3,786	5.0	51,394
1965 . . .	128,459	59.5	73,034	1,946	71,088	4,361	66,726	3,366	4.4	52,058
1966 . . .	130,180	59.8	75,017	2,122	72,895	3,979	68,915	2,875	3.7	52,288
1967 . . .	132,092	60.2	76,590	2,218	74,372	3,844	70,527	2,975	3.7	52,527
1968 . . .	134,281	60.3	78,173	2,253	75,920	3,817	72,103	2,817	3.5	53,291
1969 . . .	136,573	60.8	80,140	2,238	77,902	3,606	74,296	2,823	3.4	53,602

(continued)

TABLE 2.9. (Continued)

Year and Month	Noninstitutional Population	Labor Force		Employed		Civilian			Unemployed		Not in Labor Force
	Number	Number	Percent of Population	Total	Resident Armed Forces	Total	Agriculture	Nonagricultural Industries	Number	Percent of Labor Force	
						Annual Averages					
1970	139,203	84,889	61.0	80,796	2,118	78,678	3,463	75,215	4,093	4.8	54,315
1971	142,189	86,355	60.7	81,340	1,973	79,367	3,394	75,972	5,016	5.8	55,834
1972*	145,939	88,847	60.9	83,966	1,813	82,153	3,484	78,669	4,882	5.5	57,091
1973*	148,870	91,203	61.3	86,838	1,774	85,064	3,470	81,594	4,365	4.8	57,667
1974	151,841	93,670	61.7	88,515	1,721	86,794	3,515	83,279	5,156	5.5	58,171
1975	154,831	95,453	61.6	87,524	1,678	85,846	3,408	82,438	7,929	8.3	59,377
1976	157,818	97,826	62.0	90,420	1,668	88,752	3,331	85,421	7,406	7.6	59,991
1977	160,689	100,665	62.6	93,673	1,656	92,017	3,283	88,734	6,991	6.9	60,025
1978*	163,541	103,882	63.5	97,679	1,631	96,048	3,387	92,661	6,202	6.0	59,659
1979	166,460	106,559	64.0	100,421	1,597	98,824	3,347	95,477	6,137	5.8	59,900
1980	169,349	108,544	64.1	100,907	1,604	99,303	3,364	95,938	7,637	7.0	60,806
1981	171,775	110,315	64.2	102,042	1,645	100,397	3,368	97,030	8,273	7.5	61,460
1982	173,939	111,872	64.3	101,194	1,668	99,526	3,401	96,125	10,678	9.5	62,067
1983	175,891	113,226	64.4	102,510	1,676	100,834	3,383	97,450	10,717	9.5	62,665

[a] Not strictly comparable with prior years.

Source: *Employment and Earnings,* U.S. Department of Labor, Bureau of Labor Statistics, May 1984.

least *one* member in the household is working. While it is unfortunate that a teenager, say, is unemployed, this person may be part of a family in which both parents (and a teenage sibling) are working. In fact, there are *many* unemployment rates; there is an unemployment rate for heads of households, one for teenagers, one for men, one for women, and so on. The overall unemployment rate (and the civilian labor force unemployment rate) obscures this fact. There is a tendency to think of all the unemployed as being heads of households.

Perhaps more important is the fact that *most of the unemployed will eventually find jobs.* When someone loses a job, he or she does not usually accept the first offer or immediately find employment at a job that pays a considerably lower wage. Instead, the unemployed person embarks on a *job search*, which takes time. As a consequence, there will always be a changing portion of the labor force that is in the **frictional unemployment** category, or between steady jobs. We analyze the job search model in more detail in Chapter 14. Now it will suffice to say that a large number of the measured unemployed may well be *voluntarily* unemployed; hence, measured unemployment is a poor measure of involuntary unemployment.

On the other hand, there are those who maintain that the present method of measuring unemployment *underestimates* both the amount of true unemployment and the degree of suffering and hardship attendant upon being unemployed. These people point out that discouraged workers (there may be millions of them when the economy is in a slump) are not counted as unemployed, but they should be. These economists also (correctly) note that losing a job is one of the most serious tragedies that can befall a person and his or her family, and that cold unemployment statistics cannot possibly do justice to the trauma associated with first losing a job and then being unable to find another one.

POLICY CONTROVERSY
Are Our Measures of GNP, Inflation, and Unemployment Good Enough to Justify Stabilization Policy?

When real GNP is not rising rapidly enough, or when the inflation rate is too high, or when the unemployment rate is deemed excessive, the government pursues a stabilization policy. At a minimum, our measures of these macroeconomic variables should be valid. But are we *truly* measuring real GNP, inflation, and unemployment? What if real GNP is rising but the community's economic welfare (well-being) is falling? Suppose real GNP is falling or remaining constant and economic welfare is rising? In such circumstances, stabilization policy that attempts to increase real GNP may well decrease economic welfare! Or suppose our measures overstate the amount of unemployment and the degree of suffering associated with it. A stabilization policy that tries to reduce the amount of measured unemployment may well create more unemployment or more inflation. Suppose our measures exaggerate the rate of inflation and . . . well, you get the picture. Unless our measures are valid, we may well be caught up in a fetish of pursuing a policy that causes numbers and indices to behave nicely while the world around us crumbles. Let's be more specific.

Does Real GNP Measure Output Accurately?

GNP may not even be a valid measure of output. After all, the rule that goods and services must be sold on the market eliminates from measurement a considerable amount of production. Homemakers' services, do-it-yourself activities around the home, and the underground economy (where earnings from otherwise legal activities are not reported to the Internal Revenue Service) slip through the GNP measurement net. Thus, GNP dramatically understates output.[16]

Another GNP accounting rule is that only *final* goods should be counted. Yet many government purchases of goods and services might be considered intermediate goods. For example, government expenditures on national defense, an internal police force, and jails may be thought of as expenditures on intermediate goods that are useful only to protect assets and to permit others to produce goods and services. If this is so, then GNP overstates production and economic welfare.

Does Real GNP Measure Welfare Accurately?

Suppose a technological breakthrough in production occurs and permits the nation to produce the same quantity of goods by using less labor time. In effect, more *leisure* will be available: people can spend less time working on jobs or working around the house and more time having fun or contemplating nature. Community welfare will rise, but GNP will remain constant. The fact is that in the United States the average work week has fallen dramatically over the past 100 years and leisure has increased. Real GNP, therefore, dramatically understates community welfare.

On the other hand, suppose output rises by $10 billion but it is accompanied by a significant amount of pollution that causes health problems or reduces recreational activities (fishing, boating, and swimming, for example, are no longer enjoyable in polluted lakes and rivers). Real GNP will rise, but community output may have fallen; at the very minimum, real GNP will overstate national economic welfare.

Of course, by ignoring *production* in the underground economy or around the house, real GNP also understates community economic *welfare*.

Another serious problem is that real GNP may be rising, and even welfare may be rising for many; but what about those people whose economic lot is unchanged or worsening through time? Suppose that real GNP rises for fairly long periods but

---

[16] The underground economy has been estimated at anywhere between 3 and 25 percent of GNP. That is quite a range, we must admit, but underground activities by definition are difficult to measure. See Carol S. Carson, "The Underground Economy: An Introduction," in *Survey of Current Business*, U.S. Department of Commerce, Bureau of Economic Analysis, May 1984, pp. 21–37, and July 1984, pp. 106–119.

that many living in ghettos or places such as Appalachia are unaffected (or adversely affected) during this period of general improvement in living standards? Can we really say that the *community's* welfare has increased?

Finally, consider the case in which a nation experiences a mild winter and a mild summer during a one-year period. In the next year, an extremely cold winter and a sizzling summer occur. Now, either GNP will rise (if people spend more on energy to remain equally comfortable and spend the same amounts on other goods and services) or remain constant (if they spend more on energy but less on other goods and services). But economic *welfare* will surely fall, if only because more of the nation's natural resource wealth must be used. Reflect a moment on the fact that, although national disasters or "acts of God" may occur, our measure of GNP would still be rising. One sometimes wonders if GNP is even remotely related to national welfare.

Some have suggested that even though our measure of real GNP may be biased, the bias may be constant through time, and the *changes* in real GNP will therefore provide accurate information. This may be true. Still, it must be admitted that the degree of leisure has not remained constant through time; it has increased. Moreover, the *value* of leisure has probably risen because of the availa-

bility of better and cheaper transportation and recreational equipment. Also, the size of the underground economy and the quantity of do-it-yourself activities have surely increased over time as inflation has pushed many people into higher marginal tax brackets. Then too, the amount of crime has increased over time (except in recent years, when it has declined); people are spending more money on safety and anticrime devices, which may cause GNP to rise and welfare to remain constant or fall.

Other Problems

We know now that GNP is a very imprecise measure of both output and welfare. After nominal GNP is derived, this figure is then divided by a price index. In a previous section we indicated some of the problems associated with measuring inflation. Thus, real GNP is calculated by dividing a price index—a number that we are not too sure about—into nominal GNP—a number in which we have even less faith. Now, it is possible that the errors may cancel each other; but then again, they may not. And yet when this number called real GNP is not rising at a rate deemed sufficient, we engage in stabilization policy.[17]

---

[17] We will analyze the conceptual problem of combatting measured unemployment by stabilization policy in Chapter 14.

CHAPTER SUMMARY

1. Macroeconomics is concerned with the analysis of economic aggregates and their interrelationships.
2. An economy's performance may be measured by its real GNP, its inflation rate, and its unemployment rate.

3. When an economy is not performing well, governments engage in stabilization policy and use monetary policy, fiscal policy, and other miscellaneous policies.
4. Considerable disagreement exists among economists concerning macroeconomic analysis and stabilization policy. There is less disagreement among economists with respect to purely scientific propositions than with ideological propositions, however.
5. GNP can be broken down into the following aggregates: consumption, investment, government purchases of goods and services, and net exports.
6. Real GNP, adjusted for depreciation, is a measure of an economy's output in the current period; real national income is a measure of an economy's income generated from production. Aggregate expenditures are related to national output and national income.
7. Real GNP is nominal GNP adjusted for changes in the price level.
8. Two measures of inflation are the implicit GNP price deflator and the CPI. Each is an imperfect measure of inflation.
9. Unemployment, employment, the labor force, and the unemployment rate are, in practice, very difficult to measure. The measured unemployment rate is an imperfect measure of involuntary unemployment.
10. Because GNP, unemployment, and inflation are difficult to measure, ideology can and does creep into the analysis and into the formation of policy.
11. If the measures of economic performance are invalid, stabilization policy may be a snare and a delusion.

GLOSSARY

Consumer Price Index (CPI) A measure of inflation that measures the cost of purchasing a representative basket of consumer goods and services through time.

fiscal policy Changes in government expenditures and tax rates in order to achieve national economic goals.

frictional unemployment The temporary unemployment of persons in the labor force who are between steady jobs.

gross national product (GNP) The market value of all final goods and services currently produced between two periods.

implicit GNP price deflator A broad measure of inflation that is a weighted average of price deflators of the major GNP components; nominal GNP divided by real GNP.

inflation A sustained increase in the aggregate price level through time.

macroeconomics The study of economic aggregates and their interrelationships.

monetary policy   Control over the money supply by the monetary authorities in order to achieve national economic goals.

net national product (NNP)   Gross national product minus depreciation.

nominal GNP   The market value of all final goods and services currently produced per year, measured in the prices of the current period; GNP not adjusted for price level changes.

overall unemployment rate   The ratio of unemployed persons to the labor force (the sum of the unemployed, the civilian employed, and the resident Armed Forces personnel).

policy instruments   Elements of such tools as fiscal policy and monetary policy, such as the personal tax rate or the money supply, that are used to achieve national economic goals.

real GNP   Nominal GNP adjusted for changes in the price level; the annual market value of all final goods and services currently produced but measured in the prices that existed in an arbitrarily selected base year.

stabilization policy   Governmental activities that attempt to achieve such national economic goals as full employment, economic growth, price stability, and balance-of-payments equilibrium.

transfer payments   Money receipts that are not accompanied by the production of a good or service.

value added   The market value of a firm's output minus the cost of the inputs it purchased from other firms.

QUESTIONS AND PROBLEMS FOR REVIEW

2.1   The CPI measures the cost of an unchanging, representative basket of goods and services through time. Suppose the following occur: (a) inflation, (b) an increase in the relative price of energy, and (c) a decrease in the relative price of food. What does the law of demand predict concerning household purchases of food and energy? If households respond predictably, will the CPI overstate or understate the hardships associated with increases in the overall price level?

2.2   Suppose that quality improvements occur in both automobiles and office equipment, but that the implicit GNP price deflator is adjusted only for improvements in the quality of automobiles. Other things constant, will the GNP price deflator reflect true inflation or an inconsistent measurement technique? Why?

2.3   Suppose that an economic slump occurs and that (a) many minorities stop looking for jobs because they know that the probability of finding a job is low, and (b) many people who become laid off start doing such work at home as growing food, painting and repairing their houses and their autos, and so on. Which of these events implies that the official unemployment rate overstates unemployment, and which implies the opposite?

2.4   What happens to the official measure of GNP if
      a. A man marries his maid?

b. An addict marries her supplier?

c. Homemakers perform the same jobs but switch houses and charge each other for their services?

What happens to economic welfare in each of these cases?

2.5 Consider country A and country B. Suppose that both countries have an *average* temperature of 70 degrees. In country A the temperature never falls below 69 degrees or rises above 71 degrees; in country B the temperature seldom rises above 30 degrees in the winter and seldom falls below 110 degrees in the summer. Other things constant, which country will have a higher GNP? In which country will community *welfare* be higher?

2.6 Using Table 2.1, calculate the percentage of GNP contributed by each of its four components for the year 1929 and every third year thereafter. Construct a table containing that information. Have there been any significant changes or trends?

2.7 Consider the following table for an economy that produces only four goods:

Goods and Services	1972 Price	1972 Quantity	1985 Price	1985 Quantity
Pizza	$ 4	10	$ 8	12
Cola	12	20	36	15
T-shirts	6	5	10	15
Business equipment	25	10	30	12
GNP				

Assuming a 1972 base year:

a. What is nominal GNP for 1972 and for 1985?

b. What is real GNP for 1972? For 1985?

c. What is the implicit GNP price deflator for 1972? For 1985?

d. What is the CPI for 1972? For 1985?

2.8 Construct a value-added table for various stages in the production and sale of bread.

REFERENCES

Business Conditions Digest, a monthly publication of the U.S. Department of Commerce, Bureau of Economic Analysis.

Carol S. Carson, "The Underground Economy: An Introduction," in *Survey of Current Business*, U.S. Department of Commerce, Bureau of Economic Analysis, May 1984, pp. 21–37, and July 1984, pp. 106–117.

Economic Report of the President, annual publication of the Council of Economic Advisors.

Employment and Earnings, a monthly publication of the U.S. Department of Labor, Bureau of Labor Statistics.

John W. Kendrick, *Economic Accounts and Their Uses* (New York: McGraw-Hill, 1960).

Richard Ruggles and Nancy O. Ruggles, *The Design of Economic Accounts* (New York: National Bureau of Economic Research, 1970).

Survey of Current Business, a monthly publication of the U.S. Department of Commerce, Bureau of Economic Analysis.

3

GNP, INFLATION, AND UNEMPLOYMENT

A PRELIMINARY INVESTIGATION

C hapter 2 was concerned with measuring the three indicators of macroeconomic performance: real GNP, the rate of inflation, and the unemployment rate. That chapter defined each of these important aggregates and indicated that there are problems in measuring them, which in turn lead to problems in developing a stabilization policy.

In this chapter, we will show how these three indicators of macroeconomic performance are interrelated. We want to stress right from the beginning, however, that this is just a preliminary investigation. Indeed, one of the most important events in recent economic history was the appearance of empirical evidence (soon followed by theoretical justification) indicating that the relationships derived in this chapter are, occasionally, *reversed*. But that is getting ahead of our story. For now, let's concentrate on a reasonable explanation of how real GNP, the rate of inflation, and the unemployment rate are likely to move in response to economic events.

THE NATURAL RATE OF GROWTH OF REAL GNP

Various studies show that in the United States, between 1889 and 1985, real GNP grew at an average annual rate of approximately 3 percent. We can call this long-run secular trend rate the **natural growth rate.** To be sure, this growth rate was very uneven: sometimes the economy grew more rapidly than 3 percent per annum, sometimes less rapidly. At times it even grew negatively (i.e., real GNP declined). The deviations of real GNP (gnp) from its trend are very important, and most of this chapter will deal with them; in fact, most of this text is concerned with theories of how and why the economy veers from the path generated by the natural growth rate.

Graphing the Natural Growth Rate

Figure 3.1 depicts a natural growth rate similar to that of the United States, but it does not show the deviations from the trend. Notice that the growth curve increases at an increasing rate because gnp is growing exponentially, at a rate of 3 percent per annum.

Figure 3.2 shows the natural growth rate in a more convenient form. By using a ratio (or log) scale on the vertical axis, a constant growth rate is represented by a straight line.[1]

---

[1] Along a ratio scale, equal *percentage* changes cover the same distance. For example, the vertical axis can be so graduated that a doubling of the value on that axis is always equivalent to, say, 1 inch. Of course a curve with a greater growth rate will have a greater slope.

The Natural Rate of Growth of Real GNP Is an Exponential Growth Curve

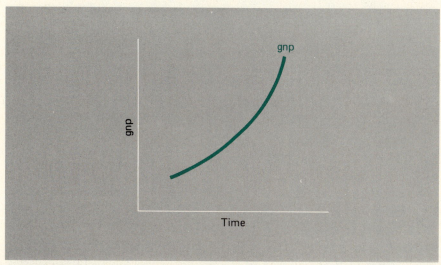

FIGURE 3.1. THE NATURAL RATE OF GROWTH OF REAL GNP
Real GNP (gnp) increases secularly at a constant annual percentage rate. In the United States this rate seems to be slightly over 3 percent per year, although that rate apparently has been falling in recent years.

Determinants of the Natural Growth Rate

Different countries apparently have different natural growth rates. For example, Japan, Singapore, and Hong Kong have natural growth rates that exceed that of the United States, while China and India seem to have negligible growth rates (when real growth rate is adjusted for population changes). It is also possible that the natural growth rate can change *within* a given country. Some people fear that the natural growth rate has fallen in the United States because actual growth has been at a rate considerably below trend since 1973. (Chapter 19 analyzes this slowdown in the growth rate in the United States.)

While there are many potential determinants of a country's natural growth rate, the main determinants seem to be population growth, technological improvements, the percentage of gnp allocated to investment, and the degree of economic incentive.

Population Growth   In the United States the annual rate of population

The Natural Rate of Growth Is Linear on a Ratio Scale

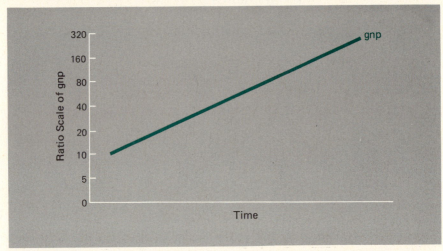

FIGURE 3.2. THE NATURAL RATE OF GROWTH OF REAL GNP
When Figure 3.1 is plotted on a ratio scale, the natural rate of growth curve is linear. The greater the growth rate, the steeper the curve.

growth from 1889 to 1985 has been approximately equal to 1.4 percent.[2] Other things constant, the greater the rate of population growth, the greater is the natural growth rate. In the United States, population increases because the number of births exceeds the number of deaths and because immigration to the United States exceeds emigration from it.

Technological Improvements Improvements in technology allow a nation to produce goods more efficiently and to reduce waste; other things constant, technological changes permit a nation to produce more final consumer goods (and/or more capital goods) from the same resources.

Technological improvements help to increase productivity; the **productivity of labor** is derived by calculating the ratio of output to the number of hours worked. Advances in technology help to increase labor's productivity per unit of time; so does labor education and training. A

---

[2] Real *per capita* annual GNP growth, therefore, has been approximately 1.6 percent. This is derived (roughly) by subtracting the annual growth in population from the annual growth of gnp. Actually, because gnp has grown by slightly more than 3 percent per year, annual real GNP per capita slightly exceeds 1.6 percent. These numbers can be derived from data in *Long-Term Economic Growth, 1860–1970*, U.S. Department of Commerce, 1973, and from the latest edition of the annual *Economic Report of the President*.

nation that devotes more resources to practical and pure research and to educating and training laborers will attain a higher growth rate (other things constant) than one that devotes fewer resources to these ends.

Percentage of gnp Allocated to Investment When a nation produces more capital goods, labor's productivity also increases. This occurs because labor can produce more with a larger quantity of machinery and because new technology is often embodied in new capital goods. A nation can increase its ratio of investment to gnp only by reducing the share of gnp allocated to the other gnp components. For example, if households decide to reduce their consumption purchases now—in order to earn interest and consume more in the future—resources will be released from the production of consumer goods and will be available for the production of investment, or capital goods. (The aggregate household decision, concerning how much income to allocate to saving, and the business investment decision are discussed in Chapters 4 and 6.)

Economic Incentives To this point we have not said much about how people respond to economic incentives. Many economists believe that most people respond to economic incentives in a predictable way. If households have incentives to save and businesses have incentives to invest, then an economy will grow; if laborers have an incentive to work (and work overtime) and develop their skills, then an economy will grow; if there are incentives to innovate and to take economic risks, such activities will be forthcoming. In short, the greater the economic incentives, the higher the natural growth rate of a nation. In Chapter 19 we analyze *supply-side economics*, a doctrine based precisely on these tenets.

THE NATURAL RATE OF UNEMPLOYMENT

The **natural rate of unemployment** is that unemployment rate to which the economy eventually returns after equilibrium is restored. It depends on the amount of frictional unemployment, price-wage rigidity, labor market rigidity, work incentives, and the composition of the labor force. In Chapter 14, we show that the natural rate of unemployment can also be thought of as the unemployment rate that exists when the inflation rate is correctly anticipated by economic agents.

Frictional Unemployment

At any moment in time there will be some small fraction of the labor force (2 to 3 percent) that is between jobs, or frictionally unemployed. People quit one job and need time to find a better one; others are laid off from one job and search for another. As long as the *individuals* who are frictionally unemployed change, a constant percentage of the labor force that is frictionally unemployed will cause no undue harm.

If frictional unemployment were the only reason for unemployment, the natural rate of unemployment would equal the percentage of the labor force that is frictionally unemployed. As we show later in the text, at times the frictionally unemployed would accept jobs sooner than normal; at other times the frictionally unemployed would remain unemployed for longer periods. Another way to state this is to note that events can occur that cause the average duration of unemployment to deviate from its normal length of time. If the average duration of unemployment were one month, then at various times the average duration of unemployment could be below one month or above one month and cause the actual unemployment rate to fall or to rise, respectively, above the natural rate of unemployment.

The natural level of real GNP is uniquely related to the natural rate of unemployment. The lower the natural rate of unemployment, the higher the natural level of real GNP, other things constant. For example, if labor market information were transmitted much more quickly in country A than in country B, then, other things constant, the average duration of unemployment and the natural rate of unemployment will be lower in country A; moreover, A's actual real GNP will be closer to its natural level of real GNP than will B's.

Determinants of the Natural Rate of Unemployment

Other potential determinants of the natural rate of unemployment are price-wage rigidities, labor market rigidities, and the strength of incentives to work.

Price-Wage Rigidities You may recall from your principles of economics course that unemployment can be interpreted as a surplus (or excess supply) of labor. Normally, if there is a market surplus for a good or service, its relative price will fall; if price impediments exist, then the surplus will remain until the relative price falls to restore an equality between quantity supplied and quantity demanded per unit of time. It follows that if the wage rate is not free to fall, then the surplus of labor (unemployment) will remain for long periods.

In a modern economy, perfect price-wage flexibility does not exist. For example, unions resist reductions in nominal wage rates, and minimum wage laws place a floor on wage rates. In the United States the Davis-Bacon Act requires that all federal government construction projects pay union wages, which puts a wage floor on such projects.

If nominal wage rates are not free to fall, then it will take the economy longer to change relative wage rates and to restore equilibrium. The natural rate of unemployment will be higher in a country with a great degree of price-wage rigidity, other things constant.

Labor Market Rigidities Market rigidities occur when laborers are not free to enter specific occupations. Government-sanctioned licensing requirements impede the movement of labor; so do union restrictions on entry into specific trades or crafts. Market rigidities prolong periods of unemployment because they reduce the employment opportunities of the unemployed. The greater the degree of market rigidity, the higher the natural rate of unemployment—and the lower the natural level of real GNP.

Work Incentives Work incentives also influence the natural rate of unemployment. If a nation institutes an unemployment compensation plan to help those unlucky enough to become unemployed, rational people who are unemployed are likely to extend their job search. The average duration of unemployment will rise and cause the natural rate of unemployment to rise and the actual level of real GNP to fall below the natural level of real GNP.

Similarly, food stamps, medical benefits, and a host of other privileges that accrue to the poor in a welfare state provide incentives for people to reject jobs. When benefits that create disincentives to work are combined with a requirement that the recipient must *say* that he or she is looking for a job, then the natural rate of unemployment and the measured rate of unemployment will rise.

A higher marginal tax rate will induce workers to substitute some leisure (which is untaxed) for income that can be earned from working. This may reduce the amount of labor time offered by workers and thereby increase the natural rate of unemployment and reduce the actual level of real GNP below the natural level.

Composition of the Labor Force Finally, one should stress that if the composition of the labor force changes so that the percentage of minorities or teenagers or women in the labor force rises, then the natural rate of unemployment may rise. This is because these groups tend to be in and out of the labor force more often and they tend to be frictionally unemployed for longer periods, perhaps because they are not primary income earners and can afford to engage in a longer job search.

Relating the Natural Rate of Unemployment to the Natural Level of Real GNP

Figure 3.3 shows the relationship between the natural rate of growth of gnp and the natural rate of unemployment. The natural rate of growth

Natural gnp Rises When Natural Unemployment Is Constant

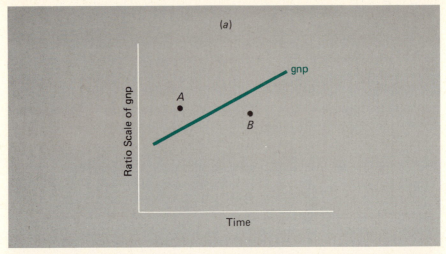

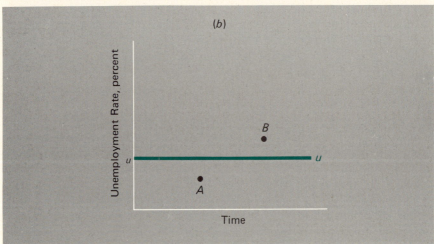

FIGURE 3.3. gnp AND THE NATURAL RATE OF UNEMPLOYMENT
Panel *a* shows a rising natural gnp through time. Panel *b* indicates a constant natural rate of unemployment.

(panel *a*) indicates a gnp that is rising at a constant annual rate. The natural rate of unemployment (panel *b*) reflects the degree of frictional unemployment, price-wage rigidity, market rigidity, and work incentives in the economy depicted in panel *a*. The natural rate of unemployment is uniquely related to an economy's level of natural real GNP. If the determinants of the natural rate of unemployment remain constant through time, the natural rate of unemployment itself will remain constant and the economy will always be on its natural gnp growth curve. If actual unemployment falls to point A in panel *b*, then actual gnp will be above natural gnp.

Relating the Rate of Inflation to the Natural Rates of Unemployment and Growth

There is widespread (but not unanimous) agreement among economists that in the long run (after economic agents correctly anticipate the money supply growth) the rate of inflation is determined only by the rate of growth of the money supply. In the long run a more rapid growth in the money supply will lead to a higher rate of inflation, but gnp and unemployment will not be affected. Because the natural rate of unemployment and the natural rate of growth are related to real, nonmoney variables, it follows that they are independent of the rate of inflation. This means that the natural growth rate and the natural rate of unemployment are consistent with *any* rate of inflation. Because the inflation rate is directly related to the growth of the money supply there is no natural inflation rate. (We analyze this in detail in Chapter 14.) For a given rate of increase in the money supply the rate of inflation will remain constant when actual gnp equals natural gnp and actual unemployment equals natural unemployment.

In the short run (before economic agents correctly anticipate the rate of money supply growth), however, the rate of inflation may be related to things other than the growth of the money supply. We turn now to a discussion of how inflation, the *actual* growth rate, and the *actual* unemployment rate might be related in the short run.

HOW INFLATION, UNEMPLOYMENT, AND REAL GNP GROWTH MIGHT BE RELATED OVER THE BUSINESS CYCLE

To this point we have been concerned with long-run trends. But the actual growth of gnp and the actual rate of unemployment deviate from their natural rates in the short run.

The Business Cycle

Frequently an event occurs that "shocks" the economy, or moves it off its natural gnp growth path. Such events might include banking panics, wars, gold discoveries, changes in tastes, interferences with international trade (such as the oil embargo placed on Western nations by Arab coun-

Actual gnp and Actual Unemployment Deviate from Their Natural Rates over the Business Cycle

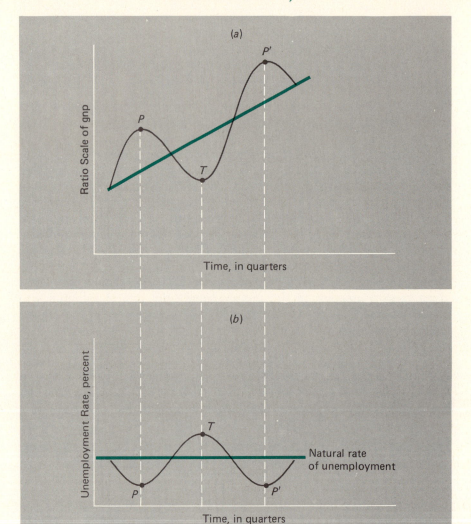

FIGURE 3.4. RELATING ACTUAL gnp AND THE ACTUAL UNEMPLOYMENT RATE TO THEIR NATURAL RATES

In a recession (from peak P to trough T) actual gnp falls below natural gnp and actual unemployment rises above the natural rate of unemployment. In a recovery (from trough T to peak P), actual gnp rises above natural gnp, while the unemployment rate falls below the natural rate of unemployment.

tries in 1973), and so on. Economists divide such disturbances into demand shocks and supply shocks. In general, the effects that these two kinds of shocks have on the economy are different, and we will return to an analysis of such shocks in Chapters 13, 14, 15, and 19.

Eventually, the economy is able to absorb a shock and return to its natural gnp path until the next shock starts the process over again. It should be stressed that the extent to which an economy is pushed off course and the time that it takes to resume that course are highly variable and depend on the magnitude and origin of the original shock. We will refer to the period during which the economy is off course as the *short run;* when the economy is back on its natural course, the *long run* is attained.

We refer to deviations from trends as **recessions** and **recoveries;** the complete cycle of recession, trough, recovery, and peak is called a **business cycle.**

Consider Figure 3.4, which shows actual gnp deviating around the trendline (or the natural rate of growth) in panel *a* and actual unemployment deviating from the natural rate in panel *b*. A recession is defined as a period during which gnp is falling and unemployment is rising; a recession occurs during the time when the economy moves from a **peak,** or the maximum value of gnp over a given business cycle, to a **trough,** the minimum value of gnp over a given business cycle.[3] You should be aware that business cycles are very irregular, both with respect to timing and magnitude. We are considering here an "ideal" business cycle.

Actual Unemployment, Actual gnp, and Inflation

Assume that an economy is on its natural-rate-of-growth path and that the natural rate of unemployment exists. Now a shock occurs and increases temporarily the general demand for goods and services. Businesses will experience a decline in their inventories and will increase their rate of output and cause actual gnp to be higher than natural gnp. In turn, the labor market is affected because an increased expansion of output causes an increased demand for labor in the short run. In order to reduce the unemployment rate below its natural rate, however, laborers must be offered incentives in the form of higher wages.[4]

Table 3.1 shows that, indeed, in the first year of a recovery gnp rises

---

[3] The last quarter before a recession begins is referred to as the peak quarter; a recession begins in the first quarter in which gnp declines—provided gnp declines for at least two consecutive quarters. The quarter when the recession bottoms out is the trough and indicates where the recovery begins.

[4] Chapter 15 shows that the relationship between a demand shock and employment (or output and the price level) may be more complicated than this paragraph implies.

TABLE 3.1. RELATING REAL GNP TO THE UNEMPLOYMENT RATE IN A RECOVERY PERIOD

Quarter and Month of Business Cycle Trough[a]	FIRST 4 QUARTERS AFTER TROUGH Real GNP (percent change)	FIRST 12 MONTHS AFTER TROUGH Industrial Production (percent change)	Civilian Employment (percent change)	Civilian Unemployment Rate (percentage point change)
1982 IV (November). .	6.1	15.7	3.6	−2.3
1949 IV (October) . . .	13.3	27.7	4.4	−3.7
1954 II (May).	7.4	14.0	2.9	−1.6
1958 II (April)	8.4	20.9	3.4	−2.2
1961 I (February). . . .	7.0	13.4	1.4	−1.4
1970 IV (November). .	4.7	6.2	2.1	.1
1975 I (March)	6.7	15.2	3.3	−1.0
1980 III (July).	4.2	9.7	1.9	−.5
Average of seven recoveries[b]	7.4	15.3	2.8	−1.5
Average of five recoveries[c]	6.8	13.9	2.6	−1.2

[a] Business cycle troughs are as determined by the National Bureau of Economic Research.

[b] Excludes 1982.

[c] Excludes 1949, 1980, and 1982.

Sources: Department of Commerce (Bureau of Economic Analysis), Department of Labor (Bureau of Labor Statistics), and Board of Governors of the Federal Reserve System. This table is adapted from Table 6.1 in *Economic Report of the President, 1984*, p. 176.

and the unemployment rate falls. These higher wages induce the frictionally unemployed to accept jobs sooner and induce some people who were not in the labor force to enter it. The *actual* rate of unemployment falls below the *natural* rate. Higher general wages mean higher general costs of production and this, in turn, leads to a higher price level. The higher price level reduces the quantities of goods and services that buyers want to purchase. Eventually, the expansion peters out and the economy is restored to its natural growth rate and to its natural unemployment rate.

In an expansion period, actual gnp rises, actual unemployment falls, and the price level tends to rise; complementary reasoning suggests that in a recession actual gnp falls below natural gnp, actual unemployment rises above natural unemployment, and the price level (or the rate at which it rises) falls. This simple analysis suggests, therefore, that in the short run there is an *inverse* relationship between the rate of inflation and the actual unemployment rate. This relationship is depicted in Figure

In the Short Run the Actual Unemployment Rate and the Rate of Inflation Tend to Move in Opposite Directions

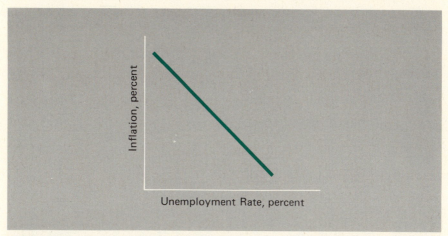

FIGURE 3.5. THE SHORT-RUN RELATIONSHIP BETWEEN INFLATION AND UNEMPLOYMENT, OR A SHORT-RUN PHILLIPS CURVE
Over a business cycle, a recession tends to increase the actual rate of unemployment above its natural rate. A recession also tends to cause the inflation rate to fall. A recovery or expansion period tends to cause unemployment to fall below the natural rate, and the rate of inflation tends to rise.

3.5; it is referred to as a short-run Phillips curve, and we return to a discussion of the Phillips curve in Chapter 14.

Similarly, an inverse relationship seems to exist between the actual unemployment rate and the ratio of actual gnp to natural gnp. If this ratio is greater than 1, the economy is growing more rapidly than its natural rate and is becoming "overheated"—and we would expect the unemployment rate to be below its natural rate; conversely, if this ratio is less than 1, the economy is in a recession and unemployment would be above the natural rate. When this ratio equals 1, the actual gnp equals the natural gnp and the actual rate of unemployment equals the natural rate of unemployment. This relationship is depicted in Figure 3.6.

THE EMPIRICAL RELATIONSHIP AMONG gnp, UNEMPLOYMENT, AND INFLATION

Table 3.2 shows actual gnp, potential gnp, the ratio of actual gnp to potential gnp, the actual unemployment rate, the benchmark unemploy-

The Ratio of Actual gnp to Natural gnp Affects the Actual Unemployment Rate

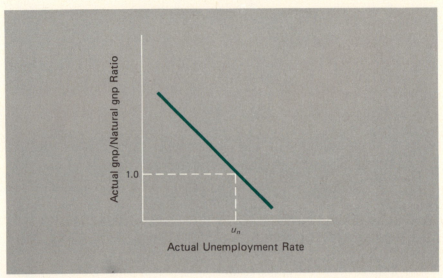

FIGURE 3.6. THE ACTUAL gnp TO NATURAL gnp RATIO AND THE UNEMPLOYMENT RATE

When the ratio of actual real GNP to natural GNP falls below 1, the economy is in a recession and the actual unemployment rate rises above its natural rate U_n. When the ratio of actual real GNP to natural real GNP rises above 1, the economy is in a recovery or expansion phase and the actual unemployment rate falls below the natural unemployment rate.

ment rate, and the change in the implicit GNP price deflator (a measure of inflation) for the period 1952–1980.[5] Note that for many years, but not all, a large change in the ratio of actual gnp to potential gnp is associated with a significant change in unemployment in the opposite direction and a significant change in inflation in the same direction. This, of course, implies that inflation and unemployment move in opposite directions.

The empirical relationships between the actual gnp/potential gnp

---

[5] Potential gnp is an estimate of what we are calling natural gnp, and the benchmark unemployment rate is an estimate of what we are calling the natural rate of unemployment; these estimates were compiled by the Council of Economic Advisors. Since 1981 the council has stopped releasing these estimates because the estimates are thought to be unreliable—they had to be revised frequently. We present them here merely as an indication of what can be done statistically.

TABLE 3.2. ACTUAL AND NATURAL gnp AND UNEMPLOYMENT, AND INFLATION, 1952–1980
(billions of dollars, except where noted)

Year	Actual gnp	Potential gnp	Ratio of Actual gnp to Potential gnp	Actual Overall Rate of Unemployment (%)	Benchmark Unemployment Rate (%)	Annual Rate of Inflation (%)
1952	598.5	584.9	1.02	2.9	4.0	1.4
1953	621.8	608.2	1.02	2.8	4.0	1.6
1954	613.7	629.7	.97	5.4	4.0	1.2
1955	645.8	651.4	1.01	4.3	4.0	2.2
1956	668.8	673.9	.99	4.0	4.0	3.2
1957	680.9	697.2	.98	4.2	4.0	3.4
1958	679.5	721.3	.94	6.6	4.0	1.7
1959	720.4	746.2	.97	5.3	4.1	2.4
1960	736.8	771.9	.95	5.4	4.1	1.6
1961	755.3	798.6	.94	6.5	4.1	0.9
1962	799.1	826.4	.97	5.4	4.1	1.8
1963	830.7	857.1	.97	5.5	4.2	1.5
1964	874.4	90.3	.98	5.0	4.3	1.5
1965	925.9	925.0	1.00	4.4	4.4	2.2
1966	981.0	960.8	1.02	3.7	4.5	3.2
1967	1007.1	996.3	1.01	3.7	4.4	3.0
1968	1051.8	1031.7	1.02	3.5	4.4	4.4
1969	1078.8	1068.3	1.01	3.4	4.4	5.1
1970	1075.3	1106.2	.97	4.8	4.5	5.4
1971	1107.5	1145.5	.97	5.8	4.6	5.0
1972	1171.1	1186.1	.99	5.5	4.7	4.2
1973*	1254.7	1234.9	1.02	4.8	4.9	5.8
1974	1248.1	1277.5	.98	5.5	5.0	8.8
1975	1233.4	1320.6	.93	8.3	5.1	9.3
1976	1300.9	1365.1	.95	7.6	5.1	5.2
1977	1371.9	1411.4	.97	6.9	5.1	5.8
1978	1437.4	1459.3	.98	6.0	5.1	7.4
1979	1483.5	1504.6	.99	5.8	5.1	8.6
1980*	1480.4	1548.5	.96	7.0	5.1	9.2

* The method of calculating potential gnp was revised after this period; therefore, data for this year and subsequent years are not consistent with the previous years.

Source: Economic Report of the President, 1979, 1981, and 1984.

ratio and the unemployment rate has been dubbed **Okun's law,** after its discoverer, the late Arthur M. Okun.[6] Okun estimated that a 1-percentage-point change in the actual gnp/potential gnp ratio is associated with a 0.33-percentage-point change in unemployment in the op-

---

[6] Arthur M. Okun, "Potential GNP: Its Measurement and Significance, " in Arthur M. Okun, ed., *The Political Economy of Prosperity* (Washington, D.C.: Brookings Institution, 1970), pp. 132–145.

posite direction. For example, if the actual gnp/potential gnp ratio falls from 100 to 97, the unemployment rate rises by about 1 percentage point. Recent estimates place the responsiveness of unemployment to the actual gnp/potential gnp ratio slightly higher, at 0.42 of 1 percentage point.[7]

The main exceptions to the inflation-unemployment trade-off seem to be in the 1974–1975 period and in 1980, when *both* inflation and unemployment increased while the ratio of actual gnp to potential gnp fell significantly, signaling recessions. A simultaneously significant increase in inflation *and* unemployment is referred to as **stagflation,** and this very important phenomenon has led to a revolution in macroeconomic analysis—and qualifies much of what has been concluded in this preliminary, investigatory chapter. We analyze stagflation in Part IV, and we address such qualifications then.

CHAPTER SUMMARY

1. Each country seems to have its unique natural rate of growth of real GNP, or secular growth rate. This growth rate may change in a given country over time.
2. A country's natural growth rate depends on its population growth, its rate of technological change, the percentage of its gnp devoted to investment, and the strength of economic incentives.
3. Uniquely related to a country's natural level of gnp is its natural rate of unemployment, which depends on frictional unemployment, the degree of price-wage rigidity, labor market rigidities, the strength of incentives to work, and the composition of the labor force.
4. In the long run, the rate of inflation is primarily (and directly) related to the rate of growth of the money supply. In the short run, there are nonmonetary determinants of the rate of inflation. Any rate of inflation can be consistent with the natural gnp growth rate and the natural unemployment rate.
5. The business cycle consists of peak, recession, trough, and recovery periods. During the four phases of a business cycle, actual gnp and actual unemployment differ from their natural rates. Business cycles are not regular in either timing or magnitude.
6. The business cycle can be considered as a short-run deviation from the long-run natural growth rate. The rate of inflation often increases

---

[7] Robert J. Gordon, "Inflation, Flexible Exchange Rates, and the Natural Rate of Unemployment," in Martin N. Bailey, ed., *Workers, Jobs, and Inflation* (Washington, D.C.: Brookings Institution, 1982), p. 94.

in the recovery and peak periods, and it often decreases in the recession and trough periods.

7. When actual gnp exceeds natural gnp, the actual unemployment rate is less than the natural unemployment rate; when actual gnp is less than natural gnp, the actual unemployment rate exceeds the natural unemployment rate; and when actual gnp equals natural gnp, the actual unemployment rate equals the natural unemployment rate.

8. For a given rate of increase in the money supply, the rate of inflation will remain constant when actual gnp equals natural gnp and actual unemployment equals natural unemployment.

9. There is no natural rate of inflation. In the short run, an inverse relationship may exist between the inflation rate and the actual unemployment rate; and in the short run, an inverse relationship also may exist between the ratio of actual gnp to natural gnp and the actual unemployment rate.

10. Data indicate that, with notable exceptions, an inverse relationship between the inflation rate and the actual unemployment rate does exist. Again with notable exceptions, an inverse relationship between the ratio of actual gnp to potential gnp and the actual unemployment rate has also been empirically established.

GLOSSARY

business cycle   Short-run deviations from the natural rate of gnp growth that create the following phases: recovery, peak, recession, and trough.

natural growth rate   The long-run secular annual percentage rate of change in real GNP.

natural rate of unemployment   The unemployment rate to which the economy eventually returns after equilibrium is restored and which depends on the amount of frictional unemployment, price-wage rigidity, labor market rigidity, work incentives, and the composition of the labor force. Also, the unemployment rate that exists when the inflation rate is correctly anticipated.

Okun's law   An empirical relationship between changes in the ratio of actual gnp to potential gnp and changes in the unemployment rate.

peak   The maximum point of an expansion; after the peak, real GNP falls and a recession begins, if real GNP falls for at least two consecutive quarters.

productivity of labor   The ratio of the value of real output to the number of labor hours worked.

recession   A phase of the business cycle in which real GNP is falling and the unemployment rate is rising.

recovery   A phase of the business cycle, after the trough, when real GNP rises and the unemployment rate falls.

stagflation   The simultaneous existence of a high rate of inflation and a high rate of unemployment.

trough The minimum point of a recession; after the trough quarter, real GNP rises.

QUESTIONS AND PROBLEMS FOR REVIEW

3.1 Define the natural rate of growth, list the determinants of the natural rate of growth, and indicate how each determinant affects the natural growth rate.

3.2 Define the natural rate of unemployment, list the determinants of the natural rate of unemployment, and explain how each determinant affects the natural rate of unemployment.

3.3 Explain how the natural rate of unemployment is related to the natural level of gnp.

3.4 Explain how specific changes in the natural rate of unemployment affect the level of natural gnp.

3.5 Explain why there might be an inverse relationship between the rate of inflation and the actual unemployment rate in the short run.

3.6 Discuss why there might be an inverse relationship between (a) the ratio of actual real GNP to natural real GNP and (b) the actual unemployment rate, in the short run.

3.7 Suppose that country A has a labor force of 100 people. In January, Mr. Miller, Mr. Pulsinelli, and Ms. Hooper are unemployed; in February those three find jobs but Mrs. Stevenson, Mr. Conn, and Mr. Romano become unemployed. Suppose further that every month the previous three that were unemployed find jobs and three different people become unemployed. For country A:
   a. What is the unemployment rate?
   b. What is the frictional unemployment rate?
   c. What is the average duration of unemployment?

3.8 Continuing Problem 3.7, suppose that country A institutes an unemployment compensation program so that, on average, people are induced to spend *two* months finding a job after they become unemployed.
   a. What is the new average duration of unemployment?
   b. What will be the new unemployment rate?
   c. Does the now higher unemployment rate reflect a great reduction in community welfare?
   d. Would it be a mistake for policymakers to react to the new, higher unemployment rate?

3.9 Using the data from Table 3.2, plot the relationship between the annual rate of inflation and the actual overall rate of unemployment. What do the data suggest about this relationship?

3.10 Using the data from Table 3.2, plot the relationship between the ratio of actual gnp to potential gnp and (a) the rate of inflation, and (b) the actual overall rate of unemployment. What do the data suggest about these relationships?

REFERENCES

Martin N. Bailey, ed., *Workers, Jobs, and Inflation* (Washington, D.C.: The Brookings Institution, 1982).

M. G. Mueller, ed., *Readings in Macroeconomics* (New York: Holt, Rinehart and Winston, 1971).

Arthur M. Okun, *The Political Economy of Prosperity* (Washington, D.C.: The Brookings Institution, 1970).

Paul A. Samuelson, *Economics*, 11th ed. (New York: McGraw-Hill, 1980), chap. 14.

PART II

HISTORICAL

PERSPECTIVE

The Evolution of Macroeconomics
from the Classical
to the Neoclassical-Keynesian Synthesis

4

THE CLASSICAL MODEL: PART 1

The classical model was the first systematic and rigorous attempt to explain the determinants of such economic aggregates as the price level and the national levels of output, income, employment, consumption, saving, and investment. It also attempted to show how these variables were interrelated and how and where money fit in.

Classical economics covers the time span from the 1770s to the 1930s and can be divided roughly into two periods. The term *classical model* was coined by John Maynard Keynes, a Cambridge University economist, who used the term to refer to the way in which previous economists (who did not have the benefit of his insights) had analyzed economic aggregates.[1]

The first period covers the works of such intellectual giants as Adam Smith (1723–1790), David Hume (1711–1776), David Ricardo (1792–1823), John Stuart Mill (1806–1873), and Thomas Malthus (1766–1834). These economists, and many of their contemporaries, waged an economic revolution against **mercantilism,** an economic doctrine that maintained:

1. A nation's wealth and power are determined by its store of such precious metals as gold and silver, or "money."
2. A nation's wealth can and should be increased by the direction of the state.

Many (but not all) of the classical economists used their influence to promote capitalism; they placed their faith in free markets instead of government. Classical economists (in the main) believed that a nation's true economic wealth was derived from the industriousness of its people. If people were allowed to pursue their own economic self-interest, the state needed only to maintain a competitive economy and provide for internal and external security. These economists not only argued in favor of a free domestic marketplace; they also argued forcibly and effectively against laws that restricted international trade.

The classical economists' deemphasis on the importance of money and their faith in competitive markets will be evident as the classical model is analyzed in this chapter and in the next.

The second period of classical economics begins around 1870 and includes the works of the *neoclassical economists*. They differed from their economic ancestors by introducing a mathematical approach that enabled them to refine the earlier economists' models. They also began a general equilibrium analysis that considered *all* markets simultaneously; and they refined the economic tool referred to as *marginal anal-*

---

[1] John Maynard Keynes, *The General Theory of Employment, Interest and Money* (London: Macmillan, 1936).

ysis. Neoclassical economists include W. Stanley Jevons (1835–1882), Carl Menger (1840–1921), Leon Walrus (1834–1910), Alfred Marshall (1842–1924), A. C. Pigou (1877–1959), and many others.

The classical and the neoclassical economists were among the most brilliant individuals of their time; their impact on the ideas and intellectual controversies of their eras and their influence on economic policy was truly enormous. Even Copernicus, the astronomer, contributed to the classical model, and there is strong evidence that Malthus influenced Charles Darwin's thinking about evolution.

Although the classical model can be divided into the classical and neoclassical periods, we will follow Keynes's approach and merely refer to "the" classical model. The model discussed in this chapter and in Chapter 5 is a combination of the Cambridge University oral tradition of macroeconomics and a reconstruction of it by Keynes. Because Keynes oversimplified the classical model, however, we devote a section to what the classical economists really said in the next chapter.

SAY'S LAW

The fundamental conclusion of the classical model is usually summarized in what is referred to as **Say's law.** Jean Baptiste Say (1767–1832) was the French popularizer of classical thinking, and he immortalized himself by coining the dictum: *Supply creates its own demand.* A catchy phrase, but what does it mean?

Say's law is that the very process of producing specific goods (supply) is proof that other goods are desired (demand); people produce more goods than they want because they want to trade them for other goods. The implication of this, according to Say, is that no general glut[2] (or overproduction) is possible in a capitalist, or market, economy. From this it seems to follow that the full employment of labor (and other resources) is the norm in such economies.

Underlying Say's law is the premise that wants are unlimited and, further, that the primary goal of economic activity is consumption for oneself or for one's family—either in the present or in the future. An increase in the supply of one commodity can be interpreted as an increase in the demand for another. If a more or less self-sufficient family wants to increase its consumption, it can do so by producing more and trading off its surplus of one good in order to get more of another.

---

[2] Specific gluts (surpluses) are possible, but such surpluses are no more likely than specific shortages. Both result from imperfect information, and both are resolved by relative price changes. Implicit in Say's law is the generalization that for every surplus there is an equal shortage—at current prices. Those goods for which a surplus exists will experience a relative price reduction; a relative price rise will occur for those goods for which a shortage exists.

All this seems reasonable enough in a simple barter economy in which households produce most of the goods they need and trade for the rest, but what about a more sophisticated economy in which people work for others? Can this complication create the possibility of unemployment? And does the fact that laborers receive money income, some of which can be *saved*, lead to unemployment? No, said the classical economist to these two questions. Much of the remainder of this chapter is devoted to an analysis of how the classical model, which indeed predicts the full employment of resources for a capitalist economy, justifies their answer.

Assumptions of the Classical Model

The major assumptions of the classical model are:

1. *Pure competition exists.* No single buyer or seller of a commodity or an input can affect its price by his or her own actions. As a consequence, each transactor is a price taker. Another consequence (and a seemingly paradoxical one) is that prices, interest rates, and wages are free to move to whatever levels supply and demand dictate. In other words, although no *individual* buyer can set a price, the *community* of buyers or sellers can cause prices to rise or to fall to an equilibrium level.
2. *Economic agents are motivated by self-interest.* One implication of this second assumption is that businesses want to maximize their total profits, and households (consumers and workers) want to maximize their total economic well-being (classical economists referred to this as utility maximization behavior).
3. *Economic agents do not suffer from* **money illusions.** That is, buyers and sellers react to changes in relative (not absolute) prices, and to changes in real (price-level-adjusted) wages and interest rates, and not to changes in nominal values. For example, suppose a given consumer has purchased a specific basket of goods and services over the year and that in the next year all prices—including her income— doubles. Because relative prices have not changed, the classical model predicts that she will buy the identical basket of goods and services— other things constant.

The Two Theories on Which Say's Law Rests

Armed with these assumptions, classical economists were able to develop the two foundation blocks on which Say's law rests: the classical theory of the aggregate demand for and the aggregate supply of labor, and their theory of the level of effective aggregate demand for goods and services. In this chapter, we show how the classical theory of the aggregate supply of and the aggregate demand for labor demonstrates part 1 of Say's law: a full-employment output will be *produced;* and part 2 of Say's law: a full-employment output will be *purchased.* These two lines of defense assure full employment in a competitive, capitalist system. This chapter will conclude with a discussion of the classical aggregate supply curve for goods and services and a Policy Controversy.

SAY'S LAW, PART 1: A FULL-EMPLOYMENT OUTPUT WILL BE PRODUCED

The Aggregate Production Function

A production function relates various output levels to various quantities of inputs, or factors of production, given the current state of the arts or technology. In equation form (a bar over a letter implies that the variable in question is constant),

$$y = f(\overline{K}, N, \overline{A}) \tag{4.1}$$

WHERE y = real output per unit of time
$\overline{K}$ = capital stock
N = quantity of labor per unit of time
$\overline{A}$ = land services

We are concerned with the *short run,* and in macroeconomics the capital stock and the quantity of land services are, by definition, fixed in the short run. Also, N is a variable between zero and the size of the labor force, N_f. It follows that in the short run a functional relationship exists between N and y, or

$$y = f(N) \tag{4.2}$$

and that y is a variable between zero and y_f, where y_f is the full-employment real-output level.

According to the classical economists, such a production function will eventually increase at a decreasing rate; increases in labor, other factors of production and technology constant, eventually cause the **marginal physical product of labor (MPP$_n$)** to decrease. The marginal physical product of labor is defined as the change in output resulting from a unit change in labor, other things constant. This technological relationship between factors of production and outputs was deduced by the classical economists and is called the **law of diminishing returns.** This law states that if one factor of production increases by equal increments while other factors of production are held constant, then eventually total output will increase at a decreasing rate or (what is mathematically equivalent) the marginal physical product of the variable input eventually will fall.

Figure 4.1 shows a production function. This production function exists for the whole economy and a similarly shaped production function exists for each individual firm. In panel *a*, total output increases at a decreasing rate; in panel *b*, the marginal physical product of labor declines.[3]

The Aggregate Demand for Labor and the Aggregate Supply of Labor

In sophisticated, highly specialized economies, most laborers work for an employer; a relatively small percentage of the population is self-employed. Consequently, a labor market evolves in which buyers and sellers of labor transact voluntarily. The following analysis of the aggregate (or total, or summed) demand for labor and supply of labor involves a money-using economy; but buyers and sellers of labor are concerned with *real* wage rates. Recall that real wage rates are inflation adjusted; real wage rate equals nominal wage rate divided by price level, or

$$w \equiv \frac{W}{P} \qquad (4.3)$$

A rise in real wage rates occurs if nominal wage rates rise more rapidly than the price level or if nominal wage rates fall more slowly than the price level is falling. The real wage rate falls when the nominal wage rate rises less rapidly than the price level, or when the nominal wage rate falls more rapidly than the price level is falling.

For ease of exposition, a national market for only one skill will be considered; hence, a national wage rate will be established. The aggregate demand-for-labor curve can be derived by summing all the individual firm labor demand curves; the aggregate supply-of-labor curve can be derived by summing all the individual labor supply curves.

The Aggregate Demand for Labor   The aggregate demand for labor is derived by summing all the individual firm demand-for-labor curves. We discuss each in turn.

The Firm's Demand for Labor   Assuming that labor is the firm's only variable input, output can be increased only by adding more labor to fixed capital and land services. According to the law of diminishing

---

[3] Those of you who have studied calculus will observe that the MPP curve is the graph of the first derivative *(dy/dN)* of the total output curve (production function). The slope of the total output curve is the marginal physical product of labor.

As More Labor Is Employed, Other Things Constant, Total Output Eventually Will Increase at a Decreasing Rate

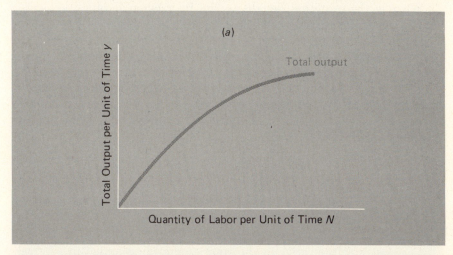

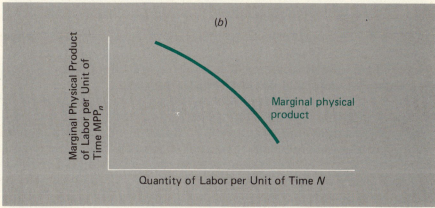

FIGURE 4.1. THE LAW OF DIMINISHING RETURNS
In the short run, higher levels of output require increased employment of labor because other factors of production are held constant. This eventually leads to diminishing returns; that is, total output will increase at a decreasing rate (panel *a*) and the marginal physical product of labor will fall (panel *b*).

returns, the marginal physical product of labor eventually will fall as a firm employs more labor, other inputs remaining constant.

A profit-maximizing firm purchasing labor will continue to expand its employment of labor until the marginal benefit equals the marginal cost of doing so. The marginal cost of hiring labor services for the competitive firm is the going wage rate. The individual firm finds marginal cost for purchasing labor services constant and equal to the going nominal wage rate W.

What is the marginal *benefit* to the firm when it purchases labor services? Is it the marginal physical product of labor? Not exactly, because the marginal physical product is in physical units and the wage rate is in money units. We must compare apples with apples, money with money. The marginal benefit is equal to the value of the marginal physical product of labor, which equals the marginal physical product of labor multiplied by the selling price of the output in a competitive market. Note that now the marginal benefit, like the marginal cost, is in money units. That is,

$$MB = VMP_n \equiv MPP_n \times P \tag{4.4}$$

WHERE MB = marginal benefit
VMP_n = **value of the marginal physical product of labor,** where the subscript n represents labor
MPP_n = marginal physical product of labor
P = selling price of the good produced, assumed to be given to individuals

The VMP_n curve eventually will slope downward. As the firm hires more labor, MPP_n eventually falls (due to the law of diminishing returns); P is constant (because the firm is a perfectly competitive seller, or a price taker); and the VMP_n will therefore fall.

Having identified the firm's marginal benefit and marginal cost of hiring services, it is necessary to explain how much labor the firm will employ to maximize its total profit. The firm will hire labor up to the quantity at which its marginal cost (equal to the constant money wage) equals its marginal benefit (equal to the decreasing VMP_n) from doing so. Algebraically,

$$W = MPP_n \times P \tag{4.5}$$

Equation 4.3 can be rewritten as

$$\frac{W}{P} = MPP_n \tag{4.6}$$

This last equation indicates that in the equilibrium (profit-maximizing) condition the real wage rate *(W/P)* must equal the marginal physical product of labor.

Suppose the nominal wage rate were now to fall by one-half. What would happen to the quantity of labor demanded? The classical economist would reply, "That depends on what happens to the price of the commodity in question." If the price of the good produced by the firm is also reduced by one-half, the firm would not hire more or fewer laborers, because both sides of equation 4.5 are multiplied by one-half, and the left side of equation 4.6 does not change. Neither equation is affected. Neither, therefore, is the equilibrium of the firm. Before the firm can be induced to hire more labor services per unit of time, the VMP_n must exceed W. This will happen only if price rises relative to the nominal wage rate.

If the nominal wage rate were to rise, the firm's equilibrium would be disturbed only if the price of the good produced were to rise at a different rate. If the nominal wage rate rises more rapidly than the price of the good produced rises, the real wage rate rises and the employer will purchase less labor. As less labor is employed, the MPP_n will rise, and therefore the VMP_n will rise; the employer will reduce the labor it employs until the VMP_n is driven up sufficiently to equal the new, higher real wage rate.

In short, the firm's quantity demanded for labor is inversely related to w, the *real wage rate*; the firm does not suffer from money illusion. One way to interpret this relationship is as follows: Before the firm voluntarily will hire more labor hours per unit of time (other things constant), the real wage rate must fall in order to offset the declining marginal physical product of labor. In fact, the competitive firm's marginal physical product curve *is* the demand curve for labor. The inverse relationship between real wage rates and the quantity of labor demanded by a firm is indicated in Figure 4.2. Remember that each lowercase letter (such as w) represents a *real* value (whereas W represents a nominal value). Since $w \equiv W/P$, it is clear that the real wage rate rises when W increases relative to P, and falls when P rises relative to W.

Each point on this demand-for-labor curve represents a *potential* equilibrium (profit-maximizing) position for the employer. The curve shows the equilibrium quantity of labor that will be purchased, per unit of time, at every real wage rate. The curve indicates that the quantity demanded per unit of time depends on the real wage rate and not on the nominal wage rate.

The Economy's Total Demand for Labor   The horizontal summation of all demand curves for labor yields the aggregate demand-for-labor curve in this highly simplified economy. This curve shows that for all firms in the economy a reduction in the real wage rate is required to induce an increase in the quantity demanded of labor, per unit of time, other things constant. What was true for the individual firm is true for all firms collectively. This negatively sloped aggregate demand-for-labor curve results from the diminishing marginal product of labor.

This curve shifts to the right if the productivity of labor increases owing to technological discoveries, capital investment, or improvements in land or in labor (due to education and training). Such changes would

The Firm's Quantity Demanded of Labor Is Inversely Related to the Real Wage Rate

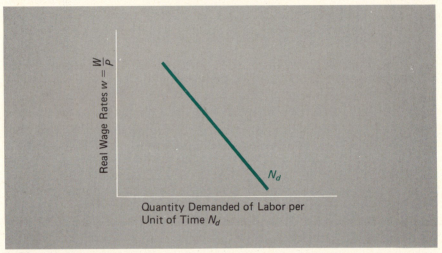

FIGURE 4.2. THE FIRM'S DEMAND-FOR-LABOR CURVE

In the short run, the firm increases output by adding more labor to other fixed factors of production. Eventually, the law of diminishing returns takes effect, and the marginal physical product of labor falls. As a consequence, a firm requires lower real wage rates—which offset a diminishing marginal physical product of labor—before it will voluntarily purchase more labor.

An aggregate demand-for-labor curve is derived by summing all the individual firms' demand-for-labor curves. The aggregate demand-for-labor curve will also indicate an inverse relationship between real wage rates and the quantity of labor demanded per unit of time, other things constant.

---

shift the aggregate demand-for-labor curve to the right; the quantity demanded of labor by businesses would be greater, at every wage rate, than previously.

The Aggregate Supply of Labor   According to the classical theoreticians (and most of us, too), work is irksome. Indeed, a laborer experiences *increasing marginal disutility* (or irksomeness) as he or she works more hours per day, per week, or per month. If this is so, then why do people work? Because they receive income that can be used to buy goods and services that have utility.

   A Worker's Supply of Labor   The rational seller of labor, therefore, compares the marginal disutility (or cost) of working one more unit of time to the marginal utility (or benefit) that can be obtained by spending (or saving) the income derived from working one more unit of time at the going wage rate. In equilibrium, the rational worker will supply labor time up to the quantity at which the marginal utility obtained from the (constant) wage rate is just equal to the marginal disutility incurred by working that last unit of time.

Suppose the market money wage rate doubles. Will a laborer previously in equilibrium now work more? The answer, according to the classical economist, depends on what happens to the price level; if the price level also doubles, the worker will not work more because to do so would leave him or her worse off economically. Why? The increasing marginal disutility of working one more unit of time would be greater than the constant marginal utility gained from working that additional unit. (Because prices have doubled too, the marginal utility of a doubled nominal wage rate has not changed.)

The only way that a rational worker can be induced to work more hours per unit of time is for the *real* wage rate to rise. Thus, the quantity of labor offered by the representative worker in this model is directly related to the real wage rate; laborers do not suffer from money illusions. Here is one interpretation of such a relationship: before a worker voluntarily will work more hours per unit of time (other things constant), the real wage rate *must rise* to offset the increasing marginal disutility from working. At every point along the supply-of-labor curve, the laborer has worked up to the point where the marginal benefit (extra utility from income) from working that last hour is exactly equal to the marginal cost (extra disutility) from doing so; at every point on the labor supply curve the worker is potentially maximizing his or her total utility. This is depicted in Figure 4.3.

The Economy's Supply of Labor By summing the individual supply-of-labor curves horizontally, an aggregate supply-of-labor curve can be derived. This curve will shift if workers' attitudes toward labor change, if the composition of the labor force changes, if the population changes, or if marginal tax rates change.

Determination of the Equilibrium Wage Rate

Figure 4.4 shows both the aggregate supply of labor and the aggregate demand for labor. In a purely competitive labor market, the equilibrium real wage will be at a point of intersection of the supply and demand curves. Consider real wage w_1 in Figure 4.4. Why will it not be the equilibrium wage rate? Inspection of Figure 4.4 indicates that at w_1 the quantity of labor supplied (4000 units of labor per unit of time) exceeds the quantity of labor demanded (3000 units of labor per unit of time); hence, a surplus of labor exists at w_1. A surplus of labor is more commonly referred to as unemployment. What will happen? Buyers of labor

Individual Laborers Require a Higher Real Wage Rate Before They Will Increase Their Work Week

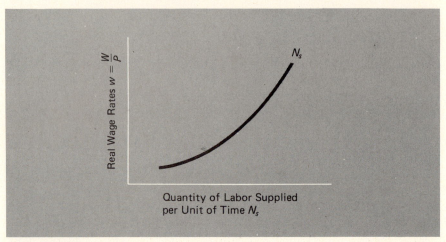

FIGURE 4.3. A SUPPLY-OF-LABOR CURVE

As an individual works more hours per unit of time, his or her marginal disutility rises. Before he or she will voluntarily offer more labor per unit of time, the real wage rate must rise to offset this increased marginal disutility. At every point on this curve, the individual is potentially maximizing his or her welfare, or total utility.

An aggregate supply-of-labor curve can be derived by summing all the individual supply-of-labor curves. The aggregate supply-of-labor curve also indicates a direct relationship between the real wage rate and the quantity of labor supplied per unit of time.

are maximizing total profits at w_1; they have hired labor up to the quantity at which the real wage w just equals the MPP_n—at 3000 units of labor.[4] On the other hand, sellers of labor are not able to realize their intentions; they want to sell 4,000 units of labor but can only sell 3,000 units per unit of time at real wage w_1. For some laborers, the marginal benefit of the real wage will exceed the cost (or marginal disutility) of working the last unit of time. These involuntarily unemployed laborers will compete with employed laborers for jobs and drive money wage

---

[4] Or the money wage W just equals the VMP_n. If $W = MPP_n \times P$, then $W/P = MPP_n$; in a one-commodity world, P is the price of the commodity. In a multicommodity world, P is a weighted average of all the prices of the goods and services produced in the economy.

The Aggregate Supply of Labor and the Aggregate Demand for Labor Determine the Equilibrium Real Wage Rate

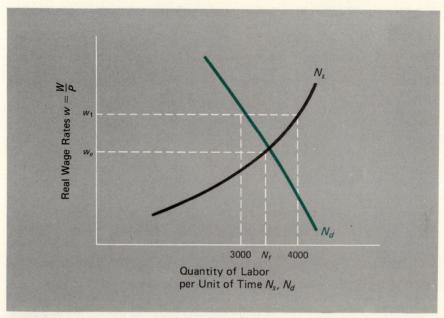

FIGURE 4.4. THE EQUILIBRIUM WAGE RATE

As long as nominal wage rates are free to change, eventually the real wage rate will be established at the point of intersection of the aggregate supply-of-labor curve and the aggregate demand-for-labor curve. At any real wage rate above w_e, such as w_1, a surplus of labor exists and unemployed laborers will offer to work for lower nominal wage rates. Nominal wage rates will fall relative to the price level until the unemployment is eliminated. Complementary reasoning implies that at any real wage rate below w_e a shortage will exist and buyers of labor will compete for scarce labor and drive the nominal wage rate up relative to the price level.

rates downward; this decrease in money wages will force real wages down toward w_e. Unemployment will exist at any real wage rate above w_e, and therefore classical economists reasoned that *any real wage rate above w_e could only be temporary.*

At any wage rate below w_e, the quantity of labor demanded exceeds the quantity of labor supplied and a shortage of labor exists. Sellers will be able to realize their intentions; they will (and can) work up to the quantity at which the marginal utility obtained from the last unit of time worked is just offset by the marginal disutility suffered from working it. On the other hand, buyers will not be able to realize their intentions and hence will not be able to maximize total profits. For buyers, the real wage rate will be less than the MPP_n; alternatively stated, the money wage rate will be less than the VMP_n.[5] Buyers of labor, competing for labor, will drive the nominal and the real wage rates upward until w_e is reached.

Labor for Hire and Full Employment

What is the implication of the classical analysis of the aggregate supply of labor and aggregate demand for labor? Full employment is achieved. Why? In Figure 4.4, N_f represents full employment; all those labor hours beyond N_f that might be offered by laborers are *voluntarily* withheld. For those extra hours, workers feel that the marginal disutility outweighs the marginal utility derivable from the real wage. Any involuntarily unemployed laborers will *eventually* (watch out for that word!) find jobs because such a surplus of labor will cause real wage rates to fall until the quantity of labor demanded rises and the quantity of labor supplied falls. Full employment of labor results.

Consider Figure 4.5, which shows the aggregate production function in panel *a* and the aggregate supply of and demand for labor in panel *b*. In panel *b*, the equilibrium quantity of labor N_f is established at real wage rate w_e, and N_f units of labor are offered and purchased per unit of time. That equilibrium quantity of labor is consistent with an economy-wide maximum rate of output of y_f, as panel *a* indicates. Thus, the classical theory of the aggregate supply of and the aggregate demand for labor implies that businesses will produce an output requiring the full employment of labor. *Wage rate flexibility assures that in a competitive market a full-employment output will be produced by business.*

Note that if, for some reason, the real wage rate were temporarily established above or below w_e, the economy would be at less than or greater than the "normal" or natural rate of unemployment. Similarly, the corresponding output rate would be at a smaller or larger rate than the natural rate of output (which would be y_f in Figure 4.5). For example, consider real wage rate w_1 in panel *b*; at that rate only N_1 units of labor will be hired by employers and the unemployment rate will exceed the natural rate of unemployment. Consistent with N_1 units of labor is output rate y_1, which is below the natural output rate y_f. Similar reasoning indicates that at a wage rate below w_e laborers might be *temporarily*

---

[5] Can you verify this? *Hint:* Pick a real wage rate below w_e and show how many units of labor will be offered by sellers. Then determine what the MPP_n is for that quantity of labor, and compare it to the real wage rate you selected. Remember that the demand-for-labor curve is the MPP_n curve.

A Full-Employment Output Will Be Produced

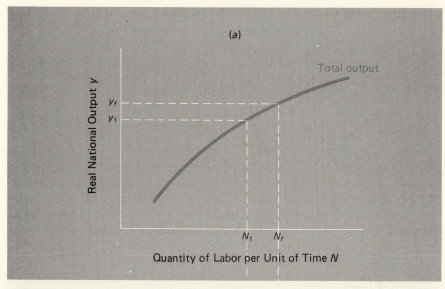

(a)

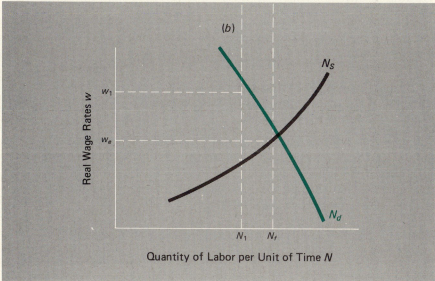

(b)

FIGURE 4.5. DETERMINING AGGREGATE OUTPUT

First, the equilibrium level of employment is established in the labor market. The production function then indicates the maximum (and therefore the most efficient) level of output consistent with that employment level.

Note that at a higher-than-equilibrium wage rate, such as w_1, a less-than-full-employment situation exists and national output will be less than the full-employment level. As long as real wage rates are free to change, however, this is only a temporary situation. Eventually, the full-employment output y_f will be produced.

fooled into supplying more hours than N_f and the actual unemployment rate would be temporarily less than the natural unemployment rate—and the output rate temporarily would exceed the natural rate.

> **When the economy is not yet in equilibrium, it is possible that the actual unemployment rate can be less than or greater than the natural unemployment rate. Therefore, the actual rate of output can be greater than or less than the natural rate of output during periods of disequilibrium.**

Our conclusion with respect to full employment, therefore, is true only in equilibrium. If the economic system is shocked—if something happens (such as a gold discovery or a banking crisis or an international payments disequilibrium) to disturb equilibrium, and disequilibrium temporarily exists—the economy can deviate from the full-employment (natural) level of output.[6] As we will see, Keynes and legions of Keynesian economists believe that periods of disequilibrium are long and frequent—and therefore worthy of consideration. The classical economists (with the exception of Malthus and Karl Marx and a few others) were more concerned with comparing the old equilibrium position with the new equilibrium position. That is, classical economists were more concerned with the long-run effects of shocks, and they tended to neglect disequilibrium periods.

SAY'S LAW, PART 2: A FULL-EMPLOYMENT OUTPUT WILL BE PURCHASED

The previous section indicated how the classical economists demonstrated that a full-employment output eventually will be produced even in an economy where laborers rent their services to entrepreneurs for money. But what assures that this full-employment output will be *purchased*? This question is addressed now.

Say's Law and National Income Accounting

National income accounting demonstrates that the market value of all final goods and services produced during the income period is identical to the incomes generated from their production. Because income forms

---

[6] To be more precise, we should point out that for the classical economist "full" employment meant only frictional unemployment. Shocks, therefore, cause the actual unemployment rate to diverge from the frictional unemployment rate.

the basis of the demand for final goods and services, national income accounting provides at least some superficial support for Say's law. In a money economy, supply creates its own *potential* demand: any output (supply) automatically will create sufficient purchasing power to clear markets.

Consider Figure 4.5 again. A competitive labor market assures full employment in panel *b*, and the maximum output rate consistent with that full-employment rate is y_f. Businesses will produce y_f because that is the most profitable output. Given a set of prices for these final goods and services, the value of national income is determined. Weighting final goods and services (y_f) by their respective prices yields nominal national income (NNP, assuming investment is measured in net terms). Thus, by establishing equilibrium in the labor market, national output of final goods and services is automatically determined. Weighting those final goods by their respective market prices automatically generates sufficient income, and hence purchasing power, to clear markets of those goods.

A nagging question persists, however. What guarantees that this purchasing power will actually be *expended*? In short, what if people save a part of their income?

Saving   First, it is necessary to interpret saving. Why do people save? Saving represents a provision for future consumption. People save for their retirement, to accumulate down payments for expensive durable goods, for future emergencies, and so on. People save to "even out" their consumption over time; they save to free themselves from the discipline of consuming only what their income happens to be in a particular period. Individuals typically have incomes that vary over their lifetimes. Saving permits households to have a more nearly constant level of consumption through time.

Even granting that saving will ultimately be spent, there is still a short-run problem. *During the period in which some income is saved*, the supply-created potential demand (the purchasing power or income) is not fully expended. The result is that the aggregate demand for consumer goods and services is insufficient to purchase all the goods and services produced. Unemployment results as producers react to rising inventories by producing less and employing fewer workers.

Saving creates a situation in which purchasing power, generated in the form of income derived from producing goods and services, is not all spent on those goods and services. Consequently, saving represents a *leakage* from the circular flow of income and it contracts the economy. Saving seems to be a formidable foe of Say's law; if not offset, it can lead to unemployment.

Investment   The classical economists were aware of the potential danger of saving. Classical theoreticians believed, however, that *investment* has precisely the opposite effect on the economy that saving has.

Investment spending is the demand for additional plant and equipment and inventory accumulation. When investment takes place, incomes and purchasing power are created, but there is no corresponding increase (at least in the short run) in the output of final *consumer* goods and service. Investment, therefore, is potentially an effective antidote to saving. Investment is an injection into the circular flow of income and is a potentially expansionary element in an economy.[7]

Saving and Investment   The problem, then, is not that people save. *What is important is the extent to which household planned saving is offset by business planned investment.* If at full employment planned saving exceeds planned investment, the economy will contract and unemployment will occur. If planned investment exceeds planned saving, then a short-run rise in the price level will result. If planned saving is exactly equated with planned investment, however, employment will remain full and prices will be stable.[8] The key variables, then, are planned saving of households and planned investment of businesses. The classical economists felt that these were both determined primarily by the rate of interest. In turn, the rate of interest is the mechanism in market economies that assures that saving and investment plans are equated.

Saving and Investment, Credit Markets, and the Interest Rate

In a money economy, credit markets arise because (1) different households have different preferences for present-versus-future consumption, and (2) businesses can make investments in plant, equipment, and/or inventory that are profitable enough to enable them to pay interest to lenders. **Interest** is the amount of money that lenders receive when they extend credit; the **interest rate** is the ratio of the annual interest to the amount lent. For example, suppose that $100 is lent and, at the end of the year, $110 must be paid back. The interest paid is $10 and the interest rate is 10 percent (because $10/$100 = 0.10).

---

[7] Indeed, a fully employed economy that suddenly allocates massive resources to investment goods production will temporarily experience a rise in the price level unless saving plans by households increase accordingly. This is because in a full-employment situation an increase in investment goods output necessitates a reduction in the output of consumer goods—households will have fewer consumer goods to purchase, but their purchasing power is constant. They compete for consumer goods by bidding prices higher. This is why inflation tends to accompany war periods.

[8] This conclusion requires a constant money supply, as Chapter 5 points out.

At the heart of the interest rate phenomenon lies the trade-off between present purchasing power and future purchasing power. The interest rate is the price that must be paid for credit and, like other prices, it performs an allocating (or rationing) function. The interest rate helps society decide how to allocate the production of goods and services through time.

Also, like other prices, the interest rate provides information. At a national level, the rate of interest reflects the community's rate of time preference for goods and services. Other things constant, a relatively high interest rate indicates that the community is impatient and wants to consume more in the present. For ease of exposition, we will refer to this type of community as **present-oriented.** Other things constant, a relatively low rate of interest reflects a patient, **future-oriented** society that is willing to forgo present consumption for more future consumption. Future-oriented societies tend to grow more rapidly than present-oriented societies. In future-oriented societies, the national saving and investment ratios are relatively high and the economic growth rate will reflect this capital expansion.

The interest rate provides essential information at the individual level. The market rate of interest indicates the rate at which a household can trade present for future purchasing power. For example, assuming that the market rate of interest is 5 percent, each household has the option of choosing, say, $100 worth of purchasing power today or $105 worth of purchasing power next year ($100 × 1.05) or $110.25 worth of purchasing power two years from now ($100 × 1.05 × 1.05), and so on into the future. If Mr. Longardo values $1.00 of today's consumption so highly that he requires $1.06 worth of consumption one year from now to make him indifferent between spending the $1.00 now or $1.06 one year hence, he will spend the $1.00 now; his *personal* trade-off between present and future consumption (6 percent) is greater than society's trade-off (the 5 percent market interest rate), so he will spend the $1.00 now. If Ms. Capra is indifferent between $1.00 of consumption today and $1.03 of consumption one year from now, her personal interest rate is 3 percent. She will save the $1.00 and purchase the $1.05 worth of goods next year that a 5 percent market rate of interest permits.

The interest rate, therefore, allows people to compare present values to future values because, by its very nature, it reflects the trade-off between present purchasing power and future purchasing power. Different households have different time preferences for consumption, and given their tastes for trading present for future consumption, they will prefer to save and to lend some percentage of their incomes. At that same rate of interest some households will prefer to be net borrowers. They will prefer to consume more than their income in the present, knowing that they must forgo future consumption because they must pay back interest and principal (the amount they borrow).[9]

Similarly, different businesses have different profit expectations; at a given interest rate, corporation *A* will *borrow* if it expects to earn a profit rate higher than that interest rate or it will *lend* if it expects to earn a profit rate that is less than that interest rate.

Because households have different rates of time preference for consumption and because businesses have different profit expectations, at any given interest rate some economic units will be net lenders and others will be net borrowers. This means that some households will be net lenders and others will be net borrowers, and that some businesses will be net lenders and that others will be net borrowers. For ease of exposition, however, in the next section we will assume that only households are savers (lenders) and only businesses are borrowers (investors).

The Aggregate Saving Curve and the Aggregate Investment Curve Determine the Market Interest Rate

The Aggregate Saving Curve   Given income, the main determinant of saving plans per unit of time is the real rate of interest. How are real saving plans and the real interest rate related? According to the classical economists, there is a direct relationship between the real rate of interest *r* and the amount that is saved out of a given level of income, other things constant. If the real interest rate rises, individual households will save more and consume less out of a given level of income. If the real interest rate falls, a household will save less and consume more out of a given level of income.

The classical economists maintained that households would prefer to consume now rather than later because of the uncertainties of life: spend now because you may not be around later, or you may not be able to enjoy consumption later. Interest is an inducement to households to forgo present consumption; households are offered *more* future consumption if they forgo consumption now. The higher the real interest rate, the more a given amount of saving will enable a household to consume in the future. Therefore, as the real rate of interest rises, households will consume less and save more as people substitute more future consumption for a given quantity of present consumption. When the interest rate falls, people substitute more present consumption for less future consumption.

---

[9] Because different consumers have different rates of time preference, a supply of and a demand for loanable funds will exist, and an interest rate will be established—even if there is no business sector. Those who are more present-oriented will borrow from those who are more future-oriented, and a market interest rate will be established.

We have noted that a given household, regardless of its rate of time preference, will tend to save more at higher interest rates than it will at lower rates. For the community as a whole, the higher the interest rate the greater will be the number of households whose personal trade-off between present and future consumption is less than the interest rate. The conclusion is that a higher percentage of income will be saved at higher real interest rates for the community as a whole; as the real interest rate rises, the community will save more and consume less out of its given level of national income. Figure 4.6 shows the community or aggregate saving curve as a positive function of the real interest rate.

Note that this saving curve was derived by holding the level of income constant. This curve will shift to the right if real national income rises; it will shift to the left if the real national income falls. That is, if real income rises, we would expect the community to save more (and consume more) at every real interest rate. If the community's real income falls, we would expect it to save less (and consume less) at every real interest rate. The saving curve also shifts to the left if the community becomes more present-oriented and to the right if it becomes more future-oriented.

Loanable Funds and Saving

The classical economists felt that the saving curve could be considered as a loanable funds curve. That is, they felt that new saving would automatically become a part of the supply of funds that could be lent to borrower-businesses. The classical position is that money is merely a medium of exchange; hence, people do not want to hold it. Dollars saved *and held* forgo interest; **hoarding** (holding money not wanted to finance transactions), therefore, is irrational in normal times. It is one thing to hold dollars for a short period in order to cover the noncoincidence of money receipts and payments; it is quite another to hold dollars in idle balances indefinitely. After the desired money balances are acquired, therefore, new saving becomes a part of the supply of loanable funds either by household deposits in banks or by household bond purchases.

Finally, it should be stressed that the classical economists viewed interest as a consumer's reward for abstinence from present consumption. Therefore, it is legitimate to ask: who would be willing to reward households for their abstinence? Businesses that wish to spend more than their income in order to invest in plant and equipment and earn profits will pay for the privilege.

The Aggregate Investment Curve

According to classical economists, given profit expectations of businesses, the most important determinant of business investment is the

The Community Saves More and Consumes Less as the Real Interest Rate Rises

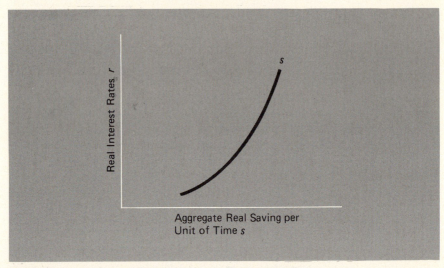

FIGURE 4.6. THE AGGREGATE SAVING CURVE

Assuming a constant level of national income, the community will save more and consume less as the real interest rate rises. A higher interest rate induces households to substitute more future consumption for present consumption.

Because hoarding occurs only in abnormal times (in normal times the gains from hoarding are negligible and the costs of doing so are measured in forgone interest earnings), the saving curve can be thought of as a supply of loanable funds curve.

The community saving curve shifts when the level of national income changes or if the community changes its rate of time preference for consumption. For example, if the level of national income rises or if the community becomes more future oriented, the saving curve will shift to the right—the community will save more at every real interest rate.

rate of interest. Rational profit-maximizing businesses will borrow money to carry out investment projects up to the point at which the marginal benefit equals the marginal cost of doing so. What is the marginal cost and what is the marginal benefit?

The marginal cost of borrowing money is, of course, the rate of interest. For any individual firm, the rate of interest is a constant.

The marginal benefit of borrowing money is the expected rate of return on the investment project. Given an interest rate of, say, 10 percent, a firm will carry on investment projects up to the point where the expected rate of return is 10 percent. If an investment project is expected to yield 12 percent, the project will be carried out and greater than "normal" profits of 2 percent will be earned, after the 10 percent interest has been paid. For that project yielding exactly 10 percent, normal profits will be earned and all costs will be covered, after the interest has been paid. But if an investment project is expected to yield only 8 percent, the project won't be undertaken; it can't even pay off the principal on the loan.

The classical economists maintained that the marginal profitability of investment projects declines as firms in an industry carry out more investment projects.[10] Why? Because the first few investment projects have locational or other advantages. Or, as more and more of a given type of investment is carried out, the supply of the final product increases. Given the demand for the final product, price falls and (other things constant) so does the profitability of marginal investment projects. Also, as an industry gets larger and larger (as firms carry on more and more investment projects), the prices of inputs specific to the industry may rise. Other things constant, marginal profits will fall.

The demand for loanable funds to carry out investments is inversely related to the rate of interest. One way to interpret this demand curve is as follows: before firms will voluntarily carry out more investment projects, the rate of interest must fall to offset decreasing marginal profitability.

Loanable Funds and Investment   A given firm will borrow more funds and carry out more investment projects the lower the interest rate is. For the business community as a whole, as the rate of interest falls, a larger number of firms will observe a market rate of interest that is less than their expected profit rate on a marginal investment project. The lower the market rate of interest, the more firms there will be that become net borrowers. The aggregate demand-for-loanable-funds curve, or the aggregate net investment curve, is indicated in Figure 4.7. It shows an inverse relationship between the rate of interest and the total quantity demanded for loanable funds.

Note that at every point on that curve firms have carried out investment projects up to the quantity at which the expected rate of return on borrowed money is just equal to the interest rate. Hence, every point on the curve is a potential profit-maximizing or equilibrium point.

---

[10] The classical economists referred to this phenomenon as the diminishing marginal product of capital; increases in capital, other things constant, also obey the law of diminishing returns.

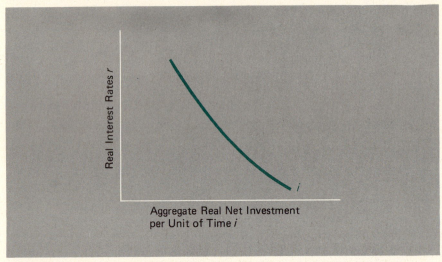

Real Interest Rates r

Aggregate Real Net Investment
per Unit of Time i

FIGURE 4.7. THE AGGREGATE REAL NET INVESTMENT CURVE i

Because of a diminishing marginal physical product of capital for business, a lower rate of interest is required to induce them to borrow additional funds and to carry out additional investment projects.

The aggregate real net investment curve will shift if profit expectations change. If profit expectations increase, the i curve will shift to the right; businesses then intend to invest more at every rate of interest.

This curve shifts if profit expectations change. An increase in profit expectations shifts the curve in Figure 4.7 to the right; the quantity demanded for loanable funds is higher at every rate of interest. A decrease in profit expectations shifts the investment curve to the left because there is a decrease in the quantity demanded for loanable funds at every rate of interest.

Aggregate Saving, Aggregate Investment, and Say's Law

Consider Figure 4.8, which shows the aggregate saving and aggregate investment curves (or the aggregate supply-of- and the aggregate demand-for-loanable-funds curves).

At r_1, the quantity of loanable funds supplied (500) exceeds the quantity of loanable funds demanded (400). In other words, a surplus of loanable funds exists at r_1. While borrowers are able to realize their intentions

A Full-Employment Output Will Be Purchased

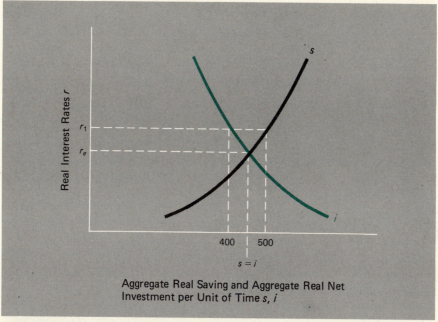

FIGURE 4.8. DETERMINATION OF THE REAL INTEREST RATE r

As long as household saving plans do not equal business net investment plans, disequilibrium exists. For example, at r_1 a surplus of loanable funds exists, so households competing for interest earnings will bid interest rates down toward r_e.

The real interest rate will adjust until household real saving plans and business real net investment plans are equated. At that point, every dollar saved, which is a leakage from the income stream, comes back as a dollar invested and is an injection into the income stream. The result is that aggregate spending, which consists of consumption expenditures and investment expenditures, is sufficient to assure full employment. A full-employment output will be purchased.

(they are maximizing total profits at that interest rate), lenders are not. Competition among lenders, some of whom can't earn any interest at all on their savings, will drive interest rates down toward r_e. As a result, investment spending will rise (because more investment projects are profitable at lower interest rates) and the quantity of saving will fall.

At any interest rate below r_e, the quantity of loanable funds demanded exceeds the quantity supplied, and a shortage of loanable funds exists. Lenders are able to realize their intentions, but borrowers cannot.

Competition among borrowers will force interest rates up, and scarce loanable funds will go to the highest bidders—in general, the most profitable businesses.

Note that we have also just explained the classical theory of the interest rate. The equilibrium rate of interest will be set at the point of intersection of the aggregate supply-of- and the aggregate demand-for-loanable-funds curves. Alternatively, the interaction of aggregate saving and investment plans determines the interest rate.

Planned Saving, Planned Investment, and Say's Law

Before we lose the forest for the trees, we should recapitulate. It has just been demonstrated that interest rate fluctuations establish the equality of planned saving and planned investment. Every dollar that leaves the income stream as a dollar saved (and is a potential drag on the economy) automatically reenters as a dollar invested. Hence, saving does not refute Say's law; dollars saved by households are spent by businesses for investment. Full employment requires only that sufficient expenditures be made; it is not required that expenditures be made by a specific group or combination of groups. Thus, *the saving-investment analysis concludes that the full-employment output will be purchased.* Say's law remains valid even when household saving in a money economy is taken into account.

AGGREGATE SUPPLY OF OUTPUT

To this point all of the economic analysis has been in real terms. As a consequence we can *interpret* such variables as the wage rate and the interest rate without reference to monetary phenomena.

For example, consider the classical interpretation of the wage rate. To classical economists, the wage rate was the result of the interaction of the marginal productivity of labor (the position of the labor demand curve) and laborers' attitudes toward work (the position of the supply-of-labor curve). Note, therefore, that changes in such nonmonetary variables as capital expansion and the work ethic determine the wage rate.

Consider also the classical economists' interpretation of the rate of interest. To them, the interest rate was the result of the interaction of society's rate of time preference for consumption (the position of the aggregate saving curve) and the marginal productivity-of-capital curve (the position of the aggregate net investment curve). Change in nonmonetary variables, such as technology and the degree to which a community is future-oriented, determine the interest rate.

All of this is in keeping with the classical tradition in deemphasizing

Aggregate Supply Is Independent of the Price Level

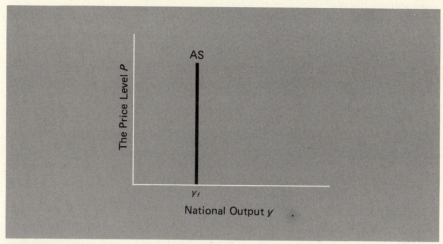

FIGURE 4.9. THE AGGREGATE SUPPLY (AS) CURVE

Because there are forces (price-wage flexibility and interest-rate flexibility) that assure long-run full employment, long-run national output will be independent of the price level. The AS curve is vertical at the full-employment output level y_f; the full-employment output level depends on such nonmonetary phenomena as the determinants of the aggregate production function and of the supply of labor curve.

money as a source of a nation's wealth or real income.[11] What then *is* the role of money in the classical model? As the next chapter emphasizes, money, appropriately enough, determines only such monetary variables as the money wage, the nominal interest rate, and the price level.

There is no reason, therefore, to assume that national output is affected by such a monetary phenomenon as the price level, at least not in the long run. We would expect the **aggregate supply (AS)** of output curve—the relationship between various price levels and the levels of national output that the business community is willing to produce, other things constant—to be vertical. National output will be at the full-employment level, and its specific level will be determined by such nonmoney factors as the determinants of the aggregate production function and the determinants of the aggregate supply of labor. Figure 4.9

---

[11] Recall that wealth is a stock concept that is measured at a given moment of time; wealth equals assets minus liabilities. Income is a flow concept, measured per unit of time. A nation's income is the value of its output *per unit of time.*

shows the classical aggregate supply curve; it is vertical at the full-employment level of output, and this curve can shift if the full-employment output level itself changes.

We want to stress that *the AS curve is a long-run curve and it is vertical in equilibrium.* Disequilibrating shocks could cause the quantity of national output to vary, temporarily, with the price level. In the long run, however, price-wage and interest rate flexibility assure a full-employment level of national output. We elaborate on these conclusions in Chapter 5.

POLICY CONTROVERSY
Policies with Diminishing Returns?

The classical economists deduced the law of diminishing returns, and this fact of nature formed the basis of their theories of economic growth. Here we analyze the Adam Smith–Thomas Malthus growth model and the David Ricardo–Karl Marx growth model.

The Smith-Malthus Model

According to the Smith-Malthus model, population increases over time, but land remains constant. If we assume a constant labor force/population ratio, then population increases geometrically but the "means of subsistence" (output) increases arithmetically. That is, the law of diminishing returns causes output to increase at a decreasing rate, as panel *a* in Figure 4.5 shows. Increases in population lead to shifts in the supply-of-labor curve in panel *b* of Figure 4.5.

Malthus maintained that wages would hover around the subsistence level because lower-than-subsistence wages lead to starvation and to a decrease in the supply of labor, while higher-than-subsistence wages lead to population increases and to increases in the supply of labor.

The belief that misery and poverty were the long-run fate of the masses and that "the poor we always have with us" helped to frame nineteenth-century economic policy.[12] The classical economists, in general, argued for the repeal of the Corn Laws, which were duties (taxes) on imported grain. By importing grain, the food shortages resulting from the law of diminishing returns operating in the agricultural sector could be partially offset; in the main, the classical economists argued in favor of free trade, domestically and internationally.

Some of Malthus's policies for thwarting the implications of the law of diminishing returns were more extreme. They were controversial in his time; today they seem downright bizarre. The following quotation is one of Malthus's more extreme policy prescriptions for minimizing the misery that the ill-fated poor would suffer:

> To act consistently therefore we should facilitate, instead of foolishly and vainly

---

[12] This belief also contributed to the reputation of economics as "the dismal science."

endeavouring to impede, the operations of nature in producing this mortality; and if we dread the too frequent visitation of the horrid form of famine, we should sedulously encourage the other forms of destruction which we compel nature to use. Instead of recommending cleanliness to the poor, we should encourage contrary habits. In our towns we should make the streets narrower, crowd more people into the houses, and court the return of the plague. In the country we should build our villages near stagnant pools, and particularly encourage settlements in all marshy and unwholesome situations. But above all we should reprobate specific remedies for ravaging diseases; and those benevolent, but much mistaken men, who have thought they were doing a service to mankind by projecting schemes for the total extirpation of particular disorders. If by these and similar means the annual mortality were increased from 1 in 36 or 40, to one in 18 or 20, we might probably every one of us marry at the age of puberty, and yet few be absolutely starved.[13]

Malthus, in order also to minimize the suffering of the masses, argued against poor laws, which provide welfare to the poverty stricken:

Among the lower classes of society, where the point is of the greatest importance, the poor-laws afford a direct, constant, and systematical encouragement to marriage by removing from each individual that heavy responsibility which he would incur by the laws of nature for bringing beings into the world which he could not support. Our private benevolence has the same direction as the poor-laws, and almost invariably tends to encourage mar-

riage and to equalise as much as possible the circumstances of married and single men.[14]

In fairness to Malthus we should point out that he lived in the period before sustained economic growth permitted a decent life for the "masses." It is the miracle of sustained economic growth that is new on the human scene—and that *still* escapes most of the world outside Western civilization—that makes Malthus's policies seem so cold and heartless today. Moreover, he also preferred that people exercise "moral restraint" to limit population.

The Ricardo-Marx Model

The Ricardo-Marx model of economic growth also incorporates, as an essential ingredient, the law of diminishing returns. In their formulation, however, it is capital accumulation (hence the term *capitalism*) that increases relative to other factors of production over time. Diminishing returns to capital implies a reduction in the profit rate and the interest rate; real wage *rates* rise but total labor real wage *incomes* fall, according to Marx, because the reserve army of the unemployed eventually grows as capital replaces labor in the production process.

Marx believed that the policy capitalists would follow was imperialism (new markets must be found in other countries to help prevent the reduction in the profit rate) and increased labor exploitation (to preserve profit margins). Marx's policy for laborers was to join the progressive forces and help bring about the inevitable transformation of capitalism into socialism and then into full communism.

[13] Thomas Robert Malthus, *An Essay on the Principle of Population*, reprinted in Leonard Dalton Abbott, ed., *Masterworks of Economics* (New York: McGraw-Hill, 1973), vol. 1, pp. 225–226.

[14] Ibid., p. 228.

CHAPTER SUMMARY

1. The classical economists waged an intellectual revolution against mercantilism, which was the doctrine that maintained that (a) a nation's wealth and power was measured by its stock of precious (monetary) metals and (b) the state could and should pursue policies to increase the sovereign's holdings of such previous metals.
2. Classical economists stressed the nonmonetary determinants of a nation's wealth, and most of them placed their faith in free markets rather than in state economic policy.
3. Classical economists believed—with varying degrees of enthusiasm and with differing interpretations—in Say's law, which states that supply creates its own demand.
4. Say's law implies that there are forces within capitalism which assure that, in the long run, a full-employment output will be produced and will be purchased.
5. Wage-rate flexibility assures that in the long run full employment will be attained. Unemployment, or a surplus of labor, will cause nominal wage rates to fall relative to the price level. This reduction in the real wage rate will restore labor market equilibrium of full employment.
6. The classical economists interpreted the wage rate as the result of the interaction of the marginal productivity of labor and laborers' attitudes toward work.
7. Through the production function, the full employment of labor generated in the labor market determines the full-employment output level.
8. Changes in the interest rate assure that planned household saving (which is a leakage from the income stream) is converted into equal business-planned investments. Total spending, which includes household consumption expenditures and business investment expenditures, therefore, will be sufficient to purchase a full-employment output.
9. In the long run, the level of national output is independent of the price level; the classical long-run aggregate supply curve is vertical at the full-employment level of national output.
10. The position of the classical long-run aggregate supply curve is dependent on such nonmoney variables as the determinants of the aggregate production function and the supply of labor.

GLOSSARY

aggregate supply (AS) The relationship between various price levels and the levels of national output that businesses will produce voluntarily.

future-oriented Having a marked preference for future consumption over present consumption.

hoarding According to the classical economists, hoarding takes place when people hold money above and beyond what they need to finance transactions.

interest The amount of money that lenders receive when they extend credit.

interest rate The ratio of interest to the amount lent.

law of diminishing returns A technological statement relating inputs to outputs; if one factor of production increases by equal increments while other factors are held constant, eventually the marginal product of the variable input will fall.

marginal physical product of labor (MPP_n) The change in total output resulting from a unit change in the quantity of labor employed; the slope of the aggregate production function.

mercantilism An economic doctrine which asserts that a nation's wealth and power are measured by its store of precious metals and that the state can and should increase its holdings of such wealth.

money illusion A money illusion exists if economic agents change their behavior in response to changes in nominal values, even if there are no changes in real (inflation-adjusted) values.

present-oriented Having a marked preference for present consumption over future consumption.

Say's law A dictum of J. B. Say that supply creates its own demand; by producing goods and services, an equal means and the willingness to purchase other goods and services are created.

value of the marginal physical product of labor The marginal physical product of labor multiplied by the selling price of output.

QUESTIONS AND PROBLEMS FOR REVIEW

4.1 List some nonmoney determinants of a nation's economic wealth and power.

4.2 What is the classical, nonmonetary interpretation of the wage rate?

4.3 What is the classical, nonmonetary interpretation of the interest rate?

4.4 What causes the saving curve, the net interest curve, the aggregate demand-for-labor curve, and the aggregate supply-of-labor curve to shift?

4.5 Why is the classical aggregate supply curve vertical only in the long run?

4.6 Consider Figure 4.1. Suppose a technological change occurs, or that the nation's capital stock increases. What happens in panel *a*? In panel *b*?

4.7 Consider Figure 4.5. Assume that for various reasons the real wage rate can depart from the equilibrium rate. Derive a short-run aggregate supply curve, assuming that the price level rises but nominal wage rates remain constant.

4.8 Consider Figure 4.5 again. The Reverend Thomas Malthus believed that there was a tendency for population to increase exponentially but for the means of subsistence (national output) to increase at a decreasing rate.

    a. Show the Malthusian doctrine using Figure 4.5 as a base.

    b. How is the law of diminishing returns related to the Malthusian doctrine?

4.9   According to Malthus, the real wage rate would tend to hover around the subsistence level because lower real wages lead to starvation and therefore to decreases in the supply of labor, while above-subsistence wages induce people to propagate and thereby lead to increases in the supply of labor.

    a. Was Malthus correct? Why or why not?

    b. Show, using Figure 4.5, how changes in technology can offset the law of diminishing returns and Malthus's predictions.

REFERENCES

Irving Fisher, *The Theory of Interest* (New York: Macmillan, 1930).

John Maynard Keynes, *The General Theory of Employment, Interest and Money* (London: Macmillan, 1936).

R. T. Malthus, *An Essay on the Principles of Population*, reprinted in Leonard Dalton Abbott, ed., *Masterworks of Economics*, vol. 1, (New York: McGraw-Hill, 1973).

A. Marshall, *Principles of Economics* (New York: Macmillan, 1890).

A. Marshall, *Money Credit and Commerce* (London: Macmillan, 1925).

J. S. Mill, *Principles of Economics* (London: J. W. Parker, 1848).

D. Patinkin, *Money, Interest, and Prices*, 2d ed. (New York: Harper & Row, 1965).

J. G. K. Wicksell, *Interest and Prices*, translated by R. F. Kahn (London: Macmillan, 1936).

5

THE CLASSICAL MODEL: PART 2

The previous chapter stressed that in the classical model real variables determine other real variables. For example, planned real saving and planned real investment determine the real rate of interest; real wage rates are determined by the marginal productivity of labor and laborers' attitudes toward work; and national output depends on the employment level.

This chapter analyzes the determination of such monetary variables as the money wage rate, the nominal interest rate, and the general price level. As you may have perceived by now, the classical model states that such monetary variables are determined only by the quantity of money—in the long run.

In this chapter we discuss:

1. The classical quantity theory of money
2. The shape and position of the classical aggregate demand curve
3. How aggregate supply and aggregate demand determine the general price level
4. The neutrality of money in the classical model
5. The role that monetary policy and fiscal policy play in the classical model
6. A controversy over classical monetary policy (see the Policy Controversy section at the end of this chapter)

THE QUANTITY THEORY OF MONEY

The *quantity theory* of money was the dominant macroeconomic theory for centuries. It was largely supplanted by Keynesian analysis in the 1930s, but a version of the quantity theory has recently made a comeback (as Chapter 11 will show). Quantity theorists dealt with such questions as the determinants of the (1) general price level, (2) interest rate, (3) demand for money, and (4) supply of money. Moreover, quantity theorists did not agree on the answers to these questions. For these reasons, it is not precise to write about "the" quantity theory of money; it is more accurate to write about the quantity theory framework.

In its simplest form (known as the *crude quantity theory*) the quantity theory is that changes in the general price level are determined by changes in the quantity of money in circulation. Two alternative versions of this crude quantity theory are:

1. The Cambridge equation.
2. The equation of exchange.

The Cambridge Equation

Alfred Marshall and his colleagues at Cambridge University in England developed the **Cambridge equation,** which states

$$M = kPy \qquad (5.1)$$

WHERE M = the nominal money supply (the value of coins, currency, and demand deposits held by the nonbank public[1])
P = the general price level
y = national output
k = the ratio of *actual* money balances held to nominal national income

The product Py can be thought of as nominal national output (GNP or NNP) because it equals the output of all the final goods and services weighted by their respective prices. $Py = P_1 y_1 + P_2 y_2 + \cdots + P_n y_n$ for n final goods; the y's are quantities of final goods and are equivalent to the q's analyzed in national income accounting in footnote 8 of Chapter 2.

The Cambridge equation is an equation derived from three other equations. First,

$$L_1 = kPy \qquad (5.2)$$

which states that the *quantity of money demanded* L_1 is equal to k multiplied by nominal national income. The second equation is

$$M = \overline{M} \qquad (5.3)$$

The money supply is **exogenously determined,** and it does not depend upon variables in the model but is determined by such outside forces as the central bank or by gold discoveries. (A bar written above a variable means that it is exogenously determined. Exogenously determined variables are constants in our models.)

The final equation is an equilibrium condition,

$$M = L_1 \qquad (5.4)$$

which states that the quantity of money supplied equals the quantity of money demanded.

Equation 5.1 is derived by substituting the demand for money function (equation 5.2) into the right-hand side of the equilibrium condition

---

[1] A rather narrow concept of the money supply that, until recently, was one of the official definitions of money used by the Federal Reserve of the United States (the Fed).

(equation 5.4) and the supply of money function (equation 5.3) into the left-hand side of the equilibrium condition.

The Equation of Exchange

Across the Atlantic, the American cousins developed an equation that is mathematically equivalent to the Cambridge equation. Irving Fisher of Yale University developed the **equation of exchange:**

$$MV = Py \qquad (5.5)$$

where V is the actual income velocity of money (the average number of times each monetary unit is spent on final goods and services per unit of time).

A moment's reflection indicates that MV is equal to total expenditures on final goods and services; the money stock multiplied by the average number of times each monetary unit is spent must be total expenditures. Py can be thought of as total business receipts from the sales of final goods and services. Thus, $MV = Py$ says that total expenditures on final goods and services by households and businesses equal total business receipts, a statement that is definitionally true. National income accounting indicates that the market value of final goods and services is identical to national income: $Py = Y$.

Multiply both sides of equation 5.5 by $1/V$, so that $M = (1/V)P_y$. Compare this to equation 5.2 and it is clear that $1/V = k$ and $V = 1/k$; velocity and the ratio of nominal money balances to nominal national income are the reciprocals of each other. The equation of exchange and the Cambridge equation are mathematically equivalent, and they are both true by definition; k is that value obtained *ex post* after dividing M by Py in equation 5.1; and V is that value obtained *ex post* after dividing Py by M in equation 5.5.

Both the American and British formulations of the equation of exchange can be transformed from identities into testable theories. *If it can be demonstrated that V and k are ratios desired by the community and that they are stable—or that they at least change predictably—then the truism has become a theory.*

The Classical Theory of the Demand for Money

Because it lends itself readily to the development of a theory of the demand for money, consider the Cambridge (or Marshallian) version. Let k now represent the community's *desired* ratio of money balances to the level of *nominal* national income. The classical economists believed this ratio to be stable (hence, we can now speak of the *quantity theory*). Why? To them, money is merely useful as a medium of exchange; because it is non–interest-bearing, money is not desired for its own sake. Money produces nothing and earns no interest; therefore, rational people use it only to make transactions for goods and services. They called this the **transactions motive** for holding money. Both Fisher and Marshall also recognized the existence of a **precautionary motive** for holding money— meaning that people hold a pool of readily available purchasing power in order to meet emergencies. But, for ease of exposition, economists typically lump these two motives together and refer only to the transactions motive.

Rational businesses and rational households try to keep their individual k's to a minimum,[2] because holding idle money balances imposes an opportunity cost on holders—forgone interest earnings. Why do people hold money at all? Businesses and households typically *receive* money on dates that do not necessarily correspond to the dates on which they want to *spend* it. Were there a perfect coincidence of money receipts and payments, money would be received and spent instantaneously.[3] Moreover, because people want to hold a pool of readily available purchasing power in order to meet emergencies, by holding money they receive precautionary security. By assumption, the *extra* benefit of holding additional dollars for these motives eventually declines. An individual's optimal k will, therefore, be established where the decreasing marginal benefit of holding one more unit of money is just offset by the constant marginal cost (forgone interest earnings) from doing so. Holding more dollars beyond the optimal k leaves an individual economically worse off, because beyond that point the marginal benefit is less than the marginal cost.

Each individual probably has a different k. An individual's k depends on frequency of income,[4] credit arrangements with creditors, use of credit cards, and the individual's degree of insecurity. According to the classical economists, however, an overall stable k is found for the community *as a whole*. That is, the determinants of k do not change significantly during the long-run adjustment period.[5] Classical economists believed the com-

---

[2] This is equivalent to a maximum V in the American equation of exchange approach. Minimally held money balances (a minimum k) translate into a maximum annual turnover rate for money (a maximum V).

[3] If nonmoney interest-earning assets, such as bonds, could be purchased and sold at zero transaction costs, money would also be held for only very short periods—according to the classical economists.

[4] The more often one gets paid, the closer the correspondence between receipts and disbursements and the less the reason for a transactions motive; hence, the lower k is.

[5] Both American and British classical economists believed that changes in V (or k) could be quite significant and disruptive in the short run. For example, changes in "confidence" were thought to create business cycles. Classical economists, in the main, were more concerned with the long-run results of shocks, and they tended to deemphasize short-run effects.

munity k to be somewhere between one-fifth and one-fourth, although significant short-run deviations from that range were acknowledged by them.

The conclusion of the previous chapter was that price, wage, and interest rate flexibility assure full employment. As a consequence, the economywide output level of final goods and services is equal to its maximum potential level. It follows that the classical economists would have predicted a constant y in the long run; y is constant at the full-employment level. Thus, we let $y = \bar{y}$.

As the price level (or nominal national income) rises, the community wants to hold proportionally more in cash balances in order to finance its transactions. Because k is assumed constant, according to equation 5.2, L_1 will rise proportionally. If the price level doubles, the community will want to hold twice as much money in order to make the same transactions. For example, assume that nominal national income is $100 per annum and that the community wants to hold a $20 cash balance—$15 to satisfy its transactions motive and $5 to meet its precautionary motive. This means that $k = 0.2$. If the price level doubles while y remains constant, then L_1 will double to 40. Why? In order to make the same transactions at a price level that is twice as high, $30 is now required. Moreover, the community will now require $10 in money balances in order to remain equally secure; a higher price level lowers the purchasing power of a constant money balance. In short, a doubling of the price level causes nominal national income to double to $200; in turn, desired money balances also double, to $40. *Real* income and k remain constant. Consider Figure 5.1, which shows a community demand-for-money curve.

Note that the implicit classical assumption is that *the community wants to hold a constant quantity of real (price-level-adjusted) balances for transactions purposes*—at the economy's full-employment output level.[6]

The Classical Theory of the Price Level   We are now ready to analyze the classical theory of the price level. In the Cambridge version,

$$M = kPy \qquad (5.1)$$

Because k and y are assumed to be constant in the long run (k is at a minimum, y is at the full-employment maximum level), exogenous increases in M lead to proportional increases in the price level.[7]

---

[6] The demand-for-money equation is $L_1 = kPy$; dividing both sides by P yields $L_1/P = ky$; real money balances demanded (L_1/P) equal a constant proportion of real national income (output).

[7] Exogenous increases in M also lead to proportional increases in nominal national income because $M = kY$.

The Community's Quantity Demanded of Money Is Proportional to the Level of Nominal National Income

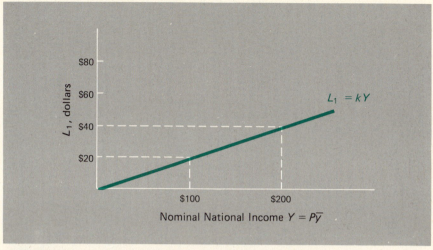

FIGURE 5.1. THE COMMUNITY DEMAND FOR MONEY

Along the horizontal axis, nominal national income rises from left to right; because y is constant, nominal national income increases as the price level rises. Along this curve, k, which is the slope, is constant and equal to 0.2. As the price level doubles, nominal income rises from $100 to $200 and L_1 doubles from $20 to $40.

Similarly, in the equation of exchange,

$$MV = Py \tag{5.5}$$

where V and y are constant, so exogenously determined changes in M lead to proportional changes in P.

Consider Figure 5.2, which shows how changes in the money supply lead to a proportional change in the level of nominal national income, and therefore to a proportional change in the price level.

At point A equilibrium exists at nominal national income $1000, given a money stock of $200 and a k equal to 0.2.[8] Assume that now an exogenous increase in the money supply occurs—owing to (say) a gold discovery—and the money stock increases 50 percent, to $300. At $Y = $1000, $300 = $M > L_1 = $200, and a surplus of money exists; the com-

---

[8] Equilibrium requires that $M = L_1$; substituting gives $200 = 0.2Y$, so $Y = $1000.

A 50 Percent Increase in the Money Supply Causes Nominal National Income to Rise by 50 Percent

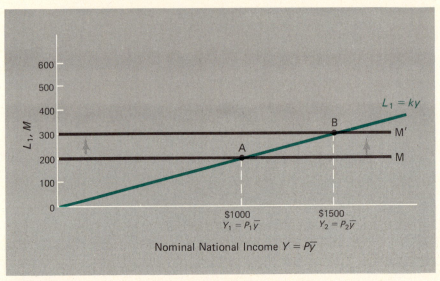

FIGURE 5.2. AN INCREASE IN THE MONEY SUPPLY

An exogenous increase in the money supply from $200 to $300 causes a movement from A to B. Start at A, where the level of nominal national income is $1000 and equilibrium exists. Now the money supply increases to $300; at Y_1 = $1000, a surplus of money exists and so people spend more. Because the economy is at full employment, prices rise and nominal national income rises to $1500; at point B equilibrium again exists.

Note that uniquely associated with a money stock of $200 and a constant y is price level P_1; uniquely associated with nominal national income $1000 is P_1. Similarly, uniquely associated with Y = $1500, given a money stock of $300 and a constant y, is price level P_2. Can you demonstrate that $P_2 = 1.5\ P_1$?

munity is now holding more money than it *wants* to hold. Because money is only a medium of exchange, national spending will rise. Because national output is at its full-employment maximum, however, increased spending causes a shortage of goods and services. Classical economists referred to this as a situation in which "too much money is chasing too few goods." A shortage of goods induces buyers to bid up prices, so the price level rises. Note, however, that as the price level rises the quantity demanded for money also rises; people want more money to finance the same transactions because goods and services cost more to purchase. Eventually a 50 percent increase in the money supply will cause the level of nominal national income to rise by 50 percent.[9]

This process can be viewed in another way. Equilibrium requires that the community voluntarily hold the existing money supply, whatever its level might be. An increase in the money supply temporarily upsets this equilibrium; the community is temporarily holding more than it desires in order to make transactions and to remain equally secure. *While it is possible for individuals to rid themselves of excess balances, the whole community cannot.* As a consequence, something must happen to induce the community to hold more money voluntarily. Because people will wish to hold more money as the price level rises, the price level must rise before equilibrium is restored. This approach to equilibrium analysis is mechanistic, and is therefore less preferable than one that stresses human behavior. (On the other hand, we'll try anything to get our point across.)

Summary and Appraisal of the Quantity Theory[10]   According to the crude quantity theory:

1. National output is constant at the full-employment output level. While some classical economists maintained that this was true even in the short run (indeed, some apparently believed that this was the case at every instant), the more sophisticated classical economists believed that there was a *long-run* tendency toward full employment.
2. Income velocity of money V, or its reciprocal k, was constant. Here again, although some classical economists seemed to believe that V was always constant, the more sophisticated classical economists maintained that *significant* variation in V or k could arise in the short run, as a result of changes in business and household "confidence" in the economy or in the banking structure. The sophisticated classical economists believed that V was stable in the long run; significant departures caused disruptions, but when "normal" times were restored, the normal V was restored too. Other sophisticated economists maintained that V was exogenously determined by factors that were not explicitly considered in the macroeconomic model.

---

[9] See footnote 8 to help you see why the new level of nominal national income is $1500, owing to an increase in M from $200 to $300.

[10] A very readable summary, and a fine historical development, of the quantity theory can be found in Thomas M. Humphrey, "The Quantity Theory of Money: Its Historical Evolution and Role in Policy Debates," in Thomas M. Humphrey, *Essays on Inflation*, 4th ed. (Richmond, Va.: Federal Reserve Bank of Richmond, 1983). A more rigorous treatment of the quantity theory can be found in Laurence Harris, *Monetary Theory* (New York: McGraw-Hill, 1981) chaps. 3, 4, and 6.

3. Because of 1 and 2, the general price level will vary *proportionally* with changes in the stock of money in circulation. This follows from the contention of the classical economists that the community wants to hold a constant quantity of *real* money balances for transactions purposes, at the economy's full-employment level of real national output (income). While some classical economists believed that the proportion was *exact* and that this proportional relationship *always* existed, the more rigorous classical economists believed that there was only a tendency toward proportionality in the long run.

4. Money supply increases cause increases in the price level; the direction of causation runs from money supply changes to price level changes. Thus, money supply changes *precede and cause* general price level changes. This proposition follows from the assumption that the nominal money supply is exogenously determined.[11] It should be noted that not all classical economists agreed with this proposition, or with its implication. Some prominent economists (and some prominent modern Keynesian economists, too) argued that the money supply could well be an endogenous variable that expands in boom times and contracts in recessions; the money supply expands and contracts automatically with the "needs of trade."[12]

5. Changes in the price level are due *predominantly* to changes in the money supply. The price level is a monetary phenomenon, and, in the long run, changes in the price level do not result from changes in real variables.

6. A higher price level is the adjustment mechanism that restores equilibrium after an increase in the money supply shocks the economy into disequilibrium. The economy will remain in disequilibrium until increased spending increases the price level sufficiently to induce people to hold, voluntarily, the now higher money stock. Some classical economists (such as Wicksell) believed that a temporarily lower interest rate resulted from an increased money supply; an interest rate that is below the marginal rate of return of capital induces increased demand for investment (and consumption) goods, thereby imparting an *indirect* mechanism that drives the price level

---

[11] Note that the desired *real* stock of money is an *endogenous* variable; it is determined by the public's demand for real money balances, which in turn is related to such variables as the coincidence of payments and expenditures, the stage of development of the banking system, the use of credit, and so on.

[12] Marshall and Fisher (and others), however, believed that in "normal times" banks would hold zero or near zero excess reserves (see a textbook on the principles of economics or on money and banking). As a consequence, the money supply would normally be at or near the maximum level consistent with the central banks' required reserve ratio. This issue resurfaces in Chapter 18, when we discuss the empirical foundation of the *modern* quantity of money—or "monetarism."

upward. They noted, further, that a higher price level increased business (and household) transactions demand for money, which in turn led to a drain on bank reserves and eventually to a higher interest rate—one that was again equal to the marginal product of capital.

7. Changes in the money supply affect only such *monetary* variables as the price level, nominal wages, and the nominal interest rate. This statement, again as far as the more sophisticated classical economists were concerned, was a long-run proposition and is referred to as the **neutrality of money.** Because this important issue deserves more systematic treatment, we postpone it until a later section in this chapter.

8. Although we have not stated so explicitly, the classical economists believed that changes in the money supply led to temporary disequilibrium disturbances *only to the extent that they were unanticipated.* (The Policy Controversy at the end of this chapter deals with this issue at greater length.)

DETERMINING THE PRICE LEVEL VIA AGGREGATE DEMAND AND AGGREGATE SUPPLY CURVES

The Aggregate Demand Curve

Another way in which the classical model can be presented, in order to demonstrate the classical economists' theory of the price level, is via the *aggregate supply (AS)–aggregate demand (AD)* approach. This is a particularly fruitful approach because it not only yields insight into the workings of the classical model, it also enables us to compare (in later chapters) the classical model with more modern economic models that also analyze the economy via an aggregate demand–aggregate supply formulation. Just remember, however, that we are applying modern tools to an old model; the classical economist did not really use these AS-AD tools *as such.*

The Equation of Exchange   Recall the equation of exchange:

$$MV = Py \qquad (5.5)$$

If we hold M constant (i.e., total expenditures are constant) and divide both sides of the equation of exchange by y, the result is

$$\frac{MV}{y} = P \qquad (5.6)$$

Note that, given a constant numerator MV, increases in national output y lead to a lower price level; given total money expenditures (or nominal national income), a larger output can only be sold at lower prices. Similarly, reductions in y, given a constant nominal national income or constant aggregate expenditures, will cause the price level to rise, as the same money expenditures "chase" fewer goods. In short, for a given level of nominal national income, an inverse relationship exists between the price level and the level of national output. We can refer to this relationship as the **aggregate demand (AD)** curve; the AD curve shows the quantity demanded of domestic national output at each and every price level.

The AD curve is shown in Figure 5.3; the curve is downward-sloping from left to right and indicates the inverse relationship between the price level and the quantity demanded of domestic output.

International Trade The classical economists were intimately concerned with another reason for a negatively sloped AD curve: international trade. A lower domestic price level, other things constant, will induce domestic residents to substitute domestically produced goods for imported goods; moreover, a lower domestic price level, other things constant, will encourage foreigners to import more goods made by domestic producers; therefore, domestic exports rise. In short, a relatively lower domestic price level will encourage exports and discourage imports and thereby increases the quantity demanded of domestically produced national output.[13]

Shifts in the AD Curve

When the AD curve was derived using the equation of exchange, MV was held constant. It follows, therefore, that a change in either M or V will shift the AD curve. For example, an increase in the money supply or an increase in velocity (a decrease in k) will shift the AD curve upward; the price level will be higher at any level of national output.[14] This is because increased spending, or an increased ability to spend, causes people to compete for a given output quantity, and this lifts the price level upward.

Complementary reasoning suggests that a reduction in M or V will lead to a decrease in AD; the price level would be lower at every quantity of national output.

When the AD curve took into account international trade consider-

---

[13] We leave it to you to demonstrate why exports fall and imports rise as the domestic price level rises.

[14] If $MV/y = P$, then an increase in the numerator requires a higher P at every y; or, equivalently, a higher numerator requires a larger y for each P.

A Lower Price Level Leads to an Increase in the Quantity Demanded for National Output

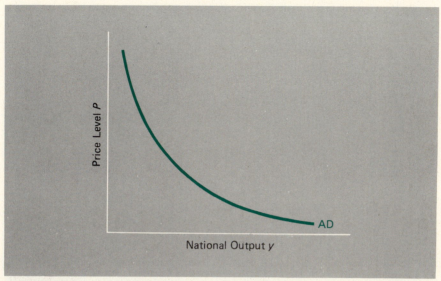

FIGURE 5.3. THE AGGREGATE DEMAND CURVE

From the equation of exchange, or by analyzing the implications of international trade, an aggregate demand (AD) curve can be derived. The AD curve is negatively sloped and indicates that lower general price levels, with other things constant (such as the price of inputs), increase the quantity demanded for domestic national output.

ations, the foreign price level was implicitly held constant; the AD curve was derived by changing domestic prices *relative* to foreign prices. If the foreign price level rises, other things constant, the domestic AD curve will shift to the right. Foreigners will want more of the domestically produced goods, and so there will be an increase in the demand for domestic goods. Similarly, if the price level falls in foreign countries, other things constant, there will be a decrease in the domestic AD curve; the domestic AD curve will shift to the left.

AD and AS Determine the Price Level

Consider Figure 5.4, which utilizes the AS curve derived in Chapter 4 and the AD derived in this chapter. Given those curves, the equilibrium price level will be determined at P_e, the point of intersection of the two curves. At any higher price level, such as P_1, a surplus of national output

Aggregate Demand and Aggregate Supply Determine the Domestic Price Level

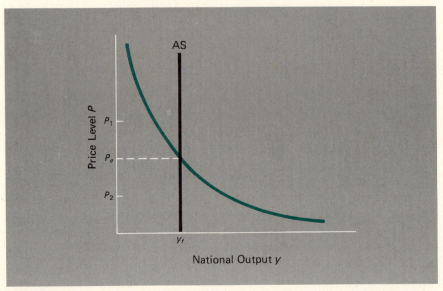

FIGURE 5.4. DETERMINATION OF THE DOMESTIC PRICE LEVEL

At P_1, a surplus of national output exists and so sellers, competing for sales, will lower prices until the quantity demanded of goods and services rises sufficiently to assure that a full-employment output is produced. At P_2, a shortage of national output exists and buyers, competing with each other for goods, will drive the price level up until the quantity demanded of national output equals the full-employment output.

In the long run, equilibrium will be at P_e. The price level is demand determined in the long run because Say's law assures a vertical AS curve in the long run.

---

exists and the price level will fall; at P_1 the community wants less than the full-employment output level. A national surplus of goods and services exists, causing the price level to fall, which in turn causes an increase in the quantity demanded of domestically produced output. In the long run, Say's law assures a full-employment output level.

At all price levels below P_e, such as P_2, the quantity demanded of domestic national output exceeds the full-employment output level. A shortage of national output exists at P_2; therefore, buyers (both domestic and foreign) compete for the goods and drive the domestic price level upward, to P_e.

At P_e, the quantity of AS equals the quantity of AD $(AS_q = AD_q)$ and equilibrium is said to exist; the domestic price level will neither rise nor fall.

Note that, given the vertical AS curve, the price level is *demand-determined*; the price level is determined mainly by M, in the long run. This is because V was assumed constant in the long run. Thus, shifts in AD are likely to result from changes in the money stock. We leave it to you to show, graphically and verbally, how an increase in the money supply will cause the price level to rise and a decrease in the money supply will lead to a lower price level.

Note that the AD curve will also shift if foreign price levels change relative to the domestic price level. Presumably other nations experience inflation or deflation when *their* money supply rises or falls, and so we again conclude that the domestic price level depends on the quantity of money in circulation—domestic and international.

Real Variables Determine Real Values and Money Determines Nominal Values

Consider Figure 5.5, which nicely summarizes the classical model graphically. The economy can be divided into the real world and the money world; panels *a* and *b*, on the left side of Figure 5.5, indicate the workings of the real world. As noted in Chapter 4, the real wage rate w_e is established in panel *a* and the equilibrium (full-employment) quantity of labor N_f is also established. Panel *b* shows the aggregate production function; given N_f, the economy will produce the full-employment output level y_f.

Panels *c* and *d* indicate the money world. Panel *c* depicts the classical AD-AS curve framework derived in the last section; note that the coordinate system in panel *c* is rotated so that we can show how y_f, derived from panel *b*, appears as a vertical curve, AS, in panel *c*.

Panel *d* needs some explanation. The real wage rate is defined as $w = W/P$, or as the nominal wage rate divided by the price level. In principle there is an infinite number of combinations of nominal wage rates and price levels that are consistent with any real wage rate. Panel *d* shows all the combinations of money wage rate and price levels that indicate the real wage rate w_e.[15]

---

[15] A higher real wage rate would bring forth a ray from the origin (in panel *d*) that has a steeper slope; a lower real wage rate would generate a ray from the origin with a lesser slope. This is because the slope of such a line *is* the real wage rate. The slope is $\Delta W/\Delta P$, which equals W/P on a ray from the origin.

The Money Supply Determines Only Nominal Values

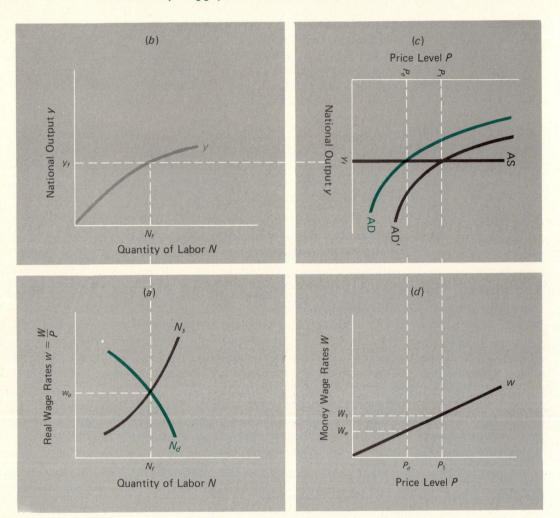

FIGURE 5.5. RELATING MONEY VALUES TO REAL VALUES

The full-employment output level y_f is determined by the real variables in panels a and b. The quantity of money in circulation determines the position of the AD curve in panel c; AD therefore determines the price level because AS is vertical. A unique AD curve exists for every money supply; therefore, a unique price level exists for each money supply.

The real wage rate is determined in panel a. A unique money supply determines the position of the AD curve and, therefore, AD determines the price level. Given a real wage rate of, say, w_e, a price level of P_e necessitates a money wage rate of W_e, and a higher money stock leads to AD' and P_1, and therefore to money wage rate W_1. It follows that, given the real wage rate, the money supply determines the nominal wage rate.

When the price level is demand-determined and the AD curve shifts only due to changes in M, there exists a unique price level for every money supply. Real output y_f is consistent with *any* price level. If the real wage rate is known—it is determined in panel *a*—and the price level is known, then the money or nominal wage is determined. The money supply, therefore, also determines the nominal wage. The next section deals with why a specific nominal wage, given the real wage and the price level, will be *in fact* eventually established in the labor market.

THE NEUTRALITY OF MONEY

To the classical economist, "money does not matter" because it serves only as a medium of exchange. One way to give content to that oft-repeated expression is to note that changes in the supply of money (given the demand for money) *in the long run* change only the price level and the money values; money supply changes leave relative prices unaltered after the new equilibrium position is restored. This is an example of comparative statics analysis. Start from equilibrium, introduce a shock such as a change in the money supply, work out the theoretical implications, and then compare the new equilibrium position with the old. This technique ignores the *dynamic* process of moving from the original equilibrium to the new equilibrium. If the time lag between the shock and the restoration of equilibrium is long, and if the magnitudes of the changes in the variables are large, then the value of the comparative statics analytic technique can be questioned. Some classical economists took precisely that position, and so they concentrated on a detailed analysis of the dynamic process of how equilibrium is restored. As we will see, Keynes also was vitally concerned with the short-run dynamics of *dis*equilibrium.

The classical economists believed that, in the long run, a change in the money stock will leave the following unchanged:

1. *Relative* prices of goods and services
2. Real wages
3. Real interest rate
4. Employment, output, and the composition of output

Goods and Services

Unless something significant such as a change in tastes or a change in the cost of production occurs, a change in the stock of money should not change relative prices. For example, suppose that 1 pound of peaches has a relative price equal to a pair of shoes; they both cost, say, $3.

Suppose the money supply increases, other things constant, so that 1 pound of peaches now costs $6. If a pair of shoes now costs only $5, the relative price of shoes has fallen; *if, however, there has not been a change in the real supply or real demand for shoes, a shortage of shoes will now exist at the new set of relative prices.* The price of shoes, therefore, will rise toward $6. Similar reasoning indicates that if the price of shoes rises to, say, $7, a surplus of shoes will exist and the prices of a pair of shoes will fall to $6.

Real Wage Rates

Consider again Figure 5.5. Panel c shows that an increase in the money supply shifts the AD curve upward to AD' and the price level rises to P_1. Unless money wage rates rise *exactly* to W_1 in panel d, real wage rates will have risen or fallen. Suppose that money wage rates rise to a level below W_1. This results in a lower real wage rate. Note, however, in panel a that because neither the supply of labor nor the demand for labor has shifted, a real wage rate below w_e creates a shortage of labor. Employers compete for scarce labor and drive nominal wage rates upward to W_1. Complementary reasoning indicates that if nominal wage rates increase above W_1, a surplus of labor will exist and nominal wage rates will fall as unemployed laborers compete for jobs. Nominal wage rate W_1 is required for equilibrium; in the long run, the nominal wage rate must be exactly equal to W_1.

The conclusion is that because neither the supply of labor nor the demand for labor has changed—each depends on nonmonetary phenomena—a change in the money supply will leave real wage rates unaltered in the long run.

The Real Interest Rate

Because the saving (supply of loanable funds) and the investment (demand for loanable funds) curves are in real terms, we would not expect them to shift as a result of a change in the money supply. In other words, unless a change in the money supply changes the community's rate of time preference for consumption or the marginal productivity of capital, the real interest rate will not change. Money supply changes, therefore, will cause changes only in nominal interest rates.[16]

---

[16] The nominal interest rate equals (approximately) the real interest rate plus the inflation rate. Stated alternatively, the real interest rate approximately equals the nominal interest rate minus the inflation rate.

Employment, Output, and the Composition of Output

If the real wage rate does not change (with a money-stock change), then the level of employment will not change; given the full-employment quantity of labor, national output will again be at the full-employment level when equilibrium is restored. If the real interest rate remains constant, then the share of national output allocated to consumer goods and to investment goods will not be altered.

Money is neutral in the long run because (after short-run adjustments) employment, national output, and the composition of output are unaffected by changes in the supply of money.

MONETARY POLICY AND FISCAL POLICY IN THE CLASSICAL MODEL

Because the classical model predicts that full employment will eventually be restored after the economy has been shocked, it would appear that the role of monetary policy and fiscal policy is limited.

As long as the quantity of money in circulation is stable, the general price level will remain stable. Monetary authorities need only do what they can do to stabilize the money stock. Such a conclusion is consistent with the classical tradition of limited governmental activities in the economic system. Still, some early classical economists (Hume and Cantillon, for example) and later neoclassical economists (such as Pigou) recognized that wage rates (and some prices) tend not to fall when a surplus of labor exists, that is, wage rates are "sticky downward." Others suggested that if the time lag between a shock and the restoration of equilibrium is long, monetary policy might reduce the length of the adjustment period.

Monetary Policy in the Classical Model

Assume that the economy is in a full-employment equilibrium position and that such disequilibrium-creating shocks as a general increase in thriftiness or an increase in the nation's demand for imports relative to exports occurs. (The latter would lead to gold outflows and a reduced domestic money stock.) Assume further that prices can *rise*, but that they are inflexible downward. These shocks can create, temporarily, an increase in the amount of frictional unemployment if relative wage rates do not change. Equilibrium requires a new set of relative prices; some wage rates and prices should be higher, others lower, or the real interest rate should fall (in the case of an increase in thriftiness).

Suppose that the government attempts to reduce the length of the adjustment period by employing monetary policy. If the money supply is (somehow) increased, then the price level will rise *but prices and wage rates will not all rise at the same rate.*[17] Prices and wage rates will rise more rapidly in those areas not directly affected by the initial shock than they will in the surplus areas. By a judicious use of monetary policy, therefore, the proper set of relative prices can be attained so that full-employment equilibrium can be restored. In effect, monetary policy induces inflation, which causes prices and wages in the nonsticky downward areas to rise relative to prices and wages in the sticky downward areas. We conclude that if an event causes domestic AD to *fall*, and if certain prices and wages are sticky downward, an inflationary monetary policy can change relative prices and relative wages so as to restore the economy to full employment more quickly. (We call this our "one cheer for inflation" lecture.)

Fiscal Policy in the Classical Model

Fiscal policy, on the other hand, is viewed less favorably in the classical model; its potential as a stabilizer of the economy is slight or redundant. Suppose the government attempts to offset the unemployment resulting from a disequilibrium-creating change in the economy, prolonged by price-wage stickiness downward, by increasing public expenditures.

In order to discern the effect of an increase in real government expenditures, it is important to know how the real government purchases of goods and services (g) is financed. There are basically three ways to finance government expenditures: taxing, borrowing, and printing money.

Taxing If government expenditures are financed by taxing the community, the net effect is small because higher taxes will reduce household consumption expenditures and business investment expenditures. When the government taxes people and spends the funds, the money supply will be unaltered and increased real G, or g, will be mostly offset by decreased real C, or c, and decreased real I, or i. The composition of national output changes, however, as the community gets more publicly provided goods and fewer private goods. (We will return to this discussion in Chapters 7 and 18.)

---

[17] Note that money is nonneutral in this case because the money supply was increased when the economy was *not* in equilibrium.

An Increase in *g* Financed by Borrowing Leads to Offsetting Reductions in *c* and *i* If Full Employment Exists

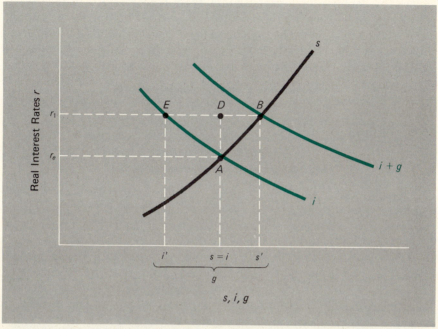

FIGURE 5.6. AN INCREASE IN *g* FINANCED BY BORROWING, GIVEN FULL EMPLOYMENT

If the government increases its real expenditures *g* by borrowing, the demand-for-loanable-funds curve shifts rightward from *i* to *i* + *g*. This causes the real interest rate to rise from r_e to r_1, which causes saving to rise from *s* to *s'* (and consumption to fall by an equal amount) and net investment to fall from *i* to *i'*. The net result of an increase in *g* financed by borrowing is that *c* + *i* fall by the increase in *g*, assuming an initial full-employment situation.

Borrowing If the government finances its real expenditures by borrowing from the public, the money supply will remain constant. The supply of loanable funds is unaffected, but the demand for loanable funds increases as the government sells bonds to private purchasers.

Figure 5.6 assumes an initial full-employment situation and shows an increase in the demand for loanable funds, given the supply of loanable funds, resulting from an increase in *g*. At the initial equilibrium real interest rate r_e, a shortage of loanable funds now exists. Competition for scarcer loanable funds drives the real interest rate up to r_1.

Note that the increase in borrowed funds, equal to g in this case, causes the demand for loanable funds to shift by g; the $(i + g)$ curve is parallel to the i curve, and the horizontal distance between them equals g at every interest rate. The distance B–E, therefore, equals g. Comparing the new equilibrium position B to the previous equilibrium position A, we can see that community real saving has increased from s to s'.

> *If national output (and national income) are assumed to be constant at the full-employment level, community real consumption must fall by the amount that community real saving has increased.*

Community real consumption, therefore, falls by the distance B–D. At the higher real interest rate r_1, net real investment falls to i', or point E on the i curve. Real net investment falls from i to i', or by the distance D–E.

What is the *net* result of an increase in g financed by borrowing, starting from a full-employment situation? Note that the increase in g equals the distance B–E, but that consumption falls by B–D and real net investment falls by D–E. Because $g = B–E = (B–D) + (D–E)$, the increase in g is completely offset by a reduction in c and in i. Thus, through a change in the real interest rate, in the long run the *composition* of national output changes—more publicly provided goods, fewer private goods—but the *level* of national output remains constant. This example of government expenditures causing higher interest rates, which in turn crowd out private expenditures, is discussed again in Chapter 7.

What if we assume, however, that an *unemployment* situation exists initially? An increase in g financed by government borrowing increases the demand for loanable funds as before. The increase in g will increase national income and lead to an increase in saving; that is, the *supply*-of-loanable-funds curve will *also* increase. Fiscal policy can *potentially* increase output and employment in the short run, although the magnitude of the changes is not certain. Also uncertain is the effect on the interest rate—because *both* the supply and the demand for loanable funds have increased. (We return to a discussion of the effects of financing g by borrowing in the Policy Controversy section of Chapter 17.)

In the long run, full employment will be established anyway. Financing g by borrowing in order to eliminate temporary unemployment, therefore, will change the *composition* of output. The public sector will expand at the expense of the private sector as a by-product of eliminating temporary unemployment. The potential short-run gain in higher employment and higher output must be paid for by a permanent change in the composition of output in the long run.

Printing Money   If g is financed by printing an equivalent amount of money, the price level will rise and output will expand toward the full-employment level. But these benefits really are due to an increase in the money supply and are not due to fiscal policy.

So why use fiscal policy? Such a combination of fiscal and monetary policy (printing money to pay for publicly provided goods) results in an expanded public sector relative to the private sector. While such a change in the composition of national output might be desirable on other grounds, it isn't apparent that it is desirable when the goal is *stabilization of the economy*.[18] Different goals should be separated conceptually. Increasing the employment level is one goal; increasing the proportion of resources allocated to the public sector is quite another.

---

[18] If the public sector expands relative to the private sector, community welfare will rise or fall—even if the *level* of national output remains constant—depending on what goods the government provides to the community. We elaborate on this in the Policy Controversy in Chapter 17.

POLICY CONTROVERSY
Classical Policy for a Prince[19]

As a practical matter, monetary policy was very difficult to implement during the classical era because most advanced economies were on some form of international metallic standards. (An international gold standard is discussed in Chapter 20.) When a country is on a metallic standard, there are three basic ways in which its domestic money supply can change: international trade imbalances, new discoveries of the money metal, and debasement of the domestic currency by the prince (ruler). The first two are clearly not under the control of the prince; the third is.

The prince can debase (or lower the real value of) a currency by (1) decree, (2) increasing the nominal face value of coins without changing their precious metal content, and (3) cutting a hole in the center of the coin or using a cheaper metal alloy to replace some of the precious metal content of the coin.

The classical economists argued about whether an increase in the money supply, when it is unexpected, immediately raises prices. Some maintained that if households and businesses are *not aware* of the increased money supply (for

---

[19] Based on an article by Filippo Cesarano, "The Rational Expectations Hypothesis in Retrospect," *The American Economic Review*, vol. 73 (1983), pp. 198–203.

whatever reason it occurs), such real variables as employment and national output can increase, because prices won't rise.

The controversy revolved around whether the prince can gain (personally or in achieving his goals for the state) by *unannounced* currency debasement. Some classical economists theorized—and they offered true anecdotes as evidence—that when currency debasement is *announced*, households and businesses take actions in their own self-interest which thwart the prince's policy. If the public knows, say, that the prince will call in coins and reduce the quantity of precious metal in each coin, the public will hoard as many of the coins as possible; the hoarded coins will retain their value during the ensuing increase in the price level. (This controversy anticipates the modern rational expectations approach discussed in Chapter 15.)

It should not be concluded that the classical economists recommended unannounced debasement as a regular policy. Rather, they believed that such a policy should be used only in emergencies, when government bond sales, increased taxes, or sales of the prince's property were not feasible.

CHAPTER SUMMARY

1. The quantity theory of money, which was the dominant macroeconomic theory for several centuries, maintains that in the long run the price level is determined only by the quantity of money in circulation.

2. Two alternate and equivalent versions of the classical quantity theory existed: the American equation of exchange and the British Cambridge equation, which are converted into theories by proclaiming V and k to be desired, and stable, values.

3. Both versions assumed that in the long run the demand for real money balances was constant and that the level of national output was at the full-employment level. Given these assumptions, changes in the quantity of money will change the price level proportionally.

4. An increase in the money supply is the cause, an increase in the price level is the effect, not vice versa. The money stock is exogenously determined by the condition of an economy's trade balance, by discoveries of gold or silver mines, and by the policy of the central bank.

5. An unexpected change in the money stock shocks the economy, and a period of disequilibrium exists. The mechanism that brings the economy back into equilibrium (the adjustment mechanism) is a change in the price level. For example, an increase in the money supply will eventually cause prices to rise until the price level rises

sufficiently to induce the community to hold the (now higher) existing money supply.

6. From the equation of exchange and international trade considerations the aggregate demand curve can be derived. This curve shifts if the supply of or the demand for money changes. It also shifts if the price levels in foreign countries change relative to the domestic price level.

7. The price level is established (in the long run) at the intersection of the aggregate demand curve and a vertical (at a full-employment level of national income) aggregate supply curve. Because the AS curve is vertical in the long run, the price level is determined by demand.

8. In the long run, changes in the supply of money change only such monetary values as the price level, nominal wage rates, and nominal interest rates. In the long run, changes in the money supply do not change such real variables as the level of employment, the level of national income, real wage rates, and the real rate of interest. Money is, therefore, said to be neutral in the long run.

9. The role for monetary policy is limited in the classical mode. Monetary authorities need only stabilize the money supply to avoid inflation. But if nominal wages are sticky downward, a contracting shock to the economy can cause prolonged unemployment, and by increasing the money supply, a new set of relative prices can be established which will restore a full-employment equilibrium.

10. When one considers how fiscal policy is financed, the classical economists maintained, it becomes evident that fiscal policy can change only the composition of national output and not the level of national output.

11. Some classical economists believed that unless the money supply is changed without the knowledge of economic agents, people will take actions in their own self-interest that counter the monetary policy goals.

GLOSSARY

aggregate demand (AD)   A relationship between various price levels and various quantities of national output demanded per unit of time, other things constant.

Cambridge equation   An equation developed by Alfred Marshall and other economists at Cambridge University, England, which indicates that the general price level depends on the quantity of money in circulation.

equation of exchange   The American version of the Cambridge equation, developed by Irving Fisher of Yale University.

exogenously determined   The value of a variable is exogenously determined if it is not affected by variables in the model under consideration. The money supply is exogenously determined, for example, if household and business behavior cannot affect it but if a central bank or discoveries of new gold mines can.

neutrality of money   Money is neutral if changes in its quantity affect only nominal values and if real variables—such as employment, national output, and the composition of national output—do not change when the money supply changes.

precautionary motive   People hold money in order to make unplanned expenditures, or to avoid bankruptcies if cash flow problems arise; they forgo interest earnings but, in exchange, receive the benefit of security.

transactions motive   People hold money because they want to make purchases during non–income-receiving periods; they forgo interest but get the benefit of convenience.

QUESTIONS AND PROBLEMS FOR REVIEW

5.1   Suppose that the demand for money is not constant. What can we say now about changes in the price level when the money supply changes?

5.2   Suppose the level of national output is not constant. What can we say now about changes in the price level when the money supply changes?

5.3   Which is a better analytic tool: comparative statics or dynamic disequilibrium analysis?

5.4   Explain what determines the shape and the position of the AD curve.

5.5   Assume that gold is money in some economy. If gold has significant use value (for jewelry, industrial use, and so on), will gold be neutral?

5.6   Throughout this chapter we have stressed that money is neutral in the long run. Does that mean that money is not neutral in the short run? If it isn't, *how* can changes in the money supply affect real variables in the short run? What are the policy implications of short-run nonneutrality of money?

5.7   Assume the values for k are
     a. 0.2
     b. 0.25
     c. 0.333
     What are the corresponding values of V? When k rises, what happens to V? What is the reason for this?

5.8   Suppose that people in our economy start to use credit cards more often. What happens to k and V? What is the intuitive reason for your answer?

5.9   Suppose that Mr. Smith receives a monthly income of $1000 at the first of each month, spends all of his income every month, and spends the same amount each day. What is the value of his average cash balances? What is his k? Now assume that he gets paid the same income, but now he is paid $500 on the first of the month and $500 in the middle of each month. What is his average cash balance? What is his k? What happens to k when people get paid more often?

5.10 Given $L_1 = kPy$; if $k = 0.2$, $P = 4.0$, and $y = \$100$ billion, then
   a. What are desired nominal money balances?
   b. What are real nominal money balances?
   c. Show that real money balances equal a constant portion of real income, using these figures.

5.11 In the equation of exchange, $MV = Py$, assume that $V = 5$ and $y = \$100$ billion. Determine P for each of the following:
   a. $M = \$80$ billion
   b. $M = \$100$ billion
   c. $M = \$160$ billion
   d. $M = \$200$ billion
   What can you conclude from your answers to this question?

5.12 In the equation $w = W/P$, assume a one-commodity economy (wheat). Suppose that W is measured in dollars per year, P is measured in dollars per bushel of wheat, and w is six bushels of wheat per year. Indicate combinations of W and P that satisfy this equation and therefore will lie on a line such as w_e in panel d of Figure 5.5.

REFERENCES

Filippo Cesarano, "The Rational Expectations Hypothesis in Retrospect," *The American Economic Review*, vol. 73 (1983).

Irving Fisher, *The Purchasing Power of Money* (New York: Kelly and Millman, 1963) (first published in 1911; 2d rev. ed., 1922).

Lawrence Harris, *Monetary Theory* (New York: McGraw-Hill, 1981).

David Hume, *Essays: Moral, Political, and Literary*, ed. T. H. Green and T. H. Grose (London: Longmans, Green, 1875).

Thomas M. Humphrey, *Essays on Inflation*, 4th ed. (Richmond Va.: Federal Reserve Bank of Richmond, 1983).

Alfred Marshall, *Money, Credit and Commerce* (London: Macmillan, 1923).

Henry Thornton, *An Enquiry into the Nature and Effects of the Paper Credit of Great Britain* (London: Hatchard, 1802).

J. G. K. Wicksell, *Interest and Prices*, trans. R. F. Kahn (London: Macmillan, 1936).

6

THE SIMPLE KEYNESIAN MODEL

Economic events have a way of changing economic theory. Economists (and other theoreticians as well) cling to their models with an almost religious fervor when those models predict reasonably well. Recurrent doubts and theoretical inelegance are rationalized until economists are confronted with overwhelming evidence that something is woefully amiss. The Great Depression, which was worldwide and lasted from 1929 until the late 1930s, seemed to provide incontrovertible evidence that there were no mechanisms within capitalism that automatically brought the economy back to full employment—at least, not in any time frame that could be called short run. Indeed, in Great Britain a deep recession and high unemployment level existed for approximately five years *before* the worldwide Great Depression began. The classical vision of a stable, self-regulating economy was due to be challenged.

In 1936, John Maynard Keynes published a book[1] that was to revolutionize economic thinking. In his book (commonly referred to as *The General Theory*), Keynes criticized previous economic thinking (which he called "the classical model") on empirical and theoretical grounds. He then replaced it with his own version of how the macroeconomy works. The remainder of this chapter will focus on Keynes's criticisms of the classical model and a simplified version of his model which replaced the classical paradigm in the hearts and minds of many (but certainly not all) economists.

KEYNES'S CRITICISMS OF THE CLASSICAL MODEL

The most fundamental criticism of any model is an assertion that the model fails to explain or predict. Moreover, a model can properly be criticized if it is logically inconsistent. Keynes made no secret of his desire to bring about a revolution in economic thinking, and he knew that such a revolution must first take place in the ivory towers of academia. As a consequence, Keynes was not content merely to point out where the classical model failed as a predictor of economic reality. As a shrewd tactician in the game of intellectual warfare, he realized that he must also show how the logic of the model is flawed and then replace it with a better one.

---

[1] John Maynard Keynes, *The General Theory of Employment, Interest and Money* (London: Macmillan, 1936). In the remainder of this text, we will cite a more recent edition, published by Harcourt Brace Jovanovich in 1964.

Recall that the classical model rested on two foundation blocks:

1. Wage rate adjustments assure that labor surpluses (involuntary unemployment) are eliminated.
2. Interest rate adjustments bring planned saving and planned investment into equality, and, as a result, no general insufficiency of aggregate spending will exist.

We now turn to Keynes's (and Keynesian) criticisms of these foundation blocks. If they can be shaken loose, the classical model will fall.

The Aggregate Supply of Labor and the Aggregate Demand for Labor

Keynes had no serious quarrel with the classical theory of the aggregate demand for labor. Buyers of labor (employers) suffer from no "money illusion" and are concerned only with the money wage rate *relative* to output price (the real wage rate). Businesses purchase additional labor only if the real wage rate falls. On the other hand, Keynes rejected the classical formulation of the aggregate supply-of-labor curve. Recall that classical theory states that the aggregate supply-of-labor curve is upward sloping and reflects the direct relationship between the real wage rate and the overall quantity of labor supplied. Such a formulation predicts that during periods when wage rates are relatively constant and prices are rising, some laborers will withdraw some (or all) of their labor because the *real* wage rate is falling. Keynes noted that actual observation did not support this prediction.

Keynes then offered some theoretical reasons to explain why the supply of labor is not directly related to the real wage rate. For one thing, people are "locked in" to mortgage and other long-term debt payments. It simply won't do for a person to withdraw *some* labor just because the going real wage rate now has a marginal benefit insufficient to outweigh the marginal disutility. Such considerations must be suspended when fixed debt payments must be made. Keynes also rejected the notion that laborers can bargain for the length of the workweek; surely some rigidity exists with respect to the workweek. Finally, according to Keynes, individual unions are concerned largely with their unions' wages relative to *other* unions' wages. In periods of generally rising prices, all unions are equally adversely affected and, hence, will not withdraw their labor.

For these reasons, rising prices, given money wage rates, will not induce a reduction in the total hours of labor offered per week, even though the real wage rate falls. The classical supply-of-labor curve, therefore, is suspect.[2] It appears that the quantity of labor supplied is not determined by the *real* wage rate. Added to this is the fact that in the *real world*, prices and wages are sticky (inflexible) downward because of unions, minimum wage laws, and a welfare society. This makes involuntary unemployment a distinct possibility. Even the classical economist would have agreed with this last point. And so Keynes dismissed the classical theory of the aggregate supply of labor on both empirical and theoretical grounds. In his model, therefore, he assumed downward price-wage rigidity.

Saving and Investment Curves

Having crumbled one foundation block of the classical model, Keynes turned to the other. Remember that it is the interest rate that brings saving and investment into equality. Recall the classical position:

1. Saving is directly related to the real interest rate, and investment is inversely related to the real interest rate.
2. Saving (and therefore consumption) and investment are *primarily* determined by the real interest rate, and thus these curves are stable.

Keynes rejected both of these assertions.

Saving and the Interest Rate   Suppose that individuals set a target for retirement. Let's say that Mr. Smith wants to have $50,000 when he retires. If the interest rate rises (or falls), he must save less (or more) to achieve his saving goal. Thus, a theoretical reason exists for assuming that saving and interest rates are *inversely* related! Moreover, said Keynes, saving (and consumption) is not primarily determined by the interest rate but is a function of real income. In effect, the classical economist held constant the most important determinant of the consumption-saving decision—real income. If full employment usually prevails, then it is legitimate to hold income constant and to claim that saving and consumption are primarily determined by the interest rate. But because the *issue* is whether or not there can be full employment, it is not proper to hold income constant. To assume a constant national

---

[2] Modern economists derive labor supply curves by analyzing the trade-off between leisure and income. Such a technique presents the possibility of labor supply curves that are perfectly inelastic (vertical) or even backward-bending (showing fewer labor hours offered at very high real wage rates as wealthier laborers now can afford to "buy" more leisure). Vertical or backward-bending labor supply curves may exist for individuals, but they are unlikely to exist for *aggregate* labor supply curves which incorporate higher participation rates for women and teenagers (and the elderly) at high real wage rates. Thus, while some individuals might prefer to work less at higher wage rates, this effect will be offset as more women and teenagers respond to higher real wage rates.

income because full employment is assumed is to assume one's conclusions.

Thus, every time community real income changes the classical saving (and consumption) function will shift. In short, according to Keynes, the saving curve is volatile (it fluctuates) because the most important determinant of saving—income—is not constant. When the Keynesian model is discussed later in this chapter, you will observe that real saving and real consumption are functions of real disposable income and not of the real interest rate.

Investment and the Interest Rate   Here, again, said Keynes, the classical economist held constant the most important determinant of investment—profit expectations. An inverse relationship exists between investment and the interest rate, *other things constant*. What is held constant are profit expectations, but profit expectations are subject to quick and violent change. As a consequence, the investment curve also fluctuates: it shifts every time profit expectations change.

Profit expectations, by definition, equal expected revenues less expected costs. Anything that increases expected revenues or decreases expected costs will increase expected net profits. Anything that decreases expected revenues or increases expected costs will decrease expected net profits.

Saving, Investment, and the Interest Rate   If neither saving nor investment is primarily determined by the interest rate, interest rate fluctuations cannot bring them into equality. If both schedules are volatile, can one be sure that saving-investment equality assures full employment? Keynes answered, "No." For example, assume that a recession is brought on by, say, an increase in general thriftiness. According to the classical model, saving increases are offset by investment increases that result from a decline in the real interest rate. But it is not legitimate to hold profit expectations constant during a recession. If profit expectations fall, significant interest rate reductions might be ignored by business investors. In short, will businesses invest more in plant and equipment at precisely the time they have excess capacity due to a recession? To Keynes the answer to this question was evident.

Money Supply and Money Demand

Recall that the supply of and the demand for money determine the price level in the classical model because the annual output of final goods and services y is constant (based on the classical prediction of full employment). In addition, because money is only a medium of exchange, the income velocity of money V is also constant. In a basic version of the equation of exchange,

$$M\bar{V} = P\bar{y} \tag{6.1}$$

It follows that M and P are proportionally related (this, you will recall, is the crude quantity theory of money). If the assumption of a constant y is rejected, however, M and P are no longer proportionally related; changes in M can change either P or y, or both, as long as V is relatively constant (or moves predictably). This is a tenet of a modern quantity theory of money, called *monetarism*, which is discussed in Chapter 18.

Actually, as will be shown in Chapter 7, Keynes also believed that V was not constant. Indeed, he showed how changes in M may lead to changes in V in the *opposite* direction. Hence, changes in M might not affect either P or y—a somewhat different version of the notion that "money doesn't matter." In fact, such a formulation implies that money supply changes may not even affect *nominal* income. This implication goes beyond even the classical model in belittling the influence of money.

The Long Run versus the Short Run

Keynes and his legion of followers criticized the patience (some would say the insensitivity) of classical (and modern) economists who are prepared to wait for relative price changes to move the economy toward full employment. In the meantime, what about all the human suffering endured by the unemployed, by the bankrupt, and by their families? This is a question guaranteed to discomfit those who believe in a "self-regulating economy." How long do people have to wait? How long is the long run? Frustrated with classical prescriptions to leave the economy to its own devices and to wait for long-run adjustments, Keynes was prompted to offer his oft-quoted dictum: "In the long run we are all dead." This dictum has become almost as famous as Say's law.

Some classical economists clung tenaciously (as do their modern-day intellectual descendants) to a belief in a self-regulating economy that was inherently stable. Apparently, the Great Depression, which was both severe and prolonged, left no impression on them.[3] Nor did three other worldwide depressions and thirteen smaller recessions that occurred between 1870 and 1929—the heyday of free enterprise in the United States. Table 6.1 indicates the time intervals of these business cycle contractions, as established "officially" by the National Bureau of Economic

---

[3] Real national income fell by 25 percent during the period 1929 to 1933, and the unemployment rate got as high as 25 percent. We elaborate on the Great Depression in Chapter 18.

TABLE 6.1. BUSINESS CYCLE EXPANSIONS (PEAKS) AND CONTRACTIONS (TROUGHS), 1870–1929

Trough	Peak
December 1870	October 1873
March 1879	March 1882
May 1885	March 1887
April 1888	July 1890
May 1891	January 1893
June 1894	December 1895
June 1897	June 1899
December 1900	September 1902
August 1904	May 1907
June 1908	January 1910
January 1912	January 1913
December 1914	August 1918
March 1919	January 1920
July 1921	May 1923
July 1924	October 1926
November 1927	August 1929

Source: U.S. Department of Commerce, Bureau of Economic Analysis, *Business Conditions Digest*, July 1982, p. 105.

Research. In the face of business cycle evidence, one can only marvel at the ability of classical theory to resist contradiction.

THE BASIC KEYNESIAN MODEL

It was apparent to Keynes and his followers that a new way of looking at the economy was necessary. Keynes was tired of waiting for full employment to return and was interested in what could be done in the meantime. Keynes's analysis dealt also with the determinants of *real national income y* or real national output in the short run. Recall that real national *income* and real national *output* are equal, but that real national output is viewed from the expenditures side and real national income is viewed from the income side. Recall also that the short run is defined as a period of time during which technology, the capital stock, natural resources (land), and the size of the labor force are constant but employment and output are variable (and functionally related).

The Keynesian model is concerned with how real national output is determined and how it changes at production levels below the full-employment level. Two important implications result from concentrating economic analysis on those periods when high unemployment of labor and considerable excess capacity exist.[4] These two implications are:

1. National output *y* can be increased over broad ranges without causing the price level to rise; increases in total expenditures lead only to increases in output because each firm has a great deal of excess capacity. Competition of firms, each of which is operating at levels considerably below full capacity, keeps prices from rising. Because we have already noted that Keynes assumed that prices and wage rates are sticky downward, this implies that over broad ranges of output the price level remains constant. As a consequence, all variables in this chapter (and for most of the next chapter) are expressed in *real* terms. Recall that the classical aggregate supply (AS) curve, which represents the relationship between various levels of national output and various price levels, is vertical. In the simple Keynesian model, price-wage constancy implies an AS curve that is *horizontal* at the current price level; different levels of national output are produced at the same price level.

2. This led Keynes to concentrate on the aggregate expenditures on goods and services as the prime mover in the economy. As total expenditures change, national output will change in the same direction.

In this chapter we first discuss Keynes's short-run theory of the equilibrium level of real national output *y* and how *y* changes, at less than full-employment levels, in a closed, private economy.[5] Then we make the Keynesian model more realistic and take government activities into account. A discussion of multiplier analysis follows, and then the chapter concludes with a section that analyzes fiscal policy in the simple Keynesian model.

Preliminaries

According to Keynes, any level of national income is possible in the short run, up to and including full employment, because there are no mechanisms to assure the full employment of labor. The key question is: What determines the equilibrium level of national income or employment?

---

[4] A considerable amount of excess capacity exists, for instance, when the economy is producing only 70 percent—or less—of what it is capable of producing; at such times much labor and much capital are idle.

[5] Closed because we ignore international transactions (which are discussed in Chapter 20) and private because we ignore the role of government (which is discussed in the next section of this chapter).

Because Keynesian analysis deals with the short run, a functional relationship exists between national output and the employment level; in the short run, output can be changed only by varying the amount of labor employed. Because national income equals the value of national output, national income and national output are, by definition, the same. Output levels are directly related to the unemployment level; therefore, a short-run functional relationship exists between the level of employment and *real national income*, or *y*. A theory of the determination of the equilibrium national output level, therefore, is also a theory of the determination of the equilibrium employment level, and vice versa.[6]

Out of the possible levels of national output and national employment, businesses select that level which is the most profitable. The most profitable level depends on the **aggregate expenditures (AE) curve** for goods and services, which is defined as total expenditures made by all sectors in the economy at each level of national income during some period of time.[7] Because businesses attempt to maximize profits, they adjust output to whatever level that aggregate expenditures make most profitable. The essence of Keynes's model is that aggregate expenditures arc the prime mover in the economy; the **aggregate output (AO) curve**, which shows the value of national output at each and every level of national income, is passive and dances to the tune of changes in aggregate expenditures.

What specifically are aggregate expenditures? They are the value of the expenditures on final goods and services by households *C*, plus the value of business expenditures on final goods and services for plant, equipment, and inventories *I*, plus the value of publicly provided goods and services *G*, plus the value of net exports of goods and services *X − M*, *at each level of national income.* See Chapter 2 for the precise definitions of these terms. In that chapter we discussed *actual* expenditures on these categories; here we are concerned with *planned* expenditures. Previously we were concerned with measurement; now we are concerned with behavior. Thus,

$$AE = C + I + G + X - M \qquad (6.2)$$

---

[6] Keynes solved for the equilibrium employment level and derived from it the equilibrium level of national income. Modern economists find it convenient to solve for equilibrium *y* and deduce from it equilibrium employment. Clearly, if indeed a short-run functional relationship does exist between employment and *y*, no conflict exists between these two approaches. This text follows the convention of modern economists and determines the equilibrium level of *y*.

[7] Keynes referred to this concept as *aggregate demand*, but modern economists have appropriated that term for the relationship between the quantity demanded for domestic output at different price levels—as indicated in Chapter 13. In order to avoid confusion, we have accepted the modern terminology and changed Keynes's.

In a closed, private economy,

$$AE = C + I \qquad (6.3)$$

In these equations, I can represent gross investment or net investment, in which case GNP or NNP, respectively, is derived.

Because Keynes's theory of how national output and employment are determined is essentially a theory of aggregate expenditures, each of the individual components of aggregate expenditures is discussed in turn.

Keynes's Consumption Function

Keynes realized that annual community (or individual) consumption is determined by many variables, but he chose to emphasize just one—real disposable income. As a result, Keynesians have derived a rather simple consumption function. Keynes's theory contains three propositions regarding the consumption function, and each is empirically testable:

1. *Real consumption (and real saving) is a stable function of real disposable income.* Because consumption (or saving) and income are related in *real* terms, no money illusion exists; consumers buy an identical bundle of goods and services if national income and all prices change at the same rate. Note that real consumption or saving depends on real disposable income y_d. In a closed, private economy $y_d = y$ because taxes and transfers are ignored; y_d and y, therefore, can be used interchangeably in a closed, private economy. Finally, Keynes assumed a *stable* (nonfluctuating) relationship between real consumption (and real saving) and real disposable income. This proposition is a radical departure from the classical model, which assumed that national income was constant at the full employment level and that real saving and real consumption are determined primarily by the real interest rate. So far, Keynes's relationship between real consumption and real income has not been specified. The test for proposition 1 is whether or not there is a high correlation between real income and real consumption (and real saving).

2. *As real disposable income rises (for the group or for the individual), both real consumption and real saving also rise.* In effect, this means that income increases will be partially consumed and partially saved. Keynes referred to the ratio of a change in consumption to a change in income as the **marginal propensity to consume (MPC)** (where Δ is our notation for a change). Thus,

$$MPC = \frac{\Delta c}{\Delta y} \qquad (6.4)$$

The **marginal propensity to save (MPS)** is defined similarly:

$$MPS = \frac{\Delta s}{\Delta y} \tag{6.5}$$

Proposition 2 can be restated as follows: The MPC and the MPS must be between zero and 1. That is, $0 < MPC < 1$ and $0 < MPS < 1$. Because income changes can be only spent or saved, $MPC + MPS = 1$.

Consider the following example. Disposable income rises from $100 billion to $110 billion, and consumption rises from $80 billion to $87 billion. A $10 billion increase in disposable income leads to a $7 billion increase in consumption (and therefore to a $3 billion increase in saving). The $MPC = \Delta c/\Delta y = \$7$ billion/$10 billion $= 0.7$, and the $MPS = \Delta s/\Delta y = \$3$ billion/$10 billion $= 0.3$. Note that $MPC + MPS = 1$.

3. *As real disposable income rises, the percentage of income devoted to consumption (c/y), or the* **average propensity to consume (APC),** *falls, and the percentage of income devoted to saving (s/y), or the* **average propensity to save (APS),** *rises.* Note that $1 = APC + APS$, because income can be only spent or saved.

Keynes's third proposition says that the APC is inversely related to the level of real disposable income. This hypothesis reflects Keynes's belief that present wants are relatively limited; higher and higher incomes eventually allow people to satisfy their basic current desires, and further income increases won't lead to much additional consumption. Only so many goods can be consumed concurrently; thus Keynes was an "underconsumptionist" (following Malthus and Marx).

Assuming a linear consumption function, Keynes's consumption function can be specified mathematically. The simple Keynesian consumption function can be written as

$$c = c_0 + by \quad \text{where} \quad c_0 > 0 \quad \text{and} \quad 0 < b < 1 \tag{6.6}$$

for a closed, private economy in which $y_d = y$. Note that c_0 is the vertical intercept of the consumption function (it is the value of consumption when the economy approaches zero income),[8] and according to Keynes's proposition 3, c_0 must be positive.[9] Note that b is the slope of the

---

[8] An intercept value greater than zero means that there are nonincome determinants of consumption, such as wealth; a change in wealth will change the vertical intercept, and the consumption line will shift.

[9] Dividing equation 6.6 by y yields $c/y = c_0/y + b$. If $c_0 = 0$, then the APC, c/y, equals the MPC, b, which is a constant. Thus, a zero vertical intercept implies a constant APC (equal to the MPC) as y rises. Can you verify that c/y falls as y rises if $c_0 > 0$ in the equation derived in this footnote?

The Keynesian Consumption Function Has Specific Properties

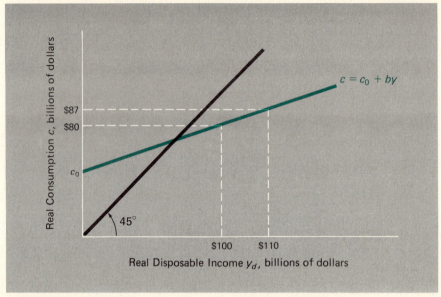

FIGURE 6.1. THE KEYNESIAN CONSUMPTION FUNCTION

This is a typical Keynesian consumption function because real consumption is related to real disposable income, the vertical intercept C_0 is positive and therefore the APC falls as income rises (use the 45° line, which has a slope of 1, to demonstrate this proposition to yourself), and the slope is between zero and 1 (use the 45° line for reference to help you see this).

consumption function and is the MPC; according to Keynes's second hypothesis, b must be between zero and 1. A typical Keynesian consumption function is illustrated in Figure 6.1.

Keynes's Investment Function

In addition to consumption, the other element included in a closed private aggregate expenditure analysis is investment. The essential nature of an investment or capital good is that it yields a stream of revenues through time. The decision as to whether or not to purchase a capital asset involves comparing the current price of the asset to the revenue stream that will flow in the future. Somehow the value *today* of a future revenue stream must be calculated so that it can be compared to today's cost of purchasing capital.

The key to the problem involves the concept of **discounting,** the process of finding the present value of money in the future. We have already indicated in Chapter 4 that the rate of interest provides a means of translating the value of the future purchasing power into present purchasing power; the market interest rate reflects the trade-off between present and future consumption. It should come as no surprise, therefore, that discounting is intimately related to the interest rate.

The value today of any amount of money in the future is given by the equation

$$V_p = \frac{R_1}{(1 + r)} + \frac{R_2}{(1 + r)^2} + \frac{R_3}{(1 + r)^3} + \cdots + \frac{R_n}{(1 + r)^n} \qquad (6.7)$$

WHERE V_p = present value; the value today of the asset
      R_1 = the amount of money to be received one year hence
      R_2 = the amount of money to be received two years hence
      R_n = the amount of money to be received n years hence
      r = the market rate of interest, or the discount rate

It should be stressed that the R's in equation 6.7 are *net* revenue streams; from the gross receipts that a capital asset yields in a given future income period are subtracted such expenses as maintenance and operation costs and depreciation. Also, an important ingredient in the analysis is that *because these net revenue streams are projected into the future, they are, of necessity, merely subjective estimates that are susceptible to large changes in very short periods of time.* Also, the R's are not necessarily equal to each other, and some may equal zero.

Suppose that an investment project yields a net revenue stream such that $R_1 = 0$, $R_2 = \$200$, and $R_3 = \$500$. Assuming that the correct discount rate is 10 percent, the present value of that investment project is

$$V_p = \frac{R_1}{(1 + r)} + \frac{R_2}{(1 + r)^2} + \frac{R_3}{(1 + r)^3}$$

or

$$V_p = \frac{0}{1.1} + \frac{\$200}{1.21} + \frac{\$500}{1.331}$$

$$V_p = 0 + \$181.81 + \$375.66 = \$557.47$$

Let's interpret what a present value of $557.47 for that particular revenue stream means. Suppose you have $557.47 *right now,* and you put it in an investment plan that earns 10 percent per annum. Suppose you draw nothing from it in year one and allow your funds to accumulate 10 percent per annum interest, and then you draw down $200 at the end of year two, allowing the balance to earn a rate of 10 percent per annum. At the end of year three you draw out $500 from your investment plan—

and *nothing* will be left in your pool. Thus, it would take exactly $557.47 *right now* to generate a revenue stream of $R_1 = 0$, $R_2 = \$200$, and $R_3 = \$500$, if the interest rate was 10 percent per annum.

The Marginal Efficiency of Capital Borrowing liberally from Marshall and Fisher, Keynes applied the concept of discounting to the investment decision. He noted first that the **supply price** of a capital asset is the price that would just induce a manufacturer of capital goods to produce an additional (new) unit of capital.[10]

Keynes then defined the **marginal efficiency of capital (MEC)** "as being equal to that rate of discount which would make the present value of the series of annuities given by the returns expected from the capital-asset during its life just equal to its supply price."[11]

We can understand the investment decision facing the entrepreneur through equation 6.7. First, we can ascertain the marginal cost of producing one more unit of capital (the supply price) and substitute that known value for V_p in equation 6.7. The net revenue streams R_1, R_2, and so on, for the n periods that reflect the life of the asset are then estimated. That leaves us with r—in this case, *some percentage*—in the equation as the unknown. Solving for r gives the marginal efficiency of capital, which is a percentage or discount rate that is to be compared to the *actual* market rate of interest.

If the marginal efficiency of capital exceeds the market rate of interest, then the capital asset in question is profitable and the entrepreneur will purchase the asset. This is true because, if the marginal efficiency of capital (a percentage) makes the V_p of the asset just equal to its cost, then applying a *lower* discount rate (the *market* rate of interest) means that the *actual present value* of the asset must exceed the cost of producing the asset.

Similar reasoning implies that, if the marginal efficiency of capital is less than the market rate of interest, then the present value (or economic worth) of the capital asset will be less than the cost of producing another unit, and entrepreneurs will not acquire it.

The Firm's MEC Curve According to Keynes, the marginal efficiency of capital falls for a given type of capital as more of it is produced during a specific time. This is because

---

[10] By the *supply price*, Keynes meant the replacement cost of the capital good, and he stressed that the supply price was *not* the *market price*—the price at which the asset could actually be purchased in the market. We can also think of the supply price as the marginal cost of producing a unit of capital.

[11] Keynes, op. cit., p. 135.

1. The stream of revenues, or prospective yield, falls as more of a specific capital asset is accumulated because the supply of the final good produced will increase relative to its demand, other things constant.
2. The marginal cost of producing a specific type of capital rises (the supply price rises) as the demand for it increases.

The first of these reasons predominates in the long run, while the second of these reasons is more important in the short run, according to Keynes.

Assuming a decreasing marginal efficiency of capital for a specific capital asset, it is easy to derive a marginal-efficiency-of-investment curve. The profit-maximizing entrepreneur will carry out investment projects up to the point where the marginal efficiency of capital just equals the market interest rate; at that point, the economic value of an additional unit of capital will just equal the marginal cost of producing another unit.

Starting from equilibrium, where a finite quantity of a specific capital asset will be purchased during some specified time period, a reduction in the market interest rate will mean that *now* for an additional unit of capital, its present value will exceed its supply price, and capital accumulation—investment—will take place. This increased capital stock will now lower the net revenue stream and increase the supply price of capital until the (now lower) marginal efficiency of capital again equals the new (lower) market interest rate.

In short, the firm's marginal-efficiency-of-capital curve will be negatively sloped. This reflects the fact that a larger capital stock reduces the marginal efficiency of capital; therefore, a lower interest rate is required to induce businesses to acquire more capital, other things constant. The firm will, potentially, be maximizing at each point on the MEC curve.

According to Keynes, we can aggregate all the MEC curves for the different types of capital in order to derive an aggregate investment curve.[12] Such a curve is shown in Figure 6.2.

You should realize that the aggregate investment curve is extremely volatile and that Keynes himself emphasized this point. The investment

---

[12] Actually, the aggregation process is not so simple, because what is true for one firm is not true for all firms: if *many* firms try to accumulate more of a specific type of capital, they will drive the supply price upward, whereas *one* firm will not. Some economists, therefore, refer to a marginal-efficiency-of-*investment* curve which shows less investment at each interest rate than the mere summation of all the marginal-efficiency-of-capital curves would show.

The Aggregate Investment Curve Is Negatively Sloped

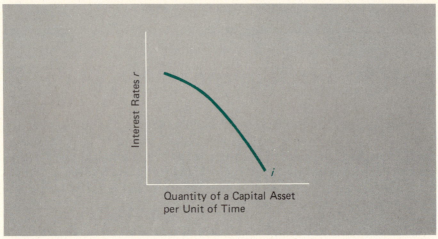

FIGURE 6.2. AGGREGATE INVESTMENT CURVE

As the quantity of a specific type of capital acquired by a firm (or all firms) increases, the MEC for that capital asset falls. The profit-maximizing firm will compare the MEC of an additional unit of capital with the market interest rate and will acquire capital up to the point where those two percentages are equal. Therefore, the MEC curve is a good proxy for a firm's (or all firms') investment demand curve.

curve shifts whenever businesses change their expectations concerning the future. Remember:

> *For a given interest rate, the present value of a capital asset depends on the asset's net revenue stream which will accrue in the future.*

Because the future is unknown—and unknowable—the projected net revenue stream is subject to great changes as expectations regarding the future change. Every time the net revenue stream changes, the investment curve will shift. A change in expectations that increases the net revenue stream will shift the investment curve to the right; investment will be higher than previously at any interest rate. A reduction in the value of the net revenue stream causes the investment curve to shift to the left, and investment will be less than previously at any rate of interest. This is shown in Figure 6.3.

The Aggregate Investment Curve Is Extremely Volatile

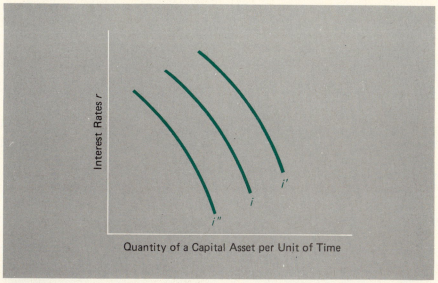

FIGURE 6.3. A SHIFTING AGGREGATE INVESTMENT CURVE

The aggregate investment curve, according to Keynes, is extremely volatile; it shifts every time the net revenue stream is expected to change. If the net revenue stream rises, the aggregate investment curve shifts to the right; the aggregate investment curve shifts to the left if profit expectations fall.

It is hard to exaggerate, according to Keynes, the importance of the fact that the investment function is extremely volatile and is therefore subject to violent upward or downward shifts in the short run. As we will see, such volatility in the aggregate investment function causes the AE curve to be volatile; in turn, a volatile AE curve makes capitalism subject to periods of boom and bust.

Investment and National Income   We have concluded that an inverse relationship exists between the *interest rate* and aggregate investment. But we are trying to derive an aggregate expenditures curve, which relates total spending (both consumption and investment) to differing levels of *national income.* In order to do so, we must relate aggregate real investment to national income.

Real net investment is either related to the level of real national income or it is not. If related, real national income increases probably induce more net investment. Boom times are associated with high real

Aggregate Investment May Be Directly Related to National Income

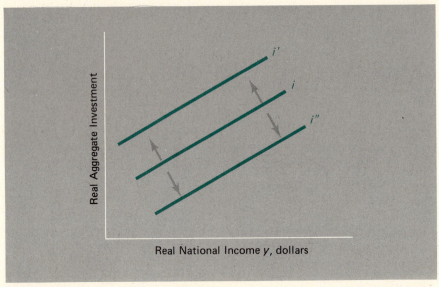

FIGURE 6.4. INDUCED INVESTMENT
In this graph, higher levels of real national income induce higher levels of real aggregate investment, and a systematic relationship exists between them. This curve is volatile; it shifts every time interest rates or the next revenue stream (expectations) changes, as the arrows indicate. The curve i' is consistent with a lower interest rate, or higher net revenue streams, than the other two curves.

national income and high real net investment; recessions are associated with relatively low levels of i and y. In this case a direct relationship exists between i and y. This **induced investment** relationship appears in Figure 6.4.

On the other hand, it is possible to conceive of a situation in which the level of real national income is high but the business outlook is bleak; a high y and a low i then coexist. Or a low y can be associated with high business confidence; then a low y and a high i appear. Thus the true relationship might therefore be between i and the *expected rate of change* of y. If so, no systematic relationship exists between i and the *level* of y; i is then *autonomous* (independent of y). An **autonomous investment** curve appears in Figure 6.5.

It is important to stress again that the induced and autonomous investment curves are both extremely volatile. According to Keynes, the

Aggregate Investment May Be Unrelated to National Income

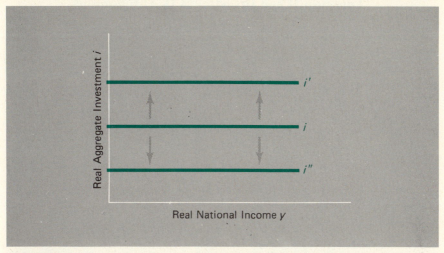

FIGURE 6.5. AUTONOMOUS AGGREGATE INVESTMENT

These graphs indicate that no systematic relationship exists between real aggregate investment and real national income. The i functions are parallel to the horizontal axis. These i curves lie above the horizontal axis; hence, investment is positive. If investment equals zero, the i curve lies on the horizontal axis; a negative investment implies an i curve that is below the horizontal axis. The curve shifts as the net revenue stream (expectations) changes and as the interest rates change; hence, it is very volatile, as the arrows indicate; the i'' curve reflects a higher interest rate or a lower net revenue stream than the other two curves.

i function, unlike the consumption function, shifts significantly and often because net investment depends on subjective evaluations of the future. Are we headed for boom or bust, inflation or recession? Every time businesses change their profit expectations, the investment function shifts (upward if the profit expectations become more favorable, downward if they become less favorable). Technological changes also affect the net investment curve, and such changes are hardly systematic or predictable.

How, then, do interest rate changes fit into Keynes's model? If the interest rate falls (given expectations), the autonomous investment curve in Figure 6.5 shifts upward; the net investment is higher at every income level. A higher interest rate shifts that curve downward. Thus, a given autonomous investment curve implicitly holds the interest rate con-

The Aggregate Expenditures Curve Is Parallel to the Consumption Function When Investment Is Autonomous

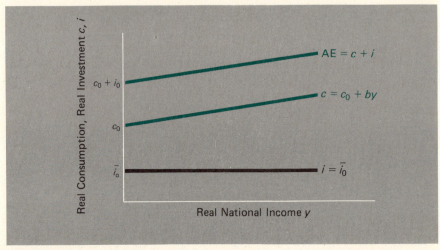

FIGURE 6.6. CONSTRUCTING AGGREGATE EXPENDITURES IN A CLOSED, PRIVATE ECONOMY

In this graph, positive autonomous net investment is added to the consumption function. Because net investment is autonomous, the aggregate expenditures curve is parallel to the consumption function. Because net investment is positive, the aggregate expenditures curve lies above the consumption function. Note that planned real consumption and real investment are plotted on the vertical axis; real national income is plotted on the horizontal axis.

stant. The interest rate, therefore, helps to determine the *position* of the autonomous investment curve and, as the next section shows, helps to determine the position of the aggregate expenditure curve. We postpone Keynes's theory of how the interest rate *itself* is determined until the next chapter. For the remainder of this chapter, we assume that the interest rate is exogenously determined.

Aggregate Expenditures in a Closed, Private Economy

Assuming that real net investment is autonomous, or independent of the level of y, an aggregate expenditures curve for a closed, private economy can be derived. Since $AE = c + i$, the aggregate expenditures function is formed by adding a constant i to the consumption function. As long as autonomous investment is nonzero, the aggregate expenditures curve is parallel to the consumption function.[13] The construction of an AE curve for a closed, private economy is illustrated in Figure 6.6.

Aggregate Output

The aggregate output (AO) curve shows the level of real national output at every level of real national income.[14] Businesses, as a group, are willing to produce any output level (less than and up to full employment) if they expect to be able to sell their products. Producers in the aggregate will produce $1 trillion worth of goods and services—*thereby generating $1 trillion worth of national income in the form of wages, interest, rent, and profits*—if they expect to be able to sell them. If businesses in the aggregate produce $1.5 trillion worth of goods and services, they automatically create $1.5 trillion of income, and so on. Figure 6.7 shows an AO curve for the economy; the value of real national output is plotted on the vertical axis, and the values of real national income are plotted on the horizontal axis. The AO curve is a 45° line—it has a slope equal to 1[15]—because the value of national output equals the value of the income generated from that production, as Chapter 2 indicated.

The AE and AO Curves
Determine Equilibrium National Income

All the tools necessary to determine the equilibrium level of real national income for a closed, private economy have now been developed. The equilibrium level of real national income is at the intersection of the aggregate output and aggregate expenditure curves; that point represents the most profitable (or least unprofitable) output rate for businesses as a whole.

Consider Figure 6.8. AE cuts AO at y_e; hence, it is the most profitable rate of output for businesses. At any higher output rate (such as

---

[13] If $c = c_0 + by$ and $i = i_0$ (investment is constant and equal to i_0) and AE = $c + i$, then AE = $c_0 + by + i_0$. Rearranging gives AE = $(c_0 + i_0) + by$. Comparing this function to the consumption function, it is clear that they have the same slope b (the MPC); if $i_0 \neq 0$, then they have different vertical intercepts. Therefore, they are parallel. If $i_0 = 0$, then AE equals the consumption function.

[14] Keynes referred to this curve as the *aggregate supply curve,* but we have adopted the modern terminology and have used that term to describe the relationship between various levels of domestic national output and different domestic price levels. See footnote 7.

[15] If the same measurement scale is used on both axes.

The Aggregate Output Curve Is a 45° Line

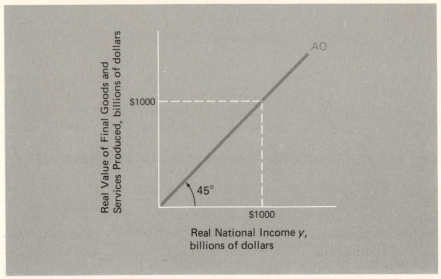

FIGURE 6.7. THE AGGREGATE OUTPUT (AO) CURVE
The AO curve shows real national output at each and every level of real national income. Because the value of real national output equals real national income, the AO curve is a 45° line and has a slope of 1.

y_1), business expectations are unfulfilled. Businesses, in the aggregate, have overestimated what they profitably can produce and sell; they have created a surplus of final goods and services. An undesired increase in inventories occurs, and businesses therefore reduce output and employment in order to increase profits.

Any rate of output consistent with a national income level less than y_e creates a shortage of final goods and services, that is, the quantity of AE (AE_q) exceeds the quantity of AO (AO_q). An undesired decrease in inventories occurs because businesses, in the aggregate, have underestimated what they can sell, and they have not, therefore, maximized profits.

Only at y_e does $AE_e = AO_q$; only at those unique income and output levels is there no unwanted inventory change; y_e is the most profitable output level. Note how AO_q adjusts to the AE curve. In that sense, AE is the prime mover and AO is passive. Whenever the AE curve shifts,

Equilibrium National Income Occurs at the Intersection of the AE Curve and the AO Curve

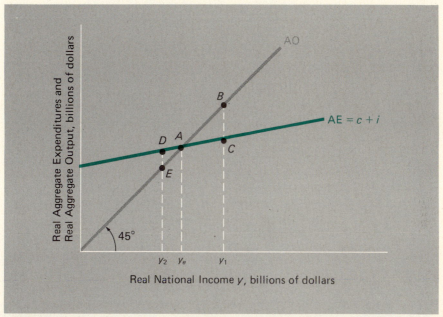

FIGURE 6.8. EQUILIBRIUM NATIONAL INCOME DETERMINATION

Equilibrium exists at point A, where $AE_q = AO_q$, and that is the most profitable output level for businesses. At a higher level of national income, such as y_1, $AO_q > AE_q$, and a surplus of goods and services exists. Unplanned inventories $(B - C)$ occur, and businesses therefore reduce output—causing real national income to fall to y_e. At a lower level of national income, such as y_2, $AE_q > AO_q$, and a shortage of goods and services exists. Inventories will fall involuntarily by $D - E$. Businesses will increase output, and real national income will rise to y_e.

both AE_q and AO_q will adjust until they are equated—at the point of intersection of the AE curve and the AO curve.

Equilibrium of Planned Saving and Planned Investment

Equilibrium in a closed, private economy can be found in another manner. Recall that $y = c + s$, by definition. Hence, if y and c are known,

Equilibrium National Income Can Be Derived by Two Approaches

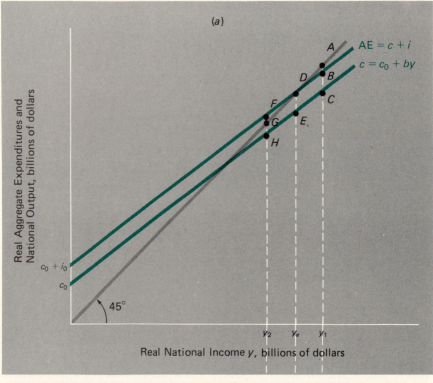

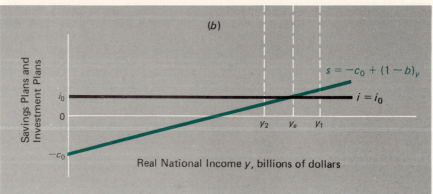

FIGURE 6.9. DERIVING EQUILIBRIUM NATIONAL INCOME

The equilibrium level of national income will occur where $AE_q = AO_q$ in panel *a* and (what amounts to the same thing in a closed, private economy) where saving plans equal investment plans in panel *b*. As a comparison of these two panels shows, at any level of national income above y_e, $AO_q > AE_q$ and $s > i$; and at any national income level less than y_e, $AE_q > AO_q$ and $i > s$.

then s is determined by $s = y - c$. It follows that a saving curve can be derived by subtracting consumption from the 45° AO curve (because $AO_q = y$).[16] Saving equals $AO_q - c$. A typical Keynesian saving curve and an autonomous investment curve are plotted in panel b of Figure 6.9. Can you see how panel b is derived from panel a in that graph?

In Figure 6.9, observe that in a closed, private economy, if $AE_q > AO_q$ (at all levels of income less than y_e), then $i > s$.[17] At all levels of income greater than y_e, inspection shows that $AO_q > AE_q$ and $s > i$.[18] Only at y_e does $AO_q = AE_q$ and $s = i$ (saving and investment both equal $D - E$). Therefore, in a closed, private economy, the equilibrium condition is that $AE_q = AO_q$, or $i = s$.

Comparing Goods-Market Equilibrium in the Classical Model and the Basic Keynesian Model

If y_1 is full employment, the equilibrium position (Y_e) in Figure 6.9 is seen to occur at less than full employment. This is Keynes's fundamental conclusion. Keynes wanted to demonstrate that full-employment equilibrium, contrary to the classical assertion, was not the general (or even the usual) case. The general case is equilibrium with unemployment. Full-employment equilibrium is only one special case that is unlikely to occur, and if it were to occur, nothing guarantees that the economy would remain there.

Because this conclusion is so fundamental to Keynesian economics, and because it is so at odds with the classical conclusion, we will now

---

[16] Because

$$y = c + s \tag{1}$$

then

$$s = y - c \tag{2}$$

We know that

$$c = c_0 + by \tag{3}$$

Substituting (3) into (2) gives

$$s = y - (c_0 + by) \tag{4}$$
$$s = y - by - c_0 \tag{5}$$
$$s = -c_0 + (1-b)y \tag{6}$$

[17] At y_2 in panel a of Figure 6.9, saving $= G - H$; investment $= F - H$.

[18] In panel a of Figure 6.9, at y_1, saving $= A - C$; investment $= B - C$.

compare the determination of goods-market equilibrium in both models, using Keynesian tools.[19]

The Classical Model   First consider the determination of goods-market equilibrium in the classical model, using Keynesian garb. The demand for final goods and services, both consumption and investment, depends on the rate of interest. As Chapter 4 indicated, both real consumption and investment expenditures are inversely related to the real interest rate. The aggregate expenditures curve, given these assumptions, is independent of national income so that in Figure 6.10 AE is parallel to the horizontal axis. Its position depends on the rate of interest; if the interest rate rises the AE curve shifts downward, and if the interest rate falls the AE curve shifts upward.

The aggregate output curve depends on the level of employment, which is determined to be at the full-employment level in the labor market. In Figure 6.10, therefore, the supply of national output is vertical at the full-employment level of real national income. We use the Keynesian 45° AO curve only as a line of reference.

Consider point A, at the intersection of the AE curve and the *vertical* AO curve. Point A, even though it is an intersection point, *cannot* be an equilibrium position under classical assumptions. At point A, aggregate expenditures equal $500 billion, but the value of output consistent with the full-employment output is $650 billion and is determined at point B. (Remember, the 45° line has a slope of 1 and therefore y_f also must be valued at $650 billion.) At point A, therefore, the value of real national output exceeds the value of real national expenditures for that output; in the classical model that means that saving plans exceed investment plans, so a surplus of loanable funds exists. The interest rate will fall, causing consumption and investment to rise and the AE curve to shift upward; this process will continue until AE shifts to AE′ and goods-market equilibrium is established at a level of national income that is consistent with full employment. Note, therefore, that equilibrium will occur at some point on the AO curve; the exact point on the AO curve depends on the level of national income that is consistent with full employment, which itself depends on the size of the labor force, labor participation rates, technology, and so on. (See Chapter 4.)

The Keynesian Model   Consider Figure 6.11, which shows that the aggregate consumption expenditures on goods and services depends on

---

[19] Note that neither Keynes nor the classical writers performed their analysis with these "Keynesian" tools. This section is based on Laurence Harris, *Monetary Theory* (New York: McGraw-Hill, 1981), especially chap. 8.

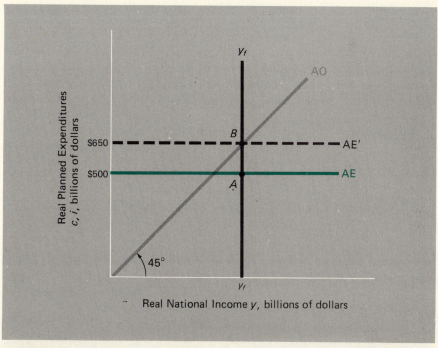

FIGURE 6.10. GOODS-MARKET EQUILIBRIUM IN THE CLASSICAL MODEL

In the classical model, AE is determined by the real interest rate; hence, it is autonomous of real national income. The vertical y_f curve shows the full-employment level of national income (at least in the long run). The equilibrium level of national income will eventually be established at the point on the 45° line that is consistent with the full-employment level of national income. At point A, $AO_q > AE_q$, a surplus of goods and services exists, and inventories rise. In the classical model such a situation causes the interest rate to fall (because planned saving exceeds planned investment), which causes the AE curve to shift to AE'.

the level of real national income (not the interest rate). To be sure, investment still depends on the rate of interest (although Keynes believed that the elasticity of investment with respect to the interest rate is quite low), but it is autonomous with respect to national income. Assume again that the y_f curve indicates the full-employment aggregate supply

In the Keynesian Model Equilibrium Can Exist at Any Point on the 45° Line

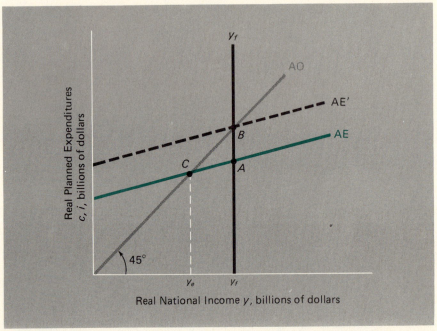

FIGURE 6.11. GOODS-MARKET EQUILIBRIUM IN THE KEYNESIAN MODEL

In the Keynesian model, there are no mechanisms that move the economy toward full employment. Equilibrium, therefore, can be determined at *any* point on the 45° line; it will be established where the AE curve intersects the 45° line.

of output, but note that the 45° AO curve *now* is an integral part of the Keynesian goods-market equilibrium model.

Consider point A at the intersection of the AE curve and the vertical y_f curve. Note that at y_f, however, the level of total expenditures A is less than the value of goods and services produced B, so $AO_q > AE_q$ and a surplus of goods and services exists. This will cause real income to fall to y_e, where $AO_q = AE_q$ and a less-than-full-employment equilibrium exists. At point C there will be *no* tendency for the income level to change, unless the AE curve shifts. Not that, according to Keynes, the AE curve will *not*, in general, shift upward to AE'. Under certain conditions, such as price-wage flexibility, however, there might be a tendency for AE to shift to AE' in the Keynesian model, but we postpone that discussion and will refer to it in Chapter 7.[20]

Recessionary and Inflationary Gaps

Figure 6.11 is also useful because it conveys additional information. The *equilibrium* level of real national income, given the aggregate expenditure curve AE, is at y_e, but the full-employment level of real national income is at y_f. The economy, therefore, has excess capacity and a recession exists. More precisely, in Figure 6.11 a **recessionary gap** equal to the distance *B–A* exists. A recessionary gap is defined as the amount by which the quantity of national output exceeds the quantity of aggregate expenditures (or, $AO_q - AE_q$) at the full-employment level of national income. That this is truly a recessionary gap can be seen by imagining an upward shift in the AE curve to AE'; note that AE' intersects AO at point *B*, and consequently the equilibrium level of real national income is also equal to the full-employment level of real national income.

Consider Figure 6.12, which shows a recessionary gap equal to the distance *B–A* (when the aggregate expenditure curve is AE) and an **inflationary gap** equal to the distance *D–B* (when the aggregate expenditure curve is AE''). An inflationary gap exists if, *at the full-employment level of real national income*, $AO_q < AE_q$. Given an aggregate expenditures curve of AE'', there exists an inflationary gap that can be eliminated by a downward shift in the AE curve, through point *B*. AE' is such a curve.

In an inflationary gap situation, household and business planned expenditures for goods and services exceed the economy's ability to produce goods and services. Households and businesses, competing for goods and services, drive prices upward, and inflation results. Thus, for Keynes, inflation arose when the economy was at or very near the full-employment output rate and planned expenditures exceeded the economy's production capacity. However, in the decade of the 1970s it was not uncommon, in the United States and elsewhere, for high unemployment rates and high inflation rates to exist *simultaneously*. For example, in 1974 the unemployment rate was 5.5 percent and the inflation rate was 12.2 percent; in 1979 they were 5.8 percent and 13.3 percent, respectively. Keynes's theory of inflation—indeed, his whole approach to macroeconomics—was then challenged. We return to this discussion in Chapter 13.

---

[20] Point *C* is examined in more detail in Chapter 15, where we discuss the "post-Keynesian" criticism of mainstream Keynesian doctrine.

Recessionary Gaps and Inflationary Gaps Depend on Where the AE Curve Is Located Relative to the Full-Employment Level of National Output

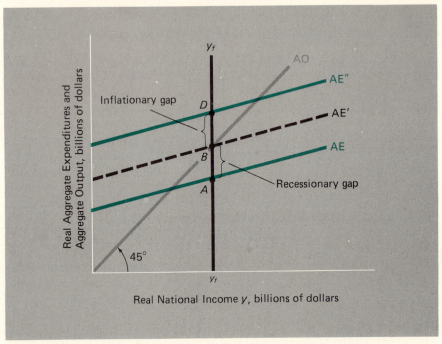

FIGURE 6.12. INFLATIONARY AND RECESSIONARY GAPS

Assuming that y_f is the full-employment output level, a recessionary gap exists if the aggregate expenditures curve is AE; the recessionary gap equals $B - A$. An inflationary gap exists if the aggregate expenditures curve is AE''; the inflationary gap is equal to the distance $D - B$. If the aggregate expenditures curve is AE', a full-employment, price-stable equilibrium exists.

Multiplier Analysis

The existence of inflationary gaps and recessionary gaps suggests the justification for and the direction of policy. If inflationary and recessionary gaps can be eliminated, the economy can reach that most desirable of situations: a full-employment price-stable equilibrium.

It is one thing to construct graphs such as those in Figure 6.12 and then "eliminate" undesirable gaps by shifting AE curves in a textbook or on a blackboard. It is quite another to determine the proper "real world" quantities involved. This section deals only with the theoretical relationship between shifts in the AE curve and changes in the equilibrium level of real national income. Clearly, before a successful monetary policy or fiscal policy can be conducted, policymakers must have a firm grasp of the amounts by which shifts in aggregate expenditures actually change national income. We explore this relationship now.

The **multiplier effect** is the result of *shifts* in the AE curve. It indicates that every $1 shift in the aggregate expenditures curve causes the equilibrium level of national income to change by more than $1. Every $1 shift downward (decrease) in the aggregate expenditures curve causes the equilibrium level of national income to fall by more than $1.

To understand how the multiplier effect works, consider an equilibrium position that is disturbed by a $1 million increase in autonomous investment for, say, machines. Recall that

$$AE = (c_0 + i_0) + by \qquad (6.8)$$

where $(c_0 + i_0)$ is the vertical intercept of the aggregate expenditures curve. The AE curve shifts (upward or downward) every time that intercept changes. If autonomous net investment changes or if the vertical intercept of the consumption function c_0 changes, the aggregate expenditures curve shifts and national income changes by a multiple of the shift in AE. Now, what effect will this $1 million upward shift in AE, resulting from the increase in autonomous net investment of $1 million, have on the level of national income? Because one group's expenditure is another group's income, national income has *already* increased by $1 million; the people who built and sold the machine for $1 million have just received an income increase. According to Keynes's theory of the consumption function, those in the machinery sector will spend some of this income increase in consumption goods and save some. Assuming a marginal propensity to consume of 0.75, the machine builders will increase their consumption by $750,000 and increase their saving by $250,000. Again, because one group's expenditure is another's income, community income now rises by $750,000—for those people who produced the $750,000 worth of goods purchased by the machine builders. Note that *already*, after only two rounds of transactions, total national income has increased by $1.75 million. A $1 million increase in aggregate expenditures due to an increase in autonomous investment has caused national income to rise by $1.75 million. Moreover, the process is not yet completed, because the group receiving an increase in its income of $750,000 will spend some and save some; the amount that it spends on consumption will become income for still another group, and so on. Thus every $1 million upward shift in the AE curve will cause the level of income to rise by more than $1 million. As is demonstrated in the mathematical appendix to this chapter, the multiplier equals $1/(1 - b)$, where b = MPC, the slope of the consumption function. In our example, $b = 0.75$, so the multiplier is 4; every $1 million shift in aggregate expenditures causes the level of national income to change by $4 million. Another example, showing a step-by-step procedure, is shown in Table 6.2. Note that at the new equilibrium, planned saving and planned investment are equal, but both are larger than previously. Figure 6.13 is a graphical representation of the multiplier effect.

As the multiplier equation shows, the multiplier is directly related to the MPC.

ADDING GOVERNMENT TO THE BASIC KEYNESIAN MODEL

By taking into account the activities of government, the basic Keynesian model is affected in two ways. First, the government makes expenditures in the form of (1) real government purchases of goods and services g and (2) real public transfers to persons t_r.[21] Second, the government taxes households t_x.

Government expenditures affect the AE curve directly, while personal taxes and transfers affect the AE curve indirectly, through the consumption function. For ease of exposition, let's assume that g, t_r, and t_x are autonomous with respect to national income.[22]

Now the AE equation becomes

$$AE = c_0 + b\,(y - t_x + t_r) + i_0 + g_0 \qquad (6.9)$$

Equation 6.9 shows that the consumption function is altered by the introduction of real taxes and real transfers into the analysis. Remember, consumption depends on *disposable income*, which falls with taxes and rises with transfers, other things constant. Rearranging equation 6.9 yields

$$AE = (c_0 - bt_x + bt_r + i_0 + g_0) + by \qquad (6.10)$$

---

[21] A transfer is a money flow that has no corresponding productive activity associated with it. Government transfers include welfare payments, Social Security payments, and other public transfers to persons.

[22] In effect, we assume that personal taxes and transfers to persons are *lump sums*; they remain constant at every level of national income. As will be shown presently, this assumption implies that the addition of these complications to the basic Keynesian model leaves the AE slope unaffected. In the mathematical appendix to this chapter this assumption is relaxed, and it is shown that the AE slope—and therefore the multiplier—is altered when taxes depend on the level of national income.

TABLE 6.2. THE MULTIPLIER EFFECT OF A $100 BILLION-PER-YEAR INCREASE IN i—THE MULTIPLIER PROCESS[a]

Round	Increase in Income (billions of dollars per year)	Increase in Planned Consumption (billions of dollars per year)	Increase in Planned Saving (billions of dollars per year)
1 ($100 billion per year increase in i)	100 ⟶	80	20
2	80 ⟶	64	16
3	64 ⟶	51.2	12.8
4	51.2 ⟶	40.96	10.24
5	40.96 ⟶	32.768	8.192
.	.	.	.
.	.	.	.
All later rounds	163.84	131.072	32.768
TOTALS ($\Delta c + \Delta i$)	500	400	100

[a] This table traces the effects of a $100 billion annual increase in investment spending on the level of national income. If we assume a marginal propensity to consume of 0.8, or four-fifths, such an annual increase will eventually elicit a $500 billion annual increase in the equilibrium level of national income.

A comparison of this equation with the previous equation for aggregate expenditures in the basic Keynesian model *without* government,

$$AE = (c_0 + i_0) + by \qquad (6.8)$$

indicates that

1. The introduction of taxes causes the vertical intercept of the AE curve to fall by bt_x, or by the MPC times the amount of autonomous taxes. The vertical intercept of the AE curve shifts by only MPC (Δt_x) because the rest of the lump sum tax $[(1-\text{MPC})\,\Delta t_x]$ would have been saved. A *change* in autonomous taxes will cause the AE curve to shift by $-b\,\Delta t_x$. Thus, an increase in autonomous taxes will cause the AE curve to shift downward by $b\,\Delta t_x$, and a decrease in taxes will cause the AE curve to rise by $b\,\Delta t_x$.
2. The introduction of transfers causes the vertical intercept of the AE curve to rise by bt_r and not by the full Δt_r because some of the transfer will be saved. A change in autonomous transfers causes the vertical intercept of the AE curve to change by $b\,\Delta t_r$; an increase in transfers causes the AE curve to shift upward by $b\,\Delta t_r$, and a decrease in transfers causes the AE curve to shift downward by $b\,\Delta t_r$.
3. Changes in autonomous government expenditures cause the vertical

The Multiplier Effect Can Be Depicted Graphically

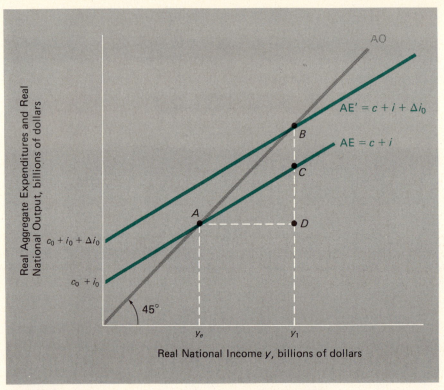

FIGURE 6.13. GRAPHING THE MULTIPLIER EFFECT

If the AE curve shifts upward from AE to AE', owing (here) to an increase in autonomous investment Δi, the equilibrium level of national income rises from y_e to y_1. The change in national income equals the distance $D - A = \Delta y$; the change in autonomous net investment equals the distance $B - C = \Delta i$. The multiplier equals $\Delta y / \Delta i = (D - A)/(B - C)$.

intercept of the AE curve to shift dollar for dollar—as do changes in autonomous consumption (c_0) and autonomous investment (i_0).

The implication of the above is that the autonomous government expenditure multiplier, M_g, will be equal to $1/(1 - b)$, which is also the autonomous investment multiplier and the autonomous consumption multiplier. On the other hand, because multipliers deal with shifts in the AE curve, and because changes in autonomous taxes and autonomous transfers shift the AE curve by *less than* $1 for each $1 change, their multipliers will be less than $1/(1 - b)$. The tax multiplier is $M_{tx} = -b/(1 - b)$, and the transfer multiplier is $M_{tr} = b/(1 - b)$; note that taxes are merely the negative of transfers.

STABILIZATION POLICY

The basic Keynesian model implies that recessionary gaps and inflationary gaps are the general case and that a full-employment, price-stable equilibrium is a special, but unlikely, case. Household consumption and business investment are largely endogenous variables, but government expenditures, the tax structure, and public transfers are largely exogenous, in the sense that they can be controlled by policymakers and not by households or businesses. Stabilization policy can be conceived of as the discretionary activity of policymakers with respect to changes in g, t_x, and t_r. Changes in these exogenous variables will shift the AE curve and lead to multiple changes in the equilibrium level of national income. By some combination of monetary policy and fiscal policy, the aggregate expenditures curve can be shifted in desirable directions to eliminate recessionary and inflationary gaps.

Eliminating Recessionary Gaps by Fiscal Policy

In order to eliminate a recessionary gap, the aggregate expenditures curve must be shifted upward sufficiently. Some combination of increased government spending, increased public transfers, and decreased taxes can do precisely that. If a **balanced budget** $(g + t_r = t_x)$ existed initially, a **budget deficit** $[(g + t_r) > t_x]$ would now exist. Thus, government deficit spending (financed by borrowing) is required to eliminate recessionary gaps; Keynes flew to the United States during the Great Depression to tell President Franklin Delano Roosevelt precisely that.[23] This created a problem for Roosevelt, who ran for president on a balanced budget platform. Roosevelt eventually got the hang of deficit spending, however. So has virtually every United States president since then. The federal government has run deficits in all but five years since the mid-1930s.

It is interesting to note that if government expenditures rise by the same amount that taxes rise (a previously balanced budget remains balanced), national income will rise by $\Delta g = \Delta t_x$. This is true because the government expenditure multiplier exceeds the (absolute value of the) tax multiplier $[M_g = |M_{tx}| + 1]$ or because (what amounts to the same

---

[23] If the budget is already in deficit, a recession calls for a larger deficit; if the budget is initially in surplus, a recession can be combated by a smaller surplus. What is important is that a recessionary policy to fight recessions requires that g and/or t_r rise and t_x fall.

thing) the *net* impact of an increase in g and an equal increase in t_x is to shift the AE curve upward. Intuitively, some of what was taxed and spent by the government would have been saved by taxpayers; therefore, net withdrawals will be less than net injections (Δg). This Keynesian assertion is challenged in Chapter 17.

Eliminating Inflationary Gaps by Fiscal Policy

If an inflationary gap exists, the AE curve must shift downward in order to bring the economy to a full-employment, price-stable equilibrium. Fiscal policy requires some combination of decreased g and decreased t_r and increased t_x. In other words, a **budget surplus** $[(g + t_r) < t_x]$ or a smaller deficit is called for in times of inflation, in order to "cool down" the economy. In practice, politicians have been more enthusiastic about deficit spending than they have been about running budget surpluses. The facts are that since the 1950s the United States government has increased taxes *and* government purchases of goods and services *and* public transfers dramatically; but because it has increased g and t_r more rapidly than it has increased t_x, it has typically run budget deficits.

So far, we have not said anything about the role of monetary policy in the basic Keynesian model. This is because we have not treated the role of money explicitly in the Keynesian model. We turn to that topic in the next chapter, where we also discuss Keynes's views on monetary policy.

CHAPTER SUMMARY

1. The Great Depression undermined confidence in the classical model and paved the way for the Keynesian model.
2. Keynes disputed the classical economists' theory of the supply of labor, criticized their theory of the rate of interest, and concluded that a full-employment, price-stable equilibrium was a special case; the general case is that of recession or inflation.
3. In the basic Keynesian model the price level is held constant, and the model determines the equilibrium level of real national income at levels less than and up to the full-employment income level.
4. Aggregate expenditures, which represent the amount of spending by all the relevant sectors in the economy at each level of national income, are the primary determinant of the equilibrium level of national income.
5. The Keynesian consumption function maintains that (a) real consumption is a stable function of real disposable income, (b) the marginal propensity to consume is between zero and 1, and (c) the average propensity to consume falls as the level of real national income rises.

6. The marginal efficiency of capital is that rate of discount that equates the supply price of capital to the present value of the expected net revenue stream associated with the capital asset. Profit maximizers acquire capital (invest) up to the quantity at which the marginal efficiency of capital equals the market rate of interest. Aggregate investment is inversely related to the interest rate.

7. The AE curve in a closed private economy represents the sum of the consumption curve and the autonomous (or induced) investment curve. The equilibrium level of national income is established at the intersection of the AE curve and the AO (45° line) curve.

8. Shifts in the AE curve lead to multiple changes (in the same direction) in the equilibrium level of national income. The main determinant of the multiplier is the slope of the AE curve, which equals the MPC when investment is autonomous and when the model deals with a closed, private economy.

9. Inflationary gaps and recessionary gaps occur when the AE curve does not intersect the AO curve at the full-employment level of national income. A full-employment, price-stable equilibrium requires that such gaps be eliminated. In principle, such gaps can be eliminated by monetary policy and by fiscal policy.

10. If a recessionary gap exists, sound fiscal policy requires that policy-makers run government budget deficits (or reduced surpluses); if an inflationary gap exists, fiscal policy requires government budget surpluses (or reduced deficits).

GLOSSARY

aggregate expenditures (AE) curve A curve that represents total expenditures by all the relevant sectors in the economy at each and every level of national income during some period of time.

aggregate output (AO) curve A curve that represents the national output at each and every level of national income; the AO curve is a 45° line, and therefore has a slope equal to 1.

autonomous investment Investment that is independent of the level of national income.

average propensity to consume (APC) Total consumption divided by total income; the percentage of income devoted to consumption.

average propensity to save (APS) The percentage of income devoted to saving; total saving divided by total income.

balanced budget When government purchases of goods and services plus public transfers equal government revenues; $g + t_r = t_x$.

budget deficit When $(g + t_r) > t_x$.

budget surplus When $(g + t_r) < t_x$.

discounting The process of finding the present value of future amounts of money.

induced investment   Investment that varies directly with the level of national income.

inflationary gap   The amount by which AE_q is larger than AO_q at the full-employment level of national income.

marginal efficiency of capital (MEC)   The rate of discount which would make the present value of a capital asset equal to its supply price; a percentage that is akin to a profit rate.

marginal propensity to consume (MPC)   The percentage of a change in income that is consumed; the change in consumption divided by the change in income; the slope of the consumption function.

marginal propensity to save (MPS)   The percentage of a change in income that is saved; the change in saving divided by the change in income; the slope of the saving function.

multiplier effect   When the aggregate expenditures curve shifts, the equilibrium level of national income changes by a multiple of the amount by which the AE curve shifts; the ratio of a change in the equilibrium level of national income to the shift in the AE curve.

recessionary gap   The amount by which AO_q is larger than AE_q at the full-employment level of national income.

supply price   The price that would just induce a manufacturer to produce an additional unit of capital; the marginal cost of producing capital.

QUESTIONS AND PROBLEMS FOR REVIEW

6.1   In the basic Keynesian model, suppose that MPC = 0.8. If income increased from $80 billion to $100 billion, consumption would be expected to increase by how much? By how much would saving be expected to increase? Is the sum of your two answers equal to the change in income?

6.2   Keynes argued that laborers are "locked into" debt payments, that rigidity exists with respect to the work period, and that each union is concerned largely with its wages relative to other unions' wages. Do you believe that these arguments are valid today? Consider the effects that such things as the existence of variable-rate mortgages and indexing have on the validity of Keynes's arguments.

6.3   The simple Keynesian consumption function can be written as

$$c = c_0 + by$$

Although the MPC is constant, show algebraically how the APC would, nevertheless, change as y changed, if $c_0 > 0$.

6.4   If the consumption function is written as

$$c = \$20 + 0.8y$$

determine the level of c and the level of s for y = $50, $150, and $250. Compute associated APC ratios.

6.5   If the consumption function is

$$c = \$20 + 0.8y$$

and the level of investment is

$$i = \$10$$

determine the level of aggregate expenditures for $y = \$50$, $\$150$, and $\$250$. Determine the level of y that makes $s = i$.

6.6 If the net revenue stream of a capital asset is in nominal terms, would the present value of the net revenue stream change necessarily if the net revenue stream itself changed? Consider the effect of changes in the level of prices on the relevant discount rate r in your answer.

6.7 Suppose that the equilibrium y is not equal to the y value that can be produced at full employment. What variables would be expected to change in the basic Keynesian model? In the classical model?

6.8 (Use the information in questions 6.3 through 6.5 to answer this question.) If aggregate output is equal to national income, determine the level of aggregate output for $y = \$50$, $\$150$, and $\$250$. Determine the level of y that makes the level of aggregate expenditures equal to the level of aggregate output. For your answer, does $s = i$?

6.9 Suppose that the consumption function is

$$c = \$20 + 0.8y$$

and the level of investment is

$$i = \$10$$

as above. If i changed to $\$12$, what variables would be expected to change in the basic Keynesian model? Determine the ratio of the change in y to the change in i that caused the change in y. Is your answer consistent with the value of the multiplier?

6.10 Suppose that the consumption function is

$$c = \$20 + 0.8(y - t_x + t_r)$$

the level of investment is

$$i = \$10$$

and the levels of government expenditures and taxes are

$$g_0 = t_x = \$5$$

Determine the level of y that makes the level of aggregate expenditures equal to the level of aggregate output. What is the effect on the equilibrium level of y of adding

$$g_0 = t_x = \$5$$

to the Keynesian model?

REFERENCES

William Branson, *Macroeconomic Theory and Policy* (New York: Macmillan, 1978).

Dudley Dillard, *The Economics of John Maynard Keynes* (Englewood Cliffs, N.J.: Prentice-Hall, 1948).

Alvin H. Hansen, *A Guide to Keynes* (New York: McGraw-Hill, 1953).

Laurence Harris, *Monetary Theory* (New York: McGraw-Hill, 1981).

John R. Hicks, "Mr. Keynes and the Classics: A Suggested Interpretation," *Econometrica*, vol. 5 (1937).

John Maynard Keynes, *The General Theory of Employment, Interest, and Money* (New York: Harcourt Brace Jovanovich, 1964).

Lawrence R. Klein, *The Keynesian Revolution*, 2d ed. (New York: Macmillan, 1966).

Robert LeKachman, *The Age of Keynes* (New York: Random House, 1966).

———, ed., *Keynes and the Classics* (Boston: Heath, 1965).

MATHEMATICAL APPENDIX
TO THE KEYNESIAN MODEL

Equilibrium Determination

The typical Keynesian consumption function is

$$c = c_0 + by \tag{A.6.1}$$

where $c_0 > 1$ and $0 < b < 1$ and c_0 and b are both known.

Assume that investment is autonomous so that

$$i = \bar{i}_0 \tag{A.6.2}$$

and that $\bar{i}_0$ is known. Assume a closed, private economy. The equilibrium level of real national income or output cannot be determined yet. Under these conditions, this system of equations is indeterminate; it contains two equations and three variables (c, i, and y), and a third equation is necessary. As is often the case, the missing equation is the equilibrium condition. Equilibrium requires that

$$AO_q = AE_q \tag{A.6.3}$$

Since $AO_q = y$ and $AE_q = c + i$ (in a closed, private economy), substitution yields

$$y = (c_0 + by) + \bar{i}_0 \tag{A.6.4}$$

Subtracting by from both sides gives

$$y - by = c_0 + i_0 \tag{A.6.5}$$

Factoring gives

$$y(1 - b) = c_0 + i_0 \tag{A.6.6}$$

Dividing both sides by $1 - b$ yields

$$y = \frac{c_0 + i_0}{1 - b} \tag{A.6.7}$$

where c_0, i_0, and b are known constants and y is the equilibrium level of real national income.

Consider now an open economy, so that

$$AE = c + i + g + (x - m) \tag{A.6.8}$$

Let g and $(x - m)$ be autonomous (independent of the level of real national income) so that

$$g = \bar{g}_0 \tag{A.6.9}$$

and

$$(x - m) = (\overline{x - m})_0 \qquad \text{(A.6.10)}$$

where g_0 and $(\overline{x - m})_0$ are both known.

By using the framework in equations A.6.1 to A.6.7 you should be able to derive the following result:

$$y = \frac{c_0 + i_0 + g_0 + (x - m)_0}{1 - b} \qquad \text{(A.6.11)}$$

where y is the equilibrium level of real national income in an open economy which also takes into account government purchases of goods and services.

Equilibrium Determination Through the Leakages = Injections Approach

In a closed, private economy

$$AE \equiv c + i \qquad \text{(A.6.12)}$$

and national income y can be spent on consumer goods or it can be saved. Thus,

$$y \equiv c + s \qquad \text{(A.6.13)}$$

In equilibrium, the AE curve intersects the AO curve; therefore,

$$AE_q \equiv c + i = c + s \equiv AO_q$$

and

$$s = i \qquad \text{(A.6.14)}$$

Thus, leakages (planned saving) equal injections (planned investment).

If we consider an open economy and take into account government activities, then

$$AE \equiv c + i + g + (x - m) \qquad \text{(A.6.15)}$$

and

$$y + t_r - t_x \equiv c + s \qquad \text{(A.6.16)}$$

Equation A.6.16 indicates that earned income, which is increased by transfers and decreased by taxes, is either consumed or saved. Isolating y gives

$$y \equiv c + s - t_r + t_x \qquad \text{(A.6.17)}$$

In equilibrium, $AE_q = y = AO_q$, so

$$c + i + g + (x - m) = c + s - t_r + t_x \qquad \text{(A.6.18)}$$

Rearranging and eliminating c from both sides yields

$$i + g + x + t_r = s + t_x + m \qquad \text{(A.6.19)}$$

Note that in equation A.6.19 all the injections into the economy are on the left-hand side and all the leakages from the economy are on the right-hand side.

Multipliers

First consider a closed, private economy. Equation A.6.7 indicates that in such an economy the equilibrium level of real national income equals the sum of the autonomous real consumption plus autonomous real investment, divided by $1 - b$. If real investment changes, by Δi, real national income will change, by Δy.

Thus,

$$y + \Delta y = \frac{c_0 + i_0 + \Delta i_0}{1 - b} \qquad \text{(A.6.20)}$$

and

$$y + \Delta y = \frac{c_0 + i_0}{1 - b} + \frac{\Delta i_0}{1 - b} \qquad \text{(A.6.21)}$$

Subtracting A.6.7 from A.6.21 gives

$$\Delta y = \frac{\Delta i_0}{1 - b} \qquad \text{(A.6.22)}$$

$$\frac{\Delta y}{\Delta i_0} = \frac{1}{1 - b} \qquad \text{(A.6.23)}$$

and

$$M_i = \frac{\Delta y}{\Delta i} = \frac{1}{1 - b} \qquad \text{(A.6.24)}$$

where M_i is the investment multiplier. A moment's reflection will indicate that $M_i = M_{c0} = M_g = 1/(1 - b)$, where M_{c0} is the consumption multiplier and M_g is the government expenditure multiplier.

Note that because $0 < b < 1$ (by assumption), $0 < 1 - b < 1$, and therefore $1/(1 - b) > 1$. Thus, an increase in i (or g or c_0) leads to a *larger* increase in y, and a decrease in i (or g or c_0) leads to a larger decrease in y.

Let's consider now the tax multiplier. Assume that taxes are lump sum, or autonomous of income, so that $t_x = \bar{t}_x$; also assume that $t_r =$

$\bar{t}_r$. For ease of exposition, assume that we are dealing with a closed economy. The consumption function now is

$$c = c_0 + b\,(y - t_x + t_r) \qquad \text{(A.6.25)}$$

or

$$c = (c_0 - bt_x + bt_r) + by \qquad \text{(A.6.26)}$$

Using the framework in equations A.6.1 through A.6.7, we conclude that in equilibrium

$$y = \frac{c_0 - bt_x + bt_r + i_0 + g_0}{1 - b} \qquad \text{(A.6.27)}$$

If taxes change, so will real national income. Thus

$$y + \Delta y = \frac{c_0 - bt_x - b(\Delta t_x) + bt_r + i_0 + g_0}{1 - b} \qquad \text{(A.6.28)}$$

and

$$y + \Delta y = \frac{c_0 - bt_x + bt_r + i_0 + g_0}{1 - b} + \frac{-b\,\Delta t_x}{1 - b} \qquad \text{(A.6.29)}$$

Subtracting A.6.27 from A.6.29 yields

$$\Delta y = \frac{-b\,\Delta t_x}{1 - b} \qquad \text{(A.6.30)}$$

$$\frac{\Delta y}{\Delta t_x} = \frac{-b}{1 - b} \qquad \text{(A.6.31)}$$

and

$$M_{t_x} = \frac{\Delta y}{\Delta t_x} = \frac{-b}{1 - b} \qquad \text{(A.6.32)}$$

Similar reasoning would indicate that the transfer multiplier is

$$M_{t_r} = \frac{b}{1 - b} \qquad \text{(A.6.33)}$$

When Real Taxes Vary Directly with Real National Income

Assume that real taxes vary directly with real national income. In particular, assume a proportional tax structure so that

$$t_x = ty \qquad \text{(A.6.34)}$$

If we assume that personal transfers are lump sum so that $t_r = \bar{t}_r$, then the consumption function is now written

$$c = c_0 + b(y + t_r - ty) \qquad \text{(A.6.35)}$$

which can be rewritten as

$$c = (c_0 + bt_r) + b(1 - t)y \qquad \text{(A.6.36)}$$

Equation A.6.36 is extremely instructive because it indicates that the *slope* of the consumption function falls from b to $(1 - t)b$. (Remember that $0 < b < 1$ by assumption.) Consequently, the slope of the aggregate expenditures curve also falls, which means that all the multipliers are smaller. For example, assume that taxes are lump sum and that the marginal propensity to consume b equals 0.75; in that case the government expenditure multiplier, the consumption multiplier, and the investment multiplier all equal 4. If the marginal propensity to tax t equals 0.2, then the marginal propensity to consume now equals

$$b(1 - t) = 0.75(1 - 0.20) = 0.6$$

and the multiplier now equals

$$\frac{1}{1 - 0.75(0.80)} = 2.5$$

Thus, by assuming a marginal propensity to tax of 0.20, the government expenditure (and consumption and investment) multipliers fall from 4 to 2.5.

7

THE EXPANDED KEYNESIAN MODEL

Chapter 5 contained a simplified version of the classical demand-for-money function. It maintained that money was only a medium of exchange; therefore, businesses and households hold as little money as possible and for as short a time as possible. The ratio of desired money balances to nominal national income was believed to be constant at its minimum; therefore, velocity is a constant at its maximum. To the classical economists, the public holds a constant (minimum) fraction of its nominal income in non–interest-earning cash balances; the quantity of money demanded is directly related to the price level.[1] It was considered irrational to *hoard*—to hold money above the minimum desired for transactions purposes—because money per se earns no income.

Because for many classical economists money was no more than a medium of exchange, they believed that in the long run the size of the money supply determines only the price level; it does not affect relative prices. Money is neutral, and it does not affect such variables as output and employment. These variables are maintained at their full-employment levels, according to the dictates of Say's law. Unemployment was defined as a surplus of labor at the current real wage rate. In a free market, this surplus is eliminated as the money wage rate and the real wage rate are driven down by laborers competing for jobs. Lower real wage rates increase the quantity of labor demanded and decrease the quantity of labor supplied. The real wage rate falls until equilibrium— full employment—is restored. As a consequence, a full-employment output level is assured. Similarly, an insufficient level of effective aggregate expenditures for goods and services was interpreted as indicative that a surplus of loanable funds existed. If planned real saving exceeds planned real investment, a surplus of loanable funds exists at the prevailing real interest rate; and an unfettered loanable funds market results in a falling real interest rate that decreases the quantity saved and increases the quantity invested. This process continues until equilibrium—an equality of planned saving and planned investment—is restored. As a consequence, the full-employment output is purchased.

Keynes assigned a more important role to money in the economy. This chapter explains Keynes's demand-for-money theory and his theory of the interest rate. It then reveals an important Keynesian insight: *the real interest rate is the link between the real world and the money*

---

[1] If output is constant, as the classicists assumed. If output varies, then the quantity demanded of money varies directly with *both P* and *y*—or with their product, nominal national income.

PART II HISTORICAL PERSPECTIVE

world. This analysis evolves toward a Keynesian-neoclassical synthesis that will require a more elaborate model. This more complicated model will "cost" in terms of intellectual effort, but it will yield a high return because it provides an efficient means to

1. Demonstrate aggregate equilibrium (a simultaneous equilibrium in both the money market and the product market)
2. Examine monetary and fiscal policies and their interaction
3. Compare the Keynesian and the classical models

As in the previous chapter, the price level in this chapter is assumed to be constant when we discuss the Keynesian model. As a consequence, when we discuss the Keynesian model a change in nominal values is equivalent to a change in real values. When we discuss the *is-lm* model later in this chapter, we will be more careful and stress that we are dealing with *real* values.

KEYNES'S DEMAND FOR MONEY FUNCTION

The Precautionary Motive

Irving Fisher and Alfred Marshall, as Chapter 5 indicated, were aware that there also existed a precautionary motive for holding money. According to them (and as emphasized by Keynes), people want to hold a pool of readily available purchasing power to meet unexpected financial obligations. In order to avoid being forced to sell a bond or to wait for the bond market to open in a financial emergency, businesses and households voluntarily forgo some interest earnings in order to gain a measure of security. The rational individual therefore compares the marginal cost of forgone interest income to the marginal benefit of security resulting from holding additional money.

Fisher and Marshall believed that, like the nominal transactions demand for money, the nominal precautionary demand for money was a function of the level of nominal income. After all, as the price level rises, a constant amount of cash balances is worth less and the degree of security of money holders will fall. A doubling of the price level will lead to a doubling of the nominal transactions and precautionary money holdings. For this reason, early twentieth-century neoclassical economists such as Marshall and Fisher and more modern economists typically lump the transactions and the precautionary demands for money together and refer to them as L_1. As you will recall, the equation is

$$L_1 = kY \qquad (7.1)$$

WHERE L_1 = the desired quantity of money to hold for nominal transactions and precautionary motives

k = the ratio of desired nominal cash balances to nominal national income[2]

Y = nominal national income, equal to Py

Some neoclassical (and modern) economists also recognized that the precautionary demand for money *might* be inversely related to the interest rate. That is, higher interest rates increase the marginal cost of holding money, and rational individuals might be inclined to economize on their cash balances by forgoing some security or by paying the brokerage and search costs necessary to earn interest. For ease of exposition, however, we will ignore that complicating factor.

Keynes's Speculative Demand for Money

Keynes was intrigued by the precautionary demand for money. It implied that money is used other than as a medium of exchange. Keynes noted that the precautionary motive is an *asset* demand for money. If the precautionary demand for money is one exception to the "money is only a medium of exchange" rule, then there might be another exception.

Keynes developed another and entirely different motive for holding money and called it the **speculative demand for money.** He maintained that rational people voluntarily hold money above that desired for L_1. Why would Keynes call "rational" behavior that the classical economists called *irrational*?

Money and Other Financial Assets Financial assets are available in many forms: money, bonds, common stocks, savings accounts, certificates of deposit (CDs), commodities futures, and so on. Until quite recently, interest earnings could not be obtained by holders of money; this is *still* the case for currency and some checking account balances, but interest earnings are possible from some transactions accounts (e.g., negotiated orders of withdrawal, or NOW, accounts). Nonetheless, it is typically true that the interest rate that can be earned on transactions accounts is less than that which can be earned on nonmoney financial assets. It is thus meaningful to distinguish between money and nonmoney financial assets. A more important reason to distinguish between these two types of financial assets is as follows:

---

[2] Of course, dividing equation 7.1 by the price level P gives $L_1/P = k\,(Y/P)$, which indicates that real L_1 balances are proportional to real national income.

Capital gains or losses are possible for holders of nonmoney financial assets, but no capital gains or losses are possible on money itself, which is, by definition, the most liquid of all assets.

A $100 bill represents a claim on 100 nominal dollars today or in the future; $100 worth of bonds can change *in nominal value* over time as market interest rates change. Following tradition, we find it convenient to refer to all those assets from which one can receive a capital gain or loss as *bonds*. Thus, you should be aware that we are using the term *bonds* in a much wider context than you might have used it in other courses.

The essence of Keynes's speculative demand-for-money motive is that at certain times money is a financial asset superior to bonds. If wealth is constant, then a change in the demand for money to hold as money is equivalent to an opposite change in the demand for bonds. For example, if the community wants to hold more money, it must do so by selling bonds; if it wants more bonds, it must purchase them with money. Money can be superior to bonds when there is risk involved in bond-holding (capital loss) and especially when the risk outweighs the benefit from earning interest. Let us examine this proposition in more detail before we derive Keynes's speculative demand-for-money function.

The yield on an income-earning asset is *inversely* related to its price. The nature of a bond is that it offers a fixed, predetermined nominal revenue stream (for example, $100 per month for ten years, at which time the face value is paid to the holder). After a bond is purchased in a primary market it may be sold (and bought by another party) in a secondary market. As the supply of and the demand for a bond change, its price will change and so, therefore, will its yield. Conversely, as interest rates change, so will bond prices. That is, as interest rates change, the present value of a bond changes, and the market price (but not the maturity value) of a bond will equal its new present value. A given revenue stream from a bond has a market value that varies inversely with the current market interest rate. The interest rate reflects the opportunity cost of purchasing a particular revenue stream associated with the given bond.

Because bonds offer fixed income streams, the prices of previously issued bonds vary inversely with the rate of interest. When interest rates rise, previously issued bond prices fall and bondholders experience capital losses. It is the possibility of a capital gain or loss—that is, risk—that distinguishes bonds from money. Note again that money yields a zero interest return (if held in coins or currency) and a small interest return (if held in an interest-earning transactions deposit), but that no capital gain or loss is possible. Money, after all, is the medium of exchange. Bonds, on the other hand, can (and frequently do) change value in terms of the medium of exchange as supply and demand for bonds change. Bonds are therefore less liquid than money. They may have to be converted into money at a lower value than the original purchase price. Moreover, such a conversion requires brokerage fees and a bond market that is in session.[3]

For simplicity's sake, Keynes (modern economists follow suit) conducted his theoretical analysis using a special type of bond called a **consol,** or a nonmaturing bond. Consols are traded on British bond markets, and they offer a perpetual, fixed income stream to their holders. The present value of a consol is given by the equation[4]

$$V_p = \frac{R}{r} \tag{7.2}$$

WHERE R = annual net revenue stream that lasts into perpetuity
r = market interest rate

If a consol pays \$100 per annum and the going market rate of interest is 10 percent, the consol is worth \$1000. If the market rate of interest rises to 20 percent, that same consol is then worth only \$500; if the interest rate falls to 5 percent, the consol that pays \$100 per year is then worth \$2000. The present value of a consol, therefore, is inversely related to the interest rate, and it is possible to earn capital gains or to take capital losses on consols in a secondary market. (See footnote 4 and equation 6.7 to see why an inverse relationship exists between the price of *maturing* bonds and the market interest rate.)

The Speculative Demand-for-Money Curve   Armed with this information concerning the riskiness of bonds, it is now possible to derive Keynes's speculative demand-for-money curve. According to Keynes, people voluntarily hold or demand money above and beyond that desired for L_1 (transactions and precautionary motives) because money is, on occasion, a safer form (than bonds) in which to store wealth. Let us refer

---

[3] For Keynes, money and bonds are substitutes *only for each other*; neither is a direct substitute for those assets we refer to as real goods and services.

[4] Equation 6.7 shows the present value of *any* income stream. If $R_1 = R_2 = \cdots = R_n$, and if n is infinite, then equation 6.7 reduces to equation 7.2. Note also how equation 6.7 indicates that there is an inverse relationship between the *price* of an income-earning asset (bonds in this chapter) and the interest rate—given the revenue stream (R_2). The nature of a bond is that the revenue stream is a constant.

to this demand for money (beyond L_1 motives) as L_2. But when are bonds risky, and when are they safe? When will L_2 rise or fall?

According to Keynes, people cling to the notion of a **natural rate of interest**; that natural rate of interest is the rate to which the interest rate usually returns.[5] The essence of Keynes's theory is that (other things constant) the farther market rates depart from a "natural rate," the greater are the expectations that the actual rate will return to the natural rate. Thus, relatively high interest rates lead many to expect that those rates will fall; relatively low interest rates lead many to suspect that interest rates soon will rise.

Because the price of bonds varies inversely with the interest rate, people believe they know when bonds are safe and when they are risky. When interest rates are very high (and bond prices are therefore very low), the risk of purchasing bonds is low because if interest rates *do* change, they are expected to fall and to create capital gains. In this situation, Keynes predicted a low overall community L_2: very few want to hold money because they prefer to hold bonds, from which they expect interest earnings and a capital gain. On the other hand, when interest rates are very low (and bond prices are therefore very high), the risk of holding bonds is high because if interest rates do change, they will tend to rise toward their perceived natural rate and bondholders will therefore experience capital losses that will offset interest earnings. If interest rates are expected to rise so that the capital loss just equals the interest earnings from the bond, then speculators will be indifferent between holding money and holding bonds—under conditions of certainty. If the interest rate is expected (with certainty) to rise so much that the capital loss exceeds the interest earnings, then speculators will prefer to hold money; if the interest rate is expected to rise just slightly, so that the capital loss is less than the interest earnings, then speculators will prefer to purchase bonds. Note that this model is constructed under conditions of certainty; expectations as to what will happen to the interest rate are held with certainty. However, *different* people have different expectations.

This analysis implies that low interest rates induce a desire for higher L_2 demand for money, and therefore an inverse relationship exists between L_2 and r. This is shown in Figure 7.1. Note that this is a *community* speculative demand-for-money curve. If each person has an expectation of future interest rates that he or she holds with certainty, then that person will hold either all bonds or all money in his or her wealth

---

[5] Of course, different people have different notions about what the natural rate is. Otherwise, there would be no gambling, which requires a difference of opinion. Presumably, the natural rate of interest is the classical equilibrium rate—that which reflects the marginal productivity of capital and society's rate of time preference for consumption.

An Inverse Relationship Exists Between L_2 and the Interest Rate

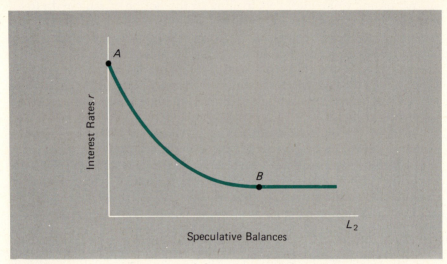

FIGURE 7.1. THE COMMUNITY SPECULATIVE DEMAND FOR MONEY
This figure shows that L_2 (the demand for money to hold over and above L_1) is inversely related to the interest rate. Only at point A, where $L_2 = 0$ (the L_2 curve becomes perfectly inelastic) do the Keynesian and classical models agree. As the interest rate falls from A, more people become convinced that the interest rate is below the natural rate and that the risk of bondholding is rising. It follows that lower interest rates induce people to hold more L_2. At point B, interest rates are at a (subjective) minimum. Here, virtually everyone is convinced that interest rates will rise; bonds are extremely risky, and people are prepared to hold limitless money balances. To the right of point B, the curve (the L_2 function) is perfectly elastic; the curve is horizontal in that range and reflects the fact that at such a low interest rate bonds are so risky that the public is prepared *to hold* limitless amounts of money. Note that because the price level is assumed constant, changes in *nominal* values are also changes in *real* values.

portfolio. (Remember, money held for L_1 balances is *already* netted out, and L_2 balances are money held above L_1 balances.) But because there are *many* speculators and many different expectations (each assumed to be held with certainty), it is possible to derive a smooth (continuous) community speculative demand-for-money curve.

To the classical economists, the L_2 curve would be the same as the vertical axis because as long as interest rates are positive, $L_2 = 0$. Keynes's position is that $L_2 = 0$ only at point A where interest rates are so high that virtually everyone is convinced rates will fall. At point A in Figure 7.1, all money balances will be used for transactions and precautionary motives, and none will be held for speculative motives. With no speculative demand, the classical and Keynesian models become the same model.

As the interest rate falls (causing bond prices to rise), the quantity of L_2 demanded will rise; some people will want to take their capital gains (by selling bonds) and hold money. Lower and lower interest rates convince more and more people that the interest rate is below the natural rate; drops in the interest rate induce a greater quantity demanded for money to hold in L_2 as bonds become progressively riskier. Finally, the speculative demand-for-money curve becomes, at least theoretically, perfectly horizontal (at point B). Virtually everyone is convinced that the market rate is below the natural rate and can only rise; bonds are so risky that speculators are prepared to hold limitless quantities of money. As will be seen later, this implies that a subjective floor exists on interest rates; interest rates won't fall below the level of point B in Figure 7.1.

Liquidity Preference and the Classical _k_ Because the curve in Figure 7.1 indicates a preference for money over bonds, the curve is also referred to as a **liquidity preference function.** It is important to realize that as the economy moves from point A to point B in Figure 7.1, the classical k rises (velocity falls). (See Chapter 5.) Assume that the level of national income equals $100 billion and that L_1 equals $20 billion as a result. The ratio of _desired_ money balances to national income, or k, is 20 percent (20/100) and the reciprocal of k—velocity—equals 5. Assume that the market rate of interest falls and some people believe that the market rate is now below the natural rate. They perceive that bonds are now relatively more risky and they prefer to hold fewer bonds and more money; some people want to substitute money for bonds in their portfolios. Suppose that the community now wants to hold _another_ $5 billion in money in order to meet L_2, the speculative motive. The _desired_ ratio of money balances to national income is $25 billion/$100 billion = 0.25, and velocity now equals 4. As we move from point A to point B the level of national income remains constant, but desired money balances rise; as a consequence, the community's desired k rises and velocity falls. In effect, Keynes notes that k and V are functions of the rate of interest and hence are not constant. This is a fundamental Keynesian conclusion to which we make reference in later chapters.

Liquidity Preference and Uncertainty: The Tobin Analysis

The Keynesian liquidity preference analysis implies that each individual wealthholder is either a bondholder _or_ a moneyholder (after L_1 balances are netted out). Whether a particular individual is a bondholder or a moneyholder depends on his or her (certain) expectations concerning the interest rate. There are no mixed portfolios; no one holds money (beyond L_1) *and* bonds simultaneously. James Tobin, a Nobel Prize laureate from Yale University, has demonstrated that if *uncertainty* is introduced, then (1) a mixed portfolio for an individual can be predicted, and (2) there will be an inverse relationship between the interest rate and L_2 balances for individuals *and* for the community.

We consider a simplified version of Tobin's analysis now.[6] Assume that no individual has any reason to believe that the interest rate is likely to move in a particular direction, but that many people believe that it will change in some direction. Tobin's contribution is to assume that most people are **risk averse;** people tend to prefer less risk to more risk, *other things constant.*

Consider an example. Suppose you are offered two options. In option 1, you get $1.00 free. In option 2, a (fair) coin is tossed; if the toss is heads, you win $1.50, and if the toss is tails, you win $0.50. Note that both of these options have the same expected value, or mathematical expectation.[7] If you are risk averse, you will choose option 1; the risk-averse prefer the sure thing, other things constant. In order to induce a risk-averse person to take option 2, he or she would have to be offered better "terms"—perhaps $1.75 if the coin is heads and $0.50 if the coin turns up tails. In fact, the amount by which the expected payoff must rise gives a clue as to *how* risk averse an individual is; risk aversion varies directly with the expected value required to induce an individual to select option 2 over option 1.

Let's now return to Tobin's analysis. If Mrs. Patullo holds her wealth in money, she neither benefits nor gains if interest rates change. The value of money remains constant.[8] Other things constant, Mrs. Patullo would always prefer money to bonds, if she is risk averse. *But other things are not constant.* Bond holding involves risk, but it also yields interest earnings. The higher the interest rate—assuming she thinks that it is equally likely to rise or to fall regardless of its level—the more risk she is willing to assume. That's another way to say that the higher the interest rate, the higher the percentage of her wealth she will hold in bonds and the smaller the percentage she will hold in money; conversely, the lower the interest rate, the lower the percentage of her wealth she will hold in bonds and the higher the percentage she will hold in money. For her, an inverse relationship exists between i and L_2. If most people

---

[6] See James Tobin, "Liquidity Preference as Behavior Towards Risk," *Review of Economic Studies,* 25 (February 1958), pp. 65–86, for the original and more rigorous presentation.

[7] The mathematical expectation is $(1/2)($1.50) + (1/2)($0.50) = $0.75 + $0.25 = 1.00.

[8] At least the *nominal* value of her money stays the same. The real value of her money is inversely related to the price level, but that is equally true for the value of the bonds she owns. Thus, we still end up with the proposition that bonds are riskier than money.

are risk averse, the community's L_2 will also be inversely related to the interest rate.

In short, Tobin dispenses with the assumption of certainty, and by applying the concept of risk aversion, he can account for the fact that individuals hold mixed money/bond portfolios (i.e., individual demands for money are inversely related to the interest rate).

Another Household Decision

In the classical model, households had one key question to answer: How much income should be allocated to consumption and saving? Once a household saved, those funds automatically became a part of the supply of loanable funds because money saved would not be hoarded by rational people. Keynes's and Tobin's analyses, however, indicate that another important question is necessary for households to answer: what *form* will saving take? That is, households must decide what portion of their wealth (if any) is to be held in bonds and what portion in money. Keynes, who was a successful speculator, noted that at times money was superior to bonds as an asset form. He therefore provided a rational motive for hoarding. The realization that households have this additional decision led Keynes to a radically different theory of the rate of interest. According to the classical theory, the rate of interest resulted from the first decision (the consumption/saving decision). According to Keynes, the interest rate results from the second decision—the money/bonds decision.

KEYNES'S THEORY OF THE RATE OF INTEREST

The classical theory of the rate of interest is that it is determined at the point of intersection of the saving and net investment curves. Keynes contended that neither saving nor investment was primarily determined by the rate of interest, and he replaced the classical theory of interest with his own theory.

The Equilibrium Interest Rate

Assume that the national money supply M is determined by the monetary authorities. Keynes's theory is that (given the level of national income) the market rate of interest will be determined at the intersection of the (net) supply of money and the liquidity preference (L_2, or his demand for money) curves.[9] This can also be viewed alternatively: the

---

[9] You may recall that for the classical economist, the supply of and the demand for money determine the price level (see Chapter 5).

In the Keynesian Model the Interest Rate Is Determined by the Net Money Supply and the Speculative Demand for Money

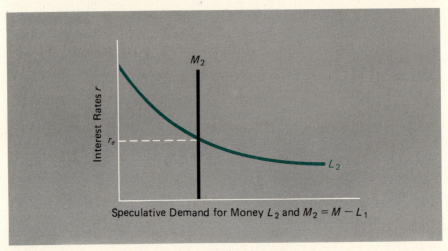

FIGURE 7.2. INTEREST RATE DETERMINATION

In this figure, L_2, the demand for money to hold above L_1 (transactions and precautionary motives), and M_2 (the money supply M determined independently by the monetary authorities, minus the amount desired for L_1) determine the equilibrium interest rate r_e. At any interest rate above r_e, a surplus of liquidity exists, and individuals will attempt to rid themselves of excess money balances by purchasing bonds. This activity will force bond prices up and the interest rate down. At any interest rate below r_e, a shortage of liquidity will lead to bond sales, which reduce bond prices and raise the interest rate.

equilibrium rate of interest is the one at which the given money supply minus the amount demanded for L_1 equals the amount demanded for L_2; in Figure 7.2, M_2 is the *net* money supply $M - L_1$, or the amount available for L_2.

Consider any interest rate above r_e, the equilibrium rate. By inspection, it can be seen that the quantity of money demanded is less than the quantity supplied; $L_2 < M_2$. A surplus of liquidity exists. People are holding more money than they wish to hold. *Individuals can change* the amount of money they hold, but *the community cannot.* Individuals can rid themselves of excess money balances by purchasing bonds; bond purchases force bond prices up, and therefore interest rates fall. Complementary analysis indicates that below r_e a shortage of liquidity exists, and this will lead to bond sales which will force bond prices down and interest rates up toward r_e. Equilibrium is achieved by changes in bond prices and the resulting change in the interest rate; if the money supply and the money demand are not equated, bond prices and the interest rate will change until they are. Recall that in the classical model, if the supply of and the demand for money are not equated, the price level and nominal national income adjust. Thus, in the classical model the supply of and the demand for money determine the price level; in the Keynesian model, the supply of and the demand for money determine the interest rate. In the classical model the interest rate analysis deals with flows (saving and investment per unit of time), and interest is perceived as a reward for postponing known consumption for more (but a vague and unspecified amount of) consumption at a later—unspecified—date. In Keynes's model, interest rate analysis deals with stocks (the net money supply and the demand for an L_2 stock of money), and interest is viewed as a reward for parting with liquidity.

Changes in *M* Lead to Changes in *r*

Now let's see how changes in the money supply can affect the interest rate. Consider Figure 7.3. Note how an increase in the net money supply, a rightward shift from M_2 to M_2', causes the interest rate to fall from r_e to r_1. If the Federal Reserve (the U.S. central bank) buys bonds from the public or from depository institutions, it may be able to affect *directly* the price of bonds and therefore interest rates.[10] Deposit expansion money multipliers will take effect, and the money supply will increase. Increased excess reserves will encourage depository institutions to increase lending, which can be done only at lower interest rates. Complementary reasoning indicates that Fed bond sales will reduce M_2 to M_2'' and raise interest rates to r_2.

KEYNES AND MONETARY POLICY

Consider Figure 7.4. Note that in the **liquidity trap** (horizontal) region of the L_2 curve changes in the (net) supply of money have no effect on the interest rate. Fed purchases of bonds are welcomed by the public, which considers bonds risky and is prepared to hold an infinite amount of money. Similarly, depository institutions are happy to sell bonds—and hold excess reserves. As a consequence, monetary policy is ineffective because banks cannot be forced to lend excess reserves.

---

[10] This is possible if the Federal Reserve (Fed) is a relatively large buyer in the market. The Fed's ability to do so, however, is limited in the horizontal range of the L_2 curve, called the *liquidity trap*, where interest rates are already so low and bond prices so high that bonds are risky to the point that the public is only too willing to sell to the Fed. We analyze monetary policy in detail in Chapter 16.

Changes in the Net Money Supply Usually Change the Interest Rate

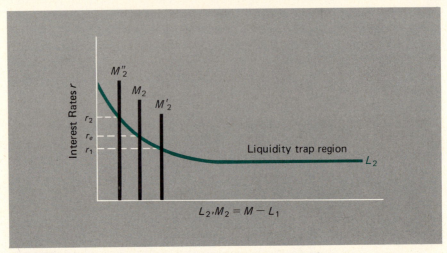

FIGURE 7.3. HOW THE INTEREST RATE CHANGES
Changes in the nominal money supply, given the speculative demand-for-money curve and given a fixed price level, will alter the real interest rate. Specifically, central bank open-market purchases of bonds will increase the nominal money supply and cause the interest rate to fall (except in the liquidity trap). Central bank open-market sales of bonds will decrease the money supply and cause the interest rate to rise (except in the liquidity trap).

According to Keynes, expansionary monetary policy is ineffective in periods of recession, and certainly during depressions, because interest rates are already low during such periods. The demand for business loans will be quite low anyway, because profit expectations have depressed desired investment expenditures. For monetary policy to be effective, small changes in the money supply should lead to significant changes in the interest rate, which in turn should lead to significant changes in net investment. Thus, $\Delta M \rightarrow \Delta r \rightarrow \Delta y$. But in a recession, when interest rates are already quite low and the economy is in the flatter ranges of the speculative demand-for-money curve, changes in the money supply lead to only *very small* changes in the interest rate. Moreover, in a recession investment plans have been greatly curtailed, and it takes very large reductions in the interest rate to encourage increased investment; the rate of interest must fall greatly to offset the reduction in profit expectations during a recession. For these two reasons—an L_2 curve that is insensitive to changes in the money supply and an investment curve

In the Liquidity Trap the Interest Rate Is Insensitive to an Increase in the Net Money Supply

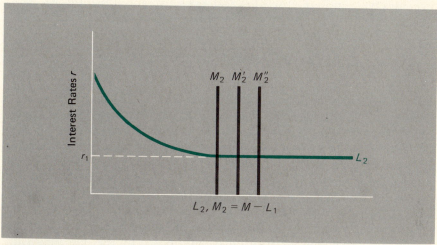

FIGURE 7.4. THE LIQUIDITY TRAP

In the liquidity trap (or horizontal) range of the liquidity preference function, increases in the money supply do not lower the interest rate. At r_1, the interest rate is so low that virtually all speculators believe that it is below the natural rate and will rise, causing the price of bonds to fall. Bonds are so risky that the public is prepared to hold an infinite quantity of money and banks are prepared to hold excess reserves. Keynes believed that the Great Depression *approached* (but was not) a liquidity trap situation.

that is insensitive to changes in the interest rate—monetary policy is not considered by Keynesians to be effective during a recession.[11]

Keynes maintained that monetary policy is effective only to the extent that it affects the aggregate expenditures (AE) curve. Because monetary policy is ineffective in a recession or in a depression, Keynes favored fiscal policy, which shifts the AE curve upward directly by increases in government purchases of goods and services and indirectly by decreases in taxes or increases in transfers that cause consumption to rise.

On the other hand, there is a role for monetary policy in combating

[11] This can be shown using the equation of exchange: $\uparrow MV \downarrow = \bar{Y}$ (recall that a $\bar{Y}$ means that Y remains constant). Increases in M are offset by decreases in V (k rises as the community merely holds new money), and Y remains constant.

inflation. Central bank bond sales on the open market can decrease the supply of money and cause interest rates to rise. While depository institutions cannot be forced to lend excess reserves, they *can* be forced to meet reserve requirements.[12] Interest rates rise and cause the AE curve to shift down so that inflationary pressures will abate.

A TOTAL-DEMAND-FOR-MONEY CURVE

It is now possible to derive a total-demand-for-money curve: $L = L_1 + L_2$. This curve, illustrated in Figure 7.5, indicates the money demanded for all three motives (transactions, precautionary, and speculative) as a function of the rate of interest. The total-demand-for-money L function is derived by adding the L_1 and L_2 demands *horizontally*. The L_1 curve is independent of the interest rate; it is primarily determined by the level of Y, as the classical economists maintained and as *we have assumed*.[13] Thus, the L_1 curve remains constant as r changes and appears as a line parallel to the vertical axis. The shape of this curve is determined by the L_2 demand curve, and its position is determined by the position of the L_1 demand curve.

The Derivation of the *lm* Curve

Keynesians have found it convenient to recast the previous analysis in terms of an **lm curve,** the locus of all points that indicates equilibrium real interest rates and real national income levels in the monetary sphere of the economy. This neoclassical-Keynesian curve incorporates the two notions that L_1/P depends on real national income (the classical assumption) and that L_2/P depends on r (the Keynesian assumption). The *lm* curve is derived by assuming the real money supply is constant; the curve relates real national income levels to real interest rates. It is important to stress that *at every point on the lm curve equilibrium exists in the money market* because the total demand for real money

---

[12] Still, a higher interest rate will reduce L_2; therefore, k will fall and V will rise. To some extent, then, decreases in M will be offset by increases in V; $MV = Y$, making the effect of a change in M on Y somewhat indeterminate. In short, Keynesians doubt the efficacy of monetary policy because V moves perversely. When M is increased, V falls; when M is decreased, V rises. The effects of fiscal policy seem to be more straightforward to the Keynesians.

[13] Actually, modern economists believe, and some empirical evidence shows, that the amount that people hold for transactions balances is also (somewhat) inversely related to the interest rate. Businesses, especially, economize on transactions balances at relatively high interest rates. See William J. Baumol, "The Transactions Demand for Cash: An Inventory Theoretic Approach," *Quarterly Journal of Economics*, 66 (November 1952), pp. 545–556, and James Tobin, "The Interest-Elasticity of the Transactions Demand for Cash," *Review of Economics and Statistics*, 38 (August 1956), pp. 241–247. We return to this issue in Chapter 11.

The Position of the Total-Demand-for-Money Curve Is Determined by the Level of National Income, and Its Shape Is Determined by the L_2 Curve

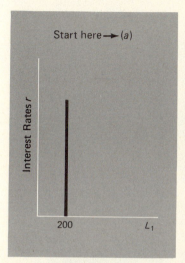 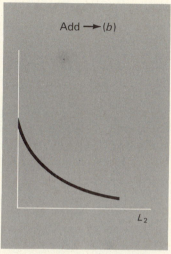 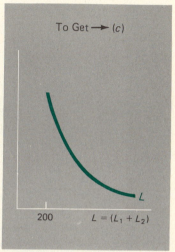

FIGURE 7.5. THE TOTAL-DEMAND-FOR-MONEY FUNCTION

Add panel *a* to panel *b* horizontally to derive panel *c*, the total-demand-for-money function. This curve indicates the money demand for all motives as a function of the rate of interest. Note that the *position* of the curve in *a* and *c* depends on the level of national income; the quantity demanded for L_1 balances, 200, is related to some specific level of national income. A change in national income will shift the curve in *a* and in *c*; increases in national income will shift the L curve to the right; decreases in national income will shift L to the left. The *shape* of the L curve is determined by the L_2 curve.

$(L_1 + L_2)/P$ and the real supply of money M/P are equated—hence the name *lm* curve.

Mathematically,

$$\frac{\bar{M}}{P} = L\left(\frac{Y}{P}, r\right) \qquad (7.3)$$

WHERE $\bar{M}$ = constant nominal money supply
$\bar{M}/P$ = real money supply
r = real interest rate

Figure 7.6 derives an *lm* curve. If the real money supply is constant, real national income changes will lead to real interest rate changes. In particular, if the level of real national income rises, there will be an

The *lm* Curve Shows All the Combinations of Real Interest Rates and Real National Income Levels That Satisfy the Money Market Equilibrium Condition

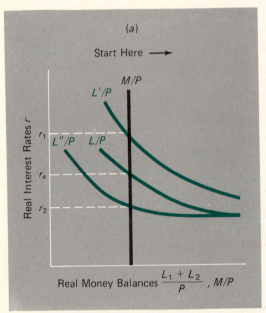

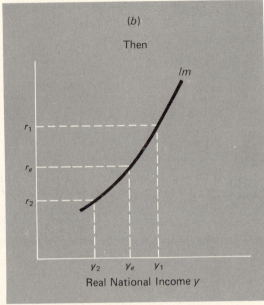

FIGURE 7.6. DERIVING THE *lm* CURVE

Given a fixed real money supply and a constant price level, a change in the demand for money leads to a change in the nominal and real rate of interest. As panel *a* shows, increases in the level of real national income from y_e to y_1 cause an increase in the total real demand for money (transactions plus precautionary) from L/P to L'/P, which causes an increase in the real interest rate from r_e to r_1. Complementary reasoning shows how a reduction in real income from y_e to y_2 causes r to fall from r_e to r_2, because L/P falls to L''/P. Panel *b* relates the different real income levels to the changes in real interest rates, given the nominal money supply and the price level; panel *b* shows the *lm* curve.

increase in the total demand for real money because L_1/P increases. Given the fixed supply of money, a shortage will exist because at r_e the quantity of real money demanded exceeds the available M/P, and a scramble for liquidity ensues. As people sell bonds in order to become more liquid, bond prices fall and real interest rates rise.

Complementary reasoning indicates that, given M/P, a reduction in real national income to y_2 will reduce L_1/P. Therefore, the total-demand-for-real-money function falls, shifting leftward to $(L/P)''$. Now at r_e a surplus of liquidity exists because the real quantity of money demanded is less than the available real supply $\bar{M}/P$, and money holders will purchase bonds, driving bond prices up and real interest rates down. Therefore, given the real money supply, increases in real national income will cause real interest rates to rise; decreases in real national income will cause real interest rates to fall. Note that in Figure 7.6 the lm curve is upward sloping, from left to right, and that real national income changes lead to real interest rate changes in the same direction, given $\bar{M}/P$. Also, it should be stressed that at each point on the lm curve the real demand for and the real supply of money are equated, that is, $(L_1 + L_2)/P = \bar{M}/P$.

A Closer Look at the *lm* Function

The Classical Range   Figure 7.6 indicates the general shape of the lm function; it will be useful to take a closer look at the shape of this important curve. Consider Figure 7.7. As the economy moves from point C to point A, what is happening? Higher real national income levels lead to an increase in L_1/P, which in turn leads to a rightward shift in the total-demand-for-real-money curve L/P. Given a constant $\bar{M}/P$, this higher real income can be financed only by offering holders of L_2/P higher interest rates to encourage them to part with liquidity. As real interest rates rise, the opportunity cost of holding money rises, and bonds become less risky; hence, some money moves from L_2/P to L_1/P and velocity rises. Eventually, sufficiently high real national income levels induce real interest rates that are high enough to move *all* L_2/P balances into L_1/P balances. At that point, point A, $L_2/P = 0$ and velocity is at a maximum. Hence, *given* $\bar{M}/P$, real national income is at its maximum. The vertical region above point A on the lm curve is referred to as the **classical range** because the classical economists maintained that money was only a medium of exchange; they assumed that $L_2/P = 0$. The classical range indicates the maximum real national income level that can be reached, given the real money supply. Velocity is at a maximum and money becomes a bottleneck to further expansion of real national income.

You should realize that the reason real national income and national output are at a maximum is not because the economy is at full employment. It isn't. Rather, national output and real national income are constrained because velocity is at a maximum and more money is required for any further expansion.[14]

---

[14] Remember, prices and wages are assumed to be constant. In theory, a fixed nominal money supply could finance *any* level of national output with *lower price levels* because a decrease in the price level increases the real money supply $\bar{M}/P$.

The *Im* Curve Has a Classical Range and a Keynesian Range

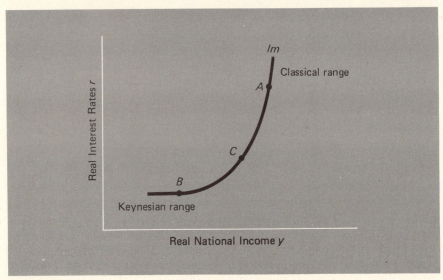

FIGURE 7.7. A CLOSER LOOK AT THE *Im* FUNCTION

In the classical range, the total M/P (real balance) is held in the form of L_1/P (transaction balance) and velocity is at a maximum. In the Keynesian range, reductions in national income create excess balances as L_1/P falls, but because interest rates are already low, wealth holders are prepared to hold these money balances. As a consequence, velocity is very low in the liquidity trap (Keynesian) range. In the intermediate range, r and y are inversely related; as we move up the *Im* curve in the intermediate range, velocity rises because more L_2/P balances are coaxed out and used to finance transactions.

The Keynesian Range Now consider what happens in Figure 7.7 as the economy moves from point C to point B. Lower levels of real national income lead to a reduction in L_1/P, creating excess cash balances at the prevailing interest rate. With these excess balances resulting from a surplus of liquidity, bond purchases are made which force bond prices up and real interest rates down. Eventually, however, very low real interest rates make bond purchases so risky that the holders of $\overline{M}/P$ are prepared to hold these excess money balances. Thus, in the horizontal region around point B (the liquidity trap), lower real income levels reduce the demand for L_1/P, but these balances are *not* used to purchase bonds; they are merely *held* in the form of L_2/P; therefore, *interest rates do not fall*. Because a lower real national income no longer leads to a lower interest rate, the *lm* curve becomes parallel to the horizontal axis. This is referred to as the **Keynesian range,** because it results from Keynes's liquidity trap hypothesis. Note that as the economy moves from point C to point B, velocity continuously falls (k rises) as the community holds more and more cash balances in the form of L_2/P.[15]

Shifts in the *lm* Curve

The *lm* curve was derived for a constant money supply and a constant price level. It follows that a change in the nominal money supply will shift the *lm* curve. If the nominal, and given the price level therefore the real, money supply were to rise, a surplus of liquidity would *now* exist at any given y (real income level) on the *lm* curve, and r would fall (except in the liquidity trap) as people use these excess balances to purchase bonds. The conclusion is that an increase in M/P will cause the *lm* curve to shift to the right, by $(\Delta M/P)/k$. Complementary analysis indicates that a reduction in M/P will cause the *lm* function to shift to the left by $(\Delta M/P)/k$. This is shown graphically in Figure 7.8. (We stress again that, because the price level is assumed constant, changes in nominal values are equivalent to changes in real values.)

A Problem

According to Keynes, the interest rate is a monetary phenomenon; it is determined by the real supply of and the real demand for money. Yet changes in the real interest rate can affect real aggregate expenditures (and therefore real national income) through changes in real net investment. Also, changes in aggregate expenditures, by changing L_1/P [and therefore $L/P = (L_1 + L_2)/P$], change the interest rate. It follows that the rate of interest is the link between the monetary world and the real world; by changing the real money supply, such real variables as employment and output may vary. And when employment, output, and real income change, the real interest rate changes. (Clearly, money is not neutral in this model.)

But a problem exists. According to Keynes, the real interest rate helps to determine real national income y. On the other hand, according to the theory of the transactions and precautionary motives for holding money, when y increases, so does L_1/P. This means that, given a fixed real money supply, an increase in real national income will cause an

---

[15] This can be shown through the equation of exchange. Because $V = (Y/P)/(M/P)$, if Y/P falls and M/P is constant, V must fall. Using the Cambridge approach, you should be able to see why k rises.

The *lm* Curve Shifts When the Real Money Supply Changes

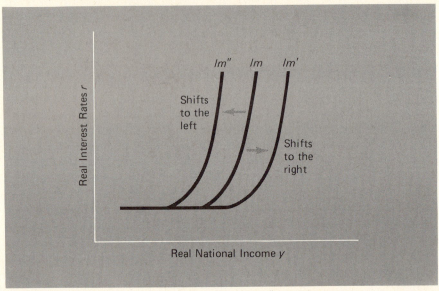

FIGURE 7.8. CHANGES IN *M/P* LEAD TO CHANGES IN *lm*

Given the price level, changes in the *nominal* money supply change the *real* money supply. This figure indicates that real money supply changes lead to shifts in the *lm* curve. If the real money supply were increased, the *lm* curve would shift downward from *lm* to *lm'*; any given real national income level would be associated with a lower level of real interest rate (except in the Keynesian range). If the real money stock were to fall, the *lm* curve would shift upward from *lm* to *lm''*; any given real national income level would be associated with a lower level of real interest rate. Note that for a given change in *M/P* the *lm* curve will shift by $(\Delta M/P)/k$.

increase in the real rate of interest. This is indicated by an upward-sloping *lm* curve.

Does the rate of interest help to determine the level of income, or does the level of income help to determine the interest rate? The problem is that this **neoclassical-Keynesian synthesis** model includes a real demand for money that is a function of two variables—the real interest rate and real income. The equilibrium condition is that the real supply of and the real demand for money must be equated. The model has two variables—real national income and the real interest rate—and one equation—$M/P = (L_1 + L_2)/P$. Consequently, the model is not determinate. Unlike a pure Keynesian model where the supply of and the demand for real money determine the real interest rate, the neoclassical-Keynesian synthesis model (which incorporates the classical model assumption that L_1/P is a function of y) yields a situation in which the real supply of and the real demand for money determine *combinations* of real interest and real income that satisfy the equation $M/P = (L_1 + L_2)/P$, given M/P. What is needed is another equation relating r and y, and that equation is provided by the equilibrium condition in the *product market* (aggregate expenditures = aggregate output). In the next section, combinations of r and y that satisfy the product-market equilibrium are determined. Aggregate equilibrium, the simultaneous equilibrium in both the money and the product markets, is then discussed. In other words:

Equilibrium y *and* r *are determined* simultaneously *by the interaction of the money market and the product market, for a given price level.*

DERIVING THE *is* CURVE

The *lm* curve is the locus of all the combinations of real interest rates and real national income levels that satisfies the equilibrium condition in the money market. The **is curve** is the locus of all the combinations of interest rates and national income levels that satisfies the equilibrium condition in the product market. Before we can derive the *is* curve, we must digress and recall the relationship between interest rates and net investment, which is called the aggregate investment curve. (Remember again that because we are holding the price level constant, changes in nominal values are equivalent to changes in real values.)

The Aggregate Investment Curve

Recall from Chapter 6 that Keynes's marginal efficiency of capital curve for a firm is inversely related to the interest rate; more investment projects are profitable at a lower interest rate than at a higher interest rate. By summing all the marginal efficiency of investment curves, we can derive an aggregate investment curve, which shows the amount of total investment at each possible interest rate; it, too, is negatively sloped. Remember, however, Keynes stressed that this aggregate investment curve is extremely volatile. It shifts every time profit expectations—which are formed by considering what will happen in the unknowable future—change.

The *is* Curve Shows All the Combinations of Interest Rates and National Income Levels That Satisfy the Product-Market Equilibrium Condition

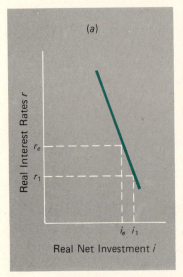

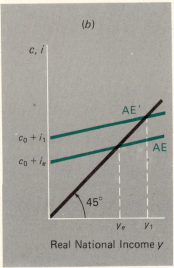

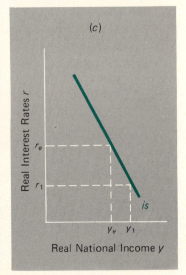

FIGURE 7.9. DERIVING THE *is* CURVE

Here it is shown how a change in the real rate of interest leads to a change in the quantity of real net investment (because businesses find it profitable to do so) in panel *a*. This causes a shift in the aggregate expenditures in panel *b* and thereby causes the equilibrium level of real national income to change. These changes are summarized in panel *c*, where it is shown how real interest rate changes lead to changes in real national income. Thus, an inverse relationship between *r* and *y* exists in the product market. The *is* curve will shift if the investment curve *i* or the consumption curve shifts. Chapter 17 shows that the *is* curve also shifts through fiscal policy actions.

Deriving the *is* Curve from the Aggregate Investment Curve and the Aggregate Expenditures—Aggregate Output Framework

Consider Figure 7.9. It shows that a reduction in real interest rates causes an increase in the quantity of real investment (a movement along the aggregate investment curve) in panel *a*. This increase in autonomous real net investment causes the aggregate expenditures curve to shift upward, and real national income rises with a multiplier effect from y_e to y_1. This is shown in panel *b*. In panel *c* the relationship is summarized: a reduction in the real rate of interest leads to a multiple (of the change in investment) increase in the level of real national income. By a series of alterations in the interest rate, the *is* curve is derived. It is depicted in panel *c*. Note that at every point along the *is* curve equilibrium exists in the product market ($AE_q = AO_q$); therefore, at every point planned investment equals planned saving in a closed, private economy (without international transactions and without government activities); hence the name *is* curve.

The *is* curve will shift if the *i* curve shifts or if the consumption curve shifts. If profit expectations rise, or if the community becomes less thrifty, the *is* curve will shift to the right (i.e., the level of real national income will be higher at any real rate of interest because each of these changes will cause aggregate expenditures to rise and cause real national income to rise). Also, if we depart temporarily from a private economy, an increase in real government expenditures (other things constant) will increase aggregate expenditures; therefore, real national income will be higher at every real rate of interest. A decrease in real autonomous consumption (increase in real autonomous saving), a decrease in profit expectations (which shifts the *i* curve leftward), and a decrease in real government expenditures will shift the *is* curve leftward. We return to a discussion of shifts in the *is* curve in Chapter 17 when we discuss fiscal policy.

AGGREGATE EQUILIBRIUM: PUTTING *lm* AND *is* TOGETHER

The *lm* curve represents all combinations of equilibrium real interest rates and real national income levels in the money market. The *is* curve represents all such combinations in the product market. If both curves are plotted on the same coordinate system, **aggregate equilibrium** (simultaneous equilibrium in both the money and the product markets) will exist at their point of intersection. Consider Figure 7.10. In this figure, aggregate equilibrium will exist at point *E*, which is the point common to both curves.

is Equilibrium and *lm* Disequilibrium

To demonstrate that aggregate equilibrium will exist at point *E* in Figure 7.10, let's first consider a disequilibrium position, such as point *A*. At point *A* equilibrium exists in the product market because *A* is a point on the *is* curve. (Remember, all points on the *is* curve represent equilibrium in the product market.) It is important to note that at point *A*, $y = y_A$ and $r = r_1$.

What about the money market? Point *A* cannot be an equilibrium position in the money market because it is not on the *lm* curve. What

Aggregate Equilibrium Exists at the Point of Intersection of the *is* Curve and the *lm* Curve

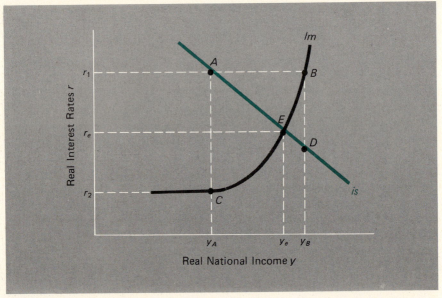

FIGURE 7.10. AGGREGATE EQUILIBRIUM

In this figure, aggregate equilibrium exists at point E because equilibrium exists in both the money market and the product market simultaneously. At any higher real interest rate–real national income combination on the *is* curve, such as at point A, the product market will be in equilibrium but a surplus of liquidity (an excess supply of money) will exist in the money market. This will cause real interest rates to fall, which will cause net investment to rise, which will cause real national income to rise; the economy moves toward point E. Similar reasoning indicates a movement from point D to point E. At point C, equilibrium exists in the money market, but in the product market aggregate output is less than aggregate expenditures and a shortage of goods and services exists. This will cause real national income to rise, which in turn will cause the real interest rate to rise through an increase in L_1/P, driving the economy toward E. Similar reasoning indicates a movement from B to E.

is the situation in the money market at point A? In order to see, consider point B, at which r is also r_1 but $y = y_B$. At point B, equilibrium exists in the money market because B is on the *lm* curve, and $(L_1 + L_2)/P = M/P$. (Remember, all points on the *lm* curve represent equilibrium in the money market.)

Now compare A (y_A, r_1) and B (y_B, r_1). At B (y_B, r_1), $(L_1 + L_2)/P = M/P$; but since $y_B > y_A$, L_1/P at B must be greater than L_1/P at A. Since both points A and B are at interest rate r_1, L_2/P is the same at both points, because L_2/P depends *only* on the interest rate. It follows that at B, $(L_1 + L_2)/P$ is larger than at A. Since at B, $(L_1 + L_2)/P = M/P$ and M/P is constant, we conclude at A that $M/P > (L_1 + L_2)/P$; a surplus of money, or liquidity, exists in the money market at point A. Holders of M/P are holding more money than they want to hold at A, so individuals will attempt to rid themselves of excess money by purchasing bonds, driving bond prices up and real interest rates down. A reduction in real interest rates leads to an increase in real net investment and causes a multiple expansion in y. As y increases and r decreases, L_1/P and L_2P increase, until $(L_1 + L_2)/P = M/P$ and the money market is driven to equilibrium. In short, the economy moves toward point E; real interest rates fall from r_1, and national income rises above y_A.

Similar analysis indicates that at point D equilibrium exists in the product market but a shortage of liquidity exists in the money market. This will cause individuals to sell bonds, forcing bond prices down and real interest rates up. In turn, a higher real interest rate will reduce real net investment, and therefore national income will fall. As y falls and r rises, L_1/P and L_2P fall until $(L_1 + L_2)/P = M/P$ and the money market reaches equilibrium.

Im Equilibrium and *is* Disequilibrium

Consider point C in Figure 7.10. At that point equilibrium exists in the money market but a shortage exists in the product market. Why? Consider point A, which incorporates the same level of real national income but a *higher* real interest rate. Because A is on the *is* curve, equilibrium exists in the product market by definition. But because the real interest rate is higher at A than at C $(r_1 > r_2)$, aggregate expenditures must be higher at point C than at point A. If $AE_q = AO_q$ at point A, then $AE_q > AO_q$ at point C and there must be a shortage of final goods and services at C. Businesses will find it profitable to increase output, which in turn causes real national income to rise. (Remember, in the Keynesian model increases in AE leave the price level constant.) The increase in real national income causes an increase in the demand for L_1/P balances, so the real interest rate will also rise. The level of real national income and the real interest rate will rise until point E is reached.

Similar analysis reveals that a surplus of final goods and services exists at point B; at B, $AE_q > AO_q$. This will cause producers to reduce their output levels, which in turn causes real national income to fall. As a result, L_1/P demand falls, causing the real interest rate to fall. The level of national income and the interest rate fall until point E is reached.

At point E equilibrium exists in both the money and the product markets; hence, aggregate equilibrium exists.

CHAPTER SUMMARY

1. Keynes accepted the classical transactions demand for money as a function of income. He also accepted the neoclassical notion of the asset demand-for-money concept of the precautionary motive, which is also related to income.
2. Keynes expanded on the notion of the asset demand for money and developed the speculative demand for money, which posited an inverse relationship between the quantity of money demanded and the interest rate.
3. Because the nominal value of money is constant but the nominal value of bonds is inversely related to the interest rate, money is more liquid and less risky than bonds.
4. Given certainty about future interest rates, individual wealth holders decide to hold their wealth in the form of bonds or in money. Because different people have different notions about what the natural rate of interest is, a continuous community speculative-demand-for-money curve can be derived.
5. According to Keynes, the market interest rate is determined at the intersection of the speculative-demand-for-real-money curve and the (net) supply-of-real-money curve. Increases in the net real money supply decrease the real interest rate, and decreases in the net real money supply increase the real interest rate when the speculative-demand-for-real-money curve is given.
6. At some very (relatively) low interest rate, virtually everyone is convinced that the market rate of interest is below the natural rate of interest and bonds are considered extremely risky. Money is far superior as an asset at this low interest rate, and the speculative-demand-for-real-money curve is perfectly elastic (horizontal). Increases in the real money supply are held by the public, and the interest rate will not fall in this liquidity trap.
7. A total-demand-for-real-money curve can be derived by adding a vertical curve for L_1/P (as a function of the real interest rate) to the speculative-demand-for-real-money curve. The position of this curve is determined by the level of real national income; its shape is determined by the L_2/P curve.
8. By varying the level of real national income and holding the real money supply constant, an lm curve is derived. An lm curve is the locus of all combinations of real interest rates and real national

income levels that satisfy the money market equilibrium condition: $M/P = (L_1 + L_2)/P$. The *lm* curve has a vertical classical range where velocity is at a maximum; higher levels of real income cannot be financed because of an insufficient real money supply. It also has a horizontal Keynesian range which reflects the liquidity trap. The *lm* curve shifts to the right if the real money supply rises, and it shifts to the left if the real money supply falls.

9. By varying the real interest rate, real net investment will change and the aggregate expenditures curve shifts, causing real national income to change. By such a procedure, a downward-sloping curve is derived. An *is* curve is the locus of all the combinations of real interest rates and real national income levels that satisfy the product market equilibrium condition for a closed, private economy: $s = i$. The *is* curve shifts if the aggregate investment curve or the consumption curve shifts; the *is* curve also shifts as fiscal policy changes.

10. Aggregate equilibrium—simultaneous equilibrium in the product market and the money market—exists at the intersection of the *lm* and the *is* curves. At any other real interest rate–real national income combination, a surplus or a shortage exists in one or both markets.

GLOSSARY

aggregate equilibrium   Simultaneous equilibrium in both the product market and the money market; the point of intersection of the *is* and *lm* curves.

classical range   The vertical section of the *lm* curve along which velocity is at a maximum and all real money balances are used to satisfy the transactions motive; higher real interest rates cannot elicit additional L_1/P balances, and so the real national income level cannot rise further, for a given money supply and a given price level.

consol   A nonmaturing bond.

***is* curve**   The locus of all combinations of real interest rates and real national income levels that satisfy the equilibrium condition in the product market; in a closed, private economy the product market equilibrium condition is $s = i$.

Keynesian range   The horizontal portion of the *lm* curve which reflects the liquidity trap portion of the speculative-demand-for-money curve; in the Keynesian range, reductions in the level of real national income create surplus L_1/P balances that are merely held in L_2/P balances; therefore, the real interest rate doesn't fall.

liquidity preference function   A relationship between interest rates and the amount of money desired to hold above transactions and precautionary motives; a relationship that indicates a preference for money over bonds, depending on the level of the interest rate.

liquidity trap   The horizontal range of the liquidity preference function curve along which virtually everyone is convinced that market real interest rates are below the natural rate and money is an asset far superior to bonds; in the liquidity trap, the real demand for money is perfectly elastic with respect to the real interest rate.

lm **curve** The locus of all the combinations of real interest rates and real national income levels that satisfy the money market equilibrium condition: $M/P = (L_1 + L_2)/P$.

natural rate of interest That interest rate to which the market rate of interest eventually returns.

neoclassical-Keynesian synthesis A model that incorporates elements of both the neoclassical model and the Keynesian model.

risk averse Preferring less risk to more risk, other things constant; risk-averse individuals must be compensated before they will voluntarily assume risk.

speculative demand for money An inverse relationship between real interest rates and the quantity of real money demanded to hold above L_1/P balances. The speculative demand for money is also referred to as the *liquidity preference function*.

QUESTIONS AND PROBLEMS FOR REVIEW

7.1 Basically, Keynes accepted both the classical transactions demand for money as a function of income and the neoclassical precautionary demand for money as a function of income. Is "income" in real terms or nominal? Does it make a difference?

7.2 Explain why an inverse relationship between the quantity of money demanded and the interest rate would be expected only if the interest rate were the real interest rate.

7.3 Since the nominal value of money is constant and the nominal value of bonds is inversely related to the interest rate, money is considered to be more liquid and less risky than bonds. Would this consideration still be true if changes in the nominal interest rate reflected only changes in the expectations of the future level of prices?

7.4 It is widely believed that increases in the net nominal money supply result in decreases in the nominal interest rate and decreases in the net nominal money supply result in increases in the nominal interest rate. If the demand for money is a function of the level of *prices*, as well as nominal income, explain why such changes in the net nominal money supply would not necessarily result in changes in the real interest rate.

7.5 If increases in the real money supply are held by economic units and the real interest rate does not fall because of the liquidity trap, what implications can be made about the effectiveness of monetary policy? Do you think that economic units would hold all increases in the real money supply? What rationale exists for a single economic unit to hold an increase in money?

7.6 Assume that aggregate equilibrium exists at the point of intersection of the *lm* and *is* curves. What is expected to happen to the equilibrium values of the real interest rate and real national income if the real money supply increases, under the assumption that a vertical curve for *lm* exists? What is expected to happen under the assumption that the *lm* curve is not vertical?

7.7 Assume that aggregate equilibrium exists at the point of intersection of the *lm* and *is* curves. Compare the changes in the equilibrium values of the real interest rate and real national income, for changes in fiscal policy, if (a) the intersection of the *is* and *lm* curves is in the vertical range of the *lm* curve, and (b) if the intersection of the *is* and *lm* curves is in the horizontal range.

7.8 If the consumption function is

$$C = \$20 + 0.8(y - t_x + t_r - g_0)$$

what is implied about consumer reaction to an increase in government expenditure for consumption goods or services? Do you think that implied reaction is reasonable? What implications does your answer make about the effectiveness of fiscal policy?

7.9 Assume that the effects of changes in the money supply are not neutral— that is, that such changes have real effects. What would be implied about comparative levels of aggregate welfare if the economy were in long-run equilibrium prior to changes in the money supply?

7.10 Suppose that in a closed, private economy the consumption and investment functions are written as

$$c = \$20 + 0.8y$$

and

$$i = \$10 - 2r$$

and $M = 25$. Determine the equilibrium values for y and r. (Note that this problem requires an understanding of the appendix to this chapter.)

REFERENCES

William J. Baumol, "The Transactions Demand for Cash: An Inventory Theoretic Approach," *Quarterly Journal of Economics*, vol. 66 (1952).

William Branson, *Macroeconomic Theory and Policy* (New York: Macmillan, 1978).

Alvin H. Hansen, *A Guide to Keynes* (New York: McGraw-Hill, 1953).

Laurence Harris, *Monetary Theory* (New York: McGraw-Hill, 1981).

John R. Hicks, "Mr. Keynes and the Classics: A Suggested Interpretation," *Econometrica*, vol. 5 (1937).

John Maynard Keynes, *The General Theory of Employment, Interest, and Money* (New York: Harcourt Brace Jovanovich, 1964).

David Laidler, *The Demand for Money* (New York: Dun-Donnelley, 1977).

Dennis H. Robertson, "Mr. Keynes and the Rate of Interest," in Dennis H. Robertson, *Essays in Monetary Theory* (London: Staples Press, 1940).

James Tobin, "The Interest-Elasticity of Transactions Demand for Cash," *Review of Economics and Statistics*, vol. 38 (1956).

———, "Liquidity Preference as Behaviour Toward Risk," *Review of Economic Studies*, vol. 25 (1958).

MATHEMATICAL APPENDIX
TO THE NEOCLASSICAL-KEYNESIAN SYNTHESIS

The *lm* Curve

The classical neo-Keynesian demand-for-real-money function is

$$l = (y, r) \tag{A.7.1}$$

WHERE l = quantity demanded of real money balances, or
$l = (L_1 + L_2)/P$
y = real national income
r = real interest rate

Assume that the specific form of l is

$$l = a - dr + fy \tag{A.7.2}$$

WHERE a = a known constant term
d = the coefficient relating l to r; assume that it is a known constant term
f = the coefficient relating l to y; assume that it is a known constant term

Equation A.7.2 implies that l is negatively related to the real interest rate and directly related to the level of real national income, other things constant.

The real money supply is

$$\frac{M}{P} = \frac{\bar{M}}{P} \tag{A.7.3}$$

WHERE M = nominal money supply
P = price supply

$M/P = \bar{M}/P$ implies that the real money supply is constant.

Equilibrium in the money market requires that the quantity demanded of real balances equals the quantity supplied of real balances; so

$$\frac{M}{P} = l \tag{A.7.4}$$

Substituting equations A.7.2 and A.7.3 into A.7.4 yields

$$\frac{\bar{M}}{P} = a - dr + fy \tag{A.7.5}$$

Solving for r gives

$$r = \frac{a - (\bar{M}/P)}{d} + \left(\frac{f}{d}\right)y \tag{A.7.6}$$

Note that on the right-hand side of equation A.7.6 only y is a variable; y is an *endogenous variable* and all the other letters represent known constants. Consequently, there is no unique solution for r. Instead, r varies directly with the variable y. By choosing values for y, a functional relationship between y and r can be derived, and at all such combinations of y and r equilibrium will exist in the money market (by equation A.7.4).

Equation A.7.6 is the *lm* function, and it (here) is linear; its intercept is $[a - (\bar{M}/P)]/d$, and its slope is f/d.

Shifts in the *lm* Curve

Any change in a, the real money supply $(\bar{M}/P)$, or d (the coefficient relating real money balances to the real interest rate), shifts the *lm* curve. If the real money supply increases, the *lm* curve shifts rightward; if the real money supply falls, the *lm* curve shifts leftward.

If d falls—the community wants to hold more real money balances at every real interest rate—the *lm* curve shifts upward. This is because if d rises the real interest rate will be higher at every level of real national income. If d rises—the community wants to hold fewer real money balances at every real interest rate—the *lm* curve shifts downward. This is because if d falls the real interest rate will be lower at every real national income level. In effect, if the demand-for-real-money balances rise, *lm* shifts upward; and if the demand-for-real-money balances fall, *lm* shifts downward.

Changes in the Slope of the *lm* Curve

The slope of the *lm* curve rises if the f/d ratio rises and falls if the f/d ratio falls. If the f/d ratio rises, this means that the community's demand for money has become relatively more responsive to changes in real national income than to changes in the real interest rate. If the f/d ratio falls, this means that the community's demand for money has become relatively less sensitive to changes in real national income than to changes in the real interest rate.

The *is* Curve

Assume that real net investment is inversely related to the real interest rate so that

$$i = i_0 - hr \tag{A.7.7}$$

WHERE i_0 = the intercept of the real aggregate investment curve
           h = the coefficient relating (negatively) the real interest rate to real net investment

Assume further (ignoring international transactions) that the remaining equations are

$$c = c_0 + b(y + t_r - t_x) \tag{A.7.8}$$

$$g = \overline{g}_0 \tag{A.7.9}$$

$$t_x = \overline{t}_x \tag{A.7.10}$$

$$t_r = \overline{t}_r \tag{A.7.11}$$

$$AE = c + i + g \tag{A.7.12}$$

Using the framework developed in the appendix to Chapter 6, we find that the equilibrium level of real national income is

$$y = \frac{c_0 + i_0 + g_0 + bt_r - bt_x - hr}{1 - b} \tag{A.7.13}$$

Rewriting equation A.7.13 gives

$$y = \frac{c_0 + i_0 + g_0 + bt_r - bt_x}{1 - b} - \frac{h}{1 - b}r \tag{A.7.14}$$

Note that equation A.7.14 is the *is* function and that it does not have a unique solution because r is an endogenous variable—the other letters are all known constants. By choosing values for r, a functional relationship between r and y can be derived, and at all such combinations equilibrium exists in the product market.

Equation A.7.14 is linear; its intercept equals $(c_0 + i_0 + g_0 + bt_r - bt_x)/(1 - b)$ and its slope equals $-h/(1 - b)$. Because the *is* curve has a negative slope, it will be downward-sloping from left to right. Because in our *is-lm* framework r is on the vertical axis and y is on the horizontal axis, however, the actual slope is the reciprocal of $-h/(1 - b)$, namely, $-(1 - b)/h$.

Shifts in the *is* Curve

Because the horizontal intercept of the *is* curve is $(c_0 + i_0 + g_0 + bt_r - bt_x)/(1 - b)$, *is* will shift rightward any time there is an increase in autonomous consumption, autonomous investment, or autonomous government expenditures, or if there is a decrease in autonomous taxes. Also, the *is* curve will shift rightward if the marginal propensity to save $(1 - b)$ falls. In all the cases the equilibrium level of real national income is higher for a given real interest rate. We leave it to you to determine what causes a leftward shift in the *is* curve.

The Slope of the *is* Curve

The slope of the *is* curve is $-(1 - b)/h$, so it depends on the marginal propensity to save $(1 - b)$ and the coefficient relating the real interest rate to real net investment h. The higher the marginal propensity to save, the smaller the slope becomes, because a given change in the real interest rate will alter to a lesser extent the level of real national income. The greater the responsiveness (elasticity) of real net investment to the real interest rate—given the marginal propensity to save—the larger the slope of the *is* curve, because a given change in the real interest rate will cause the level of real national income to change by a greater amount.

Aggregate Equilibrium

Aggregate equilibrium requires that equilibrium exist in both the money market and in the product market. This condition is met by substituting equation A.7.6 into equation A.7.14 and assuming (for simplicity) that $P = 1$. Thus

$$y = \frac{c_0 + i_0 + g_0 + bt_r - bt_x}{1 - b} - \frac{h}{1-b}\left[\frac{a - \bar{M}}{d} + \frac{f}{d}y\right] \qquad \text{(A.7.15)}$$

yields the unique aggregate equilibrium level of real national income.

Multiply both sides of equation A.7.15 by $1 - b$:

$$(1 - b)y = c_0 + i_0 + g_0 + bt_r - bt_x - h\left[\frac{a - \bar{M}}{d} + \frac{f}{d}y\right] \qquad \text{(A.7.16)}$$

Remove brackets:

$$(1-b)y = c_0 + i_0 + g_0 + bt_r - bt_x - \frac{h}{d}(a - \bar{M}) - \frac{hf}{d}y \qquad \text{(A.7.17)}$$

Add $(hf/d)y$ to both sides of the equation:

$$\left(1 - b + \frac{hf}{d}\right)y = c_0 + i_0 + g_0 + bt_r - bt_x - \frac{h}{d}(a - \bar{M}) \qquad \text{(A.7.18)}$$

Divide both sides by the coefficient of y:

$$y = \left[\frac{1}{1 - b + \frac{hf}{d}}\right]\left[c_0 + i_0 + g_0 + bt_r - bt_x - \frac{h}{d}(a - \bar{M})\right] \qquad \text{(A.7.19)}$$

Note that y is now entirely in terms of known constants so a unique solution exists; the value for y given by equation A.7.19 is the aggregate equilibrium value.

The aggregate equilibrium real interest rate can be found by substituting the aggregate equilibrium y, found from equation A.7.19, into equation A.7.6.

8

THE EXPANDED NEOCLASSICAL-KEYNESIAN SYNTHESIS

The *is-lm* framework enables us to consider simultaneously the relationship between the goods market and the money market. It enables us, therefore, to identify the equilibrium levels of real national income and the real interest rate—what we have been referring to as aggregate equilibrium.

The *is-lm* diagram, however, does not provide a complete picture of the Keynesian model or of the neoclassical-Keynesian synthesis. It does not explicitly treat conditions in the labor market. In this chapter we introduce the Keynesian labor market and demonstrate how Keynes's model is able to show simultaneous equilibrium in the money market and in the product market, and involuntary unemployment in the labor market. Stated differently, this chapter explains why there will be no tendency for the interest rate or the level of national income to change even though involuntary unemployment exists.

In order to demonstrate this important conclusion—a conclusion that fundamentally contradicts the classical model—Keynes found it necessary to make three assumptions. If any one of these assumptions is true, there can be *is-lm* equilibrium and labor market disequilibrium.[1] The three assumptions are:

1. Nominal wage rates are sticky downward.
2. The *lm* curve is horizontal (i.e., a liquidity trap).
3. The aggregate investment curve is interest insensitive.

In this chapter we will extend the neoclassical-Keynesian synthesis to incorporate the Keynesian labor market, and we will show how each of these three Keynesian assumptions is sufficient to explain a stable level of national income and involuntary unemployment. We also show that if these assumptions are relaxed, the Keynesian model implies that the level of national income will adjust until full employment is established. In the process we will derive new tools that we will find useful in later chapters.

EQUILIBRIUM IN ALL THREE MARKETS

Let's consider a case that Keynes believed to be extremely unlikely: equilibrium in all three markets—the product market, the money market, and the labor market. Figure 8.1 presents a series of diagrams that we will use throughout this chapter. Panel *a* shows the *is-lm* framework developed in Chapter 7, while panels *b* and *c*—which require that you

---

[1] This chapter is based on Chapter 8 in Laurence Harris, *Monetary Theory*.

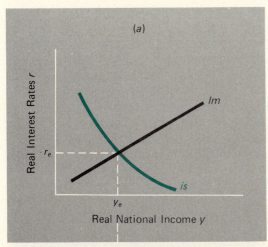

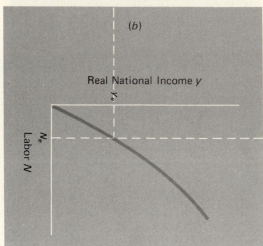

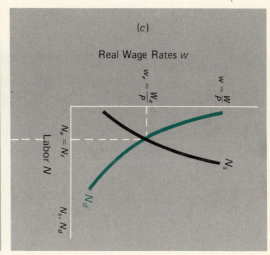

FIGURE 8.1. MACROECONOMIC BLISS

By coincidence, the full-employment quantity of labor N_f established in the labor market in panel c equals the amount of labor that is employed as a result of the level of income that is established in the is-lm framework in panel a. Keynes believed that such a situation was unlikely, and if it occurred, it would be short-lived.

rotate your textbook—show the labor market and the aggregate production function (developed in Chapter 4).

Note first that equilibrium has been reached in the *is-lm* diagram in panel *a*; according to Keynes, the product and money markets predominate and the labor market merely adjusts to the equilibrium level of national income that is established there. The equilibrium level of national income is at y_e in panel *a*; from there the employment level of N_e is found from the aggregate production function in panel *b*. The employment level determined, we then consider the labor market in panel *c*. Happily, the equilibrium level of national income established in panel *a* generates an employment level that coincidentally is consistent with the full-employment level N_f, found at the intersection of the aggregate supply-of-labor curve and the aggregate demand-for-labor curve in panel *c*.

According to Keynes, this situation is unlikely to occur, and if perchance it did, nothing guarantees that the economy would remain in such a blissful state. Keynes, you will remember, maintained that the aggregate investment curve is extremely volatile. When it shifts, the *is* curve will shift and the economy will experience an expansion or contraction. (Keynes was mostly concerned with the contraction during the Great Depression.)

NOMINAL WAGE RATES THAT ARE STICKY DOWNWARD

Keynes believed that, in the real world of the twentieth century, nominal wage rates are not likely to fall by very much. This is true because of minimum wage laws, union monopsonistic power, and a welfare state that expands the options of the unemployed (beyond the "work, beg, or starve" options).

Consider Figure 8.2, which shows what Keynes believed was a typical situation. The equilibrium level of income established in panel *a* generates an employment level of N_e in panel *b* which is less than the full-employment level N_f established in the labor market in panel *c*. Because Keynes believed that the product market dominates the labor market, unemployment exists. Note, however, that an inconsistency exists. How can conditions in the product market be stable when involuntary unemployment exists? The answer is that in panel *c* nominal wage rates (and therefore real wage rates) are too high. If nominal wage rates cannot fall below W_1, then real wage rates are set at w_1, which exceeds w_e, and a surplus of labor—unemployment—exists. The amount of unemployment equals $N_f - N_e$, and the unemployment rate equals $(N_f - N_e)/N_f$. (Remember that N_f is the size of the labor force and labor is a variable up to that level.)

If Nominal Wage Rates Are Sticky Downward, *is-lm* Equilibrium Coincides with Involuntary Unemployment

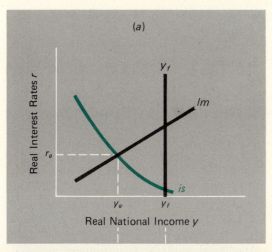

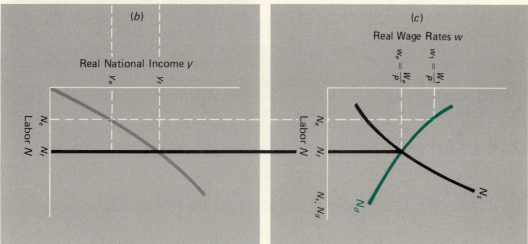

FIGURE 8.2. INVOLUNTARY UNEMPLOYMENT DUE TO STICKY NOMINAL WAGE RATES

The equilibrium level of national income y_e is established in panel a. The employment level that is consistent with that level of national income is N_e, established in panel b. The actual employment will be N_e, because the product market dominates the labor market; the actual employment level will be less than the full-employment level N_f in panel c.

This is a conclusion that even classical economists would have accepted: if real wages are not free to fall, involuntary unemployment can exist.

PRICE-WAGE FLEXIBILITY AND THE KEYNESIAN RANGE

Keynes did not rely solely on price-wage rigidity. He showed that unemployment could result even if prices and wage rates were free to fall.

Price-Wage Flexibility Without the Liquidity Trap

According to Keynes, an *economywide* reduction in wage rates (due to unemployment) will cause the price level to fall *at the same rate* that wage rates are falling. Because wage rates in the short run are the primary component of marginal cost, general wage rate reductions will increase (temporarily, until prices fall) the supply of goods and services throughout the economy. Given product demand, general wage rates and general prices fall (and rise) *together*; and there is no reason to believe that wage rates will fall more rapidly than the price level will fall. It follows that even if nominal wage rates fall, *real* wage rates will not fall; laborers can change only nominal wage rates. Because real wage rates don't fall, the original unemployment rate remains unaltered, and Keynes was able to demonstrate the simultaneous existence of price-wage flexibility and unemployment; that is, there is no automatic adjustment to full employment.

Still, Keynes pointed out, a reduction in the price level could (outside the Keynesian range) have *some* effect on the economy. The nominal money supply is held constant, but a lower price level increases the real money stock and creates an excess of liquidity, which *could* (outside the liquidity trap) lead to increased bond purchases, which causes bond prices to rise and the real interest rate to fall. In turn, a lower real interest rate leads to more investment and a higher level of real national income and employment.

In effect, the *lm* curve shifts downward due to what is now called the **Keynes effect** (or the interest rate effect). This is shown in Figure 8.3. Note that because y_e is less than y_f, unemployment exists, and this causes nominal wage rates to fall, which causes the price level to fall. This shifts the *lm* curve downward because a lower price level increases the real money supply, given a constant nominal money supply. (Remember that the *lm* curve was derived for a given price level; if the price level changes, the *lm* curve is expected to shift.) In effect, a lower price level will reduce the transactions demand for money, L_1, and the community will now have excess money balances at income level y_e. People

If Price-Wage Flexibility Exists, the *lm* Curve Will Shift Until a Full-Employment Level of National Income Is Established

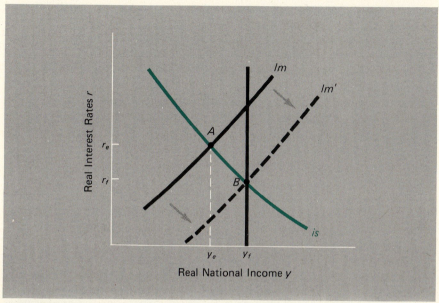

FIGURE 8.3. THE KEYNES EFFECT ASSURES FULL EMPLOYMENT

Assume that aggregate equilibrium exists at point *A*. The actual real income level y_e is less than the full-employment output level y_f, and so a situation similar to that in Figure 8.2 exists. Assume now, however, that perfect price flexibility exists. Because unemployment exists at y_e, nominal wage rates fall, which causes the price level to fall, too. A lower price level, given the nominal money stock, means that real money balances rise. Because an excess of liquidity exists, wealth owners will purchase bonds and cause bond prices to rise and the real interest rate to fall. In short, the Keynes effect occurs and the *lm* curve shifts to the right. A lower interest rate increases autonomous net investment, and the AE curve shifts upward, causing real national income to rise. The process will continue until *lm* shifts to *lm'*. At point *B*, a full-employment equilibrium output exists and the community voluntarily holds the existing real money stock.

purchase bonds with these excess balances; this drives bond prices up and the interest rate down. The *lm* curve shifts downward when the price level falls because the interest rate will be lower at any level of national income (assuming no liquidity trap). In principle, price flexibility will shift the *lm* curve sufficiently to assure full employment; as long as some unemployment exists, nominal wage rates and prices will fall, and therefore the *lm* curve will shift rightward. The classical model is, apparently, vindicated.

Price-Wage Flexibility and the Liquidity Trap

In a depression, however, interest rates are *already* very low and bonds are extremely risky. Consequently, *excess balances that result from a lower price level will merely be held.* Thus Keynes's liquidity trap prevents the Keynes effect from eliminating unemployment through lower interest rates and higher net investment. This is shown in Figure 8.4.

In Figure 8.4, panel *a* shows the equilibrium level of real national income established at y_e, where the *is* curve intersects the *lm* curve in the latter's Keynesian range. The equilibrium level of real national income is less than the full-employment level y_f, and the employment level is established at N_e, which is less than N_f. As unemployment-induced wage rate and price reductions occur, the *lm* curve shifts to the right, but in the Keynesian range the equilibrium level of y is unaffected. Excess money balances are merely held in L_2 (speculative) balances because bonds are so risky.

Panel *b* shows the employment level N_e used to produce y_e, and panel *c* shows that the *real* wage rate remains at w_1, above the equilibrium wage rate w_e. This is the case because, even though nominal wage rates are free to fall, prices fall at the same rate that nominal wage rates are falling. Again, the product market predominates, and a surplus of labor results even if price-wage flexibility exists—in the Keynesian range (liquidity trap).

AN INTEREST-INSENSITIVE AGGREGATE INVESTMENT CURVE

Assume now that the aggregate investment curve is very insensitive to the interest rate; technically, aggregate investment is very inelastic with respect to the real interest rate.

Assume price-wage flexibility, that consumption is given, that the real aggregate investment curve is given, and that they generate an *is* curve with the shape and position of that in Figure 8.5—because of low investment sensitivity to real interest rates. Note that we also assume no liquidity trap in this analysis. Unemployment exists; therefore, the *lm* curve shifts downward.

Figure 8.5 shows that an intersection of an *lm* curve (here *lm"*) and the given *is* curve consistent with full employment exists only at a *negative* interest rate. Real investment is so insensitive to real interest rates that a negative interest rate, r_4, is required to induce enough in-

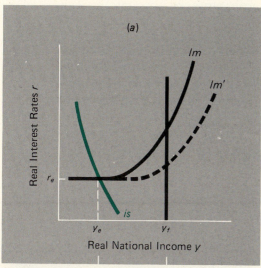

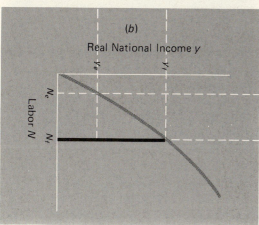

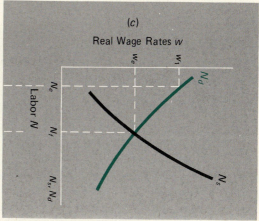

FIGURE 8.4. THE LIQUIDITY TRAP AND UNEMPLOYMENT

In panel *a*, the equilibrium level of real national income is established at y_e, which is less than y_f. Employment equals N_e, which is less than N_f, and the real wage rate in panel *c* is above w_e, and so involuntary unemployment exists. Wage rates and prices will fall at the same rate; therefore the real wage rate remains constant. A lower price level shifts the *lm* curve to *lm'* in panel *a*, but because the real interest rate is already low in a depression, people hold extra real money balances in order to avoid the risk of capital losses on bonds that will result when the real interest rate rises to its natural rate.

vestment (given consumption) to generate a full-employment level of real national income. Note that the Keynes effect can only bring the level of real national income to y_2. As long as *nominal* interest rates cannot be negative, the *lm* curve will never cross the horizontal axis and enter the fourth quadrant.[2] Not enough investment projects are forthcoming at a zero interest rate to assure full employment. Presumably, this situation could occur in a depression, when profit expectations are so dismal that businesses expect negative returns on their investments in capital. If, in fact, nominal interest rates cannot be negative, we have a third example in which a stable level of real national income is consistent with involuntary unemployment.

PRICE-WAGE FLEXIBILITY AND THE PIGOU EFFECT

The first case we analyzed concerning involuntary unemployment is different from the second two because it assumes nominal wage rate inflexibility, and it is not inconsistent with the classical conclusions. The second two cases are similar in that they directly contradict the classical model. Even if price-wage flexibility exists, these cases imply an equilibrium level of real national income at which there is involuntary unemployment.

The neoclassical economists, however, were not content with this conclusion. A. C. Pigou of Cambridge University demonstrated that a falling price level *also* increases the wealth of currency (paper money and coins) holders *without decreasing anyone else's wealth.* Consider people who own real estate worth $100, a bond worth $100, and a $100 bill. As prices fall, the value of the real estate falls at the same rate as the price level, and so real estate owners are not affected. Bondholders reap capital gains because the present value of a nominally fixed revenue stream increases. On the other hand, bond issuers experience capital losses; they have fixed nominal obligations which are worth more at a lower price level. Because bondholders benefit only at the expense of bond issuers, no *net* wealth effect is apparent. On the other hand, those people who hold $100 bills (or other currency denominations or coins)

---

[2] Recall that the real interest rate equals (approximately) the nominal interest rate minus the inflation rate. If the price level is *falling* (the inflation rate is negative), a negative *real* interest rate requires a negative *nominal* interest rate. For example, if the price level is falling at 2 percent per year, the nominal interest rate must be below a negative 2 percent per year for the real interest rate to be negative. Nominal interest rates will never be negative, however, because lenders would not lend at negative nominal (or real) rates. For example, you would not lend $100 and accept *less than* $100 in the future, regardless of how fast prices were falling, because you would be better off holding the $100; $100 in the future is always worth more than an amount less than $100 in the future. (Unless the original $100 bill were *dated*, as Keynes himself proposed on occasion, so that it is not worth $100 in the future.)

Investment Insensitivity to Interest Rates Prevents Full Employment Even If Price-Wage Flexibility Exists

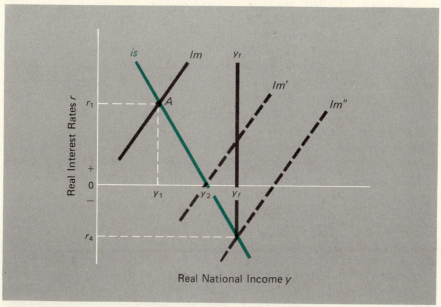

FIGURE 8.5. AN INTEREST-INSENSITIVE *is* CURVE

In this model, price-wage flexibility exists, consumption is given, and the liquidity trap is absent. If the aggregate investment curve is insensitive to real interest rates, a *negative* real interest rate (here r_4) is required for the economy to reach a full-employment level of real national income. At point A an unemployment equilibrium exists, so the *lm* curve shifts because of the Keynes effect; but given the shape and position of the *is* curve, the maximum level of real national income that this effect will generate is y_2, which is less than y_f. This assumes that a negative real interest rate cannot obtain.

are now wealthier; the purchasing power of money rises as the price level falls.

In other words, as the price level falls currency holders are wealthier from what is called the **Pigou** (or wealth) **effect.** An increase in the wealth of some, which is not offset by a decrease in the wealth of others, will shift the consumption function upward; households will consume more at every income level now that they are wealthier. There is less incentive to save and to acquire wealth for retirement or for future consumption. This upward shift in the consumption function causes the *is* curve to shift to the right; national income will be higher at any given interest rate. The Pigou effect, then, leads to a shift in the *is* curve. When the price level falls, the *is* curve shifts to the right, because national income will be higher at every interest rate. When the price level rises, the *is* curve shifts to the left, because net wealth will fall, which will cause people to consume less at every level of national income. National income will be lower at every interest rate.

The Pigou effect is indicated in the *is-lm* framework in Figure 8.6. Note that as long as unemployment exists, wages and prices will fall at the same rate and the *is* curve will shift to the right. This process will continue until a full-employment national income is established at y_f. Nothing analogous to a liquidity trap exists in the product market. Also, because the *is* curve shifts owing to a shift in the *consumption* function, an aggregate investment curve that is insensitive to the interest rate cannot prevent the economy from attaining a full-employment level of national income. The increase in consumption resulting from the Pigou effect will pick up the slack.

The conclusion, therefore, is that even the neoclassical-Keynesian synthesis predicts full employment—if price-wage flexibility is assumed. Note, of course, that even if this theoretical conclusion is valid, it still does not argue that capitalism always leads to full employment, or that economic policymakers should pursue price-wage flexibility. The fact is that in modern economies price-wage flexibility does not exist; monopolistic and monopsonistic power exists, and many prices and wages are not set by competitive market forces. Moreover, the social costs involved in making a modern economy perfectly competitive are so high that price-wage flexibility is politically impossible. Such a system would require vigorous antitrust policy against both corporations and unions; elimination of all tariffs and import quotas; elimination of government subsidies to businesses and farm-support programs; elimination of licensing arrangements for professional and nonprofessional occupations; a drastic reduction in unemployment compensation and in welfare payments; and any other changes necessary to make the economy more competitive. Virtually every sector of a modern economy would be altered. Such a system is almost unimaginable; it has never existed in the past and probably will never exist in the future.

Even if such an economic system (some would call it heaven, others would think it hell) could be brought about, the theoretical model analyzed gives no clue as to *how much* prices and wages would have to fall before equilibrium would exist in the product market, in the money market, and in the labor market. We don't have empirical estimates concerning how sensitive the *is* and the *lm* curves are to changes in the price level. Nor does our model tell us how much time it would take for price-wage flexibility to restore the economy to full employment or how

A Combination of the Keynes Effect and the Pigou Effect Can Assure Full Employment Even If a Liquidity Trap Exists

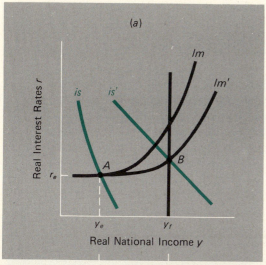

(a)

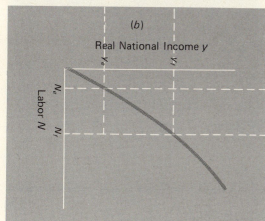

(b)

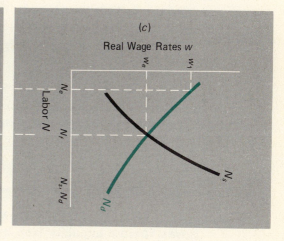

(c)

FIGURE 8.6. THE PIGOU EFFECT AND THE KEYNES EFFECT

Start at point A, where equilibrium at less than full employment exists. Nominal wage rates and the price level fall and cause the lm curve to shift rightward because the real money supply rises, given the nominal money supply. Because the economy is mired in the liquidity trap, however, the level of real national income remains at y_e. But a lower price level increases the wealth of currency holders without reducing the wealth of others, so the consumption curve shifts upward and causes the is curve to shift rightward. A falling price level occurs as long as unemployment exists, so is and lm will shift rightward until a full-employment equilibrium, such as point B, exists. Note that even if there were no Keynes effect, the Pigou effect would assure full employment.

much economic upheaval such price-wage flexibility would bring about as the economy adjusts to disequilibrating shocks.

Unfortunately, economists are unable to run controlled experiments in a laboratory to provide this information. The experiment would be an interesting one.

THE STABILITY OF THE PRIVATE SECTOR

Regardless of whether or not the Pigou effect is an important empirical phenomenon, it has powerful theoretical implications. In effect, it maintains that there is a mechanism—one not explicitly acknowledged as important by all pre-Pigou classical economists—that restores the private sector to its natural rate of unemployment and to its natural growth rate.

In Chapter 18 we try to assess just how stable or unstable the private sector is. If the private sector is stable—that is, if there are mechanisms that drive the economy, in a short period of time, toward the natural rate of unemployment and toward the natural growth rate of GNP—then stabilization policy is largely unnecessary. In such an economy disequilibrating shocks to the macroeconomy will be absorbed and the economy will soon be back on its natural growth path. On the other hand, if the private sector is basically unstable, then no mechanisms drive the economy toward a full-employment equilibrium and some combination of monetary policy and fiscal policy is required in order to achieve national economic goals.

The next three chapters analyze three possible sources of economic instability in the private sector. Chapter 9 analyzes the consumption function; Chapter 10 discusses the investment function; and Chapter 11 analyzes the demand-for-money function.

POLICY CONTROVERSY
Was There a Liquidity Trap During the Great Depression?

There are important policy implications to a liquidity trap. The existence of a liquidity trap, other things constant, makes a private economy more unstable because a trap prevents the interest rate from falling to levels that would induce increases in consumption and investment sufficient to assure full employment. The ability of the interest rate mechanism to assure full employment is thereby impaired.

Another policy implication is that if

a liquidity trap exists, monetary policy is completely ineffectual within the trap while fiscal policy is potentially very powerful. If a liquidity trap does *not* exist, then (1) fiscal policy will crowd out (some) private consumption and investment spending, and (2) monetary policy is potentially effective.

In Chapter 11 we indicate that empirical evidence points to a negative relationship between interest rates and the demand for money. Here we are concerned with the *magnitude* of that relationship. In particular, is there any evidence that a liquidity *trap* exists? Was there a liquidity trap during the Great Depression? Keynes himself, in *The General Theory*, noted that he knew of no example of a liquidity trap, but he did not rule out the possibility that it could be important in the future.[3]

Several studies have concluded that a liquidity trap has *not* existed in the United States, at least not during the twentieth century.[4]

Examination of actual data on the real money supply and long-term interest rates for the period 1929 to 1941 also leads one to conclude that no liquidity trap existed in this country during the Great Depression. Casual observations, or graphical exposition, of those data indicates a negative relationship between those variables; the curve relating them does not become parallel to the horizontal axis, it appears as a negatively sloped curve throughout.

H. W. Pifer decided to test the liquidity trap hypothesis more directly.[5] Pifer tested the proposition that the demand for money approaches infinity when the rate of interest approaches some minimum value, using a nonlinear estimating technique. He concluded that the minimum interest rate value that generates a demand for money that approaches infinity is not significantly different from zero and doubts that a liquidity trap exists at a positive interest rate.

Lest you think that for once empirical studies provide conclusive evidence, we hasten to point out that Robert Eisner maintains that Pifer used an incorrect statistical test; Eisner subjected Pifer's model to other statistical criteria. Eisner estimates that a liquidity trap, in the sense that the demand for money approaches infinity, exists at a real interest rate of approximately 2 percent.

Although on balance there seems to be little evidence of a liquidity trap, we cannot rule out completely the possibility of its existence. Once again, we reaffirm the belief that economic concepts are difficult to measure, and economic hypotheses are difficult to validate or reject by resorting to empirical tests.

---

[3] John Maynard Keynes, *The General Theory of Employment, Interest and Money* (London: Macmillan, 1936), p. 207.

[4] See Martin Bronfenbrenner and Thomas Mayer, "Liquidity Functions in the American Economy," *Econometrica*, vol. 28 (October 1960), pp. 810–834; and David Laidler, "The Rate of Interest and the Demand for Money: Some Empirical Evidence," *Journal of Political Economy*, vol. 74 (December 1966), pp. 543–555.

[5] H. W. Pifer, "A Non-linear, Maximum Likelihood Estimate of the Liquidity Trap," *Econometrica*, vol. 37 (April 1969), pp. 324–332.

CHAPTER SUMMARY

1. This chapter adds the Keynesian labor market to the *is-lm* framework, which analyzed the product market and the money market.

2. According to Keynes, the product market dominates the labor market. The equilibrium level of real national income is determined in the product and money markets, and the amount of labor required to produce that level of income will then be employed. The labor market, therefore, can potentially be in disequilibrium even if the product market and the money market are in equilibrium.

3. In the Keynesian model, it is possible for all three markets to be in equilibrium simultaneously. Keynes believed such an occurrence to be extremely unlikely, and, even if it did occur, nothing guarantees that this simultaneous equilibrium would continue. In particular, an unstable aggregate investment curve implies an unstable *is* curve.

4. If nominal wage rates are sticky downward, the neoclassical-Keynesian synthesis shows the simultaneous existence of product market equilibrium, money market equilibrium, and labor market disequilibrium (involuntary unemployment).

5. The neoclassical-Keynesian synthesis can also show *is-lm* equilibrium and involuntary unemployment under the assumption of price-wage flexibility if a liquidity trap exists. If the *is* curve intersects the *lm* curve in the latter curve's Keynesian range, an *is-lm* equilibrium will exist alongside involuntary unemployment.

6. The Keynes effect is a shift in the *lm* curve resulting from a change in the price level, given a fixed nominal money supply. According to Keynes, if involuntary unemployment exists, *wages and prices will fall at the same rate.* This will cause the *lm* curve to shift to the right. If a Keynesian range (liquidity trap) exists, however, price-wage flexibility still cannot assure full employment.

7. If the aggregate investment curve is interest rate–insensitive, the *is* curve may be shaped and positioned so that a negative real interest rate will be required to induce a sufficient quantity of net investment to assure full employment—even if price-wage flexibility exists and no liquidity trap exists.

8. The Pigou effect occurs when changes in the price level, given a constant nominal currency wealth, change the level of net wealth in the economy, which in turn shifts the consumption curve and the *is* curve.

9. The Pigou effect counteracts a liquidity trap and an interest-insensitive aggregate investment curve. It follows, therefore, that if price-wage flexibility exists, the neoclassical-Keynesian synthesis predicts equilibrium in the product, money, and labor markets at full employment.

10. For a modern nation to attain price-wage flexibility, much social upheaval would be required, and such changes are not politically feasible. Moreover, the model presented here does not indicate how long it would take price-wage flexibility to restore the economy to full employment; nor does it give any clue as to by how much prices and wages would have to fall in order for Pigou effects and Keynes effects to restore the economy to full employment.

11. On balance, there is little empirical evidence to support the existence of a liquidity trap.

GLOSSARY

Keynes effect   A shift in the *lm* curve resulting from a change in the price level, given a constant nominal money supply; the change in the real money supply resulting from a change in the price level which potentially changes the real interest rate and the level of real national income.

Pigou effect   A shift in the *is* curve resulting from a change in the price level, given a constant level of nominal currency wealth; the change in the price level changes the community's real net value of currency, which shifts the consumption curve and, therefore, the *is* curve, so that the real interest rate and the level of real national income change.

QUESTIONS AND PROBLEMS FOR REVIEW

8.1   What is the most important difference between the Keynesian labor market, as described in Chapter 8, and the classical labor market, as discussed in previous chapters?

8.2   Explain how the labor market, in the Keynesian model, can be in disequilibrium even if the product market and money market are in equilibrium.

8.3   It is, indeed, possible for the product, money, and labor markets to be in simultaneous equilibrium. Keynes believed, however, that it would be extremely *un*likely. Why did the classical economists believe that it would be *likely?*

8.4   Where nominal wages are sticky downward, the neoclassical-Keynesian synthesis assumes the possibility of the simultaneous existence of product market and money market equilibrium and labor market disequilibrium. To the extent that the unemployed have entrepreneurial skills, what is the longer-run effect on unemployment?

8.5   Does the liquidity trap explain the unwillingness of investors to invest (purchase capital), *or* of lenders to lend?

8.6   Suppose that a negative rate of interest is required to induce a sufficient level of investment to assure full employment, even where wage flexibility exists. Explain why a negative rate of interest would never exist, even in nominal terms.

8.7 Where changes in the price level, given a constant nominal money supply, change the level of net wealth in the economy, the consumption function shifts. What effect would changes in the rate of interest have on the level of wealth? What effect would such changes have on the consumption function?

8.8 What effect on employment would be expected for a change in the productivity of capital? Would the effect always lead to more or less employment under any conditions? What, then, would determine the direction of the effect on employment?

8.9 If economic units are in long-run equilibrium, under what conditions could government fiscal policy cause aggregate economic welfare to increase?

8.10 Suppose that an economy is in equilibrium where money is full-bodied (i.e., money has a value in nonmoney uses equivalent to its value as a medium of exchange). What would be expected to happen to relative prices, outputs, employment, and the rate of interest if the economy substituted money that is representative (i.e., where money has a negligible value but can be converted into full-bodied money at a fixed rate) for money that is full-bodied?

REFERENCES

Martin Branfenbrenner and Thomas Mayer, "Liquidity Functions in the American Economy," *Econometrica*, vol. 28 (1960).

William Branson, *Macroeconomic Theory and Policy* (New York: Macmillan, 1978).

Laurence Harris, *Monetary Theory* (New York: McGraw-Hill, 1981).

John R. Hicks, "Mr. Keynes and the Classics: A Suggested Interpretation," *Econometrica*, vol. 5 (1937).

John Maynard Keynes, *The General Theory of Employment, Interest, and Money* (New York: Harcourt Brace Jovanovich, 1964).

David Laidler, "The Rate of Interest and the Demand for Money: Some Empirical Evidence," *Journal of Political Economy*, vol. 74 (1966).

H. W. Pifer, "A Non-linear, Maximum Likelihood Estimate of the Liquidity Trap," *Econometrica*, vol. 37 (1969).

Arthur C. Pigou, "The Classical Stationary State," *Economic Journal*, vol. 53 (1943).

———, "Economic Progress in a Stable Environment," *Economica*, vol. 14 (1947).

PART III

SOURCES OF PRIVATE SECTOR INSTABILITY

9

THE CONSUMPTION FUNCTION

SOURCE OF STABILITY OR INSTABILITY?

The Pigou effect discussed in Chapter 8 has two important implications for macroeconomic theory. First, to the extent that consumption is determined by real wealth, the private sector has an adjustment mechanism—changes in the price level—that helps to stabilize the economy around the natural rate of unemployment and at the natural growth rate. Second, the Pigou effect asserts that consumption depends on wealth, and this assertion has led to empirical testing and to new theories that incorporate wealth as a determinant of the consumption function.

Two such theories are the permanent income hypothesis and the life cycle hypothesis; these hypotheses are analyzed in this chapter and each explains an apparent contradiction among bodies of data. The relative income hypothesis is also analyzed in this chapter. We begin with a brief review of the Keynesian consumption function and then discuss how the consumption function has evolved since Keynes's presentation.

A REVIEW OF THE KEYNESIAN CONSUMPTION FUNCTION

As you will recall from Chapter 6, the Keynesian[1] consumption function is

$$c = c_0 + by \qquad (9.1)$$

where $c_0 > 0$ and $0 < b < 1$.

The implications of this formulation are that (1) real consumption is primarily determined by real disposable income, (2) the marginal propensity to consume (the MPC), b, is between zero and 1, and (3) the average propensity to consume (the APC), c/y, falls as real disposable income rises; this last implication sometimes is referred to as the **absolute income hypothesis.**

It was not long before this simple Keynesian consumption function began to crumble. When it was used to predict post-World War II aggregate expenditures for the U.S. economy, the forecast was high unemployment, while the actual result was excessive demand, a high level of employment, and inflation. Based on the Keynesian consumption function, the forecasts seriously underestimated consumption expenditures.

---

[1] Note that we are referring to equation 9.1 as the "Keynesian" consumption function. *Keynes's* consumption function was more complicated, in that it recognized that (for upper-income groups) changes in the money value of wealth were potentially an important determinant of consumption, and he believed that (due to spending habits) the short-run marginal propensity to consume (MPC) would be less than the long-run MPC. Both of these contentions are supported in this chapter.

A Statistical Estimate of the
Keynesian Consumption Function

On the other hand, data collected over time (time series data) using annual data for the 1929–1941 period indicated the following consumption function (in billions of dollars):

$$c = 47.6 + 0.73y_d \qquad (9.2)$$

This consumption function seemed to meet all three requirements of the Keynesian consumption function. The correlation between real consumption and real disposable income was very high; the estimate of the vertical intercept ($47.6 billion) was determined to be (statistically) greater than 1, so that the APC falls as income rises; and the MPC (0.73) was found to be significantly above zero and significantly below 1 (statistically).

Kuznets's Consumption Function

Simon Kuznets, a Nobel laureate, presented data for 15 overlapping decades during the period from 1869 to 1969 that contradicted the consumption function derived from the 1929–1941 period.[2] In particular, although Kuznets found a high correlation between real consumption and national income (net disposable income) and an MPC between zero and 1, his data indicated that the consumption function was

$$c = 0.88y \qquad (9.3)$$

Note that the estimated vertical intercept is not significantly different from zero; hence the APC (and also the MPC) remained (relatively) constant (at 0.88) throughout those years. During that period, therefore, real national income quadrupled but the APC remained (relatively) constant; this evidence strongly contradicted Keynes's absolute income hypothesis.[3]

Lest you think that Kuznets's results were due to faulty estimates or to bad data, let us hasten to add that annual U.S. national income data for the period from 1929 to 1983 also show a constant APC; over

---

[2] Simon Kuznets, *Uses of National Income in Peace and War* (New York: National Bureau of Economic Research, 1942).

[3] Ibid., p. 30. Kuznets's startling disclosure was later verified by Raymond Goldsmith, *A Study of Saving in the United States,* vol. 1 (Princeton, N.J.: Princeton University Press, 1955), p. 22. Goldsmith estimated saving (independently of consumption and income) and estimated *personal* income; he concluded that the saving/personal income ratio in the United States over that same period was constant, at about one-eighth (or 12.5 percent).

that period, real disposable income increased by a multiple of about 4.8 but the APC remained constant at about 0.9. However, consumption functions based on annual observations for shorter periods (10 to 15 years) typically show "Keynesian" consumption functions such as that in equations 9.1 and 9.2.

Contradiction Between Short-Run and Long-Run Consumption Functions

It is important to be perfectly clear on this point. Consumption functions based on data collected for long periods of time (long-run consumption functions) differ from short-run consumption functions in two basic ways:

1. The long-run consumption functions indicate a greater slope (MPC)—about 0.9 versus about 0.75 for short-run functions.
2. The long-run consumption functions show a zero vertical intercept, while the short-run functions tend to show a positive vertical intercept; that is, long-run consumption functions show a constant APC as real income rises, and short-run functions show an APC that varies inversely with real income.

The apparent contradiction between short-run and long-run consumption functions can be resolved by the permanent income hypothesis, the life cycle hypothesis, the consumption drift hypothesis, and the relative income hypothesis.

THE PERMANENT INCOME HYPOTHESIS

The **permanent income hypothesis (PIH)**, developed by Milton Friedman, can be distilled into two basic statements:

1. Currently measured annual real income is a poor clue as to the economic status of an individual, a family, or a nation.
2. Individuals or families base their consumption on their economic status, not on their current annual real income.

Consider the first statement. Suppose all you know about a person is his or her income for one year. How much information concerning that person's economic status do you really have? Probably not much. For example, that individual might be a college student whose current income vastly understates what he or she will earn in the future (one hopes). Current income for most young people generally *understates* their economic status or permanent income.

Or suppose the worker in question is retired; his or her accumulated wealth and economic status may well exceed the economic status that the individual's current annual income suggests. Or, during the period when a person's income is measured, that person could be *temporarily* on strike, ill, or injured. Likewise, such groups as the self-employed, farmers, or salespersons often have an exceptionally good or an exceptionally bad year economically.

In short, it is important to know an individual's normal long-term *permanent* income before you categorize his or her economic status.

Now consider statement 2, which, in effect, says that people base their consumption on their permanent income and largely ignore deviations from that permanent income if they expect the deviations to be only temporary.

College students, anticipating higher income levels in the future, will tend to spend more than will people whose permanent incomes equal the college students' temporarily low income. Workers on strike or who are temporarily ill will not radically reduce their consumption to match what is expected to be a temporary income reduction. Instead, they will spend accumulated assets. This point is very important because:

Keynes's consumption function maintains that current income constrains current consumption, but the PIH maintains that wealth is the true constraint on current consumption.[4]

Friedman's Model

We now consider that model more formally. (All the variables are in real terms.)

$$y \equiv y_p + y_t \tag{9.4}$$

$$c \equiv c_p + c_t \tag{9.5}$$

$$c_p = k(y_p) \tag{9.6}$$

WHERE y = measured income; actual income
y_p = permanent income; normal income

---

[4] Permanent income is closely related to wealth for Friedman, who defines permanent income as the amount that can be spent currently and leaves wealth unaltered. That amount is rTW, where r is the interest rate and TW is total wealth. Total wealth is composed of both nonhuman wealth (real estate, stock, bonds, and so on) and human wealth (the present value of future labor earnings). If your wealth is $10,000 and the interest rate is 10 percent, you can spend $1,000 per year and leave your wealth unaltered. Your permanent income, therefore, is $1,000.

y_t = transitory income; nonrecurring income changes that make measured income higher or lower than normal

c_p = permanent consumption; normal consumption

c_t = transitory consumption; nonrecurring consumption changes that make measured consumption higher or lower than normal consumption

k = the marginal *and* average propensity to consume permanent income.

Identity 9.4 incorporates the first statement of the PIH. (Note that equations 9.4 and 9.5 are identities ($\equiv$); they are true by definition.) If **transitory income** is important, then **measured income** is a poor clue to permanent income. If y_t is positive, then measured income exceeds **permanent income.** This situation will exist for all those people who have had an exceptionally good year and for workers who are at the peak earning stage of their careers. If y_t is negative, then measured income will be less than permanent income; this will be the case for all those people who have had an exceptionally low-income year, for students, for young workers, and for retirees.

Identity 9.5 merely states that consumption, too, can be defined as being composed of a transitory component and a permanent component.

Equation 9.6 incorporates statement 2; permanent consumption depends only on permanent income. Note that equation 9.6 is an equation ($=$) and not an identity; it is a testable hypothesis, and it makes Friedman's model operational. Equation 9.6 directly contradicts Keynes's absolute income hypothesis (which maintains that the APC falls as real income rises); in equation 9.6 the vertical intercept is zero, and therefore k = MPC = APC and k is a constant; that is, k is invariant to the level of permanent income. As permanent income rises, permanent consumption rises proportionally (because k is constant)—hence the name **proportionality hypothesis.**

Friedman suggests that k, the marginal (and average) propensity to consume permanent income, depends not on the level of national income, but rather it is a function of the interest rate (k and r are directly related), the ratio of nonhuman wealth to permanent income (k and the ratio of nonhuman wealth to y_p are directly related because nonhuman wealth is perceived by noncompetitive lenders as being superior collateral to human wealth), and such other variables as income variability, age, and family size.

Measuring Permanent Income

We have stated that equation 9.6 makes the permanent income hypothesis operational because that equation is a testable hypothesis. This is not technically true; permanent income is not directly measurable. Equation 9.6 says that *if* permanent income and permanent consumption were measured, then it would be seen that permanent consumption is proportional to permanent income. According to Friedman, the average propensity to consume permanent income, or k, is approximately 0.9; he maintains that this percentage is suggested by empirical observation, not by logic.

It is only because empirical analysis deals with *measured* income, not permanent income (and permanent consumption), that real-world data occasionally show a declining APC as real (measured) income rises.[5]

Permanent income is difficult to measure because there are difficulties in deciding which part of current measured income is transitory and which part is permanent. Difficulties arise in the determination of what the individual's (or family's, or country's) future income will be; difficulties arise also in the determination of the human and nonhuman wealth of the subjects involved. Even if we could amass an impressive amount of economic information about a family or a country, we still have the problem that *people themselves may not know what their permanent income is.*

The Adaptive Expectations Hypothesis   Friedman has proposed a simple method for estimating permanent income that may approximate the method by which people themselves estimate their permanent income; this method is now referred to as the **adaptive expectations hypothesis.** This theory maintains that permanent income is related systematically to present income and past income.

Assume, as Friedman does, that an estimate of *permanent* income can be made from what actual *measured* income has been in the past and what it currently is. In a complex model a proxy for permanent income can be derived by using a weighted average of measured incomes over many periods and by assigning relatively larger weights to the more recent years. A more complicated model would also take into account the growth of permanent income through time; and Friedman has done this, too.

Let's now derive a very simple adaptive expectations model in which an individual (or a community) already has an estimate of permanent income. The model shows how an adjustment in expected permanent

---

[5] Budget study, or cross-section, data also suggest a falling APC; for a given year, if we observe the average propensity to consume *measured* income of low-income families and compare it to the average propensity to consume *measured* income of high-income families, it appears that low-income families have a higher APC. The PIH can account for this by an application of the two basic statements with which we started this section.

income can be made as a result of comparing this (previously established) permanent income to current income.

Assume that this year's estimate of permanent income y_p equals last year's estimate of permanent income y_{p-1} plus some fraction z of the amount by which this year's measured income differs from last year's estimate of permanent income $y - y_{p-1}$.

Thus,

$$y_p = y_{p-1} + z(y - y_{p-1}) \tag{9.7}$$

where $0 < z < 1$. (Remember, all variables are still in real terms.)

Equation 9.7 suggests that if this year's measured income is the same as last year's estimate of permanent income (i.e., if $y - y_{p-1} = 0$), then the estimate of permanent income will not be revised. If this year's measured income exceeds last year's estimate of permanent income (i.e., if $y - y_{p-1} > 0$), then the estimate of permanent income will be revised upward by z (a fraction) times the difference. If this year's measured income is less than last year's estimate of permanent income (i.e., if $y - y_{p-1} < 0$), then the estimate of permanent income will be revised downward by z times the difference.

Presumably, z will be a function of income variability; such groups as farmers, salespeople, and those who own their own businesses will not be unduly influenced by changes in measured income and will have correspondingly lower z's; groups such as teachers, clerks, secretaries, and the like will perceive changes in measured income as being more important, and they will have correspondingly higher z's.

Permanent Consumption as a Function of Permanent Income   We are now ready, using a simple adaptive expectations model, to relate permanent consumption to permanent income. Substituting equation 9.7 into equation 9.6 yields

$$c_p = k[y_{p-1} + z(y - y_{p-1})] \tag{9.8}$$

Rearranging yields

$$c_p = ky_{p-1} + kz(y - y_{p-1}) \tag{9.9}$$

Equation 9.9 yields important conclusions, even though it is based on a very simple theory of how people behave.[6] It suggests that *individuals (or a community) will respond only slightly to changes in measured*

---

[6] Equation 9.7 can be rearranged to yield $y_p = zy + (1 - z)y_{p-1}$, which suggests that this period's estimate of permanent income is a weighted average of this year's measured income (which has a weight of z) and last year's estimate of permanent income (which has a weight of $1 - z$). Note that the weights sum to 1; $z + (1 - z) = 1$.

income if they do not know to what extent that change is permanent or transitory. By assumption, people change their consumption only in response to changes in permanent income; transitory income changes will have no effect on consumption, given sufficient assets.[7] Note that permanent consumption depends on permanent income, *and permanent income depends only partly on current income,* according to equation 9.7. Equation 9.9 indicates that the average propensity to consume *permanent* income is high; it equals k, which, as we have already indicated, Friedman maintains is 0.9. If current income is different from permanent income, then the resulting change in consumption will be only a fraction of k, or zk; the marginal propensity to consume deviations from permanent income is relatively small. Another way to state this is to say that the short-run MPC is smaller than the long-run MPC.

The PIH suggests that the private economy is inherently stable for two reasons. First, because permanent income is a wealth concept, then, to the extent that the PIH is valid, it provides support for the Pigou (wealth) effect. This means that price flexibility is capable of restoring the economy to a full-employment equilibrium after the economy has been shocked. Second, when the economy strays from its natural growth path during booms and recessions, the PIH implies that consumers will respond only in part to such transitory changes in national income. Temporary booms, therefore, will not be fueled by large increases in consumption; and temporary recessions will be cushioned somewhat by consumers who maintain most of their consumption expenditures. Stated differently, the PIH implies that the APC falls in booms and rises in recessions; this countercyclical tendency is inherently stabilizing.

The PIH Resolves the Data Contradiction

We are now in a position to show how the permanent income hypothesis can resolve the apparent inconsistency in the short-run and long-run consumption-income data. As you will recall, data over a short period of time show an APC that varies inversely with national income (consistent with Keynes's absolute income hypothesis), but data over a long period of time show an APC that is invariant to national income (consistent with Friedman's PIH proportionality assumption).

---

[7] If measured income falls and is perceived as being only a temporary or transitory phenomenon, then people will draw down on their assets to maintain their permanent consumption level. If these assets are quite small, however, they may be *forced* to consume less than their c_p; in such a case *current income*, not wealth (which includes a human component), is the budget constraint. This is one reason that k is a function of the ratio of nonhuman wealth to permanent income. Whether current income or wealth is the true constraint is seen as a crucial issue in Chapter 15, where we discuss post-Keynesian economics.

Consider Figure 9.1, which shows the familiar 45° line aggregate output (AO) curve and a long-run consumption function that has a zero vertical intercept and a slope equal to 0.9.[8] Assume that we start at point A (y_1, c_1), and assume that the nation's real measured disposable income rises from y_1 to y_2. Will consumption rise from c_1 to c_2? That is, will the economy move from point A to point B? The PIH says no, unless the increase in measured income is perceived as a permanent increase. If the community is not sure, then it will increase its estimate of permanent income only slightly, to y_p (not shown in Figure 9.1), and consumption will rise by k times *this* increase in income (or by $c_3 - c_1$) and not by the larger increase, $k(y_2 - y_1) = c_2 - c_1$.

Stated alternatively, if income rises from y_1 to y_2, the economy will move from point A to point B if the increase is perceived as being permanent. Because A and B are both on the long-run consumption function (and on a ray from the origin), the APC remains constant. If the community is not sure whether the income increase is permanent, or if it is sure that some portion of the change is only temporary, the economy will move from A to C (along the short-run consumption function) and the APC will fall.[9] In the long run, the community will know whether or not the income increase was permanent or temporary, and the economy will move to B or A, respectively. To Friedman, the "long-run" consumption function, which includes the points A and B, is the true consumption function; the short-run consumption function, which includes the points A and C, exists only because the community is not sure whether a change in measured income is permanent or temporary or if they perceive part of the change as being temporary. The short-run and long-run consumption function data are thus reconciled.

THE LIFE CYCLE HYPOTHESIS

The **life cycle hypothesis (LCH)**, developed by Modigliani, Ando, and Brumberg, assumes that people allocate their income between consump-

---

[8] The long-run consumption function, according to the PIH, will exhibit a constant APC if the determinants of k do not change systematically, or if they change, but the changes offset each other.

[9] If $k = 0.9$, then the APC equals 0.9 at both point A and point B. At point C national income is the same as it is at point B, but consumption is less; therefore, the APC must be less at C than at B. Note also that the slope of the short-run consumption function is smaller than the slope of the long-run consumption function and that short-run consumption function would have a positive vertical intercept if we extend the dashed short-run consumption function line to the vertical axis.

The Amount by Which Consumption Responds to a Change in Income Depends on the Extent to Which the Change Is Perceived as Permanent

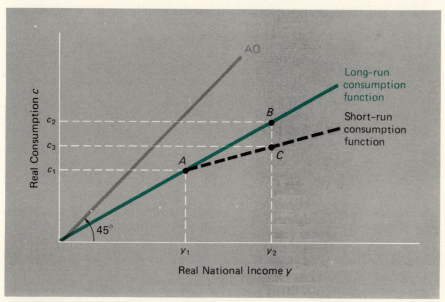

FIGURE 9.1. RECONCILING SHORT-RUN AND LONG-RUN CONSUMPTION FUNCTIONS

If measured real income rises from y_1 to y_2, real consumption will rise from c_1 to c_2 if the income change is perceived as permanent. The economy moves from A to B and the average propensity to consume (APC) remains constant at $\overset{.}{B}$. If the community is not sure whether the change is permanent, it will increase its consumption only by k times its upwardly revised estimate of permanent income y_p. The economy moves from A to C and the APC falls. If the increase in income proves to be permanent in the long run, consumption will rise to c_2 and the APC will return to k; if the increase in income is only temporary, the level of national income will return to y_1, consumption will return to c_1, and the APC will return to k. Friedman's model, therefore, interprets the curve that includes the points A and C as a short-run consumption function; note that that curve has a smaller slope than the long-run consumption function and that if the short-run curve were extended to the left it would have a positive vertical intercept.

tion and saving to maximize *lifetime* economic well-being, or utility. As was the case for the PIH, the LCH assumes that people want to free themselves from the discipline of consuming, in a given period, an amount based on their income in that period. People save, therefore, in order to insulate themselves from negative transitory changes in income and (especially) for retirement. Essentially, people save during their working years in order to consume during their retirement period.[10]

In order to derive an LCH model, let's make the following simplifying assumptions:

1. Individuals know for certain the age at which they will die D and the age at which they will retire R. (The known retirement period, therefore, equals $D - R$.)
2. Planned consumption c is the same every year of the remaining life expectancy.
3. Planned consumption depends on a constant annual labor income y_L and on inherited nonhuman wealth W_{NH}, and no interest is earned on W. That is,

$$c = b(W_{NH}, y_L) \qquad (9.10)$$

4. No planned bequests are made to heirs; therefore, lifetime labor earnings and inherited wealth will be totally consumed during the person's lifetime. Lifetime savings plus inherited wealth equal consumption during the retirement years.

The Micro LCH Model

Let's first derive the micro implications of our simple LCH model. Consider the case of a woman who currently is age A and who has not yet retired (i.e., $R > A$). Her lifetime consumption constraint is

$$c(D - A) = W_{NH} + (R - A)y_L \qquad (9.11)$$

which says that the total annual (constant) consumption for the remainder of her life is equal to her present nonhuman wealth plus what she will earn from her labor for the remainder of her working life.

Solving equation 9.11 for annual consumption yields

$$c = \left(\frac{1}{D - A}\right)W_{NH} + \left(\frac{R - A}{D - A}\right)y_L \qquad (9.12)$$

---

[10] Franco Modigliani and Richard E. Brumberg, "Utility Analysis and the Consumption Function," in Kenneth K. Kurihara, ed., *Post-Keynesian Economics* (New Brunswick, N.J.: Rutgers University Press, 1984); and Albert Ando and Franco Modigliani, "The Life Cycle Hypothesis of Saving: Aggregate Implications and Tests," *American Economic Review*, vol. 53 (March 1963), pp. 55–94.

or

$$c = aW_{NH} + by_L \qquad (9.13)$$

WHERE $a = 1/(D - A)$
$\quad\quad\quad b = (R - A)/(D - A)$

Note that a and b are the marginal propensity to consume nonhuman wealth and the marginal propensity to consume labor income, respectively. These marginal propensities to consume are clearly a function of age; they vary directly with age (or position in the life cycle). Also, they vary with life expectancy and working life expectancy, or (what amounts to the same thing) with the length of the retirement period. We can also think of a and b as parameters that can be estimated empirically.

Equation 9.12 indicates that this woman's consumption depends on both labor income and nonhuman wealth; if either changes, then her consumption will change.[11] If neither changes, c will remain constant each year. The MPC for nonhuman wealth rises with age; for example, if a positive windfall is received at a later age, she will consume a higher percentage in each remaining period than if she received the windfall at an earlier age.

The Macro LCH Model

So far we have applied the LCH to individual behavior. Our major concern, however, is with the macroeconomy. What are the macro implications of the LCH?

Assume an economy that produces a constant annual real GNP and one in which the population is also constant. Each person will go through his or her own life cycle by saving during the working life period and dissaving (consuming more than income) during the retirement years. Under these conditions, in the aggregate, national saving equals zero at any given time; saving by workers equals the dissaving of retired people.

If the population is growing, then there will be a higher proportion of the population working than in retirement; hence, positive aggregate saving requires a positive growth rate of population. It follows that aggregate saving (and aggregate consumption) depends on the age composition of the population. It also depends on the average retirement age; the higher the retirement age, given a life expectancy, the higher the

---

[11] The careful reader will note that human wealth has been ignored. You should realize that, in fact, Modigliani and Ando *have* treated it explicitly. They separate labor income into current labor income and expected future labor income; the latter can be thought of as a proxy for human wealth. We have not done so here in order to keep the model as simple as possible.

aggregate saving and the lower the consumption out of a given level of real GNP.

Let's now consider the economywide consumption/disposable income ratio (APC). Dividing equation 9.13 by real disposable income y_d gives

$$\frac{c}{y_d} = a\frac{W_{NH}}{y_d} + b\frac{y_L}{y_d} \qquad (9.14)$$

Empirical evidence indicates that the ratio y_L/y_d has been relatively stable for nearly a century in the United States, although it rises in recessions and falls in expansions. We have learned in this chapter that the ratio c/y_d (i.e., the APC) also is unstable over the business cycle but is stable in the long run; it rises in recessions and falls in expansions. It follows that if the ratio of real nonhuman wealth to real disposable income (i.e., W_{NH}/y_d) is constant in the long run, the LCH will have empirical support. In fact, that is the case: the W_{NH}/y_d ratio is relatively stable in the *long run.*

Both the ratio of real labor income to real disposable income and the ratio of real nonhuman wealth to real disposable income, however, vary over the business cycle, so their combined *short-run* effect on the APC may be difficult to determine. The difficulty is that the W_{NH}/y_d ratio rises in mild recessions but probably falls in depressions.[12] This can lead to discrepancies in short-run APC calculations.

It is important to realize that the LCH assumes that consumption is stable through time (as long as the nation's age composition does not change significantly) and *does not vary with changes in income that are expected to be temporary.* This implies that the consumption function is a stabilizing (i.e., a countercyclical) element in the private sector. The LCH further assumes that consumption depends importantly on wealth, which, because of the Pigou effect analysis, also implies that the consumption function is a stabilizing influence in the private sector.

THE STABILITY OF THE CONSUMPTION FUNCTION

Both the PIH and the LCH imply that the consumption function is stable, and the proponents of the two hypotheses have produced empirical evidence to support their models. Consumption expenditures on durable goods, however, are relatively volatile and do change significantly over

---

[12] Michael K. Evans, *Macroeconomic Activity: Theory, Forecasting, and Control* (New York: Harper & Row, 1969), pp. 36–37.

the course of the business cycle, and in a procyclical manner. That is, expenditures on consumer durables rise during boom periods and fall during recessions. Figure 9.2 shows the annual growth rate in real (1972) dollars for total personal consumption expenditures and its various components for the period 1959 to the first quarter of 1984 in the United States. Note that the total personal consumption expenditure curve, the services expenditure curve, and the nondurable goods expenditure curve are quite smooth (these variables tend to grow at a constant percentage rate), but that the durable goods expenditure curve does indeed vary systematically over the five business cycles (the shaded areas, where P = peak and T = trough) that occurred during that period.

Consequently, durable goods expenditures add an important degree of instability to the consumption function. Forecasters and policymakers, therefore, must take such an unpredictable and important component of aggregate demand into account.

The proponents of the PIH and the LCH have indicated that durable goods expenditure volatility is somewhat overstated. This is because (by definition) there is an important difference between the value of *actual consumption* (or the *use value* of the services of a durable good) and the value of the *expenditure* on the durable goods in the period of purchase. For example, suppose you buy an automobile for $10,000 in 1985; the use value of the flow of services from the automobile, in 1985, will be considerably less than $10,000. Proponents of the PIH and the LCH suggest, therefore, that most of the price of a newly purchased durable good should be allocated to saving, and only a small amount should be allocated to the value of the services of that durable good during the period in question.

To be sure, such a (justifiable) correction in durable goods consumption "expenditures" would make the durable goods expenditure curve less volatile. Still, if in fact people time their purchases of durable goods to coincide with the business cycle (e.g., if people hold off purchasing wanted durable goods during recessions and purchase them when they receive positive windfalls), then aggregate expenditures are procyclical. In short, actual expenditures is a source of instability, even if *true* consumption is quite stable. We return to this point in the next chapter when we analyze the so-called "accelerator effect" that results from expenditures on capital goods, which are also durable goods (have long lives).

THE CONSUMPTION DRIFT HYPOTHESIS

Arthur Smithies also attempted to reconcile short-run consumption functions that show an inverse relationship between the APC and real

Real Expenditures on Durable Goods Is the Most Variable Component of Total Real Consumption Expenditures

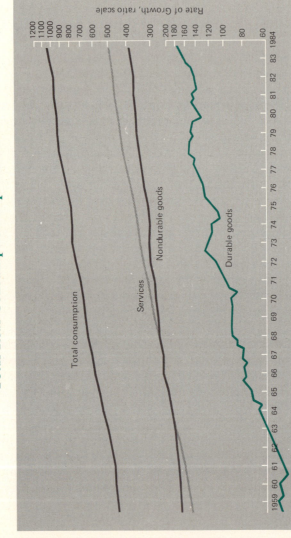

FIGURE 9.2. THE COMPONENTS OF THE CONSUMPTION FUNCTION

Real expenditures on durable goods are volatile and procyclical. The other components of total real consumption expenditures show a relatively smooth upward trend through time. The vertical axis is a ratio (log) scale, so that the slope of a curve gives its growth; a straight line would indicate that the variable is growing at a constant *percentage* through time. (From *Survey of Current Business*.)

national income with Kuznets's data that show that in the long run the APC is invariant to real national income.[13] Smithies argued that Keynes was right. The APC *does* fall as real national income rises, *other things constant*. But other things are not constant. Between 1869 and 1929 real national income quadrupled and *would have* caused the APC to decrease. But during that same period other changes (in urbanization, standard of living, and wealth) took place that would have caused the APC to rise. In short, as real national income rises, the consumption function shifts upward sufficiently to offset a declining APC; this theory is called the **consumption drift hypothesis.**

The Urbanization Effect From 1869 to 1929 the U.S. economy became increasingly industrialized as people left farms to live in cities and as immigrants came to this country and settled (mostly) in the cities. Many studies show that farmers—perhaps because their incomes are so variable—seem to have lower APC's (higher APS's) than nonfarmers. As the composition of the economy changed, therefore, the APC increased, other things constant. At any level of real national income, consumption rises (the APC rises), and this is equivalent to a shift upward in the consumption curve.

The Standard-of-Living Effect Through time, innovations in consumer goods take place and living standards rise. Many people perceive that they "need" more goods and services; last year's luxuries become this year's necessities. Keeping up with the Joneses is a lot more expensive than it used to be because it now requires the purchase of such "necessities" as a car, a stereo, a video cassette recorder, and oodles of other modern-day toys. This means that consumption will be higher at every level of national income and that the consumption curve shifts upward.

The Wealth Effect As time passes, community saving bears factories, houses, railroads, dams, bridges, and improved technology. Each generation leaves the next generation title to most of this acquired wealth (assuming that the economy grows), and the increase in wealth induces later generations to consume more at every level of real national income; the wealth effect shifts the consumption curve upward.

Consider Figure 9.3, which shows that the consumption curve shifts upward at the same time that real national income rises. Start with point A, which corresponds to real national income y_1 and real consumption c_1. Assume that real national income rises to y_2. If that were the *only* change, then the economy would move to point B and the APC would

---

[13] Arthur Smithies, "Forecasting Postwar Demand: I," *Econometrica,* vol. 13 (1945).

As Real National Income Rises, the Consumption Function Shifts Upward by Just Enough to Leave the APC Unaltered

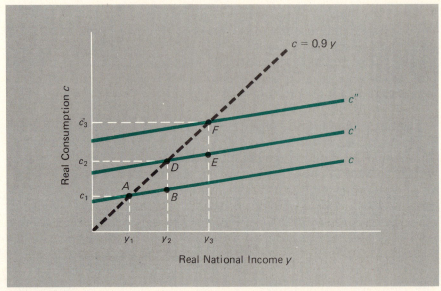

FIGURE 9.3. THE CONSUMPTION DRIFT HYPOTHESIS

As real national income rises, the economy moves along a consumption function and the average propensity to consume (APC) falls. However, the urbanization effect, the standard-of-living effect, and the wealth effect simultaneously shift the consumption curve upward—increase the APC—by just enough to offset the decline in the APC. The net result is that, as real national income rises from y_1 to y_2 to y_3, the economy moves from A to D to F, all points along a ray from the origin that has a slope of 0.9. By coincidence, therefore, the consumption function appears to be $c = 0.9y$.

fall, because A and B are on a consumption curve that has a positive vertical intercept. But other things are *not* constant. As income rises to y_2, the urbanization effect, the standard-of-living effect, and the wealth effect occur and shift the consumption curve upward simultaneously, from c to c'. The economy moves from point A to point D, and those points are (coincidentally) on a ray from the origin that has a slope equal to 0.9. Similarly, real national income then rises to y_3 which, other things constant, moves the economy from point D to point E and the APC falls. But the three effects occur simultaneously, and they shift the consumption curve upward to c''; the economy moves, therefore, from A to D to

F, all points which lie on a ray from the origin that has a slope equal to 0.9.

In short, from 1869 to 1929 the rise in real national income *would have* decreased the APC, but the urbanization effect, the standard-of-living effect, and the wealth effect caused the APC to rise. The *net* effect was a standoff, and the APC remained constant.

The consumption drift hypothesis has been criticized for its strong reliance on coincidence—especially since data from 1929 to the present also show a constant APC. Friedman's permanent income hypothesis, moreover, directly incorporates the wealth effect; permanent income is, after all, akin to wealth.

THE RELATIVE INCOME HYPOTHESIS

James Duesenberry was also to reconcile short-run consumption functions with a long-run consumption function.[14] Duesenberry's theory is referred to as the **relative income hypothesis,** and his theory seems more psychological than economic in nature.

Duesenberry's model assumes that (1) one person's consumption is dependent on other people's consumption, and (2) consumption relations are irreversible over time.

Both of these assumptions depart considerably from generally accepted economic assumptions. The first assumption allows Duesenberry to theorize that an individual's APC depends on his or her percentile position in the income distribution (i.e., the individual's *relative* income) and not on absolute real income. The second assumption leads Duesenberry to hypothesize that when income falls, people will continue to base their consumption partly on their previous peak income.

The relative income hypothesis for the community can be represented as

$$\frac{c}{y} = a - e\left(\frac{y}{y^p}\right) \tag{9.15}$$

WHERE   *a* and *e* are constants and $e > 0$
           y = current real national income
           y^p = previous peak real national income

If we consider only long-run patterns and assume that the economy is growing at some constant natural growth rate, then (1) previous peak real national income will equal last year's real national income (i.e., y^p

---

[14] James S. Duesenberry, *Income, Saving, and the Theory of Consumer Behavior* (Cambridge, Mass.: Harvard University Press, 1949).

$= y_{-1}$) and (2) the y/y^p ratio will be constant. For example, if the economy is growing at 3 percent per annum, then $y/y^p = 1.03$. If y/y^p is constant, then c/y, the community's APC, also remains constant.

This conclusion is consistent with the microeconomic implications of the relative hypothesis. If an individual's APC depends on his or her percentile position in the distribution of income and not on absolute real income, then all those people whose *relative* income position is unaltered through time (even though their absolute real income rises) will maintain the same APC. Others will rise or fall in the income distribution, but in the aggregate their APC changes will cancel out. Therefore, through time the *community* APC remains constant (assuming no change in the *overall* distribution of income); and this is not surprising, because the APC is independent of absolute real national income.

Equation 9.15 also can explain why the APC rises in a recession. In a recession the ratio y/y^p falls, and that equation indicates that the community APC rises. This phenomenon results from Duesenberry's assumption that consumption relations are irreversible. When real national income falls, many people try to maintain the consumption level that they enjoyed in the previous peak period; if real national income falls more rapidly than consumption falls, the APC rises.

Although the relative income hypothesis is intriguing, it has not gained wide acceptance—perhaps partially because economists are reluctant to accept a psychologically oriented theory. More substantively, it seems *unlikely* that (1) an individual's consumption is *completely* dependent on other people's consumption, and (2) consumer behavior is truly irreversible; surely people will adjust their consumption downward over time once they perceive an income reduction as being permanent. Still, as long as there is *significant* irreversibility in consumption the relative income hypothesis can contribute to an understanding of consumption expenditures.

POLICY CONTROVERSY
Are Temporary Tax Changes an Ineffective Policy Tool?

Both the permanent income hypothesis and the life cycle hypothesis seem to predict that income tax changes proclaimed as *temporary* will be ineffective because they have only minor effects on permanent or lifetime income. On the other hand, there are theoretical reasons to believe that income tax changes labeled as temporary might indeed have important effects on consumption and on aggregate expenditures. Alan S. Blinder[15] lists the following:

1. A temporary reduction in taxes may induce households to "save" largely by purchasing durable goods, which will significantly affect the economy. Note that the increase in *expenditures* would exceed the increase in *consumption*, as pointed out earlier in this chapter. Similarly, a temporary rise in taxes may induce households to postpone their purchase of durable goods, even though "consumption" won't be reduced by as much.

2. Some households currently may not be able to spend as much as they wish because they cannot borrow on their future earnings. Such liquidity-constrained households may spend *all* of the reduced income tax—whether it is temporary or permanent. Similarly, liquidity-constrained individuals will be *unable* to ignore temporary tax increases. We return to liquidity-constrained consumer behavior in Chapter 15.

3. People may not *believe* that tax changes are temporary; presumably, they base their consumption on what they believe the government *will* do rather than on what the government *says* it will do. This third point is probably more important with respect to tax increases than to tax reductions; the government is more likely to be deceptive about the temporary nature of a tax increase than of a tax reduction.

4. If people are very shortsighted (or, to put it more objectively, if they have very high subjective discount rates), they may respond significantly to temporary tax changes.

A moment's reflection will indicate that the issue regarding the significance of the effect on the economy of tax changes labeled as temporary is an empirical question. Accordingly, we turn now to the data.

In 1966 and 1967 the U.S. federal budget went more deeply into deficit as the United States tried to produce more "guns" (the Vietnam war) *and* "butter" (the War on Poverty). An accommodating expansionary monetary policy also led to an increase in the rate of inflation. The Johnson administration proposed a temporary tax (to finance a temporary war) in the form of a tax surcharge, which was to be removed later. A tax surcharge is a tax on a tax; people were to calculate their tax liability in the normal way and then add a certain percentage of that amount to their tax liability in the form of a surtax. The Johnson surtax was enacted in June 1968 and was scheduled to be removed in 1969.

William L. Springer[16] analyzed the effects of the 1968 temporary tax surcharge and concluded that they were minimal. The permanent income hypothesis predicts that a tax increase expected to be temporary will reduce consumption only slightly. If consumption falls less than disposable income, the average propensity to consume should rise, or (stated

[15] See Alan S. Blinder, "Temporary Income Taxes and Consumer Spending," *Journal of Political Economy*, vol. 89 (February 1981), pp. 29–30.

[16] William L. Springer, "Did the 1968 Surcharge Really Work?" *American Economic Review*, vol. 65 (September 1975), pp. 644–659.

alternatively) the average propensity to save should fall. Springer found precisely that. The overall 1967 APS was 7.3 percent. The APS rose slightly in the second quarter of 1968, but then it fell to around 6 percent in the third and fourth quarters of 1968, and to 5.3 percent in the first two quarters of 1969 when the major tax increase took effect. When the surcharge was removed, the saving rate (APS) rose; in 1970 it was 7.9 percent. It seems that the 1968 tax surcharge confirms the prediction of the permanent income hypothesis.

In early 1975 taxes *fell* temporarily as a tax rebate of up to $200 per family was granted. The evidence is that (as the PIH predicts) most of the rebate was saved *initially*; Alan S. Blinder's estimate is that

the 1975 rebate led to a rapid increase in the APS (from 6.4 percent to 9.7 percent) in the second quarter of 1975 and then to a decrease in the APS in late 1976 and early 1977.[17]

Although the available evidence supports the contentions of the PIH and the LCH, the issue is far from settled; many more studies of temporary tax changes must be made before a consensus can be reached on this issue. Also, economists are far from agreement on the *magnitude* of the difference in the impact on the economy that a temporary-versus-permanent tax change elicits.

---

[17] Blinder, op. cit., pp. 27 and 45 (table 5).

CHAPTER SUMMARY

1. Time series data collected for a fairly short period suggest that the APC varies inversely with the level of real disposable national income. Time series data calculated for longer periods suggest that the APC has remained constant over time as real disposable national income rose.
2. The permanent income hypothesis (PIH) indicates that (*a*) currently measured real income is a poor clue to economic status, and (*b*) people base their consumption on their economic status and not on their current real income.
3. The PIH suggests that the major constraint on current consumption is wealth, not (as Keynes maintained) current income.
4. The PIH predicts that the APC and the MPC will be equal and that they are invariant to the level of real income; they depend on the interest rate, the ratio of nonhuman wealth to permanent income, income variability, and certain life cycle variables.
5. Permanent income can be estimated by the adaptive expectations model, which uses a weighted average of previous income levels and current income as a proxy for permanent income; higher weights are assigned to the more recent years.

6. The PIH explains the discrepancy between the short-run consumption function and the long-run consumption function by noting that it takes time for the community to determine whether or not a change in income is permanent or temporary. In the long run this information will be known, and the community APC will return to its normal rate; but in the meantime the APC will depart from its normal rate and the departure will depend on the direction of the income change.

7. The life cycle hypothesis (LCH) assumes that people prefer a smooth lifetime consumption pattern to one that constantly adjusts to changes in current income. Current income, after all, is subject to transitory changes and falls to zero (nearly) in the retirement period.

8. The LCH maintains that consumption depends on labor income and on nonhuman wealth. People are viewed as savers during their working years and dissavers during their retirement years.

9. The LCH predicts that the aggregate saving ratio will be positive only if the economy is growing or if population is growing. The theory also predicts that this ratio depends on the average retirement age. The LCH predicts a constant saving (or consumption) to income ratio in the long run, but a ratio that varies over the business cycle in the short run.

10. Both the PIH and the LCH suggest that total consumption expenditures exert a stabilizing effect on the economy. Consumer expenditures on durable goods, however, are procyclical.

11. The consumption drift hypothesis reconciles short-run and long-run consumption functions by assuming that through time, in the United States, wealth and urbanization and standards of living have increased and caused the consumption function to shift upward just enough to offset a declining APC (due to an increase in real national income). The relative income hypothesis maintains that the APC depends on *relative* income, not absolute income, so that the APC should be invariant to national income in the long run.

12. Evidence concerning changes in taxes that are labeled "temporary" supports the permanent income hypothesis: such changes have little effect on the economy.

GLOSSARY

absolute income hypothesis   The theory that the average propensity to consume varies inversely with the level of real disposable income.

adaptive expectations hypothesis   The theory that people base their expectations for next year's values on a weighted average of actual values from previous periods.

consumption drift hypothesis A theory that reconciles short-run and long-run consumption functions; a theory that maintains that even though real national income quadrupled between 1869 and 1929 and would have caused the APC to fall, other effects occurred which increased the APC so that the net effect was to leave the APC unaltered.

life cycle hypothesis (LCH) The theory that people try to maximize their lifetime utility by maintaining a relatively constant level of consumption over their lifetimes.

measured income Actual income in a period; the sum of permanent income and transitory income.

permanent income Normal income, measured by a weighted average of past and present income; or the amount that can be consumed in a given year without altering wealth.

permanent income hypothesis (PIH) The theory that consumption depends on what real income normally is, instead of what current real income is.

proportionality hypothesis The theory that the APC remains constant as real income rises; real consumption changes proportionally to changes in real income.

relative income hypothesis A theory that reconciles short-run and long-run consumption functions by assuming that an individual's APC depends on that person's relative income and not on his or her absolute income, and by assuming that consumption relations are irreversible.

transitory income Income that is nonrecurring.

QUESTIONS AND PROBLEMS FOR REVIEW

9.1 Milton Friedman has indicated that if equations 9.4, 9.5, and 9.6 are correct, and if the correlation between permanent income and transitory income, the correlation between permanent consumption and transitory consumption, and the correlation between transitory income and transitory consumption all equal zero, then

$$b = k \left(\frac{\text{Var } y_p}{\text{Var } y} \right)$$

WHERE b = the MPC (slope) of the measured consumption function
k = the MPC (slope) of the permanent consumption function
Var y_p = variance (a measure of variability) of permanent income
Var y = variance of measured income

Use this equation to explain the discrepancy in the value of short-run and long-run MPC's.

9.2 Assume that you have collected budget study (cross-sectional) data on 1000 people, *all* of whom have a permanent income of $10,000 but many of whom have had positive or negative transitory income changes during the year in question. Assume all 1000 have a $k = 0.9$.
   a. Graph the measured consumption function that results, assuming

that sufficient numbers of people are in each measured income class so that positive and negative transitory consumption effects cancel out.

b. Use the equation in question 9.1 above to verify your results.

9.3 Assume that you have collected budget study data on 1000 people, *none* of whom has received any transitory income in the period in question. Assume that there are many people in each measured income (and therefore permanent income) class and that each has a $b = 0.9$. Assume that positive and negative transitory consumption effects cancel out in each income class.

a. Graph the measured consumption function that results.

b. Use the equation in question 9.1 to verify your results.

9.4 Assume that you have collected budget study data from 17,000 people and that this group is very heterogeneous: different occupations, races, ages, health circumstances, sexes, and so on. If you group this sample by income classes and then graph the average consumption and average income for each income class, you can derive a group MPC. (Those of you who have had statistics know how to regress average consumption on average income for the income classes.) Now suppose you form subgroups which become progressively more homogeneous: eliminate those over age 50 and under age 30; then from that group eliminate women; from the group that remains, eliminate blacks; and so on. Every time you eliminate a subgroup and make the remaining group more homogeneous, you graph average consumption and average income and calculate MPC, or slope.

a. As the remaining group becomes more and more homogeneous, what should happen to the ratio in the parentheses in question 9.1 above?

b. What should happen to b in the equation in question 9.1 above?

9.5 During any given year, a disproportionate number of people in the lower measured income classes will have received negative transitory income, and a disproportionate number in the upper measured income categories will have received positive transitory income. Another way to state this is to say that for many in the lower-income classes, measured income will be less than permanent income; and for many in the upper-income classes, measured income will exceed permanent income. Also, young laborers and retirees will tend to be concentrated in the lower-income classes; these groups, too, will have measured incomes that are lower than their permanent incomes.

If people base their consumption only on their permanent income, then explain how the PIH can account for the fact that cross-sectional budget study data always show a declining APC as one moves from lower- to higher-income classes.

9.6 Get a copy of the *Economic Report of the President, 1985,* and turn to page 261, where you will find real consumption and real disposable personal income data for (most of) the period 1929–1984. Graph (or do a regression analysis) for (*a*) the entire period, and (*b*) the years 1970 to 1983. Are your results similar to what pre-World War II researchers found?

9.7 Assume that we start at point A and income falls to y_2:

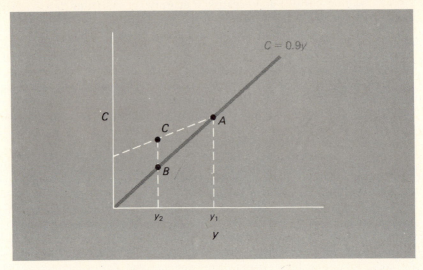

a. What is the APC at point A?
b. If the reduction in income is expected to be permanent, will the economy move to point B or to point C?
c. If the community is uncertain as to whether the reduction in income is permanent, will the economy move to point B or to point C?
d. What is the APC at point B?
e. Given your answer to (d), what must be true about the APC at point C?
f. How can the relative income hypothesis also account for the conclusion reached in (e) above?

9.8 If data collected for each of several fairly short periods suggest that the APC decreases as the level of real disposable national income increases, how can it be that time series data collected for a fairly long period suggest that the APC remains constant as real disposable national income increases?

9.9 List some expenditures that would be considered as consumption in the Keynesian model but as saving in the PIH model.

9.10 Does the PIH model indicate that consumption is influenced by the rate of interest? If the rate of interest affects the present value of a net revenue stream, would not the rate of interest affect both human and nonhuman wealth?

REFERENCES

Gardner Ackley, *Macroeconomic Theory* (New York: Macmillan, 1961).
Albert Ando and Franco Modigliani, "The Life Cycle Hypothesis of Saving: Aggregate Implications and Tests," *American Economic Review*, vol. 53 (1963).

Alan S. Blinder, "Temporary Income Taxes and Consumer Spending," *Journal of Political Economy*, vol. 89 (1981).

James S. Duesenberry, *Income, Saving, and the Theory of Consumer Behavior* (Cambridge, Mass.: Harvard University Press, 1949).

Michael K. Evans, *Macroeconomic Activity: Theory, Forecasting and Control* (New York: Harper & Row, 1969).

Milton Friedman, *A Theory of the Consumption Function*, National Bureau of Economic Research, report no. 63 (Princeton, N.J.: Princeton University Press, 1957).

Raymond Goldsmith, *A Study of Saving in the United States*, vol. 1, National Bureau of Economic Research (Princeton, N.J.: Princeton University Press, 1955).

John Maynard Keynes, *The General Theory of Employment, Interest, and Money* (New York: Harcourt Brace Jovanovich, 1964).

Franco Modigliani and Richard E. Brumberg, "Utility Analysis and the Consumption Function," in Kenneth K. Kurihara, ed., *Post-Keynesian Economics* (New Brunswick, N.J.: Rutgers University Press, 1954).

Arthur Smithies, "Forecasting Postwar Demand: I," *Econometrica*, vol. 13 (1945).

William L. Springer, "Did the Surcharge Really Work?" *American Economic Review*, vol. 65 (1975).

10

INVESTMENT EXPENDITURES

STABLE OR UNSTABLE?

In the previous chapter we saw that the consumption function was a source of both stability and instability for the private sector. Consumption expenditures are thought to be largely independent of temporary changes in current income and are dependent on wealth. Still, if households wish to hold a stock of durable goods that is a constant portion of their permanent income, slight increases in permanent income will lead to significant increases in durable good *expenditures* (even though the current *services* from durable goods increase only slightly). This means that household expenditures on durable consumer goods are procyclical; such expenditures rise in boom times and fall in recessions, therefore, they provide an element of instability to the consumption function.

A similar conclusion is reached here with respect to business expenditures on capital goods. If businesses want to maintain a stock of capital goods that is a constant multiple of their annual permanent sales, then investment expenditures will be procyclical, and such expenditures will be an important source of instability to the private sector.

In this chapter we review Keynes's theory of aggregate investment and analyze the simple accelerator theory of investment. Then a more sophisticated accelerator theory—one that makes use of the adaptive expectations model—is examined. We conclude with a survey of recent empirical studies on investment behavior.

KEYNES'S INVESTMENT MODEL RECALLED

You will recall from Chapter 6 that, according to Keynes, a business contemplating the purchase of a capital good compares the current interest rate with the marginal efficiency of capital (MEC) of the capital good. The marginal efficiency of capital is that rate of discount that makes the present value of the net revenue stream of the capital good just equal to the supply price of the capital good. If MEC > i, the investment is expected to be profitable and will be made. If MEC < i, then the capital good will not be purchased, because the investment is expected to be unprofitable.

According to Keynes, aggregate net investment is inversely related to the interest rate, because as the interest rate falls more investment projects will have an MEC that exceeds the interest rate.

Keynes's model assumes an inverse relationship between investment expenditures and the interest rate, *other things constant*. But, argued Keynes, other things are not likely to remain constant. The essence of Keynes's investment model is that the investment curve is extremely volatile. When business confidence changes, so do profit expectations (and the net revenue streams associated with capital), and therefore the investment curve shifts. Investment expenditures are based on what businesses believe will happen in an unknowable future. Figure 10.1 shows that investment expenditure is indeed volatile, and procyclical.

To maintain that the relationship between investment expenditures and the interest rate is unstable is to argue, in effect, that there are *more important* determinants of capital goods expenditures other than the interest rate. One would not expect to find a strong empirical relationship between net investment and the interest rate, and in fact that often is the case. We consider other determinants of capital goods expenditures now.

THE SIMPLE ACCELERATOR MODEL

An Industry in Equilibrium

Assume that for some industry (and for all firms in that industry) a stable level of annual sales exists. Each firm will adjust its capital stock so as to maximize its profits. The optimal capital stock for a firm will be that amount that is sufficiently large to meet the firm's production quota but not so large that much capital is idle much of the time.[1] Suppose that for the industry (and for each firm in it) the ratio of the real value of capital k to the ratio of real output y is A, and that $A = 4$; this means the accelerator is 4:

$$A = \frac{k}{y} = 4 \tag{10.1}$$

Equation 10.1 says that firms in the industry hold a capital stock that is valued at four times the value of annual sales—all in real terms. Stated alternatively, the optimal capital/output ratio for that industry is 4. The capital/output ratio is the ratio of the value of the capital stock to the value of the output produced.

In equilibrium the optimal capital stock has been attained; *net* investment is zero and gross investment will be constant and equal to depreciation.

An Increase in Final Goods Demand

Suppose now that there is an increase in the demand for this industry's output. Its sales increase (through a reduction in its inventory). The

---

[1] Some businesses that are seasonal (such as those in resort and recreational areas) will in fact have much idle capital during the slow season. Still, even those businesses must be concerned with an optimal stock of capital. Too little or too much capital will generate less-than-minimum profits for those firms also.

Gross Private Domestic Investment Expenditures Are Highly Variable, and Procyclical

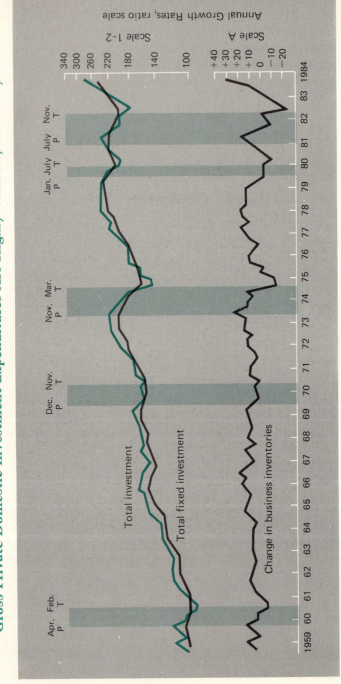

FIGURE 10.1. ANNUAL RATES OF GROSS PRIVATE DOMESTIC INVESTMENT EXPENDITURES AND ITS COMPONENTS, IN 1972 DOLLARS, UNITED STATES 1959–1983

A ratio (log) scale is on the vertical axis so the slope of each curve equals its growth rate. These graphs show that investment expenditures on both total fixed investment and on business inventories are highly volatile; moreover, total expenditures on investment are procyclical because expenditures on total fixed investment are procyclical. The shaded areas show recession periods (P = peak and T = trough). [From *Business Conditions Digest* (U.S. Department of Commerce, Bureau of Economic Analysis, June 1984), p. 42.]

previous capital stock will no longer be optimal for firms in that industry. Investment is necessary to expand each firm's capital stock and to produce the higher level of output required to meet higher sales. That is, both gross and net investment must rise.

If we assume that the *marginal* capital/output ratio is also 4, then every $1 increase in output will require a $4 expenditure on capital goods. Thus,

$$A = \frac{\Delta k}{\Delta y} = 4 \tag{10.2}$$

Assume for simplicity that the desired capital stock can be attained in one income period. In the next income period net investment is again zero, and gross investment again equals depreciation. Investment is now slightly higher because the newly added capital goods also depreciate.

This is an important conclusion because it implies that a once-and-for-all permanent increase in the demand for final goods leads to a one-time increase in net investment. If the amount of net investment is to remain constant, then annual sales must increase by a constant amount. Once the rate of increase of annual sales begins to slow down, the absolute level of net investment will decline.

This means that a once-and-for-all increase in the demand for final goods will lead to a large increase in the demand for capital goods in the first year, and then to a decrease in net investment and to a contraction in the output of the industries producing capital goods in the following year.

We want to stress that in this simple accelerator model, first developed by John Maurice Clark in 1917, the change in investment spending is due to the *change* in the desired level of output and is not related to a permanent *level* of desired output.[2] An increase in y results in a greater (accelerated) relative increase in gross investment. Hence the name **accelerator hypothesis.** Moreover, the greater the rate of change in the desired level of output, the greater the rate of change of investment expenditures.

Table 10.1 presents the simple accelerator model. It assumes an accelerator of 4 and a life of 10 years for the capital good in question. We start in equilibrium in time period one, so that the demand for *new* capital goods is zero and the total annual demand for capital is 40; with a total capital stock of 400 and a useful capital life of 10 years, the firm

---

[2] John M. Clark, "Business Acceleration and the Law of Demand: A Technical Factor in Economic Cycles," *Journal of Political Economy*, vol. 25 (March 1917), pp. 217–235. Note that although this theory was known to Keynes, he ignored it and instead stressed changes in business confidence as a determinant of investment.

TABLE 10.1. THE SIMPLE ACCELERATOR MODEL

Income Period	Annual Sales ($) Total Gross Output	Total Capital Stock	Annual Replace-ment	Annual Demand for New Capital i	Total Annual Demand for Capital
1	100	400	40	0	40
2[a]	110	440	40	40	80
3	110	440	44	0	44
4	110	440	44	0	44
5[b]	115.5	462	44	22	66
6	115.5	462	46.2	0	46.2
7	115.5	462	46.2	0	46.2

[a] A 10 percent increase in the demand for final output.

[b] A 5 percent increase in the demand for final output.

in question must purchase 40 machines per year to replace its depreciating capital stock. In the second period the demand for output rises by 10 percent to 110 and levels out until the fifth period, when it rises by 5 percent, to 115.5, and levels off at that quantity.

The table indicates that a once-and-for-all increase in the demand for output will increase the demand for *new* capital (net investment) only once. A *permanently* higher annual level of net investment requires that the demand for output continue to increase annually. For example, in Table 10.1 an annual net investment of 40 machines requires that output demand increase by 10 machines per year.

The conclusions reached here can be indicated more precisely, and we do so in the next section.

Relating Capital Goods Changes to Net Investment

A change in the capital stock is what we mean by net investment; therefore,

$$\Delta k = k - k_{-1} = i \tag{10.3}$$

WHERE $\quad k =$ the value of the existing capital stock
$k_{-1} =$ the value of the capital stock in the previous period
$i =$ the level of net investment

Substituting equation 10.3 into equation 10.2 yields:

$$A = \frac{k - k_{-1}}{\Delta y} \tag{10.4}$$

or

$$A = \frac{i}{\Delta y} \qquad (10.5)$$

Then

$$i = A(\Delta y) \qquad (10.6)$$

where A equals the accelerator, which is assumed to be equal to 4 in this example.

Equation 10.6 shows that the level of net investment equals some multiple (here, $A = 4$) of the *change* in output, and not of the level of output. It further indicates that the larger the change in desired output—given the level of output—the greater is the level of investment.

The simple accelerator model helps to explain:

1. The relationship between a change in the demand for a product and the demand for capital equipment required to produce the good.
2. Why the demand for capital goods is more volatile than the demand for final goods.
3. Why small changes in the demand for final goods cause large expansion (positive net investment for the economy) and then contraction (negative net investment for the economy) in the output of the capital goods industries.
4. Why investment goods expenditures are procyclical. If net investment is proportional to the *change* in output, then when the economy is expanding net investment expenditures rise, and when the economy is contracting net investment expenditures decline. Because investment expenditures are procyclical, they contribute to the instability of the aggregate expenditures (AE) curve and therefore to the instability of the private sector.[3]

Criticisms of the Simple Accelerator Theory

The simple accelerator model is not without its critics. The following are major criticisms of that model.

1. The model assumes full-capacity production in the industries producing consumer goods. To the extent that producers of consumer goods have excess capacity, an increase in demand generates less required capital expansion. Excess capacity, moreover, must exist in

---

[3] Gross investment expenditures are procyclical for similar reasons. Specific industries with especially long-lived capital assets are believed to be even more sensitive to output changes—they have higher accelerator values.

the capital goods industries if these industries are to supply the increased demand for capital goods. In short, a *full* accelerator effect requires, simultaneously, zero excess capacity in the consumer goods sector and much excess capacity in the capital goods sector!

2. The theory assumes a constant accelerator; the capital/output ratio is assumed to be determined by technological considerations. Clearly, if technology changes, the capital/output ratio changes. More importantly, we know from micro theory that a firm's optimal resource mix depends on the relative prices of inputs. Thus, if the price of capital changes relative to other inputs (labor, in particular), the capital/output ratio will change as firms substitute resources in order to produce a given output level most profitably. To the extent that inputs can substitute for each other, this ratio is a variable, and the model is less useful as a predictive device and as an instrument of policymakers. We return to this discussion later in this chapter.

3. The simple accelerator model does not distinguish between permanent changes in desired output levels (sales) and temporary changes. If current sales rise but this phenomenon is perceived as temporary, businesses will not react by increasing their purchases of capital by as much as they would if a sales increase were seen as permanent. Businesses (and policymakers), therefore, must have some means of deciding whether or not a change in the demand for final goods is temporary or permanent. To ignore this distinction is to assume, implicitly, that *all* changes in sales are perceived as permanent. That is unlikely, and in fact little empirical evidence exists to support the simple accelerator model in which a strong relationship exists between net investment and a multiple of last period's change in national output. We now turn to a discussion of more sophisticated accelerator models.

MORE SOPHISTICATED ACCELERATOR MODELS

Distinguishing Between Changes in Actual and Permanent Sales

One major problem with the simple accelerator model is that it does not distinguish between temporary and permanent changes in a firm's or an industry's output (sales). By borrowing from the adaptive expectations hypothesis discussed in the previous chapter, we can show how businesses, like households, can adapt to changes in sales when it is not known whether or not such changes are permanent.

If y^p represents expected permanent output for firms, then, following the adaptive expectations model,

$$y^p = y^p_{-1} + j\,(y_{-1} - y^p_{-1}) \qquad (10.7)$$

Equation 10.7 indicates that this period's expected permanent sales equal last period's expected permanent sales plus some fraction j of the difference between last period's actual sales y_{-1} and last year's expected permanent sales y^p_{-1}. If last year's expectations were fulfilled (i.e., if $y_{-1} - y^p_{-1} = 0$), then firms will not revise their estimate of permanent sales. If last year's sales exceeded expectations (i.e., $y_{-1} > y^p_{-1}$), then permanent sales will be revised upward by a fraction j of the difference. If last year's sales were less than expected, the estimate of permanent sales will be revised downward by the same fraction of the difference. The fraction j will presumably depend on whether the industry in question is a mature (stable) industry or one that is growing or declining. (This is analogous to the permanent income model in the previous chapter, where we indicated that individual households have different z's, and the differences depend on whether their incomes are stable or variable.)

Equation 10.7 can be rearranged so that

$$y^p = jy_{-1} + (1 - j)y^p_{-1} \tag{10.8}$$

This equation shows that permanent expected output (or sales) is a weighted average of last year's actual sales and last year's expected sales.

Let $k^\star$ represent the desired (indicated by the asterisk) capital stock. We can now write the accelerator model as

$$k^\star = Ay^p \tag{10.9}$$

which says that the desired capital stock equals the capital/output ratio (A, the accelerator) times permanent expected output. Recalling equation 10.3,

$$\Delta k = k - k_{-1} = i$$

we can also note that

$$i^\star = k^\star - K^\star_{-1} \tag{10.10}$$

If

$$k^\star = k^\star_{-1} = k - k_{-1} \tag{10.11}$$

then

$$i^\star = i \tag{10.12}$$

Note that $k - k_{-1}$ is the *actual* change in the capital stock. If the actual change equals the desired change in the capital stock—if the entire desired change can be accomplished in one period—then the desired net investment level equals the actual net investment level in one period.

Using equation 10.9, equation 10.10 can be written as

$$i^* = i = Ay^p - Ay^p_{-1} \tag{10.13}$$

or

$$i = A(\Delta y^p) \tag{10.14}$$

Equation 10.14 should be contrasted with equation 10.6. Equation 10.14 indicates that the level of current net investment equals the capital/output ratio A times the change in *permanent expected income or sales*. Equation 10.6 maintains that current net investment level depends on *actual* income or sales.

The more sophisticated accelerator model embodied in equation 10.14 suggests that the economy is somewhat more stable than it is if the economy is characterized by equation 10.6. This is because actual changes in output or sales are typically greater than permanent changes in output or sales. We can draw an analogy here:

> *The simple accelerator model of equation 10.6 is similar to Keynes's consumption function, which states that current consumption is dependent on current income. The more sophisticated accelerator model embodied in equation 10.14 is similar to Friedman's permanent income hypothesis adjusted for adaptive expectations.*

We can extend the analogy to the permanent income hypothesis even further. If A is constant in equation 10.14, then *expenditures* for capital will be more volatile than changes in the *services* (hours of use) from the capital stock—just as expenditures on consumer durable goods were more volatile than the consumption of the services of durable goods.[4]

If current sales rise, the level of net investment depends only on the extent to which the increase is expected to be permanent. Still, the expected *permanent* increase will lead to a net investment level equal to a multiple of the expected permanent increase. In short, net investment expenditures are *still* volatile, although not so volatile as the simple accelerator model implies.

---

[4] Another analogy between household expenditures and business expenditures provided by the permanent income hypothesis is: businesses and households time their replacement of capital goods to coincide with boom times. See Martin S. Feldstein and David Foot, "The Other Half of Gross Investment: Replacement and Modernization Expenditures," *The Review of Economics and Statistics*, vol. 53, no. 1 (February 1971), pp. 49–58.

An example of a more sophisticated accelerator model is indicated in Table 10.2. Note how the desired capital stock approaches 440 and annual net investment approaches zero.

The Flexible Accelerator

One major problem with both the simple accelerator model and the more sophisticated accelerator model just presented is that they assume (as in equation 10.11) *that firms can actually attain the desired change in the capital stock in one period.* This seems unlikely; certainly, all firms cannot do so at all times. It takes time to complete investment projects, so it is possible that there are physical limitations to the economy's ability to attain its desired capital stock change in one, or even several, years. There are economic reasons that suggest a time lag in investment, too; even if an investment project could be speeded up, the *cost* of doing so may make the game not worth the candle. The **flexible accelerator hypothesis** explicitly takes into account the fact that there may be time lags between increases in expected permanent output and net investment and that more traditional economic variables are determinants of investment spending. One such model[5] maintains

$$ k = k_{-1} + a(\text{k}^\star - k_{-1}) \qquad (10.15) $$

where $0 < a < 1$.

Equation 10.15 says that the actual capital stock at the *end* of the current period equals last year's capital stock plus some fraction a of the difference between the desired capital stock and last period's capital stock. In other words, firms can only realize a fraction of the desired change in their capital stock during any period of time; time lags exist for investment projects.[6]

Assume that $a = 0.4$ in equation 10.15. If a change in permanent expected output elicits a $100,000 increase in capital equipment expenditure, then only $40,000 will be purchased in the first year; $24,000 [or 0.4 ($100,000 − $40,000)] in the second year, and so on.[7]

---

[5] L. M. Koyck, *Distributed Lags and Investment Analysis* (Amsterdam: North Holland, 1954).

[6] Note that $a = 1$ in the nonflexible accelerator models discussed previously; i.e., firms can acquire 100 percent of their desired capital stock change in a single period of time.

[7] Of course, such a formulation means that the goal will never *actually* be reached; the $100,000 (in real terms) total investment expenditures can only be approached asymptotically.

TABLE 10.2. A MORE SOPHISTICATED ACCELERATOR MODEL

Income Period	Annual Final Goods Output	Expected[a] Permanent Output y^p	Desired Capital Stock[b]	Net[c] investment Level i
1	100	100.00	400	0
2[b]	110	100.00	400	0
3	110	105.00	420	20
4	110	107.50	430	10
5	110	108.75	435	5

[a] From equation 10.8, or $y^p = jy_{-1} + (1-j)y^p_{-1}$. We assume that $j = 0.5$.

[b] Assuming $A = 4$, then desired capital stock $= 4y^p$.

[c] $i = k^* - k_{-1}$, from equation 10.10.

[d] An increase in the demand for output of 10 percent.

Substituting equation 10.9 into equation 10.15 yields

$$k = k_{-1} + a(Ay^p - k_{-1}) \tag{10.16}$$

which says that the capital stock at the end of this period will equal last year's stock plus a fraction of the difference between the capital/output ratio times the permanent expected output (the desired capital stock) and last year's capital stock.

Rearranging equation 10.16 and recalling equation 10.3 gives

$$i = k - k_{-1} = a(Ay^p - k_{-1}) \tag{10.17}$$

This implies that the larger the gap between the desired capital stock and the actual capital stock, the greater is net investment. It also indicates that actual current net investment depends on:

1. a, a proxy for the speed at which firms are able, or are willing, to adjust their capital stock to desired levels.
2. A, or the capital/output ratio. If A is thought of as a *desired* ratio, rather than a mechanical relationship between output and the capital stock "needed" to produce that output, then the flexible accelerator model can be synthesized with Keynes's investment model and neoclassical investment models. (We do so later in this chapter.)
3. y^p, or the permanent expected sales or output, which is formed by an adaptive expectations process.
4. k_{-1}, last year's capital stock.

The flexible accelerator model suggests, therefore, that a change in any of these variables can affect current net investment.[8] It is thus more comprehensive and more theoretically appealing.

Determinants of the Capital/Output Ratio

If we treat A, the **capital/output ratio,** as a desired value rather than as a technological necessity, we will be back in the mainstream of neoclassical and Keynesian analysis. After all, inputs can be substituted for each other; therefore, the optimal capital/output ratio depends on the price of capital relative to the prices of other inputs.

As the neoclassical and Keynesian investment models suggest, businesses acquire capital assets only with the expectation of profit. In particular, a new investment project will be carried out only if the marginal efficiency of capital is at least equal to the interest rate. Modern economists have changed the terminology. Today we say that capital will be purchased only if the **marginal product of capital (MPK)** is at least equal to the real **user cost of capital.**

The MPK is the ratio of the value of the additional output (resulting from the addition of capital) to the cost of the capital. The MPK, therefore, is a percentage. The real user cost of capital is the cost to the firm of using a specific unit of capital over a specific period, and it is equal to the sum of the interest rate and the actual rate of depreciation of the capital; the user cost, too, is a percentage.

If the MPK exceeds the user cost, capital will be purchased; businesses will purchase capital up to the quantity at which the MPK equals the user cost.

Clearly, if the MPK rises relative to user cost, firms will substitute capital for other inputs and the desired capital/output ratio will rise; if the MPK falls relative to the user cost, the capital/output ratio will fall as firms substitute noncapital inputs for capital.

The MPK of a specific capital good is increased when (other things constant) the marginal physical product of capital rises—resulting from, say, an improvement in technology or an increase in the relative price of the specific final consumer good.

The user cost of capital falls if the real interest rate falls, if taxes on business income fall relative to labor income taxes, or if depreciation allowances for tax purposes are increased.

Equation 10.17 indicates that a given percentage change in the desired capital/output ratio A is just as important as that same percentage

---

[8] Gross investment depends on these variables plus the true rate of depreciation or obsolescence.

change in expected permanent output y^p, with respect to investment changes. This implies that a variable capital/output ratio adds an additional source of instability to investment expenditures and therefore to the instability of the AE curve and to the private economy.

Empirical Investigations

Numerous empirical studies have attempted to unearth the determinants of gross and net investment expenditures. An early review of such studies by Dale Jorgenson[9] of Harvard University concluded that net investment is in fact related to such variables as a constant times national output, the after-tax user cost of capital, and the previous period's capital stock. By allowing for a lagged response of capital expenditure to income changes, moreover, the predictive power of investment models can be improved. The evidence shows that a change in output affects net investment expenditures most strongly after a two-year lag; the impact in the first year is less than in the second, and the impact in the first two years is stronger than in subsequent periods.

A study by Peter K. Clark concluded that "output is clearly the primary determinant of nonresidential fixed investment" and that (in the short run, at least) "the effect of moderate variations in taxes and interest rates is likely to be negligible. . . ."[10] His study supports a "sophisticated" accelerator model, which takes into account what we have referred to as permanent output or sales. Surprisingly, other studies also show only weak support for the user cost of capital as a determinant of investment spending, and that the inclusion of user cost variables does not improve upon accelerator models.

A more recent study by Ben S. Bernanke of Stanford University, however, supports the contention that user costs are, in fact, important determinants of the short-run demand for capital. He points out that since 1979 real interest rates have been relatively high and that "it is plausible to conclude that high real interest rates are a major source of the recent sluggishness in capital expenditure."[11] As a consequence, the two recent recessions (see Figure 10.1 for the dates) can be thought of as

[9] Dale W. Jorgenson, "Econometric Studies of Investment Behavior: A Survey," *Journal of Economic Literature*, vol. 9 (December 1971).

[10] Peter K. Clark, "Investment in the 1970s: Theory, Performance, and Prediction," *Brookings Papers on Economic Activity*, 1979:1 (Washington, D.C.: The Brookings Institution, 1979).

[11] Ben S. Bernanke, "The Determinants of Investment: Another Look," *American Economic Review*, Papers and Proceedings, vol. 73, no. 2 (May 1983), p. 71.

a cause—and not a result—of the low demand for capital goods. Bernanke concludes that

> the marginal revenue product of capital, as in earlier studies, is seen to be important (at least for equipment). However, real interest rates, acting both through the cost of capital and the discount factor for future returns, are also a powerful influence.[12]

We conclude that both (1) the neoclassical model, which stresses more traditional variables such as real interest rates and after-tax earnings, and (2) an accelerator model that emphasizes permanent expected output as a variable, contribute to an understanding of investment expenditures and to a model's predictive ability. In other words, the flexible accelerator hypothesis model, which is a combination of these two models, seems to provide the best explanation for investment spending.

---

[12] Ibid., p. 74.

POLICY CONTROVERSY
Does the Multiplier-Accelerator Interaction Make Investment Expenditures Unstable?

Paul Samuelson analyzed the relationship between the multiplier effect (discussed in Chapter 6) and the accelerator effect (discussed in this chapter).[13] In particular, he presented a mathematical model that indicates period-by-period values of (1) current governmental expenditures financed by deficit spending; (2) current consumption induced by previous expenditure, based on various assumptions for the marginal propensity to consume; (3) current investment induced by changes in consumption, assuming various values

for an accelerator; and (4) total national income resulting from these values, other things constant.

Table 10.3 is adapted from several tables in Samuelson's original article. Combinations of various marginal propensities to consume MPC b and accelerators A are used to calculate the period-by-period values of national income, given a $1 *per period* government expenditure financed by deficit spending.

The second column in Table 10.3 shows the results of a $1 permanent (annual) increase in government expenditures g, given a marginal propensity to consume of 0.5 and an accelerator of zero. The result is that the national income will approach asymptotically the value

---

[13] Paul A. Samuelson, "Interactions Between the Multiplier Analysis and the Principle of Acceleration," *Review of Economic Statistics*, vol. 21 (May 1939), pp. 75–78.

TABLE 10.3. VALUES OF NATIONAL INCOME FOR A $1 INCREASE IN GOVERNMENT EXPENDITURES PER PERIOD, FOR VARIOUS COMBINATIONS OF THE MPC b AND THE ACCELERATOR A

Time Period	$b = 0.5$ $A = 0$	$b = 0.5$ $A = 1$	$b = 0.5$ $A = 2$	$b = 0.6$ $A = 2$	$b = 0.8$ $A = 4$
1	1.00	1.00	1.00	1.00	1.00
2	1.50	2.00	2.50	2.80	5.00
3	1.75	2.50	3.75	4.84	17.80
4	1.875	2.50	4.125	6.352	56.20
5	1.9375	2.25	3.4375	6.6256	169.84
6	1.9688	2.00	2.0313	5.3037	500.52
7	1.9844	1.875	.9141	2.5959	1,459.592
8	1.9922	1.875	−.1172	−.6918	4,227.704
9	1.9961	1.9375	.2148	−3.3603	12,241.1216
10					

$1/(1 - b)$ per $1 increase in g, where b is the marginal propensity to consume. This, of course, is consistent with the traditional multiplier analysis.

Columns 3 and 4 indicate that for an MPC of 0.5 and for small values of the accelerator (1 and 2, respectively), the national income will result in damped oscillatory movements around the value $1/(1 - b)$ per $1 increase in g. (In that table, $g = 1 per time period.) For example, consider column 3, where MPC = 0.5 and $A = 1$. National income oscillates; it rises above and falls below $2, with the oscillations getting smaller through time.

Column 5 shows that for an MPC of 0.6 and an accelerator of 2, a constant (here $1) level of government expenditures will result in explosive, ever-increasing oscillations around the value $1/(1 - b)$.

Column 6 shows that for an MPC of 0.8 and an accelerator of 4, a constant level of government expenditures will re-

sult in ever-increasing national income. A constant reduction in the level of governmental expenditures will result in ever-decreasing national income.

In general, we can conclude (from the mathematical implications of Samuelson's models) that the higher the accelerator value and the higher the marginal propensity to consume, the more unstable is the economy. As b and A rise, the oscillations around the multiplier value increase; at very high values of b and A, national income rises (or falls) exponentially as g rises (or falls). The policy implication is that the higher the values of b and A, the more necessary is stabilization policy. However, because the evidence is mixed regarding the magnitude of *both* the accelerator effect and the multiplier effect, the multiplier-accelerator *interaction* effect remains controversial, and it cannot be used to justify an activist stabilization policy.

CHAPTER SUMMARY

1. In a stable, mature industry, firms will establish an optimal capital/output ratio that (usually) exceeds the number 1. Net investment will be zero and gross investment will equal depreciation, and the optimal capital stock will be maintained.

2. If firms maintain a fixed capital/output ratio, or accelerator, then increases in output require capital expenditures. Changes in sales and output, therefore, lead initially to even greater net investment purchases because the capital/output ratio exceeds 1. When the new, permanently higher desired capital stock level is reached, net investment returns to zero.

3. The simple accelerator model explains (a) the relationship between a change in the demand for final goods and a change in the demand for capital goods used to produce final goods; (b) why the demand for capital goods is more volatile than the demand for consumer goods; (c) why small changes in the demand for consumer goods cause a large change in the demand for capital goods; and (d) why investment goods expenditures are procyclical.

4. Criticisms of the simple accelerator model include the following: (a) A full accelerator effect requires that the producers of final goods have zero excess capacity and that producers of capital goods have much excess capacity; (b) the capital/output ratio is not a technological constant but varies with the relative price of capital because other inputs can be substituted for capital; and (c) it does not sufficiently distinguish between increased (or decreased) sales that are expected to be permanent and those that are expected to be temporary.

5. A more sophisticated accelerator model uses an adaptive expectations model to help distinguish between the effects of permanent and temporary changes in sales. If businesses do not know whether or not a change in sales is permanent, they will adjust gradually. The more sophisticated accelerator theory suggests that the economy is more stable than it would be if it were characterized by the simple accelerator model, but it still suggests that investment expenditures are volatile.

6. The flexible accelerator model assumes an adjustment period between a change in the demand for final goods and a change in the capital stock. It incorporates the distinction between permanent and temporary changes in sales and emphasizes that the capital/output ratio is not constant; investment expenditures depend, moreover, on such user cost variables as the real interest rate and the annual percentage depreciation rate on capital goods.

7. The capital/output ratio depends on the price of capital relative to other inputs that can be substituted for capital in the production process. The marginal product of capital is compared to the user cost of capital in order to determine the optimal quantity of capital to use. If the marginal product of capital rises relative to the user cost of capital, the capital/output ratio will rise.

8. Until quite recently, empirical evidence suggested that in the short run the simple accelerator model explained investment spending better than user cost variables suggested by traditional theory. Recent evidence suggests that the real interest rate is indeed an important determinant of net investment; and the two recent recessions can be thought of as being largely induced by relatively high real interest rates. Recent evidence indicates that the flexible accelerator model, which is a combination of both models, seems to provide the best explanation for investment spending.

9. For relatively small values of the marginal propensity to consume and of the accelerator, multiplier-accelerator analysis indicates a "business cycle–type" oscillation around the value $\Delta g\,[1/(1-b)]$.

10. If the marginal propensity to consume and the accelerator are large, multiplier-accelerator analysis indicates a highly unstable economy.

GLOSSARY

accelerator hypothesis   The theory that net investment expenditures depend on the *change* in output because firms maintain a fixed capital/output ratio.

capital/output ratio   The ratio of the value of the capital stock to the value of output produced; also called the *accelerator*.

flexible accelerator hypothesis   A theory that maintains that both the accelerator hypothesis—amended to emphasize permanent expected output—and user cost of capital variables are important determinants of net investment expenditures.

marginal product of capital (MPK)   The ratio of the value of the additional output (resulting from the addition of capital) to the cost of capital.

user cost of capital   The cost to a firm of using a specific unit of capital for some specified period; it includes the actual annual rate of depreciation and the real interest rate; it is influenced by the tax structure; and it is expressed as a percentage.

QUESTIONS AND PROBLEMS FOR REVIEW

10.1   Give your reasons for agreeing or disagreeing with the following statement: Even if the assumptions associated with the simple accelerator model are true for any firm, to the extent that changes in outputs for *all* firms sum to zero, the implications of the simple accelerator model are trivial for the economy in the aggregate. When is it likely that changes in outputs for all firms sum to zero?

10.2   Suppose that the optimal capital/output ratio is equal to 3. If output is expected to increase by $5 million, then net investment is expected to increase by how much? Is the increase in net investment then also expected to affect output because of the multiplier effect?

10.3   Suppose that firms establish an optimal capital/output ratio that exceeds the number 1, where net investment is zero and gross investment is equal to depreciation. If the demand for output for one firm increases and the demand for output for another firm decreases, does the simple accelerator model explain the aggregate effect?

10.4   If firms maintain a fixed capital/output ratio, then increases in output require multiple changes in net investment. Would you expect that the time rate of change in capital expenditure would be dependent on the rate of interest?

10.5   If there is no excess capacity in the capital goods sectors, explain what effects would be expected for prices of final goods, rates of interest, and the distribution of employment if there were an increase in the demand for final goods output.

10.6   The simple accelerator model is considered to explain why investment goods expenditures are procyclical. Does the simple accelerator model explain why investment goods expenditures are more or less procyclical, depending on the *stage* of the business cycle?

10.7   What implications do the assumptions of an adaptive expectations model, with respect to adjustment periods between a change in the demand for final goods and a change in the capital stock, have for the stability of the economy?

10.8   If the marginal product of capital rises relative to the user cost of capital, the capital/output ratio is expected to rise. What would be the effect on wage rates and unemployment?

10.9   One criticism of the simple accelerator model is that a full multiplier effect requires zero excess capacity for final goods producers and significant excess capacity for capital goods producers. What rationale is given for such conditions to be expected? Does that rationale involve differences in abilities to perceive what is going on?

10.10 Describe the recent empirical evidence which suggests that the real rate of interest is important in the determination of the level of net investment. What policy implications are suggested as a result of this evidence?

REFERENCES

Gardner Ackley, *Macroeconomics: Theory and Policy* (New York: Macmillan, 1978).

Ben S. Bernanke, "The Determinants of Investment: Another Look," *American Economic Review*, Papers and Proceedings, vol. 73 (1983).

John M. Clark, "Business Acceleration and the Law of Demand: A Technical Factor in Economic Cycles," *Journal of Political Economy*, vol. 25 (1917).

Peter K. Clark, "Investment in the 1970s: Theory, Performance, and Prediction," *Brookings Papers on Economic Activity*, 1979:1 (Washington, D.C.: The Brookings Institution, 1979).

Martin S. Feldstein and David Foot, "The Other Half of Gross Investment: Replacement and Modernization Expenditures," *Review of Economics and Statistics*, vol. 53 (1971).

Dale W. Jorgenson, "Econometric Studies of Investment Behavior: A Survey," *Journal of Economic Literature*, vol. 9 (December 1971).

John Maynard Keynes, *The General Theory of Employment, Interest, and Money* (New York: Harcourt Brace Jovanovich, 1964).

L. M. Koyck, *Distributed Lags and Investment Analysis* (Amsterdam: North Holland, 1954).

Paul A. Samuelson, "Interactions Between the Multiplier Analysis and the Principle of Acceleration," *Review of Economic Statistics, vol. 21 (1939).*

11

THE DEMAND FOR MONEY

STABLE OR UNSTABLE?

n Chapter 9 we examined the consumption function, and in Chapter 10 we analyzed the investment function; in each case our concern was with the stability or instability of these functions. Stated alternatively, Chapters 9 and 10 were concerned with stability (i.e., the frequency and magnitude of shifts) in the *is* curve.

In this chapter we are concerned with the demand for money function and, therefore, with the stability of the *lm* curve. In Chapter 16 we examine the *relative* stability of the *is* and *lm* curves, and there we show that the way monetary policy should be conducted depends on which of those curves is relatively more stable.

In this chapter we first present the official definitions of money and then trace the evolution of the theory of the demand for money from classical to modern times. In particular, we show how, through time, more potential determinants of the quantity of money demanded have been added to the theoretical money demand curve. It is important to see how each of these potential determinants is related to the quantity of money demanded (i.e., inversely or directly) and how sensitive changes in the quantity of money demanded are to changes in these determinants (i.e., the elasticity of the demand for money with respect to these determinants).

It is also important to estimate the *stability* of these relationships. For example, even if the demand for money were relatively interest rate–inelastic and if monetary policy could affect the market interest rate, if the relationship between the interest rate and the quantity of money demanded were unstable it would still be difficult to use monetary policy to achieve economic goals. Stated in terms of Chapter 7, even if the Keynesian liquidity preference curve were not perfectly elastic, a *shifting* liquidity preference curve would make it difficult for policymakers to determine by how much the money supply should be changed in order to meet policy objectives.

Because the elasticity of specific determinants of the demand for money and the stability of these relationships is important, we conclude this chapter with a survey of the empirical studies of the demand for money.

WHY IT IS IMPORTANT TO DEFINE MONEY AND MEASURE THE MONEY SUPPLY

Because changes in the total money supply and the growth rate of money affect important economic variables, they can also affect the attainment of ultimate national economic goals. High employment, price stability, economic growth, and an equilibrium in international payments are all, directly or indirectly, related to changes in the total supply of money and to changes in the growth of money. The optimal quantity and optimal growth of money, therefore, are those magnitudes which enable the nation to achieve these goals. Later chapters indicate how elusive these concepts of an "optimal" quantity and the "optimal" growth rate of money actually are.

Monetary policy—changing the supply of money by the Fed in order to achieve national economic goals—requires a meaningful definition of the money supply. In particular, monetary policy requires the following:[1]

1. A close correspondence must exist between the *theoretical* definition of money and the *empirical* (or measurable) definition of money, because the real world doesn't allow the perfect measurement of theoretical constructs.

2. The Fed must be able to control the empirically defined money supply and to meet the targets that it sets for the money supply with the tools at its disposal. The Fed cannot achieve ultimate national goals directly; what it *can* do is use its powers to alter some money-like variables. The problem of setting monetary targets (or goals for the growth rate of money) is discussed in Chapter 16; the tools that the Fed can use to alter the money supply are also analyzed in Chapter 16.

3. The empirical definition of money must be closely and predictably related to ultimate national goals. It is not very useful to the nation if the Fed achieves its monetary growth rate targets unless such an achievement alters economic variables in a desired direction.

In short, a successful monetary policy requires that the Fed properly measure the money supply and effectively control its growth rate. We concentrate on money measurement now and leave the problem of money control to a later chapter.

There is honest disagreement over the proper *definition* of money and the "best" *measure* of the money supply. The two basic approaches to measuring the money supply are the transactions approach, which stresses the role of money as a *medium of exchange,* and the portfolio, or liquidity, approach, which stresses the role of money as a temporary *store of value.*

---

[1] See Bryan Higgins and Jon Faust, "NOWs and Super NOWs: Implications for Defining and Measuring Money," *Economic Review* (a publication of the Federal Reserve Bank of Kansas City), vol. 68, no. 1 (January 1983), pp. 3–18, for an excellent discussion of the main topics in this section.

The Transactions Approach

The **transactions approach** to measuring money emphasizes money's function as a medium of exchange. Proponents of this approach claim that the essence of money is that it (and only it) is accepted as a means of payment for other goods and services. They stress that this is the important difference between money and other assets. All assets serve as a store of value; only a few are accepted as a medium of exchange.

Given this theoretical preference for the definition of money, the transactions approach suggests the following rule:

Only an asset that serves as a medium of exchange should be included in the empirical measurement of the money supply.

Such assets would include the coins and paper currency that circulate and are generally accepted as a means of payment. Also included would be transactions accounts upon which checks may be written.

Regarding the second criterion for monetary policy, proponents of the transactions approach assert that the Fed *can* control the supply of money that is used to make transactions. Many economists (some dating back to the nineteenth century) believe that money thus defined has a reliable and predictable relationship to national economic goals. Households and businesses hold money in order to finance anticipated (and regular) expenditures in the near future; people hold money to spend. This transactions motive for holding money is not to be confused with money held in order to finance an uncertain amount of expenditures at some unknown future time. This latter reason for holding money to meet emergencies is referred to as the precautionary motive (discussed in Chapters 5 and 7). Economists typically lump the two motives together because in practice they are difficult to differentiate.

Traditionally, assets held in such forms (coins, currency, transactions accounts) have not earned interest and therefore have been subject to the opportunity cost of forgone interest. For this reason, people can be expected to minimize the amount of money they hold as a medium of exchange. If the total money supply were to increase (as a result of monetary authorities' actions or new discoveries of those metals used as money), then the community would be expected to increase its spending. In turn, this increase in spending might well increase national output, national income, employment, and the price level. A decrease in the money supply would lead to a predictable reduction in community spending, with predictable effects on the variables associated with national economic goals. The transactions approach has been adapted by "monetarists," who are discussed in Chapter 18. A warning: *We have assumed other things constant, i.e., that money supply changes have not been exactly offset by money demand changes.* Stated alternatively, we are analyzing changes in the supply of money relative to the demand for money when we change the supply of money and hold other things constant.

The Portfolio, or Liquidity, Approach

The **portfolio approach** was pioneered by J. R. Hicks and James Tobin (whose work we analyze later in this chapter). In this approach, each person in the community selects some desirable asset portfolio (composition) consisting of money, financial assets, and nonfinancial assets; money is the most liquid of all the assets in the portfolio. The community is in equilibrium when no one has an incentive to rearrange his or her portfolio. Of course, these assets have different degrees of liquidity (and therefore risk), and people have different feelings about how much risk they wish to assume. Other things being constant, the higher the risk associated with a financial asset, the greater must be the expected rate of return before people will hold that asset voluntarily. In equilibrium, each individual is satisfied with his or her particular portfolio; however, portfolios differ among individuals according to their diverse desires for liquidity and their disparate expectations concerning future events.

If the Fed changes the supply of money (other things constant), the community's equilibrium is disturbed. An increase in the money supply means (immediately) that the community is now more liquid than it wants to be. It is reasonable to assume that this increase in liquidity—an increase in the proportion of the public's portfolio held in money—will cause further portfolio adjustments until a new equilibrium is established. The community might now be inclined to hold assets that are less liquid. If it purchases financial assets with its newfound liquidity, a series of events ensues which causes market interest rates to fall. This leads to increases in investment and to increases in household expenditures on durable consumer goods. If the community spends its excess liquidity on nonfinancial assets, community spending will increase directly. In either case, national income, employment, national output, and the price level may increase. One can imagine that the results would be precisely the opposite were the Fed to reduce the community's liquidity (lower its ratio of money to total assets) by reducing the money supply. A warning: Once again we have analyzed changes in the money supply holding other things constant. If money supply increases also lead to offsetting increases in the *demand* for liquidity, then our conclusions are invalid.

Using a liquidity definition of money and a portfolio adjustment approach to explain the role of money in the economy leads one to broaden the definition of money beyond the transactions approach. The liquidity approach includes in the measurement of money those assets that are highly liquid (i.e., those assets that can be converted into money quickly, without loss of nominal dollar value and without much cost). In general, any asset that guarantees to the holder a fixed nominal dollar value in the future is a candidate for inclusion in the liquidity measure of money. Another way to say this is that any asset for which no nominal capital gain or loss is possible qualifies as a perfectly liquid asset and is therefore money. Those assets for which only slight capital gains or losses are possible are highly liquid and are called **near monies.** As will be seen shortly, it is not clear where the dividing line between money and near money should be.

HOW THE FED MEASURES THE MONEY SUPPLY

The Fed uses both the transactions approach and the portfolio or liquidity approach when it measures the money supply. Each approach is discussed in turn.

M1: The Transactions Approach

Consider Table 11.1; it shows what specifically is included in using the transactions approach and the specific components of **M1** (as of June 1985). The $165.2 billion figure in the table represents the value of coins and paper currency outside the U.S. Treasury, the Federal Reserve banks, and the vaults of commercial banks. The paper currency consists of $1, $2, $5, $10, $20, $50, and $100 denominations; $500, $1000, $5000, and $10,000 bills were all discontinued in 1945. If high inflation rates return, we might see them again.

Currency **Currency** consists of the following:
   Coins Minted by the U.S. Treasury Coins are credit money because the value of the metal in each coin is normally less than the face value of the coin. From time to time, the market value of the metal used in coins has risen so high that the coins have disappeared from circulation. Individuals have held the coins or melted them down and sold the metal, in spite of the fact that this practice was and is still illegal.
   Federal Reserve Notes Issued by the Federal Reserve Banks and U.S.
   Notes Issued by the U.S. Treasury Until 1960 all $1 bills were issued by the Treasury and were called silver certificates. There are several hundred million dollars' worth of silver certificates still in circulation. The remainder of the paper bills in circulation are Federal

TABLE 11.1. THE FED'S MEASURE OF MONEY AS A MEDIUM OF EXCHANGE: M1, JUNE 1985

M1 Component	Amount (billions)
Currency	$165.2
Transactions accounts	
Demand deposits	259.8
Other checkable deposits	161.3
Traveler's checks	6.0
Total M1	$592.3

Reserve notes. Federal Reserve notes are printed by the Bureau of Engraving and Printing under contract to, and issued by, the various Federal Reserve banks.

Both on a per capita basis and as a percentage of M1, currency has increased in significance in the United States. In 1973, for example, the amount of currency in circulation per capita was about $325. In 1985 it had risen to about $688. As a percentage of M1, it has risen from 20.5 percent at the end of 1960 to about 28 percent at the end of 1985.

We are not sure why there has been such a large expansion of the use of currency in the 1970s and 1980s; perhaps one major reason is the increased size of the underground economy, which was discussed in Chapter 2.

Transactions Accounts Transactions accounts include demand deposits at commercial banks and other checkable deposits (OCD's).

Demand Deposits in Commercial Banks Money-and-banking texts used to emphasize the distinction between commercial and all other depository institutions. The distinction was at one time crucial because commercial banks were defined as the only type of financial (depository) institution allowed by law to accept demand deposits (checking accounts). This was a reasonable definition until 1981; such is not the case today, however. Demand deposits at commercial banks nevertheless remain the largest component of the M1 money supply.

The term **demand deposit** is used because such a deposit can be converted to currency on demand (immediately) or used to make a payment to a third party. The checking account deposit does not, however, have legal-tender status.[2] Nonetheless, demand deposits are clearly a

---

[2] *Legal-tender status* refers to something that, when offered in payment for a debt, must be accepted—as mandated by law.

medium of exchange in this economy. The physical check itself is not money—it is the account balance that is money. That is why one refers to demand deposits, or transaction account balances, rather than to checks as a part of the money supply.

Other Checkable Deposits   Of growing importance in all definitions of the money supply are other checkable deposits in commercial banks and thrift institutions. These consist of the following:

1. *Negotiable Orders of Withdrawal (NOW) Accounts*   These are interest-bearing savings accounts on which checks may be written, and they are issued by thrift institutions. Until 1981, **NOW accounts** were authorized only in New England, New York, and New Jersey. Since 1981, all states have allowed NOW accounts or their equivalent. Business corporations are not permitted to have NOW accounts.

2. *Super-NOW Accounts*   As of July 5, 1983, thrift institutions were allowed to offer **Super-NOW accounts** which allow unlimited checking. They require a minimum deposit of $2500 and there are no interest rate ceilings on these accounts.

3. *Automatic-Transfer-System (ATS) Accounts at Commercial Banks*   An **ATS account** is a combination of a savings account, on which interest is paid, and a regular checking account, on which no interest is paid. Usually, the account holder keeps a relatively small (or no) balance in the checking account but writes checks freely on this account. Whenever there is a negative balance in the checking account, an automatic transfer is made from the interest-earning savings account. In effect, the ATS account is the commercial banks' version of the NOW account, although commercial banks can now offer NOW's too. Both offer a way to earn interest on checking account funds, and both are prohibited to business corporations.

4. *Credit Union Share Draft (CUSD) Accounts*   Credit union members are usually allowed to write a type of check called a share draft on their profit-earning "shares" or deposits. A **CUSD account** is similar to a negotiable order of withdrawal.

5. *Demand Deposits at Mutual Savings Banks*   Mutual savings banks are nonprofit thrift institutions. Any profits remaining after operating expenses are paid are kept in a surplus account or distributed to depositors. Mutual savings banks offer savings accounts, time deposits, and NOW accounts, but only a few states allow mutual savings banks to offer demand deposits.

Traveler's Checks   These checks are paid for by the purchaser at the time of transfer. The total quantity of traveler's checks outstanding, issued by institutions other than banks, is part of the M1 money supply.[3] American Express, Citibank, Thomas Cook, and other institutions issue traveler's checks.

M2: The Portfolio, or Liquidity, Approach

The narrowest definition of the money supply, M1, does not include the so-called near monies, which are slightly less-liquid assets than currency, transactions accounts, and traveler's checks. To the extent that an individual's willingness to spend depends on his or her total liquidity, the inclusion of near monies in the money supply provides a "better" definition of the money supply for the purpose of explaining changes in economic activity. This somewhat broader definition of the money supply is officially designated as M2 by the Fed and is outlined in Table 11.2. **M2** consists of M1 plus the following:

1. Savings and small-denomination time deposits at all depository institutions
2. Overnight repurchase agreements at commercial banks
3. Overnight Eurodollars held by U.S. residents (other than banks) at Caribbean branches of member banks
4. Balances in money market mutual funds
5. Money market deposit accounts

Savings Deposits   Savings deposits in all depository institutions (e.g., commercial banks, mutual savings banks, savings and loan associations, and credit unions) are part of the M2 money supply. A savings deposit is a type of **time deposit.** It is called a time deposit because, in principle, the owner of the deposit must give 14 days' notice prior to making a withdrawal. Savings deposits also include the money market deposit accounts (introduced on December 14, 1982) which allow limited checking privileges (six checks per month) and unceilinged interest rates. Savings deposits may be statement or passbook deposits.

   Statement Savings Deposits   A statement savings deposit is similar to a checking account because the owner (depositor) receives a monthly statement or record of deposits and withdrawals and the interest earned

---

[3] Banks place the funds that are to be used to redeem traveler's checks in a special deposit account, and they are therefore already counted as transactions accounts. Nonbank issuers, however, do not place these funds in transactions accounts. Improvements in data collection have made it possible to estimate the size of nonbank traveler's checks, and in June 1981 they were included in M1 for the first time.

TABLE 11.2. THE MEASURE OF MONEY AS A TEMPORARY STORE OF VALUE: M2, JUNE 1985

Components	Amount (billions)
M1	$ 592.3
Savings deposits	295.8
Small-denomination time deposits	883.6
Overnight RPs	50.3
Overnight Eurodollars	12.4
Money market mutual funds	175.4
Money market deposit accounts	475.2
Total[a]	$2476.9

[a] M2 is not equal to the sum of its components for a technical reason. See any H-6 Series, a Federal Reserve statistical release.

during the month. With the statement savings account, deposits and withdrawals can be made by mail.

Passbook Savings Accounts A passbook savings account requires that the owner physically present a paper passbook each time a deposit or withdrawal is made. The passbook is marked to record the deposits and withdrawals. In the United States, passbook savings deposits are more popular than statement savings deposits.

Small-Denomination Time Deposits Time deposits include savings certificates and small certificates of deposit. To be included in the M2 definition of the money supply, such time deposits must be less than $100,000—hence the name *small*-denomination time deposits. The owner of a savings certificate, or a certificate of deposit (CD), is given a receipt indicating the amount deposited, the interest rate to be paid, and the maturity date. A CD is an actual certificate that indicates the date of issue, its maturity date, and other relevant contractual matters.

A variety of small-denomination time deposits are available. They include six-month money market certificates, as well as floating-rate (varying with market rates) certificates of 2½ years' maturity or more.

Overnight Repurchase Agreements at Commercial Banks (REPO's, or RP's) A repurchase agreement may be made by a bank to sell Treasury or federal agency securities to its customers, coupled with an agreement to repurchase them at a price that includes accumulated interest. REPO's help to fill a gap because businesses are not allowed to use NOW accounts; REPO's can be thought of as a financial innovation that bypasses regulation. Because they pay interest on *overnight* deposits, REPO's allow businesses to earn interest on what are, in effect, transactions accounts, in much the same way that NOW accounts allow households to earn interest on transactions accounts.

Overnight Eurodollars Eurodollars are dollar-denominated deposits in foreign commercial banks and in foreign branches of U.S. banks. The phrase *dollar-denominated* simply means that, although the deposit might be held at (say) a Caribbean commercial bank, its value is stated in terms of U.S. dollars rather than in terms of the local currency. The term *Eurodollar* is inaccurate because banks outside continental Europe also participate in the Eurodollar market, and because banks in some countries issue deposits denominated in German marks, Swiss marks, British sterling, and Dutch guilders. Those deposits not denominated in U.S. dollars, of course, are not included in the U.S.'s M2 value.

Money Market Mutual Fund Balances Many individuals and institutions keep part of their assets in the form of shares in **money market mutual funds.**[4] These mutual funds invest only in short-term credit instruments. The majority of these money market funds allow depositors to write checks, provided that the size of the check exceeds some minimum, such as $250, $500, or $1000.

Money Market Deposit Accounts These are accounts issued by banks and thrift institutions. They have no minimum maturity, allow limited checking privileges, and pay an interest rate comparable to the money market mutual fund rate.

Other "official"—and broader—definitions of the money supply include M3 and *L*, and incorporate other assets that are less liquid but are potential substitutes for money.

What Is the "Best" Definition of the Money Supply?

Is there a "best" definition of the money supply? Is it M1, M2, M3, or *L*? No answer can be given to such an important question. It turns out that for different purposes, different definitions of the money supply are best. For example, if one wishes to know which money supply is most

---

[4] First introduced by Merrill Lynch in 1975, they are pools of funds contributed by investors. The institution, or "fund," invests the pooled money in such short-term instruments as Treasury bills, bank CD's, and commercial paper.

easily controlled by the Fed, it was widely believed (until only a few years ago) to be the narrowest definition, or M1. On the other hand, the money supply which seems to correlate best with economic activity is one of the broader definitions, M2 or M3—although the results are mixed. The appropriate definition depends on the question being asked. Also, the best definition will change as technology changes financial instruments and as practices of the financial sector of the economy change.

EVOLUTION OF THE THEORY OF THE DEMAND FOR MONEY[5]

Classical economists, in the main, stressed that money was a medium of exchange, and with this mindset they viewed money as something to *spend* rather than as an object that had properties making it desirable to *hold*. After all, a medium of exchange is something that is to be transferred, or circulated. If money is merely a medium of exchange, then, ideally, the demand for money to hold would approach zero and the velocity of money would approach infinity.

Irving Fisher, a classical economist (whom you will recall from Chapter 5), improved somewhat on the typical classical conception of the role of money in an economic system. He recognized that there were limitations on the velocity of money (why the demand for money did not approach zero) and even discussed why velocity changes—and he noted that short-run variations in the velocity of money can set the business cycle in motion. Still, by framing the equation of exchange in terms of velocity (i.e., the $MV \equiv Py$ approach), Fisher put economists on the wrong track and "analysis tended to center on statistical measures of the aggregate transactions velocity of money, rather than on cost and yield considerations affecting the money-holding choices of individual optimizers."[6] Fisher's foundation was even less useful than we first indicated; Fisher's equation of exchange identity was really

$$MV = PT$$

where V is not the *income* velocity of money, but rather the average number of time each unit of money turns over in financing *all transactions* (on intermediate goods and on purely financial transactions as well), and T is the total number of such transactions.

---

[5] This section is based largely on Thomas M. Humphrey, "Evolution of the Concept of the Demand for Money," reprinted in *Essays on Inflation*, 4th ed. (Federal Reserve Bank of Richmond, 1983), pp. 245–255.

[6] Ibid., p. 247.

The Cambridge Approach

A handful of neoclassical economists who taught at Cambridge University in Great Britain during the period 1917–1930 made significant advances in the theory of the demand for money:

1. They concentrated on the (national) income, or final goods, velocity of money instead of the transactions velocity of money; thus, Fisher's equation of exchange was transformed from $MV \equiv PT$ to $MV \equiv Py$. The Cambridge economists, therefore, shifted the emphasis from transactions to income, and this was the first step in viewing money as more than merely a medium of exchange.

2. They formulated the famous Cambridge k, or the ratio of desired money balances (M_d for this chapter) to the level of national income. As you will recall from Chapter 5, k is merely the reciprocal of the income velocity of money; but by formulating the equation of exchange as

$$M_d = kY$$

the Cambridge economists were led to think in terms of money as something to *hold*. Money became a utility-yielding asset, and economists were shifted to the right track:

The demand for money can be analyzed like the demand for any other good that yields services.

---

3. They distinguished between the supply of money M (believed to be exogenously determined) and the quantity demanded for money M_d. Thus, a determinate model was developed because there are three variables (M_d, M, and Py) and three equations:

$$M_d = kPy \qquad (11.1)$$

$$M = \overline{M} \qquad (11.2)$$

$$M_d = M \qquad (11.3)$$

Equation 11.1 is the demand for money, equation 11.2 is the constant money supply, and equation 11.3 is the equilibrium condition. Moreover, Py equals nominal national income and is an income constraint presented explicitly.

4. Their analysis is easily reformulated as a theory of the demand for

real money balances. By dividing both sides of equation 11.1 by *P*, we get

$$\frac{M_d}{P} = ky \qquad\qquad (11.4)$$

which indicates that the quantity of real balances demanded is a constant proportion of real national income. This, of course, is the quantity theory of money (see Chapter 5), which states that the demand for nominal money balances is proportional to nominal national income and that the demand for real money balances is proportional to real national income. The demand for real money balances, like the demand for other goods and services, is dependent on real, not nominal, values.

The Cambridge innovators, however, failed to see the full implications of their analysis. Instead, they followed tradition and emphasized that *k* (like velocity in the American version) was constant in the long run and that short-run changes in *k* led to business cycles. Like their American cousins, the Cambridge economists concentrated on the determinants of *k* which they believed to be related to the degree of development of the banking system and credit institutions, as well as to the "confidence" that households and businesses placed in the banking system and the economy.

Believing that *k* was constant in the long run led the classical economists to the conclusion that money supply changes might affect real variables in the short run, but that in the long run only the price level changes—in direct proportion to the change in the money supply. We are left, ultimately, with a theory that maintains that the quantity of nominal money demanded depends on the level of nominal income, or on the price level.

Keynes's Contribution

As Chapter 7 indicated, Keynes separated the demand for money *L* into (1) L_1 balances to satisfy transactions and precautionary motives, and (2) L_2 balances to satisfy the speculative motive, or the asset demand for money. Keynes's analysis of the speculative balances was an improvement over the Cambridge approach because it maintained that *bonds and money are substitutes for each other.* The demand for money, like the demand for other goods and services, depends on its opportunity cost; that is, there is a substitution effect as well as an income effect for money.

In the specific Keynesian formulation, you will recall, people compare the interest income forgone (from bonds) by holding money with the expected capital gain or loss from holding bonds. For example, people compare, say, $100 of interest they could earn by purchasing bonds for $1000 with the expected change in the price of bonds resulting from expected changes in the interest rate. If the price of the bond is expected to rise or to fall by less than $100, an individual will hold bonds; if the price of the bond is expected to fall by more than $100 (because the interest rate rises by such a large amount), then the bondholder will hold money.

By assuming (1) that people have a notion as to what the natural rate of interest is, (2) that different people have different notions about what the natural rate of interest is, and (3) that each person is uncertain as to the interest rate change will be, Keynes was able to show that each *individual* holds L_2 balances in either all money *or* all bonds. But the *community* will have a continuous L_2 curve, with the quantity of desired L_2 balances varying inversely with the interest rate. (See Chapter 7.) You will recall from Chapter 7 that James Tobin demonstrated that by assuming uncertain expectations about the future interest rate and assuming that most people are risk averse, both the community *and* the individual L_2 functions are negatively sloped with respect to the interest rate. That is, an individual (and the community) will hold a *mixed* portfolio of money and bonds.[7] Tobin demonstrated, therefore, that the demand for money as an asset varies inversely with changes in the opportunity cost of money, that is, on interest income from bonds. His approach also extends the portfolio approach first suggested by John R. Hicks, which we discuss in the next section.

Keynes's contribution, then, was to add another determinant of the quantity of money demanded: the current interest rate relative to the expected natural rate. By doing so, he forced theoreticians to consider the *cost* of holding money. Keynes's point of view was also different; he maintained that the demand for money was unstable because it was a function of the expected future interest rate, which varies with market conditions. Moreover, Keynes maintained that a liquidity trap existed; at some very low interest rate, bonds become so risky that holding money becomes a perfect substitute for holding bonds and the demand for money becomes infinitely elastic with respect to the interest rate. In the liquidity trap, which presumably exists in a depression, the demand for money becomes insatiable, and if the central bank increases the money supply, the public will merely hold it.

Both of these Keynesian assertions—an unstable demand for money and an infinitely interest-elastic demand for money—imply that mone-

---

[7] James Tobin, "Liquidity Preference as Behavior Towards Risk," *Review of Economic Studies,* vol. 25 (February 1958), pp. 65–86.

tary policy is difficult to use to attain national economic goals. Note, therefore, that as the theory of the demand for money changes, so do the policy implications.

Hicks's Contribution

John R. Hicks was an important founder of the portfolio approach (which interprets the demand for money as part of the choice of an optimum portfolio of assets) discussed earlier in this chapter. Hicks was the first to suggest, in 1935, that the demand for money be treated as an exercise in asset choice, in much the same way that the demand for any consumer durable would be derived.[8] Instead of treating money as a medium of exchange that is spent, Hicks suggested that the demand for money *to hold* depends on total wealth (the budget constraint) and on the expected rates of return on other assets (substitutes for money).

The demand for money, in Hicks's model, is constrained by wealth, not income, unlike the classical and Keynesian models.[9] Moreover, the expected rates of return on nonmoney assets represent the opportunity costs of holding money. Hicks's analysis is considered to be a fundamental advance in the theory of the demand for money because it treated the demand for money like the demand for any other good, and because it provided the foundation for future advances in the theory of the demand for money. He even provided the first step in analyzing the demand for *transactions* balances. According to Hicks, people compare the conversion costs (brokerage fees, opportunity cost of time, effort, and so on) of transferring cash into income-earning assets (and vice versa) to forgone interest earnings in order to decide their optimal money balances for transactions. Thus, even the transactions demand for money varies inversely with the interest rate. Hicks's influence on later developments in the theory of the demand for money will be apparent in the next few sections.

Friedman's Contribution

Milton Friedman, using Hicks's portfolio approach as a starting point, treats money like any other capital good that is desirable to hold because

---

[8] John R. Hicks, "A Suggestion for Simplifying the Theory of Money," *Economica*, vol. 2 (February 1935), pp. 1–19.

[9] The choice of wealth, not income, as a budget constraint on money holding is interesting and reflects the fact that Hicks was dealing with a *stock* variable: the quantity demanded for money to hold. The optimal stock of money to hold depends on a stock variable—wealth. For the classical economist and for Keynes, money was used to finance a *flow* of transactions or spending; hence, they naturally selected a flow variable—income—as a budget constraint.

it yields a flow of services.[10] Friedman also followed Hicks in assuming that wealth is the relevant constraint on the demand for money, but he substituted permanent income (discussed in Chapter 9) as a proxy for wealth.[11] His theory of the demand-for-money function, however, is more complete than the previous theories. Friedman believes that holding money yields a return in the form of intangible services that facilitate exchange and provide security for financial (and other) emergencies. The return on money is to be compared to returns on other assets. Unlike Keynes's portfolio approach, however, Friedman maintains that *many* assets, not just bonds, are potential substitutes for money.

Friedman's demand-for-real-money function is

$$\frac{M_d}{P} = f(r_b, r_e, \dot{p}, y_p, h, u) \tag{11.5}$$

WHERE P = price level

r_b = expected real rate of return on bonds

r_e = expected real rate of return on equities

$\dot{p}$ = expected percentage rate of change of price level, or expected inflation rate

y_p = permanent income

h = ratio of nonhuman wealth to human wealth

u = a catchall variable that includes such things as tastes or confidence

An important contribution of Friedman, and one that is worth elaboration, is the inclusion of $\dot{p}$, the expected inflation rate, as a determinant of the real quantity of money demanded. Continuing the analogy of money as a capital asset, $\dot{p}$ can be thought of as an inverse measure of the expected rate of depreciation in the purchasing power of money. Viewed alternatively, $\dot{p}$ can be thought of as the rate of return to holding such commodities as autos, houses, machinery, and so on, whose prices rise with the price level. Other things constant, the higher the expected rate of inflation, the lower the demand for money.

The variable h, the ratio of nonhuman wealth to human wealth, is important because people cannot easily convert their human wealth into money (or into other assets), but people can convert nonhuman wealth

---

[10] Milton Friedman, "The Quantity Theory of Money—A Restatement," in *Studies in the Quantity Theory of Money*, Milton Friedman, ed. (Chicago: University of Chicago Press, 1956), pp. 3–21. Also, see Milton Friedman, "The Demand for Money: Some Theoretical and Empirical Results," *Journal of Political Economy*, vol. 67 (August 1959), pp. 327–351, and see Chapter 9 in this text, where we discuss Friedman's permanent income hypothesis.

[11] Recall that Friedman's permanent income hypothesis is broad enough to consider human as well as nonhuman wealth.

into money more easily. It follows that a person with a higher h ratio, other things constant, can more easily substitute nonmoney assets for money, and a lower h will be associated with a lower demand for cash balances. The reasoning is as follows. As Chapter 9 indicated, individuals with a high h ratio will have a higher average propensity to consume because they will be able to use nonhuman wealth as collateral for spending; individuals with the same permanent income but a lower h ratio will have a lower average propensity to consume because they cannot (as easily) use human wealth as collateral for consumption loans. Other things constant, then, a person with a higher h ratio will be better *able* to attain a higher level of satisfaction because it will be easier to select the optimal asset portfolio, including durable consumer goods. A person with a low h ratio, on the other hand, will be "liquidity constrained" and will *not be able* to choose the asset portfolio that maximizes economic welfare. People with low h ratios, therefore, will hold smaller quantities of cash balances because they will be straining to purchase less liquid assets (including consumer durables) in order to move closer to their most desired asset portfolio. Stated differently, the marginal benefit to holding money relative to other assets will be higher for a person with a high h ratio than for a person with a low h ratio.

The variables r_b and r_e represent expected rates of return on nonmoney assets; as they rise, therefore, the demand for money falls.

It should be noted that P, a variable on the left-hand side of equation 11.5, represents the price level. Actually, Friedman proposes that P should really be thought of as a variable measuring *permanent* prices, P_p. In other words, individuals will not change their demand for money as a result of changes in the price level that are expected to be temporary; instead, they will attempt to change their money holdings only in response to changes in the price level that are expected to be permanent. The analogy between permanent prices and permanent income is evident. Moreover, the permanent price level can also be estimated via the adaptive expectations model examined in Chapter 9, as Chapter 12 shows.

Friedman has also argued that the *empirical* evidence shows that the rate of return (interest rates) on nonmoney assets, and the other independent variables in equation 11.5—except for permanent income—are not important determinants of the demand for money. In other words, Friedman suggests that in practice, for forecasting and policymaking, real money balances (adjusted for *permanent* prices) can be thought of as being determined only by permanent income.

Friedman maintains that his demand-for-money function, in either the theoretical form in equation 11.5 or in his practical, empirically suggested version, is stable. Just as Friedman suggested that the consumption of goods and services is a stable function of permanent income,

Harper & Row
STUDY-AID

School is tough enough.
Get an edge on studying this semester with STUDY-AID.

STUDY-AID is a new computer program for the Apple, the Macintosh, and the IBM PC (and most IBM PC compatible) computers keyed directly to your text.

After reading each chapter in the text, you can use STUDY-AID to review how much you have learned with various types of exercises and self-tests. Automatic scoring enables you to check your progress as you learn.

To purchase a copy, check with your local college bookstore. To order by mail or telephone, complete the card or call Soft Productions, Inc. at (219) 255-3911. Be sure to indicate the type of computer disk you want and to include your method of payment. If the order card has been removed, mail your order to Soft Productions, Inc., P.O. Box 1003, Notre Dame, IN 46556. Be sure to indicate the title and author of the text and the type of computer disk you want (Apple, Macintosh, or IBM) and to include your method of payment.

(Cut along dotted lines and mail card below.)

Offer available in the
U.S. and Canada only.

NO POSTAGE
NECESSARY
IF MAILED
IN THE
UNITED STATES

BUSINESS REPLY MAIL
FIRST CLASS   PERMIT NO. 4501   NOTRE DAME, IN

POSTAGE WILL BE PAID BY ADDRESSEE

Soft Productions, Inc.
P.O. Box 1003
Notre Dame, IN 46556

so too is the demand for money balances a stable function of permanent income. Because neither permanent income nor the expected permanent price level is overly affected by temporary, cyclical changes, the private sector is inherently stable.

The Baumol-Tobin Contribution

As indicated previously, John R. Hicks believed that even the *transactions* demand for money was sensitive to the interest rate. Hicks's hypothesis was that transactions balances are held to avoid the costs of converting bonds into money and vice versa. In the mid-1950s, William J. Baumol and James Tobin applied an approach originally developed to determine the optimal quantities of inventories of goods a firm should maintain to determine the optimal quantity of money "inventories" that individuals would hold.[12]

Consider a simple example in which Ms. Romano must decide how to allocate her monthly paycheck among (1) currency and demand deposits (M1) which earn no interest and (2) a savings deposit (M2) that pays a monthly interest rate. By holding M1 balances she avoids, to some degree, what Baumol refers to as "brokerage costs" which include her transportation costs and the opportunity cost of her time. If, however, she keeps funds in the savings deposit account, she earns interest but she incurs brokerage costs every time she goes to the depository institution to convert part of her *time deposits to currency or demand deposits* in order to make transactions.

Baumol and Tobin recognize two costs of holding money:

1. The opportunity cost of holding money instead of keeping it in a savings account where it will earn interest
2. Brokerage costs

The Baumol-Tobin model suggests that transactions money is held only to minimize the total costs of a given volume of transactions.

If Ms. Romano incurs high brokerage costs (because the opportunity cost of her time is high or because she must travel a great distance to a depository institution) and interest earnings are low, she will make only *one* trip to a depository institution. At the beginning of the month she will deposit her paycheck (earned from her work in the previous month) in a depository institution and convert it into a demand deposit or into currency. Next month she will do the same thing. Suppose, however,

---

[12] William J. Baumol, "The Transactions Demand for Cash: An Inventory Theoretic Approach," *Quarterly Journal of Economics*, vol. 66 (November 1952), pp. 545–556, and James Tobin, "The Interest Elasticity of Transactions Demand for Cash," *Review of Economics and Statistics*, vol. 38 (August 1956), pp. 241–247.

Ms. Romano's situation changes (she moves closer to town, the opportunity cost of her time falls, or interest rates on savings accounts rise), and she now discovers that interest earnings exceed brokerage costs. She will now make more than one trip per month to the depository institution. In the first trip she will convert her paycheck into demand deposits, currency, *and* savings deposits; but this means that she must now make a second trip later in the month to convert savings balances into currency and demand deposits.

If Ms. Romano's monthly income is $1000 and she makes only one trip to the depository institution (assuming she spends the same amount of her M1 balances every day), her average daily balance is $500. If she makes two trips, then she converts her check at the beginning of the month into $500 in M1 balances and $500 in savings balances, and in the middle of the month she makes her second trip and converts the $500 savings balances into M1. Consequently her average daily M1 balance is reduced to $250. Her interest earnings equal $500 $(\frac{1}{2})/(r_m)$, where r_m is the monthly interest rate. Note that Ms. Romano has done *two* things simultaneously: she has increased the number of trips to the depository institution and she has lowered her average daily money balances (M1). Because the number of trips and the average daily money balances are functionally related, Ms. Romano's decision is either to optimize her number of trips *or* to optimize her average daily money balances; if one of these is done, then the other is accomplished automatically.

If Ms. Romano were to make three trips, she would find that the interest earnings from making three trips (or, alternatively, from holding even smaller average daily balances) would be more than the interest earnings from making two trips. If she makes three trips, evenly spaced throughout the month, and still spends the same amount each day, she will earn interest on the (approximately) $666 she leaves in the savings account for one-third of a month on the first trip, and on the $333 she leaves in the savings account (for another one-third of a month). On the third trip, she withdraws $333 and spends it evenly during the last third of the month. Her average daily money balances fall to $333 ÷ 2 = $166 as her trips rise to three. Her *total* interest earnings have increased (beyond the interest earnings she obtained from leaving $500 in a savings account for one-half month when she made two trips), *but* the *marginal* interest earnings are less for the third trip than for the second. For the same reason—additional trips to the depository institution increase her average daily balances in the savings accounts by smaller amounts— marginal interest earnings fall for additional trips. This information is shown in Table 11.3, where we assume a monthly income y of $1000 and a monthly savings account interest rate r_m of 1 percent. The concepts in that table are defined precisely in the footnotes.

TABLE 11.3. THE EFFECT OF NUMBER OF CONVERSIONS ON MARGINAL BENEFIT

Number of Conversions, or Trips n^a	Average M1 Balances^b	Total Monthly Interest Earnings^c	Marginal Benefit^d
1	$500	0	—
2	250	$2.50	$2.50
3	166	3.33	0.83
4	125	3.75	0.42
5	100	4.00	0.25

^{a} n = number of trips per month.

^{b} Average M1 balances = $y/2n$.

^{c} Total monthly interest earnings = $yr_m(n-1)/2n$.

^{d} Marginal benefit equals the change in total monthly interest earnings resulting from one more trip.

We conclude that her marginal benefit from trips to a depository institution falls as the number of trips per month increases; if we assume that her brokerage costs per trip are constant, she will increase her number of trips to the bank (alternatively, she will decrease her average daily cash balances) up to the point where the marginal benefit equals the marginal cost of doing so. For example, if her brokerage costs are more than $2.50, she will only make one trip; if they are $0.42, she will make four trips, and so on.

The Baumol-Tobin Model   Stated formally, the problem reduces to minimizing the sum of the two costs involved in holding money balances: opportunity costs of interest earnings and brokerage costs. Total transactions costs, therefore, equal

$$TC = bn + \frac{rC}{2} \qquad (11.6)$$

or

$$TC = b\left(\frac{y}{C}\right) + \frac{rC}{2} \qquad (11.7)$$

WHERE $n = \dfrac{y}{C}$

b = brokerage costs per trip

TC = total cost of holding money

n = number of conversions into cash

r = interest rate

C = average transfer from savings to M1

y = income per unit of time

It can be demonstrated[13] that the average value of the cash with-drawal C that minimizes total costs is

$$C = \sqrt{\frac{2by}{r}} \qquad (11.8)$$

Equation 11.8 shows that desired average value of the cash with-drawal is directly related to brokerage costs and to income, and that desired cash balances are inversely related to the interest rate. It also implies that the income elasticity of the demand for real money balances (the percentage change in desired real balances divided by the percentage change in income) is equal to 0.5.[14] Because the income demand for real balances is inelastic, this model implies that people *economize* on their real cash balances as their real income rises.

Equation 11.8 also implies that the interest elasticity of the demand for real transactions balances is -0.5, implying that a 1 percent increase in the real interest rate reduces the demand for real transactions balances by 0.5 percent. (See the equation in footnote 14.)

Summary of the Baumol-Tobin Inventory Model   The Baumol-Tobin analysis is important because:

1. It emphasizes that the demand for *transactions* balances—like the demand for asset balances (L_2 in previous chapters) and the demand for commodities—is determined by rational behavior.
2. It indicates that transactions balances are desired because it is too costly for people continually to convert in and out of money—and not because of the services that money balances give to holders. When combined with Tobin's portfolio approach to the asset demand for money, which indicates that the speculative motive implies that households will hold *both* money and time deposits, we have quite a sophisticated theory of the total demand for money.
3. It shows that the total demand for money depends on the interest rate, independently of whether or not the speculative motive is cor-

---

[13] To minimize total costs of transactions, Equation 11.7 is differentiated with respect to C, and set equal to zero. Thus

$$\frac{\delta TC}{\delta C} = \frac{-by}{C^2} + \frac{r}{2} = 0$$

Solving for C yields equation 11.8.

[14] Writing equation 11.8 in exponential form yields

$$C = (2by^{1/2})(r^{-1/2})$$

Thus a 1 percent increase in real income y (or a 1 percent increase in transactions costs b) increases the demand for real cash balances by 0.5 percent.

rect. We now have *two* reasons (speculative motive and interest opportunity costs) for believing that the *lm* curve is positively sloped (nonvertical). In Chapter 18 we show that this implies that shifts in the *is* curve—due to changes in private spending or fiscal policy—will change national income and the interest rate in the short run. This is an important implication for the monetarist-nonmonetarist debate analyzed in that chapter.

4. It has implications that are empirically testable; the model implies that the income elasticity of the demand for money is 0.5 and the interest elasticity is -0.5.

EMPIRICAL EVIDENCE CONCERNING
THE DEMAND FOR MONEY

In 1973 Stephen Goldfeld published his analysis of post–World War II quarterly data on the demand for money (the 1973 M1 definition) and found the following:[15]

1. The real income elasticity of demand for real M1 balances is positive, but less than 1; it ranges from 0.19 in the very short run (one quarter) to 0.68 in the long run (over two years).
2. The interest rate elasticity of demand is negative; it ranges between -0.045 in the very short run to -0.16 in the long run. The interest rates used were the rate on time deposits and the rate on commercial paper, which are both *short-term* interest rates.
3. The demand for nominal money balances is proportional to the price level; therefore, the demand for money is a demand for real balances, and no money illusion exists.

In 1976 Goldfeld published another study that confirmed the above results. He found a long-run real interest elasticity of real money demand of -0.19 and a long-run real income interest elasticity of real money demand of 0.56.[16] In the 1976 study Goldfeld also found that his demand-for-money function, which explained the 1952–1973 data very well, suddenly started to *overestimate* the demand for money (hence the title of his article). His equation predicted a declining ratio of M1 to national income (due to rising interest rates), but the actual ratio was *even lower* than the predicted reduction. In recent times the instability of the pre-

---

[15] Stephen M. Goldfeld, "The Demand for Money Revisited," *Brookings Papers on Economic Activity*, 3 (Washington, D.C.: The Brookings Institution, 1973).

[16] Stephen M. Goldfeld, "The Case of the Missing Money," *Brookings Papers on Economic Activity*, 3 (Washington, D.C.: The Brookings Institution, 1976).

viously stable demand for money function has continued. More precisely, equations such as Goldfeld's continued to underpredict that ratio from 1974 to late 1982, but from late 1982 to 1983 the actual ratio *exceeded* the predicted value. Stated differently, velocity at first rose faster than expected and then *fell* unexpectedly in 1982–1983.

In short, the ratio of M1 to national income (or its inverse, the velocity of M1) has been relatively unstable since 1974. This fact will loom large in Chapter 16, where we discuss the problems of monetary policy and where we try to determine why the demand for money has become more unstable.

POLICY CONTROVERSY
Is M1 Still a Measure of the Transactions Concept of Money?[17]

We indicated earlier in this chapter that one necessary condition for a successful monetary policy is a close correspondence between the theoretical definition and the empirical definition of money. In recent years there has been a controversy over whether M1, the empirical definition, corresponds adequately to the transactions concept of money.

A number of financial innovations experienced in the 1970s seem to have blurred the distinction between M1 and other assets. Money market mutual funds, introduced in 1975, had grown to over $175 million by 1985. Repurchase agreements and overnight Eurodollars deposits are now used extensively by corporations to earn interest on very short-term balances that are used mostly for transactions.

More important, perhaps, are the NOW accounts and the Super-NOW's. The NOW accounts are just like checking accounts, and the Super-NOW's offer unlimited checking privileges. These instruments prompted the redefinition of the narrowest (transactions) measure of money.

In 1979 the narrowest definition of money was called M1, and it included currency and demand deposits at commercial banks. In 1980 the narrowest definition of money was called M1A; it included currency, demand deposits at commercial banks, *and* traveler's checks issued by new bank corporations. Also in that year M1B was defined; it included the components of M1A *and* NOW accounts, ATS accounts, and credit union share accounts. The Fed again has changed its narrowest definition of money; M1 is now the narrowest definition, and it is roughly equivalent to M1B (it adds demand deposits at mutual savings banks). In December 1982 the money market deposit account was introduced, and it was included in M2—under money market mutual funds. The money market

---

[17] See "NOWs and Super NOWs: Implications for Defining and Measuring Money," cited in footnote 1. Also see John A. Tatom, "Money Market Deposit Accounts, Super NOWs and Monetary Policy," *Review*, vol. 65, no. 3 (March 1983), Federal Reserve Bank of St. Louis, pp. 5–25.

deposit account was an immediate success, attracting more than $138 billion in deposits during the first 14 weeks it was offered. When Super-NOW accounts were introduced in January 1983, they were included in M1 under "other checkable deposits."

By now it is clear that financial innovations have made the job of defining money difficult. They have also blurred the distinction between transactions accounts and other slightly less liquid assets. If a significant portion of M1 now consists of money that is *not* used to finance anticipated short-run expenditures, then changes in M1 may not be closely and predictably related to changes in total spending.

What is at issue here is not a mere classification question. It may be that financial innovations, as they arise, cause distortions in the measures of M1, M2, and M3. As people move away from one credit instrument to another (seeking higher interest earnings), the various M's move in different directions, or some move while others remain constant. Thus we get changes in the various money measures, *but nothing essential may be happening to consumer or business expenditures.* The interpretation of change in the various money measures becomes difficult; if the Fed cannot attain its growth-rate targets for M1 or M2, then its ability to reach ultimate national economic goals is hampered; or if the Fed attains its targets, the expected changes in the national economy may not follow. We return to the issue of monetary control in Chapter 16. Right now you need only be aware of the seeds of the problem—the difficulty of separating the transactions definition of money from the liquidity definition, or of distinguishing between the function of money as a medium of exchange and its function as a temporary store of value.

CHAPTER SUMMARY

1. Monetary policy requires, at a minimum, (a) a close correspondence between the theoretical definition of money and the empirical definition of money, (b) the ability to control the empirically defined money supply, and (c) a close and predictable relationship between the empirical definition of money and ultimate national economic goals.

2. There are two major approaches to defining money and measuring the money supply: (a) the transactions approach, which emphasizes money's role as a medium of exchange and which is empirically defined as M1; and (b) the liquidity, or portfolio, approach, which emphasizes that money, although it is the most liquid of all assets, is just one of several types of assets which can be used as a store of value. Near monies are good substitutes for money, and the empirical definition using the liquidity approach concept of money is M2.

3. Classical economists tended to concentrate on money as a medium of exchange and were led to think of money as something that was spent. They concentrated, therefore, on velocity and its determinants.

4. The Cambridge neoclassical economists (*a*) emphasized the *income* velocity of money as being superior to the concept of transactions velocity, (*b*) developed the Cambridge *k*, which is the ratio of money balances that people *desire to hold* to national income, (*c*) introduced national income as a budget constraint on money balances and distinguished between an exogenously determined money supply and the demand-for-money curve, and (*d*) formulated a demand for money in real terms.

5. Keynes helped to originate the portfolio approach to money demand. He stressed the asset demand for money and suggested that money and bonds were substitutes, and he maintained that the desirability of one relative to the other depends on the difference between the current interest rate and the expected natural interest rate.

6. Tobin extended Keynes's analysis and developed a portfolio approach. By introducing the concept of risk aversion and by assuming uncertainty, Tobin was able to demonstrate that (with respect to the asset demand for money) *individuals* will have a mixed portfolio, which consists of both money *and* bonds.

7. John R. Hicks was the originator of the portfolio theory, and he stressed that the demand for money should be analyzed just like the demand for any other capital good. He stressed that *wealth* is the true budget constraint on the demand for money and that the demand for money depends on the rates of return on other assets. He also took the first step in noting that the *transactions* demand for money is also a function of the interest rate.

8. Milton Friedman extended Hicks's portfolio model and substituted permanent income as the wealth-proxy constraint; he also added the rate of inflation as a determinant of the demand for money. In his truncated model, the real demand for money is a stable function of real permanent income.

9. The Baumol-Tobin model stressed that transactions money is demanded because it is too costly for people continually to convert other assets into spending money. It concluded that the demand for transactions balances is inversely related to the interest rate. This relationship has important policy implications.

10. Empirical evidence indicates that real money balances are (*a*) directly related to real national income and (*b*) inversely related to real interest rates. Since 1974 the traditional demand-for-money function has become relatively unstable, and this also has important policy implications.

11. Recent financial innovations have caused problems in both the measurement and the control of money supply.

GLOSSARY

ATS accounts Automatic-transfer-system accounts that are a combination of savings accounts on which interest is paid and regular checking accounts on which no interest is paid.

credit union share draft (CUSD) accounts Profit-earning accounts on which credit union members may write checks.

currency The value of coins minted by the U.S. Treasury and any of the Federal Reserve notes issued by the Fed and by the U.S. Treasury.

demand deposits Deposits in a depository institution that are payable on demand and transferable by check, and on which no interest is paid.

M1 The transactions measure of money; the sum of the values of currency, transactions accounts, and traveler's checks issued by nonbank institutions.

M2 The liquidity measure of money; the sum of the values of M1, savings deposits, small-denomination time deposits, overnight REPO's, overnight Eurodollars, money market mutual funds, and money market deposit accounts.

money market mutual funds Pools of funds contributed by savers which are used by certain financial institutions to purchase such short-term instruments as T-bills, CD's, and commercial paper; each saver accumulates shares in such funds and has limited check-writing privileges.

near monies Assets that are highly liquid but are not money because they are not a medium of exchange or because it is possible to receive a (slight) capital gain or loss on them.

NOW accounts Interest-bearing savings accounts accepted by thrift institutions and on which checks may be written.

portfolio approach A belief that the essence of money is that it has a constant nominal value and that such assets should be included in the empirical definition of money.

repurchase agreement A contractual arrangement whereby a bank sells securities to its customers under an agreement to buy them back at an agreed lower amount.

Super-NOW accounts Savings accounts accepted by thrift institutions which allow unlimited checking, and pay market interest rates.

time deposit A savings deposit on which an owner must give notice prior to making a withdrawal.

transactions approach A belief that the essence of money is that only it is used as a means of payment for other goods and services and that only such an asset should be included in the empirical definition of money.

QUESTIONS AND PROBLEMS FOR REVIEW

11.1 State the three requirements of effective monetary policy. Discuss the consequences of the absence of each.

11.2 Assuming that the correspondence between the theoretical definition of money and the empirical definition of money is significant, compare the effects associated with conducting monetary policy by changing M1 with those associated with conducting monetary policy by changing M2 on (a) equilibrium national income and (b) equilibrium rates of interest.

11.3 Classical economists were particularly concerned with velocity and its determinants. State the determinants. In what way are such determinants changing in today's economy?

11.4 The length of payment periods is often thought to affect velocity. Suppose that the length of payment periods changes so that the present value of the future payments remains the same. Do you still think that such a change would affect velocity?

11.5 Explain why you agree or disagree with the following statement: To the extent that the money supply is endogenously determined, monetary policy is less effective.

11.6 Keynes suggested that money and bonds were substitutes, depending on the difference between the current rate of interest and the expected natural rate of interest. Distinguish between the effects of such differences on previously issued bonds and currently issued bonds.

11.7 Explain why the introduction of the concept of risk aversion under uncertainty leads to the conclusion that rational individuals will have a mixed portfolio consisting of money and bonds.

11.8 Friedman extended Hick's model, substituted permanent income as the wealth-proxy constraint, and added the rate of inflation as a determinant of the demand for money. If the real demand for money is a function of real permanent income, what effect on the demand for money is expected for a change in the rate of inflation, if real permanent income remains the same?

11.9 If transactions money is demanded because of the cost associated with the conversion of other assets into spending money, it is thought that the demand for transactions money is inversely related to the rate of interest. What important policy implications are suggested by this relationship?

11.10 Explain why the existence of instability in the traditional demand-for-money function has important policy implications.

REFERENCES

William J. Baumol, "The Transactions Demand for Cash: An Inventory Theoretic Approach," *Quarterly Journal of Economics*, vol. 66 (1952).
Milton Friedman, "The Quantity Theory of Money—A Restatement," in Milton Friedman, ed., *Studies in the Quantity Theory of Money* (Chicago: University of Chicago Press, 1956).

————, "The Demand for Money: Some Theoretical and Empirical Results," *Journal of Political Economy*, vol. 67 (1959).

Stephen M. Goldfeld, "The Demand for Money Revisited," *Brookings Papers on Economic Activity*, 3 (Washington, D.C.: The Brookings Institution, 1973).

————, "The Case of the Missing Money," *Brookings Papers on Economic Activity*, 3 (Washington, D.C.: The Brookings Institution, 1976).

John R. Hicks, "A Suggestion for Simplifying the Theory of Money," *Economica*, vol. 2 (1935).

Bryan Higgins and Jon Faust, "NOWs and Super NOWs: Implications for Defining and Measuring Money," *Economic Review*, vol. 68 (1983), Federal Reserve Bank of Kansas City.

Thomas M. Humphrey, *Essays on Inflation*, 4th ed. (Richmond, Va.: Federal Reserve Bank of Richmond, 1983).

David Laidler, *The Demand for Money* (New York: Dun-Donnelley, 1977).

John A. Tatom, "Money Market Deposit Accounts, Super NOWs, and Monetary Policy," *Review*, vol. 65 (1983), Federal Reserve Bank of St. Louis.

James Tobin, "The Interest Elasticity of Transactions Demand for Cash," *Review of Economics and Statistics*, vol. 38 (1956).

————, "Liquidity Preference as Behaviour Towards Risk," *Review of Economic Studies*, vol. 25 (1958).

PART IV

STAGFLATION

12

A RECONSIDERATION OF THE LABOR MARKET

Since the time of the classical economists and Keynes, theoretical advances have been made in the analysis of the labor market. In this chapter we concentrate on some of the changes that have occurred in the derivation of the supply-of-labor curve. In particular, we first review the demand-for-labor analysis discussed in previous chapters and then show how the supply of labor is now derived as a trade-off between real income and leisure. We next show how price expectations can play a role in determining how many labor hours workers are prepared to offer. Then various labor supply curves are developed; each is dependent on the specific assumptions about how price expectations are formed. The material in this chapter provides the foundation for deriving the aggregate supply function in the next chapter.

A MODERN LABOR MARKET ANALYSIS

The Demand for Labor Recalled

As indicated in Chapters 4 and 6, Keynes and the classical economists were in basic agreement about the nature of the demand for labor. Both felt that no money illusion existed regarding the demand for labor and that in a competitive market employers were concerned with the real wage rate $(w = W/P)$ that had to be paid relative to the marginal physical product of labor MPP_n. In equilibrium the real wage rate equals the MPP_n; at that point the employer is maximizing total profits. Alternatively, in equilibrium the money wage rate W equals the value of the marginal product of labor VMP_n. By definition,

$$VMP_n \equiv MPP_n \cdot P \tag{12.1}$$

The equilibrium condition is

$$VMP_n \equiv MPP_n \cdot P = W \tag{12.2a}$$

or

$$MPP_n \cdot P = W \tag{12.2b}$$

Stated in real terms, the equilibrium condition is

$$\frac{W}{P} = MPP_n \tag{12.3}$$

The job of employers is relatively simple because they have the correct information with respect to the money wage rate they must pay, and they also know the price of the good or service they are selling. This means that at any given time an employer knows the real wage rate that must be paid; it is found by dividing the going rate by the price of the good or service that is being produced. As we shall see later, laborers

The Nominal Demand-for-Labor and the Real Demand-for-Labor Curves Are Both Downward-Sloping, Reflecting the Law of Diminishing Returns

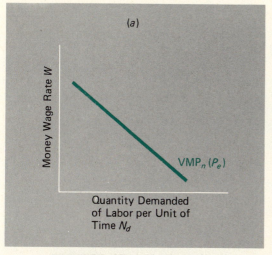
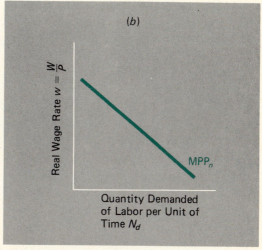

FIGURE 12.1. THE DEMAND FOR LABOR AND THE LAW OF DIMINISHING RETURNS

In panel *a*, the demand for labor is in nominal terms; the value of the marginal product of labor falls because price is constant, and the marginal physical product of labor falls as the quantity of labor employed increases, owing to the law of diminishing returns. In panel *b*, the demand for labor is in real terms; the demand for labor is the marginal physical-product-of-labor curve.

have a more difficult task. Laborers know the money wage rate, but to determine their current real wage rate they must have information concerning all the prices of the goods they purchase. This issue is raised in the next section.

The Nominal and Real Demand for Labor

Consider Figure 12.1. Panel *a* depicts the money or nominal demand for labor facing a typical firm. It is downward-sloping because, given selling price P_e, before an employer will voluntarily hire more labor the money wage rate must fall to offset a declining value of the marginal product of labor (diminishing marginal returns). In panel *b* the real demand for labor is depicted. It is negatively sloped because employers will not voluntarily hire more labor unless the real wage falls to offset the de-

A Change in Selling Price Results in a Shift of the Nominal Labor Demand Curve and a Movement Along the Real Labor Demand Curve

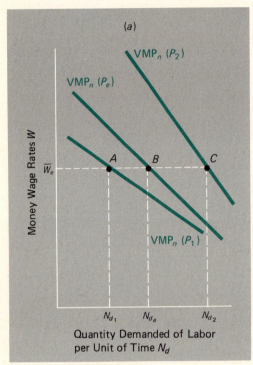

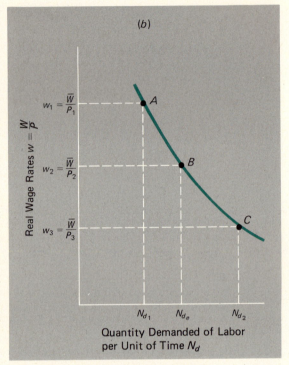

FIGURE 12.2. A CHANGE IN PRICE, GIVEN THE NOMINAL WAGE RATE

In panel a a change in price, given the money wage rate W_e shifts the VMP_n curve downward or upward depending on whether price falls or rises. At the same money wage rate, the quantity demanded of labor varies directly with the price level. This conclusion is also indicated in panel b because at the same money wage rate a higher selling price means a lower real wage rate and therefore, a higher quantity demanded of labor, other things constant.

clining marginal physical product of labor. Both curves provide the same insight.

The Effects of Changes in Price on the Demand for Labor

Look now at Figure 12.2, which shows how a change in price, other things constant, affects the nominal and the real demand-for-labor curves. Because the nominal demand-for-labor curve is the VMP_n curve, and because $VMP_n \equiv MPP_n \cdot P$, an increase in price (from P_e to P_2) causes the VMP_n curve to shift upward (because each laborer's MPP_n is now valued at a higher price), and a decrease in selling price (from P_e to P_1) causes the VMP_n curve to shift downward (because each laborer's MPP_n is now valued at a lower price). In other words, a given MPP_n is worth more or less at a higher or lower price; hence, the nominal demand-for-labor curve shifts as selling price changes. Note that $P_1 < P_e < P_2$.

In panel b in Figure 12.2 a change in price, other things constant, results in a movement along the real demand-for-labor curve. This is because the real wage rate w equals the money wage rate divided by selling price. If the selling price changes and the money wage rate is constant, the real wage rate changes.

A moment's reflection will indicate to you that if money wage rates change but price does not, *neither* curve shifts; a change in the money wage rate, other things constant, results in a movement along the nominal demand-for-labor curve. A change in the nominal wage rate, given the selling price of output, leads to a movement along the real demand-for-labor curve. For example, assume that the nominal wage rate rises and the selling price of output is constant. This means that the real wage rate also rises, because the nominal wage rate and the real wage rate move in the same direction if selling price is constant. A rise in the real wage rate results in a decrease in the quantity demanded of labor, or a movement up the real demand-for-labor curve. Similarly, if the nominal wage rate falls, given selling price, the real wage rate falls and this leads to a movement down a given real demand-for-labor curve.

What happens when *both* price and wage rates change *at the same rate*? Consider Figure 12.3, which indicates how each curve is affected by a proportional increase in prices and wage rates. In panel a the VMP_n shifts upward due to an increases in price; but because the money wage rate has also increased, we move up the new nominal demand-for-labor curve. We start at point A; price rises so we move to point B; the money wage rate rises so we move to point C. Note that the quantity demanded of labor is unaltered, at N_{d_e}. In panel b nothing happens; a proportional change in the nominal wage rate and in price results in neither a shift nor a movement along the real demand-for-labor curve because the real wage rate is unaltered. If we start at point A and prices and nominal wage rates change proportionally, we end up at point A.

The Aggregate Demand for Labor

In order to derive an aggregate demand curve, we add, horizontally, all the firm demand curves. Of course, we can derive both an aggregate nominal demand-for-labor curve and an aggregate real demand-for-labor curve.

We now turn to the derivation of labor supply curves.

MODERN SUPPLY-OF-LABOR CURVES

Recall from Chapter 4 that the classical economists maintained that a positively sloped labor supply curve reflected the fact that a worker experiences increasing marginal disutility as he works more hours per unit of time. Assuming some initial balance between hours worked and pay, before a worker will voluntarily work longer hours per unit of time the real wage rate must rise to offset increasing marginal disutility. Every point on the labor supply curve is a potential equilibrium; the worker would have worked until the marginal disutility for additional work was just offset by the extra utility gained from extra income.

The modern approach to the supply of labor incorporates two important notions:

1. Workers receive utility both from real income and from leisure. An individual worker maximizes total utility subject to the constraint that the worker's real income equals the real wage rate times the hours worked. The more hours worked, the fewer hours available for leisure; hence, there is a labor-leisure trade-off.
2. A worker cannot easily calculate his or her real wage rate, which depends on the prices of the (perhaps) hundreds of different goods and services that he or she purchases annually. All a worker really knows is the money wage rate; the real wage rate rises and falls as the price falls and rises.

The information required to ascertain one's exact real income would involve extremely high search costs. Additionally, the worker has no way of knowing what the price level will be in the future; as a consequence, workers typically enter into wage negotiations with some *expectations* about what the price level will be over the length of the contract period. We amend our notation so that

$$W = \text{nominal or money wage rate}$$

$$w^e = \text{expected real wage rate}$$

$$p^e = \text{expected price level}$$

We can now note that

$$w^e \equiv \frac{W}{P^e} \qquad (12.4)$$

A Proportional Change in Prices and Money Wage Rates Affects the Nominal and the Real Demand-for-Labor Curves Differently

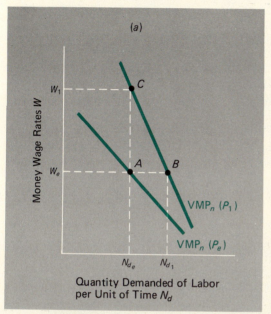

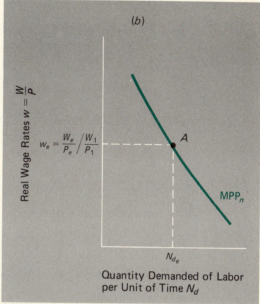

FIGURE 12.3. A PROPORTIONAL CHANGE IN W AND P

In panel a, we start at point A, which shows that when the money wage rate is W_e and the price level is P_e, N_{d_e} units of labor will be hired. An increase in price to P_1 shifts the nominal demand-for-labor curve to the right; at W_e, the quantity demanded of labor rises to N_{d_1}; however, money wage rates have also increased, to W_1. We end up at point C, which indicates that a proportional change in money wage rates and selling price leaves the quantity demanded of labor unaltered, at N_{d_e}. Can you determine what happens in panel a if prices and money wage rates *fall* proportionally?

In panel b, a proportional change in money wage rates and selling price causes nothing to change. We start at point A and we get neither a shift in the curve nor a movement along the curve because the real wage rate is unaltered.

---

or, what is its equivalent,

$$W \equiv P^e \cdot w^e \tag{12.5}$$

A distinction has now been made between w, the *actual* real wage, and w^e, the *expected* real wage, because

$$w = \frac{W}{P} \tag{12.6}$$

Note by comparing equations 12.4 and 12.6 that $w = w^e$ only if $P = P_e$. That is, there is a difference between the actual real wage and the expected real wage whenever the actual price level is not what a worker expects it to be.

The ratio of the actual real wage to the expected real wage equals the ratio of the expected price level to the actual price level. Dividing equation 12.6 by equation 12.4,

$$\frac{w}{w^e} = \frac{W/P}{W/P^e} = \frac{P^e}{P} \tag{12.7}$$

and multiplying through by w^e gives

$$w = \left(\frac{P^e}{P}\right) \cdot (w^e) \tag{12.8}$$

Then W/p^e in equation 12.4 can be substituted for w^e in equation 12.8 to yield

$$w = \left(\frac{P^e}{P}\right)\left(\frac{W}{P^e}\right) \tag{12.9}$$

or, alternatively, by multiplying both sides of equation 12.9 by P, and recalling that $wP = W$,

$$W = P^e\left(\frac{W}{P^e}\right) \tag{12.10}$$

Equations 12.9 and 12.10 are useful because they will enable us to derive a supply curve for labor as a function of the real wage w or of the nominal wage W, while at the same time allowing us to specify the role that price expectations play in the labor supply process. Price expectations become important when we discuss equilibrium in the next section.

Deriving the Modern Supply-of-Labor Curve

We are now ready to derive the supply-of-labor curve, given a competitive market, by the modern approach. Given a person's tastes for leisure hours F and for expected real income y^e, and given the expected real wage rate w^e, that person will select the optimal quantity of labor hours to offer per unit of time so as to maximize his or her total utility U. U varies directly with y^e and F:

$$U = U(y^e, F) \tag{12.11}$$

Assume that there is decreasing marginal utility for both income and leisure. The worker's budget constraint is

$$y^e = \left(\frac{W}{P^e}\right)(H - F) \tag{12.12}$$

where H represents the total number of hours available either for work or leisure. Thus, if N_s equals the number of hours worked per day,

$$N_s = H - F \tag{12.13}$$

Equation 12.13 means that once the optimal trade-off between income and leisure (for a given expected real wage rate) is determined, the optimal quantity supplied of labor is automatically determined. For example, assume that $H = 20$ hours per day (assuming the laborer must sleep 4 hours). If a laborer maximizes total utility by choosing 12 hours of (nonsleeping) leisure and an expected real income of y_1^e, that laborer *simultaneously and necessarily* has chosen to work 8 hours per day when the expected real wage rate is w_1^e, because $y_1^e = 8 (w_1^e)$.

Indifference Curves   Figure 12.4 contains the real income-leisure indifference curve analysis. Curves U_1, U_2, and U_3 are called **indifference curves;** an indifference curve shows all the combinations of the values represented on the vertical and the horizontal axes that indicate a given level of satisfaction U. In Figure 12.4 a specific indifference curve shows all the combinations of real income and hours of leisure that indicate a specific level of utility. Each indifference curve is negatively sloped because as a worker receives more of either of these "goods," he or she must receive less of the other; otherwise, the worker's total utility would rise. Note that $U_4 > U_3 > U_2 > U_1$; can you explain why?

Not only is each indifference curve negatively sloped, but as we move from left to right the curve becomes flatter.[1] For example, as someone receives more leisure (and works less), the *marginal* benefit, or personal valuation of an extra unit of leisure, falls and the marginal benefit from a given amount of income rises. For example, an individual at point Z on indifference curve U_1 is working long hours and is not experiencing much leisure; one more unit of leisure will be valued highly. This individual values one more hour of leisure so highly that he or she would be willing to sacrifice income of (say) $20 by not working. In other words,

---

[1] Technically, indifference curves are convex with respect to the origin. Also, while we are being technical, indifference curves cannot intersect because a contradiction would result. Can you see why?

A Worker Offers the Amount of Labor That Maximizes His or Her Total Utility

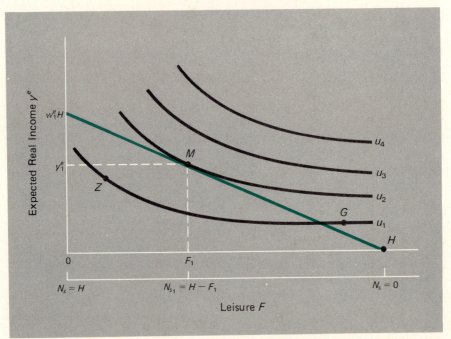

FIGURE 12.4. SELECTING THE OPTIMAL WORKDAY
Given an expected real wage rate of w_1^e and given the worker's preferences for work and leisure as indicated by the indifference curves, the worker will choose that combination of leisure and income that maximizes his or her total utility. The worker chooses income y_1^e, and F_1 hours of leisure. By implication, when the expected hourly real wage is w_1^e, the worker chooses to work $H - F_1$ hours per day, as equation 12.13 indicates. Note that when $F = 0$, $N_s = H$, and when $F = H$, $N_s = 0$, and when $F = F_1$ then $N_{s_1} = H - F_1$.

at point Z the indifference curve is fairly steep; the value of real income lost is fairly high for a unit increase in leisure.

At a point such as G, however, our individual is working very little and has much leisure time. The marginal benefit of more income is relatively high and the marginal benefit of one more hour of leisure is small. As a consequence, the worker would be willing to sacrifice only, say, $3 of income for one more hour of leisure. In other words, at point G the indifference curve is relatively flat.

The Budget Constraint In Figure 12.4 the line $w_1^e HH$ is the **budget constraint line** facing a worker if the expected real wage rate is w_1^e. The worker can maximize income by enjoying no leisure at point $w_1^e H$; the value of real income at this extreme is $20w_1^e$ in our example, or Hw_1^e in general terms. On the other hand, by not working at all, the worker can enjoy H hours of nonsleeping leisure. By connecting point $w_1^e H$ and point H with a straight line, the budget constraint is defined. The worker can choose any combination of real income and leisure on (or below) the budget line, but cannot choose any combination above the budget constraint line.

Choosing the Optimal Work Day, Given the Expected Real Wage Rate

In Figure 12.4 a worker maximizes total utility subject to the budget constraint at point M, which is a point on the highest utility curve. At M the slope of the budget constraint line (which equals $-w^e$) equals the slope of the indifference curve. In short, our worker will maximize total utility by working $H - F_1$ hours and enjoying F_1 hours of leisure, if the expected real hourly wage rate is w_1^e and his preference for work and leisure are those depicted by the indifference curves in Figure 12.4.

At point M the rate at which a laborer *can* substitute leisure for real income—the real wage rate, indicated by the slope of the budget constraint line—is just equal to the rate at which the laborer is *willing* to substitute leisure for real income (i.e., the slope of indifference curve U_2).

Changes in the Real Wage Rate Induce Changes in the Quantity of Labor Supplied

In Figure 12.5 the real wage rate is changed and the budget constraint rotates around point H; the higher the expected real wage rate, the steeper the budget constraint. Given the worker's preference map (i.e., his indifference curves), Figure 12.5 indicates that the worker will substitute real income for leisure as the expected real wage rate rises. In order to maximize total utility, as the real wage rate rises more hours are worked and less time is allocated to leisure.

When the expected real wage rate is w_1^e, the laborer will offer to work $N_{s_1} = H - F_1$, as point M depicts. If the expected real wage rate falls to w_2^e, the new budget constraint line rotates downward around point H and the worker maximizes total utility at point R and now offers to work $N_{s_2} = H - F_2$, a smaller number of hours than previously. If the anticipated real wage rate rises to w_3^e, the budget constraint line rotates upward around point H and the worker maximizes total utility at point A; a higher expected real wage rate induces the worker to offer to work longer hours, $N_{s_3} = H - F_3$.

In panel b we have summarized the information contained in panel

The Quantity of Labor Supplied Varies Directly with the Anticipated Real Wage Rate

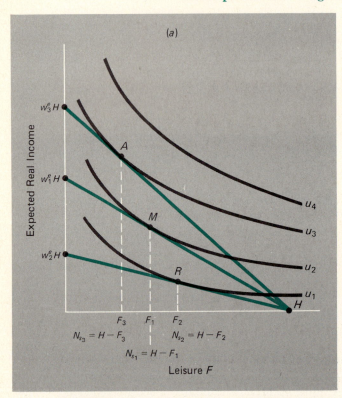

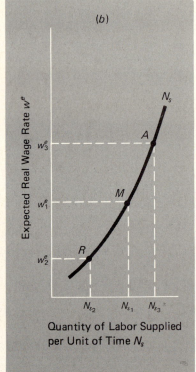

FIGURE 12.5. DERIVING THE LABOR SUPPLY CURVE

When the real wage rate is w^e, the worker maximizes total utility at point M, offering $N_{s_1} = H - F_1$ units of labor. If the real expected wage rate falls to w_2^e, the worker's utility maximization point is R, offering $N_{s_2} = H - F_2$ hours of labor, which is a smaller amount. If the real expected wage rate rises to w_3^e, the worker maximizes total utility at point A, and the quantity of labor offered is $N_{s_3} = H - F_3$, a larger amount.

Panel b summarizes the information from panel a to show a positively sloped labor supply curve; higher expected real wage rates induce a worker to offer more labor hours per day, other things constant.

a and in the process we have derived the worker's supply-of-labor curve. The curve indicates that higher expected real wage rates are required to induce a worker to substitute real income (i.e., work more hours per day) for leisure.

By adding all the individual workers' supply-of-labor curves we can derive an aggregate supply-of-labor curve.[2]

EQUILIBRIUM IN THE LABOR MARKET

Now that we have derived an aggregate supply-of-labor curve and an aggregate demand-for-labor curve, we are in a position to discuss equilibrium in the labor market. We know that the aggregate demand for labor is a functional relationship between the real wage rate and the quantity demanded of labor; stated alternatively, there is a functional relationship between the nominal wage rate and the quantity demanded of labor when the price level is given.

From the analysis of the labor supply curve, we know that a functional relationship exists between the real wage rate and the quantity of labor that laborers in the aggregate will offer. However, recalling equation 12.9,

$$w = \left(\frac{P^e}{P}\right)\left(\frac{W}{P^e}\right) \tag{12.9}$$

it is clear that in the labor market the expected future (or currently perceived) price level is an important determinant of the quantity of labor offered for sale. Alternatively, recall equation 12.10:

$$W = P^e\left(\frac{W}{P^e}\right) \tag{12.10}$$

which indicates that the nominal supply-of-labor curve also depends on the expected (future) or perceived (present) price level.

In equilibrium, given the actual price level P (note that each producer knows its own individual selling price) and the currently perceived or expected (if we are dealing with the future) price level P^e (relevant to sellers of labor), real or nominal wage rates will adjust to equate the quantity supplied and the quantity demanded of labor.

In order to demonstrate the process by which equilibrium is reached, it is convenient to start from an equilibrium position and introduce a shock. Specifically, assume that the money supply is exogenously increased as a result of the Fed's actions and that this causes an increase in the price level. What happens in the labor market depends on what

---

[2] Income effects might induce a worker—at very high real wage rates—to work *less* now that the worker can afford to purchase leisure. While a backward-bending labor supply curve is possible for an individual worker, an *aggregate* supply-of-labor curve is unlikely to be backward-bending because higher anticipated real wages will doubtless increase labor participation rates for women, teenagers, and senior citizens, and thereby offset income effects that might exist for individual workers.

The Classical Assumption Results

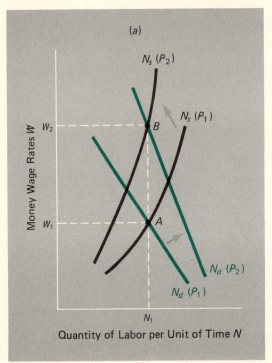

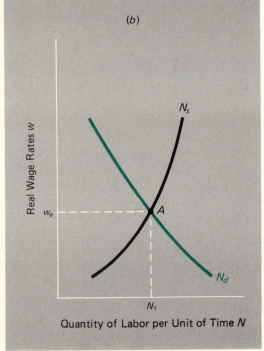

FIGURE 12.6. AN INCREASE IN THE PRICE LEVEL FROM P_1 TO P_2
Given classical model assumptions, an increase in the price level is immediately and correctly perceived by both workers and employers. Panel b is unaffected; neither the real demand for labor nor the real supply of labor is affected, so the economy remains at point A.

In panel a, an increase in the price level from P_1 to P_2 causes the nominal demand-for-labor curve to increase to $N_d(P_2)$, and it causes the nominal supply-of-labor curve to decrease to $N_s(P_2)$. Nominal wage rates rise proportionally to the increase in the price level, and employment remains at N_1. The economy moves from point A to point B, but employment is unaltered.

happens to P^e, the perceived, or expected, price level. We will consider three cases:

1. An immediate perception of the price level increase by suppliers of labor; this is the *classical model assumption.*
2. No perception of the price level increase on the part of labor suppliers; this is the assumption of the *extreme Keynesian model.*

3. A delayed perception of the price level increase by labor suppliers; this is the assumption used in the Keynesian *incomplete adjustment assumption* model.

As will be demonstrated, the alternative assumptions have different implications for the labor market with respect to nominal wage rates, real wage rates, and employment. Note also that we are assuming perfect wage rate flexibility (wage rates are *free* to rise or fall even though they, in fact, may not) in each of these three cases.

The Classical Model Assumption

The classical economists assumed that the amount of labor workers offer depends on the expected *real* wage rate. If the price level rises due to an increase in the money supply, workers immediately perceive this change. In terms of equation 12.8, the ratio $P^e/P = 1$ because $P^e = P$, and for the same reason, in equation 12.9

$$w = \frac{W}{P^e} = \frac{W}{P}$$

So if money wage rates rise at the same rate as the price level, the real wage rate is unaltered. The money wage rate *will* rise proportionally because laborers immediately perceive the higher price level, and they therefore withdraw some of their labor; this resulting shortage of labor forces the nominal wage rate upward until the original real wage rate is reestablished. This is shown in panel *b* of Figure 12.6 as no change; the labor market does not deviate from point *A* in panel *b*.

With respect to the *nominal* demand for and nominal supply of labor market, depicted in panel *a* of Figure 12.6, an increase in the price level from P_1 to P_2 will increase the demand for labor while it simultaneously decreases the supply of labor. This will leave total employment (and, by implication, total output) unaltered but will cause nominal wage rates to rise proportionally to the increase in the price level.

Note that in this model it is assumed that the perceptions are correct and that prices and nominal wage rates are perfectly flexible.

The Extreme Keynesian Model

Assume again that the money supply is exogenously increased and that, consequently, the price level rises. If laborers are completely unaware of the now higher price level—because information concerning the prices of all the goods they purchase is not immediately available to them— they will not bargain for higher money wage rates. In terms of equation 12.8, the ratio $P^e/P < 1$ because P rises and P^e is constant; also, W/P^e

remains constant. The result is that the real wage falls but the amount of labor offered remains constant; and this is equivalent to an increase in the real supply of labor because the quantity supplied of labor is now higher at every real wage rate. At the same time, a higher price level *is* perceived by employers who, after all, need only keep track of the price of their own good or service. This means that the real wage rate has fallen, and employers increase their quantity demanded of labor; the economy moves down a *given* aggregate real demand-for-labor curve. Panel *b* in Figure 12.7 shows the result in real terms: The supply of labor rises, the demand for labor remains constant, the real wage rate falls, and employment rises (and, by implication, real output rises).

In panel *a* of Figure 12.7, a higher price level increases the nominal demand for labor because employers have perceived the change in the price level (and the reduction in the real wage rate). The supply of labor is *not* changed, however, because workers have *not* perceived the change in the price level (and the reduction in their real wage rate), and their supply curve is still dependent on the former (lower) price level, P_1. The result is a higher level of employment and a higher nominal wage rate. Note, however, that even though nominal wage rates are higher, *real* wage rates are lower because the price level has increased more rapidly than nominal wage rates have risen.

In this model we have assumed that money wage rates rise only slightly, and only because of the increased nominal demand for labor due to the correct perceptions of employers. Workers are assumed to be unaware of the change in the price level. It should be stressed that the conclusions of this model are based solely on the assumption that laborers do not perceive the change in the price level:

Nominal wage rates are assumed to be perfectly flexible; the only reason nominal wage rates don't rise proportional to the rise in the price level is that workers do not perceive that the price level has increased.

The Keynesian Incomplete Adjustment Assumption Model

The two models just discussed seem rather extreme. Because workers are faced with a difficult task when they try to ascertain the correct price level, the classical assumption of immediate and correct perception seems extreme. Equally unlikely seems the extreme Keynesian assumption that workers don't perceive any change at all in the price level. A

The Extreme Keynesian Assumption Results

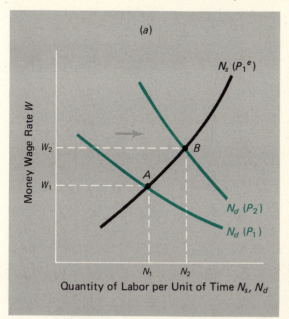

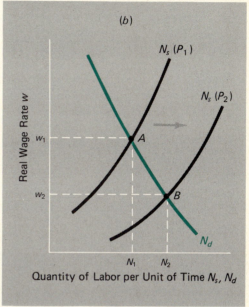

FIGURE 12.7. AN INCREASE IN THE PRICE LEVEL FROM P_1 TO P_2

Given the extreme Keynesian assumptions, an increase in the price level causes an increase in the real supply-of-labor curve in panel *b* because workers do not perceive *any* change in the price level so they offer (in effect) more labor at any given real wage rate. Employers perceive the higher price level correctly, and they increase their quantity demanded of labor from N_1 to N_2 because the real wage rate has fallen. The labor market moves from *A* to *B*.

In panel *a*, the nominal demand for labor increases to $N_d(P_2)$ because employers correctly perceive that the price level has increased from P_1 to P_2. The nominal supply-of-labor curve does not decrease because workers still perceive (incorrectly) price level P_1^e. Nominal wage rates rise from W_1 to W_2 but they rise less than proportionally to the increase in the price level, so the real wage rate falls.

more reasonable assumption, perhaps, is one which is between these two extremes.

In this model we assume that laborers adjust their perception of the price level as the actual price level changes. In effect, the assumption is that workers make incomplete adjustments to changes in the price level because they do not know if actual price changes are temporary or permanent. We have encountered this problem before when we analyzed the permanent income hypothesis (Chapter 9) and the accelerator hypothesis (Chapter 10). In those chapters we concluded that consumers adjust to changes in income that are not known to be permanent or temporary, and that businesses adjust to changes in sales that are not known to be permanent or temporary, via the adaptive expectations hypothesis. The problem now is that workers must adjust to changes in the price level that are not known to be permanent or transitory. Once again we can apply the adaptive expectations analysis.

Assume that this year's estimate of the *permanent* price level P_p equals last year's estimate of the permanent price level P_{p-1} plus some fraction J of the amount by which this year's price level P differs from last year's estimate of the permanent price level $P - P_{p-1}$. Thus,

$$P_p = P_{p-1} + J(P - P_{p-1}) \qquad (12.14)$$

where $0 < J < 1$.

Equation 12.14 suggests that if this year's price level is the same as last year's (that is, if $P - P_{p-1} = 0$), then the estimate of the permanent price level is unrevised. If this year's price level exceeds last year's estimate of the permanent price level (that is, if $P - P_{p-1} > 0$), then the estimate of the permanent price level will be revised upward, by J (a fraction) times the difference. If this year's price level is less than last year's (that is, if $P - P_{p-1} < 0$), then the estimate of the permanent price level will be adjusted downward by J times the difference.

Consider Figure 12.8. In panels *a* and *b* we start at point *A;* equilibrium exists in both nominal and real terms. The expected and actual price level is P_1. As before, we assume a Fed-induced exogenous increase in the money supply which increases the actual price level to the permanently higher level, P_3.

Workers react according to adaptive expectations; they revise their perception of the price level upward to P_2^e, which is less than P_3. In real terms (see panel *b*) the supply-of-labor curve increases, but not by as much as it did in the extreme Keynesian model, when the higher price level was totally unperceived. In the classical model workers would have adjusted their expectation of the price level immediately upward to P_3^e, and the supply of labor would not have increased at all. The result in the incomplete adjustment assumption model is an increase in employment (and, by implication, an increase in output) and a lower real wage rate. As time passes, the real supply-of-labor curve will shift back to the original supply curve because laborers will eventually adjust to the permanently higher actual price level. In the short run, therefore, the level of aggregate employment and the level of national output will rise above their original levels. Eventually, when the higher price level is completely perceived, aggregate employment and national output will return to their initial levels.

The Keynesian Incomplete Adjustment Assumption

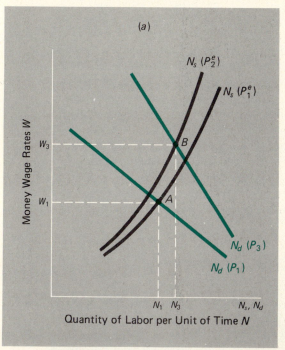 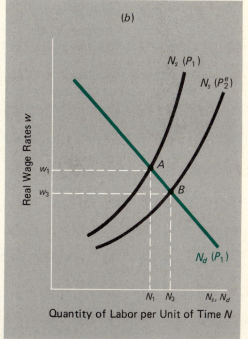

FIGURE 12.8. A RISE IN THE PRICE LEVEL FROM P_1 TO P_3

In panel b, the supply of labor increases only slightly, because laborers perceive price level P_2^e, which is between P_1 and the actual price level P_3, so employment rises slightly from N_1 to N_3 and the real wage rate falls slightly to w_3.

In panel a the demand for labor rises to $N_d(P_3)$ because employers correctly perceive price level P_3. The supply-of-labor curve decreases slightly, but not completely, because workers perceive only part of the higher price level; they perceive level P_2^e, which is between P_1 and P_3; $P_1 < P_2^e < P_3$. Money wage rates rise by less than they would have if P_3 had been correctly perceived, but by more than they would have if they were completely unperceived. Employment rises to N_3 because the real wage rate has fallen.

Panel a indicates what happens in nominal terms. Employers perceive the higher price level immediately, so the demand for labor increases to $N_d(P_3)$, a curve consistent with the actual price level, P_3. Because workers only partially adjust to the price level, to P_2^e, they (partially) reduce their supply of labor and the labor supply curve decreases to $N_s(P_2^e)$, a curve consistent with workers' (incompletely) upwardly revised perception of the price level. Consistent with panel b, panel *a* shows an increase in employment and a higher nominal but lower real wage rate. Eventually the supply-of-labor curve will decrease until it is consistent with a correctly perceived price level; at that time, employment will return to its original level and nominal wage rates will have increased proportional to the actual change in the price level.

Reasoning by analogy, a Fed-induced exogenous *decrease* in the money supply—given our adaptive expectations approach—will lead to a temporary *reduction* in aggregate employment and national output and to a temporary reduction in money wage rates and a temporary increase in real wage rates. We leave it to you to work out the analysis and the graphical exposition.

We again stress that throughout this chapter we have assumed that wage rates are perfectly flexible; in the models where wage rates *do not* rise immediately and proportionally to increases in the price level, this is due to the assumption that workers do not immediately *perceive* changes in the price level. We now relax the assumption of perfect wage flexibility.

INFLEXIBLE WAGE RATES

Many economists believe that wages are not perfectly flexible. Keynes himself believed that wages are inflexible. As we indicated in Chapter 6, Keynes believed that in times of rising prices and constant money wage rates, workers would not reduce the amount of labor they offered because they were locked into debt payments. Moreover, said Keynes, in such times labor union leaders would not strike because *all* real wage rates would fall and the hierarchy of union wage rates would not be upset; at least in times of mildly rising prices, therefore, unions would not withdraw labor. It follows, therefore, that *even if a higher price level is correctly perceived*, aggregate employment and national output might rise in response to a higher price level and a lower real wage rate.

Keynesians also stress that a welfare state which incorporates minimum-wage laws, unemployment compensation, and welfare disincentives to work creates wage rates that are sticky downward. If this is so, then aggregate employment and national output can be *below* their natural levels for prolonged periods. For example, if a shock occurs that induces a recession, relative wage rate reductions are required (at least in some industries). If nominal wage rates are sticky downward, real wage rates won't fall and unemployment will be higher than need be, for longer periods. Therefore, even if perceptions are correct, employment will be below its natural level, as will real national output.

In recent years Keynesian economists have found other reasons for assuming that wage rates are not perfectly flexible. One is that in the unionized sector of the labor market wage rates are typically set by long-term labor contracts that cover periods of two or three years. To the extent that such labor contracts are not completely indexed by cost-of-living adjustments, money wage rates will not adjust upward or downward as the demand for labor rises or falls, respectively. We again conclude that aggregate employment and national output will vary directly with the price level.

In the nonunion remainder of the labor market, where *explicit* long-term labor contracts are not signed, an *implicit* agreement is often made between buyers and sellers of labor. In order to maintain good *reputations* (working relations), both workers and employers (allegedly) implicitly agree not to take advantage of temporary situations during which one group has the upper hand. For example, in temporary recessions, when the demand for workers decreases, employers usually refrain from reducing money wage rates and from replacing their labor pool with unemployed workers who would gladly work for lower nominal wage rates. Instead, employers reduce output and reduce the amount of overtime, or put "their" workers on temporary layoff. Employers also save training costs attendant on hiring new workers frequently.

Workers, for their part of the "implicit contract," do not take advantage during boom periods by demanding higher nominal wage rates or quitting their jobs to work elsewhere for higher wages. Relocation costs to workers help to dampen their demand for higher wage rates.

The result is that good reputations are beneficial to both workers and employers. Such a quid pro quo arrangement generates good labor relations, higher long-run profits for businesses, and higher long-run incomes for laborers. Such an implicit labor contract also implies sticky nominal wage rates, and so aggregate employment and national output will vary directly with the price level.

CHAPTER SUMMARY

1. The real demand-for-labor curve indicates an inverse relationship between the quantity of labor demanded and real wage rates, other things constant. The nominal demand-for-labor curve shows an inverse relationship between the money wage rate and the quantity demanded of labor, other things constant.
2. An increase in selling price, other things constant, shifts the *nominal* demand-for-labor curve upward; a decrease in selling price, other things constant, leads to a downward shift in the nominal demand-for-labor curve. Concerning the *real* demand-for-labor curve, an increase in selling price and a decrease in selling price, other things

constant, lead to an increase in quantity demanded of labor and to a decrease in quantity demanded of labor, respectively; the real demand-for-labor curve *does not shift* as selling price changes.

3. A proportional increase in wage rates and selling price causes (a) the nominal demand-for-labor curve to shift upward but the quantity of labor demanded to remain unaltered, and (b) neither a shift nor a movement along the real demand-for-labor curve.

4. Employers need only be concerned with one price, the selling prices of their own goods or services, but workers must be concerned with the prices of the many goods that they purchase. Given the nominal wage rate, which is known by both groups, employers know "their" real wage rate but workers perceive the real wage rate imperfectly.

5. A real supply-of-labor curve can be derived by assuming different expected real wage rates on the part of workers and an indifference curve analysis that indicates workers can trade real income for leisure. Workers maximize their total utility by offering an optimal quantity of labor per unit of time. The optimal quantity supplied of labor depends on the expected real wage rate and the worker's relative tastes for leisure and real income.

6. In equilibrium, wage rates have adjusted so as to equate the quantity supplied of labor with the quantity demanded of labor. The manner in which a change in the price level affects conditions in the labor market depends on the extent to which the change is perceived by laborers.

7. In the classical model, workers immediately and correctly perceive changes in the price level; therefore, neither aggregate employment nor national output is affected. Nominal wage rates rise proportionally to the increase in the price level.

8. In the extreme Keynesian assumption model, an increase in the price level is not perceived at all by workers. As a consequence, aggregate employment and national output will vary directly with the price level and real wage rates will fall. Nominal wage rates rise slightly, but incompletely.

9. By applying the adaptive expectations model, it can be shown that workers will adapt slowly and incompletely to changes in the price level. In the short run, therefore, aggregate employment and national output will vary directly with the price level, real wage rates will fall, and nominal wage rates will rise less than proportionally to rises in the price level. This model leads to conclusions that are between those in items 7 and 8 above.

10. The previous models assumed complete wage rate flexibility. For various reasons, wage rates may not be perfectly flexible. If not, then aggregate employment and national output will vary directly with the price level, even if perceptions are correct for everyone.

GLOSSARY

budget constraint line   A line that shows all the combinations of goods that a person or group can purchase, given their resources; a point on a budget constraint line shows the maximum of one good a person can purchase, given a quantity of the other, with a fixed level of resources.

indifference curve   A curve that shows all the combinations of goods which yield the same level of total utility.

QUESTIONS AND PROBLEMS FOR REVIEW

12.1   The quantity of labor demanded is inversely related to the real wage rate. How would the demand for labor be affected by an increase in the productivity of labor? By an increase in the demand for the output?

12.2   Although it is often maintained that employers need only be concerned with the selling price of their own good, it can be argued that changes in the selling prices of other goods affect an employer's opportunity costs. How do such changes affect opportunity costs and why might the effects be important?

12.3   Show that a contradiction would result if indifference curves were drawn as below:

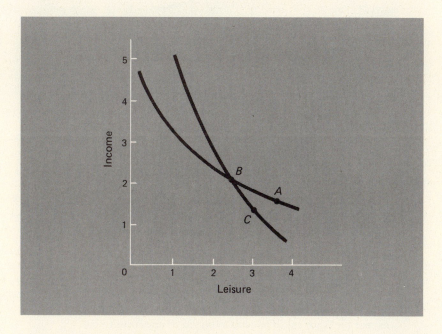

12.4   To the extent that individuals prefer more than less, can you compare the associated utility levels of the combination 14 hours of leisure and $10,000

with the combination of 9 hours of leisure and $15,000? Can you make such a comparison if you are told that the combination of 12 hours of leisure and $8,000, and the combination of 9 hours of leisure and $15,000, yield the same utility?

12.5 Various combinations on the individual indifference curves below all yield the same utility, although different from that which separate indifference curves yield. If the wage rate is $5 per hour, what is the optimal leisure/income combination?

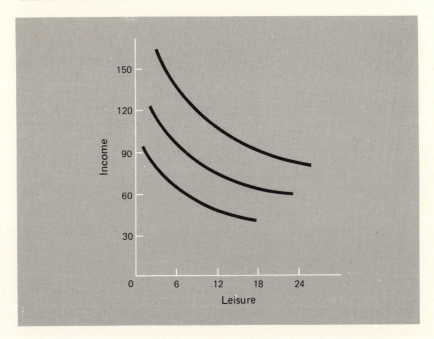

12.6 It is argued that in equilibrium (in a perfectly competitive market) the money wage equals the value of the marginal *product* of labor, or

$$W = \text{VMP}_n \equiv P \times \text{MPP}_n$$

If output is sold in an *imperfectly competitive market*, the money wage equals the marginal *revenue* product, which is less than VMP_n. On what, therefore, does the validity of the alternative assumptions rest?

12.7 The statement that in equilibrium wage rates have adjusted so as to equate the quantity supplied of labor with the quantity demanded of labor is true only under conditions of perfect competition in labor markets. To the extent that monopsony power exists, equilibrium wage rates do not occur at the intersection of supply and demand. What differences would you expect for labor markets characterized by monopsony?

12.8 In the extreme Keynesian model, a change in the price level is not perceived perfectly by all workers. As a consequence, it is thought that aggregate employment and national output will vary directly with the price level. In order for such a consequence to occur, what bias in the perception must be assumed? Do you think that this bias exists for the supply of labor?

12.9 The adaptive expectations model is associated with conclusions that are between those in the classical model and the extreme Keynesian model. Do you think that it is more important to examine the *logic* of the theories or to *empirically verify* the assumptions in order to decide on the validity of the alternatives?

12.10 For various reasons wage rates may be thought to be inflexible. Do you think that wage rates may be more flexible in one direction than the other? What importance does the possibility of more flexibility in one direction than the other have on the choice of policy?

REFERENCES

Armen A. Alchian, "Information Costs, Pricing, and Resource Unemployment," *Western Economic Journal*, vol. 7 (1969).

William H. Branson and James M. Litvak, *Macroeconomics*, 2d ed. (New York: Harper & Row, 1981).

Milton Friedman, "The Role of Monetary Policy," *American Economic Review*, vol. 48 (1968).

———, "Nobel Lecture: Inflation and Unemployment," *Journal of Political Economy*, vol. 85 (1977).

John Maynard Keynes, *The General Theory of Employment, Interest, and Money* (New York: Harcourt Brace Jovanovich, 1964).

Edmund S. Phelps, "Money Wage Dynamics and Labour Market Equilibrium," *Journal of Political Economy*, vol. 76 (1968).

Edmund S. Phelps et al., *The Microeconomic Foundations of Employment and Inflation Theory* (New York: Norton, 1970).

Edmund S. Phelps and J. B. Taylor, "Stabilizing Powers of Monetary Policy Under Rational Expectations," *Journal of Political Economy*, vol. 85 (1977).

13

THE MODERN THEORY OF INFLATION

Although the rate of inflation has abated in the United States, at least temporarily, the fear of renewed inflation continues to be a major concern. Indeed, inflation is a worldwide phenomenon and a major problem in many countries. This chapter is devoted to an analysis of inflation. In particular, we discuss:

1. Three modern theories of how the price level is determined
2. Four leading theories of inflation, which include the monetary, demand-pull, cost-push, and federal government deficits theories
3. A Policy Controversy concerning price-wage controls as a means of combatting inflation

In order to discuss **inflation,** which is defined as a sustained increase in the price level over time, it is important to know how the price level is determined. You will recall from Chapter 5 that according to the classical economists the price level was determined by the interaction of the supply of and the demand for money. This can be shown easily using the equation of exchange:

$$MV = Py \tag{13.1}$$

WHERE M = the money supply (narrowly defined as the value of currency plus the value of checking account balances)

V = income velocity, or the ratio of nominal national income to *desired* money balances; V is inversely related to the demand for money

P = the price level

y = the value of real output of final goods and services per year

According to the classical economists, y is constant at its full-employment level (owing to Say's law). As a consequence, P is determined by the value of M, the nominal money supply, and V, a factor that indicates the demand for money. From this theory of the price level, the classical theory of inflation is easily demonstrated. Classical economists believed that velocity was constant, so changes in the money supply led to proportional changes in the price level. To them, inflation was a monetary phenomenon: increases in the money supply led to increases in the price level.

Many modern economists believe that the classical theory of how the price level is determined and the classical theory of inflation are too simple. We turn now to the modern and widely accepted theory of how the price level is determined. Then we discuss various theories of why the price level rises. The leading theories of inflation can be better understood after we understand the modern theory of how the price level is determined.

AGGREGATE DEMAND AND AGGREGATE SUPPLY CURVES

The *is-lm* framework developed in Chapter 7 was couched in real terms; the real interest rate and the real level of national income were derived simultaneously through the interaction of the product and money markets. In the *is-lm* model, the price level was assumed to be constant; hence, changes in nominal and real values were equivalent. The *is-lm* framework therefore is not suitable for analyzing the determination of the price level. For this reason, an aggregate demand curve and an aggregate supply curve are now derived by varying the price level. As Chapter 5 indicated, the *aggregate demand (AD) curve* relates different quantities of real national output demanded to various price levels, other things constant; the *aggregate supply (AS) curve* relates the real value of the nation's aggregate output of goods and services to various price levels, other things constant. This analysis is somewhat analogous to the supply of and the demand for an individual good or service.

Aggregate Demand

Recall the section in Chapter 8 which describes the Keynes effect. The Keynes effect is that a falling price level (due to unemployment) is equivalent to an increase in the real money supply because it shifts the *lm* curve to the right. Even though the nominal money supply remains constant, a lower price level reduces the amount of money required for real transactions and real precautionary motives L_1/P; *real* money balances increase as the price level falls. Figure 13.1 shows how an aggregate demand curve can be constructed. In panel *a*, lower price levels cause the *lm* curve to shift to the right due to the Keynes effect. If the *is* curve remains constant, then excess money balances resulting from a lower real L_1 imply a surplus of money in the money market. If there is no liquidity trap, these excess balances are used to purchase bonds; and this forces bond prices up and interest rates down. A lower real rate of interest causes an increase in net investment, and real national income increases (potentially) by some multiple of the change in autonomous investment.[1] Thus, a lower price level, through its impact on the rate of interest, causes an increase in the equilibrium quantity output demanded. Panel

---

[1] This increased real income causes an increase in the quantity of real L_1 demanded; the process continues until the supply of and the demand for real money are equated and the community voluntarily is holding the existing stock of money. Of course, the AD curve can also be derived by the Pigou effect, also discussed in Chapter 8.

The Keynes Effect Can Be Utilized to Derive
the Aggregate Demand Curve

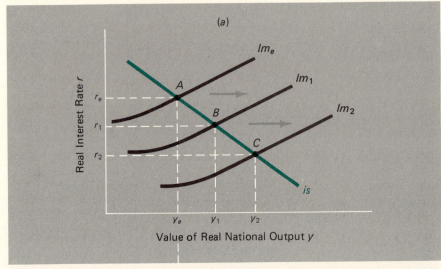

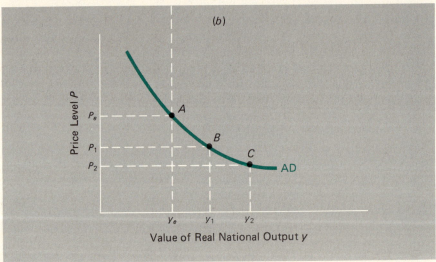

FIGURE 13.1. DERIVING THE AD CURVE

In panel *a*, lower price levels shift the *lm* curve rightward and lead to a lower real interest rate. Lower real interest rates lead to an increase in real net investment and a multiple expansion in real national output. In panel *b*, the relationship implied in panel *a* is indicated; lower price levels increase the quantity of real output demanded, other things constant.

b of Figure 13.1 traces out the equilibrium price level–output combinations resulting from the *is-lm* framework in panel *a*. Note that lm_e, lm_1, and lm_2 are associated with progressively lower price levels, P_e, P_1, and P_2, respectively.

Shifts in Aggregate Demand   What causes this aggregate demand curve to shift? Any *non–price level* change that causes either the *is* or the *lm* curve to shift will lead to a shift in the aggregate demand curve. These include changes in the money supply, shifts in the marginal efficiency-of-investment curve, shifts in the consumption function, and as you will soon see, changes in government expenditures and taxes.

Fiscal Policy Effects on the Aggregate Demand Curve   Consider Figure 13.2. In panel *a*, the initial equilibrium position is at r_e and y_e. Then the *is* curve shifts to the right by $\Delta g/(1 - b)$ as a result of expansionary fiscal policy (i.e., if, as here, government expenditures *g* increase and/or taxes t_x decrease). The effect is to cause an increase in the level of output at *any* real interest rate. However, the nominal supply of money is assumed to be constant; hence, the *lm* curve does not shift. As a consequence, a higher level of real national output and income requires a greater quantity of money demanded for real L_1 purposes. The demand for liquidity rises, and bond sales drive bond prices downward and drive real interest rates upward. Thus, a higher real interest rate "crowds out" some investment. The levels of real national income and output don't expand as much as they otherwise would have if the real interest rate had remained constant; the multiplier effect is reduced. In other words, fiscal policy *would have* expanded national output and real income to y_m but a shortage of liquidity in the money market forced real interest rates upward and crowded out private investments. Instead of real income y_m, the nation must settle for y_1. This is also indicated in panel *b*, which shows an increase in real output at the same price level P_e, from y_e to y_1 and not from y_e to y_m. The investment that was crowded out by a higher interest rate reduces *y* from y_m to y_1.

It is important to realize that point *B* in panel *b*, the combination of the new output level y_1 and the same price level P_e, is one point on a *new* aggregate demand curve. Figure 13.3 shows the results of expansionary fiscal policy on the aggregate demand curve at *all* price levels. Figure 13.2 showed the results of fiscal expansion at only *one* price level, P_e. Figure 13.3 includes the effect of fiscal policy on price level P_e (a movement from *A* to *B*) and on all other price levels as well. In short, expansionary fiscal policy shifts the aggregate demand curve to the right. It is left to you to demonstrate that a contractionary fiscal policy that

Expansionary Fiscal Policy Increases the Quantity of National Output Desired at a Given Price Level

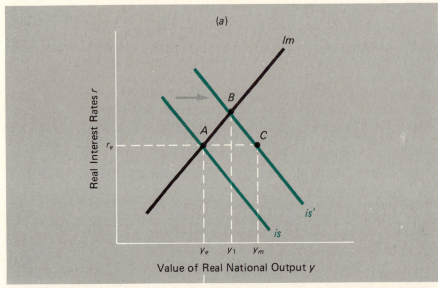

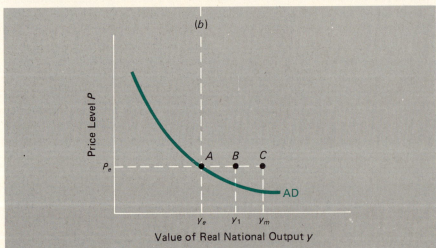

FIGURE 13.2. THE EFFECT OF EXPANSIONARY FISCAL POLICY ON THE QUANTITY OF NATIONAL OUTPUT DEMANDED

In panel *a*, an expansionary fiscal policy shifts the *is* curve rightward. Real national income increases, but not by the complete multiplier effect because an expansionary fiscal policy simultaneously raises the real interest rate and some private investment is crowded out. Panel *b* shows that a rightward shift in the *is* curve leads to an increase in the quantity of national real output demanded at the same price level P_e. If the interest rate does not rise, the quantity of national output demanded is y_m; if the interest rate rises, it is only y_1.

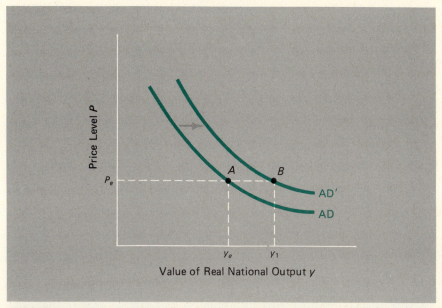

FIGURE 13.3. THE EFFECT OF EXPANSIONARY FISCAL POLICY ON THE AGGREGATE DEMAND CURVE

Figure 13.2 indicated that an increase in the *is* curve leads to an increase in the quantity of real national output demanded at the *same* price level. This figure indicates the results of increases in the *is* curve at *all* price levels. Thus, shifts in the *is* curve lead to changes in the demand for real national output; the national output demanded is different at every price level. An increase in aggregate demand results from a rightward shift in the *is* curve.

reduces g will shift the aggregate demand curve to the left by the amount that g falls times the government expenditure multiplier Mg.[2]

Monetary Policy Effects on the Aggregate Demand Curve Recall that an increase in the real money supply shifts the *lm* curve to the right by

---

[2] The aggregate demand curve also shifts if the consumption function or the autonomous net investment function shifts. These shifts would lead to a shift in the *is* curve equal to the change in autonomous expenditures times the multiplier, which in turn would cause an increase in the quantity of output demanded at any price level. In an open economy, an increase in net exports (exports minus imports) would also shift aggregate demand by a multiplier.

An Expansionary Monetary Policy Leads to a Lower Interest Rate and a Larger Quantity Demanded of National Output

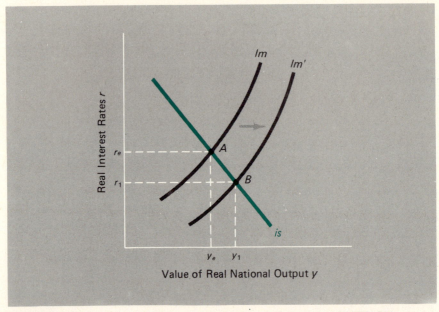

FIGURE 13.4. THE EFFECT OF AN EXPANSIONARY MONETARY POLICY

At point *A*, the supply of and the demand for money are equated. An increase in the real money supply shifts the *lm* curve rightward by $(\Delta M/P)/k$, or by the change in the real money supply divided by the ratio of money balances to national income, and initially creates an excess supply of money, or excess liquidity. This causes the interest rate to fall, which in turn causes an increase in real net investment and a multiple expansion in the level of real national output. Such an increase in real national income, however, causes an increase in the demand for real L_1 balances. This process continues until the supply of and the demand for money are again equated, at point *B*.

the change in the real money supply times $1/k$; a decrease in the real money supply shifts the *lm* curve to the left. Consider Figure 13.4, which indicates the former case. An increase in the real money supply shifts the *lm* curve to the right, from *lm* to *lm'*. The initial equilibrium position is r_e and y_e (point *A*), at which point equilibrium existed simultaneously in both the product and the money markets. A real money supply increase means that now a surplus of liquidity exists at point *A*; $M/P > (L_1 + L_2)/P$. Such an increase can result from an expansionary monetary policy pursued by the Fed (discussed in Chapter 16). The surplus of liquidity induces bond purchases and causes bond prices to rise and interest rates to fall. A lower real interest rate induces an increase in real net investment and a multiple expansion in real national income and output.[3] In turn, a higher level of real national income increases the quantity of money demanded for real L_1 purposes. This process continues until the now higher real money supply is held voluntarily by the community. The new equilibrium position is at point B, the combination of y_1 and r_1.

Figure 13.5 indicates how monetary policy affects the aggregate demand curve. Panel a reproduces Figure 13.4, while panel b indicates that an increase in the real money supply leads to an increase in the demand for national output *at the same price level P_e.*

Figure 13.6 shows how monetary policy shifts the aggregate demand curve. An increase in the money supply causes a rightward shift in the aggregate demand curve, from AD to AD'. A quantity of national output demanded is higher at every price level, including P_e.

Aggregate Supply

It is easy to discern the shape of an individual firm's supply curve. As you will recall from your principles of economics course, the firm's short-run supply curve slopes upward from left to right. Before a firm voluntarily produces more output in the short run, price must rise to offset increasing marginal costs. Marginal costs rise because of the law of diminishing returns. A firm increases its output in the short run by using more labor relative to other factors of production; this causes the marginal physical product of labor to fall, and, given nominal wage rates, the marginal cost of output rises.

A firm that has the option to produce two goods will also increase the output of one relative to the other as their relative prices change. For example, an oil refiner can increase the output of gasoline relative to heating oil. If the relative price of gasoline rises, oil refiners will increase the output of gasoline and reduce the output of heating oil; the supply of gasoline (and heating oil) is directly related to its relative price.

---

[3] Note that the *full* multiplier effect obtains, unlike the fiscal policy results, because no crowding-out effect occurs. There is, however, an effect analogous to the crowding-out effect. A lower interest rate increases the quantity of money demanded for real L_2 balances, and therefore the total quantity of money demanded rises. The ultimate increase in real national income, therefore, is less than it would have been had real L_2 not been inversely related to the real interest rate. More technically, owing to the existence of a real L_2 demand for money, the *lm* curve is not vertical; a shift in *lm* by a given amount (owing to an increase in the real money supply) would cause real national income to increase more if the *lm* curve were vertical than if it were positively sloped. We return to this issue in Chapter 18.

Expansionary Monetary Policy Increases the Quantity Demanded of National Output at the Existing Price Level

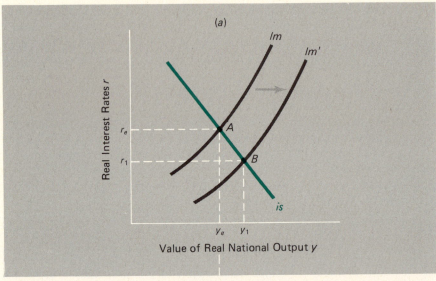

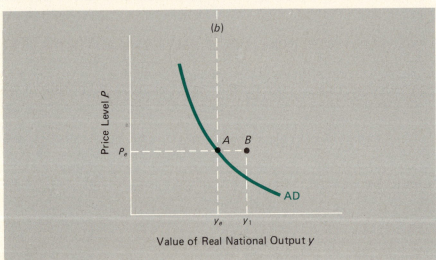

FIGURE 13.5. THE EFFECT OF AN EXPANSIONARY MONETARY POLICY ON THE QUANTITY DEMANDED OF REAL NATIONAL OUTPUT
Panel *a* reproduces Figure 13.4. Panel *b* indicates that a rightward shift in the *lm* curve leads to an increase in the quantity demanded of real national output at the current price level, from y_e to y_1.

Expansionary Monetary Policy Shifts the Aggregate Demand Curve to the Right

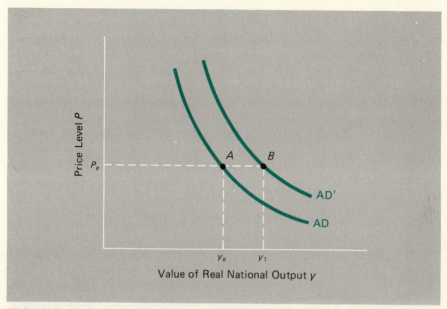

FIGURE 13.6. THE EFFECT OF EXPANSIONARY MONETARY POLICY ON THE AGGREGATE DEMAND CURVE

Panel *b* of Figure 13.5 indicated that a rightward shift in the *lm* curve causes an increase in the quantity of real national output demanded at the *current* price level. Figure 13.6 shows that a rightward shift in the *lm* curve leads to an increase in the quantity of real national output demanded at *all* price levels. That is, an increase in the *lm* curve leads to an increase in the aggregate demand for real national output.

Similar statements can be made about farms and other businesses that can produce more than one good.

The industry supply curve is derived by summing horizontally all the individual firm supply curves. This summation provides another explanation for the upward-sloping nature of supply curves. At higher relative prices, firms that are inefficient can also produce; at lower relative prices, some firms are too inefficient to operate at all. Therefore, higher relative prices increase the quantity that an industry is willing to supply, because firms that had temporarily shut down will now operate.

You may have noted that quantity supplied responds to *relative* price changes. When the price of one good rises relative to another, its quantity supplied will increase. If so, the *aggregate* supply curve (which relates total output to the price level) need not respond to changes in the price level. If all prices (input as well as output) change at the same rate, relative prices do not change and there is no reason to expect output changes. Similarly, if all prices change at the same rate, households will not change their consumption and laborers will not change the number of hours they work. Under these conditions the aggregate supply curve is unresponsive to changes in the price level. Of course, prices and wages need not all change at the same rate if tastes and technology are changing with the price level; some prices will change relative to others and some wages will change relative to others. This will cause some industries to expand and others to contract. Output and employment will increase in those industries that experience relative price increases; output and employment will contract in those industries that experience relative price decreases. Still, in this context, the overall effect is that *total* output and *total* employment are unresponsive to changes in the price level.

The Classical Aggregate Supply Curve   Such a model was the one classical economists used. Figure 13.7 shows the nominal supply of labor and the nominal demand for labor in panel *a*, which we borrowed from panel *a* in Figure 12.6. The aggregate production function is shown in panel *b*, and the classical aggregate supply curve is in panel *c*.

As the price level rises, the nominal demand for labor increases and the nominal supply of labor decreases. Both employers and workers immediately perceive the higher price level, and wages rise proportionally. Panel *a* indicates that employment remains at the full-employment level N_f. The level of real national output is determined from the production function in panel *b*; a full-employment level of real national output, y_f, consistent with N_f, is produced. Panel *c* shows that increases in the price level leave the national output level unaltered, at y_f.

In the classical model, therefore, the aggregate supply curve is vertical. We want to stress that *this* classical vertical aggregate supply curve is a *short-run* curve, because we assumed here that workers *immediately* perceive the change in the price level and because nominal wage rates are assumed to be perfectly flexible. In Chapter 5 we showed that the classical aggregate supply curve was vertical in the *long run*, after workers adjusted to such shocks in the economy as a higher price level resulting from an increased money supply.

An Extreme-Keynesian-Assumption Aggregate Supply Curve   Recall from Chapter 12 that in the extreme Keynesian model workers do not

The Classical Aggregate Supply Curve Is Vertical in the Short Run If Workers Immediately Perceive Changes in the Price Level

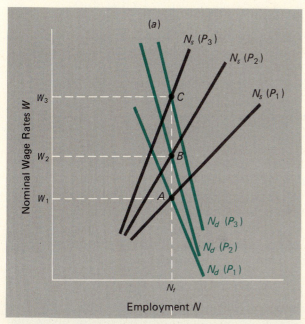

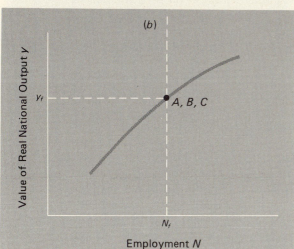

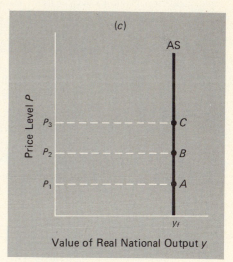

FIGURE 13.7. DERIVING THE CLASSICAL AGGREGATE SUPPLY CURVE

If workers immediately perceive a change in the price level and if wage rates are perfectly flexible, changes in the price level will leave employment and the value of national output unaltered. Hence, the aggregate supply curve is vertical, even in the *short run*, as indicated in panel c.

perceive *any* change in the price level; therefore, the nominal labor supply curve is unaltered as the price level changes. Employers, on the other hand, immediately recognize that their selling prices have risen; therefore, the nominal demand-for-labor curve varies (shifts) directly with the price level. This is indicated in panel *a* of Figure 13.8 (which we borrowed from Figure 12.7). Note that as the price level rises from P_1 to P_2 to P_3, the employment level rises from N_1 to N_f (full employment) to N_3, implying that the employment rate can depart from (below or above) the natural rate (full employment) in the short run as the price level changes.

Panel *b* indicates that, as the employment level rises from N_1 to N_f to N_3, the value of real national output rises concomitantly. Finally, panel *c* condenses the results in panels *a* and *b* and shows an aggregate supply curve that is positively sloped; higher price levels induce producers in the aggregate to increase output levels in the short run.

The Keynesian Incomplete-Adjustment-Assumption Aggregate Supply Curve Recall from Chapter 12 that a more realistic assumption is that workers may not be able to tell immediately whether a change in the price level is permanent or temporary. If we assume that workers adjust to a change in the price level gradually, according to the adaptive expectations approach, an increase in the price level causes an incomplete reduction in the nominal supply of labor. Laborers are assumed to adjust their perception of the *permanent* price level by a fraction of the change in the *actual* price level. The supply-of-labor curve therefore shifts upward, but not by so much as in the classical case, where workers are assumed to adjust immediately and perfectly to changes in the price level.

Employers, as usual, are assumed to adjust completely to changes in the price level. The result is that a given (permanent) increase in the price level will elicit increases in employment and output, but not by so much as in the extreme Keynesian model. This is all contained in the by now familiar panels *a*, *b*, and *c* of Figure 13.9; panel *a* is borrowed from panel *a* in Figure 12.8. Note that if we had assumed *no* adjustment by workers, the aggregate supply curve would go through points *A* and *B* (as in Figure 13.8) and the dashed AS' curve is less steep than the AS curve.

Our conclusion is that, unless workers immediately and correctly perceive a permanent change in the price level, and even if we assume perfect nominal wage-rate flexibility, the aggregate supply curve will slope upward, from left to right. (Of course, if we assume nominal wage rate *inflexibility*, we can also derive an upward-sloping aggregate supply curve, as our comments in Chapter 12 demonstrated.)

If Workers Do Not Perceive a Change in the Price Level, the Aggregate Supply Curve Is Upward-Sloping

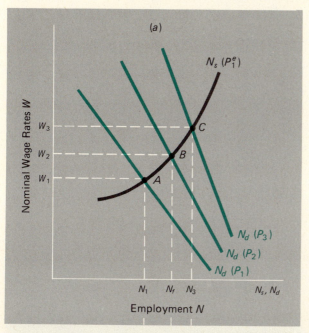

(a)

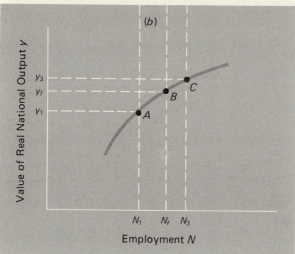

(b)

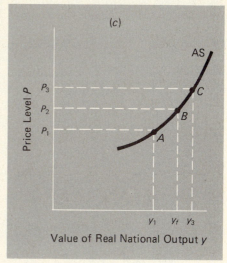

(c)

FIGURE 13.8. AS AND THE EXTREME KEYNESIAN ASSUMPTION

If workers do not observe the change in the price level, the supply-of-labor curve will not shift. Employers *do* observe the price level change, so the demand-for-labor curve shifts. If the price level rises from P_1 to P_2, total employment will rise from N_1 to N_f in panel *a*. In panel *b*, this is a movement up the aggregate production function, from A to B. The results are summarized in panel *c*.

Incomplete Worker Adjustment Leads to a Positive-Sloped AS Curve

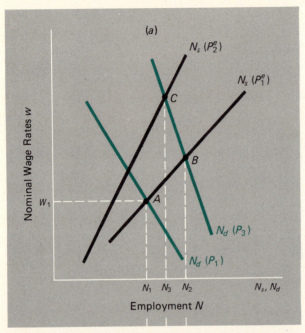

(a)

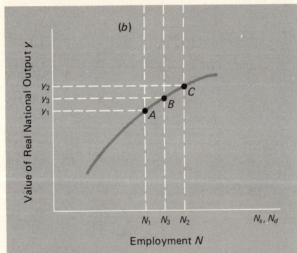

(b)

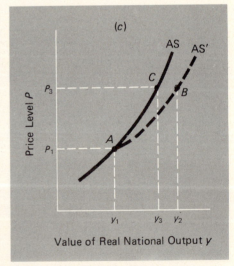

(c)

FIGURE 13.9. INCOMPLETE ADJUSTMENT AND THE AS CURVE

If the price level rises from P_1 to P_3, the nominal demand for labor increases to $N_d(P_3)$, but the nominal supply of labor decreases only partially, to $N_s(P_2^e)$ because workers perceive that the price level is $P_2 < P_3$. Employment rises to $N_3 < N_2$, and real national output rises to $y_3 < y_2$. AS is steeper than AS' because the latter curve assumes *no* perception of the higher price level by workers, while AS assumes a partial perception. Complete and perfect perception by workers means that AS would be *vertical* at y_1, as in the classical case.

Determination of the Equilibrium National Output—Price Level Combination

Figure 13.10 shows that the equilibrium national output—price level combination is determined at the intersection of the AD curve and the AS curve. Given those curves, the price level will be at P_e and the value of real national income will be y_e.

CAUSES OF INFLATION

Now that we have a theory of how a nation's price level is determined, we are in a position to discuss the cause of inflation. Although there are many cases of inflation, we will discuss the major three.

Inflation as a Monetary Phenomenon

For at least 600 years of recorded economic history, a close connection between inflation and the money supply changes has been observed. Much of the gold and silver mined in the New World was brought to the Old World during the mid-sixteenth century to the mid-seventeenth century and caused inflation in the Old World. So did other gold and silver discoveries wherever they were made. The printing of paper currency in England during the Napoleonic wars, in the American colonies during their War of Independence, in the North and the South during the American Civil War, in Russia after the Bolshevik revolution, and in Germany after World War I contributed to rapid inflation during those eras.

An Increase in the Supply of Money Relative to the Demand for Money
The relationship between the rate at which the money supply increases and the rate at which the price level rises can be understood by using simple supply-and-demand analysis. Suppose that there were a major oil discovery and the supply of oil increased relative to the demand for oil. The price of oil, relative to the prices of other goods and services, would fall. For example, if 1 barrel of oil had previously traded for 1 quart of milk or 1 gallon of cola, the *relative* price of oil would fall. Owing to the major oil discovery, 2 barrels of oil might now be required to purchase 1 quart of milk or 1 gallon of cola. Thus, an increase in the supply of oil, relative to its demand, will cause the relative price of oil to fall; it will take *more* units (barrels) of oil to purchase specific quantities of nonoil goods (1 quart of milk or 1 gallon of cola).

By analogy, we can see what happens when the supply of money is continuously increased relative to the demand for money. The relative price of money will fall; it will take more units of money to purchase

At the Point of Intersection of the Aggregate Supply and Aggregate Demand Curves, the Equilibrium Price Level–National Output Combination Is Determined

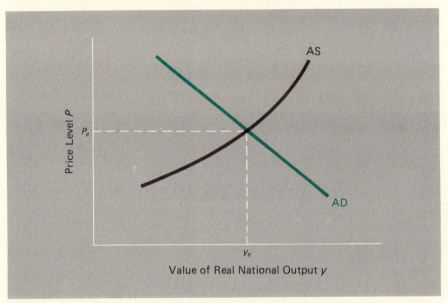

FIGURE 13.10. DETERMINATION OF THE EQUILIBRIUM PRICE LEVEL–NATIONAL OUTPUT COMBINATION
The equilibrium price level–national output combination is at the intersection of the aggregate supply curve and the aggregate demand curve.

specific quantities of nonmoney goods and services. This is what we mean by inflation.

> *It takes ever more units of money to purchase the same quantities (or units) of other goods and services.*

You will recall that classical economists believed inflation to be a monetary phenomenon. So do modern "monetarists," whose theories we discuss in detail in Chapter 18. Figure 13.11 shows the classical theory of inflation. The AS curve is vertical, and the AD curve shifts when the money supply changes relative to the demand for money. In Figure 13.11 the aggregate demand curve shifts from AD to AD′ to AD″ as the money

In the Classical Model, Inflation Is a Monetary Phenomenon

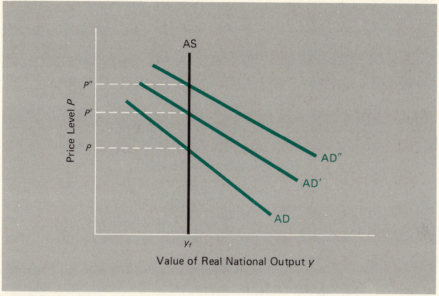

FIGURE 13.11. INFLATION IN THE CLASSICAL MODEL
Continuous increases in the money supply cause the aggregate demand curve to shift rightward from AD to AD' to AD". AS is vertical, and the net result is that only the price level increases from P to P' to P''.

supply continuously increases relative to the demand for money. As a result, the price level rises from P to P' to P''.

Money Supply Increases in a Growing Economy Modern industrialized societies experience economic growth; the potential real output of goods and services increases because of increases in the size of the labor force and increases in the productivity of labor. The proponents of the notion that inflation is a monetary phenomenon maintain that where the supply of money continuously increases relative to the potential output of final goods and services, inflation will occur. This can be seen in the equation of exchange: $MV = Py$.

If M increases relative to V (the money supply increases relative to the demand for money) *and* if M increases relative to y, P will rise. If y tends to grow at a rate of 3 percent per annum and if the money supply increases at a rate faster than 3 percent per year the price level will rise.

We return to this point in Chapter 16, where we discuss the feasibility of a monetary policy that is based on the implications of the analysis of this section.

Figure 13.12 shows how inflation results when the money supply increases faster than output.[4] The ratio of the money supply to gnp is indicated by the solid line; when this ratio rises, the money supply has increased relative to output. The white line indicates one measure of inflation, the Consumer Price Index (CPI), which was discussed in Chapter 2. Note that the curves are very similar and indicate that there is a very close relationship between (1) the rate at which money increases relative to real output and (2) the rate of inflation.

Demand-Pull Inflation

When the quantity of aggregate demand for goods and services exceeds the economy's ability to supply those goods and services (quantity of aggregate supply), the demand will "pull" price upward. Actually, two demand-pull theories of inflation have already been discussed—the classical and the Keynesian.

According to the classical model, increases in the supply of money, given velocity, lead to an increase in total money expenditures. Because the economy is already at full employment, the increased nominal demand for goods will pull prices higher. Thus, for the classical economist inflation is a demand-pull and a monetary phenomenon.

In the Keynesian model, inflation results when the quantity of aggregate real demand for final goods and services exceeds the quantity of aggregate supply at a full (or nearly full) employment level. For the Keynesians, therefore, inflation does not necessarily follow monetary expansion.

A simplified representation of Keynesian demand-pull theory is given in Figure 13.13. Output and employment can increase without any increase in the general price level, as long as the economy is *not* near the full-employment level of output. Figure 13.13 indicates an aggregate supply curve; it is horizontal in a depression and becomes vertical at the full-employment rate of output—no more can be supplied. The economy is running at full steam at output rate y_f. AD_1 through AD_4 represent possible aggregate demand curves. If aggregate demand increases from AD_1 to AD_2, then output will increase from y_1 to y_2 without any increase

---

[4] This graph was reproduced from David I. Meiselman's foreword to R. Schuettinger and E. Butler, *Forty Centuries of Wage and Price Controls* (Washington, D.C.: The Heritage Foundation, 1979), p. 8.

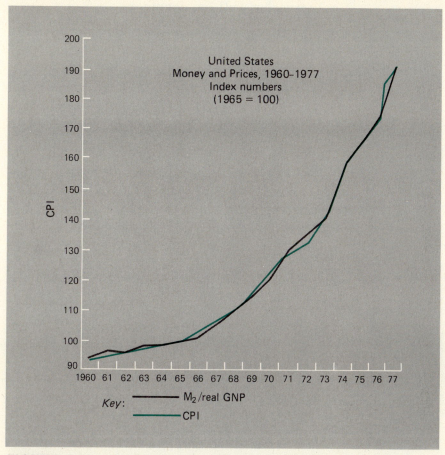

FIGURE 13.12. RELATING THE MONEY/OUTPUT RATIO TO THE PRICE LEVEL

The black line indicates the ratio of the money supply to real GNP; when it is rising, money increases faster than output. Note that the CPI, indicated by the line in color, moves in tandem with this ratio. The conclusion is that inflation results when the money supply increases faster than output increases.

in the price level. If the aggregate demand curve increases further to AD_3, output will increase to y_3, but the price level will rise somewhat. Finally, if the aggregate demand curve increases to AD_4, output will be at y_f and there will be a considerable rise in the price level. In fact, any sustained

Demand-Pull Inflation Occurs in the Keynesian Model as the Economy Approaches Full Employment

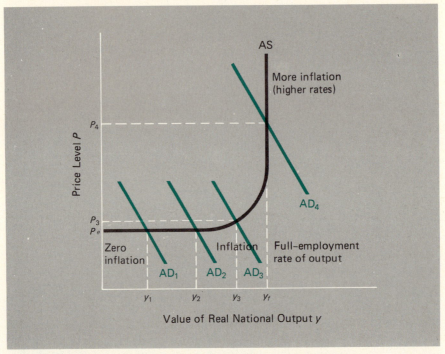

FIGURE 13.13. KEYNESIAN DEMAND-PULL INFLATION

The aggregate supply curve is AS. It is horizontal until nearly full employment is reached. When full employment is reached, it becomes vertical. More output is not possible for any sustained periods. If the aggregate demand curve for all goods and services is AD_1, output will be at y_1 per year. Aggregate demand in the economy can increase to AD_2 without any increase in the price level. When it increases to AD_3, however, there is some increase in the price level as well as an increase in output to y_3. After output rate y_f is reached, however, any sustained increases in demand, such as up to AD_4, will merely lead to increases in the price level. Increases in aggregate demand pull up prices at any point beyond the flat range of the aggregate supply curve.

increases in the aggregate demand curve that intersects the aggregate supply curve along the latter's vertical portion will produce inflation only, because no increase in output is possible. As long as the economy is not in the flat range of the aggregate supply curve, increases in demand will pull prices up; hence, the term **demand-pull inflation.**

Cost-Push Inflation[5]

Competing with the classical and the modern monetarist view of inflation as a monetary phenomenon is the cost-push theory of inflation. While cost-push theories are thought to be of recent vintage, in fact classical economists too were divided (much as their twentieth-century counterparts are) in monetarist and cost-push camps.

All of the cost-push theories discussed below, and the criticisms of these theories, were analyzed by classical economists. (If you want to do more research on this topic, consult the bibliography at the end of this chapter.)

The theory of **cost-push inflation** attempts to explain why the price level rises when the economy is not at, or near, full employment. In recent years the theory has been used to explain the moderate inflation that the United States experienced during its 1969-to-1970 and 1973-to-1975 recessions. There are essentially three causes of cost-push inflation: union monopoly power, big business monopoly power, and increases in raw materials prices.

Union Monopoly Power—or the "Wage-Price Spiral" Many people feel that unions are responsible for inflation. Their reasoning is as follows. Unions decide to demand a wage hike that is not warranted by increases in labor productivity. Because the unions are so powerful, employers must give in to union demands for higher wages. When the employers have to pay these higher wages, their marginal costs of output are higher. To maintain maximum profits, these businesses raise their prices. This type of cost-push inflation seemingly can occur even when there is no excess demand for goods, even when the economy is operating below capacity at less than full employment.

The union power argument rests in part on the assumption that unions have monopolistic market power in their labor markets. In other words, some unions are so strong that they can impose wage increases on employers even when those wage increases are not matched by increases in the productivity of their labor.

Big Business Monopoly Power—or the "Price-Wage Spiral" The second variant of the cost-push theory is that inflation is caused when the monopoly power of big business enables it to raise prices. Powerful

---

[5] This section is based on two articles by Thomas M. Humphrey, "On Cost-Push Theories of Inflation in the Pre-War Monetary Literature," and "Some Current Controversies in the Theory of Inflation," in Thomas M. Humphrey, ed., *Essays on Inflation*, 4th ed. (Richmond, Va.: Federal Reserve Bank of Richmond, 1983), pp. 19–25 and 26–37, respectively.

Cost-Push Inflation Can Account for Stagflation

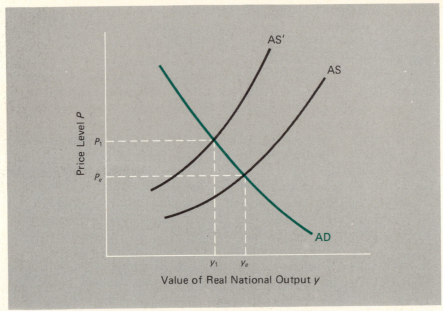

FIGURE 13.14. COST-PUSH INFLATION

If labor or raw materials costs rise continuously, AS will keep shifting leftward. If AD is unaffected, real output falls, unemployment and the price level rise simultaneously, and stagflation is said to occur.

corporations presumably can raise their prices to increase their profits. Each time the corporations raise prices to increase their profits, the cost of living goes up. Workers then demand higher wages to make up for the decline in their standard of living and thereby give the corporations an excuse to raise prices again. And so goes a vicious wage-price cycle. Note that this analysis is not consistent with the assumption that the monopolists always maximize profits. If profits are always at a maximum, a monopolist could not suddenly *raise* prices to increase profits.

Raw Materials Cost-Push Inflation From 1973 to 1978 higher and higher prices for all forms of energy led to a relatively new type of cost-push inflation. It is cost-push inflation which results because the cost of raw materials seems to keep rising all the time. Coal became more expensive, as did petroleum, natural gas, and many other basic inputs to the production processes.

Whether it be union monopoly power, big business monopoly power, or higher raw-materials prices, the resultant increased cost of production pushes prices up; hence the term cost-push inflation.

Figure 13.14 depicts cost-push inflation. Given the AD curve, a decrease in AS resulting from higher labor or raw materials costs leads to a lower level of output and a higher price level. Hence, unemployment and prices can rise at the same time; this situation, as you will recall from Chapter 3, is called *stagflation*. We return to other theories of stagflation in Chapter 15 and in Chapter 19 when we discuss supply-side economics. The supply-side economists also point to reductions in aggregate supply as the cause of stagflation; as you shall see in Chapter 19, supply-side reasons for such a shift are different from cost-push reasons. But stagflation in both cases is the result of decreases in AS.

Criticisms of Theories of Cost-Push Inflation Irving Fisher, a classical economist mentioned earlier on several occasions in this text, criticized cost-push theories on four grounds:

1. Such theories fail to distinguish between changes in relative prices and changes in absolute prices. For example, a bad harvest of wheat and other crops can only explain an increase in the relative price of food; it cannot by itself explain why all, or many, prices should rise.
2. Inflation requires an increase in the supply of money relative to the demand for money; there is no reason to believe that changes in the prices of specific goods or of union wages per se will change the supply of money relative to the demand for money. Thus, *specific price rises, given a fixed money supply and therefore a fixed nominal income, will lead to reductions in other prices.* The conclusion is that the *overall* price level will not rise.[6] For example, if the price of oil rises and there is an inelastic demand for oil, people will spend more money on oil and oil-related goods. They must therefore spend less on other goods, given nominal expenditures; prices will then fall for non–oil-related goods.
3. Inflation is defined as a *sustained* increase in the price level; special, once-and-for-all events cannot explain inflation so defined.
4. Cost-push theories lead to such inappropriate policies as price-wage controls (analyzed in the Policy Controversy at the end of this chapter).

---

[6] It is interesting to note that the secular price *deflation* during the 1873–1896 period was attributed by cost-pushers to the tremendous growth in technological change, cheapened transportation costs, new raw material sources, and increased competition, while classical monetarists claimed that the deflation was due to the failure of the money supply to grow as fast as real output. See Humphrey, op. cit., pp. 20–21.

Fisher's influence on Milton Friedman is evident if we consider Friedman's comments on the source of double-digit inflation in the 1973–1974 period. Concerning the oil price increases made by the Organization of Petroleum Exporting Countries (OPEC) and the crop failures in the United States during that period, Friedman notes:

> Are they not the obvious immediate cause of the price explosion? Not at all. It is essential to distinguish changes in *relative* prices from changes in *absolute* prices. The special conditions that drove up the prices of oil and food required purchasers to spend more on them, leaving less to spend on other items. Did that not force other prices to go down or to rise less rapidly than otherwise? Why should the *average* level of all prices be affected significantly by changes in the prices of some things relative to others? Thanks to delays in adjustment, the rapid rises in oil and food prices may have temporarily raised the rate of inflation somewhat. In the main, however, they have been convenient excuses for besieged government officials and harried journalists rather than reasons for the price explosion.[7]

The Validation Cost-Push Theory   Modern cost-push theorists, unlike their classical predecessors, emphasize the **validation theory.** The validation theory stresses price-wage inflexibility and a social commitment to full employment. If tastes change, or if a crop failure occurs, or if such supply shocks as the OPEC oil embargo or the OPEC price increase change the composition of expenditures, then (1) prices will rise for some goods and services, and (2) inflexible prices and wages will lead to a reduction in employment and output in other sectors of the economy.[8] A commitment to full employment will elicit an expansion of the money supply by the monetary authorities or to an expansionary fiscal policy; hence, specific cost increases are automatically validated by a permissive expansion of the money supply.

GOVERNMENT AND INFLATION

As indicated in Chapter 5, there are three important ways the federal government can obtain purchasing power. It can tax, borrow existing funds, or borrow (or spend directly) newly created money. This chapter

---

[7] Milton Friedman, "Perspectives on Inflation," *Newsweek*, June 24, 1974, p. 73.

[8] Structural inflation is said to occur when the *composition* of AD—but not the *level* of AD—changes due to a change in tastes, and when prices are free to rise but are inflexible downward. A change in the composition of AD will cause prices to rise for the more highly favored goods, but prices will not fall for those goods that experience decreased demand.

has made it clear that money creation leads to an increase in the *lm* curve and therefore to an increase in aggregate demand and then, in most circumstances, to inflation. In this section, the impact of federal deficits on the price level is explored. Federal deficits arise when the federal government spends more than it collects in taxes. It finances deficits either by borrowing existing funds or by borrowing newly created money.[9]

Federal Deficits and Inflation in Theory

Deficits and the Supply of Money Since the 1951 Accord between the Federal Reserve and the U.S. Treasury, the Fed no longer is required to purchase any portion of the public debt, nor is the Fed any longer directly responsible for stabilizing government security prices (and, therefore, interest rates). It follows that since 1951 there has been no *direct* relationship between federal deficits and Fed open-market operations; increased deficits will not automatically lead to increases in the money supply.

Still, it is possible that the increased demand for credit by the U.S. Treasury, as it attempts to finance deficits, will cause interest rates to rise. Thus, it is alleged in this version of the validation theory, that monetary authorities will attempt to prevent higher interest rates by buying bonds in open-market operations and thereby increase the money supply. Therefore, an *indirect* link exists between deficits and inflation when the Fed "accommodates" the Treasury by monetizing the public debt. While this may be true, it should be stressed that this link is indirect; federal deficits can only cause inflation to the extent that the Fed is willing to pay the price of increased inflation in order to keep interest rates down.[10] Moreover, in the period from 1979 to 1982, the Fed had (nearly) abandoned its attempt to stabilize interest rates, as Chapter 16 indicates. In 1983 the Fed again became interested in stabilizing interest rates at a lower level.

Deficits and the Demand for Money If inflation is caused by "too much money chasing too few goods," then the increased supply of money

---

[9] Much of what follows in this section is based on S. Hein, "Deficits and Inflation," *Review*, Federal Reserve Bank of St. Louis, vol. 63, no. 3 (March 1981), pp. 3–10.

[10] Some economists feel that such an attempt is self-defeating; an increased rate of inflation will cause nominal interest rates to rise as lenders and buyers insist on and permit inflationary premiums.

(given demand) is only part of the story. A decrease in the demand for money can (given supply) also create a situation of "too much money." Arthur Laffer (a supply-side economist discussed in Chapter 19), Milton Friedman (see Chapter 11), and others have charged that expectations of inflation reduce the demand for money because inflation imposes a tax on those who hold it. As a consequence, *velocity* rises as people try to spend money in order to convert it to other assets before prices rise. It is alleged that some recent inflation has been caused by such a decreased demand for money. As people reduce cash balances, velocity increases and a *constant* supply of money is consistent with higher price levels. To the extent that large federal deficits are "monetized" (lead to money creation) and cause inflation, *more rapid* inflation will result as velocity rises with the money supply.

Federal Deficits and Inflation: The Empirical Evidence

Regarding the size of federal deficits and the *money supply*, the evidence is that from 1955 to 1975 the growth of the federal debt and the growth of the money supply moved in tandem. In 1975, however, a clear break in this relationship occurred. The 1975-to-1980 period was the first sustained period since 1951 during which the money supply grew more slowly than the federal debt. During this period the Fed (reversing a trend) reduced the total proportion of the federal debt that it held. In short, the link between the federal debt and the money supply was broken (or, at least, loosened). When the federal debt and the money supply increased in tandem, deficits were highly correlated with inflation. But from 1975 to 1980, when the federal deficit and the money supply changed independently, the size of the federal debt was no longer so highly correlated with the rate of inflation. As a consequence, a theory that predicts future inflation and future interest rates on the basis of the size of the federal debt will not perform as well as a theory that directly predicts future inflation rates and interest rates on the basis of expected money supply increases.

Regarding deficits and the *demand for money*, the evidence is that this effect exists, but its magnitude is not very significant. Nominal interest rates would have to increase by 500 percent to induce the same amount of inflation associated with a permanent 1-percentage-point increase in the money supply growth.[11] Thus, the impact of higher nominal interest rates on the demand for money (velocity) is very slight; it follows

---

[11] Hein, op. cit.

that higher nominal interest rates resulting from higher deficits have little compounding effect on the rate of inflation due to a reduced demand for money. *Inflation is better predicted by directly observing changes in the money supply, and not by observing changes in the federal deficit.*

POLICY CONTROVERSY
Can Price Controls Combat Inflation?

Price controls have been around for a long time. Rome was using them for centuries before the birth of Christ. However, the first recorded extensive price-control program was instituted in A.D. 301 by the Emperor Diocletian. His price-control edicts set schedules for 890 different price categories, more than 200 of which were for food. Anyone caught disobeying the emperor's edict was dealt with severely—death by drowning. According to the historian Lactantius, writing in 1314, there was

> much bloodshed upon very slight and trifling accounts; and the people brought provisions no more to market since they could not get a reasonable price for them; and this increased the dearth so much that after many had died by it, the law itself was laid aside.[12]

Medieval Europe had its own set of price controls; a "just price" code was firmly established. And the colonies in the New World had price controls. In 1636 the Puritans set up wage and price limitations. Those who violated the code were officially classified with "adulterers and whoremongers."

During the American Revolution, controls were quite popular. The Continental Congress set price ceilings on October 20, 1774. It decreed "that all manufactures of this country be sold at reasonable prices" and that "vendors of goods or merchandise will not take advantage of the scarcity of goods, ... but will sell the same at rates we have been respectively accustomed to for twelve months last past." But such price controls did not prevent inflation. By November 1777, commodity prices were 480 percent above their prewar average expressed in terms of paper money, or "continentals." General Washington had great difficulty acquiring army provisions at controlled prices. This intensified the agony of Valley Forge. Partly as a result, the Continental Congress declared in June of 1778 that "It hath been found by Experience that Limitations upon the Price of Commodities are not only ineffectual for the Purposes proposed, but are likewise productive of very evil Consequences to the great Detriment of the Public Service and Grievous Oppression of Individuals."

Nonetheless, local and state price controls continued. At some town meetings, the names of those who charged higher-than-controlled prices were announced, and the guilty were condemned in patriotic newspapers. Boston declared

---

[12] L. C. F. Lactantius, *A Relation of the Death of the Primitive Persecutors*, Gilbert Burnet, trans. (Amsterdam, 1697), pp. 67–68.

that those who violated price ceilings were enemies of their country. By 1780, most controls had largely been abandoned.

This nation's most comprehensive attempt at controlling prices occurred during World War II. And, for the first time in the peacetime history of the United States, extensive wage and price controls were instituted in the 1970s by the Nixon administration. They are popular when inflation seems excessive, not only at home but also abroad. Every European country has tried them in one form or another since World War II.

In the face of cost-push inflation, a legislated maximum on both prices and wages would presumably stop inflation or at least slow or limit it. However, cost-push theories of inflation, at least in their simplest forms, are not completely accepted by everyone. After all, how can the monopoly business theory or the labor union theory of inflation predict *when* inflation will occur? In other words, how do these examples of the cost-push theory of inflation allow us to say in which future year inflation will occur or get worse? The theories say nothing about when labor unions will use their monopoly power to demand higher wages. Nor do the theories say anything about when businesses will decide to increase their profits by raising prices. In short, how do these theories explain why some periods are inflationary and others are not? Furthermore, both of these theories seem to ignore a crucial economic principle: For competitive businesses or for even a pure monopoly (but not necessarily for oligopolies), there is one profit-maximizing price. Only if cost conditions or demand conditions change will that profit-maximizing price change. Why, then, would

monopoly businesses desire to raise prices in some years but not in others? The same is true for labor unions: there is one maximizing wage rate.[13] Once that wage rate is set, an increase in it will be nonmaximizing, unless, of course, demand and/or supply conditions have changed.

Another possible reason to impose wage and price controls involves the notion of expectations, which we have alluded to in this chapter. If future inflation is anticipated, economic agents will include this anticipated rate of inflation in all of their implicit and explicit contracts. Therefore, if the forces causing inflation were reduced as a result of the monetary and fiscal policies of the federal government, economic agents may not be *aware* of the long-run impact of these policies on the rate of inflation. If wage and price controls can be seen as a clear signal by economic agents that the inflation will end, they may revise their anticipations of future inflation; and, therefore, the controls might reduce the amount of time associated with adjusting to the new, lower rate of inflation.

This scenario appears to be what occurred during the first peacetime price freeze, which began on August 15, 1971. Nominal long-term interest rates, which include whatever inflationary premium the market has decided upon, dropped when the wage-price freeze was instituted. The wage-price freeze acted as a signal to economic agents that the rate of future inflation would be lower than they anticipated. In spite of wage and price controls, however, the CPI kept rising in

---

[13] There is no general agreement on exactly what unions maximize.

1971, 1972, and 1973. When a second (60-day) price freeze was put on in June of 1973, long-term interest rates did not fall; they actually rose! From this small bit of evidence, one might argue that temporary wage and price controls can, in fact, break inflationary expectations, but only for a short time, unless the underlying sources of the inflation are reduced or eliminated. If, for example, the inflation is caused by overexpansionary monetary and fiscal policy and nothing is ultimately done to change that policy, no one will be fooled for very long by wage and price controls.

Those who have worked intimately with price controls point out that they lead to extreme disruptions in the economy. For example, according to C. Jackson Grayson, Jr., former chairman of the Price Commission, "Wage-price controls lead to distortions in the economic system, which can be minimized only in the short run. No matter how cleverly any group designs a control system, distortions and inequities will appear."[14] Grayson's point rested on some very basic economics. Equilibrium relative prices are determined by supply and demand. When the supply of something becomes relatively less or the demand becomes relatively greater, the price of the commodity relative to other prices will rise and lead, on the one hand, to an increase in the quantity supplied and, on the other, to a decrease in the quantity demanded. A government-mandated maximum price will not allow such a signaling system to work in the upward direction. To be sure, a maximum price will have no effect whenever the price determined by the forces of supply and demand is below that maximum price. When, however, for whatever reason, the market-clearing price exceeds the government-controlled price, a distortion appears. That distortion may take the form of shortages, which became painfully evident after the Nixon price-control program lingered on; or it may take the form of black markets, which were rampant in this country during World War II; or it may take the form of ingenious systems of evading or avoiding the controls (which activity per se constitutes a loss of social product). In any event, the control has the effect of distorting the flow of resources in the economy. This leads to lower economic welfare for the nation as a whole.

Moreover, some practical problems are inherent in any price-control system. Attempting to police the controls on millions upon millions of wages and prices is a task of overwhelming magnitude. During World War II, we had approximately 60,000 paid price watchers and something like 300,000 to 350,000 volunteer price watchers. The time and effort devoted to policing wage and price controls use economic resources that are not free. Moreover, although it is perhaps possible to control nominal prices, it is literally impossible to control the real price per *constant-quality* unit. In the face of a maximum nominal price, businesses can easily raise the real price per constant-quality unit of the goods they sell merely by lowering the quality. A gallon of gas that now has less octane is more expensive at the same price per gallon in terms of constant-quality units.

The rate of inflation during World War II was lower with price controls than it would have been without them. But what do we mean by the rate of inflation?

---

[14] C. Jackson Grayson, Jr., "Controls Are Not the Answer," *Challenge* (November-December 1974), p. 10.

If we mean the rate of rise in the CPI, that may have little to do with the actual rate of inflation. During World War II, the CPI rose very little because in most cases any explicit, published rise in prices was illegal! We had then what has been called a **suppressed inflation:** inflation was actually going on, but it did not show up in the official published price indices. Instead, because prices are not allowed to rise, the rationing function of price is destroyed. Because goods can no longer go to the highest bidders, society must find another way to ration goods. Typically, under price controls goods are allocated by the "first come, first served" method, which leads to long lines of people waiting for goods, or to ration-stamp or ration-coupon systems. Another sign of suppressed inflation is a deterioration of the quality of goods and services. When wage and price controls were lifted after the war, the official price index caught up with the actual price index, and, for two or three years, prices rose at a rapid rate. A basic point can be made here: there is sometimes a difference between a published price and a transactions price. The transactions price per constant-quality unit of product depends on any legal or quasi-legal arrangements made for the sale of a product, on the quality of the product, on the delivery date of the product, and on the time when the goods must be paid for.

Another question must be asked when price controls are considered in retrospect. What does a price index mean when, during periods of wage and price controls, many goods are in fact no longer available? If you go into the supermarket to buy cans of your favorite soup and they are no longer available, what comfort is it to know that their price hasn't gone up? In fact, the true price of many items during, for example, the 1971-to-1974 period of controls was actually infinite because they were unavailable. What happens to the true cost of goods when the price of even one item rises to infinity?

During the Carter administration a system of "voluntary" price controls was introduced. It consisted of numerous guidelines, formulae, and assorted strong-arm techniques that were supposed to keep prices from rising too rapidly. One such technique was the threat of withholding government contracts from firms that granted wage increases in excess of governmental voluntary guidelines. The courts ruled against the administration's ability to do that because, in effect, such actions would have changed the voluntary system into one that was totally involuntary. Clearly, the Carter administration's attempt at voluntary controls met with little, if any, success. The measured rate of change of the CPI was 9.3 percent in 1978 and 11.4 percent in 1979. If mandatory controls are again legislated by Congress (assuming they haven't been by the time you read this text), we can predict that there will be a virtual repetition of many of the events that occurred during the Nixon price-control era. Occasional shortages will mushroom into widespread shortages; halfhearted attempts at evading the controls will mushroom into a full-scale attack on them by buyers and sellers; and, finally, sporadic distaste for price controls will mushroom into overwhelming disenchantment. And the controls again will be removed.

History has a way of repeating itself.

CHAPTER SUMMARY

1. A modern (nonclassical) aggregate demand curve can be derived by the Keynes effect.

2. Shifts in aggregate demand occur because of shifts in the consumption function, the investment function, the supply of money, the demand for money, and owing to changes in government expenditures and taxes.

3. An expansionary monetary policy and an expansionary fiscal policy shift the aggregate demand curve rightward; a contractionary monetary policy and a contractionary fiscal policy shift the aggregate demand curve leftward.

4. If both employers and workers perceive a change in the price level fully and immediately, and if nominal wages are perfectly flexible, the aggregate supply curve is vertical even in the short run. Such a situation is called the classical case.

5. If employers perceive a price level change fully and immediately but workers do not perceive the change at all, the short-run aggregate supply curve is positively sloped even if nominal wage rates are perfectly flexible. Such a situation is the case of the extreme Keynesian assumption.

6. If employers perceive a permanent price level change immediately but workers adjust to such a change incompletely, by the adaptive expectations models, then the short-run aggregate supply curve will be positively sloped even if nominal wage rates are perfectly flexible. This curve will be less steep than the vertical classical curve, but it will be steeper than the curve of the extreme Keynesian assumption model.

7. There are three broad causes of inflation: (a) inflation is a monetary phenomenon, (b) demand-pull, and (c) cost-push. Case a implies that inflation occurs only when the supply of money repeatedly rises relative to the demand for money; case b occurs when AD rises repeatedly relative to a somewhat constant AS curve; and c occurs when AS decreases repeatedly relative to a somewhat constant AD curve.

8. The validation theory is that cost-push inflation can only arise if decreases in aggregate supply are validated by an expansionary monetary policy that results automatically because society is committed to a full-employment policy.

9. Federal deficits are causes of inflation only when they are validated by an accommodating monetary policy that monetizes the debt.

10. Price-wage controls cannot cure demand-pull inflation, but they might be a viable solution to cost-push inflation.

GLOSSARY

cost-push inflation   Inflation that results when aggregate supply decreases repeatedly relative to aggregate demand.

demand-pull inflation   Inflation that results when aggregate demand increases repeatedly relative to aggregate supply.

inflation   A sustained increase in the price level over time.

suppressed inflation   A manifestation of inflation during periods of price controls; long lines, quality deterioration, and cheating.

validation theory   A theory that says that cost-push inflation can only result if such pressures are validated by an expansionary monetary policy.

QUESTIONS AND PROBLEMS FOR REVIEW

13.1   Aggregate demand is believed to be determined by changes in, among other variables, government expenditures and taxes. Is aggregate demand also considered to be determined by changes in *differences* between expenditures and taxes?

13.2   Expansionary monetary policy is believed to shift the aggregate demand curve to the right. Describe the sequence of effects from an increase in the money supply to a change in aggregate demand. At what point would the classical economists have objected?

13.3   Expansionary fiscal policy is believed to shift the aggregate demand curve to the right. Would you still believe this to be the result of an equal increase in government expenditures and taxes in order to finance the purchase of goods *that consumers would have purchased anyway*?

13.4   If employers do not perceive a price level change at all but workers perceive such a change immediately, the short-run aggregate supply would be expected to be of what shape? Trace the consequences of these assumptions on national output.

13.5   Would there be any differences between the situation in which *both* employers and workers adjust to a change in the price level incompletely and the classical case in which both employers and workers adjust to a change completely?

13.6   Would the aggregate supply curve for the situation described above be more or less steep than the vertical classical aggregate supply curve?

13.7   The demand-pull explanation of inflation occurs when aggregate demand rises repeatedly relative to a somewhat constant aggregate supply curve. What importance do assumptions about unemployment have on the validity of the explanation?

13.8   The cost-push explanation of inflation occurs when aggregate supply decreases repeatedly relative to a somewhat constant aggregate demand curve. What importance do assumptions about wage inflexibility have on the validity of the explanation?

13.9 Federal deficits are believed to be a cause of inflation only when they are validated by an accommodating monetary policy that monetizes the debt. What effect would deficits be expected to have on rates of interest?

13.10 Wage-price controls may be a viable solution to cost-push inflation. Do wage-price controls have adverse welfare effects, even in this case?

REFERENCES

Milton Friedman, "A Monetary Theory of Nominal Income," *Journal of Political Economy*, vol. 79 (1971).

———, "Perspectives on Inflation," *Newsweek*, June 24, 1974.

———, "The Role of Monetary Policy," *American Economic Review*, vol. 58 (1968).

Milton Friedman and Anna J. Schwartz, *A Monetary History of the United States, 1867–1960*, National Bureau of Economic Research, no. 12 (Princeton, N.J.: Princeton University Press, 1963).

C. Jackson Grayson, Jr., "Controls Are Not the Answer," *Challenge* (November-December 1974).

Scott Hein, "Deficits and Inflation," *Review*, Federal Reserve Bank of St. Louis, vol. 63, no. 3 (March 1981).

Thomas M. Humphrey, *Essays on Inflation*, 4th ed. (Richmond, Va.: Federal Reserve Bank of Richmond, 1983).

John Maynard Keynes, *How to Pay for the War* (London: Macmillan, 1940).

Roger L. Miller and Raburn M. Williams, *Unemployment and Inflation: The New Economics of the Wage-Price Spiral* (St. Paul, Minn.: West Publishing Company, 1974).

Robert Schuettinger and Eamonn Butler, *Forty Centuries of Wage and Price Controls* (Washington, D.C.: The Heritage Foundation, 1979).

14

THE RELATIONSHIP BETWEEN INFLATION AND UNEMPLOYMENT

n Chapter 7 we developed the *is-lm* framework in real terms; the equilibrium real interest rate and the equilibrium real level of national income were derived simultaneously through the interaction of the product and the money markets. Because the price level was assumed to be constant, changes in nominal and real values were equivalent. For that reason a gap existed in Keynes's explanation of the economy: How were the level of the real value of national output and the price level related? In order to fill that gap, Chapter 13 presented aggregate supply and aggregate demand models.

Aggregate demand is the relationship between different quantities of national output demanded and various price levels, other things constant; aggregate supply is the relationship between the aggregate output of final goods and services supplied and various price levels, other things constant. Chapter 13 showed how the interaction of aggregate supply and aggregate demand simultaneously determined the equilibrium output level and the equilibrium price level, and a missing link in the Keynesian model was supplied.

Another gap in the Keynesian model is the relationship between the price level and the employment (or unemployment) level. But because a functional relationship exists in the short run between employment levels and national output levels (nonlabor factors of production assumed constant), the aggregate supply–aggregate demand approach can also eliminate *this* missing link. The first section of this chapter does precisely that: it shows how a negatively sloped **Phillips curve,** a relationship between the rate of inflation and the unemployment rate, is implicit in the aggregate supply–aggregate demand model presented in Chapter 13.

The Phillips curve is important not only because it helps to fill a theoretical gap in the Keynesian model, but because it potentially can be used for stabilization policy. If a stable trade-off between the rate of inflation and the national unemployment rate actually exists, then policymakers can select a policy to create the "optimal" combination of inflation-unemployment on the Phillips curve.

We then elaborate, in the second section of this chapter, on the implications of this short-run Phillips curve by developing a job search model that gives a commonsense explanation for a short-run trade-off between inflation and unemployment.

The third section in this chapter indicates, however, that the Phillips curve is unstable. Empirical evidence indicates that a Phillips curve trade-off between inflation and unemployment rates exists only in the short run; in the long run, the unemployment rate is independent of the rate of inflation. In the long run, the Phillips curve is vertical and its position is determined by the natural rate of unemployment, which we will define precisely later. The difference between the short-run and long-run Phillips curves is resolved by introducing the concept of inflationary expectations; changes in inflationary expectations shift the Phillips curve. Moreover, these shifts do not occur independently of stabilization policy; the Phillips curve can shift as a *direct result* of monetary policy and fiscal policy attempts to move the economy along a given short-run Phillips curve. The third section concludes that stabilization policy can work only to the extent that buyers and sellers of labor can be fooled into underestimating the rate of inflation.

THE SHORT-RUN PHILLIPS CURVE

The Phillips curve is named after British economist A. W. H. Phillips, whose 1958 article made it clear that the rate of change in money wage rates was related to the *level* of unemployment.[1] In periods of low unemployment, labor scarcity drives money wage rates upward; and in times of high unemployment, a labor surplus drives money wage rates downward (or slows their rates of increase). Phillips showed that data from the years 1948 to 1957 match rather closely data from the years 1861 to 1913. Specifically, he fitted a curve based on 1861–1913 data to observations in the 1948–1957 period and found that the old curve fit the new data amazingly well. Other economists cited this as evidence of a stable relationship between money wage-rate changes and the unemployment rate.

The Phillips curve notion changed after 1958. Price level changes were first linked to money wage-rate changes,[2] and the Phillips curve then became the inverse relationship between the rate of inflation and the rate of unemployment. Economists interpreted this new Phillips curve as a trade-off between inflation and unemployment; they observed that a stable relationship would allow policymakers to "choose" a given rate of unemployment (or inflation) and bear the cost of a necessary rate of inflation (or unemployment). In other words, a little *less* inflation had to be purchased at the price of a little *more* unemployment; or, alternatively stated, relatively low unemployment rates would generate relatively high inflation rates.

Figure 14.1 shows an illustrative Phillips curve. Point *A* shows that if policymakers in this hypothetical economy desire only a 4 percent rate of unemployment, they must accept a 12 percent rate of inflation. On the other hand, if policymakers desire a low rate of inflation, such as 2

---

[1] A. W. H. Phillips, "The Relationship Between Unemployment and the Rate of Change in Money Wage Rates in the United Kingdom, 1861–1957," *Economica*, New Series 75 (November 1958), pp. 283–299.

[2] By subtracting changes in the productivity of labor from the changes in money wage rates.

The Phillips Curve Was Believed to Offer Policymakers a Menu of Possible Combinations of Inflation and Unemployment

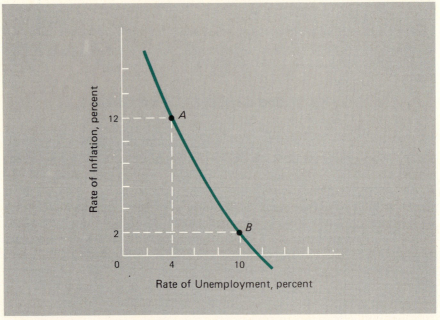

FIGURE 14.1. A PHILLIPS CURVE

This illustrative Phillips curve indicates that if society desires a 4 percent rate of unemployment, it must accept a 12 percent rate of inflation. If it desires a 2 percent rate of inflation, it must "pay" for this low inflation rate by suffering a 10 percent rate of unemployment.

percent, they must accept a relatively high unemployment rate—10 percent. A curve such as this would help policymakers decide what the "optimal" point on the Phillips curve should be. A nation such as Germany, which has had experience with extremely high rates of inflation, might place a high value on price stability and find that its optimal point is close to B. Other countries, such as the United States, might place a higher value on low unemployment (because it remembers the experience of the Great Depression) and find that *its* optimal point on the Phillips curve is closer to point A. Note, therefore, that the optimal inflation-unemployment point is ultimately subjective; it depends on the value judgments of policymakers. Nevertheless, while the usefulness of the Phillips curve is limited, a stable Phillips curve can help to set the framework for the debate among those who weigh the ill effects of inflation and unemployment differently.

Deriving the Phillips Curve from the Aggregate Supply— Aggregate Demand Model

Chapter 13 indicated that the equilibrium output level and the equilibrium price level are determined simultaneously by the interaction of the aggregate demand and aggregate supply curves. Because a functional relationship exists between the level of national output and the level of national employment (assuming nonlabor inputs constant), it is possible to derive a relationship between the price level and the unemployment level, and from there to relate sustained *changes* in the price level (inflation) to the unemployment *rate* (if the full-employment level is known).

Consider Figure 14.2. Start at point A in panels a, b, and c. The equilibrium price level is P_e, the equilibrium value of real national output is y_e, and the equilibrium employment level is N_e. Now assume that aggregate demand rises due to an increase in the money supply. At P_e, the quantity of aggregate demand AD_q exceeds the quantity of aggregate supply AS_q; therefore, a general shortage of goods and services arises. This causes an increase in the price level.

The AS Curve Has a Positive Slope Recall from Chapter 13 that an increase in the price level is perceived immediately by employers (who increase their nominal demand for labor), but that (using the incomplete adjustment assumption) workers revise their perception of the "permanent" price level upward only *partially*. Workers, consequently, are "fooled" into working longer hours in the aggregate and so N and y both rise. It is for this reason that the aggregate supply (AS) curve in panel a of Figure 14.2 is positively sloped and that the price level–employment level curve in panel c of that figure is positively sloped. Note that if workers revised their perceptions of the "permanent" price level immediately and completely, both the AS curve and the price level–employment level curves would be *vertical* at positions consistent with full employment.

Note that in Figure 14.2, panel a, the AS curve's *slope* increases as national output rises and that, in panel c, the price level–employment level curve's slope increases as the employment level rises.

The AS Curve's Slope Rises with National Output There are at least two reasons the slope of the AS curve rises as national output increases.

A Short-Run Relationship Exists Between the Price Level and the Employment Level

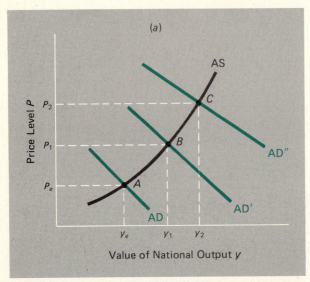

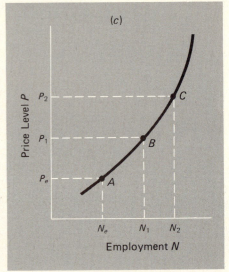

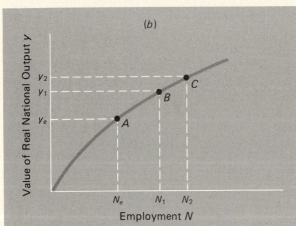

FIGURE 14.2. RELATING THE PRICE LEVEL TO THE EMPLOYMENT LEVEL

Panel *a* indicates that as aggregate demand increases from AD to AD′ to AD″, the output level and the price level both increase; the economy moves from point *A* to point *B* to point *C*. Panel *b* indicates that increases in real national output require higher levels of employment. Because a functional relationship exists between national output levels and employment levels as in panel *b*, a relationship between price levels and output levels, panel *a*, can be converted into a relationship between price levels and employment levels, as panel *c* shows.

1. **The Law of Diminishing Returns**   Assume that aggregate demand suddenly increases so that the rate of inflation rises from zero to 5 percent per year. We continue to use the incomplete adjustment assumption, so that workers are now coaxed (or fooled) into supplying an additional, say, 1 million labor hours. This extra 1 million labor hours increases real national output by, say, $20 million. In the next time period suppose that aggregate demand rises so that the rate of inflation is 10 percent per year and an extra 2 million (instead of 1 million) labor hours are then coaxed out. Because the production function in panel *b* of Figure 14.2 incorporates the law of diminishing returns, the national output curve increases at a decreasing rate. This means that 2 million labor hours will be unable to increase real national output by $40 million (twice $20 million), because the second 1 million labor hours will have a smaller marginal product than the first 1 million labor hours. In order to raise national income by another $20 million, the inflation rate must exceed 10 percent per year, so that *more* than 2 million labor hours are coaxed out. In other words, the *first* $20 million of real national output can be "purchased" with a 5 percent per year inflation rate, but the second $20 million of real national output requires that the rate of inflation *more than double*. In terms of panel *a* of Figure 14.2, unit changes in real national output require disproportionately greater changes in the price level as real national output increases, i.e., the slope of the AS curve increases as national output increases.[3]

2. **Limitation on a Worker's Ability to Substitute Income for Leisure**   Because there is a time constraint that workers face (there are only so many hours that can be worked in a day), workers cannot indefinitely increase their quantity of labor supplied proportionally to changes in the price level. Thus, a 5 percent increase in the price level might coax out additional work hours for an individual worker, but *eventually* the worker (and other workers) will have to increase work hours less than proportionally to the price level increases. This means that the AS curve will become very steep (its slope rises) as the economy approaches the absolute maximum output level.

---

[3] Note that we have implicitly assumed that every 5 percent increase in the price level fools workers into offering an extra 1 million labor hours. This is not necessarily the case. In fact, in Table 15.2 we show that a simple adaptive expectations model predicts that if the inflation rate were 5 percent per year, people would adjust their perceptions of the permanent price level upward more quickly in later years than in earlier years. This implies that if the inflation rate rises from zero to 5 percent per year, say, 1 million labor hours are coaxed out. If the inflation rate in the next year is 5 percent, *fewer* than 1 million labor hours will be coaxed out because workers will adjust their perception of the permanent price level upward more quickly. This means that *even if the marginal product of labor were constant, unit increases in real national output require disproportionately higher rates of inflation*—another reason for the slope of the AS curve to rise as real national output rises.

Because of the limits on a worker's ability to substitute income for leisure, the price level–employment level curve in panel *c* of Figure 14.2 also becomes steeper; as the labor force approaches the maximum quantity of labor hours it can offer per unit of time, the price level–employment level curve approaches a vertical line.

Finally, the Phillips Curve

Figure 14.3 derives the modern-day version of a short-run Phillips curve (i.e., a short-run relationship between the rate of inflation and the unemployment rate). Panel *a* is based on panel *c* in Figure 14.2, except that now we use index numbers for the price level and we use numbers to represent employment. If the labor force is 100 million laborers, then the full-employment quantity of labor N_f is 100 million. It is now possible to derive hypothetical rates of inflation and hypothetical unemployment rates based on the values in panel *a*. Panel *b* incorporates the inflation rates and the unemployment rates as the price level rises.

Begin at point A in panels *a* and *b*. When the price level P_e is 100 and is stable, the unemployment rate is 15 percent. This shows up as point A in panel *b*, because with a zero rate of inflation the unemployment rate is 15 percent [i.e., $(100 - 85)/100 = 15$ percent]. If the price level rises to 105, the rate of inflation is 5 percent and employment rises from 85 to 90, and the unemployment rate dips to 10 percent. That is, a 5 percent inflation rate is associated with a 10 percent unemployment rate, and inflation has "bought" less unemployment; in panel *b* this is indicated as a movement from point A to point B. We leave it to you to demonstrate how the economy can move from point B to point C in Figure 14.3.

A Caveat

Note that the Phillips curve shows an inverse relationship between the rate of inflation and the unemployment rate because of the shape of the AS curve. It is because the AS curve in Figure 14.2 is upward-sloping that the Phillips curve in Figure 14.3 is downward-sloping. Had the AS curve not embodied the assumption that workers only incompletely adjust to a higher price level (i.e., the nominal supply of labor does not shift leftward by as much as it would if the higher price level were perfectly perceived), *the Phillips curve would have been vertical*.[4]

---

[4] If we had assumed that wages are *inflexible* in the short run, we also would have derived an upward-sloping short-run AS curve and a negatively sloped short-run Phillips curve.

A Short-Run Relationship Exists Between the Rate of Inflation and the Unemployment Rate

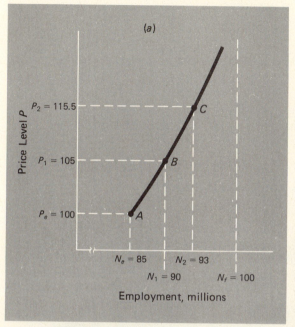

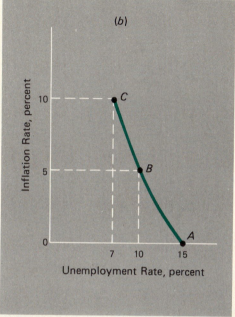

FIGURE 14.3. DERIVING THE PHILLIPS CURVE

When the price level $P_e = 100$, unemployment equals 15 percent. If the price level rises to 105 (that is, inflation is 5 percent), this causes employment to rise from 85 to 90 million and the unemployment rate is now 10 percent, as indicated in panel b at point B. If the price level then rises by 10 percent and $P_2 = 115.5$, employment rises to $N_2 = 93$; with full employment at $N_f = 100$, the unemployment rate would have been only 7 percent, as point C in panel b shows.

Thus, the higher the rate of inflation, the lower the unemployment rate; lower levels of unemployment must be "paid" for in higher rates of inflation.

> *If we interpret the classical model as implying that workers, as well as employers, correctly and immediately perceive a change in the price level and that wages are perfectly flexible, then in the classical model the Phillips curve is vertical even in the short run.*

THE JOB SEARCH MODEL[5]

The short-run Phillips curve that we have just derived requires more explanation and more fleshing out. By analyzing a simple job search model, we can

1. Understand the commonsense implications of the short-run Phillips curve
2. Relate that curve to the definitions of unemployment presented in Chapter 2
3. Understand better the Friedman-Phelps model that distinguishes between the short-run and the long-run Phillips curve

Labor-Force Stocks and Flows

In Chapter 2 the unemployment rate was defined as the ratio of the officially defined unemployed to the labor force (which includes the employed plus the unemployed). The job search model emphasizes that both the measure "unemployed" and the measure "labor force" are *stocks;* they are evaluated as of a *given* moment in time.[6] When *flows* into and out of the two stocks occur, "employment" and "unemployment," and the unemployment rate, change; a flow, as you will recall, is measured over time.[7]

Labor-Force Flows Flows *into* the labor-force stocks, called **entries,** can be either successful or unsuccessful. Successful entries are categorized as "employed," while unsuccessful entries become part of the "unemployed" category.

Flows *out of* the labor-force stock occur when people quit or are laid off from their jobs and do not look for other jobs. Also in this category are discouraged workers who (as indicated in Chapter 2) stop looking for jobs after initial searches because they believe that they cannot find employment anywhere. The important thing to remember is that if a person quits looking for a job, she or he is not in the labor force and hence is not considered unemployed. Note, then, that there is a distinc-

---

[5] A good discussion of the job search model can be found in Edwin G. Dolan, *Basic Economics,* 2d ed. (Hinsdale, Ill.: Dryden Press, 1980), chap. 16.

[6] Other stocks that have been considered in this text are wealth, the money supply, and the stock of capital.

[7] Other flows considered in this text are national income, saving plans, investment plans, aggregate demand, and aggregate supply. All are measured per unit of time.

tion between "not working" and "unemployed"; to be unemployed, you must actively be seeking employment.

Employment Flows   Flows *into* the employment stock occur when people are (a) hired for a new job, or (b) recalled to a former job; (a) + (b) equals total **accessions.**

Flows *out of* the stock of employment occur when people (c) are fired, (d) quit, or (e) retire; (c) + (d) + (e) = total **separations.**

Unemployment Flows   Flows *into* the stock of unemployed occur when (f) unsuccessful entry occurs and (g) when job separations that lead to a job search occur; (f) + (g) = total additions to the stock of unemployment. Flows *out of* the stock of unemployed result when unemployed job searchers (h) find jobs, or (i) leave the labor force by stopping their job search; (h) + (i) = total subtractions from the unemployed stock.

Changes in Unemployment   The stock of unemployed changes when total additions to unemployment differ from total subtractions from unemployment. That is, when (f + g) ≠ (h + i), the stock of unemployment changes; in particular, if (f + g) > (h + i), then the unemployment stock rises, and if (f + g) < (h + i), then the unemployment stock falls.

The Duration of Unemployment   Knowledge concerning the average duration of unemployment is important to policymakers. The same unemployment rate can be consistent with radically different average durations of unemployment. For example, if *each and every* laborer is unemployed for four weeks during the year, the unemployment rate will be about 7.7 percent. If the labor force were 100 million and 7.7 million people remained unemployed the entire year (while everyone else in the labor force worked the entire year), the unemployment rate would also be 7.7 percent. Note, however, that in the first case the average duration of unemployment of the unemployed was only four weeks, while in the second case the average duration of unemployment was one year. Policymakers view the second case as more of a problem than the first; they certainly would try to "solve" the unemployment "problem" differently in the two cases.

Another reason that information concerning the average duration of unemployment is important is that the average duration of unemployment itself affects the unemployment rate. For example, suppose that every month 4 million people out of a labor force of 100 million workers are unemployed, but that it is always a *changing* 4 million workers; those 4 million who were unemployed in January find jobs in February, but the stock of unemployed is replaced in February by a different 4 million workers. In this example the unemployment rate would be 4

The Unemployment Rate and the Duration of Unemployment Move in Tandem

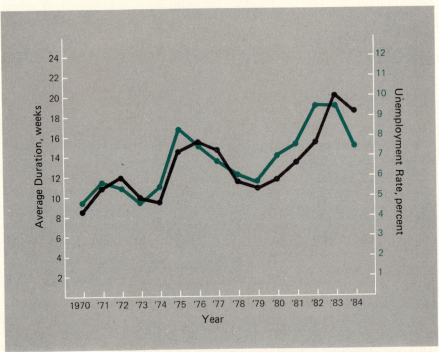

FIGURE 14.4. RELATING THE UNEMPLOYMENT RATE TO THE AVERAGE DURATION OF UNEMPLOYMENT

This figure shows that the unemployment rate and the duration of unemployment have moved together since 1970. Theoretically, changes in the average duration of employment change the employment rate, other things constant.

percent every month, and the average duration of unemployment is exactly one month. Now suppose that something occurs that induces all laborers to engage in a *two-month* job search. The average duration of unemployment rises to two months, and the unemployment rate doubles, from 4 to 8 percent. Clearly, the average duration of unemployment and the unemployment rate are directly related, other things constant. Figure 14.4 shows how the average duration of unemployment and the employment rate in the United States have, in fact, typically moved in tandem.

It is also important to recall from Chapter 2 that *frictional* unemployment arises when people are between steady jobs.

Relating Unemployment to the Job Search

We concluded in the previous section that the change in the stock of unemployment depends on flows into and out of unemployment. You should be aware that large numbers of people are involved in such flows; in any month (depending on the season) some 16 million workers experience a change in their employment status. For example, in July 1985 some 16.912 million workers experienced an employment status change; that number represents 14.45 percent of the 117.018 million people in the total labor force in that month.

Figure 14.5 shows how the labor force has grown since 1950; it also shows how the components of the labor force, employed and unemployed, have changed over that period. We are dealing with large numbers; by July 1985 the size of the civilian labor force had grown to 115.314 million. Because there are such large numbers of workers involved in employment and unemployment flows, and because they constitute a significant portion of the labor force, anything that changes the average duration of unemployment—the job search period—will have a significant impact on the unemployment rate.

The Optimal Duration of Unemployment Modern job search models predict that workers who are unemployed will behave rationally and will conduct a job search. The simple model that we shall discuss assumes, realistically, that an unemployed worker does not have perfect information about the availability of suitable jobs. What, then, is the optimal search period? Or, stated alternatively, what is the optimal duration of unemployment?

Suppose that your economics teacher, Mr. Homo Economicus, suddenly discovers on the last day of the spring semester that he is now unemployed. Will he panic and contract to deliver newspapers the next day? Not if he remembers some of the economics he has been teaching. Mr. Economicus will probably decide that he should not immediately accept any low-paying job that he can find; instead, he will decide that the best allocation of his time is to conduct a job search. More specifically, he will spend time collecting job offers. As he searches, he obtains more information, and the more time that he allocates to obtaining job offers, the higher will high wage offers become. Of course, after a while the growth in the value of wage offers he receives will start to level off.

If Mr. Economicus is like most economics teachers we know, he will have a very high opinion of his economic worth. His **reservation wage,** the lowest wage that he will accept, will therefore be quite high. As time goes by, however, Mr. Economicus (unlike his colleagues who are still teaching and who can afford the luxury of clinging to their illusions) will be forced to assess his market value more realistically. Mr. Economicus's

The Labor Force and Total Employment Have Increased Steadily Since 1950, but the Unemployment Rate Has Been Variable

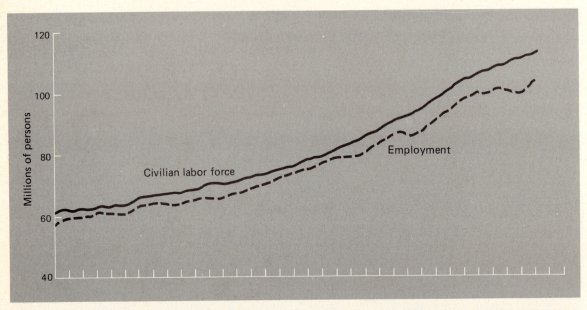

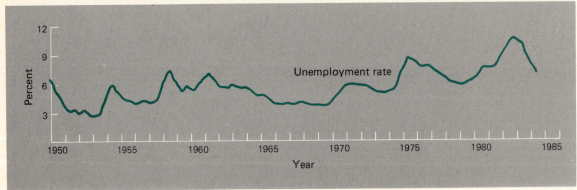

FIGURE 14.5. HISTORICAL MOVEMENT IN THE SEASONALLY ADJUSTED QUARTERLY CIVILIAN LABOR FORCE, EMPLOYMENT, AND UNEMPLOYMENT RATE

This graph was drawn from *1984 Historical Chart Book,* Board of Governors of the Federal Reserve System, p. 20.

The Optimal Duration of Unemployment Is Determined at the Point of Intersection of the Wage Offer Curve and the Reservation Wage Curve

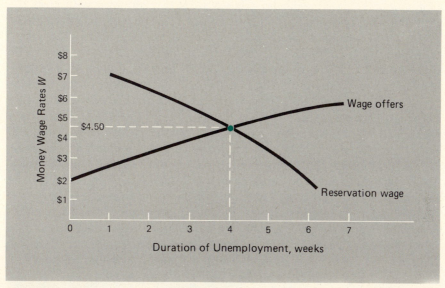

FIGURE 14.6. DETERMINATION OF THE OPTIMAL DURATION OF UNEMPLOYMENT

As time goes by, the value of wage rate offers rises, and the reservation wage declines. The intersection of these two curves determines the optimal duration of unemployment, or the optimal job search period.

reservation wage will fall for another reason: the financial (and social) pressure to get back to work will increase as time goes by because he has been spending his assets.

The Model   Somewhere a declining reservation wage curve and a rising job offer curve will intersect, and Mr. Economicus's optimal duration of unemployment will be determined.

Figure 14.6 shows a wage offer curve and a typical reservation wage curve that confront a typical unemployed worker. In that figure the optimal duration of unemployment is four weeks.

Now that we have examined the job search model, we are in a better position to understand how the short-run Phillips curve is derived, and to understand how it differs from a long-run Phillips curve.

THE LONG-RUN PHILLIPS CURVE

Unfortunately for those who wished to base economic policy on the Phillips curve, the relationship between inflation and unemployment rates proved to be unstable; the Phillips curve varied widely across countries and wasn't even stable within a given country over time. The inflation rate that was originally thought to be consistent with a specific level of unemployment did not remain fixed. After World War II, in those countries that pursued full employment as part of their stabilization policies, unemployment remained relatively high while the inflation rate *increased*. The phenomenon of simultaneous high rates of inflation and high unemployment rates, known as *stagflation*, became a worldwide problem. In effect, the Phillips curve shifted to the right, through time. Table 14.1 indicates the rates of unemployment and inflation in the United States for the years 1960 to 1984. Note that since 1967 inflation *and* the unemployment rate have increased (although not continuously). Figure 14.7 plots the data from Table 14.1. There is obviously no simple relationship between the rate of inflation and the rate of unemployment. Note that in some years *both* inflation and unemployment increased.

The Natural Rate of Unemployment

Chapter 7 examined the natural rate of *interest*. Keynes borrowed the concept of a natural rate of interest from a neoclassical economist, Knut Wicksell, in order to derive his speculative demand-for-money function. Milton Friedman and E. S. Phelps also borrowed the idea of a natural rate to develop the natural rate of unemployment.[8]

The **natural rate of unemployment** is an unemployment rate that consists of two parts: (1) frictional unemployment, and (2) unemployment due to rigidities in the economic system. *Frictional unemployment* is that unemployment experienced by people who are between steady jobs. In general, they spend a relatively short period of time between jobs when they quit or are laid off from one job until they find another. The second component of the natural rate of unemployment results from the following rigidities:

1. Union activity that restricts supply or entrance into jobs
2. Licensing arrangement granted by regulatory agencies

---

[8] Milton Friedman, "The Role of Monetary Policy," *American Economic Review*, vol. 48 (March 1968), pp. 1–17; and E. S. Phelps, "Money Wage Dynamics and Labor Market Equilibrium," *Journal of Political Economy*, vol. 76 (1968), pp. 678–711.

TABLE 14.1. INFLATION AND UNEMPLOYMENT IN THE UNITED STATES

Year	Percentage Rate of Unemployment	Annual Percentage Rate of Inflation
1960	5.4	1.5
1961	6.5	0.7
1962	5.4	1.2
1963	5.5	1.6
1964	5.0	1.2
1965	4.4	1.9
1966	3.7	3.4
1967	3.7	3.0
1968	3.5	4.7
1969	3.4	6.1
1970	4.8	5.5
1971	5.8	3.4
1972	5.5	3.4
1973	4.8	8.8
1974	5.5	12.2
1975	8.3	7.0
1976	7.6	4.8
1977	6.9	6.8
1978	6.0	9.0
1979	5.8	13.3
1980	7.0	12.4
1981	7.5	8.9
1982	9.5	3.9
1983	9.5	3.8
1984	7.4	4.0

[a] This table indicates the overall unemployment rate and the annual inflation rate (December-to-December percentage change in the Consumer Price Index) for the years 1960–1984.

Source: Economic Report of the President, Washington, D.C.: Government Printing Office, 1985, pp. 271 and 296.

3. Minimum-wage laws or laws such as the Davis-Bacon Act that require all workers to be paid union wages on government contracts
4. A welfare system that reduces incentives to work

According to Friedman, stabilization policy affects only frictional unemployment. Moreover, the effect on frictional unemployment occurs only because workers can be tricked into reducing the average duration of their frictional unemployment; workers are tricked into accepting jobs sooner than otherwise. *The Phillips curve trade-off between inflation and unemployment is, therefore, due only to a change in the average duration of unemployment for those laborers between jobs.* The trade-

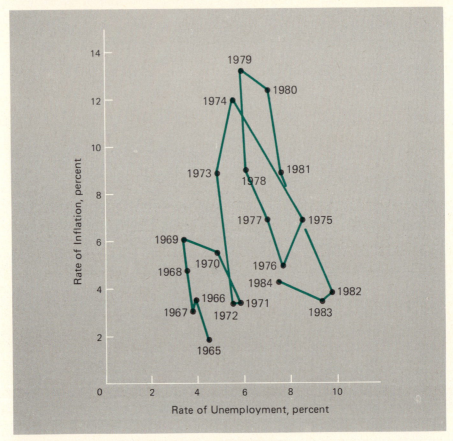

FIGURE 14.7. THE REAL "PHILLIPS CURVE"
The data from Table 14.1 are plotted in this figure, and no clear pattern emerges.
This is evidence that the Phillips curve is unstable through time.

off is the result of unanticipated changes in the rate of growth of nominal
aggregate demand. This matter is explained in greater detail in the section below.

The Friedman-Phelps Phillips Model

In the Friedman-Phelps analysis, nominal wage rate changes alter the
rate of unemployment only in the short run, because only in the short
run do laborers and employers confuse nominal wage rates with real

wage rates. Therefore, Friedman and Phelps distinguish between short-run and long-run effects of unanticipated changes in nominal aggregate expenditures.

Consider an economy in which prices have been stable and in which an unanticipated increase in the rate of growth in the money supply causes nominal aggregate expenditures to rise at a rate that results in a constant rate of inflation of 5 percent per annum. Individual employers experience a decrease in their inventories and an increase in the prices of the goods they sell. Each firm will interpret the situation (at least in part) as an increase in the demand for its own product. That is, initially each firm is aware only that its selling price has increased and is not aware that *general* inflation is occurring.

In short, each producer incorrectly interprets an increase in the nominal price of its product as an increase in the *relative* price of its product. Individual producers, therefore, are willing to pay slightly higher nominal wage rates because with their limited information the increase in nominal wage rates is perceived as a lower *real* wage rate; what matters to an individual producer is the wage rate relative to *his or her* product's selling price. As a consequence, each employer will attempt to obtain more labor and will voluntarily pay higher nominal wage rates.

On the other side of the market, frictionally unemployed laborers also have limited information. They initially know only *their* most important price—the wage rates offered to them. As a consequence, laborers view higher nominal wage rates as higher real wage rates, because they too are not yet aware that the general price level has begun to rise. They therefore respond to higher nominal and to (*perceived, but not actual*) higher real wage rates by increasing the amount of labor they are willing to offer. Those laborers who are frictionally unemployed will accept work sooner than they would have if the price level had remained stable. In terms of Figure 14.6, the wage offer curve shifts upward, the average duration of unemployment falls, and employment rises. Interestingly enough, *unanticipated inflation has led employers to perceive a reduction in the real wage and laborers to imagine an increase in the real wage.* The short-run result of inflation will be an increase in employment (because the average duration of unemployment falls). It appears that inflation has "bought" a reduction in unemployment. However, the Friedman-Phelps analysis maintains that the increase in employment is only a temporary (or short-run) situation. Once employers and laborers realize that the price level actually is rising at 5 percent per annum, they will both build this expectation into *new* labor contracts, and the unemployment rate will return to its old level. Laborers who are frictionally unemployed will accept only those jobs that "look good" after taking into account the fact that prices and wages in general are rising at 5 percent per annum.

In the meantime, however, long-term labor contracts made prior to the unanticipated inflation have allowed employers to gain at the expense of laborers (unless these contracts contained a cost-of-living clause).[9] The new wage contract will include a 5 percent inflation premium, which laborers demand and employers agree to, because all will now anticipate a 5 percent increase in the price level.

This analysis can be extended to another case in which the money supply is again unexpectedly increased and causes the level of nominal aggregate demand to rise at a rate that results in a 10 percent annual inflation rate. Long-term wage (and other) contracts were made in the expectation of a 5 percent annual inflation rate; again people will be fooled temporarily. Again laborers will increase their labor supplies, and a redistribution of income from laborers to employers will result. Once people fully anticipate the 10 percent annual increase in the price level, the new contracts will reflect this expectation, and the unemployment rate will return to its natural rate. We can now think of the natural rate of unemployment as follows:

> **The natural rate of unemployment is that rate of unemployment that exists when workers and employers correctly anticipate the rate of inflation.**

The only way that a permanent or long-run trade-off between unemployment and inflation can exist is if the money supply is continually increased at faster rates—and always unexpectedly. This is an unlikely possibility.

Complementary reasoning indicates that unanticipated reductions in the rate of growth of the money supply lead to unemployment rates temporarily *higher* than the natural rate. It would appear that less inflation is being purchased at the expense of higher employment. But again the trade-off would last only until the new contract time, when everyone would now anticipate the lower inflation rate. Lower-than-anticipated inflation therefore leads to higher unemployment only in the short run.

Short-Run versus Long-Run Phillips Curves

By distinguishing between the short-run and the long-run effects of unanticipated inflation, the Friedman-Phelps model can account for (1) the

---

[9] Once the inflation is correctly anticipated, these redistributional effects will disappear. Of course, laborers locked into long-term labor contracts might quit instead of waiting for the next contract, or go on a wildcat (union-unauthorized) strike. If so, the initial trade-off would be reversed sooner.

When the Inflation Rate Is Correctly Anticipated, the Phillips Curve Is Vertical

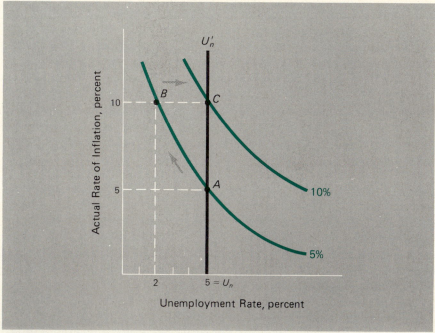

FIGURE 14.8. THE NATURAL RATE OF UNEMPLOYMENT

Here are two short-run Phillips curves: one is for a 5 percent and the other for a 10 percent anticipated rate of inflation. Each indicates that the unemployment rate is negatively related to the *actual* rate of inflation. When the actual rate of inflation differs from the anticipated rate, laborers and employers are fooled; a temporary trade-off between inflation and the unemployment rate therefore exists.

In the long-run, however, laborers and employers will adjust to a constant inflation rate, and unemployment will return to its natural rate of 5 percent (in this figure). As a result, the long-run Phillips curve is vertical and parallel to the vertical axis at the natural rate of unemployment. There is, in short, no long-run trade-off between inflation and unemployment. The natural rate of unemployment is the rate of unemployment that exists when the inflation rate is correctly anticipated.

existence of a short-run Phillips curve and (2) a shifting, or unstable, short-run Phillips curve. To see this, consider Figure 14.8, which links the natural rate of unemployment and the measured rate of unemployment to the Phillips curve. The unemployment rate is plotted on the horizontal axis and the *actual* rate of inflation is plotted on the vertical axis. It is assumed that the natural, or long-run, level of unemployment is at U_n, here at 5 percent of the labor force. One Phillips curve is labeled "5 percent," and it indicates the inverse short-run relationship between *actual* inflation and unemployment when employers and employees anticipate an annual inflation rate of 5 percent. Along that curve a temporary trade-off between inflation and the unemployment rate exists; when the actual rate of inflation differs from the anticipated rate of inflation, laborers and employers are fooled. For example, assume that the economy is actually experiencing a 5 percent rate of inflation and that buyers and sellers of labor correctly anticipate that rate of increase in the price level. The economy will be at point *A* in Figure 14.8; buyers and sellers of labor correctly anticipate the 5 percent rate of inflation and the unemployment rate is at its natural rate—here assumed to be 5 percent. Suppose that this unemployment rate is considered to be too high, and some combination of monetary and fiscal policy generates an inflation rate of 10 percent per annum. If this new inflation rate is *unanticipated* by laborers and employers, the economy will move from point *A* to point *B*. Some frictionally unemployed laborers will interpret an increase in nominal wages as an increase in real wages and will accept jobs sooner. The average duration of unemployment will fall, and therefore the unemployment rate will fall to 2 percent.

It appears that a 5 percentage point increase in inflation has been traded off for a 3 percentage point decrease in unemployment. Eventually, however, both employers and laborers will realize that the annual inflation rate is now 10 percent. New labor contracts will take this into consideration, and the frictionally unemployed will again remain unemployed for the "normal" average duration. That is, the unemployment rate returns to 5 percent (the natural rate) and the economy moves from point *B* to point *C*. Note that at point *C* the *actual* rate of inflation is correctly anticipated and that in order to reduce unemployment a still higher unanticipated rate of inflation is required.

Points *A* and *C* are part of the *long-run* Phillips curve, which can be derived by finding the unemployment rate when the inflation rate is correctly perceived. A family of short-run Phillips curves can be drawn, each with a specific anticipated rate of inflation. In the long run, when the specific anticipated rate of inflation is correctly perceived, the unemployment rate will be at the natural rate of unemployment. The long-run Phillips curve will be vertical—in the long run there is no trade-off between inflation and unemployment—and its position is determined by the natural rate of unemployment.

It should be stressed that the previous example points out that the shift in the Phillips curve was *not independent* of stabilization policy:

Attempts to move along a specific short-run Phillips curve cause the curve itself to shift. Stabilization policy can work only in the short run, therefore, because in the long run inflationary expectations will be correct.

A Rising Natural Rate of Unemployment

For the past two decades the natural rate of unemployment in the United States has been rising. According to Friedman,[10] this is due to two major factors. First of all, women, teenagers, and part-time workers have come to comprise an increasing percentage of the labor force. In general, these groups change jobs more often and experience higher average rates of unemployment. Second, unemployment insurance and other assistance to the unemployed have been made available to more categories of workers; these benefits have also become more generous in duration and amount. Consequently, the unemployed can afford to remain idle for longer periods; they wait to be recalled to their former jobs or wait for even better jobs. In terms of Figure 14.6, these benefits shifted the reservation wage curve upward. Therefore, the average duration of unemployment has risen and, other things constant, the unemployment rate has risen. Moreover, in many cases people must *say* they are looking for employment before they become eligible for welfare benefits. Such benefits, therefore, at once increase voluntary unemployment *and* measured unemployment; measured unemployment, however, is often (incorrectly) interpreted as *in*voluntary unemployment.

The Friedman-Phelps model discussed in this chapter is consistent with an economic theory called monetarism, discussed in detail in Chapter 18. For now, we can say that the monetarist theory accounts for stagflation by combining the two following increases:

1. Increases in the natural rate of unemployment due to changes in the composition of the labor force, increased government interference in the marketplace, and a welfare state that prolongs the duration of unemployment and simultaneously increases voluntary unemployment and measured unemployment
2. Increases in monetary growth to combat this rising natural rate of unemployment

---

[10] Milton Friedman, ''Nobel Lecture: Inflation and Unemployment,'' *Journal of Political Economy*, vol. 85, no. 3 (1977), pp. 451–471.

In effect, the long-run consequences of an expansion in the rate of monetary growth under such a situation are higher inflation rates and a higher natural rate of unemployment—stagflation.

POLICY CONTROVERSY
Is the Employment Rate Better Than the Unemployment Rate as an Indicator of the State of the Economy?

If employment rises, then the unemployment rate will fall, right? Not necessarily. The reason for this surprising conclusion is that the unemployment rate is defined as the ratio of the stock of the unemployed to the labor-force stock. During the expansion phase of the business cycle, employment typically will rise as flows into employment will exceed flows out of employment. On the other hand, during the expansion phase flows into the labor force also rise because the expansion attracts additional laborers into the labor market. It is possible, therefore, for both employment *and* unemployment to rise; if the net inflows into unemployment exceed the net inflows into the labor force, the unemployment rate will rise. Policymakers will conclude that the economy is contracting when in fact it is expanding.

For example, suppose that the labor force consists of 100 million people, and that 90 million people are classified as employed and 10 million are classified as unemployed; the unemployment rate in that case is 10 percent. Now suppose that an expansion occurs and attracts 1 million laborers into the labor force and one-half of them find jobs. Employment rises to 90.5 million, the labor force rises to 101 million, unemployment rises to 10.5 million, and the unemployment rate rises to $10.5/101 = 10.39$ percent.

Something akin to this hypothetical example did, in fact, occur in the United States during the period from February through April of 1984. During those three months the civilian unemployment rate remained constant at 7.8 percent and the number of unemployed rose by about 42,000. The implication is that the economy was stagnant or declining during that period. Actually, however, employment increased by some 510,000, and the economy expanded.

Some have suggested that a better indicator of the state of the economy is the ratio of total employment to the total noninstitutional population (civilians aged 16 and over, not living in mental or criminal institutions). During the 1984 February-to-April period, that ratio rose from 58.4 percent to 58.6 percent and correctly indicated the direction in which the economy actually moved.

Whether this employment ratio will replace the widely published unemployment rate in the hearts of policymakers remains to be seen.

CHAPTER SUMMARY

1. The Phillips curve is a relationship between the rate of inflation and the unemployment rate.
2. If the short-run AS curve is positively sloped, then the short-run Phillips curve will be negatively sloped.
3. If workers adjust only partially to changes in the price level in the short run, then even if wages are perfectly flexible the short-run AS curve will be positively sloped and the short-run Phillips curve will be negatively sloped. Also, if wages are inflexible in the short run, the short-run AS curve will be positively sloped and the short-run Phillips curve will be negatively sloped.
4. The average duration of unemployment can vary significantly for a given unemployment rate.
5. The longer the average duration of unemployment, the higher the rate of unemployment, other things constant.
6. Where the job offer curve intersects the reservation wage curve, the optimal job search period is established; that period also represents the optimal duration of unemployment.
7. The natural rate of unemployment equals the unemployment rate associated with the sum of frictional unemployment and unemployment resulting from price-wage rigidities and interferences with labor mobility.
8. Empirically, the Phillips curve has been unstable over time.
9. The Friedman-Phelps model indicates that the Phillips curve is negatively sloped only in the short run because in the short run both employers and laborers incorrectly perceive the rate of inflation. In the long run the actual rate of inflation is known and unemployment will be at its natural rate; therefore the long-run Phillips curve is vertical.
10. During an economic expansion, both employment and unemployment can rise because additional people are drawn into the labor force. It is possible, therefore, for the unemployment rate to rise or remain constant during an expansion. For that reason, some have suggested that policymakers use the ratio of employment to the noninstitutional population (instead of on the unemployment rate) to make their decisions.

GLOSSARY

accessions Flows into employment; total accessions equal the sum of people hired for a new job and people recalled to a former job.
entries Flows into the labor force.

natural rate of unemployment   A rate which reflects frictional unemployment plus unemployment due to rigidities in the economic system; the unemployment rate when inflation is correctly perceived by both workers and employers.

Phillips curve   A relationship between the rate of inflation and the unemployment rate.

reservation wage   The lowest wage that a worker will accept; a worker will not offer labor if the reservation wage exceeds the value of the worker's highest job offer.

separations   Flows out of employment; total separations equals the sum of people who are fired and those who quit or retire.

QUESTIONS AND PROBLEMS FOR REVIEW

14.1   If the short-run aggregate supply curve is negatively sloped because *employers* (not workers) incompletely perceive changes in prices, describe the slope of the short-run Phillips curve.

14.2   Even if workers adjust completely to changes in the price level in the short run, the short-run Phillips curve may still be negatively sloped. Explain how.

14.3   Even if wage rates are flexible, the short-run Phillips curve may still be negatively sloped. Explain how.

14.4   Explain how the average duration of unemployment may be different for a given rate of unemployment.

14.5   What effect does the average duration of unemployment have on the rate of unemployment if we hold constant the variables you used to explain question 14.4?

14.6   What is meant by an optimal duration of unemployment? What may affect such an optimal duration of unemployment?

14.7   The natural rate of unemployment is a function of, among other variables, wage-price rigidities and interferences with labor mobility. What are examples of such rigidities and interferences?

14.8   If both employers and workers incorrectly perceive the rate of inflation to the same extent, would the Phillips curve still be expected to be negatively sloped?

14.9   What explanations can you give for the empirically unstable Phillips curve?

14.10 "Unemployment" is arbitrarily defined. What differences do different definitions have with respect to policy?

REFERENCES

Armen A. Alchian, "Information Costs, Pricing, and Resource Unemployment," *Western Economic Journal*, vol. 7 (1969).

Edwin G. Dolan, *Basic Economics,* 2d ed. (Hinsdale, Ill.: The Dryden Press, 1980).

Milton Friedman, "The Role of Monetary Policy," *American Economic Review,* vol. 48 (1968).

———, "Nobel Lecture: Inflation and Unemployment," *Journal of Political Economy,* vol. 85 (1977).

Robert J. Gordon, "Recent Developments in the Theory of Inflation and Unemployment, *Journal of Monetary Economics,* vol. 2 (1976).

Thomas Humphrey, *Essays on Inflation,* 4th ed. (Richmond, Va.: Federal Reserve Bank of Richmond, 1983).

Richard G. Lipsey, "The Relationship Between Unemployment and the Rate of Change of Money Wage Rates in the U.K., 1862–1957: A Further Analysis," *Economica,* vol. 27 (1960).

Edmund S. Phelps, "Money Wage Dynamics and Labor Market Equilibrium," *Journal of Political Economy,* vol. 76 (1968).

Edmund S. Phelps et al., *The Microeconomic Foundations of Employment and Inflation Theory* (New York: Norton, 1970).

Edmund S. Phelps and J. B. Taylor, "Stabilizing Powers of Monetary Policy Under Rational Expectations," *Journal of Political Economy,* vol. 85 (1977).

James Tobin, "Inflation and Unemployment," *American Economic Review,* vol. 62 (1972).

15

OTHER EXPLANATIONS OF
STAGFLATION

RATIONAL EXPECTATIONS AND

POST-KEYNESIAN ECONOMICS

Chapter 14 indicated that stagflation, the simultaneous existence of high inflation and high unemployment rates, dealt a serious (perhaps mortal) blow to Keynesian economics. We showed there that the Friedman-Phelps model can account for stagflation by introducing an expansionary monetary policy undertaken to fight a rising natural rate of unemployment.

In this chapter two other modern theories capable of explaining stagflation are analyzed: rational expectations and post-Keynesian economics. In Chapter 19 yet another explanation of stagflation—the supply-side economics model—is analyzed.

THE RATIONAL EXPECTATIONS HYPOTHESIS

In the Friedman-Phelps model, monetary (or fiscal) policy cannot affect the long-run level of unemployment or, therefore, of output. Unemployment will return to its natural level and output to its natural level because in the long run employers and employees will fully and correctly anticipate the inflation rate.[1] Short-run departures from the natural rate of unemployment and the natural rate of output can be achieved by monetary and fiscal policies because these policies cause people to make errors when they try to anticipate the inflation rate; that is, monetary and fiscal policies can work in the short run only if people are fooled. Aside from the question of whether such short-run stabilization policy is *desirable*,[2] it nevertheless has been widely accepted that monetary and fiscal policies *can* affect employment and output in the short run.

A recent innovation in economic analysis suggests that monetary and fiscal policies cannot affect output and employment *systematically* even in the short run! This theoretical innovation, first formalized by J. F. Muth in 1961 and applied to the theory of stabilization policy a decade later, is the **rational expectations hypothesis (REH)**.[3] The REH was first

---

[1] Whether or not employers and employees fully adjust current prices and wages to expected inflation is an empirical question. If they do not fully adjust, then it is possible for the *long-run* Phillips curve to be negatively sloped. The data are mixed; both G. Perry ["Changing Labor Markets and Inflation," *Brookings Papers on Economic Activity*, vol. 3 (1970), pp. 411–441] and R. J. Gordon ["Inflation in Recession and Recovery," *Brookings Papers on Economic Activity*, vol. 2 (1972), pp. 385–421] concluded that people do *not* fully adjust. On the other hand, studies of the late 1960s and 1970s (when inflation rates and the costs of not adjusting were higher) indicate that people *did* fully adjust. See R. J. Gordon, "Wage-Price Controls and the Shifting Phillips Curve," *Brookings Papers on Economic Activity*, vol. 2 (1972), pp. 385–421.

[2] Fooling people may well leave them economically worse off and may cause a misallocation of resources. If laborers accept jobs sooner or later than they would have otherwise, they will work at jobs that are "inappropriate," in the sense that they will not be maximizing the present value of their lifetime earnings, other things constant.

[3] J. F. Muth, "Rational Expectations and the Theory of Price Movements," *Econometrica*, vol. 29 (1961), pp. 315–335.

applied to such microeconomic problems as the formation of expectations concerning the price of commodities or the price of a share of common stock traded in the stock market. In the 1970s this theory was applied to the macroeconomy by such economists as Robert Lucas of the University of Chicago, Thomas Sargent and Neil Wallace of the University of Minnesota, and Robert J. Barro of the University of Rochester. (See references at the end of this chapter.)

The REH leads to the conclusion that short-run stabilization policies have no *systematic* effect on the errors that people make about the expected inflation rate. (A **policy** can be defined as a sustained pattern of action or reaction. An example is "increase the money supply by 6 percent per annum if the measured unemployment rate is 7 percent.") But the conclusion of the widely accepted Friedman-Phelps model is that an effective stabilization policy requires that the government generate an inflation rate that is higher than that expected by buyers and sellers of labor. The essence of the REH is that the difference between the community's expected inflation rate and the actual rate is purely random. Therefore, we can say:

If stabilization policy cannot systematically influence people's expectational errors for the inflation rate, then stabilization policy cannot systematically alter real variables such as employment and output, even in the short run.

The following are important tenets of most versions of the REH:

1. Acceptance of the concepts of a natural rate of unemployment and a natural level of output, and acceptance of the Friedman-Phelps conclusion that in the long run the economy will return to these rates.

2. A rejection of the adaptive expectations hypothesis concerning how "economic agents" (households, laborers, businesses) form their expectations, because that hypothesis implies that economic agents make *systematic* forecasting errors, in the sense that they always, say, underestimate the inflation rate.

3. A rejection of the adaptive expectations hypothesis that people base their forecasts of, say, the price level only on *past* values of the price level and that people, by implication, ignore other relevant information. The REH (in one version) assumes that people have imperfect information, and it assumes that information has value but is costly; as a consequence, people will gather information—to help them in their forecasts—up to the point where the marginal cost of additional information equals the marginal benefit of that information. This

information is then used to maximize profits or utility. The REH, therefore, allows for the existence of errors that remain in forecasts, where the marginal cost of information exceeds the marginal benefit of information. The errors that remain, however, are unbiased even to the extent that they are unknown with respect to the signs of the errors.

4. The insistence that the consequences of an "event" (such as a change in the money supply) depend on whether the event is anticipated or unanticipated.

5. An assumption that prices and wages are perfectly flexible and always adjust so as to clear markets; stated differently, markets are always in equilibrium.

Rational Expectations versus Adaptive Expectations

Systematic Errors According to proponents of the REH, *the adaptive expectations model is fatally flawed because it assumes that people can make systematic errors.* Assume that the price level is initially equal to 100 and that people have adjusted completely to it. Now assume that it rises *permanently*, by 5 percent, to 105. Recall from Chapter 12 that one simple adaptive expectations model is

$$P_p = P_{p-1} + J(P - P_{p-1}) \qquad (15.1)$$

WHERE P_p = permanent price level estimate
P_{p-1} = last period's estimate of the permanent price level
J = an adjustment factor, where $0 < J < 1$, which implies that $P_p < P$ when P rises
P = actual price level

Because economic agents are not sure whether the rise in the price level is permanent or temporary, they adjust their expectations upward only partially—by the adjustment factor J.

TABLE 15.1. PERMANENT INCREASE IN THE PRICE LEVEL

Period	Actual Price Level P	Adaptive Expectations Estimate of the Price Level[a] P_p
1	1.00	1.00000
2	1.05	1.02500
3	1.05	1.03750
4	1.05	1.04375
5	1.05	1.04688
6	1.05	1.04844

[a] Assuming an adjustment factor of $J = 0.5$.

Consider Table 15.1, which assumes an adjustment factor of 0.5 (i.e., $J = 0.5$). Initially, the price level is 100 and it rises permanently to 105. Column 3 shows the adaptive expectations estimate of the permanent price level. Note that it *systematically underpredicts* the permanent price level increase; it approaches the permanent price level asymptotically.

Again assume an initial price level of 100, but now assume that the price level rises continuously at 5 percent per period. Table 15.2 shows that the adaptive expectations model again systematically underpredicts the permanent price level.

REH proponents maintain that such behavior is inconsistent with the typical analysis of how rational utility- (or profit-) maximizing agents behave. This criticism of the adaptive expectations hypothesis (and of Keynesian economics, too) has gained widespread acceptance.

Ignoring Relevant Information   The REH also takes the adaptive expectations model to task because the latter implies that people base their forecasts of the future price level only on past values of the price level; by implication, other useful information is ignored.

Consider an example from microeconomics. Assume you wanted to forecast the price of wheat. Would you base your forecast solely on the *past* prices of wheat? Suppose that you did so and that your forecast is $1.00 per bushel. Then suppose you discover that a poor harvest of wheat, due to poor weather conditions, has been projected. Would you *still* cling to your forecast of $1.00 per bushel of wheat? You would probably lose money if you made decisions based on that forecast.

The REH says that people will incur costs to discover information about the *future* supply of and demand for wheat (or the future supply of and demand for other goods, or future wage rates, or the future price level.) In fact, the REH suggests that such competitive markets as the

TABLE 15.2. PRICE LEVEL RISING AT 5 PERCENT PER ANNUM

Period	Actual Price Level[a] P	Adaptive Expectations Estimate of the Price Level[b] P_p
1	1.0000	1.0000
2	1.0500	1.025
3	1.1025	1.064
4	1.1576	1.111
5	1.2155	1.163
6	1.2763	1.220

[a] Increasing at 5 percent per period.
[b] Using an adjustment factor of $J = 0.5$.

stock market, the commodity market, and the bond market are **random walks.** This means that the *present* prices of competitively traded goods about which information is widely available has *already* been incorporated in their market price. The only thing that can change the current price is (1) unanticipated events or (2) new information. If this is so, then *past* information about such goods is irrelevant. This conclusion is entirely at odds with the adaptive expectations hypothesis. The best estimate of a random-walk value is its value right now; its future value will equal its value now plus an unpredictable random error. *REH advocates apply this conclusion concerning a particular price to the price level itself.*

It should be stressed that the REH doesn't say that *everyone* will expend time, effort, and money to gather information concerning (1) how the economy functions, (2) what specific stabilization policy is likely to be carried out, and (3) how such policy will affect the economy. The REH conclusions merely require that *some* people obtain this information and use it to their advantage.

Anticipated Changes versus Unanticipated Changes

Proponents of the REH insist that the effect a given event will have on economic variables depends on whether or not it was anticipated. Whether the event originates from the private sector or from economic policy doesn't matter; the crucial issue is whether it was anticipated or unanticipated. In order to demonstrate the significance of the difference between anticipated and unanticipated events, let's consider a **supply shock,** which is an unanticipated shift in the AS curve. (A **demand shock** is an unanticipated shift in the AD curve.) In particular, consider a supply shock that is typical of what happened in the United States (1) during 1973–1975 when Arab nations first embargoed oil to the United States and other Western nations and then quadrupled the price, and when the price of other energy sources and raw materials such as copper rose sharply, or (2) during 1978–1979 when the Iranian revolution led to worldwide oil supply disruptions and to rapidly rising energy prices.

Consider Figure 15.1, which shows an initial equilibrium at point A, where aggregate supply is AS (P^e), the price level is at P_e, and the economy is at the natural level of output, y_{n_1}. Now a supply shock occurs and the AS (P^e) curve shifts leftward to AS'. This means that producers will produce less at every price level because they must now pay higher raw-material prices and/or higher energy prices.[4] Because equilibrium output

---

[4] Up to this point the AS curve shifted only when the nominal aggregate supply-of-labor curve shifted as a result of a change in the perceived price level.

An Unanticipated Supply Shock Shifts the AS Curve by More Than an Anticipated Shock Does

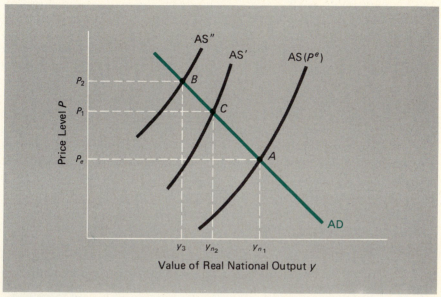

FIGURE 15.1. ANTICIPATED AND UNANTICIPATED SUPPLY SHOCKS
If a supply shock occurs due to an unanticipated increase in raw material costs, the AS curve will shift from $AS(P^e)$ to AS''. Because of the increase in raw material prices and an increased price level, workers (mistakenly) withdraw some labor. This causes output to fall to y_3, which is less than the new (lower) natural level, y_{n_2}. Unemployment will be higher than the natural rate, too. Eventually, the economy will move to point C.

   If the supply shock had been perfectly anticipated and if prices were perfectly flexible, the AS curve would shift only to AS', which reflects the higher raw material costs. The actual output level would immediately fall to y_{n_2}.

will decline, the demand for labor will also decline, and the economy will experience a lower natural level of output and a lower natural level of unemployment. The new natural level of output, shown in Figure 15.1, is y_{n_2}. Note that if the AD curve does not shift, the new long-run equilibrium price level must be at P_1, at which the AD curve intersects AS'.

   Suppose, however, that workers do not yet know what the new (lower) natural level of output is and that they react to the higher price level by reducing their supply of labor. This in turn shifts the aggregate supply curve leftward again to AS''. You should realize that the AS curve has shifted leftward for *two* reasons: (1) the cost of raw materials has increased, and (2) laborers do not have all the information about what has happened and so they mistakenly react to a higher price level by withdrawing some labor.

The shift in the AS curve to AS″ will induce a still higher price level, P_2. But because this higher price level is at an output level y_3 that is *below* the *new* natural level of output y_{n_2}, unemployment exists at point B. Wages and prices will fall, but only after laborers fully understand what has happened; and the economy eventually will settle at point C.

Note that greater unemployment than the natural unemployment level (involuntary) existed in the short run and that the output level was below the new (lower) natural output level only because the supply shock was unanticipated and because workers were misinformed about what the new natural output level would be. Because workers had incomplete information, the economy moved from A to B, and then eventually to the new equilibrium at C, in Figure 15.1.

Suppose, however, that the increase in raw-materials costs had been anticipated and that workers knew that the new natural level of output (and employment) would be lower. Given perfect information, the economy would have moved *immediately* from A to C in Figure 15.1, and the economy would not have experienced involuntary unemployment in the short run.

The economy departs only from its natural output level and its natural employment level when information is incomplete.

This conclusion has startling policy implications. If an event is anticipated, then no government fiscal or monetary policy is necessary because no departures from natural levels will result. But if the event is unanticipated, then policy is not feasible because policymakers can't anticipate future events any better than the public can. Shocks will lead to temporary departures from natural output and natural employment levels until the new information is completely assimilated; policy might even lengthen the adjustment period.

This example is also instructive because it depicts one REH explanation of stagflation—the supply-shock variety associated with the two episodes in the 1970s cited in a previous paragraph.

Stabilization Policy and the REH

We are now in a position to assess the virtues of stabilization policy as the REH advocates see it. If the REH is correct, the policy failures of the last several decades are not a result of human error or of poor policy.

REH proponents maintain that the policy objectives can never be achieved and that the deployment of policy in an effort to achieve these objectives causes more harm than good.

The first thing to realize is that when economic agents make forecasts of economic variables, they also take into account the likely monetary and fiscal policies of government. Therefore, policy objectives cannot be met because people will acquire the information necessary to discern what policies will be undertaken, and then take actions that are in their own self-interest. These actions usually will thwart the policies.[5] For example, suppose that the Fed's policy is to increase the money supply at an annual rate of 6 percent whenever the measured unemployment rate rises to 7 percent. Workers and employers *eventually* will recognize this policy and act in their own self-interest. When the measured unemployment rate reaches 7 percent, frictionally unemployed workers will realize that the Fed will now pursue an expansionary monetary policy and they will incorporate an inflationary premium into their reservation-wage curve. Similarly, union and management negotiators will incorporate an inflationary premium into their negotiations. All these actions will frustrate the Fed's monetary policy, and the unemployment rate will not fall because economic agents will not be fooled.

If an expansionary monetary policy is *announced*, it won't have any effect even in the short run because economic agents will merely incorporate inflationary premiums into their negotiations. True, an *unannounced* expansionary policy will affect real values; but the REH maintains that an unannounced policy cannot cause people to make *systematic* forecasting errors; that is, at any given time, some people will anticipate a rate of inflation that is below, and others will anticipate a rate of inflation that is above, the actual rate of inflation to which the policy of the Fed will lead. This means that some people will overpredict and others will underpredict the rate of inflation. Consequently, some laborers will lengthen their job search and others will shorten it as the Fed pursues some unannounced policy (a specific monetary expansion target, for example). In the long run, of course, everyone will learn what the policy is and there will be a vertical Phillips curve. *In the short run the Phillips curve can be negatively sloped or positively sloped.* Which it will be depends on the direction in which most people are fooled. The point is that a given Fed policy cannot systematically cause forecasting errors, so that the *unbiased* short-run Phillips curve is vertical. If this is

---

[5] One of coauthor Pulsinelli's classroom objectives is to not have students enter the room after his lecture begins. His policy is to come to class two minutes late. Students eventually incorporate his policy into their own actions and come to class three or four minutes late. Rational expectations, right?

true, then even though policy can affect output and employment in the short run, it can't affect these real variables systematically, in desirable directions.

The question that must be asked now is, what good is stabilization policy if it can only affect output and employment randomly? The REH proponents respond that stabilization policy can't do any good, and it probably does much harm because it introduces one more element of uncertainty into economic life—economic policy itself. By avoiding stabilization policy, or by faithfully following some preannounced money growth rule, the Fed can (1) eliminate the instability that the policies of the Fed create, and (2) at least prevent inflation, if the money supply growth rate is not greater than the natural rate of growth of output.

Problems with the REH

Even advocates of the REH admit that it poses some unresolved problems. For one thing, if the macroeconomic variables truly follow a random walk, then in any one-year period output and employment are just as likely to *exceed* their natural levels as they are likely to *fall short* of them. If this is so, then the REH has trouble explaining the existence of business cycles, in variables which typically show several periods below, and several periods above, their natural levels. Technically, the empirical evidence shows that if the current period's output level exceeds the natural level, the probability is high that in the next period the actual output level will also exceed the natural level. Conversely, if the actual output level is below the natural level, the next period's output is more likely to be below the natural level than it is to be above the natural level. A dramatic example of this is the Great Depression, which was both severe and persistent. We return to this important issue in Chapter 18; we merely note here that some REH advocates admit that they must do more work in this area.[6]

Another problem which the REH proponents own up to is the notion that the REH predicts that money is neutral in the short run. They can explain any nonneutrality of money as a consequence of misinformation, to be sure, but they still need to demonstrate that the *extent* of relative price changes during inflation can be accounted for solely by misinformation. Again, REH advocates admit they must do more work here, too.[7]

---

[6] See Robert J. Barro, "Rational Expectations and Macroeconomics in 1984," *American Economic Review*, Papers and Proceedings (May 1984), pp. 179–182.

[7] Ibid. Barro also notes in his paper that problems for the REH are not necessarily good news for Keynesian economists.

Criticisms of the REH

The REH is not without its critics. As noted above, the REH cannot account very well for business cycles and it can't account for the degree of nonneutrality of money that exists in the short run.

Another important criticism of the REH is that it assumes that prices and wages always adjust until markets are cleared, and that the economy is always in equilibrium. We return to this important issue in the next section of this chapter, when we analyze post-Keynesian economics.

Finally, we should point out that not *all* government policy requires that people be fooled before output and employment can be affected; only stabilization policy requires such deception. Such governmental policies as tariffs, import quotas, minimum wage laws, immigration quotas, and taxes can affect output and employment without fooling people. In Chapter 19 we analyze in detail the effects that taxes have on (1) the supply of labor, (2) household saving, and (3) business investment. Because taxes can affect these important variables, taxes can also determine the position of the aggregate supply curve. In Chapter 19 we show why proponents of supply-side economics stress the importance of high marginal tax rates as an explanation of stagflation, and we show how reductions in the marginal tax rates can cure stagflation. Here we need only point out that changes in tax rates shift the AS curve and that, along with monetarism and rational expectations, supply-side economics can also explain stagflation. We turn now to yet another theory capable of explaining stagflation—post-Keynesian economics.

POST-KEYNESIAN ECONOMICS

Post-Keynesian economists are a very diverse lot, but they share at least two related beliefs. First, they point out that the neoclassical-Keynesian synthesis discussed in Chapter 8 pushed Keynes's analysis on to the wrong track. By synthesizing Keynes's work with that of the classical economists, Keynesians have thrown out Keynes's most important insight—the crucial implications of transactions that take place when the economy is not in equilibrium. If prices and wages don't adjust instantaneously, then there will be quantity adjustments. Moreover, if transactions occur at nonequilibrium prices in one market, then an additional (beyond the normal) constraint is placed on economic agents in other markets. The analysis of the implications of off-equilibrium transactions, referred to as **disequilibrium analysis,** is an integral part of post-Keynesian methodology.

The second belief shared by post-Keynesian economists follows from the first: *Unemployment can be involuntary and prolonged*, and there are no mechanisms to restore full employment. Post-Keynesians find it striking that the classical model, the neoclassical-Keynesian synthesis, and the rational expectations model cannot account for prolonged involuntary unemployment.

The disequilibrium analysis approach was developed by Don Patinkin, who applied it to the labor market; Robert Clower, who applied it to the consumption function; and Axel Leijonhufvud, who applied it to the capital goods market.[8] Post-Keynesians have elaborated on this foundation; they include Cambridge University economists Roy Harrod, Nicholas Kaldor, and the late Joan Robinson. Rutgers University post-Keynesians include Paul Davidson, Alfred Eichner, and Jan Kregal. Hyman Minsky of Washington University is also a prominent post-Keynesian.

In the remainder of this section, we will first present a simplified example of disequilibrium analysis, and then indicate how this approach itself has been criticized.[9]

Disequilibrium Analysis

In order to understand the disequilibrium-analysis approach and the theoretical distinction between voluntary and involuntary unemployment it is helpful to begin with the classical approach of complete price-wage flexibility where all transactions are made in equilibrium. This approach is first compared to the neoclassical-Keynesian synthesis and to the REH approaches, and then all are compared to the disequilibrium approach. Although it may seem as though we have a lot of complicated work to do, you will find that the comparisons can be made with just a few diagrams.

The Classical Case Yet Again Consider Figure 15.2. Start at a full-employment equilibrium, point A in panel a and panel b. Then suppose that a demand shock occurs (due to, say, an unexpected reduction in the money supply or an unexpected event that reduces the "confidence" of businesses or consumers). This shock reduces the aggregate demand curve from AD to AD' in panel b. If prices are perfectly flexible and if producers receive the new information instantaneously, the price level will fall immediately from P_e to P_1.

---

[8] Don Patinkin, *Money, Interest and Prices*, 2d ed. (New York: Harper & Row, 1965); Robert Clower, "The Keynesian Counterrevolution: A Theoretical Reappraisal," in F. H. Hahn and F. D. R. Brechling, eds., *The Theory of Interest Rates* (New York: St. Martin's Press, 1965), pp. 103–125; Axel Leijonhufvud, *On Keynesian Economics and the Economics of Keynes: A Study in Monetary Theory* (New York: Oxford University Press, 1968).

[9] See Laurence Harris, *Monetary Theory* (New York: McGraw-Hill, 1981), especially chap. 13, for a more rigorous presentation of the material in this section.

If Prices and Wages Are Perfectly Flexible and If Information Is Perfect, All Transactions Will Take Place in Equilibrium and at the Natural Rates

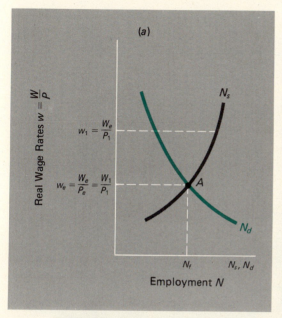

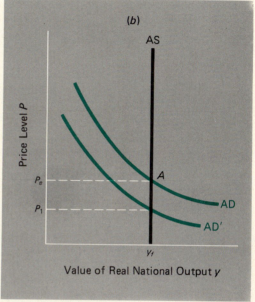

FIGURE 15.2. CLASSICAL EQUILIBRIUM ANALYSIS

An aggregate demand shock that shifts the AD curve leftward will cause the price level to fall instantaneously if prices are perfectly flexible and perfect information exists, as panel *b* indicates.

Money wage rates will fall proportionally and instantaneously in panel *a*. All transactions are made in equilibrium, at the natural rate of employment and at the natural rate of output.

In panel *a* the now lower price level P_1 and a constant money wage rate W_e indicate a higher real wage rate: $W_e/P_1 > W_e/P_e$. A surplus of labor exists at that real wage rate, but because workers and employers have perfect information and because wage rates are perfectly flexible in this model, the money wage rate immediately falls to W_1, the real wage rate remains constant, and $W_1/P_1 = W_e/P_e$.

In this example the new information is absorbed immediately by economic agents and *no transactions are made out of equilibrium*. As a consequence, employment at all times equals the natural level.

The Neoclassical-Keynesian Synthesis and the REH Cases Consider now the more realistic situation in which *either* (1) it takes time for

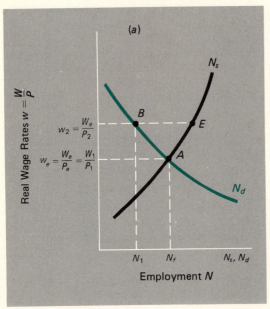
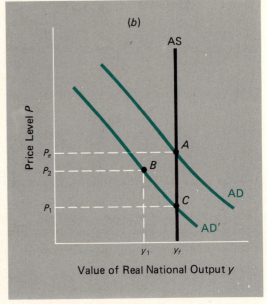

FIGURE 15.3. A DEMAND SHOCK IN THE NEOCLASSICAL-KEYNESIAN CASE AND THE REH CASE

In both the REH model and the neoclassical-Keynesian synthesis, a leftward demand shock will create temporary involuntary unemployment. Equilibrium is restored in the REH model when the correct information is transmitted; equilibrium is restored in the synthesis model because the price level falls and leads to the Keynes effect and the Pigou effect.

It is important to note that in both models transactions occur at nonequilibrium prices and at nonequilibrium wage rates. Involuntary unemployment exists, but it is temporary.

economic agents to obtain the new information about a demand shock and/or (2) prices and wage rates are not completely flexible (owing to the market rigidities discussed in Chapter 12).

In Figure 15.3 we start again at point A in panel a and panel b. An adverse demand shock again occurs. This means that the quantity of output demanded at every price level becomes smaller and so disequilibrium exists in the goods market; a general surplus of goods and services now exists at P_e. This causes downward pressure on prices. But assume that the price level falls only partially, to P_2 instead of all the way down to P_1, because of incomplete information or because of some price inflexibility. This means that the real wage rate rises to $w_2 = W_e/P_2$, assuming that nominal wage rates don't fall (or they fall incompletely). The economy is now at point B in both panels of Figure 15.3.

Unemployment now exists, and it equals $N_f - N_1$ in panel a; this is consistent with the fact that real national output is at y_1, which is less than y_f in panel b. This unemployment is *involuntary* because employers have hired only up to the profit-maximizing point, B in panel a (where the real wage rate equals the marginal physical product of labor), but workers plan to (want to) offer an amount of labor determined at point E. The problem is that real wage rates are too high, either because of nominal wage rate inflexibility or because of imperfect information. REH proponents maintain that eventually economic agents will perceive the truth and the economy will move back from B to A in panel a and from B to C in panel b. The synthesis model of Chapter 8 maintains that this situation will eventually be alleviated by the Keynes effect and by the Pigou effect as the price level falls, if there is no liquidity trap or no extreme investment insensitivity to interest rate reductions.

Note that in both models transactions have occurred at nonequilibrium prices; transactions in the labor market occur at real wage rate w_2, which is above the equilibrium real wage rate, and at P_2, which is *above* the new equilibrium price level.

The Post-Keynesian Disequilibrium Case   Post-Keynesians believe that the synthesis model and the REH model are fundamentally flawed because they do not appreciate the implications of off-equilibrium-price transactions. Both the REH model and the synthesis model apply the classical equilibrium analysis to a disequilibrium situation, and therein hangs a tale.

Consider Figure 15.4, which also begins at full-employment equilibrium and which also depicts a (leftward) demand shock. The new equilibrium price level is P_1, but imperfect information or price inflexibility will cause the price level to fall only to P_2. In panel b this is indicated as a movement from A to B. At B the value of real national output is y_1 and the price level is P_2.

According to post-Keynesians, because the demand for output is only y_1, businesses will be unable to sell the full-employment output y_f and will produce only y_1. Because the price level is (temporarily) "stuck" at P_2 and the real value of producers' sales equals only y_1, producers will want less labor—indicated as N_1 in panel a. *N_1 represents the amount of labor that producers are constrained to hire because they can only sell output y_1.* In other words, employers now have an additional constraint, called a **quantity constraint,** besides the usual ones (i.e., the real wage rate, the productivity of labor) deployed in the profit-maximization

In the Disequilibrium Model an Adverse Demand Shock Creates Involuntary Unemployment for Indefinite Periods

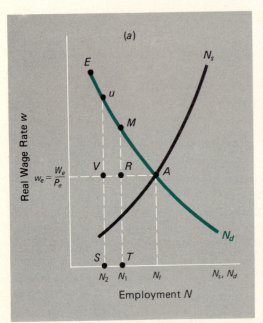

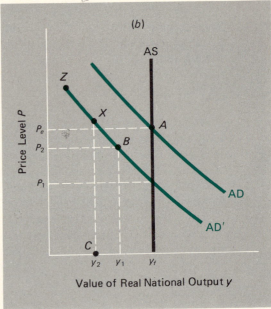

FIGURE 15.4. DISEQUILIBRIUM ANALYSIS

An adverse demand shock in panel a, combined with sticky prices or imperfect information, reduces the quantity of output sold to y_1 at the (slightly) lower price level P_2. This reduction in output that can be sold imposes an additional quantity constraint—a constraint on the quantity of labor that employers can purchase—on employers in the labor market. The effective demand for labor becomes $EUMRT$ and involuntary unemployment equal to $N_f - N_1$ exists.

Because workers cannot sell as much labor as they planned, their consumption is now constrained by their lower income; their effective demand for national output now becomes ZXC in panel b. This in return imposes an *additional* quantity constraint in the labor market, and the process continues until this multiplier effect is worked out.

models. Because their sales are limited to y_1, employers will not hire more than N_1 labor even if the real wage rate falls. The **effective demand-for-labor** curve which reflects the quantity constraint is $EUMRT$; this demand curve is vertical up to the real wage rate associated with point M and then becomes the same as the original or **planned demand**-for-labor curve. The vertical range of the effective demand-for-labor curve implies that regardless of how low the real wage rate falls, the quantity demanded of labor is constant—at N_1 in panel a in Figure 15.4—because of the quantity constraint on the amount of labor required to produce output y_1.

The amount of unemployment is $A - R$, and this is *involuntary* unemployment. Furthermore, if nominal wage rates are constant, this unemployment is somewhat permanent and will remain unchanged because there are no mechanisms to restore full employment. In fact, even if money wage rates were to fall so that the real wage fell *below* w_e, the quantity constraint facing employers would not induce them to purchase any more labor than N_1.

Post-Keynesians say that the problem is not yet fully elucidated because there will be a feedback from the labor market in panel a to the goods market in panel b. Now that some laborers are unemployed they will reduce the amount that they can afford to spend on goods and services. That is, workers will have a lower effective demand for goods and services because they are *further* constrained. Originally, workers planned to purchase goods and services based on the income associated with N_f employment. Because involuntary unemployment exists, workers are now further constrained (beyond what their income would *otherwise* have allowed) by a lower actual, current, real income. This feedback from the labor market to the market for goods and services is shown in panel b of Figure 15.4, where the new, quantity-constrained effective aggregate demand curve now becomes ZXC. In turn, this new lower output level y_2 presents a *further* constraint on the labor market because lower sales make it unprofitable for employers to hire more than N_2, the amount of labor required to produce output y_2. The new effective demand-for-labor curve is now $EUVS$.

This leads to another quantity constraint in panel b (which we have not indicated) because an even lower amount of employment will in turn lead to a lower effective demand for consumer goods and services. This feedback process between the two markets will continue, and it is, in fact, the Keynesian multiplier process. An initial reduction in autonomous expenditures leads to a reduction in employment and income, which leads to a reduction in consumption, which in turn leads to a reduction in income—and so on. As with the Keynesian multiplier, as long as the marginal propensity to consume is less than 1, the successive feedback rounds in panels a and b will get smaller.

Unlike the synthesis model and the REH model, nothing in the Keynesian model guarantees that the economy will eventually return to the natural output and the natural employment levels. Therefore, government intervention is necessary.

In summary, post-Keynesians have, to their way of thinking, remained unregenerate Keynesians and have put macroeconomics back on the right track by stressing Keynes's fundamental insight: off-equilibrium price transactions lead to quantity constraints which can account for *prolonged involuntary* unemployment, and there are no mechanisms to restore full employment. Obviously, many real-world transactions do take place at nonequilibrium prices because of price-wage inflexibilities and imperfect information. The disequilibrium model, therefore, is potentially very robust and "realistic," and its policy implications are different from those in the other models. The neoclassical-Keynesian synthesis model leaves room for economic policy if in practice the Keynes effect and the Pigou effect require *drastic* price level reductions: monetary and fiscal policy can be used to get the economy back to the natural levels sooner. The REH says that economic policy is unnecessary, not feasible, or downright harmful—depending on the circumstances. The post-Keynesian disequilibrium analysis maintains that *nothing* will restore the economy to its natural levels (the existence of which they deny), and that massive governmental intervention is necessary to increase effective demand in order to eliminate prolonged involuntary unemployment.

Stagflation and the Disequilibrium Model   The post-Keynesian disequilibrium model can account for stagflation rather easily. A supply shock occurs, and this leads to an increase in the price level and to a reduction in national output, which imposes a quantity constraint on the amount of labor that employers will hire. This increases unemployment, which decreases the aggregate effective demand for consumer goods, and so on. Note that the price level and unemployment rise simultaneously as national output falls. The duration of unemployment is uncertain, and governmental action becomes necessary.

Criticisms of the Disequilibrium Model

While the post-Keynesian model is quite challenging and obviously insightful, it has one rather dramatic flaw. The quantity constraint is not necessarily binding on economic agents if they have another option. Consider the effective demand constraint on consumers, which Friedman's permanent income hypothesis (analyzed in Chapter 9) has already anticipated.

Recall that according to Friedman consumption is constrained by permanent income and not by current income (or by what the post-Keynesians call effective demand). Consumers can, therefore, draw upon their wealth, or money holdings, or they can borrow; therefore, their consumption expenditure is not totally constrained by the amount of labor they can sell. In fact, the permanent income hypothesis predicts that this is precisely what consumers will do if they anticipate that their current income is only temporarily lower. They will borrow, or spend previously acquired assets. On the other hand, some low-income workers will have precious few assets to sell, and they may be unable to borrow funds to finance consumption because they have little collateral. Such workers will in fact base their consumption, necessarily, on their current income.[10]

Labor hiring is not necessarily quantity-constrained by business sales either. If businesses believe that sales are only temporarily lower, they may want to hire more labor (or continue to maintain the old labor force to avoid costs of rehiring and retraining) and increase their inventories, which they expect to sell when their sales increase in the future. This labor hiring, or labor-force maintenance, can be financed by borrowing or by selling previously acquired assets.

Another problem for the disequilibrium model arises from the job search model analyzed in Chapter 14. In that model temporary wage rigidity can result from workers' own decisions to withdraw their labor temporarily in order to search for a job. If this is true, and it doubtless is true that many unemployed workers do so behave, then such workers are *voluntarily* (frictionally) unemployed. Furthermore (contrary to the disequilibrium model), their income reductions cannot be viewed as an exogenous constraint on their consumption; instead, their incomes are temporarily lower *by their choice to engage in a job search*, and their consumption need not be reduced during the search period.

Finally, if prices do not adjust instantaneously, a theory of how prices are set simultaneously in the various markets (what we have called aggregate equilibrium analysis in previous chapters) is required. If there is no aggregate equilibrium, then economic agents cannot be viewed as facing market-determined prices. Agents can now affect prices by their own behavior. But now the exact process by which prices are set in interdependent markets must be explained. Some post-Keynesians are indeed prepared to throw off the yoke of tradition and accept the challenge of devising a whole new theory of aggregate equilibrium determination in interdependent markets. They have an enormous task ahead of them.

CHAPTER SUMMARY

1. The rational expectations hypothesis (REH) assumes that there are a natural level of unemployment and a natural output level around which a shocked economy eventually stabilizes.

---

[10] Even Friedman's permanent income hypothesis implicitly acknowledges this point because one determinant of the APC of permanent income is the ratio of nonhuman wealth to permanent income. The higher this ratio, given permanent income, the easier it is to borrow to finance consumption, and economic agents won't be as liquidity-constrained.

2. The REH rejects the adaptive expectations hypothesis because the latter (*a*) implies that economic agents base their forecasts on only the past values of some variable and neglect other information; and (*b*) implies that economic agents can make systematic or biased forecasting errors.

3. Because policymakers cannot cause economic agents to make systematic forecasting errors, policymakers cannot systematically affect real economic variables even in the short run.

4. REH proponents maintain that the consequences of a given economic event depend on whether or not the event has been anticipated. An anticipated economic event will cause the economy to move from one equilibrium to another immediately, and the economy will not depart from its natural levels. An unanticipated adverse demand shock causes misinformation, causes temporary unemployment, and generates an output rate that is less than the natural rate.

5. Because they believe that (*a*) policymakers cannot systematically affect real economic variables in the short run or in the long run, (*b*) anticipated events do not require economic policy, and (*c*) economic policy is not feasible when economic events are *un*foreseen, REH proponents believe that stabilization policy can cause more harm than good.

6. The REH has difficulty in explaining the existence and severity of business cycles, and the extent to which money is apparently non-neutral.

7. Post-Keynesian economists maintain that there are no natural employment and no natural output levels, and that the synthesis model and the REH model misapply aggregate equilibrium analysis to disequilibrium situations.

8. Post-Keynesian economists maintain that if transactions are made at nonequilibrium prices in one market, then quantity constraints are imposed in another market.

9. Quantity constraints imply that effective demand will be less than planned demand, and post-Keynesians believe that economic agents will base their behavior on effective demand. By implication, employment will be involuntary and of indeterminate duration because there are no mechanisms to restore full employment. As a consequence, government intervention is required to stabilize the economy around desirable levels.

10. The post-Keynesian disequilibrium model has been criticized because consumers are not necessarily constrained by their current incomes and employers are not necessarily employment-constrained by their sales, if each group has the ability to borrow or to finance expenditures by selling assets.

GLOSSARY

demand shock   An unanticipated shift in the aggregate demand curve.

disequilibrium analysis   Analysis of the transition period from one equilibrium position to another after a shock occurs; analysis of the implications for some markets when transactions are made at nonequilibrium prices in others.

effective demand   Effective demand is to be distinguished from planned demand; effective demand is a quantity-constrained demand and it reflects *actual* purchasing power generated in the current period.

planned demand   A schedule of intentions indicating the amounts that agents intend to purchase at different prices, per unit of time, other things constant.

policy   A sustained pattern of action or reaction.

quantity constraint   A constraint over and above the normal budget constraints that arise from the profit- or utility-maximizing process; if workers cannot work as much as they planned, then their effective demand will depend on their actual (lower) income and this will lead to a reduction in their purchases, which will impose a quantity constraint on producers.

random walk   The values of a variable are said to exhibit a random walk if the current value of that variable already reflects all the known relevant information that affects its value, and if its value changes only if unanticipated events occur, or if new information arises.

rational expectations hypothesis (REH)   The hypothesis that economic agents take into account all relevant information, including the policy of policymakers, when they make forecasts of economic variables. As a consequence, policymakers cannot cause agents to make systematic errors in their forecasts and policymakers cannot, therefore, influence real variables systematically, even in the short run.

supply shock   An unanticipated shift in the aggregate supply curve.

QUESTIONS AND PROBLEMS FOR REVIEW

15.1   The proponents of the rational expectations hypothesis suggest the existence of a natural rate of output around which output is observed. Do the REH proponents suggest that output systematically approaches the natural rate after a shock?

15.2   For what reasons do the REH proponents reject the adaptive expectations hypothesis?

15.3   The REH proponents suggest that policymakers cannot cause economic units to make systematic forecasting errors. If they could, real economic variables would be affected systematically. To the extent that real economic variables can be affected systematically, describe the effect on aggregate economic welfare of a successful monetary policy.

15.4   The REH proponents maintain that an unanticipated adverse shock causes misinformation and temporary unemployment that results in a rate of output that is less than the natural rate. Describe the effect of an advantageous shock.

15.5 For several reasons the REH proponents believe that stabilization policy can cause more harm than good. What harm do they believe can occur?

15.6 Is the apparent nonneutrality of money necessarily inconsistent with the REH?

15.7 What importance do the assumptions of no natural employment and no natural output levels (to which the economy returns) have on the validity of the post-Keynesian model?

15.8 In the post-Keynesian model, disequilibrium in one market has effects in other markets. What is the suggested consequence of such a disequilibrium in one market?

15.9 Explain why quantity constraints would cause unemployment to be involuntary and of indeterminate duration.

15.10 What importance do the abilities to borrow and to finance expenditures by selling assets have on the validity of the post-Keynesian model?

REFERENCES

Robert J. Barro, "Unanticipated Money Growth and Unemployment in the United States," *American Economic Review*, vol. 67 (1977).
———, *Macroeconomics* (New York: Wiley, 1984).
Robert Clower, "The Keynesian Counterrevolution: A Theoretical Reappraisal," in F. H. Hahn and F. D. R. Brechling, eds., *The Theory of Interest Rates* (New York: St. Martin's Press, 1965).
Paul Davidson, "Post Keynesian Economics: Solving the Crisis in Economic Theory," *The Public Interest*, 1980.
Robert J. Gordon, "Inflation in Recession and Recovery," *Brookings Papers on Economic Activity*, vol. 1 (1971).
———, "Wage-Price Controls and the Shifting Phillips Curve," *Brookings Papers on Economic Activity*, vol. 2 (1972).
Laurence Harris, *Monetary Theory* (New York: McGraw-Hill, 1981).
John R. Hicks, "Some Questions of Time in Economics," in Anthony M. Tang, ed., *Evolution, Welfare, and Time in Economics* (Lexington, Mass.: Heath, 1976).
John Maynard Keynes, *The General Theory of Employment, Interest, and Money* (New York: Harcourt Brace Jovanovich, 1964).
Axel Leijonhufvud, *On Keynesian Economics and the Economics of Keynes: A Study in Monetary Theory* (New York: Oxford University Press, 1968).
Robert Lucas and Thomas Sargent, "After Keynesian Macroeconomics," in *After the Phillips Curve: Persistence of High Inflation and High Unemployment* (Boston: Federal Reserve Bank of Boston, 1978).
Bennett McCallum, "The Significance of Rational Expectations Theory," *Challenge* (January-February 1980).

Hyman P. Minsky, *John Maynard Keynes* (New York: Columbia University Press, 1975).

John F. Muth, "Rational Expectations and the Theory of Price Movements," *Econometrica*, vol. 29 (1961).

George Perry, "Changing Labor Markets and Inflation," *Brookings Papers on Economic Activity*, vol. 3 (1970).

William Poole, "Rational Expectations in the Macro Model," *Brookings Papers on Economic Activity*, no. 2 (1976).

Thomas Sargent and Neil Wallace, "Rational Expectations and the Theory of Economic Policy," *Journal of Monetary Economics*, vol. 23 (1976).

G. L. S. Shackle, "Keynes and Today's Establishment in Economic Theory: A View," *Journal of Economic Literature* (1973).

PART V

STABILIZATION

POLICY

16

MONETARY POLICY

Monetary policy is the discretionary changing of the money supply by the monetary authorities in order to attain such ultimate goals as price stability, high employment, steady economic growth, and an international payments equilibrium. Up to this point in our study the money supply has been assumed to be exogenously determined. That is, the money supply has been assumed to be unaffected by the behavior of economic agents in the private sector of the economy.

In this chapter we analyze the determinants of the money supply more carefully and indicate that the money supply is determined by the interaction of three groups: the Fed, the nonbank private sector, and depository institutions (banks, savings and loan associations, mutual savings banks, and credit unions). First we develop a hypothetical economy that consists of these three groups and, by comparing consolidated balance sheets for each group, show how they are interrelated. Next we show how the nonbank private sector and the depository institution sector each can affect the money supply; in the process a theoretical money supply curve that is *endogenously* determined is developed. Following this, we show how the Fed can determine the money supply. We are then ready to discuss the issue of monetary control by the Fed. In particular, the targets and strategies of monetary policy are analyzed, and then the problems of monetary policy are considered. The chapter ends with a Policy Controversy concerning a 100 percent reserve requirement for depository institutions.

THE FED, THE NONBANK PRIVATE SECTOR, AND DEPOSITORY INSTITUTIONS

In order to appreciate the issues involved in monetary policy, it is helpful to understand how the Fed, the nonbank private sector (households and business firms), and the depository institution sector are interrelated. Consider Table 16.1, which shows hypothetical consolidated balance sheets for each of these three groups.

These hypothetical balance sheets have been simplified and include only those entries that we will analyze in this and the remaining chapters.

Definitions

We must next define some terms and then derive some equations. In the economy described by the balance sheets in Table 16.1, the money supply M (which corresponds to M1, defined in Chapter 11) equals the value of currency C, held by the nonbank private sector, plus the value of checkable deposits D the nonbank public holds in depository institutions. Thus

TABLE 16.1. CONSOLIDATED BALANCE SHEETS

Assets		Liabilities	
Consolidated Fed Balance Sheet			
Gold and foreign exchange	105	Currency held by the non-	
Government securities	200	bank sector	240
Loans to depository		Depository institution re-	
institutions	5	serves	60
Other	2	(Vault cash 20)	
TOTAL	312	(Deposits of depository	
		institutions 40)	
		Other liabilities plus	
		net worth	12
		TOTAL	312
Consolidated Balance Sheet for Depository Institutions			
Reserves at Fed	60	Deposits of nonbank private	
(Vault cash 20)		sector	600
(Deposits at Fed 40)		Loans from the Fed	0
Loans and investments	540	Other liabilities plus net	
(Loans to public 500)		worth	10
(Government securities 40)		TOTAL	610
Other assets	10		
TOTAL	610		
Consolidated Balance Sheet for the Nonbank Private Sector			
Currency	240	Bank loans	500
Checkable deposits at		Other liabilities plus	
depository institutions	600	net worth	1200
Government securities	110	TOTAL	1700
Other	750		
TOTAL	1700		

$$M \equiv C + D \qquad (16.1)$$

In Table 16.1 the corresponding figures are $840 = 240 + 600$.

Another important definition is the **monetary base B,** which is the sum of the value of currency held by the non-bank sector plus the value of depository institution reserve R.[1] In equation form, the monetary base is

$$B \equiv C + R \qquad (16.2)$$

In Table 16.1, the values are $300 = 240 + 60$.

---

[1] Actually, in the U.S. economy the monetary base would also include the Treasury-issued currency, which consists mostly of coins and a rather small amount of paper currency. These are held by the public, and by depository institutions as a vault-cash component of their reserves.

Notice that depository institutions hold **reserves,** which include their vault cash and their deposits at their Federal Reserve district banks. Banks hold reserves because (1) they accept checkable deposits from the public, the public writes checks on those deposits, and the checks in turn are usually deposited in other depository institutions; and (2) depositors occasionally withdraw currency from those checkable deposits. Prudent banking necessitates that banks have reserves on hand for those unpredictable periods when the flow of withdrawals exceeds the flow of deposits. Banks also hold reserves because the Fed requires them to do so; **required reserves** are that quantity of depository institution reserves held in the form of vault cash or on deposit with a Fed district bank, as mandated by the Fed. The Fed requires that a depository institution hold a minimum fraction of its total deposits in reserve form; this ratio of required reserves to total deposits is called the **required reserve ratio.**[2] If the **actual reserve ratio** exceeds the required reserve ratio, then actual reserves will be greater than required reserves. Required reserves minus actual reserves is defined as **excess reserves,** and at times they may be negative. In Table 16.1 the actual reserve ratio equals 0.10, calculated by dividing actual reserves, 60, by total deposit liabilities of the depository institution, 600; these deposits are assets of the nonbank private sector. This 10 percent ratio is in fact close to the actual ratio; depository institutions held 9.6 percent in May, 1985.

Another ratio that is important for the analysis in this chapter is the nonbank private sector ratio of currency to total deposits, C/D. In Table 16.1 the *currency/deposit ratio* is 0.4, calculated by dividing currency, 240, by total deposits, 600. This, too, is a realistic percentage; in June, 1985, the public held a 39 percent ratio of currency to transactions deposits.

Relationships

The monetary base, the actual reserve/deposit ratio, and the currency/deposit ratio together determine the money supply. This relationship can be derived as follows.

Recall that

$$M \equiv C + D \qquad (16.1)$$

---

[2] Actually, a more complicated model would take into account the fact that depository institutions also must hold required reserves on time deposits; the required time deposit ratio is lower than the required ratio on demand deposits.

and

$$B \equiv C + R \qquad (16.2)$$

Then, because

$$M = \left(\frac{M}{B}\right) \cdot B \qquad (16.3)$$

we can substitute equations 16.1 and 16.2 in equation 16.3:

$$M = \left(\frac{C + D}{C + R}\right) \cdot B \qquad (16.4)$$

Dividing the numerator and the denominator of the expression in the parentheses by D yields

$$M = B\left[\frac{1 + (C/D)}{(C/D) + (R/D)}\right] \qquad (16.5)$$

Equation 16.5 shows that the money supply can be defined in terms of (1) the monetary base, (2) the ratio of currency to transactions deposits held by the nonbank private sector, and (3) the ratio of reserves to transactions deposits held by depository institutions. Substituting the values from Table 16.1 yields

$$M = 300\left(\frac{1 + 0.4}{0.4 + 0.1}\right)$$

$$M = 300\left(\frac{1.4}{0.5}\right)$$

$$M = 300(2.8)$$

$$M = 840$$

Equation 16.5 also indicates that changes in the money supply vary inversely with changes in the ratio of currency to deposits, and inversely with changes in the ratio of reserves to deposits, given the monetary base. The smaller those ratios, the larger is the money supply, and the larger those ratios the smaller the money supply—given the size of the monetary base.

Finally, equation 16.5 indicates that a change in the monetary base will change the money supply by some multiple, the **money multiplier** *MM*. The money multiplier is found by

$$MM = \frac{M}{B} = \frac{1 + (C/D)}{(C/D) + (R/D)} \qquad (16.6)$$

And in Table 16.1, it equals 2.8.

AN ENDOGENOUSLY DETERMINED MONEY SUPPLY

The money supply is said to be endogenously determined if the behavior of economic agents in the private sector itself can change the money supply. The previous section indicated that the money supply and the money multiplier are each a function of the nonbank private sector's currency/deposit ratio and the depository institution sector's reserve/deposit ratio. Therefore, if these sectors change their desired ratios, the money supply will change and the money supply can be said to be, at least in part, endogenously determined. To the extent that the money supply is endogenously determined, monetary policy is more difficult because the Fed does not have complete control over the money stock. Actions by the Fed may be offset by economic agents in the private sector. Also, to the extent that the money stock is endogenously determined, we have cause-and-effect problems. To wit: Do increases in the money supply *cause* inflation, or are they the *result* of inflation? We return to this issue in Chapter 18; here our concern is merely with how economic agents in the private sector can change the money supply.

The Currency/Deposit Ratio

The currency/deposit ratio is determined primarily by such institutional factors as the lack of coincidence of receipts and disbursements by businesses and households (the classical economists referred to this as "payments habit"), the extent of credit use, the degree to which the banking system has developed, the existence of credit cards and the extent to which they are used to finance transactions, and the "confidence" that people have in the banking system.

Since 1962 the public has wanted to hold more currency. To be sure, higher prices account for an increased transactions demand for currency. Currency holdings adjusted for higher price levels, however, still indicate a 2 percent per annum increase in currency holdings since 1960. At the same time, real demand deposits have remained relatively constant. The result, as Figure 16.1 indicates, has been a rising ratio of currency to demand deposits since 1968.[3]

This is a rather extraordinary increase in the real demand for currency in light of the fact that (1) credit cards and traveler's checks are increasingly popular, (2) higher interest rates have increased the opportunity

---

[3] From Norman H. Bowsher, "The Demand for Currency: Is the Underground Economy Undermining Monetary Policy?" *Review*, Federal Reserve Bank of St. Louis, vol. 62, no. 1 (January 1980).

Since 1968, the Ratio of Currency to Demand Deposits Has Increased

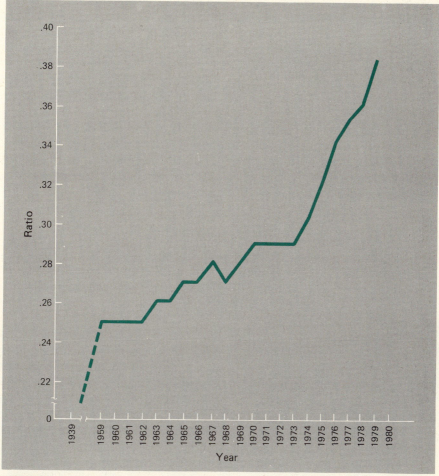

FIGURE 16.1. RATIO OF CURRENCY TO DEMAND DEPOSITS, 1959–1979

From *Review,* Federal Reserve Bank of St. Louis, January 1980, p. 12.

costs of holding currency, and (3) deposit insurance has decreased the risk of holding deposits.

Experts disagree as to why such a growth in the real demand for currency has occurred. Some point to the increase in the real value of illegal drug transactions, others to growth in the real value of underground economy transactions; and the Fed recently has expressed concern about the increased demand for U.S. currency by foreigners.

Assuming that a large currency drain is occurring, can monetary policy be hampered? Theoretically, yes. Because one of the determinants of the amount of money that the banking system can create is the public's desired ratio of currency to demand deposits, a fixed ratio of currency to deposits held by the public would make the money multiplier almost totally dependent on required reserve ratios. But if the public holds more currency, as it seems to be doing of late, the increased currency/demand deposit ratio lowers the size of the deposit expansion multiplier. An outflow of cash reduces bank reserves by an equivalent amount.

The Fed, however, receives information on currency drains promptly and can offset them easily by buying securities on the open market, as you will soon see. Although a rapidly growing underground economy potentially interferes with the Fed's ability to achieve monetary control, the Fed has the tools to offset such occurrences.

The Reserve/Deposit Ratio

The depository institution sector can affect the money stock by changing its reserve/deposit ratio. This reserve/deposit ratio is determined by (1) minimum reserve requirements set on depository institutions by the Fed, and (2) the desire of depository institutions to hold positive excess reserves.

Why a Reserve Requirement?   Early in the banking history of this country certain states imposed reserve requirements on state-chartered banks. National banks have also had a reserve requirement since 1863. Today, virtually all depository institutions have some type of reserve requirement.

What would be the economic effects of a zero-required reserve system? It might appear that such a system would be disastrous. Actually, it seems likely that depository institutions would *voluntarily* hold reserves which would be some percentage of their deposits. Depository institutions have sufficient experience to calculate the amount of funds they need to have on reserve to meet cash and deposit withdrawals. Continued profitability would require sufficient liquidity to satisfy depositors, and depository institutions would doubtless hold reserves to cover their normal expected net withdrawals. These are sometimes called *prudent reserves.* So, even in a world of zero reserve requirements, prudent reserves would not be zero.

Do Reserve Requirements Protect the Depositor?   The closing of so many banks that were in compliance with the Fed's reserve requirements during the Great Depression (several even failed in 1984 and 1985) is sufficient evidence that even with required reserves (at less than 100 percent), banks can and do fail. Only if the required reserve ratio were set at 100 percent could depositors be assured of liquidity on demand. (A 100 percent–required reserve ratio has been touted by some, and we discuss that issue in the Policy Controversy at the end of this chapter.)

Actually, the argument that reserve requirements are necessary to protect depositors is irrelevant today. Deposit insurance has eliminated the concern of a run on banks. Why, then, do we have reserve requirements?

The Reason for Reserve Requirements   Reserve requirements must be viewed as a monetary policy tool of the Fed. The Fed can directly alter required reserves (within the limits set by Congress) and thereby alter the size of the money supply. (The money multiplier is a function of the required reserve ratio.) Rarely in recent times has the Fed used changes in reserve requirements to effect monetary policy. Rather, the argument in favor of required reserves relates to the *stability* of the money multiplier. The Fed sets the minimum required reserve ratio at a level that is above the level that prudent banking requires. This means that excess reserves will typically be close to zero; therefore, required reserves will be stable. If required reserves are stable, then the money multiplier will, within certain bounds, be stable. This means that the Fed can control the money supply with greater precision. A voluntary reserve ratio would certainly be less stable than a required reserve ratio, and control of the money supply would therefore be more difficult.

The Desire to Hold Excess Reserves   Despite the fact that the Fed typically sets a required reserve ratio above what prudent banking would make necessary, depository institutions do, nonetheless, hold excess reserves. For example, as a result of the 1929–1933 depression, when over 15,000 banks were forced to close down, banks accumulated cash reserves in excess of legal requirements in order to meet unanticipated withdrawals. By 1936, excess reserves held by member banks totaled $3 billion. Fed officials felt that these excess reserves were serving no useful purpose and might later serve as the source of an undesired expansion in bank credit. On August 16, 1936, the Fed increased reserve requirements by 50 percent in an attempt to immobilize about $1.5 billion of these excess reserves. The Fed, unfortunately, did not understand the circumstances of the time. Banks *desired* to hold excess reserves as an additional source of liquidity. When the Fed increased legal reserve requirements, banks *further* restricted their loans in an attempt to make up the lost prudent reserves. Consequently, the money supply fell. In the midst of this slowdown in the growth of reserves, the Fed foolishly increased reserve requirements again, in two steps. These increases became effective on March 1 and May 1 of 1937 and absorbed another $1.5 billion in excess reserves. The money supply fell by 6 percent in 1937. A potential economic recovery was nipped in the bud.

In more recent times excess reserves have been considerably smaller; over the past ten years excess reserves have averaged less than 1 percent of total reserves. This is because (1) bank deposits are now insured, and a run on a bank is unlikely, and (2) relatively high interest rates mean a high opportunity cost to depository institutions holding excess reserves.

Still, banks do hold excess reserves, and such behavior must be explained. The reasoning is straightforward. Banks can't predict exactly what their reserve requirements are, but by law they must meet these requirements. When excess reserves are negative, a given depository institution can meet its reserve requirements by (1) borrowing from the Fed, which charges an interest rate, called the **discount rate,** and (2) borrowing from other depository institutions in what is called the federal funds market, where it also must pay an interest rate, called the **federal funds rate.**

Profit-maximizing banking requires, therefore, that depository institutions hold an optimal quantity of excess reserves. If excess reserves are too high, then earnings on loans and investments must be forgone; if excess reserves are negative, a depository institution must pay interest when it borrows funds in order to meet reserve requirements. A trade-off exists, therefore; the more excess reserves a depository institution holds, the more interest earnings it must forgo, but the less likely it is to incur the expense of borrowing reserves. Conversely, if it holds a small quantity of excess reserves, its interest earnings will be higher, but so is the probability that it will have to pay interest to borrow reserves. The interest rate that banks pay on the reserves they borrow, therefore, measures the opportunity cost of holding reserves for banks.

Depository institutions face a problem similar to that faced by households. They must decide upon the optimal quantity of money (here, reserves) to hold, and that decision is intimately related to the interest rate. For depository institutions, the higher the interest rate they can earn, the fewer reserves they will hold, other things constant. This means that, within limits, the reserve/deposit ratio, and therefore the money supply and the money multiplier, are functions of the interest rate paid on borrowed reserves (loans).

The Endogenous Determination of the Money Supply

We are now in a position to derive an endogenously determined money supply. Consider Figure 16.2, which shows a typical negatively sloped demand-for-money curve and (what is new) a positively sloped money supply curve. The money supply curve is positively sloped because as

The Interest Rate Is Determined by the Demand for Money and an Endogenously Determined Money Supply

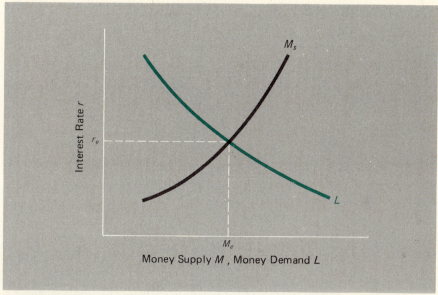

FIGURE 16.2. AN ENDOGENOUS MONEY SUPPLY

As the interest rate rises, depository institutions will hold fewer excess reserves. They will thereby decrease the reserve/deposit ratio and, other things constant, increase the money multiplier. This means that as the interest rate rises, other things constant, the money supply rises. The money supply, therefore, is at least partially endogenous because depository institutions respond to changes in the interest rate and their actions can change the money supply.

The market interest rate will be determined at the intersection of the demand-for-money curve and the supply-of-money curve.

the interest rate that banks can earn (charge) rises, other things constant, depository institutions will hold fewer excess reserves. The reserve/deposit ratio falls, and given the size of the monetary base and the currency/deposit ratio, the money supply will grow (check equation 16.5 to confirm this). The intersection of the demand-for-money curve L and the endogenously determined money supply curve M_s determines the market interest rate, as Figure 16.2 shows.

Figure 16.3 indicates that the money supply curve shifts as a result of changes in the monetary base. The extent of the shift equals the money multiplier times the change in the monetary base. The money supply itself, however, will not rise by that full amount because the demand-

An Increase in the Monetary Base Will Lead to a Lower Interest Rate and a Higher Money Supply

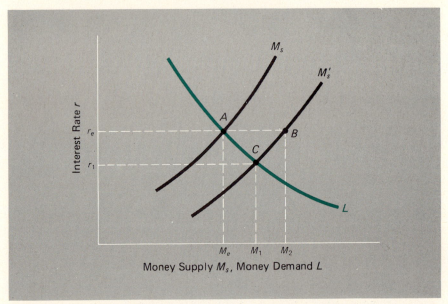

FIGURE 16.3. AN INCREASE IN THE MONETARY BASE
If the monetary base rises, the money supply curve will shift to the right, by the distance B–A. This distance equals the change in the monetary base times the money multiplier. Because the demand-for-money curve is negatively sloped, the interest rate will fall when the money supply rises. In turn, a lower interest rate lowers the money multiplier as depository institutions increase their reserves. The money supply rises from M_e to M_1, and not to M_2.

for-money curve is negatively sloped. A lower interest rate induces banks to hold more reserves, so the money multiplier falls. The interest rate falls from r_e to r_1, and the money supply rises from M_e to M_1. The conclusion is that by changing the monetary base the Fed can change the money supply. We elaborate on that point in the next section.

HOW THE FED AFFECTS THE MONEY SUPPLY

The Fed's effect on the money supply can be seen by reexamining equation 16.5. Because it is empowered by Congress to set (within limits) the *required* reserve ratio, the Fed can influence the *actual* reserve/deposit ratio of depository institutions. Moreover, the Fed can affect the federal funds rate, and it sets the discount rate. As you will soon see, the Fed also can control the monetary base. While the nonbank private sector can select its own currency/deposit ratio, the Fed can neutralize the changes in the currency/deposit ratio. The Fed, then, can influence but cannot completely control all the variables that determine the money supply and the money multiplier.

Recall that the monetary base equals the sum of the value of currency held by the public and the value of reserves. The Fed issues almost all of the currency in our economy (the U.S. Treasury issues the rest), and it can change bank reserves by (1) changing the required reserve ratio, (2) changing the discount rate, and (3) engaging in **open-market operations (OMO)**—that is, by the buying and selling of government securities (usually three-month Treasury bills).

The Fed can actually increase bank reserves by increasing the size of *any* of its assets. Consider again the simplified version of the Fed's balance sheet in Table 16.1. There we listed as Fed assets (1) gold and foreign exchange, (2) government securities, and (3) loans to depository institutions. The reason the Fed can increase depository institution reserves is that the Fed eventually "pays" for any assets that it acquires by crediting depository institutions with reserves. It "collects" on assets that it sells by debiting depository institution reserves. We will show presently how this is done when the Fed buys and sells government securities and when it lends to (or loans are repaid by) depository institutions. Gold and foreign exchange transactions are discussed in Chapter 20.

Changing Reserve Requirements

A change in reserve requirements affects the money supply in two ways: it changes (1) the levels of required and excess reserves and (2) the money multiplier.

When the required reserve ratio falls, a depository institution's *actual reserves are not immediately affected.* But required reserves fall and excess reserves rise. A lower reserve ratio also increases the size of the money multiplier because these increased excess reserves can be turned into loans and deposits. For example, as Figure 16.4 shows, given an average reserve requirement of 12 percent, $12 of reserves would be required for deposits of $100. But, as Figure 16.5 shows, a reduction in the legal reserve requirement to 10 percent would "tie up" only $10 for reserves, freeing $2 out of each $12 of reserves for use in creating additional bank loans and deposits. Note that the total amount of reserve is unaffected initially. Excess reserves rise; and therefore, the bank can increase its lending. The money multiplier would rise from 8⅓ to 10, if

Bank A

Assets		Liabilities	
Loans and investments	$88	Deposits	$100
Reserves	$12		
(Required, $12; excess, $0)			

FIGURE 16.4.

Federal Reserve Bank		Bank A	
Assets	Liabilities	Assets	Liabilities
No	change	Reserves $12 (Required, $10; excess, $2)	Deposits $100

FIGURE 16.5.

we ignore the currency/deposit ratio. (To check these multipliers, calculate the money multiplier in equation 16.5 by assuming that the currency/deposit ratio is zero.)

An *increase* in reserve requirements, on the other hand, increases required reserves; banks that previously had zero excess reserves would be forced to acquire more reserves or reduce their loans.

Consider Figure 16.6, which indicates the initial result of an increase in the required reserve ratio from 12 to 14 percent. Total reserves are initially unaffected, but required reserves rise from $12 to $14 for each $100 deposit. Assuming bank A had zero excess reserves prior to the increase in the required reserve ratio, it must now reduce its loans and investments until its deposits are no greater than the amount that the

Federal Reserve Bank		Bank A	
Assets	Liabilities	Assets	Liabilities
No	change	Reserves $12 (Required $14; deficit, $2)	Deposits $100

FIGURE 16.6.

existing amount of reserves can support. The money multiplier falls from $8\frac{1}{3}$ to $7\frac{1}{7}$ (again ignoring the currency/deposit ratio).

For at least two reasons the Fed traditionally has been reluctant to use changes in the reserve ratio as a monetary policy tool.

1. It considers this tool "too powerful." Even small changes in reserve requirements could have an enormous effect on excess reserves and therefore on deposit creation and the money supply. The Fed maintains that this tool is crude and unnecessary because open-market operations can be carried out with facility and refinement. Still it is hard to see why the Fed can't change reserve requirements by *very small* amounts, in which case this tool can be as efficient as open-market operations.

2. The Fed has felt in the past that member banks would be put at a competitive disadvantage if their reserve ratio were increased relative to the reserve ratio of other depository institutions. This concern is no longer relevant because, with the passage of the Depository Institutions Deregulation and Monetary Control Act of 1980, both member and nonmember banks (and all other depository institutions) of the same size are now subject to exactly the same reserve requirements. For this reason, it is possible that the Fed will use reserve requirement changes as a monetary policy tool more often in the future.

Changing the Discount Rate

Bank reserves change if depository institutions increase or decrease their borrowing from the Fed if the other items in the Fed's balance sheet

Miami Bank			
Assets		Liabilities	
Loans	+ $100	Deposits	$ 100
Reserves (no change)			
(Required, + $12; deficit, $12)			

FIGURE 16.7.

remain constant. In this section we show how this is done, using T-accounts.

When a bank borrows from the Fed, it borrows reserves; a bank usually borrows to cover a reserve deficiency, and not to obtain excess reserves. As a consequence (and unlike cases in which a depository institution obtains more reserves through increased deposits), a bank *borrows* reserves to finance an expansion that has *already* taken place.

In order to accommodate the demand for loans and to maximize total profits, banks normally make loans with the expectation that they will soon acquire funds from new deposits or from borrowing in the federal funds market. When a bank makes a loan with such an expectation, it creates demand-deposit liabilities *but not reserves.* In the absence of excess reserves, reserves will be insufficient to meet reserve requirements on the newly extended loans. Similarly, *individual* banks may find themselves with insufficient reserves as a result of unexpected withdrawals and losses of reserves when checks are cleared.[4] Under these circumstances, a bank may temporarily borrow reserves from its Federal Reserve bank.

Suppose that the Miami Bank makes a $100 loan to one of its customers but discovers that its reserves are not sufficient to cover the newly created deposits. For simplicity, assume that the Miami Bank had exactly zero excess reserves when it made the $100 loan. Figure 16.7 shows the results. The Miami Bank has a $100 increase in its liabilities (in the form of new deposits). Its assets also rise by $100, in the form of

---

[4] Of course, other banks probably will receive these deposits and their reserve accounts will be credited when the checks clear.

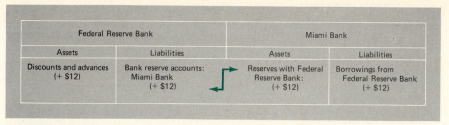

Federal Reserve Bank		Miami Bank	
Assets	Liabilities	Assets	Liabilities
Discounts and advances (+ $12)	Bank reserve accounts: Miami Bank (+ $12)	Reserves with Federal Reserve Bank: (+ $12)	Borrowings from Federal Reserve Bank (+ $12)

FIGURE 16.8.

loan IOU's. Its actual reserves are unaffected, but its *required* reserves have risen by $12 (assuming a 12 percent required reserve ratio) and it therefore has a $12 reserve deficit.

The Miami Bank may temporarily borrow $12 from its Federal Reserve bank, which extends a loan by crediting the Miami Bank's reserve account (a new $12 liability to the Federal Reserve bank) and crediting its own assets with a $12 increase in loans to depository institutions. The Miami Bank gains a $12 asset in the form of reserves and incurs a corresponding liability, "loans from the Fed." Figure 16.8 indicates how a $12 loan from the Federal Reserve bank to the Miami Bank appears in the T-accounts. Note that *no further expansion can take place* because the new reserves are all needed by the Miami Bank to cover the newly created deposits shown in the previous figure.

In order to repay the $12 loan from the Federal Reserve bank, the Miami Bank must obtain additional reserves, either by increasing its reserve deposits or by selling assets. Figure 16.9 indicates what happens to the Miami Bank's balance sheet when it sells securities. Assume that the Miami Bank sells $12 worth of assets to Ms. Harryman, who pays for them with a check drawn on *another* bank. The $12 check is sent to the Federal Reserve bank for clearing, and the Fed increases the Miami Bank's reserve account by $12. Figure 16.9 also shows the changes in the Miami Bank's balance sheet. When the check has cleared, its reserves with the Federal Reserve bank rise by $12, and its securities fall by $12 because it sold the security to Ms. Harryman.

Now that the Miami Bank has increased its reserves, it is in a position to repay its loan from the Fed. It docs so by authorizing a decrease in its reserve account at the Federal Reserve bank. The Miami Bank thereby reduces its assets (reserves with the Federal Reserve bank) and its liabilities (borrowings from the Federal Reserve bank) by $12. The Federal Reserve bank, in turn, also reduces its assets by $12 and reduces its liabilities—reserves owed to the Miami Bank—by $12. Figure 16.10

Miami Bank	
Assets	Liabilities
Securities − $12	
Reserves with Federal Reserve Bank + $12	

FIGURE 16.9.

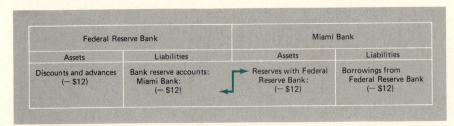

FIGURE 16.10.

shows how the Miami Bank's repayment of the $12 it borrowed from its Federal Reserve bank changes the balance sheet of both institutions.

Open-Market Operations

The Fed Purchases a $100,000 Government Security   Assume that the trading desk at the New York Fed has received from the Fed an order to purchase $100,000 worth of U.S. government securities.[5] The Fed pays for these securities by writing a check on itself for $100,000. This check

---

[5] In practice, the trading desk is never given a specific dollar amount to purchase or sell. The account manager uses personal discretion in determining what amount should be purchased or sold in order to satisfy the Federal Open Market Committee's latest directive. For expositional purposes, assume that the account manager is directed to make a specific transaction.

Federal Reserve System		Depository Institution	
Assets	Liabilities	Assets	Liabilities
+$100,000 U.S. government securities	+$100,000 Depository institution's reserves	+$100,000 Reserves	+$100,000 Transactions deposit owned by broker

FIGURE 16.11.

is given to the bond dealer in exchange for the $100,000 worth of bonds. The bond dealer deposits the $100,000 check in its transactions account at a bank, and the bank then sends the $100,000 check back to the Federal Reserve. When the Fed receives the check, it adds $100,000 to the reserve account of the bank that sent it the check. Thus, the Fed has created $100,000 of reserves. The Fed can create reserves because it has the ability to "write up" (that is, add to) the reserve accounts of depository institutions whenever it buys U.S. securities. When the Fed buys a U.S. government security in the open market, it expands total reserves and the money supply (initially) by the amount of the purchase.

Consider the T-accounts of the Fed and of the depository institution receiving the check. Figure 16.11 shows the T-accounts for the Federal Reserve after the bond purchase and for the depository institution after the bond dealer deposits the $100,000 check. The Fed's T-account (which here deals only with changes) shows that after the purchase, the Fed's assets have increased by $100,000 in the form of U.S. government securities. Liabilities have also increased by $100,000, in the form of an increase in the reserve account of the depository institution. The T-account for the depository institution shows an increase in assets of $100,000 in the form of reserves with its district Federal Reserve bank. The depository institution also has an increase in its liabilities in the form of $100,000 in the transactions account of the bond broker; this is an immediate $100,000 increase in the money supply, because the monetary base has changed by exactly that amount. The maximum potential change in the money supply will equal $100,000 times the money multiplier.

Federal Reserve System		Depository Institution	
Assets	Liabilities	Assets	Liabilities
−$100,000 Reduction in U.S. government securities	−$100,000 Depository institution's reserves	−$100,000 Reserves	−$100,000 Transactions account balances

FIGURE 16.12.

The Sale of a $100,000 U.S. Government Security by the Fed The process is reversed when the account manager at the New York Fed trading desk sells a U.S. government security from the portfolio of the Fed. When the individual or institution buying the security from the Fed writes a check for $100,000, the Fed reduces the reserves of the depository institution on which the check was written. Thus, the $100,000 sale of the U.S. government security leads to a reduction in reserves in the banking system.

Figure 16.12 shows the T-accounts after the sale of a U.S. government security by the Fed. On the left-hand side, the T-account for the Federal Reserve is shown. When the $100,000 check goes to the Federal Reserve System, the Federal Reserve reduces by $100,000 the reserve account of the depository institution on which the check is written. The Fed's assets are also reduced by $100,000 because it no longer owns the U.S. government security. The depository institution's liabilities are reduced by $100,000 when that amount is deducted from the account of the bond purchaser, and the money supply is thereby reduced by that amount. The depository institution's assets are also reduced by $100,000 because the Fed has reduced its reserves by that amount. The maximum potential reduction in the money supply will equal this $100,000 decrease in the monetary base times the money multiplier.

Adjusting the Price of the U.S. Government Securities No one is forced to deal with the Fed; it sells or purchases government securities in the open market. The Fed merely adjusts the price it offers or asks until it can buy or sell what it wants. For example, if the Fed wants to sell a U.S. government security for $100,000 and no one wants to buy it, the Fed can lower the selling price (thereby increasing the yield). If the Fed wants to buy a $100,000 U.S. security and no one wants to sell it, it raises its offered price until sellers are willing to sell at the price offered (thereby reducing the yield).

Remember that the Fed can purchase as large an amount of U.S. government securities as it wishes because it is empowered to pay for them by writing a check on itself. Also, it can adjust the price of bonds to achieve its objective because, unlike private securities dealers, it does not have to worry about minimizing capital losses or maximizing capital gains. The Fed is operated for social benefit and not for private gain. In any event, every time the Fed purchases U.S. government securities, it increases reserves in the banking system.

MONETARY POLICY STRATEGIES[6]

The Fed has at its disposal certain monetary tools: open-market operations, discounting, and reserve requirements. It also has certain ultimate goals: price stability, high employment, an international-payments equilibrium, and an acceptable growth rate in real national income. Even if these goals could be defined operationally (in a way that makes them quantifiable), it is apparent that they cannot be reached *directly* by the use of monetary policy tools. Those tools allow the Fed to affect only such **monetary instruments** as depository reserves, the discount rate, and the monetary base.

A Single-Stage Strategy

The overall problem of the Fed is to change the values of the monetary instruments to take it along the most feasible paths for reaching the ultimate goals.

The single-stage strategy for monetary policy is to aim the policy instruments directly at the ultimate goals. If the ultimate goals are not reached along these paths, the instruments can be altered along other paths that the Fed believes will lead to the ultimate goals. We will elaborate on the single-stage strategy after we analyze the two-stage strategy.

---

[6] See R. C. Bryant, "Should Money Targets Be the Focus of Monetary Policy?" *The Brookings Review* (Spring 1983), pp. 6–12.

A Two-Stage Strategy

An alternative to the single-stage strategy is the two-stage strategy. By using **intermediate targets**—such as the federal funds rate and the growth of one or more of the monetary aggregates (M1 or M2)—the overall problem is broken down into two separate stages.

In the first stage, the Fed reasons backward from desired growth rates for ultimate goals to determine the paths for intermediate targets that are consistent with the ultimate goals. For example, suppose the Fed desires to reduce the rate of inflation from 10 to 3 percent per annum over the next two years. The Fed selects some intermediate target, such as a 6 percent growth rate of M1, that it hopes will be consistent with the ultimate goal.

In the second stage, the Fed takes the intermediate-target path as given and determines the rate of change in its instruments that is consistent with the intermediate-target path. For example, the Fed might decide that, in order to "hit" the intermediate target of a 6 percent per annum rate of growth of M1, it must increase the monetary base at, say, 2 percent per annum.

Figure 16.13 shows the two-stage, or intermediate-target, approach. You should be aware that the variables listed under the targets and goals are not exhaustive; the lists are merely suggestive.

Criteria for Selecting Targets

What criteria are necessary for a variable to be a desirable target for monetary policy? Given that the Fed can choose among several variables as intermediate targets, how would it go about deciding which variable to affect? In general, there are three criteria for a good target variable: measurability, attainability, and relatedness to higher-level goals.

Measurability   To meet the measurability criterion, accurate and reliable data must be quickly available. The data should also conform to economists' theoretical definitions of these variables as closely as possible. Unfortunately, some of the intermediate-target variables (money stock and long-term interest rates) rank low on the measurability scale. As noted previously, financial innovation has blurred the meaning of "money stock"; the Fed has alternative measures of the "money stock" (M1, M2, M3, *L*). Moreover (over short periods of time), each one of these measures is subject to measurement errors that require them to be revised, and they are not always highly correlated with each other. This does not necessarily mean, however, that the Fed shouldn't set targets for these target variables.

The measurability of interest rates is also fraught with problems.

A Two-Stage Strategy Sets Intermediate Targets to Reach Ultimate Goals

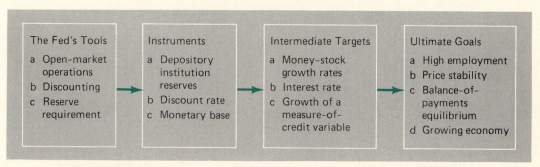

FIGURE 16.13. TOOLS, INSTRUMENTS, INTERMEDIATE TARGETS, AND ULTIMATE GOALS

These boxes indicate the chain of monetary policy. The Fed uses the tools at its disposal to reach its ultimate goals. Doing so, however, may require that the Fed set intermediate targets that it *can* affect directly.

While "the" interest rate is conceptually a weighted average of all interest rates, *measured* interest rates do not include all rates, nor do they have the proper weights. Some of these rates are also difficult to interpret. Published interest rates do not take into account the compensating balances (funds that the borrower must keep in the lender's bank) that the lender may require of the borrower, or any other restrictions that the lending institution imposes on the borrower. Credit rationing (which exists when the market interest rate is below the equilibrium rate, owing to market rigidities) also implies that the posted interest rates are inaccurate. What is the "true" interest rate to those who can't borrow at the going rate (because they have been discriminated against, or "rationed out")? Finally, nominal interest rates don't always allow one to infer readily what the real rate is. Borrowers are motivated by changes in the *real* rate of interest, to which an estimated inflation premium must be added before the nominal rate is determined. Only nominal rates are readily observable, however, because no accurate way of measuring *anticipated* inflation currently exists. The distinction between nominal and real interest rates is especially important during periods of high and variable inflation. For these reasons, among others, "the" interest rate is of limited value as a target.

Attainability The Fed must be able to attain its targeted goal; otherwise, setting the target becomes an exercise in futility. If the Fed could have encouraged conservation of gasoline and fuel oil during the 1970s, it could have helped solve the U.S. balance-of-payments problem. Targets for reduced gasoline and fuel oil use are of little value, however, when the Fed has within its control only changes in the discount rate, reserve requirements, and open-market operations.

Can the Fed in either the short run or the long run attain money-stock growth targets? It is important to know whether the Fed can achieve money growth targets by using its tools. Alternatively, we want to know if the Fed can achieve any specific interest rate target. Can the tools that affect short-term rates also affect long-term rates? Indeed, can the Fed affect *real* rates or can it affect only nominal rates? The key question is whether the Fed actually can use its tools to attain intermediate targets. Targets which are unattainable are not very practical.

Relatedness to Higher-Level Goals   It is pointless for the Fed to select and attain a target unless the target is related to a higher goal. It is not very useful to attain, say, money-stock targets unless they in turn enable the Fed to attain ultimate goals.

To take a different approach, even if the Fed attains its interest rate intermediate target, all is in vain if interest rates don't affect employment, the price level, the rate of economic growth, or the international payments situation.

Which Variable Should the Fed Target?

A school of economists dubbed monetarists (analyzed in Chapter 18) maintain that the Fed should set monetary-aggregate targets, and not interest rate targets. In this section each of these targets is assessed. Because each target has its own peculiar problems, there is honest disagreement among economists and the issue is not yet resolved.

It is crucial to understand that, in most circumstances, *both monetary-aggregate and interest rate targets cannot be pursued simultaneously.* Interest rate targets force the Fed to abandon control over the money stock; money-stock growth targets force the Fed to allow interest rates to fluctuate.[7]

Consider Figure 16.14, which indicates the relationship between the

---

[7] This statement is not technically correct. Under the (unlikely) conditions of certainty, money-supply targets and interest rate targets amount to the same thing. The full-employment, price-stable equilibrium level of national income is maintained by increasing the money supply so that the real interest rate remains constant. Also, very *broad* money-stock and interest rate target ranges could be set and met simultaneously, even under uncertainty. For example, the Fed could set a range of targets for M1 growth between 1 and 30 percent per annum, and a federal funds rate of between 1 and 35 percent. The Fed can simultaneously attain *both* targets—but to what avail? Such a policy would mean that the targeting process is a fraud.

The Fed Cannot Determine Both the Money Supply and the Interest Rate

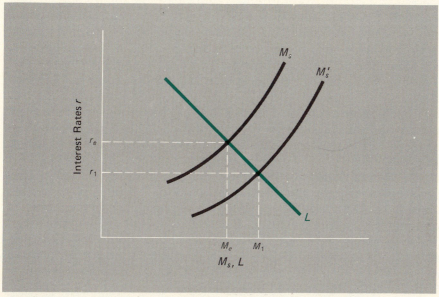

FIGURE 16.14. CHOOSING A MONETARY POLICY TARGET

This figure indicates that the Fed, in the very short run, can select an interest rate *or* a money-supply target, but not both. It cannot, for example, choose r_e and M_1; if it selects r_e, it must accept M_e; if it selects M_1, it must allow the interest rate to fall to r_1. Because these targets present a problem of mutual exclusivity, the Fed must choose one target or the other if it wants to follow a two-stage policy.

total demand for and the supply of money. Note that in the very short run (in the sense that nominal national income is fixed), the demand for money is constant; short-run money supply changes leave the demand for money unaltered. In the longer run, however, as the changed money supply causes nominal national income to change, the money demand curve will shift. In the short run, the Fed can choose either a particular interest rate or a particular money supply.

If the Fed wants interest rate r_e, it *must* select money supply M_e; if the Fed desires a lower (higher) interest rate in the short run, it must increase (decrease) the money supply. Thus, by targeting an interest rate, the Fed must relinquish control of the money supply. Conversely, if the Fed wants to target the money supply at, say, M_1, it must allow the interest rate to be r_1.

Consider now the case in which the Fed wants to reduce the present level of interest rates. If actual interest rates are above the desired rates, the Fed will continuously be forced to increase the money supply. This will only temporarily lower interest rates. The increased money stock will induce inflation, and inflationary premiums will be added to interest rates. To pursue its low-interest-rate policy, the Fed must *again* increase the money stock. Note that in order to maintain an interest rate target (lower interest rates), the Fed must abandon an independent money-stock target.

Complementary reasoning indicates that by setting growth rate targets for monetary aggregates, the Fed must allow short-run decreases or increases in interest rates when the economy experiences a recession or an expansion.

But which should the Fed target: interest rates or monetary aggregates?[8] It is generally agreed that the answer to this important question depends on the *source* of instability in the economy. If the source of instability is a variation in the *is* curve (due to variations in private or public spending), then monetary-aggregate targets should be set and pursued. On the other hand, if the source of instability is an unstable demand for (or perhaps supply of) money, then interest rate targets are preferred. Let's discuss each in turn.

Instability of *is*, Stability of *lm*   Consider Figure 16.15, which indicates a stable *lm* curve and an unstable *is* curve. This situation could arise because fiscal policy is destabilizing (a high variance in public spending)[9] or because the consumption function or the investment curve varies (a high variance in private spending). If the demand-for-money curve is relatively stable,[10] then the equilibrium level of income will vary between y_e and y_1 if a monetary-aggregate rule is followed. Remember that the *lm* curve is derived by assuming a constant money stock and that this is a nondynamic version of a monetary target.

If, however, an interest rate target is set (keep the "desired" interest rate at r_d), then the *lm* curve becomes horizontal at r_d (specifically, lm_f, in Figure 16.15); this means the money supply must always be adjusted to maintain r_d. Note that pursuit of the interest rate target causes the level of national income to fluctuate between y_2 and y_3. Since $y_3 - y_2 > y_1 - y_e$, a money-stock target is more stabilizing than an interest rate

---

[8] And, *which* interest rates or *which* monetary aggregates should the Fed target?

[9] A reason dear to the monetarist's heart.

[10] A monetarist's article of faith. For an opposite view, however, see J. P. Judd and J. S. Scadding, "The Search for a Stable Money Demand Function," *Journal of Economic Literature* (September 1982), pp. 993–1023.

If *lm* Is More Stable Than *is*, Then the Fed Should Target the Money Supply

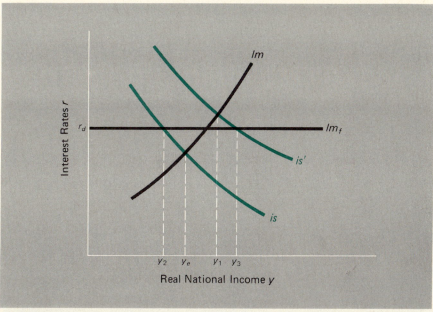

FIGURE 16.15. STABLE *lm*, UNSTABLE *is*

If the *lm* curve is stable because of a stable demand for money, then an unstable *is* curve causes the level of national income to fluctuate between y_e and y_1 when a money target is followed. On the other hand, with a shifting *is* curve an interest rate target set at r_d would cause the level of real national income to vary only between y_2 and y_3. A monetary aggregate target would therefore be more stabilizing than an interest rate target if the *lm* curve is more stable than the *is* curve.

target. The implication is that changes in the money supply to maintain a constant interest rate will be destabilizing or procyclical when the *is* curve is unstable. That is, the Fed would be prompted to increase the money supply during an inflation (to keep interest rates down) and to decrease the money supply during a recession (to keep interest rates from falling).

Instability of *lm*, Stability of *is* Consider Figure 16.16, which shows a stable *is* curve and an unstable *lm* curve. The *lm* curve is presumed unstable because the demand-for-money curve is unstable. Under a monetary target policy, the level of national income would fluctuate between

If *is* Is More Stable Than *lm*, Then the Fed Should Target the Interest Rate

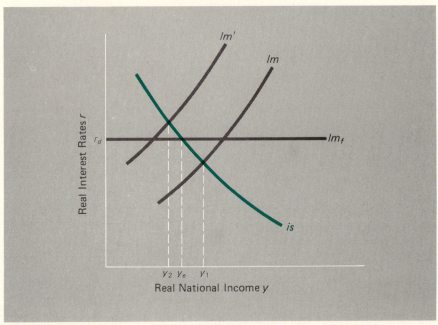

FIGURE 16.16. STABLE *is*, UNSTABLE *lm*

The *is* curve is stable, and an unstable demand-for-money relationship causes the *lm* curve to shift between *lm* and *lm'*. A monetary aggregate target will leave the money supply unaltered so that the level of national income will vary between y_1 and y_2. However, an interest rate target of r_d will leave the level of national income unaltered at y_e; an interest rate target is more stabilizing than a money-stock target if the *is* curve is more stable than the *lm* curve.

y_1 and y_2. A constant money supply would cause interest rate and national income fluctuations every time the demand for money changed. On the other hand, a policy of targeting the interest rate at r_d (a horizontal lm_f curve at r_d) would cause the Fed to increase the money supply when the demand for money increases, and to decrease the money supply when the demand for money falls. An interest rate target would therefore cause the Fed to pursue countercyclical money supply changes. In Figure 16.16 an interest rate target would leave the level of income at (or near) y_e, the point of intersection of *is* and lm_f.

The issue as to which target is "better" turns out to be an empirical one. *If* is *is more stable than* lm, *set an interest rate target;* if lm *is more stable than* is, *set a monetary-aggregate target.*

The Single-Stage Strategy Reconsidered

We are now in a better position to consider the single-stage monetary policy strategy. In the previous section we showed that the Fed must concentrate on an interest rate target *or* a monetary-aggregate target; the Fed can't choose both targets unless it is willing to tolerate wide swings in both. It was also concluded that the optimal intermediate target for the two-stage monetary strategy depends on whether the *is* curve or the *lm* curve is more stable.

This means that if the Fed targets a monetary aggregate, and hits the target, it may not achieve its ultimate goal of, say, a specific level of real national income. The goal may not be achieved as long as the *lm* curve is not vertical, if (1) the *is* curve shifts due to a supply shock or a demand shock or (2) the *lm* curve *itself* shifts due to a change in the demand for money or to a change in the price level.

Apparently, many things must remain constant if the Fed is to achieve its ultimate goals, *even if it hits its monetary-aggregate growth target.* Similarly, if the Fed targets an interest rate, then it may be able to hit this target and simultaneously not attain its ultimate goal of, say, a higher specific real national income level. This could happen if the *is* curve shifts due to a supply shock or a demand shock. Again, in order to attain an ultimate goal, many things must remain constant or changes must be predictable.

A one-stage monetary strategy is not locked into targeting one variable to the virtual exclusion of the other; a one-stage strategy will enable policymakers to make use of *all* the available information. For example, suppose the Fed's strategy is to increase the money supply by 6 percent per year, and then suddenly a very deep recession occurs. Should this information be ignored? It would seem that a growth of more than 6 percent per year in the money supply is called for in this situation. Or suppose that the Fed is targeting nominal interest rates at (the real rate of) 5 percent, and then the real interest rate rises, owing to (1) a rise in the productivity of capital, or (2) a change in tastes in favor of present consumption relative to future consumption. Should this information be ignored? It would seem that trying to peg the market or nominal interest rate forever will merely cause inflation and disruption when the real, or natural, rate changes because of some fundamental change in the economy.

In short, a single-stage monetary strategy may be superior to a two-stage strategy because:

1. It uses all the available information; sometimes the solution is obvious.
2. At times the *is* curve may be more stable than the *lm* curve, and at other times the *lm* curve may be more stable than the *is* curve. Why should we expect one curve always to be more stable than the other?
3. The two-stage strategy forces policymakers to substitute the intermediate target for the ultimate goal, and the chances are good that hitting an intermediate target will not assure attainment of the ultimate goal.

PROBLEMS WITH MONETARY POLICY

You must be aware by now that monetary policy is a tricky business, an art rather than a science. The rest of this chapter presents a more systematic discussion of the problems of monetary policy.

As we noted earlier in this chapter, there are three criteria for an intermediate-target variable: measurability, attainability, and relatedness to ultimate goals. Monetary policy is the Fed's use of the tools at its disposal to achieve its ultimate goals. But there is a long road between the Fed's tools and its goals. This road is not easy to follow, and in many ways the Fed is powerless to achieve some of these goals.

Still, the Fed is committed to doing *something*, and it does have tools. What the Fed can do is alter bank reserves and the monetary base. These, then, are the potential instruments that can be altered to achieve such intermediate targets as the various monetary aggregates and short-term interest rates. The attainment of these intermediate targets will presumably enable the Fed to reach its ultimate goals by the two-stage strategy.

This section divides problems of monetary policy into three major categories: (1) choosing the best intermediate target, (2) attaining the intermediate target, and (3) relating the intermediate target to the ultimate goal. Each is discussed in turn.

Choosing the Best Intermediate Target

By using its monetary policy tools the Fed can change the total reserves of depository institutions. Changes in reserves, in turn, affect either the money stock (one of the monetary aggregates) or short-term interest rates (Treasury bill yields or the federal funds rate). The first task is to choose between these two targets, because they are mutually exclusive.

At some times the Fed has tried to achieve the first target and at other times the second target. Indeed, at times the Fed has attempted to achieve *both* targets. In October of 1979, the Fed announced a change in its method of conducting monetary policy. The change involved placing greater emphasis in day-to-day operations on the supply of bank reserves and less emphasis on restricting short-term fluctuations in the federal funds rate. In other words, the Fed indicated that it would now (primarily) target monetary aggregates (especially M1) and not interest rates.

In recent years financial innovations have raised questions concerning the usefulness of M1 (or even M2) as an intermediate target. Nationwide NOW accounts, money market mutual funds, federally insured money market deposits, and super-NOW accounts have altered the form in which the public holds transactions and savings balances. A greater part of "narrow" money, or M1, now earns interest; eventually, a high percentage of M1 may earn interest at near money market rates. Because part of M1 is clearly a transactions account but another part has become a savings or store-of-value account, the relationship between M1 (or M2) and gross national product is now less certain.[11]

Economists are not yet sure how much time must elapse before the smoke will clear, financial innovations level off, and people adjust to the new financial accounts. In the meantime, the search continues for the "best" intermediate target. Some have suggested a return to an interest rate intermediate target because they believe that the *lm* curve is less stable than the *is* curve, and pursuing an interest rate target is therefore preferable to pursuing a monetary growth target.

In 1983, Benjamin Friedman, a Harvard economist, suggested that the best intermediate target would be a *combination* of a credit-aggregate target *and* a monetary growth target.[12] The credit-aggregate target he suggested was total net credit, a broad measure consisting of the aggregate indebtedness of all U.S. borrowers other than financial institutions. According to Benjamin Friedman, total net credit satisfies the criteria for a desirable intermediate target:

1. Data on total net credit are available on a monthly basis, and the data are as reliable as those for other potential targets.
2. The Fed can influence total net credit through open-market operations; over a year or so, the Fed should be able to meet a total net credit target.
3. Total net credit bears as close and stable a relationship to financial

---

[11] See Chapter 11.

[12] Benjamin M. Friedman, "A Two-Target Strategy for Monetary Policy," *Wall Street Journal*, January 27, 1983, editorial page.

economic activity as do any of the monetary aggregates. This relationship has persisted in the United States since at least World War I, and the relationship between credit and GNP is also strong in other Western industrialized nations.

According to Benjamin Friedman, the Fed should target both money growth and credit growth, because such a system "would draw on a more diverse and hence more reliable information base for the signals that govern the systematic response of monetary policy to emerging developments."[13]

Under such a scheme, the Fed would pick one monetary aggregate and total net credit, specify growth targets for each, and carry out open-market operations aimed at achieving both targets. A deviation in either target from its target range would warrant a change in open-market operations to alter financial institution reserves and the federal funds rate.

Clearly, economists are not yet, if they ever will be, in agreement as to what is the best intermediate target.

Attaining the Target

When the Fed shifted its emphasis to the monetary aggregates, wider interest rate fluctuations had to be accepted. But how well has the Fed succeeded in attaining monetary growth targets since 1979? Has it been able to attain its targets? Has the money supply moved smoothly toward its targets? Unfortunately for the monetarist position (which maintains that the Fed can easily control the money supply), over long periods the Fed has been unable to obtain its monetary-aggregate targets. Even when the Fed *was* able to meet its targets, the money supply grew erratically. There have been wide divergences among the rates of growth in the different measures of money, and at times the different money stock measures have changed in opposite directions. This unstable growth in the monetary aggregates led to wide variations in nominal interest rates. Table 16.2 (page 458) shows just how unstable money (then called M1B) growth was from October 1979 to January 1982. Milton Friedman has described this as an "unprecedented volatility in monetary growth" and has noted that the money supply growth from October 1978 to the policy change date of October 1979 was *more* stable than it was *after* the policy change date.[14]

The apparent inability of the Fed to generate a smooth growth in the money supply has caused problems. Erratic monetary growth caused

---

[13] Ibid.

[14] Milton Friedman, "Monetary Instability," *Newsweek*, December 21, 1981, p. 71.

short-term interest rates to hit historic highs in 1979, and over the next two years they varied between 17 percent and 6 percent. This variability is unprecedented in the century for which data exist. Friedman has argued that this erratic growth in the money stock was responsible for both the short recession between January and July 1980 and the all-too-short expansion between July 1980 and July 1981.

For the discussion at hand, however, a more fundamental problem exists. Do the data since October 1979 mean that the Fed *cannot* attain its monetary growth targets? When we realize that the Fed abandoned interest rate targets in favor of monetary-aggregate targets because the former proved unattainable, the possible unattainability of the money-stock targets is all the more distressing. It may be that neither target is attainable. If neither is attainable, then monetary policy may be a "snare and a delusion."

In October 1982 the Fed publicly abandoned M1 targets, and it appeared that the experiment with monetarism had failed. Being a particularly tenacious and resourceful lot, however, the monetarists are not about to concede defeat when they fought so hard to get the Fed to change its target from interest rates to money stocks. The monetarists have blamed the erratic growth of the money stock on the Fed.[15] Because the Fed has not brought about a *smooth* growth of M1, they maintain, there really has been no experiment with monetarism.

We return to the issue of whether or not there was an experiment in monetarism during the October 1979 to October 1982 period and to the issue of whether or not the Fed can attain monetary-aggregate growth targets in Chapter 18.

Did the Fed Really Abandon Its Commitment to Interest Rate Targets?
Some monetarist critics of the Fed have maintained that one important reason the Fed has not been able to attain its monetary growth rate targets is that it really has not abandoned its commitment to stable interest rates. Because the Fed cannot simultaneously pursue both targets, the Fed has lost some control over the money supply.

This argument has been challenged forcefully by Ralph C. Bryant, a

---

[15] The Fed, in turn, has blamed its inability to achieve its monetary growth targets on recent financial innovations in the banking industry. Such recent financial innovations may have called into question the desirability of a money-stock target. First, the measurability criterion is affected, because recent financial innovations blur the meaning of "money" and generate redefinitions of the monetary aggregates. Second, financial innovations have made the M1 and M2 monetary targets more difficult to achieve. Third, because M1 includes *savings* as well as transactions balances, the relationship between M1 and GNP (an ultimate target) is no longer so clear-cut. If you wish to pursue this topic, see the speech by Anthony M. Solomon, former president of the Federal Reserve Bank of New York, entitled "Financial Innovation and Monetary Policy," in the 1981 *Annual Report of the Federal Reserve Bank of New York*, which can be obtained by writing to the New York Fed.

TABLE 16.2. INTEREST RATES FOLLOW MONEY

Money Turning Point	Date	Interval in Weeks	Annual Rate of Change in M1B	THREE-MONTH TREASURY BILLS, WEEKS LATER		
				Three	Four	Five
Peak	Oct. 3, 1979			12.6%	12.1%	12.3%
Trough	Nov. 28, 1979	8	− 1.4%	12.1	12.0	12.1
Peak	Feb. 20, 1980	12	+ 12.1	15.3	14.8	15.6
Trough	April 30, 1980	10	− 12.4	8.2	7.7	7.5
Peak	Nov. 26, 1980	30	+ 15.0	16.2	14.6	14.3
Trough[a]	Feb. 4, 1981	10	− 13.1	14.2	14.4	13.8
Peak	April 22, 1981	11	+ 23.8	16.8	16.6	15.6
Trough	July 1, 1981	10	− 10.6	15.5	15.1	15.4
Peak	Sept. 16, 1981	11	+ 7.2	13.8	13.4	13.4
Trough	Oct. 28, 1981	6	− 5.1	10.3	10.2	10.4
Peak	Jan. 13, 1982	11	+ 24.6	13.2		

[a] Corrected roughly for NOW accounts.

Source: Adapted from Milton Friedman, "The Yo-Yo Economy." *Newsweek*, February 15, 1982, p. 72.

Senior Fellow in the Brookings Institution's Economic Studies Program, whose article on this subject has already been mentioned.[16] Consider Figure 16.17, which shows that the October 1979 decision constituted a major change in the day-to-day conduct of open-market operations. Note that before October 1979 the target *ranges* for the federal funds rate were much smaller than they were after October 1979. This indicates that after 1979 the Fed was, *in principle,* more willing to accept variations in the federal funds rate in order to achieve monetary-growth targets. More importantly, Figure 16.17 also shows that, *in practice,* the Fed permitted much greater swings in the federal funds rate after October 1979.

Money Control in a Global Setting In recent years the world's financial markets have become increasingly integrated. As a consequence, the demand for the United States dollar (or the currency of several other economic powers) has become an international phenomenon. Corporations, governments, and private citizens from all over the world can, within broad limits, *choose* the currency they wish to hold. It is becoming increasingly true that short-term changes in the *international* demand for the dollar can dominate the Fed's monetary policy. This makes the Fed's job of attaining monetary control extremely difficult.

[16] See footnote 5 in this chapter.

After 1979, the Fed Allowed More Variation in the Interest Rate

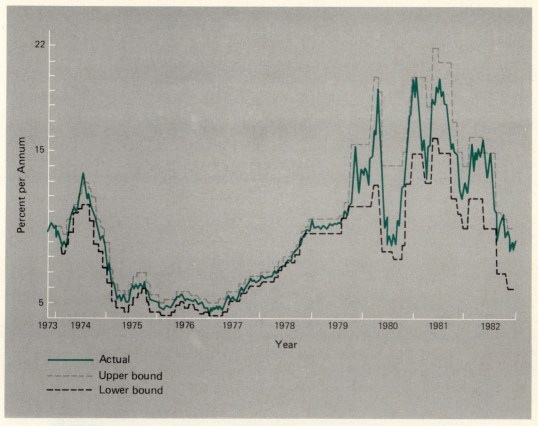

FIGURE 16.17. FEDERAL FUNDS RATE: ACTUAL PATH AND THE FED'S OPEN MARKET OPERATIONS CONSTRAINT

This figure shows that a definite change in Fed operations occurred in October 1979. After that date, upper and lower bounds (the broken lines) and actual interest rates (the solid colored line) fluctuated more than they did prior to that date.

Relation of the Target to Ultimate Goals

Even if the Fed is able to agree on the "proper" intermediate target and is able to attain the intermediate target, fundamental problems still exist. What good would it be to attain interest rate or monetary-aggregate targets if these targets are unrelated to ultimate Fed goals? This section

CHAPTER 16 MONETARY POLICY

459

discusses the problems of time lags and rational expectations, both of which indicate that achieving targets may not lead to attaining ultimate goals.

The Problem with Time Lags   The Fed may be able to attain its intermediate-target objectives only after the lapse of a period of time. If time lags are long and variable, meeting a target may worsen the economic problem that the Fed is currently trying to solve.

How does the Fed go about setting a target? Generally, the decision is based on a mixture of data on the current economic scene—the current rate of inflation, the current level of unemployment, the current level of business capital formation, and predictions about future changes in economic activity. The Fed has at its disposal models that forecast the future values of aggregate economic variables on a quarterly and yearly basis. The numerical values in these models are obtained by feeding past data into a computer that is programmed to determine whatever the current income and employment determination model indicates is appropriate. The models involved are called *econometric models* and they forecast future economic activity. Ultimately, however, the theories used in computers are devised by economists. When a particular econometric model doesn't predict well, it is not the fault of the computer.

There are, therefore, difficulties in predicting accurately the future course of economic activity. The ability to predict well depends on using a national income determination model that takes into account all the relationships necessary to make a good forecast.[17] It also depends on the availability of accurate current data. For example, the models that use changes in inventories as a variable often go awry because the data on business inventory changes never seem to be correct the first time they are collected. They are nearly always revised three or six months later. Weekly data on the money supply are also frequently revised.

The problem of information forms a part of a larger problem called *time lags*.

Time Lags for Short-Run Policies   Have you ever taken a shower, turned on the hot water, and had the water come out cold? Then, in an act of frustration, you gave the hot-water faucet another turn and got scalded? What happened was that there was a lag between the time you turned on the faucet and the time the hot water actually reached your body. Short-run stabilization policymakers face not only a similar time lag but several other time lags as well:

---

[17] The ability to forecast also depends on the ability to predict variables such as war, the outcome of political elections, relative price changes, and a myriad of other variables which the model *uses implicitly* but does not explicitly predict.

1. **The Recognition Time Lag** Before any policy can be made, there must be information on the *current* state of the economy. However, we don't know immediately what is happening to the rate of capital formation, the unemployment rate, changes in prices, and so on until after a time lag. It is crucial to obtain accurate information as quickly as possible, but sometimes accurate information about the *present* state of the entire economy isn't available for months. In other words, it is possible that we will not *recognize* that we are in a recession until, say, three months after it has begun. This is often called the **recognition time lag.**

2. **The Action Time Lag** Once it is discovered that the economy is indeed in, say, a recession, a long period may elapse before new monetary or fiscal policy can be put into effect. This is particularly true of tax cuts and tax increases that are desired for stabilization purposes. A tax cut was first suggested in the Kennedy administration in 1961. It didn't pass until 1964—a lag of three years. Monetary policy does not suffer the same **action time lag** because the Federal Open Market Committee of the Federal Reserve System meets thirteen times a year and can quickly put into effect any policy upon which it decides. It simply instructs the trading desk at the New York Fed how to proceed. The action lag, then, can be long and variable for fiscal policy but will generally be relatively short for monetary policy.

3. **The Effect Time Lag** Even if there were no recognition lag or action lag, there would still be an **effect time lag** because even a perfect economic policy variable change will not have an immediate impact upon the economy. An increase in government spending, for example, takes time to work itself out; a change in taxes does, too. A change in the rate of growth of the money supply may not have an effect for several months. Economists have spent considerable effort attempting to estimate the effect time lag. Some say that for fiscal policy the lag can extend over several years. The lag in monetary policy, on the other hand, may vary from only a few months to several years.

Taking Lags into Account Now you can see the problem inherent in trying to stabilize the economy in the short run. Assume you are a policymaker and you have just discovered that the economy has entered a recession. You try to get taxes changed to counter that recession. What kinds of problems will you encounter? First of all, the economy may have already been in a recession for several months before you detected it. Second, it may take another year or two to get Congress to put a tax-change package into effect. And third, it may take another year until the major effect of the new fiscal policy is felt in the economy. By that time, the economy may already have begun to recover. Your fiscal policy change will then be inappropriate and will only add fuel to inflationary fire.

The long and variable lags involved in short-run stabilization policy have prompted some critics of such policies to recommend that no short-run stabilization attempts be made at all. The most outspoken proponent of stable, or nondiscretionary, monetary policy is Milton Friedman. He has been a proponent of the so-called **monetary rule** for many years. This monetary rule would require that the money supply grow at a fixed annual rate that could not be altered by the Federal Open Market Committee (or anyone else, for that matter). That is why such a policy is referred to as nondiscretionary: no one has the discretion to change it. On the fiscal policy side, there are numerous advocates of a long-run commitment to a balanced full-employment budget (i.e., a budget that *would* be balanced *if* full employment existed). There would be no discretionary fiscal policy to change the direction of economic activity in the short run.

Note that the adoption of a monetary rule and long-run commitment to a balanced full-employment budget would, to a large extent, eliminate short-run stabilization policies. We return to a discussion of rules versus discretion in Chapter 18.

Coordination

Because stabilization policy can employ fiscal tools as well as monetary tools, there would seem to be a problem of coordination. What if the fiscal authorities—the president and Congress—decide on one policy and the monetary authority—the Fed—decides on another? As a matter of fact, conflicting policies have occasionally been applied by monetary and fiscal authorities. In 1968, for example, a fiscal policy of restraint was adopted by Congress in the form of a temporary income surtax. Soon after that surtax went into effect, however, the monetary authorities began what would have to be considered an expansionary policy. It seems, therefore, that unless all policymaking is put under one roof, so to speak, the problem of coordination will at times be serious.

When all is said and done, the empirical evidence suggests that monetary policy does have a significant impact on economic activity. Both Keynesians and monetarists agree on this point. The effects of monetary policy seem to be distributed over several years; the immediate effects are strong, but the effects over time are stronger still.

Yet, the variability of the effect lag combined with the recognition lag implies that timing problems surely exist. The usefulness of monetary policy as a *short-run* stabilizing agent has therefore been questioned. A boom in April may not be recognized until September, at which time the Fed tries to slow the inflation accompanying it. If, however, the boom peaks in June and the price level stops rising and employment begins to fall, September's monetary restraint will cause an even greater slump.

Rational Expectations Analysis

The rational expectations hypothesis (examined in Chapter 15) predicts problems for those who would stabilize the economy in the short run by using monetary (or fiscal) policy. The existence of the various lags makes monetary policy difficult and may destabilize rather than stabilize the economy; the rational expectations hypothesis implies that short-run stabilization is impossible. Rational expectations analysis predicts that monetary (or fiscal) policies cannot *systematically* affect (change in desired directions) such real variables as output and employment even in the short run. Even short-run departures from the natural rate of unemployment and output cannot be remedied in any systematic way by a change of policy. Rational expectations analysis also provides a rationale for throwing up one's hands and declaring, "Alas, stabilization policy is futile."

Accepted economic analysis indicates that *in the long run* neither monetary nor fiscal policy will cause the economy to deviate significantly from its natural levels of unemployment and output. Rational expectations analysis makes it doubtful that there will even be systematic departures from these rates in the short run. We are led to the tentative conclusion that monetary policy can be used only to achieve the goal of price stability. This conclusion has an appeal for at least two reasons:

1. A *monetary* variable (money supply) is to be used to control a *monetary* phenomenon (inflation).
2. *One* tool (monetary policy) is used to achieve one goal (price stability).

POLICY CONTROVERSY
Should Depository Institutions Have a 100 Percent Reserve Requirement?

Required reserve ratios are supposedly more stable and predictable than voluntary reserve ratios; hence, required reserve ratios permit easier and more consistent monetary control by the Fed. If this is true, it would seem to follow that a 100 percent reserve requirement would allow the monetary authorities even better control over the money supply. Whether a system of mandatory reserve requirement ratios causes depository institutions to vary their reserve ratios less often than would a system of voluntary reserve requirement ratios is unknown.

But it is known that a 100 percent reserve requirement system certainly allows the monetary authorities to have better control over the money supply.

A 100 percent reserve requirement would abolish multiple deposit expansion by the banking system—the money expansion multiplier would be equal to 1. Such a requirement was proposed by Irving Fisher in 1935, and it represented Fisher's notion of how to stop runs on banks.[18]

Milton Friedman, unhappy with the fractional reserve banking system, has also proposed a 100 percent reserve requirement with slight variations.[19] Recognizing that bankers would be displeased because bank earnings would fall, Friedman has suggested that the Fed pay interest at a rate equivalent to the yield on Treasury bills on bank reserves held at Federal Reserve district banks.

The major advantage of a 100 percent reserve requirement today is that it would allow the Fed more precise control over the money supply. However, it would not necessarily improve the position of depositors in terms of whether or not they had to worry about runs on banks. Deposit insurance has already eliminated that worry for the most part. In any event, with a 100 percent reserve requirement, the Fed would no longer have to be concerned about the unpredictability of excess reserves and leakages into currency. Perhaps another advantage is that with 100 percent reserves, the Fed and Congress could reduce substantially the regulation of depository institutions.

Open-Market Operations

Under a 100 percent reserve requirement system, open-market operations would work as follows: If the Fed bought $1 million of Treasury bills from depository institution A, A's reserves would rise by that much. Institution A could then increase its lending by $1 million and the money supply would rise by $1 million. However, when the $1 million is spent and deposited in, say, depository institution B, B must hold the whole $1 million to meet its reserve requirement. It follows that no more lending is possible; therefore, no further increase in deposits and the money supply will occur. The effect of a $1 million Fed security purchase is a $1 million increase in the money supply. The money multiplier is 1.

With a 100 percent reserve requirement, the Fed can change the money supply with more precision than it does today. This appeals to those who want the Fed to use its discretion in changing the money supply, *and* also to those who wish the Fed to follow a monetary rule that increases the money supply at a steady rate.

Will a 100 percent reserve requirement be imposed in the future? The probability of this is small because it represents a radical change. It would be disruptive and confusing to the banking community; and the Fed would also run into the problem of properly defining the money supply and of determining which items of a depository institution's liabilities would be considered deposits subject to a 100 percent reserve requirement.

---

[18] Irving Fisher, *One Hundred Percent Money* (New York: Adelphia Co., 1935).

[19] Milton Friedman, *A Program for Monetary Stability* (New York: Fordham University Press, 1960).

CHAPTER SUMMARY

1. The money supply depends on the monetary base, the reserve/deposit ratio held by depository institutions, and the currency/deposit ratio held by the public. The money multiplier is that amount by which a change in the monetary base is multiplied in order to determine the change in the money supply.

2. Because (a) households can select their own currency/deposit ratio, and (b) depository institutions can hold excess reserves and therefore determine their own reserve/deposit ratio, the money supply is at least partially endogenously determined.

3. Depository institutions face a trade-off between (a) their desire to hold a small quantity of reserves in order to maximize their interest earnings and (b) their desire to avoid the interest-rate costs of borrowing reserves in order to meet reserve requirement. Therefore, they will decrease their excess reserves as the interest rate they can earn rises; it follows that the money supply is, within limits, directly related to market interest rates.

4. The Fed can affect the money supply because it can (a) change the monetary base, (b) change the required reserve ratio, (c) set the discount rate, (d) affect the federal funds rate by changing the discount rate, and (e) offset changes in the currency/deposit ratio.

5. The Fed acquires assets and pays for them by increasing the reserves of depository institutions; it sells assets by decreasing the reserves of depository institutions. This means that whenever the Fed changes its assets, it changes the monetary base and, therefore, the money supply.

6. The Fed can change the amount of excess reserves in the banking system by changing the required reserve ratio; this action will change the loans made by depository institutions and, therefore, the money supply. It can also change the quantity of bank reserves by lending to depository institutions and by engaging in open-market operations; these Fed actions, therefore, can change the money supply.

7. A two-stage monetary policy strategy requires that the Fed use its tools to change its instruments, which in turn will enable it to hit such intermediate targets as a monetary aggregate or an interest rate; in turn, it is hoped that hitting intermediate targets will help the Fed attain ultimate goals. A one-stage strategy allows the Fed to use all relevant information, and it frees the Fed from ignoring either the money supply or the interest rate.

8. If the *lm* curve is more stable than the *is* curve, an intermediate monetary-aggregate target is preferable to an interest-rate target. If the *is* curve is more stable than the *lm* curve, then an intermediate

interest rate target is preferable to an intermediate monetary-aggregate target.

9. Problems with a two-stage monetary policy include choosing the best target, hitting the target, and relating the targeted value to ultimate goals. Other problems with monetary policy include the fact that the dollar has become an international currency, the time lags, the coordination of monetary and fiscal policy, and the possibility that the Fed may be unable to affect real output and employment systematically (owing to rational expectations).

10. Both Irving Fisher, the classical economist, and Milton Friedman, a modern classical economist, have called for a 100 percent reserve requirement. Such a policy would allow the Fed better control over the money supply and should please (a) policy activists *and* (b) those who prefer that the Fed follow a monetary-aggregate rule.

GLOSSARY

action time lag   The time required between recognizing an economic problem and putting policy into effect.

actual reserve ratio   The ratio of actual reserves held by depository institutions to their deposits.

discount rate   The rate that the Fed charges depository institutions when they borrow from it.

effect time lag   The time that elapses between the onset of a policy and the results of that policy.

excess reserves   Actual reserves minus required reserves.

federal funds rate   The interest rate that depository institutions pay to borrow reserves from other depository institutions in the federal funds market.

intermediate targets   Targets such as the monetary aggregates and the federal funds rate that link instruments to ultimate goals.

monetary base, B   The sum of the value of currency held by the public and the value of the depository institution reserves.

monetary instruments   Variables such as depository institution reserves, the discount rate, and the monetary base over which the Fed has control and which help it to hit its intermediate targets.

monetary rule   A rule directed at the Fed that would eliminate discretionary monetary policy and which would commit the Fed to, for example, increasing the money supply at some specific rate.

money multiplier   The amount by which a change in the money base is multiplied to determine the change in the money supply; the ratio of (a) 1 plus the currency/deposit ratio to (b) the currency/deposit ratio plus the actual reserve/deposit ratio.

open-market operations (OMO)   Purchases and sales of government securities by the Fed in order to conduct monetary policy.

recognition time lag   The time required to gather information about the current state of the economy.

required reserves   Reserves that the Fed requires depository institutions to hold.

required reserve ratio   The ratio of reserves to deposits that the Fed mandates depository institutions to hold.

reserves   The value of vault cash plus the deposits at the Fed owned by depository institutions.

QUESTIONS AND PROBLEMS FOR REVIEW

16.1   How is the money multiplier expected to be affected by an increase in the monetary base? A decrease in the reserve/deposit ratio? An increase in the currency/deposit ratio?

16.2   The money supply is considered to be at least partially endogenously determined. What is meant in this case by the description *endogenously determined*? For what reasons is the money supply considered to be at least partially endogenously determined?

16.3   Banks are thought to face a trade-off with respect to their desire to avoid the interest rate costs of borrowing reserves in order to meet reserve requirements. If interest rate costs of borrowing reserves in order to meet reserve requirements are less than interest rate revenues, would you still think that banks faced such a trade-off?

16.4   To the extent that interest rate costs of borrowing reserves changes in proportion to changes in market rates of interest, would it still follow that banks will decrease their reserves as the market rates of interest increase?

16.5   Explain why it is thought that the money supply is, within limits, directly related to market rates of interest. Does the explanation hold irrespective of the cause for the change in market rates of interest?

16.6   The Fed can change the amount of excess reserves, and therefore the money supply, by transacting government securities through open-market operations. What effect is this particular method of operation considered to have on market rates of interest?

16.7   Suppose that the balance sheet of the Fed is as given below:

Assets

Gold certificates	10
Government securities	20
Loans to commercial banks	20
Loans to the government	10

Liabilities

Fed notes	40
Deposits of commercial banks	15
Deposits of the government	5

Suppose that the combined balance sheet of commercial banks is as given below:

Assets

Cash in vault	5
Deposits at Fed	15
Loans	100

Liabilities

Deposits of the public	90
Deposits of governments	10
Liabilities to Fed	20

Let reserve requirements be equal to 15 percent of total deposits. If the Fed wanted to increase the money supply by 10, by buying or selling government securities, how many would they have to buy or sell?

16.8 Assuming the same balance sheets as given in Question 16.7, if the Fed wanted to decrease the money supply by 10 by increasing or decreasing commercial bank liabilities to the Fed, how much of liabilities to the Fed would they have to increase or decrease?

16.9 Again assuming the same balance sheets as given in Question 16.7, if the Fed wanted to increase the money supply by 10 by increasing or decreasing the reserve requirement ratio, how much of a change would they make?

16.10 What is meant by a two-stage monetary policy strategy? What actions are required in such a strategy?

REFERENCES

Norman H. Bowsher, "The Demand for Currency: Is the Underground Economy Undermining Monetary Policy?" *Review*, Federal Reserve Bank of St. Louis, vol. 62 (1980).

Ralph C. Bryant, "Should Money Targets Be the Focus of Monetary Policy?" *The Brookings Review* (Spring 1983).

———, *Controlling Money: The Federal Reserve and Its Critics* (Washington, D.C.: Brookings Institution, 1983).

Benjamin Friedman, "A Two-Target Strategy for Monetary Policy," *Wall Street Journal*, January 27, 1983, editorial page.

Milton Friedman, *A Program for Monetary Stability* (New York: Fordham University Press, 1960).

———, "The Role of Monetary Policy," *American Economic Review*, vol. 58 (1968).

———, "Monetary Instability," *Newsweek*, December 21, 1981, p. 71.

———, "The Yo-Yo Economy," *Newsweek*, February 15, 1982, p. 72.

John P. Judd and John L. Scadding, "The Search for a Stable Money Demand Function," *Journal of Economic Literature*, vol. 20 (1982).

Lawrence R. Klein et al., *Controlling Money: A Discussion*, Original Paper 29, International Institute for Economic Research (1980).

Roger L. Miller and Robert W. Pulsinelli, *Modern Money and Banking* (New York: McGraw-Hill, 1985).

Modern Money Mechanics: A Workbook on Deposits, Currency, and Bank Reserves (Federal Reserve Bank of Chicago, 1982).

Lawrence S. Ritter and William L. Silber, *Principles of Money, Banking, and Financial Markets*, 4th ed. (New York: Basic Books, 1983).

Anthony M. Solomon, "Financial Innovation and Monetary Policy," Annual Report of the Federal Reserve Bank of New York (1981).

Neil Wallace, "Some of the Choices for Monetary Policy," *Quarterly Review*, Federal Reserve Bank of Minneapolis (Winter 1984).

17

FISCAL POLICY

n Chapter 6 we analyzed fiscal policy in the simple Keynesian model. Now that we have explicitly introduced the role of money into the Keynesian model and have incorporated elements of both the classical and the Keynesian models in the *is-lm* framework, we are in a position to analyze fiscal policy more realistically. This chapter discusses fiscal policy—both in theory and in practice. It begins with a theoretical analysis of fiscal policy and then stresses the distinction between automatic and discretionary fiscal policies. This is followed by an examination of the high-employment budget and a clarification of the difference between automatic and discretionary fiscal policy. Then we discuss problems with fiscal policy; and the chapter ends with a Policy Controversy concerning the burden of the public debt.

FISCAL POLICY IN A THEORETICAL CONTEXT

Fiscal policy is the deliberate changing of levels of federal government expenditures, taxes, and borrowing to achieve such national economic goals as high employment, price stability, economic growth, and a balance-of-payments equilibrium. Fiscal policy is determined jointly by the executive and legislative branches of the federal government.

Consider Figure 17.1, in which *is* and *lm* indicate that the equilibrium level of real national income is y_e and that the equilibrium real interest rate is r_e. We can consider this a short-run equilibrium position due to misinformation (as the rational expectations proponents and the monetarists would have it) or a more permanent situation due to price-wage rigidities (as Keynesians or post-Keynesians would interpret it). Whatever the reason, because the Employment Act of 1946 and an amendment to that act (the Full Employment and Balanced Growth Act of 1978) commit the government to achieving the national economic goals listed above, fiscal policy is justified.

A Change in Government Expenditures

An increase in government expenditures can, assuming constant taxes t_x and a constant price level P, stimulate the economy; an increase in real government purchases g increases aggregate expenditures directly. If no other types of expenditures, such as consumption c, investment i, or net exports (exports minus imports, $x - m$) are reduced, this net increase in aggregate spending will lead to an expansion of output, real national income, and employment. In turn, this expansion leads to additional expansion because of induced increases in consumption. In Chapter 6

Because of National Economic Goals, Fiscal Policy Is Justified When the Economy Is Not at Its Natural Output Level

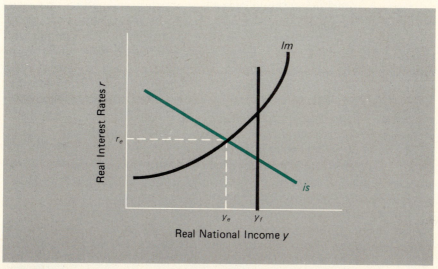

FIGURE 17.1. A NON–FULL-EMPLOYMENT EQUILIBRIUM

Aggregate equilibrium will exist at y_e and r_e. Nothing assures that y_e will be at the full-employment level of real national income y_f, because price-wage rigidities exist in modern economies. A commitment to national economic goals justifies fiscal policy.

we referred to this expansion as the multiplier effect; for a closed, private economy the ultimate change in real national income Δy is

$$\Delta y = \Delta g \left(\frac{1}{1 - b}\right) \qquad (17.1)$$

WHERE $\Delta y =$ changes in real national income

$\Delta g =$ change in real government purchases of goods and services

$1/(1 - b) =$ the multiplier

$b =$ marginal propensity to consume

So far our discussion is consistent with our analysis in Chapter 6. If we are to analyze the *pure* effects of fiscal policy, however, we must hold the real money supply constant—the *lm* curve should not shift due to a change in the real money supply. An increase in government expenditures must be *financed;* if the real money supply remains constant, an increase in real government expenditures requires either an increase in real taxes or an increase in Treasury bond sales. The effects of an increase in real taxes is analyzed in the next section. Consider now the effects of an increase in real government purchases of goods and services financed by Treasury bond sales. Suppose the Treasury sells $10 billion in bonds and uses the money received to finance $10 billion in government purchases. Note that the money supply has not changed; $10 billion of the money supply is reduced at the time of the bond sales, but it returns to its previous level when the increased government purchases of goods and services are made.

Figure 17.2 indicates the effects of an increase in government expenditures in the *is-lm* framework. An increase in government expenditures shifts the *is* curve rightward, by the amount $\Delta g[1/(1 - b)]$. At any real interest rate, the level of real national income will be higher, by the amount of the change in government expenditures times the closed private economy government expenditure multiplier.

If the real interest rate does not change, real national income will increase from y_e to y_3, where $y_3 - y_e = \Delta g[1/(1 - b)]$, and the full multiplier effect results. A change in the product market, however (a shift in the *is* curve), leads to disequilibrium in the money market. A shortage of liquidity (which exists at point C) causes real interest rates to rise to r_1 and in turn reduces business investment expenditures and household consumption expenditures. Eventually a new aggregate equilibrium level will be established at point B. In comparison with the original equilibrium (position A), both real national income and the real interest rate are higher at point B. Note, however, that the full multiplier effect does not occur; $y_1 - y_e < y_3 - y_e$. This is true because the expansionary effect of the increase in real government purchases of goods and services was partially offset by a decrease in real investment and real consumption—due to a higher real interest rate resulting from the increase in real government expenditures. This phenomenon is called the **crowding-out effect.** In other words, if we take into account how the government expenditures are *financed*, we see that the multiplier-effect analysis in Chapter 6 was oversimplified.

If government expenditures were to *fall* by $10 billion, a full multiplier effect—in the downward direction—would not result either. The *is* curve would shift to the left by the full multiplier effect, but a lower interest rate would induce more business investment expenditures and more household consumption expenditures. Some of the contraction in the economy resulting from a reduction in government expenditures would be offset by the increase in real net investment and real consumption that results from a lower real interest rate. A lower real interest rate results from a reduction in the real demand for liquidity due to a lower level of real national income.

An Increase in Government Expenditures Does Not Lead to a Full Multiplier Effect If the Money Supply Remains Constant

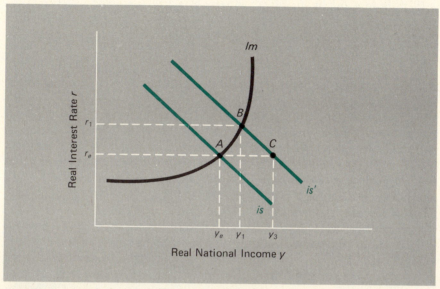

FIGURE 17.2. CROWDING OUT AND GOVERNMENT PURCHASES

An increase in government purchases shifts the *is* curve rightward by $\Delta g[1/(1 - b)]$. If the real interest rate does not change, income will increase from y_e to y_3; $y_3 - y_e = \Delta y = \Delta g[1/(1 - b)]$. An increase in real national income, however, increases the amount of real money desired for L_1 balances. In turn, this increase in the demand for money relative to the (constant) real supply of money causes a shortage of money and liquidity. Bond sales cause real interest rates to rise; a higher real interest rate causes a reduction in real investment and real consumption. Eventually, aggregate equilibrium moves from point A to point B; both the real interest rate and real national income have risen. The ultimate increase in real national income, however, is not as great as it otherwise would have been; the multiplier effect has been lessened; $y_1 - y_e < y_3 - y_e$.

A Change in Taxes

An expansionary fiscal policy can also result from a decrease in (lump-sum) real taxes; unlike government expenditures, however, a change in real taxes affects aggregate expenditures only *indirectly*. A decrease in real taxes t_x (holding g and P constant) increases the real disposable income that households have to spend on consumer goods. A real tax decrease, therefore, increases aggregate spending, but not by the amount of the tax cut. Because lump-sum real tax changes affect aggregate expenditures indirectly through shifts in the consumption function, the $AE = (c_0 + i_0 + g_0) + by$ curve (see Chapter 6) will shift only by $(\Delta c_0) = b(\Delta t_x)$; if real lump-sum taxes fall by \$100, the consumption function will shift upward by b (\$100), where b is the marginal propensity to consume, MPC, and not by the full \$100. Hence, aggregate expenditures will only increase by $b(\Delta t_x)$; the tax multiplier equals $-b(1 - b)$, or $[-1/(1 - b)] + 1$, where the absolute value of $-b/(1 - b)$ is 1 less than $1/(1 - b)$. The tax multiplier is negative because increases in real taxes decrease real disposable income, while decreases in real taxes increase real disposable income.

Consider Figure 17.3, which shows the effect of a decrease in real taxes. The *is* curve shifts to the right by the value of the decrease in taxes multiplied by the tax multiplier. If the money supply remains constant, the *lm* curve is unaffected. Note that the new aggregate equilibrium position C exists at a higher level of real national income y_1 and at a higher real interest rate.

The level of national income has risen because the tax reduction has stimulated aggregate expenditures indirectly as a result of the upward shift in the consumption function. The resulting increase in real national income (initially to y_2) increases the real quantity of money demanded for transactions and precautionary purposes L_1/P. If the real money supply is fixed, a shortage of money or liquidity now exists at the higher level of real national income, y_2, and r_e (point B). The increased desire for liquidity is met by bond sales by the public; this increases the real rate of interest; and the higher real rate of interest induces some people to part with their real speculative balances L_2/P. A higher interest rate reduces c and i, so national income expands only to y_1, and not to y_2.

Note that an *increase* in taxes will shift the *is* curve to the left, by an amount equal to the reduction in taxes multiplied by the tax multiplier. The economy will contract, but not by the full amount of the tax-multiplier effect. A lower level of real national income resulting from a downward shift in the consumption function will reduce the quantity of real money demanded for L_1 purposes and create a surplus of liquidity at the original interest rate. The real interest rate will fall and induce an increase in real consumption and real investment expenditures. The result will be that the contraction in the economy due to the tax increase will be partially offset by a lower real interest rate.

Budget Surpluses and Budget Deficits

If the federal government spends an amount that is exactly matched by tax revenues, it has a balanced budget. If expenditures exceed tax receipts, it has a budget deficit; if expenditures are less than tax revenues, it has incurred a budget surplus.

A Decrease in Taxes Does Not Lead to a Full Tax-Multiplier Effect If the Money Supply Is Constant

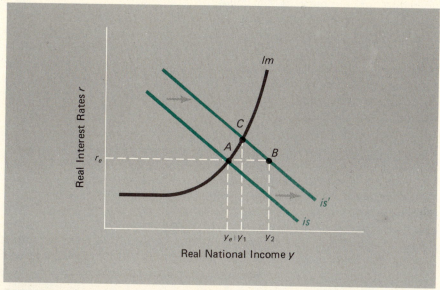

FIGURE 17.3. CROWDING OUT AND TAXES

A decrease in taxes (given g and P) shifts the *is* curve to the right, by a distance equal to the reduction in taxes times the tax multiplier. If the real interest rate doesn't rise, the new equilibrium position occurs at point B; the full tax-multiplier effect results and the change in income is $y_2 - y_e$.

A higher level of real national income increases the real demand for L_1 balances, however; because the money supply is constant, a shortage of liquidity exists at point B. Increased desire for real L_1 balances leads to the sale of bonds by the public and to higher real interest rates; higher real interest rates reduce consumption and investment and real national income falls below y_2. Eventually, some combination of a higher interest rate and a level of national income will satisfy equilibrium conditions in both the product market and the money market. In this figure, that combination exists at point C.

Suppose that the government budget is *initially* balanced and that the economy is in a recession. Keynesians suggest that fiscal policy should be expansionary. Real government expenditures should rise. But what about taxes? The previous discussion implies that if increased government expenditures are financed by increased taxes, the expansionary potential of the increased g will be *somewhat* reduced (not totally offset, because the tax-multiplier effect is less than the government expenditure multiplier effect). As a consequence, Keynesians believe that the fiscal policy prescription for fighting recession is a budget deficit (or a larger deficit, or a smaller surplus, as the case may be); some combination of increased g *and* decreased t_x will shift the *is* curve sufficiently to reduce unemployment. Of course, if the government already has a deficit, recessionary fiscal policy requires an even larger deficit.

Similarly, inflation can be countered by a fiscal policy that both reduces g and increases t_x. If the budget were balanced initially, a budget surplus would be required to fight inflation. If a surplus existed initially, then anti-inflationary fiscal policy would call for a larger surplus. If a large budget deficit existed initially, anti-inflationary fiscal policy would require a smaller deficit.

AUTOMATIC VERSUS DISCRETIONARY FISCAL POLICY

So far we have been analyzing **discretionary fiscal policy,** which is the deliberate and conscious attempt by Congress and the executive branch to create full employment and to stabilize the price level of the economy. Discretionary fiscal policy entails changes in tax *rates* and changes in transfer-payment programs, as well as changes in government expenditures for final goods and services. Moreover, all these fiscal policy changes require specific legislation.

Yet not all changes in taxes, transfer payments, and government spending constitute discretionary fiscal policy. Some changes may instead be built-in stabilizers in the economy. These kinds of changes are sometimes called **automatic**, or **nondiscretionary**, **fiscal policies.** There are several types of automatic fiscal policies that operate in the economy. When we refer to automatic fiscal policies, we are referring to **automatic stabilizers** which do *not* require new legislation on the part of Congress; Congress does not have to reenact such built-in stabilizers into law once they have been put in place. Remember, we are examining these in contrast to the discretionary fiscal policy changes that have been discussed up to now.

The main built-in stabilizers are a progressive (or proportional) income tax system, unemployment compensation, the corporate income tax, and other taxes. All these are automatically *countercyclical* in nature.

The Progressive Income Tax

The 1985 personal income tax schedule indicates that as taxable income increases, the marginal tax rate also goes up to a maximum of 50 percent. Or, as taxable income decreases, the marginal tax rate goes down. Think about this for the entire economy. If the nation is at full employment, personal income taxes may yield the government, say, $375 billion in revenues per year. But suppose that business activity starts to slow down. When this happens, workers are not allowed to put in as much overtime as before. Some workers are laid off, and some must change to jobs that pay less. Some workers and executives might take voluntary pay cuts. What happens to taxes when wages and salaries decrease? Taxes are still paid but at a lower rate than before, because the tax schedule is progressive. For example, assume that a single person who makes $30,000 taxable income a year is in the 45 percent marginal tax bracket. If the person's taxable income drops to only $20,000 a year and puts this person into, say, the 38 percent marginal tax bracket, average taxes paid as a percentage of income will also fall. As a result of these decreased taxes, disposable income—the amount remaining after taxes—falls by a smaller percentage than the fall in pretax income. Taking the progressive nature of our tax schedule into consideration, therefore, the individual feels less of a financial pinch during a recession than he or she would have felt if the tax system were not progressive. The *average* tax rate falls when less is earned.

Conversely, when the economy experiences a boom, people's incomes tend to rise. They can work more overtime and change to higher-paying jobs. However, *disposable* income does not go up as rapidly as total income because average tax rates are rising at the same time. The internal revenue service ends up taking a bigger bite. In turn, this means that consumption and aggregate demand do not increase by so much as total income increased. In this way, the progressive income tax system tends to lessen the impact of abrupt changes in economic activity.

Unemployment Compensation

Unemployment compensation works like the progressive income tax: It lessens the impact of changes in aggregate expenditures. Throughout the business cycle, automatic changes in unemployment compensation slow down and limit the size of changes in people's disposable incomes. When business activity drops, most laid-off workers become eligible for unemployment compensation from their state government. Their disposable incomes decline, but at a slower rate than national income is declining. During boom periods there is less unemployment, and consequently fewer unemployment compensation payments are made to the labor force (other things constant). Less purchasing power is being added to the economy because less unemployment compensation is paid.

The Stabilizing Impact   The impact of these two aspects of our taxing and transfer system is to lessen changes in disposable income, consumption, and the equilibrium level of national income. Previous chapters presented a model in which disposable income (take-home pay) is the main determinant of how much consumers desire to spend and, therefore, a key determinant of general economic activity. Hence, if disposable income is not allowed to fall so much as it would otherwise during a recession, the downturn will be moderated. On the other hand, if disposable income is not allowed to rise so rapidly as it would otherwise during a boom (expansion), the boom will create fewer inflationary problems. The progressive (or proportional) income tax and unemployment compensation therefore give automatic stabilization (in the sense of *lessening*, not eliminating, business cycles) to the economy. This notion is shown graphically in Figure 17.4. Real government spending is assumed to be constant. The real t_xt_x curve shows *net* taxes at different levels of national income; t_xt_x equals taxes *minus* transfers. t_xt_x is upward-sloping because taxes are directly related to national income (the tax structure is progressive); transfers are inversely related to national income, but tax receipts are greater than government transfer payments.

Fiscal Policy and a High-Employment Budget

Economists do not look only at the government's *actual* deficit or surplus when they measure *discretionary* fiscal policy. Generally, they do not think it is useful to look at current levels of taxes and expenditures or the current budget deficit or surplus that results for such purposes. Consider for a moment the following situation. Suppose the economy is nearly at full employment and the government budget is in balance. Then the economy falls into a recession, and incomes fall. Assume that neither government expenditures on goods and services nor its expenditures on the various transfer programs change. If tax *rates* are also held constant, government revenues will fall, because tax revenues depend on the level of national income. A formerly balanced budget shows a deficit, because g is now greater than t_x. The budget deficit should certainly not be regarded here as an active stimulating policy decision on the part of the government. It is a *result* of the recession and not a conscious counterrecessionary move. Therefore, to see whatever discretionary action is needed, economists make calculations to determine whether at *high employment* the present government budget *would be* in a deficit or a surplus position. The result is called the **high-employment government budget.** (In *our* example, the high-employment budget is balanced and the actual budget is in deficit.) It is defined as what the federal budget deficit or surplus would be *if the economy were operating at high employment, or at the natural rate of employment*, throughout the entire year. Figure 17.5 shows the results of such calculations for the years 1960 to 1982.

Economists, therefore, now refer to a *stimulating high-employment*

Automatic Stabilizers Generate Budget Surpluses When the Economy Expands and Budget Deficits When It Contracts

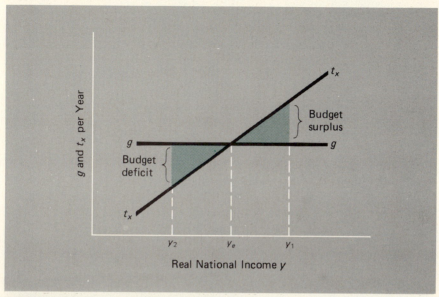

FIGURE 17.4. AUTOMATIC STABILIZERS

Assume that government real purchases of goods and services, g, and expenditures for various federal transfer programs remain constant no matter what the level of national income; they are fully autonomous and are represented by gg. Net real taxes t_x, on the other hand, vary directly with real national income because we assume a progressive tax structure. When national income increases from y_e to y_1, real taxes will exceed government expenditures, as shown by the vertical distance between gg and the tax line, $t_x t_x$. The government budget surplus, which occurs *automatically* during an expansion, can assist in offsetting possible inflationary pressures. Alternatively, when real national income falls from y_e to y_2, the resultant automatic budget deficit can help offset or alleviate the recession. Automatic stabilizers are therefore countercyclical by nature.

deficit or a *depressing high-employment* surplus. The actual budget deficit in 1980 may have been $60 billion, but the high-employment deficit was much less. Many economists therefore maintain that this deficit was stimulating but not so stimulating as it would first seem, because at a high rate, or the natural rate, of employment the deficit would have been much smaller. You should be aware that it is very difficult to define "high" or "natural" employment. Because frictional unemployment always exists, we are never at "full" employment. Other considerations,

The High-Employment Deficit Is Less Than the Actual Deficit

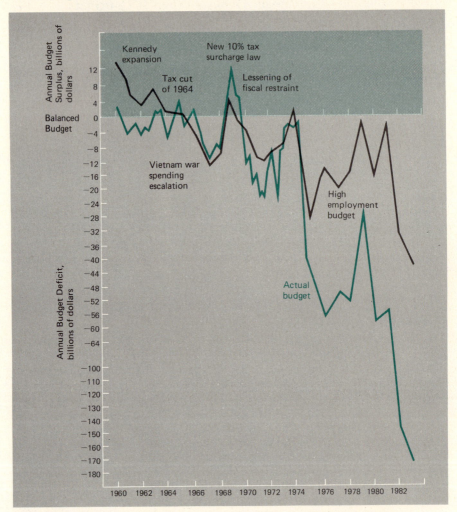

FIGURE 17.5. HIGH-EMPLOYMENT VERSUS ACTUAL BUDGET

This figure shows the actual budget surpluses and deficits of the U.S. government from 1960 to 1981. It also shows the high-employment budget surpluses and shortages. For the most part, the federal budget has been in deficit for the last two decades. The high-employment budget, however, has not been in deficit for so long a time. (From A. M. Okun and Nancy H. Teeters, "The Full-Employment Surplus Revisited," in *Brookings Papers on Economic Activity*, no. 1, Washington, D.C.: The Brookings Institution, 1970; Council of Economic Advisers, *Economic Report of the President*, Washington, D.C.: U.S. Government Printing Office, 1981; and *Survey of Current Business*, April 1982, August 1982, and August 1983.)

such as price-wage rigidities, also make the meaning and measurement of natural employment difficult. Through the years the rate of unemployment that has been identified with "natural" employment has gradually increased from 3–4 percent to 6–7 percent. Clearly, the amount of unemployment that we consider to represent natural unemployment determines the size of the high-employment deficit or surplus.

Another problem is that, through time, economic growth occurs. Consequently, the natural output level rises. If government outlays were constant, the rise in national income and tax receipts would cause the high-employment deficit to fall. Unless adjustments are made for this trend, it will appear that *discretionary* policy has been employed to reduce the high-employment deficit. Similar statements can be made about the impact of pure inflation.[1]

PROBLEMS WITH FISCAL POLICY

While the theory of fiscal policy seems easy enough, in practice fiscal policy is extremely difficult. In this section we consider such problems as time lags, choice of fiscal policy instruments, and the public choice problem.

Time Lags

In Chapter 16 we indicated that there are problems with time lags when monetary policy is used. Many of these same problems plague fiscal policy. Accurate economic data are always difficult to come by, and it takes time to obtain data—accurate or inaccurate. Inaccurate forecasting is just as troublesome for fiscal policy as for monetary policy. Different forecasting models use different estimates of the various fiscal instrument multipliers and have different estimates of the effect time lags. The problem of coordination between monetary policy and fiscal policy also remains. A model linking changes in fiscal policy instruments to changes in ultimate goals is necessary, and there seems to be just as much disagreement among economists over such a linkage as there was with monetary policy. Such difficulties would make discretionary fiscal policy a crude policy instrument even if there were no other problems. But there are other problems.

Political wrangling can make the action lag for the fiscal policy very long; this is a problem unique to fiscal policy because monetary policy

---

[1] See Alan S. Blinder and Robert Solow, "Analytical Foundations of Fiscal Policy," in Alan Blinder, ed., *The Economics of Public Finance* (Washington, D.C.: Brookings Institution, 1974) for a discussion of these and other problems with the high-employment budget.

can be put into effect virtually overnight. Although the following brief examination of the budgetary procedure is accurate, in no way does it indicate how politically difficult it is to implement fiscal policy.

It is important to realize that no single governmental body designs and implements fiscal policy.[2] The president, with the aid of the director of the Office of Management and Budget, the secretary of the Treasury, and the Council of Economic Advisers, designs, but only *recommends*, the desired mixture of G and T. It is Congress, with the aid of many committees,[3] that *enacts* fiscal policy. On the other hand, the president has veto power over congressional fiscal policy. An inherent organizational problem exists at the beginning: The power to enact fiscal policy does not rest with one institution. Disagreement as to the proper fiscal policy might (and usually does) emerge among members of the Congress, or between Congress and the president. While the procedure required for an ultimate solution is clearly spelled out in the U.S. Constitution, in practice it is sometimes a tedious and time-consuming process. During the process, hearings are called and recalled, and scores of expert witnesses testify—and disagree.

We return to considerations of political reality in a later section of this chapter when we analyze the public choice model of political behavior.

Choice of Fiscal Policy Instruments

Suppose it is agreed that fiscal policy measures are necessary. Which fiscal tools should be used? There are many possibilities. A change in government spending is possible, through either transfers T_r or government purchases of goods and services G. Even within these two major categories there are many possible choices. A change in taxes is possible with several options:

1. Permanent changes in personal taxes
2. Permanent changes in corporate taxes
3. *Temporary* changes in either 1 or 2
4. Changes in investment tax credits
5. Changes in employment subsidies

---

[2] Unlike monetary policy, which is the duty solely of the Fed. However, even though the Fed is an independent institution in theory, it too faces (and bends under) political pressure. It is still generally agreed that monetary policy is, at least theoretically, easier to implement.

[3] The House Ways and Means Committee, the Senate Finance Committee, the House and Senate budget committees—to name a few.

6. Changes in depreciation allowances

7. Any number of other possibilities

Changes in Government Purchases of Goods and Services   Changes in government expenditures are more efficient (they get more "bang for the buck," or they change national income more) than equal changes in transfers or in taxes, other things constant, because the multiplier for government purchases of goods and services is larger than the transfer multiplier or the tax multiplier. Disadvantages of changes in G are (1) the action time lag is long, because the legislature usually wrangles over the amount, the type, and the geographic location of the expenditure; (2) if the expenditure is to be made on a capital goods project, such as a highway or a public transportation system or a dam, the problem of timing arises. If started in a recession, should or could such a project be abandoned or delayed if inflation emerges before the project is completed? Are delays or reversals politically feasible?

Changes in Taxes   Because the tax multiplier is less than the government purchase of goods and services multiplier, changes in taxes are less efficient than changes in government expenditure (other things constant).

Apart from the multiplier issue, there are real problems with changing tax rates to stabilize the economy. For one thing, if tax changes are viewed as temporary, both the permanent income hypothesis (see Chapter 9) and the rational expectations hypothesis (see Chapter 15) predict that they will be ignored and therefore will be ineffective. For example, it is widely believed by economists that changes in the personal income taxes in 1964, 1968, and 1975 were designed to stabilize the economy, but in fact they merely led to offsetting changes in saving.

Permanent changes in taxes, furthermore, affect economic incentives. As the analysis of supply-side economics in Chapter 19 will show, it is believed that high marginal tax rates destroy incentives to work, save, invest, and take risks; if this is true, then increases in taxes to counter inflation can significantly reduce the natural growth rate if they are perceived as being permanent.

The Public Choice Problem

Fiscal policy would be difficult even if all the parties involved were sincere, dedicated people who had as a common goal the well-being of the nation. When one realizes that special interest groups exist and that politicians often have time horizons that reach no further than the next election, it becomes evident that there is more to fiscal policy than Figures 17.2 and 17.3 could ever hope to convey.

Recently the **public choice model** has gained wide acceptance among economists, and its proponents include James Buchanan and Gordon Tullock, both of the Public Choice School at James Mason University. (A bibliography of the Public Choice School literature can be found at the end of this chapter.) The essence of the public choice model is that policymakers act as if to maximize their own utility rather than the community's. As Tullock notes, "If bureaucrats are ordinary men, they will make most (not all) their decisions in terms of what benefits them, not society as a whole."[4]

More generally, the public choice model applies economic maximization principles to voters, candidates, elected officials, and policymakers. The implications of the public choice model are insightful and powerful. This relatively new model is being developed; some of its major tenets will be considered here.

1. Voters will be especially influenced by the state of the economy at election time. This means that policymakers, to the extent that they can actually influence the economy, will make policy changes so as to produce economic expansion right before elections. This allegedly generates a political business cycle, over which the economy peaks right before an election and bottoms out after the election. The empirical evidence of a political business cycle has not yet been firmly established.

2. Voters generally are more concerned with unemployment than with inflation, because the causes of inflation are allegedly more complex; therefore, inflation can be blamed more easily on others (i.e., on OPEC, unions, or the fastest-rising component of the CPI). This means that there will be an inflationary bias in democratic countries.

3. There is a bias toward deficits in the budgetary process. This is in part because an individual will act *collectively* with others only if he or she perceives that the benefit in doing so outweighs the cost of joining a group. Mancur Olson of the University of Maryland has argued that individuals with a common interest will not voluntarily combine and act to further their common interests *unless each individual has an incentive to participate in such collective action.*[5] More collective action will take place in small, homogeneous groups than among large, diverse groups. The existence of many **distributional coalitions** can be explained by this theory. For example, it is likely that special interest groups such as farmers, unions, and people who represent "the poor" will be able and willing to lobby for special

---

[4] Gordon Tullock, *The Vote Motive* (London: Institute of Economic Affairs, 1976).

[5] Mancur Olson, *The Rise and Decline of Nations* (New Haven, Conn.: Yale University Press, 1982).

privileges. They are small groups that tend to *gain very much individually* at the expense of many people who lose much collectively, *but lose very little individually* from the special privileges granted to others. Farm subsidies to farmers mean a lot of money to *specific farmers*, but cost very little to *specific nonfarmers* (in the form of higher food prices and taxes that must be paid to finance farm subsidies). Farmers have an incentive to organize and lobby for special privileges, and individual nonfarmers have little incentive to organize against privileges to farmers. (We return to Olson's model in Chapter 19.)

James Dale Davidson of the National Taxpayer's Union has described the incentive problem in Congress in the following way. Select 435 people (the number of congressional representatives) and give them each a credit card with a single, common account number. Further, provide that each person is responsible for 1/435 of the total monthly bill, but that each can keep what he or she buys. Clearly, such a scheme would promote much spending among the 435 people; each person has a tremendous incentive to spend more than 1/435 of the expected increase in total monthly spending. This example may well indicate what each of the 435 members of Congress faces; each member has an incentive to reduce spending that benefits *other* congresspersons' constituents, but to increase federal spending that benefits his or her *own* constituents.

Another problem is that the president—even if he or she *were* of a mind to reduce real government expenditures—usually is unable to use the veto power over legislation. Congress is able to add any amendment to a proposed bill; the amendment need not be germane to the originally proposed bill. If the president feels that a specific piece of legislation is really essential, Congress can add special-privilege legislation to the bill. The president, if he or she wants to exercise the power of the veto, *must veto the whole bill, not just the sections he or she disapproves of.*

Thus, a combination of powerful special interest groups that lobby for special privileges, and a congressional system that promotes government spending, have helped to expand the public sector at the expense of the private sector. In 1973, President Nixon indicated that he would impound funds appropriated by Congress that were to be spent on programs he disapproved of; in effect, even though Congress voted funds for specific projects, the president refused to *spend* the funds. Congress retaliated with the Budget Impoundment and Control Act of 1974, which reduced the power of the president to impound funds that have been authorized by Congress. Since then, deficits have increased, at least partially because of that 1974 Act; so has government spending as a percentage of gross national product.

In 1983, several economists and the editors of the *Wall Street Journal* called for a constitutional amendment to grant the president the power to reduce or to veto individual items in appropriations bills.[6] These people noted that many former presidents have asked for this power, and that the governors in virtually every state in the union have such power. This proposal implicitly suggests that a *balanced budget* is not the real issue, but government spending is. It is doubtful that a presidential line-item veto will soon be forthcoming.

Requiring a Balanced Budget

Because they believe that the democratic process is biased toward budget deficits, proponents of the public choice school (and some monetarists and some proponents of the rational expectations hypothesis) have called for a requirement that the federal budget be balanced.

Thirty-one state legislatures have petitioned for a convention to consider a balanced-budget amendment to the U.S. Constitution. According to Article V of the U.S. Constitution, Congress must call a constitutional convention when so petitioned by two-thirds of the states. It is not clear that a sufficient number of states (34) will petition, but even if they do not, a balanced-budget amendment to the Constitution is a possibility if congressional action is taken. Indeed, the U.S. Senate has recently passed one version.[7]

The following discussion centers around the economic implications of a balanced federal budget. It does not include the political aspects—not because they are unimportant, but because they are beyond the scope of this text. There are at least seven potential problems which an amendment requiring the federal budget to be balanced annually would create, most of which have already been examined.

1. The automatic stabilizer (nondiscretionary) aspect of fiscal policy would be impaired. In times of recession, tax receipts normally fall. A balanced budget would require that federal expenditures also fall or that tax rates be increased. Such a policy not only jeopardizes the automatic outlays for social welfare (outlays which many people deem desirable), but it runs counter to what Keynesian discretionary policy would require.
2. If a balanced-budget requirement hampered fiscal policy, a greater burden would be placed on monetary policy to stabilize the economy.

---

[6] See Henry Hazlitt, "Line-Item Leash on Runaway Spending," *Wall Street Journal*, September 9, 1983, and an editorial on the same page entitled "Take Your Pick."

[7] After the 1982 passage, one senator remarked that the Senate vote in favor of the amendment was like the desperate cry of a murderer saying, "Stop me before I kill again."

3. Congress could circumvent this requirement by placing more activities in the "off-budget" category; the illusion of solving the problem is worse than realizing that the problem exists. Off-budget expenditures are made mostly (about 85 percent) through the Federal Financing Bank (FFB), which is administered by the Treasury Department and whose assets grew from $600 million in 1974 (its first year of operation) to $106 *billion* in 1983; in 1984 it was $114.1 billion. Most of the remaining off-budget expenditures are made on the Strategic Petroleum Reserve. It's pretty clear that off-budget items provide a formidable path for circumventing "balanced" budgets.

4. Federal appropriations are not identical to actual outlays in their timing and effects, and technical problems would doubtless emerge.

5. Complications could arise for long-term projects; multiyear contracts could run into problems under a system of annual budget balancing.

6. Forecasting tax revenues and expenditure outlays is hardly a well-developed art. As a consequence, the budget process would be even more difficult than it already is.

7. Budgets can be balanced in two ways: by cutting expenditures or by raising taxes. A balanced-budget requirement might induce Congress to raise taxes, which might well interfere with economic incentives. Most state and local governments are forced to balance budgets, and their expenditures have grown more rapidly than have federal expenditures over the past 15 years. State and local governments have balanced their budgets by raising taxes.

POLICY CONTROVERSY
Is There a Public-Debt Burden?[8]

By August 1985 the public debt had reached $1.81 trillion. Technically, the U.S. public debt is defined as the total value of U.S. government debt outstanding. The public debt rises when the federal government runs a deficit and finances that deficit by borrowing. In 1984 the official deficit was $185.324 billion, and the general consensus is that the deficit will be *at least* $170 billion per year over the next five years. (Note, moreover, that we are not including off-budget spending in these deficits, which would add another $12 billion or so.) The federal deficit has increased from about 2.6 percent of national income to 6 percent in 1982 and 6.9 percent in 1983. By the end of 1984 it was about 6.3 percent.

Clearly, the federal debt is large, and in recent years it has been rising in real terms and as a percentage of national income. But does it impose a burden on the

---

[8] This section is the result of discussions with Mel Borland of the Economics Department, Western Kentucky University.

community? In order to answer that question, let's consider several hypothetical cases.

Case 1

Suppose the government taxes you $100 this year and then gives you $110 one year later. If the market interest rate is 10 percent, then you are neither better off nor worse off (assuming away the problem of your *personal* rate of time preference not being 10 percent). Or suppose the government (1) taxes you $100 this year or (2) borrows $100 from you this year and pays you $110 one year later, and then immediately taxes you $110. You would be indifferent to option 1 or 2 if the market rate of interest were 10 percent.

Continuing the second case, suppose the government (3) taxes you $100 right now or (4) borrows $100 from you now, pays you $110 one year later, and immediately borrows from you again and pays you $121 one year later. Then it taxes you $121. You are, yet again, neither worse off nor better off from option 3, or 4. *In other words, you will be indifferent between the government taxing you, or borrowing from you and taxing you in the future at a rate that incorporates market interest earnings.* Furthermore, if the government uses the money it obtains by taxing or borrowing and invests it and earns the market rate of interest, then nobody else need be affected either.

Although these examples are somewhat improbable, they contain some important insights. For one thing, note that in the second and third examples a public debt existed (it equaled $100 and then increased to $110 in the third example) and no burden was placed on anyone because the government invested the money at the market interest rate. Another insight

is that *refinancing* the public debt by borrowing again doesn't particularly change things as long as the government is earning the market interest rate and can tax people.

Of course, the government didn't accomplish anything in these examples either, so let's move on to Case 2.

Case 2

Suppose the government provides you with $110 worth of good y one year from now. Assume that it finances this transaction by (1) taxing you $100 right now, or (2) borrowing $100 from you and (a) repaying you with a $110 check one year from now that can only be used to purchase good y, or (b) taxing you $110 one year hence. In each case assume that the government buys a machine that costs $100, produces $110 worth of good y in one year, and then the machine falls apart and becomes worthless.

You again would be indifferent between being taxed $100 now or lending the government $100 and being taxed $110 one year later. The public debt has, temporarily, risen. Has there been a burden imposed on you (or society in general, if many people were involved in similar transactions)? That depends. Assume again that the market rate of interest is 10 percent per year.

If you had *wanted* to purchase $110 of good y one year from now, you not only would be indifferent to options 1 and 2, but your economic welfare would not have been altered and you would not be burdened—either by taxes *or* by the public debt.

But suppose you *would not voluntarily* have purchased $110 worth of good y one year from now? Suppose instead you would have preferred to purchase $110 of good *x*, or that you could have purchased the same quantity of good *y* at a lower price from the private sector. Note that even though you are still indifferent to options 1 and 2, each option imposes an equal burden on you.

Suppose, on the other hand, that you would have wanted to purchase $110 of good *y* one year from now, but that you would have been unable to do so without the government's intervention? This would be the case if, say, good *y* were a *true public good* (not merely a publicly provided good such as garbage collection), such as national defense or inoculation against social diseases, that would not otherwise be forthcoming from private markets in optimal quantities due to free-rider problems. In this case you would be *better off* as a result of being taxed or as a result of lending to the government and being taxed at a later date. Clearly, no burden is placed on society if the government increases the public debt and uses the money to cause the output of desired public goods to rise. This is true even if the government continually refinances the debt by borrowing every year.

In summary, if the government taxes you $100 right now and gives you $110 worth of good *y* one year hence, or if it sells you a bond for $100 right now and uses the money to provide you with $110 worth of good *y* one year hence and *then* taxes you $110, you would be indifferent between those two options. Furthermore, (1) you would be equally well off if you had purchased $110 worth of good *y* one year hence anyway; (2) you would be better off if good *y* were a public good that you had wanted to buy but couldn't; and (3) you would be worse off if good *y* were merely a publicly provided good that you

could have purchased from the private sector at a lower price or would not have purchased at all.

Case 3

Suppose the government gives *someone else* $110 one year from now. If it were to tax you $100 right now or sell you a $100 bond and pay you $110 one year hence and *then* tax you $110, you would be indifferent between the two options. Note that *you* would be equally burdened in each case, but that someone else would be better off; therefore, the *community* is not burdened. Because we "owe the debt to ourselves" the community is not burdened.

If, however, taxes and transfers destroy incentives for both you and the transfer recipient, then total employment and total output will, presumably, be lower. We have abstracted from incentive effects in the previous cases too. Incentive effects may well be present in the previous cases; they almost certainly are in this case, if taxes are related to income and are not lump-sum.[9]

Case 4

Suppose that the government finances its production of public goods, publicly provided goods, or domestic transfers by selling a $100 bond to a foreigner, paying her

---

[9] The notion that people are indifferent to, and that output is unaffected by, (1) a current lump-sum aggregate tax of $1, and (2) a current deficit of $1, is referred to as the Ricardian equivalence theorem and is named after David Ricardo who first presented it. See David Ricardo, "Funding System," in P. Sraffa, ed., *The Works and Correspondence of David Ricardo*, vol. 4 (Cambridge: Cambridge University Press, 1951); and Robert Barro, "Public Debt and Taxes," in *Money, Expectations and Business Cycles* (New York: Academic Press, 1981).

$110 one year hence. If the foreigner purchases the bond voluntarily, she does so because it offers her the highest return she can get, given risk. If risks are greater in her country, moreover, she even might be willing to accept an interest rate of return that is lower than the current domestic rate in her country. How would you like the government to finance the repayment to the foreigner? If you could earn a rate of return domestically on a private investment that is *higher* than 10 percent, you would prefer being taxed $110 one year from now to either (1) a tax of $100 right now, or (2) a $100 loan to the government that earns 10 percent accompanied by a future (one year hence) tax bill of $110.

In this case, even if we don't "owe the debt to ourselves," we would be better off if the government produced a public good. *If the government used the borrowed money to produce costly or undesired publicly provided goods, or to provide transfers to others*, we would be burdened, but less so than had we financed the debt internally. The foreigner would be better off, presumably because our government bond yields the highest rate of return she can get, adjusting for risk. Why not cash in on an economic system that is a safe haven for foreign investors?

Therefore, the general conclusion is that there seems to be no extra burden per se from a public debt when the other option is higher taxes. The real burden results when the government does not spend the money wisely. For this reason we should spend more time and effort trying to reduce wasteful government spending and less time worrying about how such spending is financed. A good allocation of our time would be to analyze the Grace Commission Report.

CHAPTER SUMMARY

1. Fiscal policy shifts the *is* curve. An increase in g, other things constant, causes the *is* curve to shift rightward, by the amount of the increase in government purchases times the government purchases multiplier. An increase in real taxes t_x causes the *is* curve to shift leftward, by the amount of the increase in taxes times the tax multiplier.

2. If changes in taxes or government expenditures leave the money supply unaltered, changes in g or t_x will not lead to a full multiplier effect. This is because as changes in g or t_x change national income, the quantity of money desired for real L_1 balances will change in the same direction. For example, if g rises, real national income will rise, which in turn causes real L_1 balances to rise, which leads to a shortage of liquidity. Real interest rates will rise, and therefore some real consumption or real investment will be crowded out.

3. Discretionary fiscal policy refers to the deliberate and conscious attempt by Congress to stabilize the economy. Automatic stabilizers,

on the other hand, are those that require no additional legislative action. Automatic stabilizers are countercyclical in nature and include a progressive income tax structure and unemployment compensation.

4. By themselves, automatic stabilizers will move the budget toward a deficit in a recession and toward a surplus in times of inflation. It follows, then, that the mere existence of a budget deficit or budget surplus does not indicate the use of *discretionary* fiscal policy. In order to measure what actual discretionary fiscal policy is and to what degree it might be necessary, economists calculate what the government budget position would be at a high-employment level of national income.

5. Implementing fiscal policy is difficult because of time lags, because there are many fiscal policy instruments from which policymakers can choose, because forecasting is difficult, and because accurate data are not available.

6. The public choice model applies economic maximization principles to voters, candidates, elected officials, bureaucrats, and policymakers. It assumes that policymakers will make most, but not all, of their decisions in terms of what benefits them, not society as a whole. If the public choice model is correct, the use of fiscal policy to stabilize the economy is thereby more difficult.

7. The public choice model predicts a political business cycle, an inflationary bias in government budget making, and budget deficits in democratic societies; and its advocates recommend a balanced-budget amendment to the Constitution.

8. If the alternative to a public debt is higher taxes, there doesn't seem to be any *special public debt* burden on society. Society is burdened by unwise government expenditures, regardless of whether they are financed by taxing or by borrowing (increasing the public debt).

9. Government expenditures can be financed (a) by taxing; (b) by borrowing from the public, from depository institutions, or from the Fed; and (c) by printing money. (See chapter appendix.)

10. If government expenditures are financed by taxing, or if they are financed by borrowing from the public or from depository institutions with zero excess reserves, then the monetary base, bank reserves, and the money supply will be unaltered. If such expenditures are financed by borrowing from depository institutions with positive excess reserves, then the monetary base and bank reserves are unaltered, but the money supply rises by the amount of borrowing. If government expenditures are financed by borrowing from the Fed or by printing money, then the monetary base and bank reserves will rise, and there will be a multiple expansion in the money supply. (See chapter appendix.)

GLOSSARY

automatic, or **nondiscretionary, fiscal policy**   Changes in the levels of federal government expenditures or net taxes that occur automatically without additional congressional action.

automatic stabilizers   Countercyclical changes in taxes and such transfers as unemployment compensation and welfare payments that occur without any new legislative action by Congress.

crowding-out effect   When increases in g or decreases in t_x occur, national income and the demand for real L_1 balances rise and cause real interest rates to rise and, therefore, some real consumption and some real investment will not be undertaken.

discretionary fiscal policy   The deliberate changing of levels of federal government expenditures, taxes, and borrowing to achieve national economic goals.

distributional coalitions   Associations such as cartels, unions, and cooperatives that are formed to gain special governmental privilege in order to redistribute money by taking small amounts from many people and giving large amounts to only a few.

high-employment government budget   What the federal government deficit or surplus would be if tax revenues commensurate with high employment, or the natural rate of employment, existed throughout the year.

public choice model   An economic theory that asserts that policymakers act so as to maximize their own utility rather than the community's; a theory that applies economic maximization principles to voters, candidates, elected officials, and policymakers.

QUESTIONS AND PROBLEMS FOR REVIEW

17.1   An increase in g, other things constant, is believed to cause the *is* curve to shift to the right. Why?

17.2   An increase in t_x, other things constant, is believed to cause the *is* curve to shift to the left. Why?

17.3   Suppose that government expenditures or taxes are changed, but the money supply is unaltered. What would be expected to happen to market rates of interest? Why?

17.4   What is meant by the description *discretionary fiscal policy?* What is meant by the description *automatic stabilizers?* Give examples of each.

17.5   Given the existence of automatic stabilizers, a recession is expected to generate a budget deficit and an expansion is expected to generate a budget surplus. If the generation of such budget deficits or surpluses are to be countercyclical in nature, what assumptions must be made about how consumers react to such budget deficits or surpluses?

17.6 How do economists distinguish between budget deficits or surpluses that occur automatically and those that are the result of discretionary policy?

17.7 Advocates of the public choice model recommend a balanced-budget amendment. For what reasons?

17.8 It may be argued that the effects of a higher public debt are the same as the effects of higher taxes. Why?

17.9 Government expenditures are financed by various methods. Distinguish between such methods with respect to their effects on the money supply. (See chapter appendix.)

17.10 If government expenditures are financed by borrowing from depository institutions, the money supply might rise by an amount that is less than that by which the money supply may rise if government expenditures are financed by borrowing from the Fed. For what reason might such a difference occur? (See chapter appendix.)

REFERENCES

S. Almon, "The Distributed Lag Between Capital Appropriations and Expenditures," *Econometrica*, vol. 33 (1965).

Robert J. Barro, "Public Debt and Taxes," in *Money, Expectations and Business Cycles* (New York: Academic Press, 1981).

———, *Macroeconomics* (New York: Wiley, 1984).

Alan S. Blinder, *Fiscal Policy in Theory and Practice* (Morriston, N.J.: General Learning Press, 1973).

Alan S. Blinder and Robert Solow, "Does Fiscal Policy Matter?" *Journal of Public Economics*, vol. 2 (1973).

———, "Analytic Foundations of Fiscal Policy," in Alan S. Blinder, ed., *The Economics of Public Finance* (Washington, D.C.: The Brookings Institution, 1974).

Karl Brunner and Allan H. Meltzer, "Money, Debt, and Economic Activity," *Journal of Political Economy*, vol. 80 (1972).

James M. Buchanan and Gordon Tullock, *The Calculus of Consent* (Ann Arbor, Mich.: University of Michigan Press, 1965).

K. M. Carlson and R. W. Spencer, "Crowding Out and Its Critics," *Review*, Federal Reserve Bank of St. Louis (December 1975).

Carl F. Christ, "A Simple Macroeconomic Model with a Government Budget Restraint," *Journal of Political Economy*, vol. 76 (1968).

Robert J. Gordon, *Macroeconomics*, 3d ed. (Boston: Little, Brown, 1984).

Henry Hazlitt, "Line Item Leash on Runaway Spending," *Wall Street Journal*, September 9, 1983, editorial page.

Roger L. Miller and Robert W. Pulsinelli, *Modern Money and Banking* (New York: McGraw-Hill, 1985).

Arthur M. Okun and Nancy H. Teeters, "The Full Employment Surplus Revisited," *Brookings Papers on Economic Activity*, no. 1 (Washington, D.C.: The Brookings Institution, 1970).

Mancur Olson, *The Rise and Decline of Nations* (New Haven, Conn.: Yale University Press, 1982).

David Ricardo, "Funding System," in P. Straffa, ed., *The Works and Correspondence of David Ricardo*, vol. 4 (Cambridge: Cambridge University Press, 1951).

James Tobin and W. Buiter, *Long Run Effects of Fiscal and Monetary Policy on Aggregate Demand*, Cowles Foundation Discussion Paper No. 384 (New Haven, Conn.: Yale University Press, 1974).

Gordon Tullock, *The Vote Motive* (London: Institute of Economic Affairs, 1976).

APPENDIX:
FINANCIAL ASPECTS OF FISCAL POLICY

Many economics texts treat monetary policy and fiscal policy as if they were separate policies, and many students think of monetary policy and fiscal policy as if they were inseparable. The truth is somewhere in between; in practice, these two policies are different but interrelated. While *pure* fiscal policy can be conducted without altering the money supply, this section examines the financial aspects of fiscal policy; it shows that the various methods of financing federal expenditures can affect such monetary variables as the monetary base, financial institution reserves, and the money stock.

Financing Federal Government Expenditures

Recall from Chapter 5 that there are three basic ways in which the federal government can finance its spending: taxing, borrowing, or printing money. This section analyzes these methods in greater detail. The impact of each of these three methods on the money supply, on the monetary base, and on bank reserves is described; the different effects of federal borrowing from the public, from depository institutions, and from the Fed are also examined.

We further analyze the different impact on the economy of financing government spending (through taxing, borrowing, or printing money) by examining the budget constraints on both the public and the federal government.

Taxing

One way to finance government expenditures is to tax the public. As taxes are collected, they are deposited in U.S. Treasury accounts at banks throughout the country; these accounts are referred to as *tax and loan accounts:* taxes are paid when privately owned demand deposits are reduced and Treasury accounts are increased by the same amount.

At this stage the money supply has fallen by the amount of the tax revenue collected because the money supply (by definition) does not include U.S. Treasury deposits. All checks written by the U.S. Treasury are written against its accounts at Federal Reserve banks. As its balances at the Fed are drawn down, the Treasury shifts funds from commercial banks to the Federal Reserve. When the Treasury shifts these funds, total bank reserves and monetary base fall by the amount of the funds shifted.

But when the Treasury spends these tax revenues by writing checks on its accounts at Federal Reserve banks, the public receives these checks. The checks are then deposited in depository institutions which in turn send the checks to the Fed for collection. When this happens, the money supply and the monetary base increase, and bank reserves increase by the amount spent by the Treasury.

The *net* effect of these transactions is that neither the money supply nor bank reserves have been altered. If the government taxes people and then spends those tax dollars, the money supply has not changed.

The Impact of Taxation Financing on the Budget Constraints of the Public and the Federal Government

Most students leave their principles of economics courses with the notion that individuals and businesses face budget constraints. No individual or business can spend without limit; the spending of both the household and the business sectors is limited by their earnings and by their ability to borrow.

It turns out that even the federal government has a budget constraint, although it has options not available (legally, at least) to the public: the federal government can print money and it can tax. In the following analysis we assume that state and local government budgets are constant and balanced. Let us look first at the budget constraints of households and businesses.

The Public's Budget Constraint   The private nonbank budget constraint is

$$\Delta L = y_d - C - \Delta Z \qquad (A.17.1)$$

WHERE ΔL = change in *desired* money balances

  y_d = disposable income; national income minus taxes plus government transfers

  C = desired expenditures by households on consumer goods and services

  ΔZ = change in net lending to the federal government (net purchases of government securities by the public)

Equation A.17.1 represents the private sector's budget constraint. It implies that (given y_d) if the public as a whole wants to increase its money balances, it must either spend less (save more) or own fewer government securities. Conversely (given y_d), if the public as a whole wants to decrease its total money balances, it can increase its consumption expenditures or its ownership of government securities.

Equation A.17.1 can be rewritten as

$$\Delta L + \Delta Z = y_d - C = S \qquad (A.17.2)$$

where S represents saving.

Equation A.17.2 indicates that the community saves by purchasing government securities or by voluntarily holding more money; annual saving by the public leads to net lending to government *or* to increased cash balances.

The Federal Government's Budget Constraint   The federal government's budget constraint can be written as

$$E = \Delta B + T + \Delta A \qquad \text{(A.17.3)}$$

WHERE E = government spending for goods and services G, *and for transfer payments Tr; E = G + Tr*

ΔB = change in the monetary base; B consists of printed money, coins, and depository institution reserves

T = tax receipts

ΔA = change in net sales or bonds to the private sector by the Treasury *and* the Fed

Note that a government budget constraint *does* exist.
Equation A.17.3 can be rewritten as

$$\Delta B + \Delta A = E - T \qquad \text{(A.17.4)}$$

which implies that government deficits must be financed by increases in B or A. Congress and the president decide the size of the deficit through their appropriations and taxation decisions, and the Fed determines how much of the deficit is financed by borrowing from the public and by increasing the monetary base.

Budget Constraints and Financing Government Expenditures by Taxing   Suppose that the government's budget is at first balanced and that it then finances increased government expenditures of, say, $1 billion by increasing taxes by that amount. Chapter 6 indicated that a balanced budget is slightly expansionary because the *net* effect of equal increases in G and T is a rightward shift in the AE curve; national income rises by $1 billion if G and T rise by $1 billion.

Analysis of the probable impact of this balanced-budget effect on the public's and the federal government's budget constraints suggests otherwise. Rewriting equation A.17.4 yields

$$\Delta B = E - T - \Delta A \qquad \text{(A.17.5)}$$

A balanced budget implies that $E - T = 0$ and that $\Delta A = 0$; therefore $\Delta B = 0$; the monetary base (high-powered money) is unaltered. This is consistent with a conclusion that we reached earlier in this chapter; an increase in government expenditures financed by an equal increase in taxes leaves the money supply unchanged.

Consider now what happens in the public's budget constraint. The increase in income resulting from the net increase in aggregate expen-

The Balanced-Budget Multiplier Is Less Than 1
If the Money Supply Is Unaltered

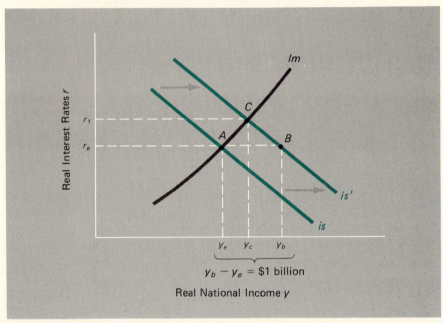

FIGURE 17.6. BALANCED-BUDGET CROWDING OUT

These curves indicate the net impact on the economy if increased real government expenditures are financed by an equal increase in real taxes, if M/P and P
are constant. A $1 billion increase in g and t shifts the *is* curve rightward by $1
billion (equal to $B - A$); aggregate expenditures are higher at every rate of real
interest. Because the real money supply is not changed, however, the *lm* curve
does not shift. As a result, the net change is a movement from A to C, and not
from A to B; real national income rises by less than $1 billion.

ditures due to a $1 billion increase in g and t means the *is* curve will
shift to the right by $1 billion; real national income will rise by $1 billion
if the real interest rate doesn't change. This is indicated in Figure 17.6.
Because $y_d - C = 0$ and $\Delta Z = 0$, total L/P remains constant in equation
A.17.2. But the level of y has increased by $1 billion. So desired L_1/P
balances rise and the *composition* of L changes.

Considering the *overall* results, we see that the money supply has
remained constant but that the community *wants* to hold more real
money balances because of the higher real national income level; that
is, the desire for L_1/P balances increases. This means that at the higher

level of real national income and the given real rate of interest (point *B* in Figure 17.6) a shortage of money exists. This will cause the real interest rate to rise, which in turn causes real investment and (perhaps) real consumption to fall. This process continues until some combination of a higher interest rate and a lower level of real national income than y_b (it is point *C* in Figure 17.6) reduces the quantity demanded of money sufficiently to make the public again want to hold the unchanged money supply. *The public's budget constraint must be consistent with the government's budget constraint;* if a government activity leaves the money supply constant but changes the demand for money, some combination of national income change and interest rate change must be forthcoming to restore equilibrium in the money market.

The conclusion is that if a $1 billion increase in government expenditures is financed by a $1 billion increase in taxes, national income will rise by less than $1 billion because the interest rate will rise.

Borrowing

Increased federal government expenditures can also be financed by borrowing from the nonbank public, from depository institutions, or from the Fed. Each is discussed in turn below.

Borrowing from the Public   The U.S. Treasury borrows from the (nonbank) public by selling bonds which the public purchases from its saving; the public will buy these bonds voluntarily if the terms (interest rates or bond prices) are attractive. By paying with a check drawn on a depository institution, the public surrenders money for a bond, which is nonmoney. As a result, the money supply, depository institution reserves, and the monetary base fall by the value of the bond sold. When the government spends these funds, however, and the public deposits its checks in depository institutions, the money supply, bank reserves, and the monetary base again rise. The *net* result (as was true in the case of increasing taxes) is that the money supply, bank reserves, and the monetary supply are not altered.

Assume that the $1 billion increase in government expenditures is financed by the Treasury borrowing $1 billion from the public. The preceding analysis indicated that the money supply remains constant. So do the amounts in equation A.17.3, the federal government's budget constraint. Because $\Delta E = \Delta A$, $\Delta B = \Delta T = 0$; put another way, increased government expenditures are financed totally by increased net sales of bonds to the private sector; therefore, taxes and high-powered money are unaltered.

On the other hand, analysis of equation A.17.1, the public's budget constraint, reveals that the public will desire to hold *more* real money balances. As Figure 17.7 shows, assuming a marginal propensity to con-

The Financial Effects of Government Expenditures Dampen
the Ultimate Change in National Income

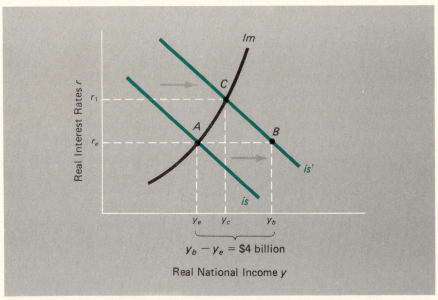

FIGURE 17.7. AN INCOMPLETE GOVERNMENT-EXPENDITURE MULTIPLIER

This figure indicates that an increase in g financed by an equal increase in borrowing, A, does not cause a full multiplier effect because of the financial impact of fiscal policy. A $1 billion increase in g and A (given a marginal propensity to consume of 0.75) causes real national income to rise to y_c and not y_b, because some private real investment and real consumption is crowded out as the real interest rate rises from r_e to r_1; real national income rises by less than $4 billion.

sume of 0.75, the increase in real government expenditures of $1 billion shifts the *is* curve rightward by $4 billion; national income would rise by $4 billion *if the interest rate were unaltered*. At point B, the combination of a higher level of real national income and the same real interest rate r_e, a shortage of liquidity exists because the higher level of national income increases the amount desired for real L_1 balances.

Moreover, before the public voluntarily will increase its Z to accommodate the government's increase in A (note that $\Delta A = \Delta Z$ of necessity), the public must be offered a higher real interest rate to part with its real L_2 balances. At point A the public was in equilibrium; an increase in

Treasury bond sales requires an increase in Z, so somehow the public must be induced to hold less money and more government bonds.

In short, the real interest rate will rise, real net investment and real consumption will fall, and real national income will fall—below y_b in Figure 17.7. This process will continue until some combination of a higher real interest rate and higher level of real national income restores equilibrium in the money market. That combination is indicated by point C in Figure 17.7. The conclusion is that once we take into account the impact on financial markets of financing increased government spending by borrowing from the public, we realize that a full government expenditure multiplier effect will not result. In our example, national income will rise by *less* than $4 billion.

Borrowing from Depository Institutions　The U.S. Treasury can borrow from depository institutions by selling them securities. As with the nonbank public, depository institutions purchase bonds and securities voluntarily if "the price is right."

The ultimate effect of Treasury borrowing from depository institutions depends on whether excess reserves do or do not exist in the banking sector.

Zero Excess Reserves　Consider first the case in which depository institutions have zero excess reserves. In such a situation, these institutions cannot purchase Treasury securities unless they sell other assets.[10] Why not? Because when a depository institution purchases a government security from the Treasury, it creates a comparably valued demand deposit for the Treasury. The depository institution must hold additional reserves against this increased Treasury demand deposit account. Given the assumption of initial zero excess reserves, excess reserves would now be negative. Therefore, depository institutions would have to reduce the public's demand deposits by selling assets equal in value to the public. Thus, the money supply (which again includes only the nonbank *public's* demand deposits) initially falls. However, as in the previous case when the Treasury spends its demand deposits, the money supply increases. The net result, again, is that the money supply, depository institution reserves, and the monetary base are unaltered.

Positive Excess Reserves　Lest you think that the money supply is never altered by fiscal policy, consider the case in which the U.S. Treasury borrows from depository institutions that have excess reserves. Assume in this example that excess reserves exceed the value of Treasury

---

[10] At least they aren't supposed to. On occasion, they do, however; they borrow the needed reserves in the Eurodollar market or from the Fed itself.

securities sales. That is, some excess reserves still exist after the depository institutions purchase Treasury securities. What happens now? This situation does not require that depository institutions sell assets to reduce the public's total demand deposits. In this case depository institutions will purchase the Treasury securities and create demand deposits for the Treasury; the Treasury will then shift its deposits to the Fed, and this allows the Treasury to draw down on its checking account with the Fed in order to finance the increased federal government expenditures.

The net result is that the money supply increases, but only by the amount of the government expenditures financed by bond sales to the depository institutions. Note, however, that total bank reserves and the monetary base are not affected. Hence, no multiple deposit expansion in the money supply occurs.

Borrowing from the Fed If the Treasury were to sell securities to the Fed, it would receive demand deposits upon which it could write checks to finance government expenditures. In exchange, the Fed holds interest-earning assets (Treasury securities) that are liabilities to the Treasury. Note, however, that when the Treasury has spent these funds, the public has received checks that it would then deposit in depository institutions; the latter would experience an equal increase in total reserves and a somewhat smaller increase in excess reserves. As a result, the money supply could expand still further by some multiple of the original debt sale. If you think this sounds like the public is getting something for nothing, you may have a point. Still, remember that the public also has increased liabilities because the Treasury's liabilities are the public's liabilities. To the extent that this process is inflationary, moreover, the public also pays for the asset (money) with a "hidden tax."

Printing Money

The U.S. Treasury is empowered to print money, but printing money is a rather crude form of financing government expenditures. It is reminiscent of the days when kings and queens called in gold and silver coins, melted them down, and either minted coins with higher face values or alloyed them with cheaper metals. Today the government prefers to debase the currency in more subtle ways. The link between open-market operations and borrowing from the Fed is less obvious as a cause of inflation than is the printing of money. In some countries where governments apparently don't have to worry about such subtle distinctions, printing money has often been an inexpensive and politically viable method of financing government expenditures.

If the U.S. Treasury decided to print money to finance government expenditures, the process would simply require it to print the money, deposit the money in its checking account with the Fed, and write checks on the account. This process is similar to the situation in which the Treasury sells bonds to the Fed: a multiple expansion of the money supply occurs. The only difference is that in the first case the Fed receives an interest-earning security as an asset; but here the Fed receives newly printed (and non–interest-earning) currency. In light of the fact that at year's end the Fed turns over most of (over $12 billion per year in recent years) its net earnings to the Treasury, this distinction is more apparent than real.[11]

We can show how printing money (or Treasury bond sales to the Fed) affects the budget constraints of the federal government and the public, and how, therefore, the economy is affected. Consider the case in which a $1 billion increase in government expenditures is financed by the Treasury printing $1 billion of new money, or by the Treasury selling $1 billion worth of bonds to the Fed. The monetary base will rise by $1 billion; $\Delta B = \Delta E = \$1$ billion, because $\Delta T_x = \Delta A = 0$, according to equation A17.3. This $1 billion increase in the monetary base will cause a multiple expansion in the money supply. Other things constant, the public is no longer in equilibrium because the real money supply has increased; a surplus of liquidity exists. Therefore, real national income will rise as the community starts spending its excess money balances. Equation A17.1 indicates that the public will desire to hold more money balances if $(y_d - C)$ rises (because $\Delta Z = \Delta A = 0$).

Two forces are at work here. First, total expenditures rise because of the increase in government expenditures and because of the increase in private spending that results from the increase in the money supply. Second, a higher level of national income will increase the amount of money desired for transactions and precautionary purposes, L_1. While it is safe to predict that national income will rise, the effect on the interest rate is uncertain because we get our increase in both the supply of *and* the demand for money.

This point in the preceding paragraph is demonstrated by the *is-lm* framework in Figure 17.8. Note that the *lm* curve shifts to the right by the change in the money base times the money multiplier. A $1 billion increase in real government expenditures shifts the *is* curve rightward by $4 billion, assuming a marginal propensity to consume of 0.75.

In Figure 17.8, the *lm* curve is shifted by just enough to leave the interest rate unaltered—at r_e. Consequently, a full government expenditure multiplier effect will be obtained. You can demonstrate to yourself that if a $1 billion increase in the monetary base caused the *lm* curve to shift by less than it did in Figure 17.8 (because of a lower money mul-

---

[11] For those of you who worry about such things, the Fed's newly acquired assets—paper currency— are the U.S. Treasury's liabilities and therefore are ultimately the *public's* liabilities. Moreover, the resulting inflation will assure that the public does not get something for nothing.

If the Money Supply Is Increased with an Increase in Government Expenditures, a Full Multiplier Effect Can Occur

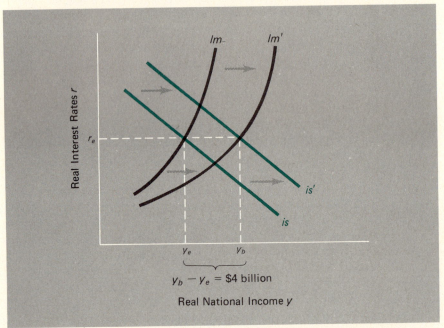

FIGURE 17.8. COORDINATING MONETARY POLICY AND FISCAL POLICY

The *is* curve shifts from *is* to *is'* by $4 billion if *g* increases by $1 billion and the marginal propensity to consume is 0.75. In this example, we shifted the *lm* to the right (due to an increase in the monetary base, which leads to a multiple expansion in the money supply) by exactly enough to generate a new equilibrium at which real national income is $4 billion higher and the real interest rate is unchanged. If the *lm* curve had shifted rightward by *less* than the amount indicated here, the equilibrium real interest rate would be higher and the equilibrium level of real national income would be less than y_b.

tiplier due to higher reserve requirements or a higher desired ratio of currency to demand deposits, for example), then the equilibrium real interest rate would be higher than r_e, and the equilibrium level of real national income would be less than y_b.

Table 17.1 summarizes how each method of financing government expenditures affects the money supply, depository institution reserves, and the monetary base.

TABLE 17.1. METHODS OF FINANCING GOVERNMENT EXPENDITURES

Method of Financing	Monetary Base and Bank Reserves Increased?	Money Supply Increased?
Taxing	No	No
Borrowing from public	No	No
Borrowing from depository institutions with		
Zero excess reserves	No	No
Positive excess reserves	No	Yes, by the amount of borrowing
Borrowing from the Fed	Yes	Multiple expansion
Printing money	Yes	Multiple expansion

18

THE MONETARIST-NONMONETARIST DEBATE

I n this chapter we analyze the debate between monetarists and non-monetarists. The tools required to understand this debate were presented in earlier chapters, and analysis of this debate is a convenient way to show how those tools are interrelated. But this is not the only reason for examining the debate. The monetarist-nonmonetarist debate sets the stage for the most important macroeconomic issue of the 1980s: Should monetary policy and fiscal policy be conducted by rules or at the discretion of policymakers?

Specifically, this chapter will discuss the initial stage of the monetarist-nonmonetarist debate, the current state of the debate, and the rules-versus-discretion issue.

THE INITIAL STAGE OF THE DEBATE

Implications of the Classical Model

Recall that according to the classical economists there are two mechanisms in private enterprise economies that assure full employment: real wage rate flexibility and interest rate flexibility. Flexible wage rates imply that labor surpluses and labor shortages will be eliminated by decreases and increases, respectively, in the nominal and the real wage rates. Also, because money is only a medium of exchange in that model, excess real money balances are spent (not hoarded), and the income velocity of money (at least in the long run) is usually at its maximum.

Assume a decrease in community consumption (an increase in community saving). Such a shift leads to a lower interest rate and to higher investment expenditures. A temporary surplus of labor ensues in the consumer-goods industry, but a temporary shortage of labor develops in the capital-goods industry. Eventually labor is reallocated, and the composition of national output changes; but full employment prevails. Note, then, how real interest rate flexibility and real price-wage flexibility are the mechanisms that drive the economy back to a full-employment equilibrium; such mechanisms seem to be able to absorb shocks, and they imply that a private enterprise economy is inherently stable.

Implications of the Keynesian Model

Keynes, however, developed the liquidity-preference function, which indicated that the amount of money that the community wanted to hold varied inversely with the interest rate[1] (or that velocity varied directly

---

[1] As well as directly with the level of real national income.

with the interest rate). The demand for money was believed to be especially interest rate–elastic during times of recession or depression, when the market interest rate was considerably below the natural interest rate. Keynes also maintained that the nominal wage rate was inflexible downward. The combination of a high interest rate elasticity of demand for money and downwardly inflexible wage rates proved to be lethal to the stability of private enterprise economies, according to Keynes. As if this combination were not enough, Keynes maintained that both household consumption expenditures and business investment expenditures were insensitive to changes in the interest rate.

Consider Figure 18.1, which indicates a decrease in autonomous aggregate expenditures in the *is-lm* framework. A decrease in autonomous household consumption (or what is more likely in the Keynesian model, a reduction in autonomous business investment) shifts a steep *is* curve—which is interest rate–inelastic—leftward. Because the demand for money is assumed to be highly interest-elastic, the *lm* curve is quite flat. The result is that (1) national income falls greatly (the multiplier effect is large), (2) the interest rate falls only slightly, and (3) the reduction in the interest rate induces only a negligible movement down the new *is* curve (aggregate expenditures are insensitive to a reduction in the interest rate).

Even if wage rates were free to fall, Keynes maintained, the economy would not return to full employment either by way of (1) the *direct* wage rate effect (market clearing), because general money wage rate reductions also lead to general price level reductions, and *real* wage rates won't fall; or (2) the *indirect* wage rate effect, which lowers the price level and increases the real money supply. The indirect effect (the Keynes effect) shifts the *lm* curve rightward, but the existence of a liquidity trap means that the community will merely *hold* more excess money balances (created by a reduction in L_1) to meet its increased speculative demand (an increase in L_2 demand) at a lower interest rate.

An Inherently Unstable Economy?   The Keynesian-classical comparison enables us to gain some insight into what determines whether or not a private enterprise economy is inherently stable or inherently unstable. In general, such an economy will be *un*stable if (1) the *lm* curve is relatively flat; that is, there is a high interest rate elasticity of demand for money; (2) the *is* curve is steep; that is, consumption expenditures and investment expenditures are insensitive to the interest rate; and (3) wage rates and prices are sticky.

If these three conditions exist, then such *exogenous* shocks as war, changes in exports relative to imports, and changes in the money supply will lead to large multiplier effects. Moreover, such *endogenous* shocks as changes in the rate of time preference for consumption, changes in

An Adverse Demand Shock Reduces National Income Greatly, Given Keynesian Assumptions

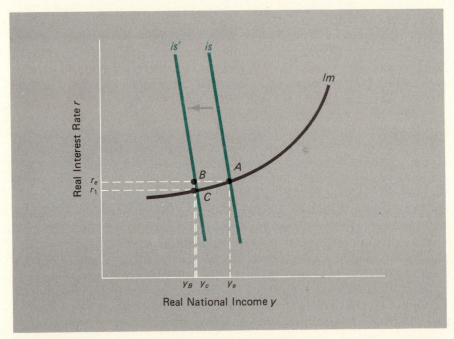

FIGURE 18.1. AN ADVERSE DEMAND SHOCK

A reduction in real autonomous aggregate household consumption expenditures shifts the *is* curve leftward and would cause the economy to move to point *B* if the real interest rate remains constant; income would fall to y_B. But the real interest rate falls slightly and induces a slight movement down the *is* curve. Nearly a full multiplier effect results from this endogenous demand shock; the new equilibrium position is found at point *C*. A shock causes real national income to fall greatly; by implication, the economy is inherently unstable.

the productivity of capital, and changes in "confidence" will also have large multiplier effects.

If the *lm* curve is relatively flat, then shocks that shift the *is* curve will not have much of an impact on the real interest rate. For example, suppose that the economy is shocked so that autonomous expenditures fall, causing the *is* curve to shift leftward. As real national income falls, so will the demand for real L_1 balances, and an excess of real money balances now exists at the original real interest rate. The real interest rate falls, but this leads to an increase in real L_2 balances, so the real interest rate reduction is somewhat cushioned; *the interest rate won't fall by so much as it would have had there been no liquidity preference.*

Continuing this analysis, if the *is* curve is steep, then changes in the real rate of interest will have to be very large before offsetting (increased) expenditures will be made. For example, if the *is* curve shifts leftward due to a reduction in real autonomous household consumption (an increase in household real saving), the real interest rate will fall (incompletely, as noted above), but real net investment is not sensitive enough to such a change (i.e., *is* is steep) to pick up the slack. Similarly, if the domestic economy's real exports fall relative to its real imports, the *is* curve will shift leftward, but an even lower real interest rate is necessary to induce the offsetting increases in real consumption expenditures and real investment expenditures required to keep the economy at full employment. However, if the *lm* curve is relatively flat, further reductions in the interest rate are difficult.

Finally, even if the *is* curve is steep and the *lm* curve is relatively flat, if prices and wages are flexible, then full employment can be restored by the Keynes effect and by the Pigou effect. As you will recall, as the price level falls, (1) the *real* (given the nominal) supply of money rises and the *lm* curve shifts rightward, because of the Keynes effect, and (2) the real value (purchasing power) of currency, and therefore wealth, rises without any offset anywhere else in the economy; consequently the *is* curve shifts rightward because of the Pigou effect. Continuing our example, then, the original shock—a leftward shift in the *is* curve—will cause real national income to fall and unemployment to rise. If wage rates are flexible, then they will fall and cause the price level to fall. In turn, a lower price level shifts the *lm* curve downward and the *is* curve rightward, until full employment is again restored. The conclusion is that price-wage flexibility is stabilizing and, therefore, that price-wage *in*flexibility means that the economy is less stable.

Policy Implications   To Keynes and his followers, the policy implications of his model were obvious. The economy is unstable and, therefore, stabilization policy is necessary. Furthermore, the very factors that make the economy unstable—a flat *lm* curve and a steep *is* curve—make fiscal policy preferable to monetary policy.

Consider monetary policy first. Figure 18.2 shows a typical (to the Keynesians) *is-lm* situation for a private enterprise economy. The economy is in a relatively flat range of the *lm* curve, and equilibrium exists at point *A*. Suppose the Fed pursues an expansionary monetary policy by purchasing government securities in its open-market operations. Because the price level is assumed to be constant, this causes the *lm* curve to shift rightward; but, because the *lm* curve is relatively flat, the real interest rate won't fall by very much. In effect, the Fed purchases secu-

Monetary Policy Is Ineffective If the *lm* Curve Is Relatively Flat and the *is* Curve Is Steep

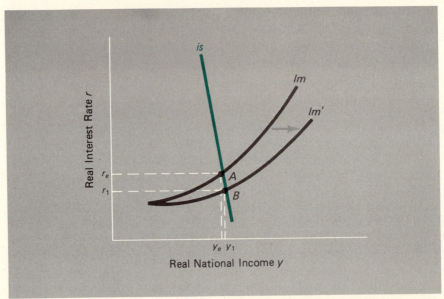

FIGURE 18.2. MONETARY POLICY IN AN UNSTABLE ECONOMY

Start in an unemployment equilibrium position at point A. The real money supply rises, causing the *lm* curve to shift rightward. Most of the increased real money supply is held in L_2 balances because the real interest rate is already relatively low. The interest rate, therefore, falls only slightly. Because the *is* curve is steep, a slight reduction in the real interest rate causes only a negligible increase in real net investment. The increase in real national income is small, from y_e to y_1; monetary policy is ineffective under such conditions.

rities from the public and from depository institutions which are only too happy to sell "risky"[2] bonds at interest rates that are already low. The public holds the increased real money supply and banks hold excess reserves. The increased real money supply, therefore, has only a small impact on the real interest rate. Furthermore, because the *is* curve is very steep the small reduction in the real interest rate has little or no impact on household purchases of durable goods or on business investment expenditures.

---

[2] Bonds are risky because interest rates are below their normal levels. The probability is high that interest rates will rise, bond prices will fall, and holders of bonds will suffer capital losses.

The net result is that the change in real national income resulting from an expansionary monetary policy is very slight, and equal to $y_1 - y_e$. Stated in the Fisher equation-of-exchange mode, an increase in the real money supply is mostly offset by a decrease in the income velocity of money. Thus, because the demand for money is inversely related to the real interest rate, velocity moves perversely. (If the money supply were reduced in order to pursue a contractionary monetary policy to fight inflation, the interest rate would rise and velocity would rise—thereby partially offsetting the effects of a reduction in the money supply.) In general, then, Keynes believed that monetary policy was virtually useless in times of depression and difficult to conduct in periods of inflation.

Now consider Figure 18.3. The *is* curve is again steep and the *lm* curve is again relatively flat; the initial equilibrium position is at point *A*; the equilibrium level of real national income is relatively low and the unemployment rate is relatively high. An expansionary fiscal policy requires some combination of increased government expenditures and reduced taxes.[3] The *is* curve shifts rightward to *is'*.

Note that a fiscal policy that causes a rightward *is* shift is extremely expansionary, precisely because the *lm* curve is relatively flat and the *is* curve is steep. In other words, a relatively flat *lm* curve means that an expansionary fiscal policy will not cause real interest rates to rise by very much; a higher real income level requires higher real L_1 balances, which are coaxed out of real L_2 balances by a slight rise in the real interest rate. Furthermore, a steep *is* curve means that the slight rise in the real interest rate won't crowd out very much private expenditure. Fiscal policy actions, therefore, are very effective and cause real national income to rise a great deal, by $y_1 - y_e$ in Figure 18.3; and nearly a full multiplier effect is achieved.[4]

Early Keynesians, then, believed that a private enterprise economy is inherently unstable and that stabilization policies are necessary. The stabilization policy that they believed would do the job best was fiscal policy.

The Monetarist Counterrevolution

Monetarism developed as a counterrevolution to the Keynesian revolution.[5] In particular, it was a reaction to the following excessive claims

---

[3] We ignore here the important question concerning how such expenditures are financed. We also ignore the important question regarding *on what* the expenditures are made.

[4] A *full* multiplier effect would occur only in the liquidity trap, or Keynesian range, of the *lm* curve.

[5] See Harry G. Johnson, "The Keynesian Revolution and the Monetarist Counter-Revolution," *American Economic Review*, vol. 61 (May 1971), pp. 1–14.

Fiscal Policy Is Very Effective When the *lm* Curve Is Relatively Flat and the *is* Curve Is Steep

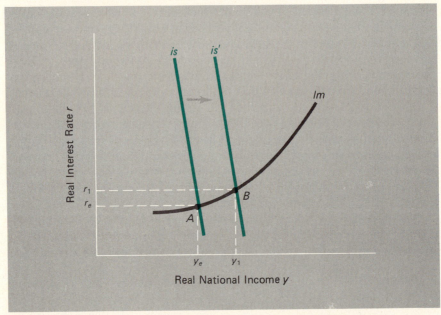

FIGURE 18.3. FISCAL POLICY IN AN UNSTABLE ECONOMY

An expansionary fiscal policy shifts the *is* curve rightward to *is'*. Because the *lm* curve is relatively flat, the real interest rate rises only slightly. Because the *is* curve is steep, a higher real interest rate crowds out only a negligible amount of real investment expenditure. The net result is that fiscal policy is very effective; the level of real national income rises from y_e to y_1, and the fiscal policy has almost a full multiplier effect.

made by the early Keynesians:

1. Money (the size of the money supply) doesn't matter.
2. A private enterprise economy is extremely unstable.
3. By judicious and continuous use of fiscal policy the economy can be fine-tuned so as virtually to eliminate the business cycle.

Monetarists, in the early stage of the debate, were defined as those economists who disputed these three Keynesian tenets. In the remainder of this chapter we will (1) indicate how the monetarist counterrevolution successfully disputed each of these claims and, in the process, contributed to macroeconomic theory and monetary theory; (2) indicate the present state of the monetarist-nonmonetarist debate; and (3) discuss the rules-versus-authority issue.

Money Does Too Matter   Perhaps the most convincing victory for monetarists was their demonstration that money does matter. On this point monetarists disagreed not only with early Keynesians but also with classical economists. To the classical economist money didn't matter because it was merely a medium of exchange. They maintained that changes in the supply of money affected absolute, not relative, prices, so money was considered by them to be neutral.[6] Monetarists maintain that changes in the money supply affect only absolute prices in the long run, but they stress more strongly than the classical economists (who often neglected short-run effects) that *in the short run* money *can* affect relative prices. This is an important distinction because, as Chapter 14 indicated, if money supply changes affect relative prices in the short run, they can cause the unemployment rate to deviate from the natural rate of unemployment. The natural rate of unemployment, you will recall, is the rate to which the unemployment level returns after inflation is perfectly anticipated, or after relative prices have been adjusted properly. Monetarists are inclined to agree with the classical economists that monetary (and fiscal) policy cannot affect the level of unemployment *in the long run*. Of course, the rational expectations model, which has monetarist origins (although many monetarists disclaim it), places in doubt the ability of stabilization policies to affect, *systematically*, real variables even in the short run. In that sense, rational expectations proponents are closer to classical economists than they are to monetarists.

Monetarists also disagree with their classical intellectual ancestors with respect to the older quantity theory of money, which maintains that money supply changes lead to exactly *proportional* changes in the price level. They reject the older quantity theory of money in favor of a more sophisticated quantity theory, which (being less restrictive) merely assumes a high positive correlation between money supply changes and changes in nominal national income in both the short run and the long run. They are not very precise in indicating just *how* changes in the money supply affect the economy, and their position is that the specific breakdown of an increase in nominal income (resulting from an increase in the money supply) between price level increases and quantity (real output) increases cannot be deduced. Instead, they maintain, the break-

---

[6] That is, changes in the money supply affected all prices, including money wages, in the same proportion. In such an instance real variables (in equilibrium) remain unaltered.

down is an empirical question. For taking such a weak position they have been severely criticized by nonmonetarists.[7]

In their classic work on the monetary history of the United States, Milton Friedman and Anna Jacobson Schwartz concluded as follows:

Throughout the near century examined in detail we have found that:

1. Changes in the behavior of the money stock have been closely associated with changes in economic activity, money income, and prices.
2. The interrelation between monetary and economic changes has been highly stable.
3. Monetary changes have often had an independent origin; they have not been simply a reflection of changes in economic activity.[8]

Monetarists further maintain that changes in nominal national income, employment, and the price level are more closely related to changes in the money supply than to changes in government expenditures or taxes. However, the *time lag* between the money supply changes and their effects on economic variables is so unpredictable, and political pressures on the Fed so great, that discretionary (deliberate) monetary policy has a *destabilizing* rather than a stabilizing effect on the economy. We return to this issue later in this chapter when we discuss the present state of the monetarist-nonmonetarist debate.

The Debate over the Great Depression Interestingly enough, both the Keynesians and the monetarists cite the Great Depression as evidence to support their theories. The monetarist view of what happened during the Great Depression is indicated in Figure 18.4. First the money supply falls from *lm* to *lm'*. This indicates that the Fed failed to do its job of providing liquidity. Between 1929 and 1933, the Fed allowed over 5000 banks to go under and thereby caused the money supply to fall by one-third—-the greatest contraction of the money supply in U.S. history.[9] Such an event created panic and caused profit expectations to plummet. Consequently, the net investment curve shifted leftward, and this in turn shifted the *is* curve leftward. That is, the decrease in the money supply from *lm* to *lm'* eventually led *is* to shift leftward to *is'* as the banking panic depressed profit expectations. Nominal interest rates were very low; this reflects the reduced demand for money for transactions and precautionary balances L_1 due to the lower level of national income. According to Friedman, the Fed believed that because interest rates were

---

[7] Johnson, op. cit.

[8] Milton Friedman and Anna J. Schwartz, *A Monetary History of the U.S.: 1867–1960* (Princeton: Princeton University Press, 1963), p. 676. These results have been duplicated for many other countries.

[9] Ibid., p. 299.

Monetarists Think That the Great Depression Was Caused by Fed Monetary Mismanagement

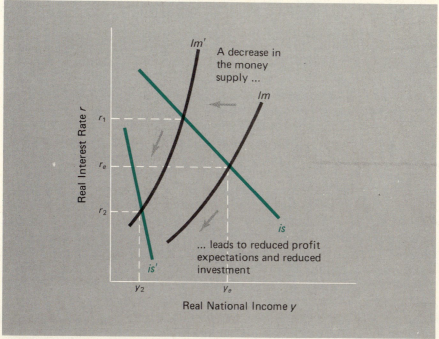

FIGURE 18.4. A MONETARIST VIEW OF THE GREAT DEPRESSION

First, the money supply fell from lm to lm'; the Fed allowed banks to go under and the money supply fell by about one-third between 1929 and 1933. This caused temporarily high interest rates at r_1. The long-run result of this reduction in the money supply was a leftward shift of the is curve because the investment curve shifted leftward owing to a reduction in profit expectations. Real interest rates fell below the original rate, r_e to r_2. Notice that no liquidity trap portion is drawn on the lm curves because monetarists deny its existence.

low, it had provided the economy with sufficient liquidity; *real* interest rates may have been relatively high, however, due to widespread expectations of a falling price level. (Remember that the real interest rate approximately equals the nominal interest rate minus the expected change in the price level. If deflation is expected, the real interest rate equals the nominal interest rate *plus* the expected rate of deflation, and real interest rate will be greater than the nominal interest rate.)

Friedman believes that the Fed is still making the same mistake: *it looks at nominal interest rates instead of at what is happening to the money supply when it wants to determine if it is pursuing a loose or a tight monetary policy.* Thus, if nominal interest rates are high today, this should be interpreted to mean that monetary policy was expansionary six months to two years ago—and not that money is *currently* tight. If the Fed reacts to high current interest rates by increasing the money supply to provide more liquidity, it will cause future nominal interest rates to be even higher. After all, the nominal interest rate is just one price among many, and it, too, will rise in times of inflation. Nominal interest rates rise as lenders add inflationary premiums to them and borrowers willingly pay the premiums.

Figure 18.5 presents the Keynesians version of the Great Depression. The *is* curve shifted leftward because the investment curve decreased to nearly zero during the Great Depression. Between 1929 and 1933, gross private investment fell by over 90 percent. Figure 18.5 also indicates that increases in the real money supply would not have been very helpful because the economy was mired in the liquidity trap. Therefore, increases in the money supply were merely held by the public, which feared capital losses from risky bonds. At the same time, banks held excess reserves in order to avoid (1) capital losses on bonds and (2) default losses on loans. Increases in the money supply, therefore, shift *lm* to *lm'*, but the real interest rate remains constant at a low level, r_1, and the level of real national income remains constant at y_1.

Inflation Is a Monetary Phenomenon   Monetarists point out that the Keynesian model (and the *is-lm* framework) cannot easily account for inflation. It certainly cannot explain stagflation, nor can it account for *high* rates of inflation (inflation at rates greater than, say, 10 percent per year).

Monetarists also insist that inflation is an important social problem.[10] They think inflation is a more important problem than unemployment, which, as you will soon see, they believe is largely *voluntary* anyway. They claim, too, that inflation is always and everywhere a monetary phenomenon, but this is a contention with which nonmonetarists strongly disagree. Finally, some extreme monetarists go so far as to claim that *only money matters*—which makes them guilty of some excesses themselves.

---

[10] Which is, perhaps, why monetarism's appeal did not spread until the late 1960s and 1970s, when inflation rates were relatively high. See the Harry G. Johnson article cited in footnote 5.

Keynesians Blame the Great Depression on the Collapse of the Investment Function

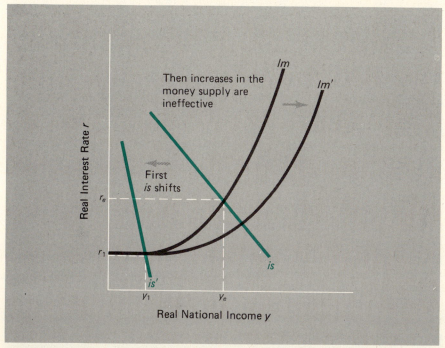

FIGURE 18.5. A KEYNESIAN VIEW OF THE GREAT DEPRESSION

First, the *is* curve shifted from *is* to *is'* as a result of a leftward shift of the investment curve. This caused the real interest rate and the level of real national income to fall dramatically. The ineffectiveness of monetary policy is then depicted. Because real interest rates were already low, implying that the purchase of bonds carried with it a high risk of capital loss, the increased real money supply (indicated by the shift from *lm* to *lm'*) was held in real L_2 balances. The banking parallel to this is that banks held excess reserves because bonds were subject to capital losses and bank loans were subject to a high default risk.

Notice that no classical range exists on the *lm* curve. Keynesians can't imagine a real-world situation in which the demand for money is totally unresponsive to real interest rate changes.

The Economy Is Stable

Monetarists, like their classical intellectual ancestors, believe that a private enterprise economy is inherently stable. In particular, they maintain that (1) the *lm* curve is steep, (2) the *is* curve is flat, and (3) prices and wage rates are flexible.

The *lm* Curve Is Steep   Milton Friedman is prepared to admit that Keynes's liquidity preference concept is a good contribution to monetary theory, but Friedman thinks that the empirical evidence shows that the interest rate elasticity of the demand for money is negligible.[11] As we indicated in Chapter 11, other empirical studies also show that the demand for money is only slightly responsive to changes in the interest rate.

Because the demand for money is relatively insensitive to changes in the interest rate, it follows that velocity is also insensitive to changes in the interest rate. Monetarists have, in fact, presented empirical evidence that velocity is constant. As indicated in Chapter 11, however, from 1974 to 1982 velocity increased more rapidly than the trend growth rate; from 1982 to 1983 velocity decreased significantly (and unexpectedly), and thereby contributed to the severity of this country's most recent recession. Chapter 11 also indicated that, according to Friedman's analysis, the demand for money is a stable function of permanent income, or wealth. Again, the monetarists claim that the demand for money is stable, and this stable demand for money adds to the stability of the economy. But, as Harry G. Johnson indicated, "a stable demand function for money is by no means inconsistent with the Keynesian macroeconomic general equilibrium model, and indeed is presumed to exist in the construction of the standard *is-lm* diagram."[12]

The *is* Curve Is Flat   Monetarists claim, and empirical evidence supports their contention, that both fixed investment expenditures and household consumption expenditures on durable goods are sensitive to changes in the rate of interest.

Furthermore (as we indicated in Chapter 9), Friedman, employing his permanent income hypothesis, argues that consumption depends on wealth. By implication, the short-run marginal propensity to consume is low; a potentially disruptive shock, if perceived as temporary, will have a small multiplier effect. The economy, according to this theory, is therefore relatively stable. Moreover, if prices and wage rates are flexible, then the Keynes effect and the Pigou effect will also help to stabilize the economy.

By linking the consumption function and the demand for money to wealth, Friedman has enriched both functions theoretically, and if he is

---

[11] Milton Friedman, "The Demand for Money: Some Theoretical and Empirical Results," in Milton Friedman, ed., *The Optimum Quantity of Money and Other Essays* (Chicago: University of Chicago Press, 1969).

[12] Harry G. Johnson, op. cit., p. 10.

correct he has gone a long way toward demonstrating that a private enterprise economy is inherently stable.

Prices and Wage Rates Are Flexible   In his presidential address to the American Economic Association in 1968,[13] Milton Friedman presented his theory of the natural rate of unemployment and demonstrated that the Phillips curve is negatively sloped only in the short run and is vertical in the long run (as we explained in Chapter 14). Friedman then showed that unemployment exists even if wage rates are flexible; his theory states that unemployment rises above, and falls below, the natural rate only temporarily and only because employers and workers are fooled. In that model Friedman also implies that the unemployment rate changes due to changes in the duration of unemployment; therefore, unemployment is perceived by Friedman as being mostly frictional and *voluntary*. (See Chapter 14.)

Fiscal Policy Is Not Effective

Far from being able to fine-tune a private enterprise economy, fiscal policy is not very effective at all, claim the monetarists. This conclusion follows from what has already been said. A steep *lm* curve and a flat *is* curve imply, at once, an inherently stable economy, a potentially important role for money, and a small role for fiscal policy.

Consider the government expenditure multiplier. In the first place, one needs to know how the increased expenditures are financed. If they are financed by borrowing from the public, the real rate of interest will rise (assuming no liquidity trap) and crowd out some investment and consumption. On the other hand, private consumption and investment *might* rise because the quantity of money demanded falls (velocity rises) as interest rates rise and leave the public with excess cash balances. The *net* effect is theoretically indeterminate and probably quite small in practice.

Moreover, it is important to ask: on what will the federal expenditures be made? If they are spent on goods or services that would otherwise have been provided by the private sector, increased competition from the public sector will cause the private sector to contract. A federally operated post office means reduced private investment in mail carrier services; more federal parks mean fewer private parks. Do increased government transfers to help the needy lead to decreased private and church

---

[13] Milton Friedman, "The Role of Monetary Policy," *American Economic Review*, vol. 58 (March 1968), pp. 1–17.

contributions? If so, the *net* impact of government activity in those areas may also be negligible.

Consider Friedman's permanent income hypothesis. If government expenditure (or tax) changes are perceived as being temporary, then people will not spend so much out of their (perceived) temporary income increases. People base their spending decisions on their permanent incomes and not on their temporarily changed incomes. If government expenditure changes or tax changes are announced as temporary, income recipients will not adjust their expenditures by much, and the multiplier effect will be lessened.

Finally, automatic stabilizers must be considered. Some of the potential increases in national income resulting from private respending of the government spending will be lessened, as some people move into higher marginal tax brackets and others receive fewer transfers in welfare payments and unemployment compensation. Again, the *net* effect of a change in government spending might be quite small.[14]

Considering all this, is it any wonder that two Keynesians who set out to measure the government expenditure multiplier concluded that the short-run (one-year) multiplier was only slightly larger than 1?[15] Or is it any wonder that different econometric models assume widely different multiplier effects in their predictions?[16]

Monetarists also point to the long lags and the political problems attendant to fiscal policy. To monetarists, fiscal policy is not a very useful tool.

THE PRESENT STATE OF THE DEBATE

By 1977 a leading nonmonetarist, Franco Modigliani, announced that the debate had reached a new plane.[17] He indicated that the issue was no

---

[14] Although it does seem unfair to criticize Keynesian models on this point; after all, automatic stabilizers are viewed favorably by Keynesians.

[15] Lawrence R. Klein and Arthur S. Goldberger, *An Econometric Model of the United States, 1929–1952* (Amsterdam: North Holland, 1955). Also see T. M. Brown, "Habit Persistence and Lags in Consumer Behavior," *Econometrica* (July 1952), pp. 355–371.

[16] For example, assuming no accommodating change in the money supply, the St. Louis Fed forecasting model (a non-Keynesian model) assumes a government expenditure multiplier of 0.7 and the Data Resources, Inc., econometric model assumes a multiplier of 1.8. These are the predicted accumulated effects on nominal GNP of a *permanent* increase in government expenditures, after one year.

[17] Franco Modigliani, "The Monetarist Controversy, or Should We Forsake Stabilization Policies?" *American Economic Review*, vol. 67 (March 1977), pp. 1–19. Modigliani was the 1985 Nobel prize winner in economics.

longer centered on whether aggregate economic activity was determined by monetary or fiscal policy variables, or whether monetary policy or fiscal policy was better suited to stabilize the economy.

Modigliani (and, he believes, most other nonmonetarists) was willing to concede that

1. Money plays an important role in determining output and prices. As Modigliani puts it,

   Milton Friedman was once quoted as saying, "We are all Keynesians now," and I am quite prepared to reciprocate that "We are all monetarists"—if by monetarism is meant assigning to the stock of money a major role in determining output and prices.[18]

2. A private enterprise economy is far less unstable than the early Keynesians believed it to be.

3. A considerable amount of humility and scaling down of the claims for fine-tuning is called for.

4. Most nonmonetarists have no *serious* objection to the notion of a long-run Phillips curve that is vertical, or (what amounts to the same thing) to the assertion that in the long run money is neutral.

What, then, are the *present* issues of disagreement? According to Modigliani,

In reality the distinguishing feature of the monetarist school and the real issues of disagreement with nonmonetarists is not monetarism, but rather the role that should probably be assigned to stabilization policies. Non-monetarists accept what I regard to be the fundamental practical message of *The General Theory:* that a private enterprise economy using an intangible money *needs* to be stabilized, *can* be stabilized, and therefore *should* be stabilized by appropriate monetary and fiscal policies. Monetarists by contrast take the view that there is no serious need to stabilize the economy; that even if there were a need, it could not be done, for stabilization policies would be more likely to increase than to decrease instability; and, at least some monetarists would, I believe, go so far as to hold that, even in the unlikely event that stabilization policies could on balance prove beneficial, the government should not be trusted with the necessary power.[19]

RULES VERSUS DISCRETION

The main issue, then, is not that monetarists prefer monetary policy and nonmonetarists prefer fiscal policy. The key difference is that nonmon-

---

[18] Ibid., p. 1.

[19] Ibid.

etarists are in favor of governmental intervention in the economy in order to stabilize it, and monetarists are not. Nonmonetarists believe that fiscal policy is an important stabilizing tool, but they are prepared to use monetary policy (or anything else), too. Monetarists insist that fiscal policy is not very effective in its ability to affect macroeconomic variables. While monetarists present evidence to indicate that monetary policy can affect macroeconomic variables, especially in the short run, their position is that attempts at "fine-tuning" an economy through monetary policy are destabilizing because the monetary policy time lags are long and variable. Moreover, monetarists believe that it would be foolish to "stabilize" market interest rates if the real interest rate rises because of (for example) (1) a rise in the productivity of capital due to an improvement in technology, or (2) an increase in the degree of present-orientedness of households. Monetarists further believe that fiscal policy also is destabilizing because its lags (also) are long and variable and because of the political problems associated with it. For these reasons, they prefer a monetary rule and a fiscal rule to policy discretion.

Many nonmonetarists, although they concede that there are mechanisms that drive a private enterprise economy to full employment, insist that those mechanisms take a long time. Because unemployment (which they believe is *in*voluntary), inflation, and bankruptcy cause much hardship, an important role exists for monetary policy and fiscal policy to restore the economy *more rapidly* to a full-employment price-stable equilibrium. Nonmonetarists also concede that there have been policy mistakes in the past, but they believe that (1) the post–World War II economy, on balance and until the 1973–1979 supply-shocks period, was relatively stable, partially because of stabilization policies, and (2) they can learn from the mistakes of the past. Nonmonetarists further believe that *any* kind of demand management policy, including monetary growth rules, leave the economy in bad shape if supply shocks occur. Any future success in dealing with unforeseeable supply shocks will have to come about through experience with policy activism.

A Monetary Rule versus Fed Discretion

Monetary policy problems that result from the various lags and rational expectations are considerable. As a consequence, and following a long tradition, monetarists favor a rules rather than a discretion approach to monetary policy. The Fed should be prohibited from using its own discretion in deciding what monetary policy should be. Instead, the Fed should be forced to follow a rule such as: increase the money supply at 4 percent per annum. This policy is seen to be better than one in which the Fed changes the money supply in response to recently observed economic events.

This policy of following a clear-cut monetary policy rule was formalized in 1936 by Henry Simons of the University of Chicago.[20] Milton Friedman also called for a money-stock growth rule in 1948,[21] and has done so in just about every year since then.

Friedman and his allies maintain that the economy is basically stable and that prices and wages are sufficiently flexible to enable it to achieve its natural rates of unemployment and output. By forcing the Fed to follow a monetary rule, a major source of macroeconomic instability (the Fed's policies) will be removed. All that the Fed need do is announce its rule and follow it. Real GNP in the U.S. economy has grown (on average, but with much variability) at about 3.3 percent per annum over the past 100 years. Also, the annual velocity of M1, in recent decades, has increased (slightly). Recall the equation of exchange:

$$MV = Py$$

If the rule is "increase the money supply at 3 percent per annum"—while y is increasing at 3.3 percent per annum and V is increasing slightly—P (the price level) will be stable in the *long run*.

While such a monetary rule has a certain appeal, it is not without its critics. For one thing, *the Fed may not be able to increase* M *at a specific rate.* A monetarist tenet is that the Fed can virtually pinpoint the money supply by controlling the monetary base.

In a recent study, Ralph C. Bryant, a senior fellow in the Brookings Institution's Economic Studies program, reached a different conclusion about the Fed's ability to attain monetary targets.[22] Consider Figure 18.6, which indicates specific M1 money **target cones**—a target range for the growth of M1 (or other monetary aggregates) over a 12-month period.[23] The colored line indicates the *actual* growth of M1. Figure 18.6 indicates that during much of the period from September 1979 to September 1980, the actual money supply was below or above the target cone; for most of the December 1980 to December 1981 period, the actual money supply was *below* the target cone; for nearly all the December 1981 to December 1982 period, the actual money supply was *above* the target cone. In other

---

[20] Henry C. Simons, "Rules versus Authorities in Monetary Policy," *Journal of Political Economy*, vol. 44 (1936), pp. 1–30. His rule: change the money supply so as to stabilize the price level.

[21] Milton Friedman, "A Monetary and Fiscal Framework for Economic Stability," *American Economic Review*, vol. 38 (1948), pp. 245–264.

[22] Ralph C. Bryant, "Should Money Targets Be the Focus of Monetary Policy?" *The Brookings Review* (Spring 1983), pp. 6–12.

[23] A target cone forms a point in the base month and projects the upper and lower bounds for the money supply target ranges for one year; hitting the target range requires staying *within* the cone.

A Monetary Rule Is Senseless If the Fed Can't Hit Its Targets

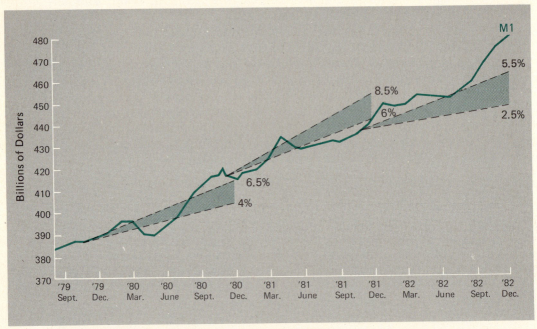

FIGURE 18.6. MISSING THE TARGET CONES

From October 1979 to October 1982, the Fed *said* that it was committed to hitting the M1 target. This figure indicates that the Fed was either unable or unwilling to hit its targets. Most of the time the actual money supply was outside the target cones.

words, even though the target ranges for the growth of M1 were relatively large, the Fed was unable to attain its targets most of the time! Bryant also indicates that the variability of weekly averages of daily M1 data is even greater; *it is even more difficult to hit M1 targets for periods of less than one month.*

Bryant suggests that "variations in nonpolicy factors influencing the money stock cannot be accurately predicted by the Fed and are therefore unexpected disturbances when they occur." He lists the following disturbances:

1. Supply-of-money disturbances
   a. Bank holdings of excess reserves
   b. Bank borrowings from the Fed

2. Demand-for-money disturbances in the form of unexpected changes in the asset preferences of the nonbank private sector for
   a. Currency
   b. Demand deposits
   c. Savings deposits

Bryant concludes that "if close control is defined as continuous prevention of sizable deviations of the actual money stock from a pre-determined target path, therefore, close control over the short run [which, according to Bryant, is one to three months] is just not possible." Moreover, Bryant presents evidence that money-stock targets weren't reached because of changes in the nonpolicy factors affecting the money supply, and not because of Fed incompetence, as some of the Fed's critics have charged.

Fed critics have argued that the Fed did not achieve its money supply targets because it was still wedded to a policy of controlling short-term interest rates. We indicated in Chapter 16, however, that Bryant also provided evidence that the Fed did allow the interest rate to vary tremendously during that period. (See Figure 16.17.)

More recently, the specific issue of whether or not a monetarist experiment was performed during the period from October 1979 to October 1982 was debated in the 1983 American Economic Association meetings, and the results published in the May 1984 *American Economic Review*, Papers and Proceedings. At that meeting, nonmonetarists pointed out that during the October 1979 to October 1982 period

1. There was a significant divergence between the growth in the various money aggregates (M1, M2), and this raises the important question of *which* money supply is to be increased at a constant rate.
2. There was a significant divergence between money growth and national income growth during that period, which (you will recall from Chapter 16) calls into question the relationship between the monetary target (rule) and ultimate goals; it also suggests that GNP, not a monetary aggregate, should be targeted.
3. The Fed was unable to attain its monetary targets, velocity was unstable, and during that period the cost (more unemployment) of attaining a lower rate of inflation was high—and roughly consistent with Okun's law (discussed in Chapter 3).

Milton Friedman's rejoinder at that conference was that in fact *a monetarist experiment was not conducted* during that period:

A monetarist policy involves not only targeting monetary aggregates, but also—as a major and central element—achieving a steady and predictable rate of growth in whatever monetary aggregate is targeted. By this essential criterion the experiment was antimonetarist . . . the volatility of monetary growth during the experiment was about three times as high as earlier. Indeed, monetary volatility was higher during the three years of the experiment than in any earlier three-year period since at least the end of World War II.[24]

While Friedman's point is doubtless relevant, we still nevertheless have some doubts about whether the Fed *can* attain a smooth rate of growth in the money supply. Also, as Modigliani has pointed out, there are two four-year stretches during the post-Korean War period in which the growth of the money stock was relatively stable: the period from early 1953 to 1957 and the nearly four years beginning with the first quarter of 1971. During both of those periods, Modigliani notes, there was well-above-average economic instability—"sharp fluctuations in output and wild gyrations of the rate of change in prices."[25] Apparently, a stable monetary growth is not a *sufficient* condition for economic stability.

Other potential problems with a fixed domestic monetary growth rule arise when we consider such a policy in a worldwide context. For example, such a rule requires flexible foreign exchange rates. A gold standard or a system of fixed exchange rates (discussed in Chapter 20) eventually would force policymakers to abandon a monetary rule. A monetary rule, in addition, could prove to be exceedingly difficult in light of the fact that over \$3 trillion of Eurodollar deposits exist, and some of these deposits can be used by domestic depository institutions to thwart such a rule. Advances in communication and electronic information transfer have increasingly made the dollar (and several other currencies) an *international* currency. The weekly international demand for the dollar can change by such large amounts that they can dwarf the effects of typical weekly Fed open-market operations. A monetary growth target will obviously be difficult to attain if the demand for money (velocity) can change greatly and swiftly. Moreover, it seems foolish to follow a monetary rule when the need for discretionary policy is *obvious* (such as in a depression). Finally, our species has gotten as far as it has because it has an inherent desire to tinker or meddle. Such a desire has been, alternatively, a boon and a bane to our welfare.

Perhaps Friedman already has implicitly conceded that the growth rate of a monetary aggregate is not a cure-all and might, in practice, be difficult to attain. Recently he has come out in favor of a monetary rule

---

[24] Milton Friedman, "Lessons from the 1979–82 Monetary Policy Experiment," *American Economic Review*, Papers and Proceedings, vol. 74 (May 1984), p. 397.

[25] Franco Modigliani, op. cit., p. 11.

which the Fed could certainly attain. *The rule would stabilize the monetary base:* The Fed should be directed to buy a fixed dollar value of bonds per week. Obviously, the monetarist-nonmonetarist debate is still evolving.

Fiscal Policy Rules versus Discretion

Monetarists think that the use of fiscal policy to stabilize the economy should also be abandoned. Instead, government expenditures should be made only in order to alter the quantity of social goods and services provided by government, and they should be financed by taxation. But there is much more to a fiscal rule than the elimination of fiscal stabilization policy and the achievement of a balanced federal budget.

The founders of this nation were very suspicious of government power and "much of their purpose in drafting the Constitution was to prevent or at least impede the development of a large and highly centralized government that would intrude on the lives of the citizens."[26] However, there is nothing in the Constitution that limits the size of the federal government, and nothing that ensures that the government will not debase the currency. Hence, a fiscal discipline rule and a monetary discipline rule are both considered to be essential by monetarists.

In the appendix to Chapter 17 we indicated that monetary policy and fiscal policy are interrelated because there are monetary implications to fiscal policy. It should not be surprising that a monetary discipline rule and a federal fiscal discipline rule are also interrelated. This is because governmental expenditures (government purchases of goods and services plus government transfers) can be financed by taxing, printing money, or borrowing. When the government borrows, this means that either future taxes must rise or **debt monetization** must occur: the Fed can accommodate this borrowing by purchasing government securities through its open-market operations in order to prevent interest rates from rising. Ultimately, this (monetizing of the federal debt) causes inflation; so, if the government prints money or if it borrows and the Fed monetizes the debt, the currency is debased. In that sense, monetary policy is merely another fiscal instrument.

According to Jerry Jordan,

The evolutionary process of economic policymaking in the twentieth cen-

---

[26] Jerry L. Jordan," Economic Policy Making in the 1980s—Evolutionary or Revolutionary?" a lecture presented to Rockhurst College, University of Missouri-Kansas City, Kansas City, Mo., on February 29, 1984; reprinted in that school's Oppenstein Brothers Foundation Lecture Series, No. 3. This section is based on that paper.

tury has given rise to a tendency for the government sectors to grow relatively large in all of the Western Democracies, for deficits in the Federal budgets to grow as a share of national income, and for the monetization of national debts to be reflected in rising trend rates of inflation. Given the existing rules according to which the political game is played, changing the policymakers or their advisors makes little difference to these long-term trends.[27]

Jordan also indicates that a balanced budget is not an effective fiscal rule. (Recall Chapter 17, where we indicated that a balanced-budget rule might well lead to an increase in off-budget spending or to an increase in taxes.) Jordan calls for *a fiscal rule that limits the ratio of government expenditures to national income* because to him the burden of government is measured by government expenditures and not by government tax receipts.

Jordan further states that a fiscal rule that limits the ratio of government expenditures to national income will not necessarily impose monetary discipline but it will help. Why? Because such a fiscal rule will eliminate one incentive to debase the currency; Fed purchases of government securities through open-market operations to accommodate government borrowing won't be necessary if such a fiscal rule is followed. An additional advantage of a limit to the ratio of government expenditures to national income is that it will force Congress to set priorities and recognize opportunity costs: If the government has reached the maximum allowed government expenditure/national income ratio, an increase in expenditures in one area requires a reduction in expenditures in another.

Similarly, a monetary discipline rule won't necessarily impose fiscal discipline, but it will help. A monetary discipline rule will impose *one* constraint on government expenditures; a monetary discipline rule would mean that increased government expenditures would have to be financed by *explicit* taxes.[28] Presumably, such a constraint would slow down the rate of government expansion.

Nonmonetarists claim that a fiscal policy rule is not feasible because it will be breached in one way or another, and it is harmful because the economy needs to be stabilized, can be stabilized, and therefore should be stabilized. It is not certain at this time whether fiscal policy rules and monetary policy rules that really have bite in them will be adopted. It

---

[27] Ibid., p. 8. As we indicated in Chapter 17, the public choice school makes these identical points.

[28] Or, if government expenditures are not monetized into an "inflation tax," then (according to Jordan and others) interest rates will rise and the public will protest.

is certain, however, that the monetarist-nonmonetarist debate will rage on.

CHAPTER SUMMARY

1. Classical economists believed that a private economy is stable because (*a*) real consumption and real investment expenditures are sensitive to the interest rate, and (*b*) relative prices and relative wage rates will adjust to clear markets.

2. Keynes believed that a private enterprise economy was inherently unstable because (*a*) the demand for money is sensitive to the interest rate, (*b*) wage rates are inflexible downward, and (*c*) consumption and investment are insensitive to the interest rate.

3. In terms of the *is-lm* model, an economy is inherently unstable if (*a*) the *lm* curve is relatively flat, (*b*) the *is* curve is steep, and (*c*) prices are inflexible, so that the Keynes effect and the Pigou effect cannot restore the economy to full employment. Under these conditions, monetary policy is ineffective and fiscal policy is powerful.

4. Early Keynesians maintained that a private enterprise economy is inherently unstable, that money doesn't matter, and that such an economy can be stabilized by fiscal policy. Demand management fine-tuning was thought to be able to eliminate the business cycle.

5. Monetarism developed as a counterrevolution to the Keynesian revolution which spawned the ideas listed in 4 above.

6. Monetarists maintained, and brought forth empirical evidence to support their claims, that (*a*) changes in the growth rate of the money supply exert a powerful influence on economic activity in the short run and on the rate of inflation in the long run; (*b*) consumption and investment are sensitive to the interest rate; (*c*) consumption and money demand are stable functions of wealth; and (*d*) monetary policy and fiscal policy are destabilizing.

7. By 1977 the monetarist-nonmonetarist debate had changed. Nonmonetarists conceded that (*a*) a private economy was not so unstable as they originally thought, (*b*) money can have a powerful effect on economic activity but is neutral in the long run, and (*c*) fine-tuning a complex economy is very difficult.

8. Nonmonetarists insist, nevertheless, that a private enterprise economy needs to be stabilized, can be stabilized by monetary policy and fiscal policy, and therefore should be stabilized. Nonmonetarists think that the inherent mechanisms that can restore the economy to full employment take too long and that therefore an important role exists for monetary and fiscal policy.

9. Monetarists favor a monetary rule and a fiscal rule instead of discre-

tionary monetary policy and discretionary fiscal policy. *Nonmone-tarists* don't believe that the Fed can attain a monetary growth target, and they believe that even if such a target were attainable, it would be undesirable. They have similar thoughts concerning a fiscal policy rule.

10. Monetary discipline rules and fiscal discipline rules are interrelated. If one is obeyed, the other is easier to obey.

GLOSSARY

debt monetization   A policy of accommodating government borrowing by an expansionary monetary policy.

monetarism   An economic school of thought that stresses that (1) the rate of growth of the money supply is important, (2) the economy is inherently stable, and (3) monetary rules and fiscal rules should replace discretionary monetary policy and discretionary fiscal policy.

target cone   A target range for the growth of monetary aggregates; a target cone forms a point in a base month and projects the upper and lower bounds for the money supply target ranges for one year.

QUESTIONS AND PROBLEMS FOR REVIEW

18.1   For what two reasons did classical economists argue that a private enterprise economy is stable? Why are both reasons necessary for such an argument?

18.2   For what three reasons did Keynes argue that a private enterprise economy is inherently unstable?

18.3   Under the classical–neo-Keynesian synthesis, monetary policy is considered to be ineffective. Why?

18.4   Alternatively, under the classical–neo-Keynesian synthesis, fiscal policy is considered to be powerful. Why?

18.5   Early Keynesians maintained that money doesn't matter. What did they mean?

18.6   Monetarists maintained that changes in the rate of growth of the money supply have a powerful effect on economic activity in the short run. Why?

18.7   Why do the monetarists maintain that discretionary monetary and fiscal policy are destabilizing?

18.8   Cite the changes in the position of the nonmonetarists that had evolved by the late 1970s.

18.9   Nonmonetarists think that a private enterprise economy should be stabilized. Why?

18.10 Does the question of whether or not to follow a monetary rule and a fiscal rule rest on value judgments or on empirical results?

REFERENCES

Leonall C. Anderson and Jerry L. Jordan, "Monetary and Fiscal Actions: A Test of Their Relative Importance in Economic Stabilization," *Review*, Federal Reserve Bank of St. Louis (November 1968).

Albert Ando and Franco Modigliani, "Impacts of Fiscal Actions on Aggregate Income and the Monetarist Controversy: Theory and Evidence," in J. L. Stein, ed., *Monetarism* (New York: American Elsevier, 1976).

T. M. Brown, "Habit Persistence and Lags in Consumer Behavior," *Econometrica*, vol. 20 (1952).

Karl Brunner, "Has Monetarism Failed? *Cato Journal*, vol. 3 (1983).

———, "Mr. Hicks and the 'Monetarists,' " *Economica*, vol. 40 (1973).

Karl Brunner and Allan H. Meltzer, "Predicting Velocity: Implications for Theory and Policy," *Journal of Finance*, vol. 18 (1963).

Ralph C. Bryant, "Should Money Targets Be the Focus of Monetary Policy?" *The Brookings Review* (Spring 1983).

Milton Friedman, "Lessons from the 1979–82 Monetary Policy Experiment," *American Economic Review*, Papers and Proceedings, vol. 74 (1984).

———, "A Monetary and Fiscal Framework for Economic Stability," *American Economic Review*, vol. 38 (1948).

———, "The Role of Monetary Policy," *American Economic Review*, vol. 58 (1968).

Milton Friedman, ed., *The Optimum Quantity of Money and Other Essays* (Chicago: University of Chicago Press, 1968).

Milton Friedman and Anna J. Schwartz, *A Monetary History of the United States, 1867–1960*, National Bureau of Economic Research (Princeton, N.J.: Princeton University Press, 1963).

Robert J. Gordon, *Macroeconomics*, 3d ed. (Boston: Little, Brown, 1984).

Harry G. Johnson, "The Keynesian Revolution and the Monetarist Counter-Revolution," *American Economic Review*, vol. 61 (1971).

Jerry L. Jordan, "Economic Policy Making in the 1980's—Evolutionary or Revolutionary?" Oppenstein Brothers Foundation Lecture Series No. 3, University of Missouri, Kansas City, Mo., 1984.

Lawrence R. Klein and Arthur S. Goldberger, *An Econometric Model of the United States, 1924–1952* (Amsterdam: North Holland, 1955).

Dwight R. Lee, *Inflation and Unemployment: The Case for Limiting Political Discretion*, Original Paper 45, International Institute for Economic Research (September 1983).

Allan H. Meltzer, "Monetary Reform in an Uncertain Environment," *Cato Journal*, vol. 3 (1983).

Franco Modigliani, "The Monetarist Controversy, or Should We Forsake Stabilization Policies?" *American Economic Review*, vol. 67 (1977).

William Poole, *Money and the Economy: A Monetarist View* (Reading, Mass.: Addison-Wesley, 1978).

Henry C. Simons, "Rules Versus Authorities in Monetary Policy," *Journal of Political Economy*, vol. 44 (1936).

Peter Temin, *Did Monetary Forces Cause the Great Depression?* (New York: Norton, 1976).

James Tobin, "The Monetary Interpretation of History, *American Economic Review*, vol. 55 (1965).

PART VI

PRODUCTIVITY GROWTH AND OPEN-ECONOMY MACROECONOMICS

19

THE PRODUCTIVITY SLOWDOWN AND SUPPLY-SIDE ECONOMICS

Most of this text has been concerned with the short run, with how the economy absorbs temporary shocks, and with how long it takes the economy to absorb these shocks. In this chapter we are more concerned with the long-run phenomena that determine the rate of growth of real GNP and the rate of growth of the productivity of labor. (Recall that in the short run the size of the labor force, the size of the capital stock, land, and technology are constant, but in the long run they all vary.)

Since 1965 there apparently has been a slowdown of these two growth rates in the United States, and this situation has been referred to as the productivity puzzle. First we relate growth, productivity increases, and aggregate supply (AS), and then we analyze the productivity puzzle. **Supply-side economics,** an economic school of thought with classical origins that proposes to combat stagflation and to increase the growth rate of real GNP and of productivity by reducing marginal tax rates, is then explored. The chapter ends with a Policy Controversy that questions the *existence* of a productivity slowdown after 1965.

GROWTH, PRODUCTIVITY INCREASES, AND AGGREGATE SUPPLY

Output Growth

In this section we provide the theoretical framework that will help you to understand the material examined in the rest of the chapter.

The average productivity of labor a is defined as the ratio of total output to total labor employed, or

$$a = \frac{y}{N} \tag{19.1}$$

The average productivity of labor times the quantity of labor employed must, by definition, equal total output. Rewriting equation 19.1 gives

$$y = aN \tag{19.2}$$

For example, if each unit of labor on average produces 2 ties per year and there are 20 laborers employed, then the total output of ties is 40 per year.

Figure 19.1 shows that the average and marginal productivity of labor decrease as the level of employment rises, owing to the law of diminishing returns.

The growth of output can be seen to be a function of the average productivity of labor and the quantity of labor employed; output varies directly with each of these two variables. If the size of the labor force increases through time, because of an increase in population or because of a rising participation rate of the population, then (other things constant) output will grow through time. In Figure 19.1, if employment rises from N_1 to N_2, output rises from y_1 to y_2.

Output will also grow if, other things constant, the average productivity of labor rises through time.[1]

In general, the *rate of growth* in output will approximately equal the sum of the rate of growth of labor plus the rate of growth of labor productivity. For example, if the labor force grows at 1 percent per year and labor's productivity grows at 2 percent per year, then output will grow at approximately 3 percent per year.[2]

Increases in Labor Productivity

The average productivity of labor will rise over time if, other things constant,

1. Technological improvements occur, or
2. The size of the capital stock increases, or
3. Quality improvements in labor occur, or
4. Resources are allocated more efficiently, for one reason or another.

Consider Figure 19.2, which shows an increase in the average productivity of labor. If a technological improvement, an increase in the capital stock, an increase in the quality of labor, or a more efficient allocation of resources occurs, then the aggregate production function shifts upward. This means that national output will be higher at every level of employment. In Figure 19.2 national output rises from y_1 to y_2 at employment level N_1.

---

[1] We can express this mathematically. The derivative of y with respect to time is $dy/dt = a\ dN/dt + N\ da/dt$. This equation says that the change in output through time dy/dt equals the average productivity of labor times the change in labor over time plus the quantity of labor times the change in the average product of labor through time.

[2] From the derivative in footnote 1, we find the differential of y:

$$dy = a\ dN + N\ da$$

which is an approximation of the change in y. Dividing both sides of this equation by $y = aN$ yields

$$\frac{dy}{y} = \frac{dN}{N} + \frac{da}{a}$$

which says that the growth in output (approximately) equals the growth in labor plus the growth in the average productivity of labor.

Owing to the Law of Diminishing Returns, Both the Marginal Productivity and the Average Productivity Decline as More Labor Is Employed

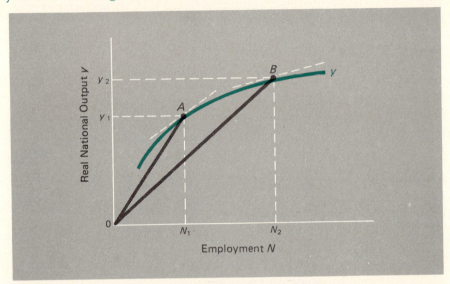

FIGURE 19.1. A TYPICAL PRODUCTION FUNCTION

As employment increases, such other things as capital and technology constant, total output will increase at a decreasing rate owing to the law of diminishing returns. This is indicated because the slope of the dashed line tangent to point A (the marginal product of labor at point A) is greater than the slope of the dashed line tangent to point B.

The slope of a line that is a ray from the origin to a point on the production function is the average product of labor. Note that because the slope of the solid line OA is greater than the slope of the solid line OB, the average productivity of labor also declines as the level of employment is increased, other things constant.

Aggregate Supply and Changes in the Marginal Productivity of Labor

Recall from Chapter 13 that *aggregate supply* (AS) relates levels of national output supplied by producers to price levels, other things constant. In Chapters 4 and 12 we indicated that in a competitive model the equilibrium condition in the labor market is that the real wage rate (W/P, or the nominal wage rate divided by the price level) must equal the marginal physical product (marginal productivity) of labor $\Delta y/\Delta N$, where Δ is the notation for a *change* in a variable. Thus, in equilibrium,

The Production Function Shifts Upward When Labor's Productivity Rises

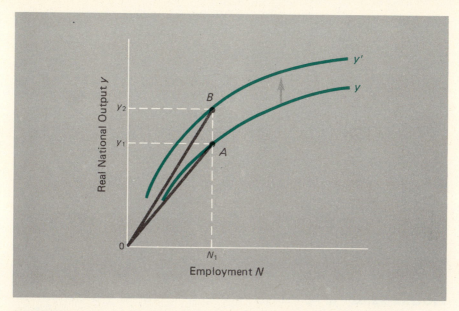

FIGURE 19.2. AN INCREASE IN THE PRODUCTIVITY OF LABOR

If the average productivity of labor rises, owing to a technological improvement, an increase in the capital stock, an increase in the quality of labor, or a more efficient allocation of resources, the aggregate production function will shift upward; national output will be higher at each level of employment. Note that the slope of the solid line OB exceeds the slope of the solid line OA.

$$\frac{W}{P} = \frac{\Delta y}{\Delta N} \tag{19.3}$$

Let $\Delta y/\Delta N = b$, so that

$$\frac{W}{P} = b \tag{19.4}$$

Multiplying both sides by P/b yields

$$P = \frac{W}{b} \tag{19.5}$$

Equation 19.5 indicates that, *given the aggregate production function, the price level varies directly with wage rates and inversely with changes in the marginal productivity of labor.*

The AS Curve Is Positively Sloped

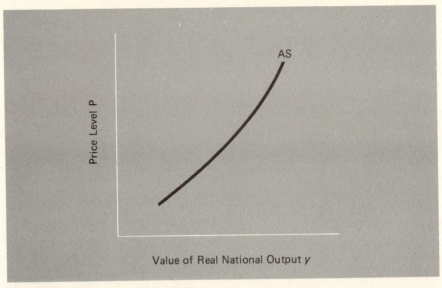

FIGURE 19.3. THE AS CURVE

The wage rate is held constant, and increases in real national output require more labor, other things constant. Because of the law of diminishing returns, the marginal productivity of labor falls, so the price level rises. The extreme Keynesian assumption model, therefore, indicates that the short-run AS curve is positively sloped.

The AS Curve Assume that wage rates are constant.[3] Increases in national output, in the short run, require higher employment levels, which (other things constant) leads to a reduction in b, the marginal productivity of labor. This means that the AS curve will be positively sloped: given the wage rate, higher output levels require higher price levels because the marginal product of labor decreases. Figure 19.3 shows a positively sloped AS curve.

Shifts in the AS Curve If the wage rate changes, the AS curve will shift. As equation 19.5 indicates, given the marginal productivity of labor, a higher wage rate will be associated with a higher price level at every level of national output. If the wage rate rises, therefore, the AS curve

---

[3] This is the extreme Keynesian assumption model of Chapters 12 and 13.

shifts upward. Intuitively, the price level will rise if wage rates rise relative to labor's marginal productivity, other things constant. Similar reasoning indicates that if wage rates *fall* relative to the marginal productivity of capital, other things constant, the AS curve shifts downward.

If the wage rate is constant and the marginal productivity of labor changes, the AS curve also shifts. For example, if the capital stock rises or technological improvement occurs, the marginal (and average) productivity of labor will rise and shift the AS curve downward; the price level will be lower at every level of national output. Similarly, if for some reason resources are now allocated more *in*efficiently, the AS curve shifts upward; the price level will be higher at every level of national output. Figure 19.4 shows shifts in the AS curve due to changes in the wage rate and due to changes in the marginal productivity of labor, other things constant.

THE PRODUCTIVITY SLOWDOWN

Over the past two decades the United States has apparently experienced a significant reduction in the rate at which labor productivity is rising. **Labor productivity** is defined as the ratio of the real value of output to the quantity of labor used to produce that output. We shall refer to the deceleration in the rate of growth of output and of the rate of labor productivity as the "productivity slowdown." The productivity slowdown is widely known because it has occurred in most of the developed nations and much has been written about it. (See the references at the end of this chapter for a partial list of such works.) There is not much agreement on the cause of the growth deceleration, and hence there is not much agreement on whether it is temporary or permanent.

The main facts in the United States seem to be the following:

1. For approximately 20 years before 1965, real output per hour of labor input—labor productivity—in the private (nongovernment), nonfarm sector grew at an average of 2.5 percent per year.[4]
2. From 1965 to 1973 private, nonfarm labor productivity grew at 2 percent per year.[5]
3. From 1973 to 1979 private, nonfarm labor productivity grew at approximately two-thirds of 1 percent (0.67 percent) per year.[6]

---

[4] Peter K. Clark, "Inflation and the Productivity Decline," *American Economic Review*, Papers and Proceedings (May 1982), p. 149.

[5] Ibid.

[6] Ibid.

The AS Curve Shifts If the Wage Rate Changes or If the Marginal Productivity of Labor Changes

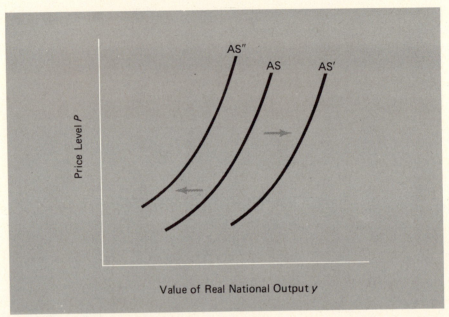

FIGURE 19.4. SHIFTS IN THE AS CURVE

The AS curve is derived by holding the wage rate and the production function constant. If the wage rate rises relative to the change in the marginal productivity of labor, the AS curve shifts upward. If the wage rate falls relative to the change in the marginal productivity of labor, the AS curve shifts downward. Changes in the marginal (and average) productivity of labor curves occur (the production function shifts) as a result of changes in the capital stock and in the quality of labor, of technological improvements, and of changes in overall resource reallocation.

4. From February 1979 to February 1984 the annual rate of growth of private, nonfarm labor productivity was 1.28 percent.[7]

There are many theories that purport to explain the productivity slowdown, but we shall analyze only those that seem to be the most

---

[7] This calculation is based on data from page 88 of the October 1981 and page 88 of the July 1984 *Business Conditions Digest,* United States Department of Commerce, Bureau of Economic Analysis.

promising. As you will see, some of these theories are not mutually exclusive; some are interrelated.

A Reduction in Innovation

In 1971 the rate of patent issuance by the United States Patent Office reached its peak of 56,000 per year. Since then that rate has fallen dramatically—to approximately 37,000 in the year 1980. Furthermore, the ratio of research and development (R&D) spending to gross national product fell from about 2.9 percent in the 1960s to a low of 2.2 percent in 1978.[8]

As we shall indicate later, technological improvement contributes importantly to labor productivity growth; the relationship between patents and technical progress or actual innovation, however, is very imprecise. Moreover, there seems to be a trend away from business patenting because of the high costs of acquiring and protecting patents relative to the gains from patents. The empirical evidence relating R&D expenditures to labor productivity growth is mixed: Some studies show a strong relationship; others indicate that R&D expenditures account for only a very small percentage of labor productivity growth.[9]

If the world is running out of innovative ideas (because diminishing returns exist for innovation, too) or if the incentives to spend on R&D are permanently depressed, then the deceleration in labor productivity growth will be permanent—to the extent that each of these factors contributes to labor productivity growth.

Inability to Measure Productivity

Some economists have claimed that the inability to measure productivity properly accounts for an *apparent* productivity slowdown. If we could measure productivity better, they claim, then we would see that in fact there has been no productivity slowdown. (We discuss one skeptic's point of view in the Policy Controversy at the end of this chapter.)

Albert Rees, an economist who chaired the Panel to Review Productivity Statistics for the National Academy of Sciences, believes that,

---

[8] Martin Neil Baily, "Will Productivity Growth Recover? Has It Done So Already?" *American Economic Review*, Papers and Proceedings (May 1984), p. 232.

[9] Edward F. Denison of the Bureau of Economic Growth and Zvi Griliches of Harvard University find that R&D contributes only slightly to economic growth; John W. Kendrick (whose work we will analyze later in this chapter) of George Washington University and Roger Brimmer of Data Resources, Inc., an econometrics firm, find reduced R&D expenditures to be a significant cause of the productivity slowdown.

although the level of productivity is difficult to measure, a slowdown in the rate of growth of productivity *has* occurred. Rees lists the following as the problems in measuring productivity:[10]

1. For service industries and for some types of construction, it is extremely difficult to measure the output. As a consequence, output proxies are used. The proxies used are "average hourly earnings of workers"; unfortunately, this "output" proxy is in fact an *input*. Because output is not measured independently of input in such cases, the overall productivity measure is biased toward showing no change.[11]

2. Because the output of the government sector and the output of nonprofit institutions are extremely difficult to measure, these important sectors are *excluded* from productivity measurements. In short, some outputs are simply ignored because they are difficult to measure.

3. Output is supposed to be measured in real terms, but for some very important classes of outputs (such as aircraft and computers) which have recently experienced rapid technological change, no price indices have been developed. Because no price indices have been developed, *real* output cannot be estimated, and, as a consequence, such outputs have been omitted from the productivity measurements. Such omissions bias the overall productivity level downward. It is generally agreed that price indices for *other* important classes of outputs do not adequately measure quality improvements. This, too, means that the level of labor productivity is understated.

4. Productivity data count hours paid rather than hours actually worked as a measure of labor input; therefore, paid holidays, vacations, and sick leave have been treated as hours worked. This measurement procedure obviously overstates the quantity of labor input and, other things constant, understates the level of labor productivity.

5. Hours worked by nonproduction workers and by supervisory workers are not measured directly; instead, rule-of-thumb estimates are made. Such rough estimates are made for some 18 percent of the workers on all private nonagricultural payrolls. It is difficult to say in which direction this procedure biases the level of labor productivity.

---

[10] Albert Rees, "Improving Productivity Measurement," *American Economic Review*, Papers and Proceedings (May 1980), pp. 340–342.

[11] Measuring inputs to try to estimate an output is a widespread and troublesome phenomenon. If you are given the opportunity to evaluate your teacher, your opinion of your teacher's ability to teach probably will be used as an estimate of his or her teaching ability, instead of some objective (output) measure of what you actually learned. Medical and business school accreditation decisions are typically based on such criteria as research by the faculty, the number of volumes in the library, physical facilities, and so on; this procedure measures the quality of *inputs*. A more direct measure of an *output* would be to test the knowledge and performance of the graduates of those schools.

6. Labor hours by all workers are *not* weighted by *quality differences*. This is a fundamental problem (one economist, as we show in the Policy Controversy section at the end of this chapter, suggests that a proper weighting indicates *no* productivity slowdown). For example, suppose a technical change occurs so that lower-skilled laborers can now be substituted for an equal number of higher-skilled laborers, but output is unaltered. A moment's reflection will indicate that such a change has increased the level of labor productivity. But because laborers are not weighted by quality differences, such a technical change will show up in the present measure procedure as no change in the labor input and no change in output and hence no change in labor productivity.

Despite these measurement problems Rees nonetheless concludes that

> the presence of errors that bias a measure downward, however, is not sufficient to cause a decrease in the measure's rate of growth. To cause such a decrease, a downward-biasing error would have to be getting larger through time. I know of nothing that suggests that this is true of the errors I have discussed, and a good deal that suggests the opposite.... In short, the lag in measured productivity growth seems to me to be entirely a real phenomenon and in no part attributable to measurement error. Indeed, if anything, the deceleration has been understated.[12]

Higher Energy Prices

Between the years 1973 and 1979 worldwide energy prices rose dramatically as a consequence of oil price increases by the Organization of Petroleum Exporting Countries (OPEC). Many economists claim that such supply shocks are a fundamental cause of the worldwide slowdown in the rate of growth of real GNP and of the declaration of labor productivity growth.

What is the link between higher energy prices and the productivity slowdown? The reasoning is that *artificially* high relative energy prices (the marginal cost of extracting OPEC oil was estimated at $1 per barrel during that period, while the spot market price of oil rose above $40 per barrel) induced producers to substitute labor and capital for energy in the production process. While this substitution is rational to private producers, it is a misallocation of resources to society. This misallocation caused the growth rates of national output and labor productivity to fall.

This theory has been criticized because energy costs are only a small percentage of total output costs; consequently, the total loss of output

---

[12] Rees, op. cit., p. 342.

associated with the output and productivity growth slowdowns seems too large to be accounted for by inefficient resource substitution.[13] To the extent that this theory is correct, labor productivity growth and real GNP growth should return to their previously higher natural growth rates in the future, because the relative energy prices are now falling in tandem with OPEC's waning economic power.

Inflation

It is maintained by many that high and varied rates of inflation have increased the variance of *relative* prices and have, consequently, reduced the ability of the price system to transmit information efficiently. This in turn has caused resources to be allocated inefficiently, and the growth rate in output per unit of labor and the growth rate of real GNP have decelerated. Inflation has also eroded the value of tax allowances for depreciation and has caused businesses (and households) to move into higher marginal tax brackets; therefore, inflation has reduced the rate of capital formation (investment) which also contributes to the productivity slowdown.[14]

Government

Many economists place the blame for the productivity slowdown and the real GNP slowdown on the government—especially on the federal government. Governmental overregulation, they allege, has caused a misallocation of resources and has reduced overall efficiency; in turn, real GNP growth and labor productivity growth have waned.

These critics also point out that governmentally mandated increased business expenditures on such environmental goods as pollution-abatement equipment necessitate a lower output of consumer and capital goods. This argument, in effect, indicates that part of the productivity slowdown is due to a measurement-of-output error, because the benefits of environmental goods are not measured as an output.

Finally, governments are also responsible for high marginal tax rates for households and for businesses; and governments have instituted a vast welfare system. These have presumably destroyed labor incentives to work, household incentives to save, and business incentives to invest. We return to this discussion in the next major section, when we discuss supply-side economics.

---

[13] Baily, op. cit., p. 233.

[14] Clark, op. cit., pp. 149–154. We elaborate on this point later in this chapter when we discuss supply-side economics.

Distributional Coalitions

A distributional coalition, you will recall from Chapter 17, is a collective that has gained political or economic power in order to redistribute income or wealth away from others to reward itself. Examples of distributional collectives include cartels; businesses with market power; unions and professional sports associations that have monopolistic power and freedom from antitrust prosecution; and associations of physicians, morticians, taxicab owners, plumbers, and others that require professional and/or governmental licensing. Distributional coalitions use their collective power to influence Congress to grant them special privilege in forms that range from licensing requirements, freedom from antitrust prosecution, direct subsidies, and such forms of indirect subsidies as tariffs and import quotas on foreign-produced goods.

Distributional coalitions are, in effect, government sponsored cartels; these coalitions receive special privileges from Congress (or from governments in general). Such special privileges convey vast benefits to the small numbers that form a coalition, but the costs of these income- and wealth-distributing privileges are so widely dispersed that many people pay, individually, only a very small price. For example, milk price supports are worth millions of dollars to a small number of dairy farmers, while millions of milk drinkers and dairy product consumers pay individually only a few cents more per gallon of milk. Because the costs to individuals outside the coalition are small, special interest groups to represent the interests of the many will not arise. How much time and effort are you willing to invest in fighting milk price supports in order to save yourself a few pennies per gallon of milk?

As Chapter 17 indicated, the concept of distributional coalitions is associated with Mancur Olson, of the University of Maryland.[15] Olson recently has applied his model to the productivity-slowdown puzzle.[16]

Olson's theory, simplified here, is that when a nation experiences political stability and unchanged borders for a long period (as the United States and other Western, developed nations have), many groups will find it beneficial and possible to form distributional coalitions. Because these coalitions have economic power, they can—to various extents—insulate themselves from competitive market forces. Specifically, such coalitions find it in their interest to set *prices* (or wages, in the case of unions and professional associations) that are above equilibrium (or market-clearing)

---

[15] Mancur Olson, *The Logic of Collective Action* (Cambridge, Mass.: Harvard University Press, 1971), and *The Rise and Decline of Nations* (New Haven, Conn.: Yale University Press, 1982).

[16] Mancur Olson, "Stagflation and the Political Economy of the Decline in Productivity," *American Economic Review*, Papers and Proceedings (May 1982), pp. 143–148.

levels and to produce at *output rates* that are below what they would be under competitive conditions. Equally important, *distributional coalitions have a rational interest in blocking transactions that are mutually advantageous to people outside their coalitions.* For example, unions have an incentive to prevent their employers from hiring nonunion laborers at a mutually advantageous, below-union wage rate. For another example, consider the amount of time and effort that OPEC, an international distributional coalition, spends to block its members from selling oil at discounted prices (below the cartel price) to willing buyers in order to maintain the viability of the cartel.

Olson also claims that decision making in such cartel-like organizations is a laborious and time-consuming process because the decisions often require new laws or unanimous-consent bargaining. Finally, says Olson, such organizations establish barriers to entry and retard innovation.

Given an increase in the number and power of such distributional coalitions, the economy becomes less flexible in response to such shocks as changes in tastes, energy crisis, high and variable inflation, or **disinflation**—a reduction in the rate of inflation. For example, if disinflation occurs, distributional coalitions will react slowly and the absolute price of their goods will remain constant and thereby raise the relative prices of their output. These higher relative prices will cause lower output rates and a higher unemployment rate (because distributional coalitions block mutually advantageous transactions and prolong the job search). Because such coalitions reduce the economic system's overall ability to adapt to change, they reduce the economy's overall efficiency. Growth rates of national output and labor productivity, therefore, will fall through time as distributional coalitions increase in number and power.

Will the Productivity Slowdown Continue?

Where do all these theories to account for the deceleration in the rate of growth of real GNP and labor productivity leave us? If Mancur Olson is correct, or if the world really is running out of innovative ideas, then the temporary growth slowdown eventually will be seen as permanent. While Olson's theory is intriguing, in our opinion diminishing returns have certainly not yet set in with respect to innovation (nor are they likely to for quite some time). Indeed, Western economies seem to be on the brink of a tremendous age of technological growth. Recent innovations in office equipment, computer technology, robotics, miniaturization, microwave energy, telecommunications, laser applications, and in scores of other areas will pay huge dividends in the future; such innovations, in turn, will spur even further technological discoveries.

Even though distributional coalitions retard *their own* technologically innovative development, they create economic incentives for *others* to innovate as a means to circumvent the power of the distributional coalitions. Witness the technological advances made in underwater diving equipment and in off-shore drilling which were the direct results of OPEC's increase in the relative price of oil. Today OPEC's power is diminishing as a direct result of these and other oil-related technological advances that are reactions to a higher relative price of oil. Witness, too, the use of robotics to substitute for high-priced union labor.[17]

If the productivity growth slowdown is caused by the high relative price of energy, inflation, excessive government involvement in the economy, or reduced expenditures on research and development, we can expect productivity growth to return to its natural rate because these causes have recently disappeared. The relative price of energy is falling in the 1980s (continuing its century-long decline), and inflation seems to have abated. Moreover, John W. Kendrick, of George Washington University, has in several forums argued that the productivity slowdown will be reversed because of measures taken since 1978.[18]

In particular, Kendrick points to the following:

1. The tax reductions and the investment tax credit that was liberalized and made permanent in the Revenue Act of 1978.
2. The accelerated cost recovery system, the indexation of personal income tax brackets, increased exemptions, lower marginal tax rates, and the increased standard deduction that began in 1985, all of which resulted from provisions of the Tax Acts of 1981 and 1982.
3. The 25 percent incremental R&D tax credit that was made permanent in 1985.
4. Reductions in capital gains taxes, reductions in government economic regulation, and increases in federal government funding of R&D.
5. The fact that in the decade of the 1980s the baby boom children will be in their thirties, and hence, on average, the labor force will be composed of a higher percentage of workers in the more productive stage of their careers.

Consider Table 19.1, which indicates Kendrick's estimates of actual values of GNP growth and its individual components, and of real product

---

[17] Still, Olson's distributional coalitions, combined with governmental regulations and market interventions that contribute to price-wage inflexibility and to resource immobility, doubtless have reduced our economy's ability to adapt to shocks. As a consequence, the *variability* in real GNP growth and in labor productivity growth may well increase.

[18] Kendrick has made this argument at a Cato Institute Conference held in Washington, D.C., in April 1984, and on the *Wall Street Journal* editorial page, August 29, 1984.

per unit of labor (labor productivity) of the two periods 1948–1973 and 1973–1981. Table 19.1 also indicates Kendrick's forecasts for those values in two future periods: 1981–1990 and 1990–2000.[19] Note that Kendrick has broken down real GNP growth into its components: (1) total factor (labor and capital input) growth and (2) total factor productivity growth, which in turn is composed of advances in knowledge, changes in labor quality, changes in quality of land, resource reallocations, volume changes (benefits from economies of scale and from capacity utilization), government regulations, and what he calls the ratio of actual to potential efficiency (which is a residual). In that table, total factor input growth plus total factor productivity growth sum to real GNP growth.

As Table 19.1 shows, Kendrick believes that the future growth rates in real GNP and in labor productivity will approach their long-term (1948–1973) natural rates.

SUPPLY-SIDE ECONOMICS

Supply-side economics refers to a theory that stresses the primacy of economic incentives to work, save, invest, and bear risk as determinants of the level of economic activity. This theory, although characterized as radical or revolutionary, is in fact firmly rooted in the classical economist's traditional preference for market solutions over governmental intervention; such a preference has long been labeled laissez-faire.

The recent reemergence of supply-side economics began in 1971 when Robert Mundell of Columbia University proposed (1) reducing marginal tax rates to encourage increased output and (2) pegging the price of the U.S. dollar in terms of gold to cure U.S. inflation.

Mundel inspired Jude Wanniski, Arthur Laffer, George Gilder, Alan Reynolds, Paul Craig Roberts, and others, who crusaded in the *Wall Street Journal* and in other forums. These latter supply-siders advocated a reduction in marginal tax rates as a means to combat the stagflation that plagued the economy in the United States (and elsewhere) during 1973–1975 and 1978–1979.

Supply-side economists have been divided into two camps: radical and mainstream.[20] Some members of the radical group have already been

---

[19] John W. Kendrick, "Long-Term Economic Projection: Stronger U.S. Growth Ahead," *Southern Economic Journal*, vol. 50, no. 4 (April 1984), pp. 945–964.

[20] Harold McClure and Thomas Willett, "Understanding the Supply Siders," in W. C. Stubblebine and T. D. Willett, eds., *Reaganomics: A Midterm Report* (New York: Institute of Contemporary Studies, 1983).

TABLE 19.1. PAST AND PROJECTED FUTURE REAL GNP AND LABOR PRODUCTIVITY GROWTH RATES AND THEIR SOURCES

	ACTUAL		PROJECTED	
	1948–1973	1973–1981	1981–1990	1990–2000
	Average Annual Percentage Growth Rates			
Labor Productivity	3.0	0.8	2.7	2.3
Real GNP	3.7	2.2	4.0	3.2
Total factor input growth[a]	1.7	2.0	2.2	1.8
Labor	(0.7)	(1.4)	(1.3)	(0.9)
Capital	(3.6)	(3.2)	(4.0)	(3.6)
Total factor productivity	2.0	0.1	1.8	1.4
	Percentage-Point Contributions to Total Factor Productivity Growth			
Advances in knowledge	1.4	0.7	1.2	1.0
Changes in labor quality	0.5	0.6	0.9	0.9
Education and training	(0.6)	(0.7)	(0.7)	(0.6)
Health and safety	(0.1)	(0.1)	(0.1)	(0.1)
Age/sex composition	(−0.2)	(−0.2)	(0.1)	(0.2)
Resource reallocations	0.4	0.1	—	—
Volume changes	0.3	−0.3	0.6	0.4
Economies of scale	(0.4)	(0.2)	(0.4)	(0.3)
Capacity utilization	(−0.1)	(−0.5)	(0.2)	(0.1)
Government regulations	—	−0.2	−0.1	−0.1
Actual/potential efficiency	−0.6	−0.6	−0.5	−0.5

[a] Total factor input growth is a weighted average of labor growth and capital growth; the weights are 0.655 for labor and 0.345 for capital, which approximate their respective shares of national income.

Source: Adapted from Table 1, J. W. Kendrick, "Long-Term Economic Projection: Stronger U.S. Growth Ahead," *Southern Economic Journal*, vol. 50, no. 4 (April 1984), p. 953.

listed. They achieved (intellectual) influence in the Reagan administration and framed what has been called *Reaganomics*. In particular, most of them insisted that:

1. A drastic reduction in marginal tax rates would *raise* tax revenues.
2. A drastic reduction in marginal tax rates would *quickly* cure stagflation so that inflation could be eliminated *without* a recession. (Inducing a recession, unfortunately, is the tried-and-true way to fight inflation.) We discuss each of these in turn.

Can a Reduction in Tax Rates Raise Tax Revenues?

Radical supply-siders argued vehemently in favor of drastic reductions in marginal tax rates for both households and businesses. To the charge that such an action would generate very large federal government deficits, the radical supply-siders responded that a drastic reduction in taxes would stimulate so much extra work effort and economic activity that national income would rise so dramatically as to *increase* tax revenues. These more zealous supply-siders maintained that so much economic activity would be induced by lower marginal tax rates that (1) households could have more consumer goods *and* (2) government could provide more national defense *and* more social welfare.[21] Such a position is doubtless appealing to politicians who apparently are relieved from making hard decisions and selecting optimal trade-off positions.

How was this economic miracle, as it were, to come about? The key is to understand the impact of marginal tax rates. The underlying assumption is that individuals in their capacities as workers, savers, and investors respond to changes on the margin. What is important to the worker contemplating more or less work is the after-tax (or take-home) pay, which is a function of that worker's marginal tax rate. What is important for the saver is the after-tax rate of return on additional saving, which is also a function of that saver's marginal tax rate. Finally, what is crucial to the firm contemplating investment in new plant and equipment is the expected after-tax rate of return. Again, that is a function of the marginal tax rate.

Tax Rates and the Labor/Leisure Choice   From labor's point of view, there is always a choice between more work (and pay) and less leisure, or less work (and pay) and more leisure. The choice at the margin is a function of after-tax earnings. The greater the marginal tax rate, the lower the after-tax wage and, hence, the lower the opportunity cost of leisure. Figure 19.5 shows this relationship. The quantity of leisure demanded is greater (the quantity of labor supplied is less) when its opportunity cost is lower (i.e., when the marginal tax rate is higher).

Ways to Increase Leisure or Reduce Work Effort   There are several ways in which individuals can respond to higher marginal tax rates. They include

1. Longer vacations
2. Fewer supplemental jobs (less moonlighting)
3. Earlier retirement
4. Greater absenteeism
5. Refusal of higher-paying positions that require more work effort or relocation

---

[21] Many economists resent the supply-siders' apparent repeal of the "there ain't no such thing as a free lunch" law, but the radical supply-side position is that a "free" lunch can arise from increased efficiency.

Work Effort Is Directly Related to the Marginal Tax Rate on Income

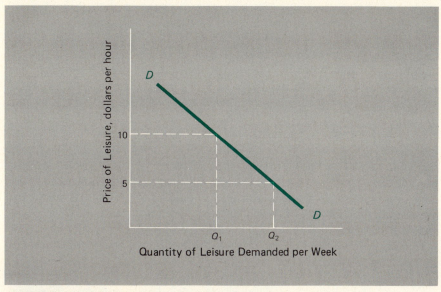

FIGURE 19.5. THE DEMAND FOR LEISURE

The demand for leisure (not working) is related to its price. Its price, however, is an individual's after-tax wage rate because when the individual does not work (that is, "buys leisure") his or her opportunity cost is the after-tax income loss. Assume that with a zero marginal tax rate the individual makes $10 an hour. The quantity of leisure demanded will be Q_1. If the individual's marginal tax rate increases to 50 percent, then the after-tax wage rate will be $5 an hour (given a pretax wage rate of $10 per hour) and the quantity of leisure demanded will increase to Q_2. It follows that as the marginal tax rate rises the quantity of labor supplied falls, because an increase in the quantity of leisure demanded is the counterpart of a decrease in the quantity of labor supplied, other things constant.

6. Lower participation rates (the ratio of those in the labor force to the total number in the group) for teenagers and older people

"Misdirected" Work Effort and Resource Misallocation   Supply-side economists advocate reductions in marginal tax rates for another reason. They believe that the lower the marginal tax rate, the fewer will be the resources that are misdirected. Individuals, in their capacities as workers and investors, put their resources in those economic activities that yield the relatively higher rates of return; but (so-called) loopholes in the tax laws increase the relative rate of return from *particular* activities. For example, individuals may invest in real estate only because of the tax advantages. From a social point of view, society often ends up having "too many" resources in certain sectors because of these "loopholes." This is tantamount to an inefficient use of society's resources.

Resources Devoted to Avoiding Taxes Another disadvantage of an income tax system with high marginal tax rates is that it encourages the use of resources to find ways to avoid taxes. Millions of dollars' worth of lawyers' and accountants' time is used each year to help high-income-earning individuals to (legally) reduce their tax liabilities. A growing quantity of resources is additionally devoted to evading tax liabilities illegally.

That part of the economy in which income is not reported is called the cash, underground, or subterranean economy. The subterranean economy is estimated to produce an output between 2 and 20 percent of the measured gross national product. Individuals engage in exchanges in cash to avoid records—cancelled checks and receipts—that could be used by the Internal Revenue Service to prove that income was earned and not declared for tax purposes.

These exchanges would be made more efficiently (at lower cost) if they were part of the normal economy; according to supply-side economists, they would become part of the normal economy if marginal tax rates were sufficiently reduced. After all, the lower the marginal tax rate, the smaller the benefit from trying to find cash deals by which income taxes are illegally avoided.

Putting It All Together—The Laffer Curve We are led to conclude that there is a relationship between tax rates and tax revenues. After some "high" marginal tax rate is reached, individuals reduce their work effort, spend more time seeking ways to reduce tax liabilities, and engage in more nonreported (nontaxed) exchanges. The relationship between tax rates and tax revenues has been popularized by Arthur Laffer of the University of Southern California. His now famous (some say infamous) **Laffer curve** demonstrates a relatively simple proposition: above some tax rate an increase in tax rates actually reduces tax revenues. Look at Figure 19.6, which measures tax rates T on the vertical axis and tax revenues R on the horizontal axis. Tax rate T_1 is the maximum rate that the government can impose before the relationship between tax rates and revenues becomes negative.

For example, at tax rate T_2, revenues will have dropped from R_{max} to R_2. Note that even though T_1 *appears* (in our graph) to be at about 50 percent, that is not necessarily the case; T_1 needs to be established empirically.

A Policy Implication of the Laffer Curve One policy implication of

A Reduction in Tax Rates Can Actually Increase Tax Revenues

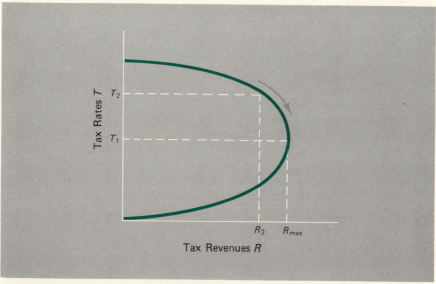

FIGURE 19.6. THE LAFFER CURVE

The Laffer curve is a representation of the relationship between tax rates and tax revenues collected. Tax revenues are on the horizontal axis and tax rates are on the vertical axis. The maximum tax revenues collectible, R_{max}, result at the tax rate T_1. If the government imposes a higher tax rate of T_2, tax revenues collected fall from R_{max} to R_2. The policy implication of the Laffer curve is that if tax rates are above tax rate T_1, then a reduction from current tax rates of, say, T_2 toward tax rate T_1 will *increase* tax revenues from R_2 toward R_{max}. This proposition (and the actual rate of T_1) rests on the empirical relationship between reductions in tax rates and changes in the amount of work effort, investment, saving, and attempts at tax avoidance and evasion.

the Laffer curve is that if the economy is already at tax rate T_2, a reduction in tax rates will actually lead to an increase in tax revenues. This implication assumes, implicitly, that work disincentives are great and that the size of the underground economy is large at very high tax rates. This reasoning was the basis for the radical supply-siders' seemingly odd notion that the economy could have more of everything—more private goods and more publicly provided goods—if only marginal tax rates were reduced sufficiently. Lower marginal tax rates will lead to increased production (more private goods) and a higher level of national income which will generate more taxes to pay for more social goods.

Can A Reduction in Tax Rates Cure Stagflation?

Radical supply-siders also insisted that a drastic reduction in marginal tax rates on corporate and noncorporate income of all kinds was just what the doctor ordered as a cure for stagflation. Extending the discussion of the previous section, they argued that in fact the combination of (1) actual tax increases and (2) inflation that caused people to move into higher marginal tax brackets (bracket creep) has so reduced work effort, saving, and business incentives to invest that the aggregate supply curve in Figure 19.3 drifted leftward; that is, a reduction in aggregate supply resulted from higher marginal tax rates.

To them it seemed that a natural way to fight stagflation (and to fight the productivity slowdown discussed in the early part of this chapter) would be to lower tax rates drastically. By doing so, inflation could be eliminated without the nation having to endure the hardship of a recession. Because reduced inflation usually requires a recession, the supply-side approach seemed novel.

Consider Figure 19.7, which shows how the supply-siders would fight stagflation. Congress enacts a drastic reduction in marginal tax rates, which in turn increases work effort, saving, and business invesment. All of this economic activity, in effect, increases the aggregate supply curve relative to the aggregate demand curve. This is indicated in Figure 19.7 as a rightward shift in the aggregate supply curve, from AS to AS'. Notice that the result is, simultaneously, a lower price level and an increase in real national output—the perfect antidote to stagflation.[22]

Mainstream Supply-Side Economics

Mainstream supply-side economists include Martin Feldstein, Chairman of the Council of Economic Advisers for the Reagan administration until his return to Harvard in 1984; Michael Boskin of Stanford University; and Michael K. Evans, founder and president of Evans Econometrics, Inc., a national consulting firm.

Mainstream supply-side economists are sympathetic to much of what radical supply-siders say, but they believe that the claims of the latter are excessive.

Mainstream supply-siders agree that the U.S. economy was in bad shape right before the first Reagan election. As Evans notes:

Indeed, the record of the U.S. economy since 1965 had been one long story of impaired performance. From 1947 to 1965, productivity increased slightly

---

[22] If prices are sticky downward, reduced marginal tax rates will permit aggregate demand to rise without the price level rising.

Supply-Side Economics Can Combat Stagflation

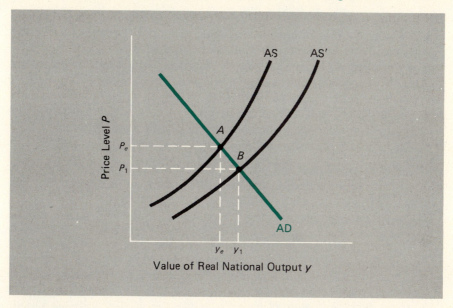

FIGURE 19.7. FIGHTING STAGFLATION WITH SUPPLY-SIDE
ECONOMICS FIRE

By reducing marginal tax rates drastically, work effort, saving, and investment
will increase and cause the aggregate supply curve to increase from AS to AS′.
The result is that the price level falls and real national output rises (or, if prices
are sticky downward, AD must rise if a surplus of y and N is to be avoided).

more than 3 percent per year while from 1977 through 1981 it actually
declined. The rate of inflation for that earlier period averaged 1.9 percent—
including the commodity inflation at the beginning of the Korean War. The
inflation rate then increased to 4.1 percent for the 1966–1972 period and 9.0
percent for the 1973–1981 period. The unemployment rate, which had averaged 4.8 percent from 1947 to 1965, rose to an average of 6.7 percent from
1975 through 1980 and surpassed 10 percent by late 1982. Even the once
highly valued dollar had lost more than half of its purchasing power by 1980
relative to now-strong foreign currencies such as the deutsche mark, the
Swiss franc, and the Japanese yen.[23]

[23] Michael K. Evans, *The Truth About Supply-Side Economics* (New York: Basic Books, 1983), p.
10.

Evans points out that this poor economic performance in the United States economy is directly tied to its declining productivity; he suggests that declining productivity is due to:

1. A sharp increase in both average and marginal tax rates on personal income after the Kennedy-Johnson tax cut in 1964
2. A sharp increase in the rate of inflation that skewed investment away from productive assets (capital) and toward such nonproductive assets as land, gold, and silver
3. The doubling of the maximum tax rate on capital gains and the curtailment of federal funding and support of R&D projects
4. The large increase in government regulatory activity during the 1970s

Evans believes that the advice that the radical economists gave to the Reagan administration, and which resulted in Reaganomics, was seriously in error. As Evans notes:

> The Reagan program, as it was structured, asked the economy to perform not one but three unnatural acts. The first was for the gross national product (GNP) to grow faster at the same time that the money supply growth was being severely restricted. The second was for the rate of real growth to increase from 1 percent to 5 percent at the same time that the rate of inflation was cut in half, from 10 percent to 5 percent. The third was to balance the budget by 1984 in spite of massive increases in defense spending and unprecedented tax cuts.[24]

Evans believes, therefore, that the Reagan economic plan was rife with logical inconsistencies, and that for the program to reach its goals of higher economic growth, lower inflation, and a balanced budget by 1984, it was necessary for the economy to experience

1. An unprecendented increase in the velocity of money over a five-year period
2. An extraordinary improvement in the rate of productivity growth
3. More than a 50 percent reduction in all government spending, excluding defense and social safety-net programs[25]

To Evans, the Reagan plan was a failure. He writes:

> Judged by any reasonably unbiased criteria, including the administration's own forecast, the program *as actually implemented* was an egregious failure. When Wall Street heard the news of the tax cut, the stock market plunged almost 20 percent in a two-month period, and the economy promptly entered a recession which was to send unemployment soaring to postwar highs and profit margins and capacity utilization to postwar lows. Whereas the rate of inflation was indeed cut in half, interest rates initially failed to decline; and

---

[24] Ibid., p. 4.

[25] Ibid., p. 7.

some yields, particularly mortgage rates, moved to new all-time peaks. The so-called real rate of interest—the nominal rate less the rate of inflation—reached levels unmatched since the early 1930s. The financial position of the federal government made a hollow mockery of the claim to return to a balanced budget as the deficit soared from $60 billion in fiscal year (FY) 1981 to $110 billion in FY 1982 and appeared headed toward $180 billion in FY 1983.[26]

To Evans, the lesson to be learned from the supply-side failure of the Reagan administration is not that supply-side theorizing is invalid. Instead, the Reagan programs contained two critical mistakes: First, taxes were cut without cutting government spending; and second, too much was promised too soon. Evans maintains that an optimal supply-side program

> can be likened to a three-legged stool: personal tax cuts, business tax cuts, and government spending cuts. Remove any one of the three legs, and the stool collapses. That is what happened with the Reagan program. Taxes were cut by an unprecedented amount but government spending in FY ... 1982 rose 4.6 percent in real terms—an amount *greater* than the average increase during the so-called big spending decades of the 1960s and 1970s.[27]

In short, one should not abandon a supply-side economics program just because the Reagan supply-side plan was poorly implemented.

Empirical Foundations to Supply-Side Economics

Radical supply-side economists presented much historical and anecdotal evidence to justify their boundless enthusiasm,[28] and mainstream supply-siders presented empirical support for their tempered enthusiasm.

Evidence that real saving is very sensitive to the real, after-tax interest rate was provided first by Michael Boskin.[29] Michael K. Evans also finds that

> a 1 percent change in the rate of return—that is, from 3 percent to 4 percent—would change the personal saving rate by about 1 percent, or $20 billion at 1982 levels of income. A 1 percent change in the rate of return could occur through a 1 percent change in the inflation rate, a 2 percent change in the

---

[26] Ibid., p. 4.

[27] Ibid., p. 20.

[28] See Arthur B. Laffer and Jan P. Seymour, eds., *The Economics of the Tax Revolt: A Reader* (New York: Harcourt Brace Jovanovich, 1979); George Gilder, *Wealth and Poverty* (New York: Basic Books, 1981); and Paul Craig Roberts, "The Breakdown of the Keynesian Model," *The Public Interest*, vol. 52 (Summer 1978), pp. 20–23.

[29] Michael Boskin, "Taxation, Saving, and the Rate of Interest," *Journal of Political Economy*, part 2 (April 1978), pp. 3–27.

interest rate, or approximately a 13 percent cut in tax rates (for example, from 50 percent to 43.5 percent.[30]

There is also empirical evidence relating work effort and tax rates. Research by Jerry A. Hausman indicates a strong supply-side response to tax changes.[31] His studies indicate that increases in income and payroll taxes reduced the labor supply of husbands by about 8 percent and of wives by almost 30 percent. The fact that men are less responsive than women to marginal tax rate changes is not inconsistent with past findings; that *both* men and women are so responsive is surprising. Hausman also unearthed a rather startling piece of evidence. He designed a very mildly progressive tax structure—with marginal tax rates rising from a low of 14.6 percent to a high of 20.7 percent—with a $4500 exemption. He estimates that this structure would yield about the same total tax revenues as the current progressive system, but he concluded that the labor supply would be only 1.5 percent less than if there were no income tax at all! Such a finding, if it can be replicated in other studies, argues strongly in favor of a "flat" tax rate system, or of a very mildly progressive structure, as a means of obtaining tax revenues.

Martin Feldstein and Lawrence Summers have argued that the slowdown in productivity in general and the decline in the rate of capital formation (investment) in the United States from 1973 to 1978 were largely attributable to the disincentive for savers to save and businesses to purchase capital equipment. The main culprit, according to Feldstein and Summers, was the interaction of inflation and the (then existing) tax system, which had lowered the after-tax rate of return on investment and on saving.[32]

In particular, Feldstein and Summers show that

1. Most firms value inventory according to the first-in, first-out accounting system (FIFO), although economic analysis suggests that inventory should be valued at its replacement cost. During periods of inflation, the FIFO method understates true production costs and, consequently, overstates profits and increases the corporations' tax liability, other things constant.

---

[30] Evans, op. cit., p. 112. See also Timothy R. Roth and Mark R. Policinski, *Marginal Tax Rates, Saving, and Federal Government Deficits* (Washington, D.C.: Joint Economic Committee, July 9, 1981), who find a strong negative relationship between marginal tax rates and personal saving and a strong positive relationship between interest rates and saving.

[31] Jerry A. Hausman, "Income and Payroll Policy and Labor Supply," Working Paper No. 610, *National Bureau of Economic Research*, 1979; reprinted in the volume, *How Taxes Affect Economic Behavior*, edited by Henry J. Aaron and Joseph A. Pechman (Brookings Institution, April 1981). Also see Evans, op. cit., p. 188.

[32] Martin Feldstein and Lawrence Summers, "Inflation and the Taxation of Capital Income in the Corporate Sector," *National Tax Journal*, vol. 32 (December 1979), pp. 445–470.

2. The current tax system permits firms to deduct depreciation of capital equipment only at the original (historical) cost instead of at replacement cost. Again, during periods of inflation, depreciation costs are understated, profits are overstated, and the firm's tax liability is overstated, other things constant.

Feldstein and Summers conclude that these two accounting features of the current tax system increased corporate tax liability in 1977 alone by $32 billion dollars (which was about 50 percent of *total* corporate taxes for that year), money that might have been used to purchase capital goods.

Similarly, Feldstein and Summers point out that the U.S. tax system, during periods of inflation, discourages saving because it lowers the after-tax return to saving. After all, people pay taxes on *nominal* interest rates, nominal dividends, and nominal capital gains—all of which rise during periods of inflation. Less saving, in turn, means fewer funds available for business expansion.

Finally, some evidence of a Laffer curve (for high-income groups, at least) has emerged. James Gwartney and Richard Stroup, of Florida State University and Montana State University, respectively, present evidence using 1982 income tax data that show that, as a result of the 1981 tax cut, the tax base increased.[33] Consider Table 19.2, which is adapted from the Gwartney-Stroup article. It shows striking evidence that although overall tax revenues fell, the tax cut decreased the tax liabilities of the relatively lower-income groups more than it decreased the tax liabilities of the relatively higher-income groups and actually *increased* the tax liabilities of the very highest income group. The explanation for this phenomenon comes straight out of the supply-side economics model. The 1981 tax reduction was across the board, meaning that tax rates fell by the same percentage for everyone. Let's follow the Gwartney-Stroup example and assume that everyone's taxes fall by 20 percent. People in the 10 percent marginal tax bracket find that their tax rate is cut to 8 percent, while people in the 70 percent bracket experience a rate of decline to 56 percent. This means that people in the 10 percent bracket change from keeping $0.90 out of every extra dollar earned to keeping $0.92 (a 2.2 percent increase), while people in the 70 percent bracket increase their take-home pay from $0.30 to $0.44 for every extra dollar earned (a 47 percent increase). People in the higher marginal tax brackets thus had a stronger incentive effect than people in lower marginal tax brackets. As a consequence, upper-income groups respond by earning

---

[33] James Gwartney and Richard Stroup, "The Redistributionist Tax Reduction," *Wall Street Journal*, June 26, 1984, editorial page.

TABLE 19.2. EFFECTS OF REAGAN TAX CUT ON THE RICH AND OTHERS

Income Grouping[a]	INCOME TAX LIABILITY (BILLIONS OF DOLLARS)		Percent Change
	1981	1982	
Bottom 50 percent	$ 21.7	$ 19.5	− 10.1
50th to 75th percentile	59.0	55.6	− 5.8
75th to 98.6th percentile	145.4	141.3	− 2.8
Top 1.3 percent	58.0	60.5	+ 4.3
TOTAL	$284.1	$276.9	

[a] The number of returns in each income grouping was virtually identical in 1981 and 1982.

Source: Adapted from J. Gwartney and R. Stroup, "The Redistributionist Tax Reduction," *Wall Street Journal*, June 26, 1984, editorial page.

more taxable income and by engaging less intensively in tax-shelter activities.

Michael K. Evans analyzed the 1981 United States income tax data and concluded that "income tax revenue would be maximized if the top rate were cut to at least 35 percent and possibly as low as 25 percent."[34]

In effect, Evans concludes that a reduction in the very high marginal tax rates will, eventually, increase tax revenues. It is reassuring that mainstream supply-side economics, which is so well grounded in traditional economic theory, is being confirmed by empirical studies.

---

[34] Evans, op. cit., p. 200.

POLICY CONTROVERSY
Is the Productivity Slowdown a Statistical Illusion?[35]

One of the themes of this text is that economic variables are very difficult to measure and, consequently, policymakers should be very careful to avoid prescribing medicine when the economy is in fact healthy. If poor data make it *seem* as if the economy is having problems, "stabilization" policy is not only unnecessary, it is harmful.

Michael R. Darby, of the University of California at Los Angeles, wrote an ar-

---

[35] Based on Michael R. Darby, "The U.S. Productivity Slowdown: A Case of Statistical Myopia," *American Economic Review*, vol. 74 (June 1984), pp. 301–322.

ticle entitled "Three-and-a-Half Million U.S. Employees Have Been Mislaid: Or, an Explanation of Unemployment, 1934–1941," published in the *Journal of Political Economy* in February 1976. There Darby showed that after 1933 (until 1941) unemployment was mismeasured because workers who were employed in government relief programs were included under the "Unemployed" category. When the approximately 3.5 million people are (properly) moved into the employed category, the data show that the unemployment rate fell from 20.6 percent in 1933 to below 10 percent in 1936. This is a much more rapid "shock absorption" than was (and still is) generally known. The implication is that poor measurement (1) overstated unemployment and its attendant misery and (2) understated the ability of the economy to recover from the monetary (or demand) shock.

Recently, Darby has again attacked a "problem" by checking the validity of a measurement. Darby notes that

the productivity panic is based upon statistical myopia, and . . . a careful analysis within the perspective of the entire twentieth century discloses no substantial variation in what is variously described as growth in total factor productivity or technical progress.[36]

Darby points out that the rate of productivity growth is not significantly different from its natural growth trend *once allowances are made for age, sex, education, and immigration to obtain a quality-adjusted labor force.* Most importantly, during the 1965–1979 period, the labor force was, on average, younger than usual. For a variety of reasons, younger people are less productive than older people (over broad ranges) so that a change to a younger (on average) labor force reduces the productivity of the labor force as a whole. In short, according to Darby, "simple demographic adjustments eliminate any secular decline in technical progress."[37]

Darby also points out that the 1973–1979 period shows a slower productivity growth rate than the 1965–1973 period because in the former period measurement error existed. In particular, the Nixon price-wage freeze led to underreporting of price increases and, consequently, to overreporting of real output increases.

Darby concludes as follows:

Taken as a whole, the evidence does not support the view that there has been a substantial, inexplicable decline in total factor productivity growth since 1965 and especially since 1973. Instead the evidence presented here indicates that there has been a surprisingly stable growth rate of total factor productivity throughout the twentieth century.[38]

If Darby is correct, no policy is necessary. Indeed, policy might create a problem where none exists.

---

[36] Ibid., p. 301.

[37] Ibid., p. 301.

[38] Ibid., p. 316.

CHAPTER SUMMARY

1. Since 1965 the rate of growth of real GNP and the rate of growth of labor productivity have decreased. The deceleration of these growth rates is referred to as the productivity slowdown.
2. Theories that purport to explain the causes of productivity slowdown include (a) a reduction in innovation, (b) an inability to measure productivity properly, (c) higher energy prices, (d) inflation, (e) government overregulation and overtaxation, and (f) the growth of distributional coalitions.
3. If the productivity slowdown is due to the fact that the world is running out of innovative ideas, or due to the rise of distributional coalitions, the productivity slowdown will be permanent.
4. On the other hand, if the productivity slowdown is due to (a) an *artificially* high relative price of energy, (b) inflation, (c) excessive government involvement in the economy, or (d) reduced expenditures on research and development, we can expect productivity growth to return to its natural rate, because the first three are likely to decline and the fourth is likely to rise in the future.
5. John W. Kendrick, an authority on economic growth, predicts that productivity growth will return to its previous rate because the Revenue Act of 1978 and the Tax Acts of 1981 and 1982 have decreased marginal tax rates for workers, savers, and businesses.
6. Supply-side economists can be divided into two groups: radical supply-siders and mainstream supply-siders. Both groups believe that marginal tax rates affect (a) the labor/leisure choice, (b) the saving/consumption choice, and (c) investment.
7. Radical supply-siders influenced President Reagan's administration and helped to create Reaganomics. In general, radical supply-siders promised too much; they promised that (a) lower tax rates would increase tax revenues so that the economy could produce more consumer goods *and* more governmentally provided goods, and (b) that lower tax rates would fight stagflation quickly so that the economy could reduce inflation without suffering a recession.
8. The Reagan economic plan, according to mainstream supply-siders, was a failure because (a) the plan reduced tax rates without also cutting government spending and (b) it promised too much too soon. The optimal mainstream supply-side policy requires (a) personal tax cuts, (b) business tax cuts, and (c) government spending cuts.
9. Empirical evidence supports the contentions that (a) work effort is directly related to real after-tax earnings, (b) real investment is directly related to the real after-tax rate of return, and (c) real saving is directly related to real after-tax interest rate earnings. Evidence

also shows that significantly lower tax rates for very high income earners will induce that group to earn more taxable income and engage less intensively in tax-shelter activities, and also provides limited evidence that a lower marginal tax rate will lead to increased tax revenues.

10. There is some evidence that, if demographic quality adjustments in the labor force are made, the growth of productivity since 1965 is not significantly less than the long-term natural productivity growth rate.

GLOSSARY

disinflation   A reduction in the rate of inflation.
labor productivity   The ratio of the real value of output to the quantity of labor used to produce that output.
Laffer curve   A curve that relates tax rates to tax revenues.
supply-side economics   An economic school of thought, with classical origins, that proposes to combat stagflation and increase the rates of growth of real GNP and of productivity by lowering marginal tax rates.

QUESTIONS AND PROBLEMS FOR REVIEW

19.1   The rate of growth of labor productivity is thought to have decreased since 1965. How is labor productivity measured?

19.2   Of the theories that purport to explain the decreased rate of growth of labor productivity, which are considered to result in permanent decreases?

19.3   Explain why inflation is thought to result in a decreased rate of growth of labor productivity. Would this explanation still hold if taxes were proportional? If taxes were regressive?

19.4   What is meant by the description, government overtaxation? Describe the difference between high "levels" of taxes and high "rates" of taxes.

19.5   Explain why distributional coalitions such as unions might not attempt to raise the wage rate above the equilibrium level or market-clearing level, even though they could.

19.6   How are the Revenue Act of 1978 and the Tax Acts of 1981 and 1982 expected to affect labor productivity?

19.7   Distinguish between the beliefs of the radical supply-siders and the mainstream supply-siders.

19.8   Why did the mainstream supply-siders think that the early Reagan economic plan was a failure?

19.9 Do you think that the supply of labor is a function of real *before-tax* wages or real *after-tax* wages? What does the empirical evidence suggest?

19.10 How would demographic quality adjustments in the labor force be expected to affect evidence with respect to the rate of growth of labor productivity?

REFERENCES

Henry J. Aaron and Joseph A. Pechman, eds., *How Taxes Affect Economic Behavior* (Washington, D.C.: The Brookings Institution, 1981).

Martin Neil Baily, "Will Productivity Growth Recover? Has It Done So Already?" *American Economic Review*, Papers and Proceedings, vol. 74 (1984).

Michael Boskin, "Taxation, Saving, and the Rate of Interest," *Journal of Political Economy*, vol. 86 (1978).

Peter K. Clark, "Inflation and the Productivity Decline," *American Economic Review*, Papers and Proceedings, vol. 72 (1982).

Michael R. Darby, "The U.S. Productivity Slowdown: A Case of Statistical Myopia," *American Economic Review*, vol. 74 (1984).

Edward F. Denison, *Accounting for Slower Economic Growth* (Washington, D.C.: The Brookings Institution, 1979).

Michael K. Evans, *The Truth About Supply-Side Economics* (New York: Basic Books, 1983).

Martin Feldstein and Lawrence Summers, "Inflation and the Taxation of Capital Income in the Corporate Sector," *National Tax Journal*, vol. 32 (1979).

George Gilder, *Wealth and Poverty* (New York: Basic Books, 1981).

James Gwartney and Richard Stroup, "The Redistributionist Tax Reduction," *Wall Street Journal*, June 26, 1984, editorial page.

Jerry A. Hausman, "Income and Payroll Policy and Labor Supply," Working Paper No. 610, (New York: National Bureau of Economic Research, 1979).

John W. Kendrick, "Long-Term Economic Projection: Stronger U.S. Growth Ahead," *Southern Economic Journal*, vol. 50 (1984).

———, "U.S. Economic Policy and Productivity Growth," *Cato Journal*, vol. 4 (1984).

Arthur B. Laffer and Jan P. Seymour, eds., *The Economics of the Tax Revolt: A Reader* (New York: Harcourt Brace Jovanovich, 1979).

Harold McClure and Thomas Willett, "Understanding Supply Siders," in W. C. Stubblebine and T. D. Willett, eds., *Reaganomics: A Midterm Report* (San Francisco: Institute for Contemporary Studies, 1983).

Mancur Olson, *The Logic of Collective Action* (Cambridge, Mass.: Harvard University Press, 1971).

———, *The Rise and Decline of Nations* (New Haven, Conn.: Yale University Press, 1982).

———, "Stagflation and the Political Economy of the Decline in Productivity," *American Economic Review*, Papers and Proceedings, vol. 72 (1982).

Mancur Olson and Hans H. Landsberg, eds., *The No-Growth Society* (New York: Norton, 1973).

Robert W. Pulsinelli and Melvin V. Borland, "How Labor Productivity Growth Projections Overstate Lifetime Earnings," *Defense Law Journal*, vol. 34 (1985).

Albert Rees, "Improving Productivity Measurement," *American Economic Review*, Papers and Proceedings, vol. 70 (1980).

Paul Craig Roberts, "The Breakdown of the Keynesian Model," *The Public Interest*, vol. 52 (1978).

Timothy R. Roth and Mark R. Policinski, *Marginal Tax Rates, Saving, and Federal Government Deficits* (Washington, D.C.: Joint Economic Committee, 1981).

20

MACROECONOMICS AND AN OPEN ECONOMY

Throughout this text we have introduced international transactions whenever it was necessary or convenient to develop economic theory or to indicate applications of theory. For example, we have already noted that

1. One major national economic goal is an international payments equilibrium.
2. One major component of GNP is *net* exports of goods and services, or $X - M$, where X is the value of exports and M is the value of imports. (See Chapter 2.)
3. One exogenous source of change of the money supply in the classical model is a change in net exports; on a gold standard, a change in net exports leads to gold flows and therefore to changes in the domestic (and foreign) money supply. (See Chapter 5.)
4. When the aggregate demand curve was derived, it was indicated that one important reason the AD curve is negatively sloped is that changes in the domestic price level lead to changes in net exports, and hence to changes in the quantity demanded of domestic output. (See Chapters 5 and 13.)
5. It was pointed out that monetary control by the Fed is difficult if the demand for money (velocity) is unstable; because the demand for the United States dollar has become a *global* phenomenon in recent years, Fed control over the dollar has become weaker. (See Chapter 16.)

Nevertheless, we have postponed the systematic integration of international transactions into macroeconomic analysis until this chapter. Specifically, in this chapter we analyze the following:

1. International accounting identities
2. International adjustment mechanisms, or mechanisms that establish an international payments equilibrium
3. International adjustment mechanisms in (a) a fixed exchange rate system and (b) a floating exchange rate system
4. Monetary policy and fiscal policy under the two types of international adjustment mechanisms
5. A Policy Controversy concerning the world debt problem

INTERNATIONAL ACCOUNTING IDENTITIES

If a family spends for consumer goods and services more than its current income, it must do one of the following:

1. Draw down its wealth. The family can reduce its money holdings or it can sell stocks, bonds, or other assets.

2. Borrow.
3. Receive gifts from friends or relatives.
4. Receive public transfers from a government, which obtained the funds by taxing or borrowing from others.

We can use the above information to derive an identity. If a family unit is currently spending more for consumer goods and services than it is earning, it must draw on previously acquired wealth, borrow, or receive private or public aid. Similarly, an identity exists for a family unit that it currently spending less for consumer goods and services than it is earning: It must increase its wealth by increasing its money holdings by lending and acquiring other financial assets; or it must pay taxes or bestow gifts on others.

Additional identities arise when we consider *all* household units. For example, given the money supply, the amount by which some households reduce their money holdings must equal the amount by which other households increase their money holdings. A moment's reflection indicates that when we consider businesses and governments, each individual unit and each individual group faces its own identities or constraints. (We discussed the government constraint in the appendix to Chapter 17.) For example, *net* lending by households must equal net borrowing by businesses plus borrowing by governments.

Even though our individual family unit's accounts must "balance," in the sense that the identity discussed previously must exist, sometimes the item(s) that brings about the equality cannot continue indefinitely. If family expenditures exceed family income and this situation is financed by borrowing, this household may be considered to be *in disequilibrium if such a situation cannot continue indefinitely.* Or, if such a family deficit is financed by drawing on previously accumulated assets, the family may also be in disequilibrium because it cannot continue indefinitely to draw on its wealth; eventually, it will become impossible for that family to continue such a life-style.[1]

Individual households, businesses, and governments, as well as the entire group of households, businesses, and governments, must eventually reach equilibrium, or a situation that *can* be maintained indefinitely. Certain economic adjustments have evolved to assure equilibrium. Deficit households must eventually increase incomes or decrease expenditures if they are to reach equilibrium. Businesses, on occasion, must lower costs and/or increase revenues (or go bankrupt) in order to reach equilibrium.

---

[1] Of course, if the family members are retired, they may well be in equilibrium by drawing on previously acquired assets to finance current deficits. After all, they do not expect to live forever. This is an important lesson: it is necessary to understand the circumstances fully before pronouncing an economic unit in disequilibrium.

When nations transact with each other, certain identities or constraints also exist. People in a nation buy goods from people in other nations; they also lend and present gifts to people in other nations.

If a nation transacts with others, an accounting identity assures a "balance," but not an equilibrium.

As is true within nations, economic adjustment mechanisms evolve to assure that economic equilibrium will eventually exist between each nation and the rest of the world. Eventually, interest rates, prices, and national incomes change until international equilibrium is reached. The adjustment mechanisms driving the international economy toward equilibrium are discussed in the following section. In this section we explain why a country's international accounts *balance*.

A country is different from a family because (1) a country's accounts take into consideration the actions of its central bank, and (2) different countries use different currencies to settle their accounts.

The balance of payments is a record of all the transactions between the households, firms, and government of one country and the rest of the world. Any transaction that leads to a *payment* by a country's residents (or government) is a deficit item; a deficit item will be identified by a negative sign when we use actual data. Deficit items include the following transactions: imports of merchandise, gifts to foreigners, use of foreign-owned transportation, tourism expenditures abroad, military spending abroad, interest and dividends paid to foreigners, purchases of foreign assets (such as stocks, bonds, and real estate), deposits made in foreign depository institutions, and purchases of gold and foreign currency.

Any transaction that leads to a *receipt* by a country's residents (or government) is a surplus item and is identified by a plus sign when actual data are considered. Surplus items include exports of goods and services, expenditures made by foreigners touring the domestic country, services rendered by the domestic country's transportation facilities, interest and dividends received from abroad, gifts from abroad, foreign military spending in the domestic country, and such loans from foreigners as foreign purchases of domestic securities, increases in foreign bank loans to domestic companies, and increases in foreign holdings of the domestic currency. Also included are domestic sales of gold.

The Current Account Balance

The current account balance is the amount by which the value of a country's exports of goods and services (including military receipts and income on investments abroad) and transfer payments (private and government) exceeds the value of that country's imports of goods and services (including military payments) and transfer payments (private and government). For ease of exposition, let us refer to the current account balance as the excess of "exports" over "imports." As long as you understand that these terms actually include items that are not normally considered exports or imports, no harm is done.

If exports exceed imports, a **current account surplus** is said to exist; if imports exceed exports, a **current account deficit** (a negative number) is said to exist. A current account deficit must be financed by borrowing from abroad (increasing liabilities to the rest of the world) or by selling assets (reducing net claims on the rest of the world). A current account surplus necessarily leads to a purchase of foreign assets (increasing net claims on the rest of the world) or a reduction in net liabilities (repayment of foreign-owned debt).

The Capital Account Balance

The capital account balance is the amount by which the value of a country's sales of such assets as capital goods, stocks, bonds, and private sales and purchases of foreign money and land to foreigners exceeds the value of that country's purchase of such assets from abroad. If the value of such sales is greater than purchases, then a **capital account surplus** (a positive number) exists; if the value of such sales is less than purchases, then a **capital account deficit** (a negative number) exists. A capital account surplus implies a net capital *in*flow; a capital account deficit implies a net capital *out*flow.

The Official Settlements Balance

The **official settlements balance** is the sum of the current account balance and the capital account balance. Because of the existence of central banks, this sum need not be zero. If both the capital account and the current account are in deficit, the official settlements balance is said to be negative; that is, the domestic country pays more foreign currency to foreigners than it receives. A negative official settlements balance must itself be financed by such official reserve transactions as:

1. Increases in liabilities to foreign officials holders
2. Gold sales
3. Use of special drawing rights with the International Monetary Fund (IMF)
4. Sales of foreign currencies
5. Use of reserves with the IMF

By definition, the official settlements balance must equal the value of the official reserve transactions. In practice, the numbers don't correspond perfectly because many private international transactions are not recorded. Because by definition the sum of the current account balance and the capital account balance must equal the value of the official reserve transactions (a number we can determine with certainty), a term labeled *errors and omissions* (statistical discrepancy) is included to reconcile the differences.

Table 20.1 shows the values of the current account balance, the capital account balance, errors and omissions, and official reserve transactions of the United States for selected years. If there were no central banks, a current account deficit would have to be financed by a capital account surplus: if the residents of the United States spent and gave more than they earned and received in gifts, this deficit would have to be made up by borrowing from the rest of the world. The existence of deficits or surpluses in the official settlements balance of the United States shows that central banks have intervened in the balancing process. Note that since 1982 the United States has had a significant, and rising, capital account *surplus*, which helps to pay for its enormous, and rising, current account deficit.

Official Reserve Transactions

A surplus or deficit in the official settlements balance must be made up by *official reserve transactions* among the central banks. Table 20.2 shows how the U.S. official settlements surplus or deficit was balanced by official reserve transactions during the years 1975 to 1984. In general, a deficit in the U.S. official settlements balance can be financed by a reduction in U.S. assets claims on foreign central banks or by an increase in borrowing from foreign central banks (an increase in liabilities to foreign central banks). Table 20.2 shows that, for the most part, our official settlements deficits have been balanced by borrowing from foreign central banks; the foreign official assets entries are positive in every year except 1979, when a U.S. official settlements surplus existed. In fact, Table 20.2 shows that for most years after 1977 the U.S. official reserve asset change was *positive*—the United States was increasing its official reserves instead of reducing them.

THE ADJUSTMENT MECHANISMS UNDER FIXED AND FLOATING EXCHANGE RATE SYSTEMS

The last section indicated that the United States currently has an international **balance-of-payments disequilibrium:** the United States is in a disequilibrium position with respect to its international transactions. It

TABLE 20.1. THE UNITED STATES BALANCE-OF-PAYMENTS ACCOUNT (billions of dollars)

	1960	1965	1970	1975	1978	1979	1980	1981	1982	1983	1984
Current account balance	2.8	5.4	2.3	18.1	−15.4	−1.0	1.9	6.3	−8.1	−40.8	−101.5
Plus Capital account balance	−5.4	−6.3	−12.4	−30.2	30.8	−11.9	−43.5	−32.7	−28.4	23.5	73.4
Plus Errors and omissions	−1.0	−0.5	−0.2	5.9	12.5	25.4	25.0	20.3	32.8	11.5	24.7
Equals Official settlements balance	−3.6	−1.4	−10.3	−6.2	−33.7	12.5	−16.6	−6.1	−3.7	−5.8	−3.4

Note: Numbers may not add due to rounding. Negative sign denotes deficit.
Sources: Economic Report of the President (various editions) and *Economic Indicators*, 1985.

TABLE 20.2. OFFICIAL RESERVE TRANSACTIONS BETWEEN THE FED AND OTHER CENTRAL BANKS (billions of dollars)

	1975	1976	1977	1978	1979	1980	1981	1982	1983	1984
Changes in U.S. official reserve assets	−0.8	−2.6	−0.4	0.7	−0.8	6.6	2.2	3.9	−0.2	1.2
Changes in foreign official assets	7.0	17.7	36.8	33.7	−13.7	15.5	5.0	3.7	5.8	3.4
Allocations of special drawing rights	0.0	0.0	0.0	0.0	1.1	1.2	1.1	0.0	0.0	0.0

Note: Numbers may not add due to rounding.
Source: Economic Indicators, 1985.

typically has a deficit in its official settlements balance, and this deficit is financed mostly by borrowing from foreign central banks. If individual families or businesses have "payments deficits," eventually they must do one of two things: increase earnings or decrease expenditures. In this section we discuss the adjustment mechanisms that would, in the absence of central-bank manipulations, move a country toward an overall international balance-of-payments equilibrium. The variables that adjust are national incomes, price levels, and interest rates.[2] These three economic variables would change, in the absence of government intervention, until a balance-of-payments equilibrium is reached among nations. There are two basic international monetary systems that allow these three adjustment mechanisms to work: a **fixed exchange rate system** and a **floating exchange rate system.** We discuss these two systems now.

Fixed Exchange Rate Systems

From 1821 to 1971 the world was on what are referred to as the classical gold standard (1821 to 1914), the gold exchange standard (1925 to 1931), and the Bretton Woods system (1946 to 1971). Each of these is a fixed exchange rate system and will be discussed briefly; then we analyze the post-1971 period. First, however, we consider the *pure* gold standard.

The Pure Gold Standard[3]   Consider a nation on a pure gold standard. In order to be on a pure gold coin system, three conditions must exist.

1. Only official gold coins minted by the government are used as money.
2. The government commits itself to purchase gold from the public on demand at a fixed price and to pay for the gold with gold coins. For instance, if you discover or in some other way obtain gold, you can sell it to the government and obtain officially stamped gold coins of a predetermined value.
3. The government will sell gold to the public at the same fixed price. If you wish, you can sell your gold coins to the government for a predetermined quantity of gold—uncoined, and, therefore, not money.

Under such a system, the supply of minted gold *coins* (the money supply) is determined by the total quantity of gold available less the amount of gold used for nonmonetary purposes (jewelry, etc.). The frac-

---

[2] Note that these are the same basic mechanisms that drive the *domestic* economy to equilibrium in the classical model, the Keynesian model, and the neoclassical-Keynesian synthesis.

[3] See M. D. Bardo, "The Classical Gold Standard: Some Lessons for Today," *Review*, Federal Reserve Bank of St. Louis, vol. 63, no. 5 (May 1981), for much of what is in the next few sections.

tion of the available gold used for nonmonetary uses depends on the purchasing power of gold in terms of all other commodities. If the price level rises, the purchasing power of gold coins falls; and this fall in the relative price of gold coins will induce people to increase the use of gold for nonmonetary purposes. A fall in the price level increases the relative price of gold coins, and a higher proportion of the available gold will be converted into gold coins—money. In the short run, the stock of gold is limited due to high production costs.[4] The demand for gold *coins* in a nation on a pure gold standard is the demand for money in that nation, and it is determined by the nation's wealth and income, tastes, and the opportunity cost of holding money (the interest rate). The supply of and the demand for gold coins (money) will determine the price level, as you will recall from the classical theory of inflation in Chapter 5.

A Pure International Gold Standard   A pure international gold standard exists when a number of countries are on a gold coin standard. Under such a system, each government agrees to buy and to sell its particular minted gold coins (the Americans might call them "dollars," the British "pounds sterling"). Of course, the coins will be of different weights, shapes, and values in the different nations. Under a pure international gold standard, exchange rates between countries are necessarily fixed. An **exchange rate** is the price of a foreign currency in terms of domestic currency. Thus, if the United States values its currency at 1 ounce of gold per $20 (U.S.), and Great Britain sets the price of its currency at 1 ounce of gold per £4 (pounds sterling), then the exchange rate will be £1 and is equivalent to $5, or, conversely, $1 is equivalent to £1 divided by 5.

Adjustment Mechanisms Under a Pure International Gold Standard Suppose that, in our two-economy model, both the United States and Great Britain are on a pure gold standard and that there is a balance-of-payments equilibrium. One way for such an equilibrium to exist is for the value of exports to equal the value of imports, in each country. Now assume that U.S. residents increase their demand for British goods, other things constant. This action will cause a current account deficit for the United States and (necessarily) a current account surplus for Great Britain. This will cause a flow of gold from the United States to Great Britain.[5] Because gold can be converted into money, the British money

---

[4] This limited supply helped to make gold a good candidate for money. Gold is also durable, storable, portable, and divisible, and it is easily standardized and recognized—all desirable attributes of money.

[5] Technically, the increased U.S. demand for British goods will raise the value of the pound sterling in terms of the dollar. At some high price of the pound sterling gold coin (the "gold export point"), it will benefit U.S. importers to convert gold dollar coins into gold bullion (nonmoney), to ship the bullion to Great Britain, and to convert it into pound sterling gold coins (British money) in order to pay for British goods.

supply will rise and the U.S. money supply will fall. The price level, as a result, will fall in the United States and will rise in Great Britain. British goods will be relatively more expensive and U.S. goods relatively cheaper; and as a consequence the United States will export more and import less, and Great Britain will import more and export less. These actions will help to establish a payments equilibrium.

In addition, the decrease in the U.S. money supply will also induce a recession in the United States; an increase in Great Britain's money supply will cause an expansion in Great Britain. Subsequently, real or nominal incomes will fall in the United States and they will rise in Great Britain. These income changes will lead to an increase in British imports (an increase in U.S. exports) and a decrease in U.S. imports (a decrease in British exports). These income effects will also help to restore international-payments equilibrium.

Finally, under a pure gold standard central banks are supposed to follow the "rules of the game," which leaves very little indeed for central bankers to do. A central bank is supposed to allow its country to fall into a recession (or allow its price level to deflate) when it has a payments deficit and to allow it to expand (or inflate) when it has a payments surplus. A central bank should raise the discount rate (the rate it charges banks to borrow) when its country is experiencing a payments deficit and lower the discount rate when its country is experiencing a payments surplus. In our example, such actions will cause U.S. interest rates to rise relative to British interest rates. This interest rate differential causes short-term capital seeking higher interest earnings to flow to the United States from Great Britain. This capital flow from Great Britain to the United States lessens the required movement of gold from the United States to Great Britain and economizes on the use of gold.

In short, under the pure international gold standard, an international-payments equilibrium is established by relative price level changes, by relative interest rate changes, and by income-level changes. Moreover, central banks are supposed to allow and encourage these adjustment mechanisms to work.

The Classical Gold Standard (1821 to 1914) The pure gold standard described in the previous section never existed. Such a system is extremely costly to operate. Discovering, mining, and minting gold are extremely costly activities. Milton Friedman estimated that the cost of maintaining a full gold coin standard for the United States in 1960 would have been more than 2.5 percent of its GNP.[6] It is not surprising, there-

---

[6] Milton Friedman, *A Program for Monetary Stability* (New York: Fordham University Press, 1959).

fore, that nations sought ways to minimize the use of gold. The most obvious way to minimize the use of gold was to find substitutes for gold as money. These substitutes included government-provided paper money and privately produced bank notes and bank deposits. In practice, therefore, during the period of the classical gold standard a nation could be on a modified gold standard by maintaining a *fixed ratio of its paper currency to gold* and by requiring its central bank to keep a fixed ratio of bank liabilities to gold—or (to save on gold again) a fixed ratio of central bank liabilities to government bank notes and gold.

During the classical gold standard period the use of gold was minimized internationally, too. International trade was financed by credit; by receiving short-term loans, a current account deficit could be financed by a capital account surplus, and the use of gold could be lessened. Similarly, long-term loans—investments by developed nations in less developed nations, for instance—also provided a means whereby a nation could finance a current account deficit by a capital account surplus. In such cases, a prolonged current account deficit is not necessarily a sign of a payments disequilibrium. Nations also minimized the use of gold by employing the currency of certain reliable countries as reserves; certain "key currencies" were used as a substitute for gold for international reserves. Thus, payments adjustments didn't actually require gold flows; in many cases, transfers from one nation to another of pound sterling or other key currencies were made in the money markets of the major cities (London, New York, Paris, and Berlin) to avoid gold shipments.

In short, the classical gold standard that existed between 1821 and 1914 evolved into a modified gold standard in which paper currency and deposits were substituted for gold domestically, and key currencies were substituted for gold internationally. Current account deficits were also financed temporarily by a short-term capital account surplus and, for long periods, by long-term borrowing that led to capital account surpluses, which also economized on gold transfers.

Another way in which the classical gold standard differed from the pure international gold standard was that nations didn't always abide by the rules of the game. Some countries simply were not willing to induce a domestic recession or to allow inflation in order to restore payments equilibrium. Central banks engage in **gold sterilization:** they neutralize the impact of gold flows on the money supply by open-market operations. A deficit nation, for example, could sterilize gold outflows by purchasing government securities in the domestic open market; a surplus nation could sterilize gold inflows by selling government securities in the domestic open market. Such actions, of course, prolonged the payments disequilibrium. Eventually, a policy of sterilizing gold flows became infeasible, and the sterilizing country had to either start abiding by the rules *or go off the gold standard completely.* This is because eventually surplus nations will prefer goods to marginal increases in gold (which earn no interest), and deficit nations will prefer gold (which is necessary to settle international accounts) to marginal increases in goods as their gold stock nears depletion.

The Gold Exchange Standard (1925 to 1933)   The classical gold standard came to an end during World War I. Only the United States remained on a gold standard, and even then the Fed frequently sterilized gold flows. Other nations abandoned their commitment to maintain a fixed price of gold.

From 1925 to 1936 the gold standard was restored internationally, as the major trading countries established a *gold exchange standard*. Under this standard, most countries held gold, dollars, or pounds sterling as reserves; the United States and the United Kingdom held only gold reserves, and each defined its unit of currency in terms of a fixed quantity of gold. Most countries also sterilized gold flows in order to insulate their economies from the consequences of adjusting to international payments disequilibria.

The Bretton Woods System (1946 to 1971)   In 1944, representatives of the major trading nations met in Bretton Woods, New Hampshire, to create a new international payments system to replace the gold standard that had been abandoned in the early 1930s. The conference had two main objectives:

1. To create a monetary system that would provide for the relief and reconstruction of the countries devastated by World War II
2. To devise a system of fixed exchange rates and a means of correcting international payments disequilibria

On July 31, 1945, a compromise was finally adopted, and President Truman signed the Bretton Woods Agreement Act on behalf of the United States. The articles of that agreement created the International Monetary Fund (IMF) to administer the articles and to lend foreign exchange to member countries with balance-of-payments deficits. Each fund member, with the exception of the United States, would establish the par value for its currency in terms of either dollars or gold. The United States was required to define the dollar in terms of gold.

Member governments were obligated to intervene to maintain the value of their currencies in foreign exchange markets within 1 percent of their declared par values. The United States, which owned most of the world's already-mined gold stock, was obligated to maintain gold prices within a 1 percent margin of $35 (U.S.) per ounce. Except for a transitional arrangement permitting a one-time adjustment of up to 10 percent in par values, members thereafter could alter par values on exchange rates only with the approval of the IMF. The articles stated that such approval would be given only if the country's balance of payments was in "fundamental disequilibrium." This term, however, was never officially defined.

The Adjustable Peg The foreign exchange system established at Bretton Woods was based on the concept of the adjustable peg. Par, or pegged, values for each currency were established in 1944 in terms of the U.S. dollar or gold. The term *par value* meant the "appropriate" foreign exchange values set at that time. Exchange rates were to be pegged to those par values. For example, if it were decided that the par value of the French franc could be 5 francs to $1, or $0.20 (U.S.) per French franc, then the foreign exchange rate would be pegged at that level. Exchange rates were, however, allowed to fluctuate under the influence of supply and demand within a narrow band. From 1944 to 1971, the band was 1 percent above and below par value. From 1971 until 1973, the band was 2.25 percent above par value to 2.25 percent below par value.

Under these rules established at Bretton Woods, governments were supposed to intervene to prevent the values of their currencies in foreign exchange markets from falling *below* the lower limits. When there was an excess quantity supplied of its currency—that is, when the lower limit was reached—the deficit country's government was obligated to buy the surplus with U.S. dollars in order to support the price of its own currency.

Other Duties of the International Monetary Fund The IMF could also lend funds to member countries with balance-of-payments deficits. Such loans could come from IMF holdings of gold and currencies obtained from the subscriptions of IMF members according to a system of quotas. Each member's quota was set by a formula that took into account its importance in the world economy.

Fixed Exchange Rate Systems in Theory

Recall the *is-lm* model of Chapter 7, which explained how the equilibrium level of real national income and the equilibrium real interest rate were determined simultaneously in a closed economy, when the price level is assumed to be fixed. We called the *is-lm* intersection point the aggregate equilibrium. For our present purposes, we will now refer to the point of intersection of the *is* curve and the *lm* curve as the **internal equilibrium.** Figure 20.1 shows the by now familiar curves of *is-lm*. Because we are concerned with international transactions and with an open economy in this chapter, we must also consider **external equilib-**

Internal Equilibrium Exists at the Point of Intersection of the *is* Curve and the *lm* Curve

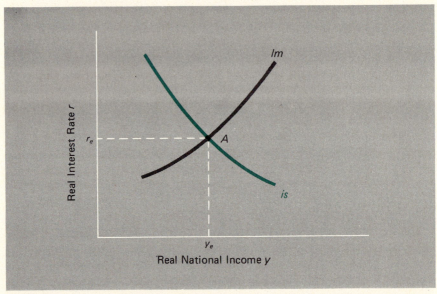

FIGURE 20.1. INTERNAL EQUILIBRIUM

Within the *is-lm* framework, product market equilibrium exists at all points along the *is* curve and money market equilibrium exists at all points along the *lm* curve. Internal equilibrium exists at point *A*, where *is* and *lm* intersect. Recall that the price level is assumed to be fixed in the *is-lm* model.

---

rium. We define external equilibrium as a situation in which the sum of a nation's current account balance and its capital account balance equals zero. Stated alternatively, external equilibrium exists when a nation's official settlement balance is zero.

The Balance-of-Payments (*bp*) Curve The **balance-of-payments (*bp*) curve** shows all the combinations of real interest rates and real national income levels that satisfy the external equilibrium condition. The balance-of-payments curve, clearly, is akin to the *is* curve and the *lm* curve. In order to derive the *bp* curve systematically, we will

1. Indicate the relevant assumptions necessary to the analysis
2. Explain why the curve is positively sloped, and what determines its degree of steepness or flatness
3. Indicate what causes the *bp* curve to shift

After the *bp* curve is mastered, we will then impose it on the *is-lm* framework and indicate how the economy will adjust until both internal equilibrium and external equilibrium exist simultaneously. This analysis of the equilibrating process assumes no government or central-bank intervention.

The Assumptions   In order to derive the *bp* curve, we make several assumptions:

1. Exchange rates are fixed.
2. The domestic price level and the international price level are fixed; this is a short-run assumption, and it will allow us to use the tried-and-true *is-lm* framework. We will later dispense with this assumption.
3. The capital account transactions that occur are due to differences between the domestic real interest rate and the international real interest rate. If the domestic real interest rate falls relative to the international interest rate (the latter is assumed constant), then capital will flow out of the domestic country, seeking higher interest earnings in other countries. In effect, we assume *positive but imperfect* international capital flows. If there were perfect international capital flows, then *no* differential (adjusting for the various risks) could exist between the domestic interest rate and the international interest rate.
4. The real exports *x* of the domestic country are fixed (constant, or exogenously determined).
5. The real imports *m* of a nation depend directly *and only* on that nation's real national income; this is because we have assumed fixed exchange rates and constant domestic and international price levels.

Derivation of the *bp* Curve   Because real exports are assumed to be constant and real imports vary directly with real national income, real imports increase relative to real exports as real national income rises. At some level of real national income, real exports and real imports will be equal. But at real national incomes greater than the one at which real exports and real imports are equal, the value of real imports will be greater than the value of real exports, and the nation then will have a current account deficit.[7] Therefore, at real incomes greater than the one at which real exports and real imports are equal, the following rule applies:

---

[7] And at real national incomes smaller than the one at which real exports and real imports are equal, the nation will have a current account surplus.

Higher real income levels require larger capital account surpluses in order to finance the larger current account deficits, if external equilibrium is to be achieved.

However, capital account surpluses require a higher domestic real interest rate r_d (given the international real interest rate). In short, if external equilibrium is to be maintained beyond some income level, higher real national income levels require higher (relative) domestic real interest rates. Stated alternatively, the *bp* curve, which shows all the combinations of real domestic interest rates and real national income levels that satisfy the external equilibrium condition, must be positively sloped. Figure 20.2 shows a typical *bp* curve.

The slope of the *bp* curve depends on the extent to which international capital flows are permitted. If international capital markets are *very* efficient, and if governments do not impede international capital flows, the *bp* curve will be parallel to the horizontal axis (have a slope of zero). There will be *no* difference between domestic and international real interest rates, and any domestic current account deficit will be financed by an infinitely small increase in the domestic real interest rate.

Conversely, if international capital markets are very inefficient and undeveloped, or if governments completely disallow capital flows, the *bp* curve will be parallel to the vertical axis (have an infinite slope) at the level of real national income at which there is a zero current account balance. To have external equilibrium under these extreme conditions, a nation must balance its current account because its capital account balance must be zero; under conditions of no capital flows, given a nation's exports, external equilibrium will exist only at the level of real national income at which real imports equal real exports.

We conclude that the slope of the *bp* curve depends on the degree of capital mobility between nations; the freer capital is to cross national boundaries, the flatter is the *bp* curve.

Points Above and Below the *bp* Curve   It is important to understand that at all points *above* the *bp* curve an external *surplus* exists; at all points above the *bp* curve the current account plus the capital account is positive.

Consider point *B* in Figure 20.3. Point *B* lies directly above point *A*, which is on the *bp* curve. At point *A*, by definition, a payments equilibrium exists. At point *B*, the level of real national income is the same as at point *A*, and therefore real imports are the same at both points; real exports are constant (by assumption). At point *B* the real interest rate is higher than at point *A*, so capital inflows will be greater at B than at point *A*. If (1) real exports and real imports are the same at points *A*

The *bp* Curve Is Positively Sloped Because Higher Levels of Real National Income Require Higher Relative Domestic Real Interest Rates to Maintain External Equilibrium

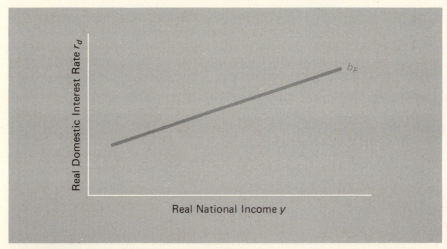

FIGURE 20.2. DERIVING A *bp* CURVE

The *bp* curve shows all the combinations of domestic real interest rates and domestic real national income levels that satisfy the external equilibrium condition. As the level of real national income rises, real imports rise relative to (fixed) real exports, so larger capital account surpluses are required to finance larger current account deficits. A capital account surplus is obtained when the domestic real interest rate rises relative to the international real interest rate. When real national income rises, therefore, external equilibrium requires a relatively higher real domestic interest rate.

and *B*, (2) capital inflows are greater at point *B*, and (3) an external equilibrium exists at point *A*, then (4) an external surplus must exist at point *B*. We leave it to you to explain why an external deficit must exist at point *C* in Figure 20.3.

Shifts in the *bp* Curve   A curve shifts when a variable that was assumed to be constant initially changes. The *bp* curve will shift if (1) the domestic price level changes relative to the international price level, (2) the exchange rate changes, (3) there is an exogenous change in real exports or a change in autonomous real imports (the community wants to import more or less at every level of real national income as a result of a change in tastes), or (4) international interest rates change. Of course, a change in *y* merely results in a movement along the *bp* curve (and *lm* and *is* curves).

At All Points Above the *bp* Curve an External Surplus Exists; at All Points Below the *bp* Curve an External Deficit Exists

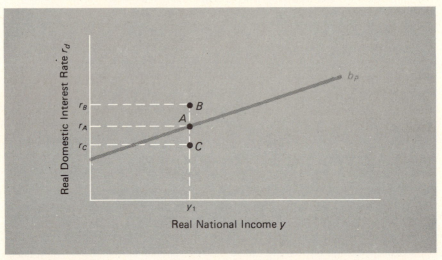

FIGURE 20.3. EXTERNAL EQUILIBRIUM AND EXTERNAL DISEQUILIBRIUM

At point *A*, an external equilibrium exists. Because points *A*, *B*, and *C* are all on a line perpendicular to the horizontal axis, each exists at the same level of real national income but at different real interest rates. At all three points, exports and imports are the same but capital flows are different. Because an external equilibrium exists at *A*, an external *surplus* exists at *B* and an external *deficit* exists at *C*.

Changes in Relative Price Levels   If the domestic price level rises relative to the international price level, domestic real imports will rise and domestic real exports will fall. This means that the current account balance will be "worse" at every level of real national income, and that a higher domestic real interest rate will be required to induce international capital flows to maintain external equilibrium at every level of real national income. We conclude, therefore, that if the domestic price level rises relative to the international price level, the *bp* curve will shift *upward*. Parallel reasoning indicates that a relative fall in the domestic price level will shift the *bp* curve *downward*. (Note, for future use, that if the domestic price level falls relative to the international price level, the resulting "improvement" in real net exports shifts the *is* curve to the right; and a relative increase in the domestic price level shifts the *is* curve to the left.)

Changes in Exchange Rates   A change in the exchange rate (initially, at least) leaves the domestic price level and the international price level unaltered. But it changes the purchasing power of one currency relative to others and the *effect* is the same as if there actually had been a change in relative price levels. We will analyze the interpretation of changes in the exchange rate more rigorously in the next section when we explore the open-economy adjustment mechanisms under a floating exchange rate international payments system. Here we merely note that if foreign exchange rates rise, it takes more units of the domestic currency to purchase a unit of foreign currency. For example, suppose the exchange rate for the dollar falls from 1/5 to 1/10 of a pound. It now takes more dollars to purchase specific British goods (remember only the exchange rate has changed; each country's price *level* has remained unaltered), and, conversely, it now takes fewer units of British pound sterling to purchase specific units of U.S. goods. The United States' real imports will fall and its real exports will rise; at any level of real national income, the U.S. current account is "improved" and it will now take a relatively *lower* U.S. real interest rate to restore external equilibrium. In short, if foreign exchange rates rise, the U.S. *bp* curve shifts downward; parallel reasoning indicates that decreases in foreign exchange rates (i.e., now it takes fewer dollars to purchase a specific unit of a foreign currency) shift the U.S. *bp* curve upward. (Be aware that if real *net* exports rise, the *is* curve will shift to the right.)

We leave it to you to explain why an exogenous increase in U.S. real exports will shift its *bp* curve downward and its *is* curve rightward, why an autonomous increase in its real imports will shift the U.S. *bp* curve upward and its *is* curve leftward and why a rise in international interest rates will shift the *bp* curve upward, and vice versa. Figure 20.4 shows a shifting *bp* curve.

The Adjustment Mechanism Under a Fixed Exchange Rate System

A Constant Price Level   Consider Figure 20.5, which imposes the *bp* curve on the *is-lm* framework. Simultaneous external equilibrium *and* internal equilibrium require some combination of a real interest rate and a real national income level that is at the point of intersection of the *is* curve, the *lm* curve, *and* the *bp* curve. In Figure 20.5, the economy is *not* in overall equilibrium. The level of real national income, established at the intersection of the *is-lm* curves (point *A*), is y_f and the domestic

The *bp* Curve Shifts If There Is a Change in the Relative Price Level, in the Exchange Rate, in Exogenous Exports, in Autonomous Import Expenditures, or in International Interest Rates

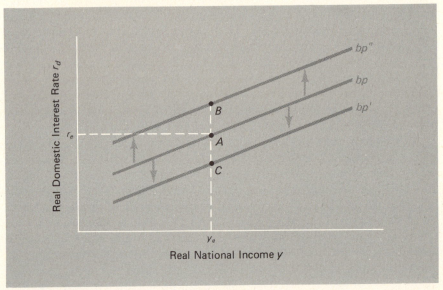

FIGURE 20.4. A SHIFTING *bp* CURVE

Start at point A on *bp*. If a country's relative price level falls, its own exchange rate falls, its exogenously determined real exports rise, its autonomous real import expenditures fall, or international interest rates fall, then its *bp* curve shifts downward to *bp'*; changes opposite to these will shift the *bp* curve upward to *bp"*.

real interest rate is r_1; at point A internal equilibrium exists. Point A is not on the *bp* curve, however, and an external *dis*equilibrium exists. In particular, because point A is below the *bp* curve (at y_f), an external deficit must exist at point A; at point A the official settlements balance is negative.

A negative official settlements balance means that such official reserve transactions as (1) gold sales, (2) foreign currency sales, and/or (3) use of IMF reserves must occur to finance the external disequilibrium. Each of these official transactions will lower the deficit country's monetary base, and there will be a multiple contraction in the money supply of the country depicted in Figure 20.5.

Because the price level is *assumed* to be fixed, a reduction in the

If Internal Equilibrium Exists Alongside an External Deficit, the *lm* Curve Will Shift Leftward

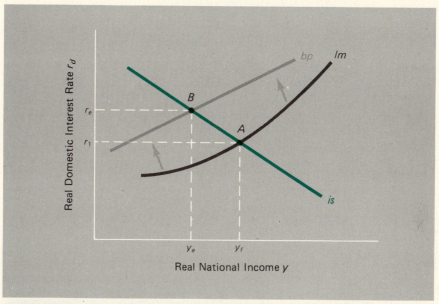

FIGURE 20.5. EQUILIBRIUM DETERMINATION IN AN OPEN ECONOMY WITH A FIXED EXCHANGE RATE

At point *A* internal equilibrium exists, but point *A* is below the *bp* curve and an external deficit exists. Consequently, the domestic nominal money supply will contract. *If the price level is fixed*, this decrease in the nominal money supply will decrease the real money supply, and the *lm* curve will shift leftward. The natural output level is at y_f, and the *actual* equilibrium level of real national income can be less than y_f, if the price level is constant.

---

nominal money supply is also a reduction in the real money supply, and the *lm* curve will shift leftward. The *lm* curve will continue to shift leftward until it passes through point *B* in Figure 20.5.[8] Figure 20.6 shows a situation in which both external equilibrium and internal equilibrium

---

[8] If the *lm* curve had shifted to the *left* of the *bp* curve, an external surplus would exist at the point where the new *lm* curve intersected the given *is* curve. This would lead to a positive change in the official settlements balance and to gold purchases, foreign exchange purchases, and/or to increased IMF reserve holdings. Each of these would increase the monetary base; a multiple expansion in the real money supply would occur and the *lm* curve would shift rightward. The process would continue until *is*, *lm*, and *bp* all intersect at point *B*, as in Figure 20.6.

Under a Fixed Exchange Rate System, If the Price Level Is Fixed, Simultaneous Internal and External Equilibrium Can Exist at a Level of Income Below the Natural Income Level

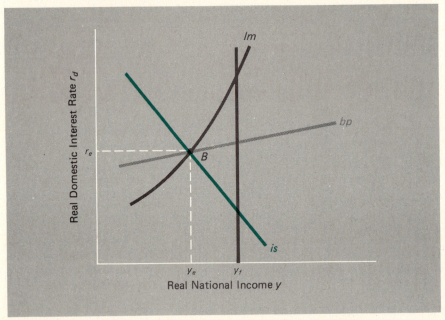

FIGURE 20.6. SIMULTANEOUS EXTERNAL AND INTERNAL EQUILIBRIUM UNDER A SYSTEM OF FIXED EXCHANGE RATES, GIVEN A FIXED PRICE LEVEL

Given the price level, external disequilibrium will shift the *lm* curve until the economy simultaneously reaches both internal equilibrium and external equilibrium. Under the assumptions of this model (fixed exchange rates and fixed price levels), the real money supply will change and the *lm* curve will shift until it passes through the point at which the *lm* curve, the *is* curve, and the *bp* curve intersect. This point *need not be* at the natural level of employment and the natural level of national income y_f.

exist simultaneously at point *B*, where the real interest rate is r_e and real national income is y_e.

It should be stressed that in this example the economy was brought to simultaneous internal equilibrium and external equilibrium only by changes in the real money supply. This is because our analysis assumed a fixed exchange rate system and also assumed that the domestic and international price levels are fixed. Because the price levels are fixed, it is quite possible that simultaneous external equilibrium and internal equilibrium can exist at a level of real national income that is below the natural level of income and below the natural level of employment. This is because the *lm* curve will shift to coincide with the intersection of the *bp* curve and the *is* curve. This situation is shown in Figure 20.6.

A Flexible Price Level If we had assumed that prices were flexible, then the flexible-price mechanism would have brought the economy to simultaneous internal equilibrium and external equilibrium *and* to the natural real income level. An internal equilibrium that exists at the natural level of real income, accompanied by an external deficit (as in Figure 20.5), leads to a multiple decrease in the domestic real money supply and to a multiple expansion in the international real money supply. In turn, the international (nondomestic) price level rises, and the domestic price level falls. This causes domestic real imports to fall and domestic real exports to rise, and this in turn shifts the *bp* curve downward *and* shifts the *is* curve rightward.[9] This process will continue until the economy is simultaneously in internal equilibrium and external equilibrium *at the natural level of national income* (as shown in Figure 20.7).

In a later section we indicate that a floating exchange rate system is yet *another* mechanism that drives the economy toward simultaneous internal and external equilibrium. A floating exchange rate shifts the *bp* curve and the *is* curve.

Stabilization Policy Under a Fixed Exchange Rate System

In Figure 20.6, *where the price level is fixed*, internal equilibrium and external equilibrium exist at a level of real national income that is *below* the natural output level. If prices are inflexible (fixed), therefore, stabilization policy may have a role to perform.

Consider monetary policy first. Starting at point *B* in Figure 20.6, suppose the Fed pursues an expansionary monetary policy by purchasing Treasury bills on the open market. This action increases the nominal money supply which, given the price level, causes the real money supply to rise. This shifts the *lm* curve rightward. This shift, however, raises the level of real national income and, therefore, raises real imports so at the new *is-lm* intersection point (not shown, but which would be below and to the right of point *B* in Figure 20.6) an external deficit exists. This

---

[9] A lower domestic price level also shifts the *is* curve rightward owing to the Pigou effect and shifts the *lm* curve rightward owing to the Keynes effect. Thus, *all three* curves will shift until the natural output level is established.

If the Price Level Is Flexible, the *bp* and the *is* Curves Will Shift Until *is*, *lm*, and *bp* Intersect at the Natural Income Level

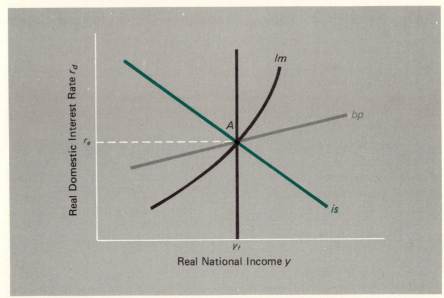

FIGURE 20.7. SIMULTANEOUS EXTERNAL AND INTERNAL EQUILIBRIUM UNDER A FIXED EXCHANGE RATE SYSTEM AND FLEXIBLE PRICES

If the price level is flexible, an external imbalance will lead to changes in the real money supply which in turn lead to changes in the domestic (and international) price level. This will cause real imports and real exports to change and shift the *bp* curve and the *is* curve rightward. These curves will shift until external equilibrium, internal equilibrium, and the natural level of real national income are all attained simultaneously.

deficit, in turn, causes the domestic money supply to fall, which shifts the *lm* curve back to its original position. The conclusion is as follows:

> *Under a system of fixed exchange rates and a fixed price level, monetary policy is ineffective.*

What then about fiscal policy? Consider Figure 20.8, which initially looked like Figure 20.6 but which now incorporates an expansionary

Fiscal Policy Can Achieve Internal Equilibrium at the Natural Income Level, But an External Surplus Will Exist Temporarily

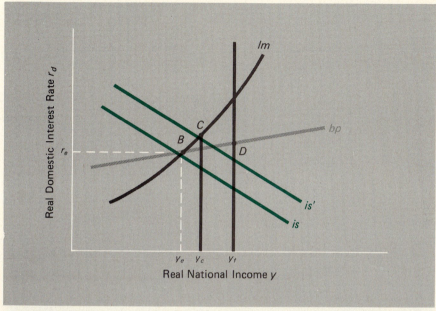

FIGURE 20.8. FIXED EXCHANGE RATES, A CONSTANT PRICE LEVEL, AND FISCAL POLICY

Start at point *B*, where internal and external equilibrium exist but the economy is operating at less than its natural income level. Because the price level is assumed to be constant, an expansionary fiscal policy is desirable. Such a policy shifts the *is* curve to *is'* and internal equilibrium is at a higher level but is still below the natural income level, at point *C*. Because point *C* lies above the *bp* curve, however, an external surplus exists. This will cause the *lm* curve to shift rightward. *Eventually*—as Figure 20.9 shows—*is* and *lm* will intersect at point *D*, or at the natural income level.

fiscal policy that raises national income to y_c but still does not achieve the natural level of income and internal equilibrium. Note, however, that point *C* lies *above* the *bp* curve; hence, an external surplus exists. This will lead to an increase in the domestic real money supply, and therefore the *lm* curve will shift rightward. *Eventually*, the *lm* curve and the *is* curve will intersect at point *D* in Figure 20.8, which is also on the *bp* curve. Figure 20.9 shows the *eventual* result of expansionary fiscal policy.

A Combination of Monetary Expansion and Fiscal Policy Is Necessary to Achieve Internal and External Equilibrium at the Natural Income Level

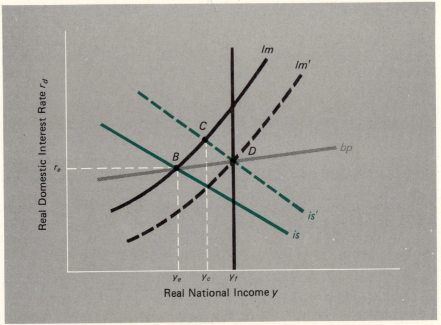

FIGURE 20.9. FIXED EXCHANGE RATES, A CONSTANT PRICE LEVEL, AND THE EVENTUAL RESULT OF EXPANSIONARY FISCAL POLICY

Start at point B. An expansionary fiscal policy eventually can cause the is curve and the lm curve to intersect at point D, which is also on the bp curve. Fiscal policy, then, is potentially beneficial in an economy characterized by fixed exchange rates and a constant price level.

We conclude this section with three observations:

1. Monetary policy is not very effective if exchange rates are fixed and the price level is constant.
2. Fiscal policy is *potentially* quite effective under a fixed exchange rate system and a constant price level, especially since fiscal policy automatically leads—by way of external disequilibrium—to changes in the real money supply in a countercyclical direction.
3. If the exchange rate is fixed but price flexibility exists, internal equilibrium and external equilibrium will *eventually* be established at the natural income level.

The History of the Bretton Woods Fixed Exchange Rate System

Immediately after the Bretton Woods system was organized, the rest of the world used about $6 billion of its gold and silver reserves to finance its deficits with the United States. Threatened with a reduction in their imports, European countries were faced with declines in their standards of living, zero economic growth, deflation, and devaluation. The United States solved Europe's balance-of-payments problems by voluntarily lending billions of dollars to Europe under the Marshall Plan (formally called the European Recovery Program). Between mid-1948 and mid-1952, the United States provided $11.6 billion in the form of grants and $1.8 billion in the form of loans to Europe. These voluntary loans averted a "dollar shortage" and allowed Europe and Japan to build their industrial bases and to reduce substantially their external deficits.

A major weakness in the Bretton Woods arrangement was that it failed to provide for a *systematic* means by which world reserves of dollars and gold could grow as world trade grew. The IMF subscriptions created a once-and-for-all increase in world monetary reserves; but the IMF could not provide for a continuous *growth* in world reserves. The only way the rest of the world could increase its foreign exchange reserves was for the United States to have deficits. In essence, the United States took on the role of a world central bank, the world was on a key currency standard, and the key currency was the U.S. dollar.

During the late 1950s and early 1960s the rest of the world *wanted* to increase its U.S. dollar reserves. The fact that they did not convert those dollar holdings into gold indicates that they did not want the United States to correct its balance-of-payments deficit by reducing its rate of inflation. A reduction in the U.S. inflation rate would have allowed U.S. exports to be more competitive in the world market; it would have also induced U.S. citizens to import less. But by the mid-1960s, the U.S. deficits were no longer matched by the desire of the rest of the world to increase dollar reserves. Dollar reserves were being *forced* on the rest of the world as a result of accelerating inflation in the United States.

If there had been no government intervention in the foreign exchange market, the excess supply of dollars would have caused the price of the dollar to fall against the pound and other currencies. However, under the IMF's fixed exchange rate system, foreign central banks were required to buy the excess supply of dollars. To prevent the pound from appreciating, for example, the Bank of England had to sell pounds to buy the dollars that were in excess supply.

If the foreign central banks had allowed their purchases of dollars to increase their money supplies, the U.S. inflation would have been exported to other countries. If this adjustment mechanism had been allowed to operate, the U.S. trade deficit would have become smaller because the rest of the world would have had a rate of inflation similar to that of the United States. But this would have required other countries to allow the Fed to determine their monetary policies. No country would have had an independent monetary policy; a country's inflation rate would have been determined by the U.S. rate of inflation.

Some central banks, notably in Germany, France, and Japan, did not permit their country's rate of monetary growth to accelerate. Instead, they sterilized the (internal) effects of their dollar purchases in the foreign exchange market by having their central banks sell bonds in their domestic open markets. Inflation was *not* imported by these countries, and, consequently, U.S. trade deficits with these countries continued.

Under the Bretton Woods agreement, though, foreign central banks technically did have the option of buying gold from the United States at $35 per ounce. Every U.S. Secretary of the Treasury during the latter part of this period spent part of his time traveling to Europe to persuade foreign central banks to purchase U.S. bonds rather than gold with their dollars. Most of the European countries and Japan honored the American requests. France did not.

The Demise of the Bretton Woods System   The United States took actions to insulate its gold stock. Although it was illegal for U.S. citizens to own gold, private foreign investors could buy gold at a fixed price of $35 per ounce in world gold markets; the United States guaranteed that it would intervene with gold sales in those markets if the price rose above $35 per ounce. This created a potential threat to the U.S. gold stock. Aside from the fact that the gold stock was used to meet obligations to member central banks, private speculators betting on the devaluation of the dollar in terms of gold also had claims on U.S. gold. In March 1968, the United States took the radical step of announcing that it would no longer sell gold to *private* holders of dollars. The gold market was thus divided into two tiers: gold held by foreign central banks (and treasuries) and gold held privately. The United States continued to honor its commitments to buy and sell gold in transactions with other central banks, but it no longer pegged the price of privately held gold. From 1968 until August 1971, however, the United States "lost" very little of its gold. The United States continued to sell gold to foreign central banks at $35 per ounce, *but it insisted that they not ask for any!*

To ensure further that the United States would not have to induce a recession in order to protect its gold reserves, the United States supported an amendment to the articles of the IMF that permitted the creation of special drawing rights (SDRs). The amendment turned the IMF into a world central bank with the ability to create international reserves. It also allowed the U.S. to buy back its dollars with such reserves, instead of gold.

On Sunday evening, August 15, 1971, President Nixon dropped a bombshell on America's trading partners. Nixon announced a radically new economic program to deal with the *overvalued* dollar. Included in the program were the following:

1. A 90-day freeze on wages and prices to reduce inflationary expectations
2. An import surcharge of 10 percent
3. A suspension of the convertibility of dollars into gold

Because the United States no longer honored its IMF obligations to sell gold at $35 per ounce, Nixon put the world officially on a "dollar standard," instead of a gold/dollar standard. In describing these actions, President Nixon acknowledged that "this action will not win us many friends among the international money traders. But our primary concern is with American workers, and with fair competition around the world." The 10 percent surcharge on imports was characterized as a "temporary" action designed to pressure other countries into appreciating their currencies so that "American products will not be at a disadvantage because of unfair exchange rates. When the unfair treatment is ended, the import tax will end as well. . . . The time has come for exchange rates to be set straight and for the major nations to compete as equals. There is no longer any need for the United States to compete with one hand tied behind her back."

The Smithsonian Agreement What finally came out of this new policy was the Smithsonian Agreement of December 18, 1971, which officially devalued the dollar by an average of 12 percent against the currencies of 14 major industrial nations. Even this devaluation of the dollar, however, was not sufficient to eliminate the excess supply of dollars on the foreign exchange market. The U.S. balance-of-payments deficit was still a substantial $10.4 billion during 1972. In early 1973, partly in reaction to the rapid expansion of the money supply in the United States during 1972, private speculators sold large amounts of dollars in the foreign exchange market. Foreign central banks purchased about $10 billion in the first three months of the year alone—compared to a deficit of $10.4 billion for the whole year of 1972—in an attempt to support the dollar. When this massive intervention failed to stabilize the dollar (even after an additional devaluation of the dollar in February), fixed exchange rates were abandoned.

The Floating Exchange Rate Is Determined by the Forces of Supply and Demand

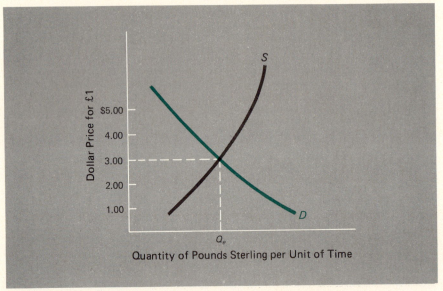

FIGURE 20.10. MARKET-DETERMINED EXCHANGE RATES

Given these curves, the equilibrium exchange rate will be established at $3; one British pound sterling will be equivalent to three U.S. dollars. At a higher sterling price, a surplus of pounds exists; at a price higher than $3 per pound, Great Britain will have a payments deficit and the United States will have a payments surplus. A surplus of pounds will cause the dollar price of the pound to fall toward $3. At any dollar price per pound below $3, a shortage of pounds exists; the United States will have a payments deficit and Great Britain will have a payments surplus. This shortage of pounds will drive the dollar price of the pound upward, toward $3 per pound.

The Floating Exchange Rate System   On March 16, 1973, the finance ministers of the European Economic Community (EEC) (the Common Market) announced that they would let their currencies float against the dollar. (Japan had begun to let the yen float against the dollar on February 12.) The communiqué argued that the official interventions in exchange markets might be useful at appropriate times in order to facilitate the maintenance of "orderly" conditions. Each nation in the EEC stated that it "will be prepared to intervene at its initiative in its own market, when necessary and desirable, acting in a flexible manner in the light of market conditions and in close consultation with the authorities of the nation whose currency may be bought or sold." In other words, the international monetary system was now on a managed float or, as it is sometimes called, a **dirty float**.

A SYSTEM OF PURE FLOATING EXCHANGE RATES

Establishing the Equilibrium Exchange Rate

Unlike a fixed exchange rate system, a system of pure floating exchange rates allows exchange rates to be set by supply and demand. In order to see how, let's consider the exchange rate of dollars for British pounds sterling. Consider Figure 20.10, which indicates the dollar price of £1 on the vertical axis and the quantity of British pounds sterling on the horizontal axis.

There is an inverse relationship between the dollar price of £1 and the quantity of pounds demanded. As the dollar price of pounds falls (that is, it takes fewer dollars to purchase £1 of British sterling), British goods are now relatively cheaper, other things constant. U.S. citizens will substitute British-made goods for American-made goods; that is, Americans will import more British-made goods. As the dollar price of £1 falls, other things constant, U.S. residents also experience an increase in their real incomes. *The same money income will allow them to purchase more goods than before, if they purchase British-made goods.* Such an increase in their real income will induce Americans to import more British-made goods. Normally, therefore, U.S. residents will purchase more British goods (increase their imports) as the dollar price of £1 falls.[10] In turn, this increase in the quantity of British goods demanded increases the quantity of British pounds demanded.[11]

A direct relationship exists between the dollar price of £1 and the quantity of pounds supplied, because a higher dollar price for pounds (i.e., a lower pound price for dollars) induces British residents to purchase more American-made goods, and British residents therefore offer more pounds on foreign exchange markets. At higher dollar prices per pound, the British can get more dollars, and therefore more American goods, for a unit of their money. At higher dollar prices per pound, therefore, Amer-

---

[10] A lower dollar price per pound might also encourage U.S. residents to be more generous to British relatives or induce U.S. residents to travel to England. The U.S. government might also be induced to give more military aid to Great Britain. Similarly, U.S. businesses might be more inclined to purchase more British-made parts and assemble them locally, or to make outright investments in England. All of these activities will increase the quantity demanded of pounds.

[11] After all, British sellers (or gift or loan recipients) want to be paid in their own currency so they can spend it locally.

ican goods are cheaper and the British import more U.S. goods.[12] Of course, larger real imports of American goods will require British residents to make greater quantities of pounds available to American sellers.

As Figure 20.10 shows, the equilibrium exchange rate will be established at $3 per £1, where the supply and demand curves intersect. At any price above $3 per £1, the quantity of pounds supplied by the British exceeds the quantity of pounds demanded by Americans; a surplus of pounds exists. (The British would experience a payments deficit, and the Americans would experience payments surplus, assuming they are the only two countries). Because a surplus of pounds exists, the price of pounds will fall; this will increase the quantity of pounds demanded by Americans and decreases the quantity of pounds supplied by the British. This process will continue until equilibrium is restored at $3 per £1.

At any price below $3 per £1, a shortage of pounds exists; the American quantity of pounds demanded exceeds the British quantity of pounds supplied. (The Americans would experience a payments deficit, and the British would experience a payments surplus.) In the absence of any government intervention (remember, this is a *pure* floating exchange rate system), a shortage of pounds will drive up the dollar price per pound; this will lead to a decrease in the American quantity of pounds demanded and an increase in the British quantity of pounds supplied.

At $3 per £1, the equilibrium exchange rate is established. Note, furthermore, that an international payments equilibrium is also established in this two-country model.

Changes in the Equilibrium Exchange Rate   Consider Figure 20.11, which shows a decrease in the demand (from D to D') for pounds. A decrease in the demand for pounds may be the result of one of the following:

1. The price level in Great Britain rises more rapidly than the U.S. level rises. If the British rate of inflation exceeds the American rate of inflation, for example, Americans will want to reduce the quantity of British-made goods they purchase at *any* dollar price for pounds. As a consequence, Americans will reduce the quantity of pounds they want at every dollar price per £1.
2. Real interest rates rise in the United States relative to Great Britain. In such a situation, American citizens will want to purchase fewer British securities at *any* dollar price per £1; the quantity of pounds demanded falls at every dollar price per £1.

---

[12] Or give more gifts to their relatives in the United States.

A Decrease in the Demand for Pounds Will Reduce the Dollar Cost of a Pound

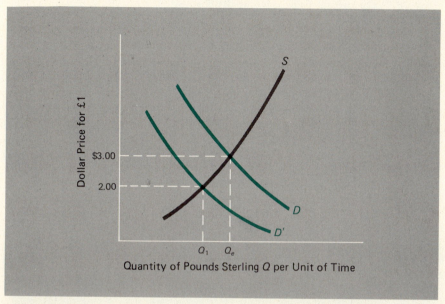

FIGURE 20.11. A DECREASE IN THE DEMAND FOR POUNDS

A decrease in the American demand for pounds, from D to D', could come about if (1) Great Britain experiences a higher rate of inflation, (2) real interest rates in the United States rise relative to those in Great Britain, or (3) real incomes fall in the United States, other things constant. Such a decrease in the demand for pounds causes a surplus of pounds at the old exchange rate. The dollar price of pounds will fall—the pound will depreciate and the dollar will appreciate—until a new equilibrium exchange rate is established at two U.S. dollars for one British pound. At the new equilibrium exchange rate, an external equilibrium is restored.

---

3. **Real income falls in the United States, other things constant.** If real incomes fall in the United States, its residents will want to import fewer goods at *any* exchange rate; the quantity of pounds demanded by Americans will fall at every dollar price per £1.

Figure 20.11 shows that the new equilibrium exchange rate will be established at $2 (U.S.) for £1. A decrease in the demand for pounds from D to D' causes a surplus of pounds at the old exchange rate; the quantity of pounds supplied by the British now exceeds the quantity of pounds demanded by Americans at the previous exchange rate. This will cause the dollar price of pounds to fall—the dollar will appreciate relative to the pound because it takes fewer dollars to purchase £1; this is called

The Dollar Has Appreciated Since 1980

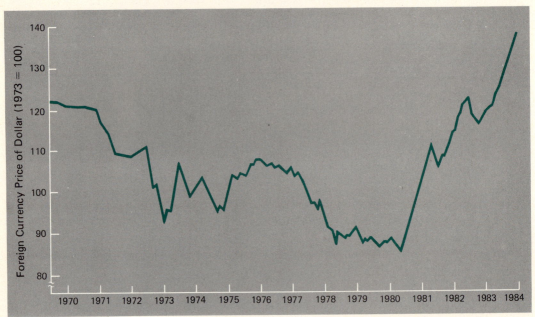

FIGURE 20.12. THE DOLLAR AFLOAT

This graph shows the real value of the dollar relative to an index of ten foreign currencies. Note that since early 1980 the dollar has appreciated and that other currencies have depreciated dramatically.

currency appreciation. Simultaneously (and of necessity), the pound will depreciate because the pound will exchange for fewer dollars; this is called **currency depreciation.** Eventually, the new exchange rate will be established where the quantity of pounds supplied by the British equals the quantity of pounds demanded by Americans. At that equilibrium exchange rate ($2 can purchase £1), an international payments equilibrium will also be restored.

Floating the U.S. Dollar   Figure 20.12 shows how the exchange rate for the dollar has fared relative to a weighted (by the extent of trade) average of ten other currencies.[13] Immediately following the March 1973 decision to float the dollar, the dollar depreciated relative to the other ten curren-

---

[13] The ten countries whose currencies are included in the weighted average are Belgium, Canada, France, Germany, Italy, Japan, the Netherlands, Sweden, Switzerland, and the United Kingdom.

cies and confirmed the belief that the dollar was overvalued. From mid-1975 to early 1977, the dollar appreciated, and then it plunged rapidly during 1978. Note that since late 1980, the dollar has appreciated quite rapidly. Although the reason for this appreciation is not totally clear, it is generally agreed that the recent dollar appreciation has occurred, at least in part, because (1) real interest rates are relatively high in the United States and because (2) political and economic instability have increased in much of the rest of the world—especially in Europe, Latin America, and the Middle East. The second explanation means that the United States is still considered to be a safe haven for investors and has become a financial refuge in troubled times. If this is true, it can account for the fact that from 1982 to 1986 the United States enjoyed (1) a large current account deficit that was financed mostly by a capital account surplus (if we include errors and omissions), and (2) an appreciating dollar on the foreign exchange markets. In effect, U.S. citizens may well be benefiting from a current account deficit because they are living in a country that is relatively stable politically and economically. Because an appreciating exchange rate raises U.S. export prices, however, U.S. exporters have complained bitterly about the appreciating dollar. It's hard to please everybody.

Floating Exchange Rates and a Fixed Price Level: The Adjustment Mechanism

At point A in Figure 20.13, internal equilibrium exists (given is and lm) but so does an external deficit—assuming that the relevant bp curve is bp in Figure 20.13. Because the exchange rate can float, an external deficit will cause the exchange rate to fall for that country experiencing the external deficit; a lower exchange rate, in turn, increases exports and decreases imports.[14] Consequently, the bp curve shifts downward and the is curve shifts rightward, and eventually they will pass through some point such as C (bp shifts to bp' and is shifts to is'), at which point both internal equilibrium and external equilibrium exist at y_2. Because the price level is constant, however, y_2 can be less than y_f.

Floating Exchange Rates and a Fixed Price Level: Stabilization Policy

Fiscal Policy Under a Floating Exchange Rate System Consider Figure 20.14. Internal and external equilibrium initially is established at y_e.

---

[14] If the exchange rate were fixed, as in the previous section, an external deficit would have led to a reduction in the nominal money supply. The lm curve, *given the price level*, would shift leftward, through point B; internal equilibrium and external equilibrium would exist at y_1, which is considerably below y_f.

If Exchange Rates Float, the *bp* Curve Will Shift Until Both Internal Equilibrium and External Equilibrium Exist

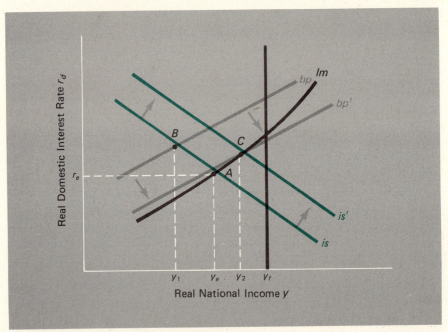

FIGURE 20.13. EQUILIBRIUM DETERMINATION WITH A FIXED PRICE LEVEL AND A FLOATING EXCHANGE RATE

At point *A*, there is an internal equilibrium but an external deficit also exists if *bp* is the existing *bp* curve (not *bp'*). The exchange rate will fall, real exports will rise, and real imports will fall, causing the *bp* curve and the *is* curve to shift rightward. Eventually, a *bp* curve (*bp'* here) and an *is* curve pass through point *C*, so internal and external equilibrium will exist simultaneously at y_2. Because the price level is fixed, however, y_2 can be below the natural income level y_f.

If the original *bp* curve had been below *bp'*, an external surplus would exist, the exchange rate would rise, exports would fall, and imports would rise; the *bp* curve would shift upward (and the *is* curve would shift leftward) until it again coincided with *bp'*.

But y_e is less than y_f, and there is an apparent role for stabilization policy. At point *A* in Figure 20.14, *lm*, *is*, and *bp* all intersect. An expansionary fiscal policy shifts the *is* curve rightward to *is'*, and the internal equilibrium position is moved to point *R*, which is at a higher level of real national income and a higher real interest rate. However, point *R* lies

Fiscal Policy Is Not Very Effective When the Exchange Rate Floats

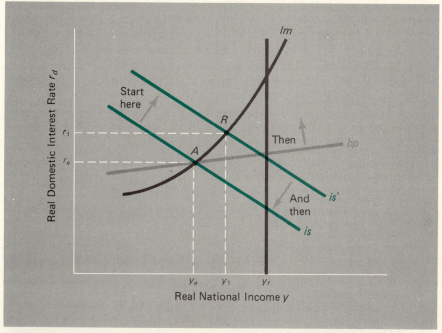

FIGURE 20.14. EXPANSIONARY FISCAL POLICY, FLOATING EXCHANGE RATES, AND A CONSTANT PRICE LEVEL

Start at point A, the intersection of is, lm, and bp, where both external equilibrium and internal equilibrium exist, but where the national income level y_e is below the natural output level y_f. An expansionary fiscal policy shifts the is curve to is', so internal equilibrium exists at point R (real income y_1 and real interest rate r_1). Point R lies above the bp curve, however, so an external surplus exists, which causes the exchange rate to rise and thereby causes the bp curve to shift upward and the is curve to shift leftward. The economy will *not* reach y_f and fiscal policy is relatively ineffective because it causes the bp curve and the is curve to shift in a countercyclical direction—when exchange rates float.

above the bp curve, and now an external surplus exists at y_1; a relatively higher domestic real interest rate, due to expansionary fiscal policy, leads to capital inflows. This leads to currency appreciation which, in turn, causes real net exports to fall; this, in turn, shifts the bp curve upward (as the arrow indicates), and the is curve shifts back to the left (as the arrow indicates). Thus, given a system of floating exchange rates, *fiscal policy sets in motion forces that counter the initial fiscal policy effects; fiscal policy is not very effective if exchange rates can float.*

Monetary Policy Under a Floating Exchange Rate System   If fiscal policy is ineffective, then perhaps monetary policy may be effective. Start at point A in Figure 20.15, where *is*, *lm*, and *bp* all intersect at r_e and y_e; y_e, however, is a level of real national income below the natural income level. Expansionary monetary policy shifts the *lm* curve rightward (remember, the price level is assumed to be constant), and the new internal equilibrium position is at point Z, where the level of real national income is higher and the domestic real interest rate is lower (compared to point A).

Because the domestic real interest rate is relatively lower, there will be an outflow of capital which will cause the exchange rate to fall; stated alternatively, point Z is below the *bp* curve, so an external deficit exists. Currency depreciation causes real net exports to rise, and this causes the *bp* curve to shift downward and the *is* curve to shift to the right. This means that the new level of real national income, where both external equilibrium and internal equilibrium exist, must be closer to y_f.

We conclude that if the price level is constant, then monetary policy is both desirable and effective under a floating exchange rate system. To the extent that the price level is flexible, stabilization policy is accordingly less essential.

ARE FIXED OR FLOATING EXCHANGE RATES BETTER?

Under a fixed exchange rate international payments system, disequilibrating changes (such as gold discoveries or changes in tastes or improvements in technology) require that resources be reallocated until a new equilibrium is restored. Such disequilibrating changes also require that resources be reallocated under a floating exchange rate system. Under both systems the basic economic mechanisms that bring about resource allocation and restore equilibrium in international payments are essentially the same: price effects, real income effects, and real interest rate changes. What is different about the two systems is the *process* by which equilibrium is restored.

Fixed Exchange Rates

Under a gold or modified gold fixed exchange rate system, gold must flow from the deficit nation to the surplus nation; under a Bretton Woods–type system, the deficit country must ultimately experience a reduction in its real money supply and the surplus country must experience an

Monetary Policy Is Potentially Very Effective When the Exchange Rate Floats

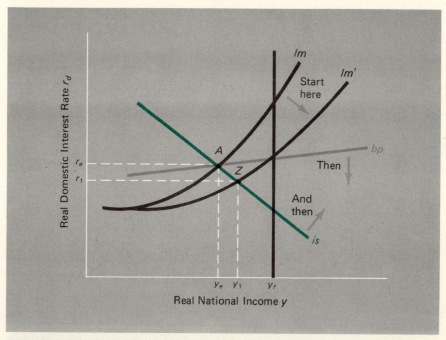

FIGURE 20.15. EXPANSIONARY MONETARY POLICY, FLOATING EXCHANGE RATES, AND A CONSTANT PRICE LEVEL

Start at point A, where internal equilibrium and external equilibrium exist at real national income level y_e, which is less than the natural income level. Expansionary monetary policy shifts the lm curve to the right, and internal equilibrium exists at point Z (or at real national income level y_1 and real interest rate r_1). Point Z is below the bp line, however, so an external deficit exists, which causes the exchange rate to depreciate; in turn, a lower exchange rate shifts the is curve rightward and the bp curve downward, causing the level of real national income to rise further. Monetary policy under a floating exchange rate system is therefore potentially very powerful.

increase in its real money supply. Under any fixed exchange rate system, then, surplus countries must inflate and deficit countries must deflate or experience recession; these are the rules of the game under a fixed exchange rate structure. In periods of a payments disequilibrium, under a fixed exchange rate standard, monetary and fiscal policies must be geared to achieve a payments equilibrium, and such other ultimate goals as less unemployment and price stability must become of secondary importance. Even if an international payments equilibrium currently exists, monetary and fiscal policy actions to attain other goals must be carried out with an eye toward how these actions will affect the balance of payments. For example, if an international payments equilibrium currently exists but unemployment is high, an expansionary monetary policy may well lead to an international payments deficit. Under a fixed exchange rate standard, therefore, monetary and fiscal policies are carried out to achieve only one goal—an international payments equilibrium. Policymakers, therefore, are not free to pursue *other* goals. Moreover, the rules of the game require that individual trading partners are not free to pursue monetary and fiscal policies that are independent of the other trading partners. Under a fixed exchange rate system a nation that is determined to pursue inflationary policies will "export" inflation to other nations. This is because an inflating country will experience a payments deficit and generate a payments surplus to other nations—which now experience an increase in their domestic money supply. A nation in the throes of a recession will export its recession to other countries, as similar reasoning will show.

In short, a fixed exchange rate system requires that each nation's other ultimate goals become secondary to one ultimate goal—an international payments equilibrium. If nations are not willing to play by the rules of the game (if they sterilize gold flows by preventing inflation or deflation in their economy), a fixed exchange rate system will not work smoothly. Such a system will be characterized by prolonged and chronic payments disequilibria and occasional (and sometimes not-so-occasional) official exchange rate (or gold price) adjustments.

Floating Exchange Rates

When a disequilibrating change occurs under a floating exchange rate system, an external equilibrium will be restored automatically, without any governmental or central bank intervention. Deficit nations will find that their currency depreciates; surplus nations experience currency appreciation. Note that *only one price*—the exchange rate—has to change. The *price level* of the several countries need not change. Moreover, because a payments imbalance will eventually disappear under a *pure float system*, nations can pursue other ultimate goals. And nations can do so independently of each other.

While a floating exchange rate system seems superior "on paper," in practice it too has problems. Under a floating exchange rate system there are "rules of the game" too. A nation must *allow* its currency to inflate or deflate. Nations are not always willing to allow their currencies to float because there are costs to doing so.

A deficit nation will experience a currency depreciation; it will take more units of its currency to import the same quantity of goods and services. But this means that the price of its imports will rise, and, other things constant, its standard of living will fall. This reduction in living standards also occurs because the currency depreciation means the producers in the deficit nation have an incentive to export more, and this will further reduce the local availability of goods and services. There will be a strong temptation for policymakers to cushion (or to offset) such a reduction in living standards by intervening in the exchange market; policymakers may put pressure on the central bank to support the deficit nation's currency by purchasing it with foreign exchange reserves (gold, or foreign currency reserves).

The surplus nation, on the other hand, will experience a currency appreciation. That nation will increase its real imports and decrease its real exports, and the payments surplus will eventually be eliminated. Such events, however, may well be seen by local producers as putting them at a competitive disadvantage in international markets for goods and services. Local producers (and their unions) may well put pressure on policymakers to make their goods more competitive on international markets by selling their currency on international exchange markets (or by placing tariffs or import quotas on imported goods that are substitutes), thereby forestalling currency appreciation. This political pressure, in fact, has occurred recently in the United States, while the dollar has appreciated.

In short, there are strong political pressures for central banks to intervene in the foreign exchange markets under a floating exchange rate system.

Fixed versus Floating Exchange Rates

When everything is said and done, fixed exchange rates become somewhat flexible, and flexible exchange rates become somewhat fixed, because political pressures are exerted to lessen the resource reallocations that are necessary to adjust to the shocks that cause disequilibrium in the international balance of payments. In that respect, we can conclude:

If nations are not willing to "pay the price" to adjust to change, it doesn't make any difference whether the world is on a fixed exchange rate system or a floating exchange rate system.

The real issues are two in number: (1) Do floating exchange rates cause *unnecessary* changes in exchange rates, and therefore unnecessary changes in real exports and real imports (and therefore in resource allocation)? To the extent that floating exchange rates cause unnecessary changes in exchange rates, more (unnecessary) disruptions in real economic variables will result under such a system, as compared to a fixed exchange rate system. (2) Are such interferences with free trade as tariffs, import quotas, and currency restrictions more likely under a fixed exchange rate system than under a floating exchange rate system?

Ultimately, these are empirical questions that only time will answer. If policymakers refuse to play by the rules of the game under either payments system, we may never know the answer to the first question. The second question really asks: Which payments system presents the greatest temptation to policymakers to resist the winds of change?

POLICY CONTROVERSY
Can the IMF Solve the World Debt Crisis?

In November 1983, the United States increased its IMF quota by $8.4 billion. Other developed nations also agreed to increase their quotas, and the total increase in IMF reserves will be $42 billion. It is expected that this money will be lent to less developed countries (LDC's) to help them meet the short-term payments due on their enormous foreign debts. How did the current world debt crisis arise? Is this IMF solution the best way to deal with the crisis? We turn to these issues now.

A Short History of the LDC Foreign Debt Crisis

In 1973, on the eve of the first oil price shock from the Organization of Petroleum Exporting Countries (OPEC), the total foreign debt, public and private, owed by the LDC's was slightly less than $100 billion. The private international banking system held 36 percent of this foreign debt. In 1979, another increase in OPEC oil prices stunned the world, and private banks (mostly in the United States) received a fortune in deposits because the OPEC

members were unwilling (some say unable) to spend all their oil earnings so rapidly. By depositing their dollars in safe Western banks, OPEC members were able to earn a fairly high rate of return. The private banks recycled these so-called "petrodollars" largely by making loans to LDC *governments*. Such loans were considered safe because "governments don't default on loans."[15] In fairness to the private banks, it should be pointed out that these loans were encouraged by the United States government and by other governments.

Borrowers were counting on continued inflation in the United States (and in other developed countries) to reduce the *real* value of such nominal-dollar-denominated debt. Unfortunately for these borrowers, the United States reduced its in-

---

[15] They apparently forgot that more than twenty nations had defaulted on their World War I debts to the United States. Only Finland paid; Britain, France, Germany (which borrowed to meet its war reparations payments to Britain and France), and Italy did not. At other times Austria, Hungary, Nicaragua, the USSR (on Czarist-initiated loans), Imperial China, and several U.S. states (in the nineteenth century) also defaulted on loans.

flation rate, and the world entered its largest recession since the 1930s. The real value of the debt did not fall, and developed nations reduced their imports and became more trade-protectionist. Higher interest rates also led to higher costs for debt restructuring (new, easier payment schedules) and for new loans that were sought to help pay old loans. By the end of 1981, the total foreign debt of non-OPEC LDC's had grown to $470 billion, and 53 percent of this debt was owed to privately owned banks.

It is estimated that by the end of 1984 the total foreign debt of the non-OPEC LDC's (including the Eastern communist bloc) was nearly $700 billion and that most of it was owed to private banks. Table 20.3 shows the total foreign debt of selected countries at the end of 1984.

TABLE 20.3. FOREIGN DEBT OF SELECTED COUNTRIES AT THE END OF 1984 (billions of dollars)

Country	Debt
Brazil	$104.4
Mexico	96.3
Argentina	48.6
South Korea	43.1
Venezuela	34.9
Indonesia	32.5
Philippines	25.5
Chile	19.9

Source: Institute of International Finance.

World Debt Crisis: Short-Term Illiquidity or Long-Term Insolvency?

A vigorous debate over how this foreign-debt problem can best be resolved has taken place. Not surprisingly, the proper solution to the problem depends on how one interprets the root of the problem. Debaters are split as to whether the world foreign-debt problem is a short-term liquidity problem or a long-term solvency problem.

Those who see the problem as a short-term liquidity problem believe that when the world recession is over, and after four or five years of world economic growth has increased LDC exports, the LDC's can pay off their loans.[16] Therefore, they believe that the IMF solution is proper.

Critics of the IMF solution are many and varied.[17] The critics see the problem as a long-run solvency problem; they all believe that most of the LDC's cannot possibly repay their debts. Table 20.4 seems to support their contention. Note that the ratio of annual debt service (interest payments plus payments of principal) to annual exports (the source of payment out of *current* earnings) is extremely high for all these nations. Note that current *imports* are also paid out of exports; the fact that these nations also run deficits on their current accounts makes their ability to repay seem very unlikely.

---

[16] This position is held by W. S. Ogden (vice-chairperson of Chase Manhattan Bank), "A Banker's View of the Foreign Debt Issue," *Wall Street Journal*, November 8, 1982; by Donald T. Regan (former U.S. Secretary of the Treasury), "The United States and the World's Debt Problem," *Wall Street Journal*, Feb. 8, 1983; and (understandably) by many private U.S. bankers and officials of the borrowing countries.

[17] See W. E. Simon (former U.S. Secretary of the Treasury), "Cut Off the International Loan Lushes," *Wall Street Journal*, April 6, 1983; Paul Craig Roberts (former assistant Treasury secretary), "The High Cost of Funding a Growing IMF," *Wall Street Journal*, February 3, 1983; Marshall Wright (Exxon Corporation vice-president), "On the Trail of a Lending Binge," *Wall Street Journal*, September 7, 1983; George Champion (chairperson of Chase Manhattan Bank, 1961–1969), "Foreign Debts: A Proposal for U.S. Banks," *Wall Street Journal*, January 1, 1983; Gustav Rains (Yale University), "For Latin American Economies: Lessons in Asia," *Wall Street Journal*, October 12, 1983; and Manuel F. Ayau (president of Universidad Francesco Marroquin in Guatemala City), "Lending Institutions Stall Latin American Progress," *Wall Street Journal*, November 18, 1983.

TABLE 20.4. SELECTED COUNTRIES AND THEIR TOTAL FOREIGN DEBT AND THEIR YEARLY DEBT SERVICE/EXPORTS RATIO[a]

Country	Total Debt (billions of dollars)	Annual Debt Service to Annual Exports Ratio (percent)[b]
Brazil	$86.3	129
Mexico	84.6	122
Argentina	38.8	179
South Korea	37.2	53
Venezuela	33.2	95
Philippines	20.7	91
Chile	17.2	116
Peru	11.2	90
Colombia	10.2	94

[a] End of 1982.

[b] The ratio of interest plus principal payments to the value of exports.

Source: Morgan Guarantee Letter and data provided by Frederick Heldring, deputy chairperson, CoreStates Financial Corporation and Philadelphia National Bank, in a lecture on August 12, 1983, to the University of Wisconsin Prochnow Banking Seminar for College Faculty Participants.

The critics also agree that the IMF is the wrong institution to solve the problem and that the cause of the problem is that *the LDC's have not used the loans productively*. The IMF prefers to extend loans to *governments*,[18] and LDC governments have used the funds to:

1. Invest in very expensive and prestigious "megaprojects" (chemical plants, hydroelectric dams) whose end products could have been imported more cheaply.
2. Subsidize inefficient state-operated or nationalized industries.
3. Support their own currencies to prevent currency depreciation on the foreign exchange market.

4. Purchase armaments for national defense.

However, the critics differ on the solution to the long-range solvency problem. Some maintain that the private banks and their stockholders (and the owners of those deposits over $100,000) should pay the price for making bad loans, in order to discourage the practice. Their solution is to require the banks to value the loans at their true value and to set aside greater reserves for bad loans. Because both of these measures would reduce current profits, the banks are fighting this solution.

Another solution suggested is that the U.S. government *itself* (not the IMF, over which the United States has less control) bail out the banks and the LDC's. The price, however, would be increased domestic bank disclosure of foreign lending, and the LDC's would have to support U.S. foreign policy. U.S. taxpayers and borrowers (who would pay higher interest rates

[18] Indeed, some critics maintain that it was the belief of banks that the IMF or a similar international agency would bail out the banks that encouraged private banks to lend to governments in the first place. See G. E. Nunn (San Jose State University), "How the Banks Got Drawn into Ponzi-style Foreign Lending," letters to the editor, *Wall Street Journal*, June 29, 1983.

if the U.S. government borrows the money to bail out the banks and the LDC's) would foot the bill.

Yet another solution offered is that the private banks accept payment of the assets of the LCD's (resources, equity in businesses) for the debt. Although this is a common solution to insolvency, the LDC's themselves might be "somewhat" reluctant to do this; the LDC's might find, however, that this solution is preferable to default and to the loss of access to foreign funds in the future.

If the critics are correct, the IMF bailout will solve the world debt crisis only temporarily. Over a longer period, the result of throwing good money after bad will be an even more severe foreign debt crisis, another problem prolonged by bad policy. By mid-1985 a free market solution seemed to be emerging. A market for the resale of LDC debt had evolved, and LDC creditors were reselling their loans at discount prices. Somewhere in the range of $100 million per month of such debt was trading at discounts ranging from 60 to 80 percent of face value. Interestingly enough, debtor countries *themselves* were purchasing some of these discounted loans. Venezuela purchased an undisclosed amount of its own debt at discounted prices. It was rumored on international financial markets that Mexico was preparing to allow foreign creditors to exchange some debt for ownership in industrial companies owned by the Mexican government. Sometimes the best policy prescription is to do nothing.

CHAPTER SUMMARY

1. As is true for individuals and families, a nation's accounts always balance. A current account deficit is financed by a capital account surplus; if the sum of the current account and the capital account are in deficit, the deficit is financed by official settlements between governments and central banks.
2. If a nation is in a balance-of-payments disequilibrium situation, such adjustment mechanisms as changes in national income, price levels, interest rates, and foreign exchange rates will restore it to payments equilibrium.
3. Fixed exchange rate systems include the classical gold standard, the gold exchange standard, and the Bretton Woods system. The latter two systems economize on the use of gold.
4. A balance-of-payments (*bp*) curve identifies all the combinations of real interest rates and real national income levels that indicate external equilibrium. The *bp* curve is positively sloped, and it shifts if a nation's relative price level changes, its exchange rate changes, its exogenously determined exports change, its autonomous import expenditures change, or if international interest rates change.
5. Under a fixed exchange rate system, if the price level is constant, simultaneous internal equilibrium and external equilibrium is

achieved because the *lm* curve will shift until it intersects the point at which the *is* and the *bp* curves intersect; but the equilibrium level of national income may occur at less than the natural income level.

6. Under a fixed exchange rate system, if the price level is constant, monetary policy is relatively ineffective but fiscal policy is potentially very effective in stabilizing the economy.

7. Under a fixed exchange rate system, if the price level can change, an external disequilibrium will cause the money supply, the domestic price level, net exports, the *bp* curve, and the *is* curve to shift until internal and external equilibrium are established at the natural real output level.

8. Under a floating exchange rate system, a country's exchange rate is set by the supply of and demand for its currency. Changes in a country's exchange rate affect the current account and the capital account; freely floating exchange rates will adjust until external equilibrium exists.

9. Under a system of flexible exchange rates and a fixed price level, fiscal policy leads to procyclical shifts in the *bp* and the *is* curves, while monetary policy leads to countercyclical shifts in the *bp* and the *is* curves. Fiscal policy is, therefore, relatively ineffective, and monetary policy is potentially very effective in stabilizing the economy under these conditions. If the price level is flexible, there is less need for any stabilization policy.

10. If nations are not willing to pay the price of adjusting to change, it doesn't make much difference whether the world is on a fixed exchange rate system or a floating exchange rate system because governments will interfere with the adjustment mechanisms under either system.

11. If the world debt crisis is a short-run liquidity problem, IMF loans to LDC governments will solve the problem. If the crisis exists because the less-developed countries did not spend borrowed funds productively, such IMF loans will prolong the crisis.

GLOSSARY

balance-of-payments (*bp*) curve The locus of all the combinations of real interest rates and real national income levels that satisfy the external equilibrium condition.

balance-of-payments disequilibrium A situation in which a nation cannot continue indefinitely its current international transactions.

capital account deficit When the value of a country's sales of such assets as stocks, bonds, and land to foreigners is less than the value of that country's purchase of such assets from the rest of the world; a net borrowing situation.

capital account surplus When the value of a country's sales of such assets as stocks, bonds, and land to foreigners exceeds the value of that country's purchase of such assets from the rest of the world; a net lending situation.

currency appreciation A nation will experience currency appreciation when its exchange rate changes so that it takes fewer units of its own currency to purchase a unit of another currency.

currency depreciation A nation will experience currency depreciation when its exchange rate changes so that it takes more units of its own currency to purchase a unit of another currency.

current account deficit When the value of a nation's exports of goods and services (and public and private transfers from the rest of the world) is less than the value of its imports of goods and services (and public and private transfers to the rest of the world).

current account surplus When the value of a nation's exports of goods and services (and public and private transfers from the rest of the world) exceeds the value of its imports of goods and services (and public and private transfers to the rest of the world).

dirty float An international payments system under which exchange rates are free to change in principle, but in practice nations intervene in order to influence exchange rates.

exchange rate The price of a unit of foreign currency in terms of its domestic currency.

external equilibrium A situation in which the sum of a nation's current account balance and its capital account balance equal zero; when a nation's official settlement balance is zero.

fixed exchange rate system An international payments system in which exchange rates are pegged at some official level and only minor fluctuations are permitted.

floating exchange rate system An international payments system under which exchange rates are allowed to rise or to fall as supply and demand conditions dictate.

gold sterilization Neutralizing the impact of gold flows on the money supply by counteracting open-market operations; i.e., gold outflows can be sterilized by Fed T-bill purchases on the open market.

internal equilibrium A situation in which a nation is simultaneously in product market equilibrium and money market equilibrium; the intersection of a nation's *is* curve and its *lm* curve, or aggregate equilibrium.

official settlements balance The sum of the current account balance and the capital account balance, plus errors and omissions.

QUESTIONS AND PROBLEMS FOR REVIEW

20.1 A nation's accounts (like an individual's or a family's) must balance. If both the current and the capital account are in deficit, they must be financed by official settlements between governments. What is the analogous scenario for individuals and families?

20.2   Changes in national income, price levels, and rates of interest can be expected to restore a balance-of-payments equilibrium. Is the combination of such changes unique, or may any of several combinations of changes be possible?

20.3   The gold exchange standard and the Bretton Woods system were attempts to economize on the use of gold. What benefit results from such an attempt to economize on the use of gold?

20.4   Explain why the *bp* curve is considered to be positively sloped.

20.5   The *bp* curve is expected to shift if a nation's relative price level rises. In which direction would it be expected to shift? Would your answer be different depending on what it was that *caused* the relative price change?

20.6   Distinguish between explanations of why simultaneous equilibria exist under a fixed exchange rate system and under a floating exchange rate system.

20.7   Why would monetary policy be thought to be relatively ineffective for a fixed exchange rate system where the price level was constant?

20.8   Why is the particular assumption with respect to price flexibility particularly important in the choice of stabilization policy techniques?

20.9   In what way might the adjustment mechanisms under a floating exchange rate system be stifled?

20.10 On what does the answer rest to the question of whether or not the world debt crisis is a short-run liquidity problem?

REFERENCES

Manuel F. Ayau, "Lending Institutions Stall Latin American Progress," *Wall Street Journal*, November 18, 1983, editorial page.

Michael D. Bordo, "The Classical Gold Standard: Some Lessons for Today," *Review*, Federal Reserve Bank of St. Louis (May 1981).

J. H. Boyd, D. S. Dahl, and C. D. Line, "A Primer on the International Monetary Fund," *Quarterly Review*, Federal Reserve Bank of Minneapolis (Summer 1983).

George Champion, "Foreign Debts: A Proposal for U.S. Banks," *Wall Street Journal*, January 1, 1983, editorial page.

Rudiger Dornbusch and Stanley Fischer, *Macroeconomics*, 3d ed. (New York: McGraw-Hill, 1984).

Milton Friedman, *Essays in Positive Economics* (Chicago: University of Chicago Press, 1953).

———, *A Program for Monetary Stability* (New York: Fordham University Press, 1959).

Milton Friedman and Robert V. Roosa, *The Balance of Payments: Free versus Fixed Exchange Rates* (Washington, D.C.: American Enterprise Institute, 1967).

Thomas M. Humphrey, *Essays on Inflation*, 4th ed. (Richmond, Va.: Federal Reserve Bank of Richmond, 1983).

Rita M. Maldonado, "Recording and Classifying Transactions in the Balance of Payments," *International Journal of Accounting* (Fall 1979).

Robert A. Mundell, "International Monetary Options," *Cato Journal*, vol. 3 (1983).

W. S. Ogden, "A Banker's View of the Foreign Debt Issue," *Wall Street Journal*, October 12, 1983, editorial page.

Gustav Rains, "For Latin American Economies: Lessons in Asia," *Wall Street Journal*, October 12, 1983, editorial page.

Donald T. Regan, "The United States and the World Debt Problem," *Wall Street Journal*, February 8, 1983, editorial page.

Paul Craig Roberts, "The High Cost of Funding a Growing IMF," *Wall Street Journal*, February 3, 1983.

Joseph T. Salerno, "Gold Standards: True or False," *Cato Journal*, vol. 3 (1983).

Dominick Salvatore, *International Economics* (New York: Macmillan, 1983).

William E. Simon, "Cut Off the International Loan Lushes," *Wall Street Journal*, April 6, 1983.

Janice M. Westerfield, "Would Fixed Exchange Rates Control Inflation?" *Business Review*, Federal Reserve Bank of Philadelphia (July-August 1976).

Marshall Wright, "On the Trail of a Lending Binge," *Wall Street Journal*, September 7, 1983, editorial page.

Leland B. Yeager, "Stable Money and Free Market Currencies," *Cato Journal*, vol. 3 (1983).

APPENDIX

ANSWERS TO ODD-NUMBERED QUESTIONS
IN "QUESTIONS AND PROBLEMS FOR REVIEW"

Chapter 2

2.1 The law of demand predicts that households will purchase less energy and more food. Because the CPI measures the cost of purchasing an *unchanging* basket, however, it will overstate the hardships of inflation.

2.3 If minorities become discouraged from looking for a job, they will not be counted as officially unemployed, and therefore the actual employment rate will understate "true" unemployment. If people perform do-it-yourself activities, they are "really" working, but they won't be counted in the labor force if they quit looking for a job; or they will be counted as unemployed if they continue their job search. Either way, such do-it-yourself activities cause the official unemployment rate to overstate the "true" unemployment rate.

2.5 Country B probably will have a higher GNP, other things constant. Community welfare will be higher in country A because, other things constant, its annual welfare is the same but its wealth (natural resources) will decline more rapidly.

2.7 a. Nominal GNP for 1972 = ($4)(10) + ($12)(20) + ($6)(5) + ($25)(10) = $560. Nominal GNP for 1985 = ($8)(12) + ($36)(15) + ($10)(15) + ($30)(12) = $1,146.

  b. Real GNP for 1972 = $560. Real GNP for 1985 = ($4)(12) + ($12)(15) + ($6)(15) + ($25)(12) = $618.

  c. Implicit GNP deflator for 1972 = $\left(\dfrac{\text{GNP}_{1972}}{\text{gnp}_{1972}} \times 100\right) = \left(\dfrac{\$560}{\$560} \times 100\right)$ = 100.

  Implicit GNP deflator for 1985 = $\left(\dfrac{\text{GNP}_{1985}}{\text{gnp}_{1985}} \times 100\right) = \left(\dfrac{\$1146}{\$618} \times 100\right)$ = 185.4.

  d. CPI for 1972 = 100 because it is the base year.

  CPI for 1985 = $\left(\dfrac{P_{1985}Q_{1972}}{P_{1972}Q_{1972}} \times 100\right) = \left(\dfrac{\$1150}{\$560} \times 100\right)$ = 205.35.

  $P_{1985}Q_{1972}$ = ($8)(10) + ($36)(20) + ($10)(5) + ($30)(10) = $1150.

  $P_{1972}Q_{1972}$ = ($4)(10) + ($12)(20) + ($6)(5) + ($25)(10) = $560.

Chapter 3

3.1   The natural growth rate is a country's long-run secular annual percentage rate of change in its real GNP. It varies directly with such factors as population growth, technological improvements, percentage of gnp allocated to investment in capital, and the degree of economic incentives.

3.3   The lower the natural rate of unemployment, the closer is actual gnp to natural gnp; the higher the natural rate of unemployment, the further below natural gnp is actual gnp.

3.5   Inflation (at least in mild amounts) tends to be associated with high levels of economic activity, and consequently with lower unemployment rates. In a recession both the inflation rate and the employment rate are apt to fall; thus, when the inflation rate falls, the unemployment rate may rise.

3.7   a. 3%

       b. 3%

       c. One month

3.9   If you plot the data in Table 3.2, you will see that no simple relationship exists between the actual overall rate of unemployment and the annual rate of inflation.

Chapter 4

4.1   Economic incentives to be productive, natural resources, skilled labor force, good climate.

4.3   The interpretation is that the interest rate resulted from the interaction between the community's rate of time preference for consumption and the productivity of capital.

4.5   Because prices, wages, and interest rates can adjust completely to shocks to the economic system only in the long run. In the short run some price-wage and interest rate inflexibility exists.

4.7   If the price level rises and money wage rates remain constant, then real wage rates will fall and employers will hire more labor. If producers can get more laborers at a lower real wage rate, then the aggregate supply curve will be positively sloped: higher price levels will lead to higher levels of national output.

4.9   a. He was apparently wrong about those western nations that have achieved sustained economic growth. These countries have had the benefits of technological improvements and stabilized populations; consequently, real incomes have increased in such countries.

       b. In Figure 4.5 a technological improvement will shift the total output curve upward in panel *a* and may cause its slope to be higher at every employment level. This causes demand for labor to rise in panel *b*, which causes the real wage rate and quantity of labor employed to rise.

Chapter 5

5.1   The price level rises if the supply of money increases *relative* to the demand for money. If the money supply rises but the demand for money rises just as fast, the price level will not change. Indeed, if the money supply rises but the demand for money rises *more* rapidly, the price level may *fall*.

5.3   It depends. If prices are inflexible and shocks are significant, dynamic disequilibrium analysis is better. If prices are very flexible, quantities can adjust quickly, and the shocks are small, then comparative statics has the advantage of simplicity.

5.5   Gold money will still be neutral for the goods that are gold-free, but it will be nonneutral for those goods that have gold components. If there is a gold discovery, all nongold goods will experience the same rate of price increase; but the price of those goods that have gold components will fall relative to other goods because the supply of gold will have risen relative to its demand.

5.7   If $k = 0.2$, then $V = 5$.
If $k = 0.25$, then $V = 4$.
If $k = 0.333$, then $V = 3$.
When k rises, V falls because $V = 1/k$.

5.9 $500, $k = 1/2$; $250, $k = 1/4$

5.11   a. $MV = P_y$; $(\$80)(5) = P(\$100)$, therefore, $P = 4$.
      b. $P = 5$
      c. $P = 8$
      d. $P = 10$

As the money supply increases, the price level increases proportionally— if V and y are constant.

Chapter 6

6.1   If the MPC $= 0.8$, then a $20-billion increase in income will lead to a $16-billion increase in consumption and a $4-billion increase in saving; the sum of the increases is $20 billion.

6.3   Dividing $(c = c_0 + by)$ by y yields $c/y = (c_0/y) + b$, where $c/y =$ APC and $b =$ MPC. Note that in this second equation, as y increases, c/y falls (if $c_0 > 0$) and b is constant.

6.5 $AE = c + i$; therefore $AE = \$30 + 0.8y$. If $y = \$50$, then $AE = \$70$; if $y = \$150$, then $AE = \$150$; if $y = \$250$, then $AE = \$230$. From these calculations, it is clear that $AE = y = \$150$, and that is the equilibrium income level. At that level, consumption equals $140 [because $c = 20 +$

0.8(150) = 140], and therefore saving equals $10, which equals investment.

6.7   In the basic Keynesian model, real income, real saving, and employment will change until equilibrium is established. In the classical model, the real interest rate, real saving, and real investment will change until equilibrium is restored.

6.9   If i rises by $2, real national income will rise until real saving rises by $2. In this example, the new equilibrium income level will be $160, and the change in income is therefore $10. The ratio of the change in income to the change in investment is $10/$2 = 5, which is the multiplier when the MPC = 0.8.

Chapter 7

7.1   Real. It makes a difference in terms of the implied values for velocity and the price level.

7.3   If changes in the nominal rate of interest reflected only changes in the expected future level of prices, the real value of bonds would remain constant, and therefore bonds would be less risky than money.

7.5   It is less effective as an attempt to cause interest rates to decrease under such conditions. To the extent that *some* economic units would not hold such money balance increases, prices would increase, and those that did hold such increases would suffer individual welfare losses.

7.7   The changes in the equilibrium values of the interest rate and the national income level, for changes in fiscal policy, would be greater if the intersection of the *is* and *lm* curves was in the vertical range and less if the intersection was in the horizontal range.

7.9   Aggregate welfare must necessarily be less after changes in the money supply than before such changes, under the stated conditions.

Chapter 8

8.1   Sticky nominal wages.

8.3   Classical economists believed that nominal wages would adjust to the level that would equate the quantities demanded and supplied of labor, given equilibrium in the product and money markets.

8.5   Although there may be some reluctance to purchase capital under such conditions, the liquidity trap, in essence, reflects the unwillingness of lenders (bond purchasers and banks) to lend.

8.7   Decreases in the rate of interest would be expected to increase the level of existing community wealth and increase consumption. Thus, if the price level falls, wealth will *rise* owing to the Pigou effect, and the present value of labor's future earnings will *rise* as the interest rate falls owing (indirectly) to the Keynes effect.

8.9 If long-run equilibrium values for the rate of interest and national income result in unemployment, and if wages are sticky downward, fiscal stabilization policy may cause aggregate economic welfare to increase. If all three markets are in long-run equilibrium, however, fiscal stabilization policy must necessarily cause aggregate economic welfare to decrease.

Chapter 9

9.1 Transitory income accounts for a higher portion of measured income in the short run than it does in the long run. Consequently, the ratio Var y_p/Var y is likely to be smaller in the short run than it is in the long run. Given $k = 0.9$, then b will be a smaller number in the short run than it will be in the long run.

9.3 a. Your graph should be a ray from the origin that has a slope equal to 0.9.

b. In that equation the ratio Var y_p/Var y equals 1, because by assumption transitory effects are zero. Therefore, $b = (0.9)^{(1)} = 0.9$.

9.5 In the lower-income categories there will be a disproportionate number whose permanent income is above their measured income and who, consequently, will borrow or sell assets to consume all, or more than all, or nearly all their measured income. The overall APC for such groups will be relatively high. In the higher-income categories there will be a disproportionate number whose permanent income is *below* this measured income and who, consequently, will be adding to their assets by saving more than usual. At relatively high income levels, therefore, the APC is likely to be relatively low.

9.7 a. At point A, the APC = 0.9

b. B.

c. C.

d. 0.9.

e. At point C, the APC > 0.9.

f. The community is trying to maintain its high level of consumption, reached at point A.

9.9 Refrigerators, cars, other durables—the nondepreciated portions, that is.

Chapter 10

10.1 If the demand for output for one firm increases and the demand for output for another firm decreases as a result of a shift in tastes, changes in outputs sum to zero and the economywide implications of the accelerator hypothesis are trivial.

10.3 It does, if the appropriate influences of the negative change in output for the other firm are incorporated in the model.

10.5 The prices for final goods and the rate of interest would increase and the distribution of employment would shift away from the consumer to the capital goods sector in the short run, assuming the optimal capital/output ratio was greater than 1.

10.7 The adaptive expectations model suggests that the economy is more stable than it would be if it were characterized by the simple accelerator model.

10.9 It would seem unlikely that significant excess capacity in the capital goods industry and zero excess capacity in final goods industries would exist *simultaneously.* Such a situation *could* exist if the capital goods industry prematurely expanded its capacity in anticipation of a boom while final goods producers failed to anticipate it.

Chapter 11

11.1 A close correspondence between the theoretical and empirical definition of money; a significantly reliable ability to control the money supply, empirically defined; and a close relationship between the empirical definition of money and national goals. Monetary policy is extremely difficult if any one of these is missing.

11.3 Length of the period between payments; real rates of interest; sophistication of the banking system; use of credit cards. Recent innovations have increased the economy of money use; therefore, velocity is rising, other things constant.

11.5 If the money supply is endogenously determined, monetary policy is difficult because economic agents can change the money supply in the opposite direction. To the extent that economic units are in long-run equilibrium and the money supply is at least somewhat endogenously determined, not only is monetary policy less effective in changing real variables, but *less* welfare loss will obtain as a result of policy!

11.7 The introduction of uncertainty into the analysis forces one to concentrate on the marginal costs and marginal benefits of taking on *extra* risk. The extra risk comes from buying more bonds with money. Hence, a portfolio develops rather than an all-or-nothing situation.

11.9 As a result, there is a second reason to expect that the *lm* curve is positively sloped (nonvertical), and therefore that shifts in the *is* curve will change both national income and rates of interest in the short run.

Chapter 12

12.1 Both would shift the demand curve to the right.

12.3 *A* is equivalent to *B*, since they are on the same indifference curve. *B* is equivalent to *C*, also since they are on the same indifference curve, though different from above. Therefore, since *A* is equivalent to *B* and *B* is equivalent to *C*, then *A* is equivalent to *C*. However, *A* is superior to *C*, since more of both goods are associated with *A* than with *C*. Conflicting conclusions cannot hold.

12.5 Six hours of leisure, $90 income.

12.7 The wage would be lower and employment less. Unemployment, however, may still be equal to 0.

12.9 In this case, the logic is sound for both arguments. The validity of alternative models is an empirical question.

Chapter 13

13.1 Yes, in the simple Keynesian model.

13.3 To the extent that increases in government expenditures are for goods that consumers would have purchased anyway, private consumption expenditures can be expected to decrease by exactly the value of the increase in government expenditures. Therefore, such increases in government expenditures are not expansionary.

13.5 No.

13.7 To the extent that unemployment exists and is reduced by increases in aggregate demand, prices do not rise.

13.9 Interest rates would increase, because lenders will put an inflationary premium on them.

Chapter 14

14.1 The short-run Phillips curve can be shown to be positively sloped.

14.3 Workers may adjust only partially to changes in the price level in the short run.

14.5 It increases the rate of unemployment as the average duration of unemployment increases.

14.7 Minimum wage laws on contracts, licensing arrangements, Davis-Bacon Act, unemployment compensation.

14.9 Differing degrees of interferences and rigidities in the labor market over time.

Chapter 15

15.1 Yes, the speed of adjustment depends on the time it takes to perceive the magnitude of the shock.

15.3 It would be necessarily *decreased* because people would be swayed from optimal job search durations.

15.5 Misallocation of resources and welfare loss to society.

15.7 The assumptions imply that the synthesis model and the REH model misapply equilibrium analysis to disequilibrium situations.

15.9 Effective demand will be less than planned demand, and economic units will base their behavior on effective demand. Because no automatic adjustment mechanisms exist to return the economy to equilibrium, involuntary unemployment is of indeterminate duration.

Chapter 16

16.1 The money multiplier is not affected by the size of the monetary base. It increases when the reserve/deposit ratio decreases. It decreases, given relevant reserve requirement ratios.

16.3 Where interest rate costs of borrowing reserves are less than interest rate revenues, banks would be expected to borrow such reserves to meet requirements, whatever the *absolute* size of the interest rate costs. If interest rate costs per unit of borrowed reserves are an increasing function of the level of borrowed reserves, the interest rate costs would increase relative to interest rate revenues as the level of borrowed reserves increased. As the trade-off changes, banks would be expected to borrow reserves to the extent that marginal interest rate benefits equaled marginal interest rate costs.

16.5 Other values held constant, the opportunity cost of holding assets in the form of money increases. As such, portfolios are expected to be adjusted to accommodate less money and more income-earning assets. If interest rates are rising as a result of an expected future increase in the monetary base, the demand for money may in fact be different than implied above.

16.7 2.

16.9 18.18 . . . %

Chapter 17

17.1 An increase in g is expected to increase aggregate spending by the amount of the increase in g times the government expenditure multiplier. This means that national income will be higher at every interest rate.

17.3 In either case, market rates of interest are typically expected to change: they will increase for an increase in g and decrease for an increase in t_x because the *is* curve shifts and the *lm* curve doesn't.

17.5 Consumers must be expected *not* to take into account the existence of a budget deficit or surplus in the determination of the present value of future tax liabilities.

17.7 They believe that the democratic process is biased toward budget deficits and inflation, and that a politically induced business cycle exists.

17.9 *Taxing:* neither the money supply nor bank reserves are expected to be altered. *Borrowing from the public:* neither the money supply nor bank reserves are expected to be altered. *Borrowing from depository institutions:* it depends on whether or not excess reserves exist in the banking system. *Borrowing from the Fed:* the money supply is expected to increase by a multiple of the original debt sale. *Printing money:* a multiple increase in the money supply is expected.

Chapter 18

18.1 Real consumption and investment expenditures are sensitive to interest rates, and relative prices and relative wages adjust to clear markets.

18.3 The *lm* curve is flat, the *is* curve is steep, and prices and wages are inflexible downward.

18.5 To say that money doesn't matter is to say that real variations cannot be affected by exogenous changes in the money supply and therefore that monetary policy is ineffective.

18.7 Time lags attendant to such policies are unpredictable. Therefore, conditions that will exist when policy effects are felt may be different from the conditions that existed when policy changes were made, and such policy effects may be perverse.

18.9 They think that the market mechanisms that *can* restore the economy to full employment take too long to do so.

Chapter 19

19.1 The quantity of output per unit of available labor.

19.3 Inflation results in higher nominal prices and wages. A progressive income tax structure imposes higher marginal tax rates at higher nominal incomes. Higher marginal tax rates reduce the quantity of labor supplied at the same real wage for a higher nominal wage. This would not hold if taxes were proportional, nor would it hold if taxes were regressive.

19.5 If the demand for labor is elastic at equilibrium, an increase in the wage rate, though possible, would necessarily result in a decrease in the total wage or payroll for those in the union, as well as a reduction in employment.

19.7 Radical supply-siders thought that lower marginal rates would *increase* total tax revenues in the short run and that inflation could be reduced without an associated recession.

19.9 Empirical evidence suggests that the supply of labor is a function of real after-tax earnings.

Chapter 20

20.1   They must borrow or spend their assets; that is, they must suffer a reduction in their own individual wealth.

20.3   There is an increase in both available inputs and final goods, to the extent that the metal is both an input and a final good, and prices would fall.

20.5   The *bp* curve is typically expected to shift to the left under such a circumstance. However, if prices rose as a result of an increase in the demand by foreigners for domestically produced goods, the *bp* curve would shift to the *right*.

20.7   Under a fixed exchange rate system, if the price level is constant, the LM curve shifts irrespective of the monetary base, according to the extent of an internal disequilibrium.

20.9   If nations are not willing to suffer the consequences of adjustment, governments may interfere with the adjustment mechanisms inherent in a floating exchange rate system.

INDEX TO GLOSSARY TERMS

Suppressed inflation, 368

Target cones, 534
Time deposits, 303
Transaction motive, 124
Transactions approach, 303
Transfer payments, 41
Transitory income, 252

Troughs, 62

User cost of capital, 274

Validation theory, 368
Value-added technique, 41
Value of marginal physical product of labor, 97

SUBJECT INDEX

Borland, Mel, 489n
Borrowing, by government, 119–121, 476–478, 501–504
Boskin, Michael, 9, 560–563
Bowsher, Norman H., 430n
Brazil, 615–616
Bretton Woods Agreement Act (1946), 584
Bretton Woods system, 584–585, 599–601
Brimmer, Roger, 547n
Britain, 581–582, 584, 591, 599, 603–606, 614n
Bronfenbrenner, Martin, 223n
Brumberg, Richard E., 238, 240n
Brunner, Karl, 7
Bryant, Ralph C., 445n, 457–458, 527–529
Buchanan, James, 486
Budget constraint line, 319
Budget constraints, 318–319, 498–501
Budget deficits, 4, 11, 161, 362–363, 476–478, 488–492
Budget Improvement and Control Act (1974), 487
Budgets
    balanced, 161, 476–478, 488–492
    high-employment, 480–483
Budget surpluses, 162, 476–478
Bureau of the Census, 32
Bureau of Economic Analysis, 132–133
Bureau of Labor Statistics, 30, 31n, 32–33
Business
    demand for labor by, 72–76
    monopoly power of, and inflation, 357–358
    as nonbank private sector, 426–429
Business Conditions Digest, 19n
Business cycles, 53, 55, 132–133

Cambridge economists, 289–290
Cambridge equation, 101–102
Canada, 606n
Capital, marginal efficiency of, 140–143
Capital account balance, 476
Capital account deficits, 577
Capital account surpluses, 577
Capital goods changes, 262–263
Capitalism, 5–11, 68, 95
Capital/output ratio, 269–270
Carter, Jimmy, 366
Certificates of deposit (CDs), 176, 286
Cesarano, Filippo, 121n
Champion, George, 615n
Checks, 283–285
Chile, 615–616
China, 614n
Civilian labor force, 33
Civilian unemployment rate, 33
Clark, John Maurice, 261
Clark, Peter K., 270, 545n, 550n
Classical economists, 5–6, 68–69
Classical gold standard, 582–584
Classical model, 68–69, 94–95, 100, 121–122

aggregate supply, 92–94, 346–347
demand-for-money function, 288
equilibrium analysis, 410–411
full-employment output produced, 71–82
full-employment output purchased, 82–92
goods-market equilibrium, 151–155
inflation, 352–353
Keynes's criticism of, 128–133
labor market equilibrium, 323
and monetarism, 510
monetary/fiscal policies, 117–121
neutrality of money, 115–117
price level determination, 109–115
quantity theory of money, 100–109
Say's law, 69–71
Classical range, 191
Clower, Robert, 410
Coins, 282, 580–581
Colombia, 616
Commerce Department, 19n
Commercial banks, 283–284, 286–287, 426–429
Common stocks, 176
Communism, 95
Competition
    maintenance of, 10
    pure, 70
Congress, U.S.
    and balanced budget, 488–489
    as fiscal policymaker, 462, 484, 487, 532, 551
    and price controls, 363, 366
    and reserve requirements, 433, 436, 464
    and stabilizers, 478
    and time lags, 461, 484
Consols, 178
Constant price levels, 591–595
Constraints, budget, 318–319, 498–501
Consumer Price Index, 30–31, 354–355, 364–366
Consumption drift hypothesis, 243, 245–247
Consumption function, 230, 248–250
    consumption drift hypothesis, 243, 245–247
    Keynesian, 136–138, 230–232
    life cycle hypothesis, 238, 240–242
    permanent income hypothesis, 232–239
    relative income hypothesis, 247–248
    stability of, 242–244
Copernicus, Nicolaus, 69
Cost-push inflation, 357–360
Council of Economic Advisers, 484, 560
Credit markets, 84–86
Credit unions, 284, 426–429, 463–464
Credit union share draft accounts, 284
Crowding-out effect, 474–477
Crude quantity theory of money, 100–102
Currency, 282–283, 427–428, 437, 504–506, 580–585
Currency appreciation, 606
Currency/deposit ratio, 430–432
Currency depreciation, 606
Current account balance, 576–577

Current account deficits, 577
Current account surpluses, 577
Current Population Study, 32

Darby, Michael R., 566–567
Darwin, Charles, 69
Davidson, James Dale, 487
Davidson, Paul, 410
Davis-Bacon Act, 50, 387
Debt, public. *See* Budget deficits
Debt monetization, 531
Debts, of less-developed countries, 4, 614–617
Deficits
    capital account, 577
    current account, 577
    government, 4, 11, 161, 362–363, 476–478, 488–
      492, 531–532
Deflation, 359n
Demand
    aggregate, 109–115, 337–343, 375–378
    effective, 414
    planned, 414
Demand deposits, 283–284
Demand for labor, 72–76, 129–130, 310–314
Demand for money, 102–104, 131–132
Demand-for-money function, 278, 300–301
    classical, 288
    empirical evidence of, 299–300
    Federal Reserve measurement of money supply,
      282–288, 300–301
    Keynesian, 175–183, 188–195, 290–292
    and money/money supply, 278–282
    neoclassical, 289–290
    recent views, 292–299
Demand-pull inflation, 354–356
Demand shocks, 404–405
Denison, Edward F., 547n
Department of Commerce, 19n
Department of Defense, 32
Department of Labor, 32
Department of the Treasury, 282–283, 361, 437, 484,
    489, 497–498, 501, 503–505, 600
Deposit/currency ratio, 430–432
Depository institutions
    government borrowing from, 503–504
    and money supply, 283–287
    100 percent reserve requirement, 463–464
    relation with Federal Reserve, 426–429
Depository Institutions Deregulation and Monetary
    Control Act (1980), 439
Depository reserves, 428, 432–434, 437–439, 445,
    463–464, 503–504
Deposit/reserve ratio, 432–434
Deposits/deposit accounts, 283–287
Depression of 1930s. *See* Great Depression
Diminishing returns, law of, 71–73, 94–95, 377
Diocletian, 363
Dirty floats, 603

Discounting, 139
Discount rate, 434, 439, 439–442, 445
Discouraged workers, 33
Discretionary fiscal policy, 478–483
Disequilibrium, 82, 115, 578, 580. *See also* Equilib-
    rium
Disequilibrium analysis, 409–417
Disinflation, 552
Disposable personal income, 26, 136–138
Distributional coalitions, 486–487, 551–552
Dollar, floating of, 606–607
Dollar-denominated deposits, 287
Domestic price level, 111–113
Duesenberry, James, 247–248
Duration of unemployment, 381–385, 393

Economic incentives, and growth rate, 49
Economic performance, measurement of, 16–18, 37–
    39
    gross national product, 18–28
    inflation, 28–32
    unemployment, 32–37
Economy
    demand for labor by, 75–76
    inherent stability of, 521–523
    state of, determined by employment/unemploy-
      ment rates, 394
    supply of labor of, 77
Effective demand, 414
Effect time lags, 461
Eichner, Alfred, 410
Eisner, Robert, 223
Employment, 5, 16–18, 32–33, 117. *See also* Un-
    employment
Employment Act (1946), 16, 472
Employment flows, 381
Endogenously determined money supply, 430–436
Energy costs, 4, 549–550
Entries, 380
Equation of exchange, 102, 109–110
Equilibrium, 5–6, 80–82, 115, 117–118, 135n. *See
    also* Disequilibrium
    aggregate, 197–200, 208
    in all three markets, 210–212
    goods-market, 151–155
    internal/external, 585–586
    in labor market, 321–328
    mathematic determination, 167–169
    national income, 147–150
    national output–price level, 351–352
    planned savings and investments, 149–151
Equilibrium exchange rates, 603–607
Equilibrium interest rate, 183–185
Equilibrium wage rate, 77–80
Essay on the Principle of Population (Malthus), 95n
Eurodollars, 287, 503n
European Economic Community, 602–603
European Recovery Program, 599

Evans, Michael K., 9, 242n, 560–564, 566
Excess reserves, 428, 433–434, 503–504
Exchange rates, 581, 591, 603
Exchange rate systems, 578, 580–614
Exogenously determined money supply, 101
Expenditures, 17
  aggregate, 135, 146–149
  government, 20–22, 158, 472–475, 485, 497–507
External equilibrium, 586

Factor shares, 25–26
Faust, Jon, 279n
Federal Financing Bank, 489
Federal funds rate, 434
Federal Open Market Committee, 442n, 463
Federal Reserve notes, 282–283
Federal Reserve system, 185, 279–282, 300–301,
    361–362, 407–408, 463–464, 497, 504–505.
    See also Money supply
  effect on money supply, 436–445
  endogenously determined money supply, 430–436
  government borrowing from, 504
  measurement of money supply, 282–288
  monetarist view, 526–531
  monetary policy problems, 454–463, 518–520
  monetary policy strategies, 445–454
  relation with nonbank sector and depository in-
    stitutions, 426–429
Feldstein, Martin, 8, 266n, 560, 564–565
Final goods demand, 259, 261–262
Financial assets, 176–178
Finland, 614n
Firms. See Business
Fiscal policy, 9–10, 17, 472, 489–492. See also Mon-
    etary policy; Stabilization policy
  automatic, 478–483
  classical model, 118–121
  discretionary, 478–483
  effect on aggregate demand, 339–341
  eliminating recessionary gaps, 161–162
  financial aspects of, 497–507
  under floating exchange rate system, 607–610
  ineffectiveness of, 523–524
  monetarist-nonmonetarist debate, 510–533
  problems with, 483–489
  rules versus direction, 531–533
  theoretical context, 472–478
Fisher, Irving, 102–103, 108n, 175, 288, 359–360,
    464
Fixed exchange rate system, 578, 580–601, 610–614
Fixed price level, and floating exchange rates, 607–
    610
Flexible accelerator hypothesis, 267–269
Flexible price levels, 595
Floating exchange rate system, 578, 580, 602–614
Flows (labor force), 380–382
Foot, David, 266n
France, 585, 599–600, 606n, 614n

Free enterprise economy, 5–11
"Free lunch," 556n
Frictional unemployment, 8, 37, 49–50, 386
Friedman, Benjamin, 455–456
Friedman, Milton, 7, 232–238, 247, 292–295, 360,
    362, 386–390, 393, 416–417, 456–457, 462,
    464, 518–519, 522–525, 527, 529–530, 582
Friedman-Phelps model, 388–390, 400–401
Full employment, 5, 80–82, 117, 214–217, 481
Full Employment and Balanced Growth Act (1978),
    16–17, 472
Full-employment output
  produced, 71–82
  purchased, 82–92
Future-oriented communities, 85

General Theory of Employment, Interest and
    Money (Keynes), 6, 68n, 128, 223, 525
Germany, 599–600, 606n, 614n
Gilder, George, 9, 554, 563n
GNP. See Gross national product (GNP)
Goals, for Federal Reserve strategies, 448, 459–462
Goldberger, A. S., 524n
Gold exchange standard, 584
Goldfeld, Stephen, 299–300
Goldsmith, Raymond, 231n
Gold standards, 580–584
Gold sterilization, 583
Goods and services
  government purchase of, 20, 22, 158
  and neutrality of money, 115–116
  public, 10
Gordon, Robert J., 400n
Government. See also Fiscal policy; Monetary pol-
    icy; Stabilization policy
  activities, adding, 24–25
  borrowing, 119–121, 476–478, 501–504
  deficits, 4, 11, 161, 362–363, 476–478, 488–492,
    531–532
  expenditures, 20–22, 158, 472–475, 485, 497–507
  and inflation, 360–363
  Keynesian model, 158–162
  printing money, 121, 504–506
  and productivity, 550
  role in free enterprise economy, 9–10
  size in free enterprise economy, 10–11
  surpluses, 162, 476–478
  taxing, 118, 475–477, 485, 497–501
Grace Commission Report, 492
Grayson, C. Jackson, Jr., 365
Great Depression (1930s), 6, 128, 132, 161, 187, 212,
    222–223, 374, 432–434, 518–521
Griliches, Zvi, 547n
Gross national product (GNP)
  components of, 19–22
  defined, 18–19
  and inflation, 28–30
  measurement of, 37–39

Output (Continued)
    and neutrality of money, 117
    real gross national product measurement of, 38
Output/capital ratio, 269–270
Output growth, 540–541
Overall unemployment rate, 33
Overnight Eurodollars, 287
Overnight repurchase agreements, 286–287

Part-time workers, in labor force, 393
Passbook savings deposits, 286
Patent Office, 547
Patinkin, Don, 410
Payments, international, 576
Peaks, 55
Permanent consumption, 236–237
Permanent income, 234–237
Permanent income hypothesis, 232–239
Permanent sales, 264–267
Perry, George, 400n
Personal consumption expenditures, 19, 22
Personal income, 26–28
Peru, 616
Phelps, E. S., 386, 388–390
Philippines, 615–616
Phillips, A. W. H., 373
Phillips curves, 57, 372–373
    long-run, 386–394
    short-run, 373–379, 390–392
Pifer, H. W., 223
Pigou, A. C., 69, 219
Pigou effect, 218–222, 230, 337n, 416
Planned demand, 414
Planned investment, 92, 149–151
Planned saving, 92, 149–151
Policinski, Mark R., 564n
Policy, in general, 17–18, 401, 462–463. *See also*
    Fiscal policy; Monetary policy; Stabilization
    policy
Policy instruments, 17
Population growth, and growth rate, 47–49, 95
Portfolio approach, 281–282, 285–287
Positive excess reserves, 503–504
Positive externalities, correction for, 10
Precautionary motive, 103, 175–176
Present-oriented communities, 85
President, as fiscal policymaker, 462, 484
Price controls, and inflation, 363–366
Price deflators, 28–30
Price indexes, 30–31. *See also* Consumer Price Index
Price levels, 104–107, 109–115, 336–337, 350–351.
    See also Inflation
  and aggregate demand, 337–343
  and aggregate supply, 343–350
  constant, 591–595
  fixed, and floating exchange rates, 607–610
  flexible, 595
Prices, 5, 16–18

Price-wage controls, 17
Price-wage flexibility
  and Keynesian range, 214–217
  monetarist view, 523
  and Pigou effect, 218–222
Price-wage relationship, 312–313
Price-wage rigidities, and unemployment rate, 50–51
Price-wage spiral, 357
Printing money, by government, 121, 504–506
Private enterprise economy, 5–11
Production function, 71–72
Productivity, 4, 48, 540
  and distributional coalitions, 551–552
  and energy prices, 549–550
  and government, 550
  and growth, 540–545
  increases in, 541–543
  and inflation, 550
  labor, defined, 545
  measurability, 547–549
  slowdowns, 545–554, 566–567
  and technological improvements, 547
Progressive income tax, 478–479
Propensity to consume, 136–137, 230–232
Propensity to save, 137
Property rights, enforcement of, 10
Proportionality hypothesis, 234
Prudent reserves, 432
Public, government borrowing from, 501–503
Public choice model, 10, 485–488
Public debt. *See* Budget deficits
Pure gold standard, 580–582
Pure international gold standard, 585–586
Puritans, 363

Quantity constraints, 413–415
Quantity of labor, 319–321
Quantity theory of money, 100–109, 132

Rains, Gustav, 615n
Random walks, 404
Rational expectations hypothesis, 8, 400–409, 411–413, 464
Raw materials cost-push inflation, 358–359
Reagan, Ronald, 9, 555, 560–563
Reaganomics, 9, 555
Real demand for labor, 311–312
Real gross national product, 26–28, 37–39, 46–48, 55–57
Real interest rates, 91, 117, 174
Real national income, 133–136, 170–171
Real taxes, 170–171
Real values, and money values, 113–115, 174–175
Real wage rates, 75–77, 79, 95, 116, 310–314, 319–321
Receipts, international, 576
Recessionary gaps, 155–156, 161–162